COLLINS

DICTIONARY OF

ARCHAEOLOGY

D0042807

COLLINS

DICTIONARY OF

ARCHAEOLOGY

Edited by Paul Bahn

HarperCollins*Publishers*

HarperCollins Publishers
P.O. Box, Glasgow G4 0NB

First published 1992

Reprint 9 8 7 6 5 4 3 2 1 0

© Paul Bahn 1992

ISBN 0 00 434158 9

A catalogue record for this book is available from the British Library.

Printed in Great Britain by HarperCollins Manufacturing, Glasgow.

INTRODUCTION

This volume is intended to be a new, up to date dictionary of use to anyone involved or interested in Archaeology. By dictionary, we mean a collection of short but useful definitions of terms and names. In other words, this is most emphatically neither an atlas nor an encyclopedia – several excellent volumes of that kind have appeared in recent years (see suggestions for further reading on page 642), and readers are advised to turn to them for extended essays on archaeological topics. Instead, the present work places important facts at one's fingertips. It is a reference book, not a textbook; it is for quick, easy consultation, not for sitting down and reading.

To do justice to the vast and varied field of world archaeology in this way is clearly far beyond the capabilities of a single scholar, and hence a first-class team of contributors was required. Even the 16 specialists involved in the project found their expertise stretched both geographically and chronologically. They were selected not only for their scholarship but also for their ability to write (only English speakers were chosen, in order to avoid the delays of translation). In addition, I purposely set out to find eight outstanding contributors of each sex. I succeeded at the start, but an unavoidable last-minute change of personnel changed the score to 9 males and 7 females. Nevertheless, I feel that this is an important step in the right direction for a subject that still tends to be dominated by the male.

A word must be said about the book's contents. All compendia inevitably attract a charge of arbitrariness, and this one will be no exception. Certainly, I have often found that any term I wished to look up in other archaeological dictionaries was frustratingly absent, but we hope that this phenomenon will be minimized in our case. However, no dictionary of this size on such a huge subject can hope to be comprehensive; any of the contributors could easily have filled the book with entries from their own areas. Choices clearly had to be made, but how?

First, it seemed sensible to leave the selections in large measure up to the individual specialists who used their expertise to assess what should be included and what could be omitted from their areas. Second, where entries concerning archaeologists were concerned, it was decided to limit them to those who are deceased: simply brain-dead did not count!

Third, we resolved to omit the self-explanatory: there seems little point in including terms such as cave or insect-analysis or figurine: anyone who needs to look up words of this kind should not be using this dictionary. More important, we have tried to escape from some of the old chestnuts of more traditional archaeological dictionaries which devote much space to agriculture or domestication, terms which are best served in encyclopedias or textbooks. Instead, we felt it important to include a wide range of technical and theoretical terms that are absent from older dictionaries but which, for better or worse, are currently of great concern to archaeology. In short, we have tried to drag the concept of the archaeological dictionary kicking and screaming into the 1990s.

A harder decision, caused by sheer pressure on space, was made to omit food resources, other than a few which are now extinct. There is certainly a case to be made for their inclusion, but much of the information normally supplied about them is better suited to dictionaries of biology or geography.

We have tried to avoid the Eurocentric nature of some other works of this kind; Europe still receives more entries than other continents, but not enormously so. We have included comparatively few entries from the post-classical/historical/colonial periods, and none at all from Industrial Archaeology: once again, sheer pressure of space is to blame.

Names beginning with La, Le or L' are to be found under the letter 'L', while those starting with El are under 'E'. Entries are listed in a simple letter-by-letter alphabetical order, with spaces and hyphens being ignored. Uncalibrated radiocarbon dates are followed by bc/ad or bp (before present), while corrected or vague dates have BC/BP/AD. To save space, only the first figure in a date is given, without the plus/minus range, so these figures should be taken only as a rough guide to true age. Illustrations have also been kept to a strict minimum, and employed only to present a shape or design.

Not every term included has been cross-referenced – e.g. all periods from the Palaeolithic onwards have an entry, but it seemed superfluous to highlight these common terms every time they occur in other entries. The same applies to a wide range of other common words.

For help in choosing suitable contributors, I would like to thank Janette Deacon, Bill Hyder, Carl Lamberg-Karlovsky, Maria Mercer and Olga Soffer; and I am particularly indebted to Andrea Stone and Adrian Lister for their expertise. The contributors would like to thank the following for help and advice at various stages of the work: Stephen Acheson, Mark S. Aldenderfer, J. Barto Arnold, Peter B. Beaumont, Robert Bednarik, Barbara Blackshear, Jane Callander, Bill Cavanagh, Angela E. Close, Paul Courbin, Janette Deacon, Francesco d'Errico, David Frankel, Michael Green, S.L. Hall, Paul Halstead, T.N. Huffman, A.J.B. Humphreys, Jim Judge, Richard Klein, Alice & Tom Kehoe, Dan Lenihan, J.D. Lewis-Williams, Gary Matlock, Aron D. Mazel, Mike McIntyre, Christa Mee, Sarah Nelson, Annette Parkes, Jim Rhoads, Susan Riches, Peter Robertshaw, Karim Sadr, Andrew B. Smith, Marion F. Smith Jr., Louise Steel, Solveig Turpin, Lyn Wadley, N.J. Walker, and the Victoria Archaeological Survey. Finally, my own profound gratitude goes to the team of contributors; to Roy Boyd, who redrew the illustrations, Barbara Bruce who drew the maps, and to Monica Thorp of HarperCollins.

Paul G. Bahn

CONTRIBUTORS

Editor and contributor: Dr Paul Bahn, Hull.

Dr Gina L Barnes	Dept of Archaeology/School of Oriental Studies, University of Cambridge *Far East*
Dr Caroline Bird	Victoria Archaeological Survey, Victoria, Australia *Australia and the Pacific*
Dr Peter Bogucki	Forbes College, Princeton University, USA *Later Periods, Central and Eastern Europe*
Dr Jan Wisseman Christie	Centre for Southeast Asian Studies, University of Hull *Southeast Asia*
Dr Philip Duke	Dept of Anthropology, Fort Lewis College, Durango, Colorado, USA *North America; theory*
Dr Christopher Edens	Peabody Museum, Harvard University, Cambridge, Mass, USA *Near East, Central Asia, India*
Dr David Gill	Fitzwilliam Museum, Cambridge *Classical Archaeology*
Dr Martha Graham	Dept of Anthropology, American Museum of Natural History, New York, USA *Mesoamerica*
Dr Edwin Hajic	Quaternary Studies Program, Illinois State Museum, Springfield, Illinois, USA *Geoarchaeology, methods, materials, techniques*
Dr John Hoffecker	Argonne National Laboratory, Argonne, Illinois, USA *Early periods, Central and Eastern Europe*
Dr Christopher Mee	School of Archaeology, Classics and Oriental Studies, University of Liverpool *Greece and the Aegean*
Dr Christopher Scarre	McDonald Institute of Archaeological Research, University of Cambridge *Later periods, Western Europe*
Dr Katharina Schreiber	Dept of Anthropology, University of California, Santa Barbara, USA *South America*
Dr Steven Snape	School of Archaeology, Classics and Oriental Studies, University of Liverpool *Egypt, the Levant*

Dr Anne Thackeray   Dept of Archaeology, University of
Stellenbosch, S Africa
Africa

Dr Joyce Tyldesley   The Quaternary Research Centre, University
of Oxford
Early periods, Western Europe

A

abacus   the top part of the CAPITAL which is in contact with the bottom part of the ENTABLATURE of a CLASSICAL building. It is thicker on capitals of the DORIC ORDER than on those of the IONIC ORDER.

Abada, Tell   a 2–3 ha 'UBAID period site in the Hamrin district of east central Iraq, where S. Jasim's recent excavations provided the first wide exposure of 'Ubaid residential architecture. The site contains three phases of occupation: the lowest corresponds to the CHOGA MAMI Transitional and 'Ubaid 1 of neighbouring regions, and also contains a little SAMARRAN pottery; the upper two levels belong to the 'Ubaid 2–3 in which a little Late HALAF POLYCHROME painted pottery appears. The domestic buildings of the village consist of rooms that are (largely) symmetrically grouped on both sides of a long and often 'T'-shaped central hall; each building may have contained an extended family household. This tripartite floor plan is found in other 'Ubaid settlements (e.g. KHEIT QASIM), and also appears in religious architecture of the 'Ubaid and URUK periods.

Abbevillian   an outdated term denoting the Early ACHEULIAN IN-DUSTRIES of western Europe, named after the type-site of Abbeville in the Somme Valley, France (see BOUCHER DE PERTHES). The Abbevillian was formerly called the CHELLEAN.

Abdul Hosein, Tepe   an ACERAMIC NEOLITHIC site in the uplands of the Zagros mountains (western Iran), excavated by Judith Pullar in the 1970s. Its sequence of architecture indicates a transition from ephemeral occupation marked by pits and scattered debris to one of rectilinear MUD-BRICK structures with green- or red-painted plaster floors. The material culture includes a range of chipped and ground stone equipment, clay figurines and geometrics (see TOKENS); the botanical evidence indicates cultivation of 2-rowed hulled barley and of emmer.

Abejas phase   a phase in the TEHUACÁN VALLEY, Mexico, beginning about 3500 to 1500 BC. The phase comes after the initial introduction of maize in the valley, when agricultural production begins to make up a significant part of the diet. See also AJUERADO PHASE.

Abercromby, John, Lord (1841–1924)   a Scottish antiquary, author of the seminal *Bronze Age Pottery of Great Britain and Ireland* (1912), which opened a new phase in the study of the British Bronze Age. In 1904 Abercromby introduced the term 'beaker' for decorated handleless drinking vessels characteristic of the Late Neolithic/Early Bronze Age, subdividing them into three types A, B and C, a classification which remained the basis of British Beaker TYPOLOGY until the 1960s.

Abeurador, Balma   a cave-site in Hérault, France, on the southern edge of the Massif Central, with 10 distinct layers of human occupation from EPIPALAEOLITHIC to Late Neolithic *c*.9000 bc to 2500 bc. Carbonized remains of lentils, peas and chick peas, morphologically

1

indistinguishable from early cultivated forms of southwest Asia, were found in AZILIAN levels dated to c.8000 bc, and have suggested incipient cultivation of these species in a formally pre-Neolithic context.

Abingdon   a Neolithic CAUSEWAYED CAMP, dating from c.3200 BC in Berkshire, England, with remains of two widely spaced concentric ditches with several entrance-gaps. Located on Thames valley river gravels, this was the first causewayed camp to be found in a low-lying location.

abri   see ROCKSHELTER.

abri Dufaure   see DURUTHY.

Abri Pataud   an Upper Palaeolithic rockshelter in LES EYZIES, Dordogne, southwest France, which has yielded a detailed stratigraphy with RADIOCARBON dates from 34 250 to c.19 000 bc. The abundant artifacts have been classed as AURIGNACIAN, Upper PERIGORDIAN (or GRAVETTIAN) and proto–MAGDALENIAN. The shelter, excavated by MOVIUS in 1958–64, was primarily a winter site, its faunal remains heavily dominated by reindeer. A number of human remains were discovered, including a 16 year-old girl of the Proto-Magdalenian. Fallen fragments in all levels indicate that the shelter's wall was always painted, engraved and sculptured.

Abri Zumoffen   see ADLUN.

Absolon, Karel (1887–1960)   a Czech archaeologist who excavated a number of major Palaeolithic sites, including DOLNÍ VĚSTONICE, ONDRATICE, PEKÁRNA, and BÝČÍ SKÁLA.

absolute dating   the process of utilizing DATING methods that allow ages to be reported in years either as years before present (bp), uncorrected for carbon flux in the atmosphere, or as calendar years (AD/BC/BP), corrected for carbon flux. A margin of uncertainty as compared with standards, usually expressed in years, is reported as well. Compare RELATIVE DATING. See also CHRONOMETRIC DATING.

absolute pollen counting   the process of counting pollen grains for each species per sample unit volume or unit weight. Because SEDIMENTATION rates may vary among sampled intervals, pollen counts are reported as a pollen influx rate for each species per sample. The pollen influx rate is the number of pollen grains of a species accumulating on a unit SEDIMENT surface area per unit time. Sedimentation rates are required to perform the calculation, and these are obtained with multiple RADIOCARBON ages through the sampled column. Using pollen influx rates circumvents the problem that relative pollen counting of species percentages is codependent on percentages of other species being counted, and therefore does not necessarily reflect changes in vegetation composition. See PALYNOLOGY.

Abu Ballas   a series of mud pans in the Western Desert of Egypt, occupied between 8500 and 5000 years ago. The CERAMICS indicate a cultural relationship with the KHARTOUM NEOLITHIC.

Abu Ghurab   the site of the SUN TEMPLE of King Niuserre of the 5th DYNASTY of Egypt, excavated by Borchardt and Schäfer in 1898–1901.

Abu Hureyra, Tell   an EPIPALAEOLITHIC (late NATUFIAN) to early ceramic Neolithic site on the middle Euphrates. A.M.T. Moore's excavation in the 1970s provides considerable detail on the beginnings of food production in this part of Syria. The Epipalaeolithic levels contained an abundance of wild einkorn, and of other wild cereals, legumes, nuts and seeds; the excavator suggests that the einkorn at least was cultivated. The ACERAMIC NEOLITHIC (PPNB) levels contain rectilinear MUD-BRICK structures with plastered and painted walls and floors, and a material culture that included stone vessels, bone tools, a variety of personal ornaments, clay figurines and a wide variety of exotic materials in addition to the chipped stone. In the 7th millennium BC, exploitation switched abruptly from gazelles to sheep and goats.

Abu Roash   a site northwest of GIZA, Egypt; the unfinished PYRAMID of King Radjedef, the immediate successor of KHUFU, is the northernmost of those associated with the capital MEMPHIS.

Abu Salabikh, Tell   Set in southern MESOPOTAMIA on an extinct watercourse just northwest of NIPPUR, Abu Salabikh was first excavated by V. Crawford in the 1960s. This work exposed part of a large building complex of EARLY DYNASTIC III date, in which were found over 500 texts including the earliest-known literary works of SUMERIAN literature (the 'Instructions of Shuruppak' and the 'Kesh Temple Hymn'). They also define a scribal tradition different from that previously known in Sumerian Mesopotamia (at Fara), remarkable for the Semitic names of many of its scribes and resemblance to the documents from KISH as well as from EBLA in Syria. I.J. Gelb has proposed the name 'Kish civilization' to identify the cultural patterns of northern BABYLONIA during the mid 3rd millennium. Nicholas Postgate and his collaborators have excavated at Abu Salabikh since the 1970s. The site is composed of eight separate mounds, six of which fall within a 100 ha area. The latter collectively date to Early URUK–Early Dynastic III times, with some later 3rd millennium occupation also occurring. Not all the mounds were inhabited simultaneously, and the settlement focus shifted through time. Major contributions of the project include: application of extensive surface scraping to reveal urban architectural layout during several periods; identification of walled house compounds of Early Dynastic I date, probably a material reflection of extended families; documentation of the layout of a major Early Dynastic III settlement; and detailed analysis of Early Dynastic pottery that entails a correction to the ceramic chronology based on the older Diyala evidence (at KHAFADJE, Tell ASMAR), and identification of regional variations in the Early Dynastic pottery of southern Mesopotamia that may archaeologically reflect Gelb's 'Kish civilization'.

Abu Shahrain   see ERIDU.

Abu Simbel   the site, in LOWER NUBIA, of two ROCK-TEMPLES constructed under RAMESSES II. The Great Temple has a façade of two pairs of colossal seated figures (approximately 22 m tall) of the king, flanking the entrance. The Small Temple has a more modest, but nonetheless impressive, frontage of standing figures of Ramesses and his principal queen, Nefertari. Both temples were dismantled and reconstructed on higher ground during the NUBIAN RESCUE CAMPAIGN.

Abusir   the site of the PYRAMIDS of the 5th DYNASTY Egyptian Kings Sahure, Niuserre, Neferirkare and (probably) Raneferef, excavated by Borchardt in 1902–08. Between these pyramids and ABU GHURAB lies the SUN TEMPLE of King Userkaf, also of the 5th Dynasty, excavated by Ricke and Haeny in 1954–57.

Abydos   a much-excavated site in UPPER EGYPT containing a series of important structures, including royal tombs of the ARCHAIC PERIOD and the TEMPLES of the early 19th DYNASTY. Abydos was considered to be the burial-place of OSIRIS, and as such became an important 'national' cemetery and place of pilgrimage, giving rise to the construction of a large number of tombs, and of monuments (including royal examples) commemorating individuals buried elsewhere, especially from the MIDDLE KINGDOM onwards.

Acacus or **Tadrat Acacus**   broken country in the Sahara Desert of southwestern Libya with many rock paintings. Exfoliated pieces of paintings incorporated into a cave deposit enabled depictions of domestic cattle to be RADIOCARBON dated to c.4800 BP (see UAN MUHUGGIAG).

accelerator mass spectrometry (AMS)   a RADIOCARBON-DATING method that utilizes an accelerator mass spectrometer to determine the actual numbers of ^{14}C atoms present in a sample, rather than the relatively small numbers of ^{14}C atoms that decay radioactively during the measurement time of the conventional β-counting method. Both methods have about the same dating age limit of about 50 000 bp. The greatest advantage of the AMS method is the sample size requirement of only 1 mg of carbon, and in some cases, as little as 100 μg of carbon. A second advantage is that actual measurement time takes about an hour, whereas conventional β-counting can take days. The cost of AMS analysis is a drawback and, if enough sample is available, the finest conventional counters can achieve a slightly greater precision. In addition to dating standard materials such as charcoal, bones and other organic residues of occupation, the AMS method allows dating of individual seeds, textiles and artifacts without totally destroying the sample.

Aceramic Neolithic   1. another term for the PRE-POTTERY NEOLITHIC. The word Neolithic was originally technological, referring to peoples using ground stone and pottery, whatever their subsistence practices. It is now exclusively used to refer to communities with food production as the central basis of subsistence. The differentiation between technology and economy became apparent with the discovery of food-producing communities in western Asia that did not use pottery; the reverse situation – i.e. foragers who use pottery – is also known but rarer, and not given a special name.
2. a transitional phase identified on a number of sites in Greece, Crete and Cyprus such as ARGISSA, SESKLO, KNOSSOS, KALAVASOS and KHIROKITIA, in which agriculture is the basis of the economy but pottery is not yet in use.

Achaeans   one of the terms used by Homer for the Greeks at TROY which may have been current in the Bronze Age, if HITTITE Ahhijawa is correctly identified as a MYCENAEAN state, but which is not attested in LINEAR B.

Achaemenids   a branch of the Persian tribes that moved into western Iran early in the 1st millennium BC (if not earlier) and settled in Fars. From there, the ruling house (who claimed descent from Achaemenes, eponymous founder of the royal line in the early 7th century BC) expanded during the 6th century BC to create a world empire that stretched from Central Asia and northern India to

THRACE and Egypt. Notable Achaemenid rulers include CYRUS II (559–530 BC), Darius I (522–486 BC) and Xerxes I (485–465 BC). The Macedonian Alexander the Great conquered the Achaemenid empire in 330 BC.

Achenheim a prehistoric French site situated 10 km to the west of Strasbourg and investigated by a number of workers since 1835. The LOESS layers have produced abundant faunal remains, including MAMMOTH, rather poor Lower Palaeolithic artifacts, MOUSTERIAN-like tools dating to the RISS GLACIATION, and some Upper Palaeolithic material.

Acheulian or **Acheulean** **1.** (*European*) the main Lower Palaeolithic TRADITION of BIFACE makers which lasted from over one million years ago until the early part of the last GLACIATION *c.*100 000 BP. Acheulian INDUSTRIES have been identified over much of Africa, across western and central Europe and as far east as India. Their tool-kits are characterized by the presence of bifaces, waste FLAKES and flake tools, with considerable local and regional variation within the same Acheulian tradition. The Acheulian takes its name from the type-site of Saint-Acheul, Amiens, in the Somme Valley, France.

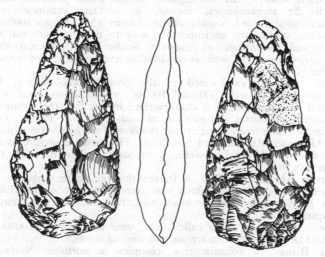

Acheulian Biface.

Acheulian **2.** (*African*) an EARLIER STONE AGE industrial COMPLEX represented throughout Africa, except for some equatorial areas, from about 1.5 million to 150 000 years ago, characterized by the production of BIFACES, especially handaxes and CLEAVERS, manufactured by HOMO *erectus* and later by early *Homo sapiens*.

Acropole of Susa structures at SUSA in lowland Khuzistan, southwestern Iran. Among the many excavations there, perhaps the most important are those named 'Acropole 2' and 'Acropole 1', dug in the 1970s by D. Canal and A. Le Brun respectively. Acropole 2 addresses the context of the large cemetery and large platform that de Morgan had exposed in Susa's initial occupation levels. Dated to the end of the 5th millennium BC, these structures and their contents imply a considerable degree of social complexity at this time in lowland Khuzistan. Acropole 1 provides a sequence of 27 levels running from the initial settlement of the place to AKKADIAN times. In this sequence may be observed the replacement of painted pottery in the local style (levels 27–23) by an URUK ceramic inventory (22–17), followed by an abrupt change in pottery (16–14); the transition between these two phases, of uncertain duration, seems to be absent from the sequence. The latter two ceramic phases correspond to important developments in writing: levels 18–17 contain tablets marked only with numbers, and TOKENS in envelopes (which themselves are often marked with numbers), while levels 16–15 contain tablets bearing PROTO-ELAMITE script. This developmental sequence of writing parallels that found at WARKA, but here represents a different language.

acropolis   see AKROPOLIS.

acroterium   see AKROTERION.

activity area   an area of a SITE in which a specific activity, such as stone tool or pottery manufacture, was practised.

actualistic study   an investigation of the actual processes through which the archaeological record, or artifacts common in the archaeological record, comes about. Under the NEW ARCHAEOLOGY, actualistic studies are an important way to develop BRIDGING ARGUMENTS and WARRANTING ARGUMENTS. Studies of ETHNOARCHAEOLOGY and TAPHONOMY, as well as replication experiments, are actualistic studies.

Adena   a COMPLEX located in the central Ohio Valley, USA, between approximately 500 and 100 BC, which shows great internal cultural variation. Adena is characterized by pottery, the construction of earthen enclosures and earthen mounds built over burials. Gravegoods are made from a variety of materials found in various parts of the American Midwest and Southeast. Habitation structures vary in size, from single-family dwellings to communal houses. See GRAVE CREEK MOUND.

Adlun or **Abri Zumoffen**   a Palaeolithic site on the Lebanese coast between SIDON and TYRE which was investigated by GARROD. Excavations have revealed an AMUDIAN INDUSTRY followed by JABRUDIAN occupation.

adobe   dried mud, often called *jacal*, used in the WATTLE-AND-DAUB method of building construction. See also MUD-BRICK.

Adrar Bous   a volcanic ring complex in northern Niger with archaeological material dating from ACHEULIAN times until about 4500 years ago. The sites offer important information on the beginnings of cattle domestication in the Sahara.

adyton or **adytum**   an enclosed room which formed the innermost sanctuary of a CLASSICAL temple. It was normally entered via the OPISTHODOMOS and was located to the rear of the CELLA.

adze   1. a stone tool made on FLAKES or PEBBLES, with steep flaking or battering along one or both sides, hafted and used for woodworking. Adzes approximately 25–40 mm long are found in small numbers in most southern African LATER STONE AGE sites, particularly those dating to the last few thousand years. In Australia several types have been recognized, but, except for the TULA, they are not clearly

defined. Australian archaeologists often use the term loosely to describe flake SCRAPERS with heavily RETOUCHED step-flaked edges. Repeated resharpening and reversal in the haft results in the production of a heavily-flaked 'slug'.
2. a tool made of ground stone found throughout the Pacific. There is a wide variety of forms, which are important cultural and CHRONOLOGICAL markers. The most widely used classification was devised by DUFF. Shell adzes are also found in MICRONESIA and POLYNESIA. See POLISHED STONE ADZE.

Adzhi-Koba　a Palaeolithic cave-site in the Crimea, Ukraine. The lower occupation HORIZON contains an ASSEMBLAGE of Middle Palaeolithic artifacts, including sidescrapers (see SCRAPER). The upper horizon contains an Upper Palaeolithic occupation, rare in the Crimea, with artifacts apparently similar to those from SYUREN' I. Adzhi-Koba was excavated by Bonch-Osmolovskij in 1932–33.

aedicula　a small Roman shrine usually projecting from a wall inside a building. Two columns supported a miniature ARCHITRAVE and above that a PEDIMENT. A small statue of a deity may have been placed inside. Wall-paintings, in particular those at POMPEII, often include aediculae in an attempt to give depth to the room.

Aegina　an island in the Saronic Gulf between the PIRAEUS and the Peloponnese. An Early Bronze Age site has been excavated at Kolonna adjoining the modern town. Over this settlement was constructed a temple of the DORIC ORDER. Elsewhere on the island was the temple of Aphaia, rebuilt in the early years of the 5th century BC. The PEDIMENTS of the new building showed the two sacks of TROY.

Aeneolithic　see ENEOLITHIC.

aeolian or **eolian** *adj.*　of the wind. The term is applied to deposits caused by, material carried by, or processes related to the wind. Aeolian deposits can easily bury archaeological deposits intact or with little disturbance, whereas aeolian erosion can cause collapse of the archaeological record and displacement of debris. Aeolian particle movement may modify archaeological debris through abrasion and create a PATINA.

Aeolic order　an architectural order defined by an ornate type of CAPITAL seems to have been widely used in the northwest part of Turkey (the ancient Aeolis) as well as the island of Lesbos. The capital was formed by two VOLUTES which are separated by a spreading PALMETTE. The ECHINUS rests below the bottom of the volutes and tends to be formed by water-lily leaves. See IONIC ORDER.

Aeolic order Capital.

aerial photography   a SURVEY tool used to locate sites, detail site structures, and map GEOMORPHOLOGY and SOILS in site vicinity. It is based on contrasting tonal patterns due to differences in soil TEXTURE, soil moisture content, organic matter content, and vegetation type and vigour. Photography is usually from an aircraft utilizing a range of film type depending on needs, and can be oblique or vertical, the latter taken with overlap to allow stereoscopic examination.

aerobic, *adj.*   denoting an environmental state where free molecular oxygen is available. An aerobic environment is not conducive to preservation of plant, animal and human remains, or of artifacts made from them, because the presence of oxygen facilitates the chemical or biochemical decay of organic structures. Compare ANAEROBIC.

Afanasievo culture   a Late Neolithic culture of southern Siberia, centred on the headwaters of the Ob and Yenisei rivers. The Afanasievo culture is known primarily from graves, in which multiple inhumations were interred in a central pit with grave-goods, above which was a low mound surrounded by a low circular wall up to 12 m in diameter. Most of these burials occur in groups of up to 20, such as at the sites of Afanasieva Gora and Karasuk III. Afanasievo pottery shows similarities to that of the slightly earlier KELTAMINAR culture of the Aral and Caspian basins.

Afontova Culture   an Upper PALAEOLITHIC culture of south-central Siberia, dating to *c*.20 000–10 000 BP. Diagnostic artifacts include WEDGE-SHAPED MICROCORES, MICROBLADES and SCRAPERS. RETOUCHED BLADES, which are common in sites of the roughly contemporaneous KOKOREVO CULTURE, are rare. The Afontova Culture was defined by Abramova in 1979.

Afontova Gora   a group of four Upper Palaeolithic open-air sites on the Yenisei River in Krasnoyarsk, south-central Siberia. At each locality, artifacts and faunal remains are buried in slope deposits overlying ALLUVIUM of the second TERRACE. Most of the occupation layers date to the late GLACIAL. Among the fauna, reindeer is generally the most abundant species, although woolly MAMMOTH and arctic fox are also common. The artifact ASSEMBLAGES contain WEDGE-SHAPED MICROCORES, MICROBLADES and SCRAPERS. Afontova Gora I was discovered and excavated by Savenkov in 1884–93; subsequent investigations by Auerbakh, Gromov and others occurred in 1912–14 and 1923–30.

African Red Slip ware   a type of red-glossed pottery (see SLIP) produced in North Africa, particularly from the 3rd to the 6th centuries AD. A range of shapes was produced. The stamped decoration included simple motifs such as PALMETTES as well as figured scenes, some of which were drawn from biblical passages. The fabric has a wide distribution, being found as far north as Britain. Its export may be linked to the demand for African olive oil.

Afunfun   early copper-working sites in Niger, of the 2nd millennium BC (4140–3660 bp), containing a series of furnaces and quantities of slag.

Agade   the city founded by SARGON of Akkad as the capital of his empire; its location is unknown, but is probably in the neighbourhood of KISH.

Agate Basin   **1.** a PALAEOINDIAN site located in eastern Wyoming, USA, probably used as a bison KILL-SITE. It shows evidence of both the killing and butchering of animals.

2. a late Palaeoindian point form recognized at its type-site.

3. an archaeological COMPLEX centred in the Northwestern Plains of North America. It is dated at the HELL GAP site to 10 500–10 000 BP. Besides the distinctive point form, the complex is characterized by its scrapers and eyed bone needles. The Agate Basin occupation at Hell Gap had evidence of POSTHOLES, possibly representing small circular structures.

agger **1.** the raised causeway which served as the foundations for the construction of Roman roads.
2. a rampart forming part of a series of fortifications.

Aggsbach an Upper Palaeolithic open-air site located on the River Danube in northeastern Austria. Artifacts and faunal remains (e.g. woolly MAMMOTH, reindeer, giant deer) are buried in deposits of LOESS yielding RADIOCARBON dates of 25 700–22 450 bp. The ASSEMBLAGES contain endscrapers (see SCRAPER), BACKED BLADES and RETOUCHED BLADES; they are assigned to the EASTERN GRAVETTIAN.

Aggtelek see DOMICA.

agora a focal point for civic life in the Greek city. The area tended to be surrounded by buildings linked to the government of the state (see BOULEUTERION, PRYTANEION) and the law-courts. It could also include markets as well as spaces for athletic events and festivals. The perimeter of the agora could be marked by boundary stones. From the HELLENISTIC period agoras throughout the Greek world could be lined by STOAS. As the civic centre the agora attracted the erection of honorific statues. One of the best understood agoras is that at ATHENS excavated by an American team. Compare FORUM.

Agrigento (*Gk* Akragas, *Lat.* Agrigentum) a Greek colony in southern Sicily traditionally founded by GELA *c.*580 BC. It became a prosperous city, probably flourishing on the rearing of horses, vineyards and olives. Its wealth is reflected in the large number of temples of the DORIC ORDER which continue to dominate the ridge forming the southern edge of the city. In the late 2nd century BC there was substantial rebuilding, with the streets laid out in a grid pattern (see HIPPODAMIAN PLANNING).

Agrileza see LAURION.

Agris helmet an Iron Age helmet discovered in the Grotte des Perrats, Agris, Charente, France, by cavers in 1981. One of the finest works of LA TÈNE art to be discovered in recent years, it was of iron, overlaid by bronze bands with decoration in raised relief covered by thin gold sheet. Further decoration of coral was fixed to the helmet with silver rivets. PALMETTES are prominent among the decorative motifs, and the helmet is attributed on stylistic grounds to the 4th century BC.

A-Group a CULTURE which emerged in LOWER NUBIA during the late 4th millennium BC and disappeared by *c.*3000 BC; it was influenced by the GERZEAN of UPPER EGYPT. The economy was based on the herding of cattle, sheep and goats, and there is a concern for burial ritual hitherto unknown among populations in Nubia.

Ahar a prehistoric site in southern Rajasthan, just south of the Aravalli Hills in western India. The settlement of Ahar falls into two distinct periods: CHALCOLITHIC (Ahar IA–C) and Iron Age (Ahar IIA–C). RADIOCARBON dates for Ahar I indicate occupation between 2500 and 1500 BC. The community lived in fairly large structures of stone and MUD-BRICK, and by the end of the period grew rice, sorghum (?and millet) as well as other crops, herded cattle and kept other animals, and SMELTED a great deal of COPPER. The latter feature, most clearly evident in Ahar IB, reflects the settlement's proximity to the copper sources in the Aravalli Hills. The pottery displays changes through time. A white-painted black-and-red ware and black on cream slipped ware are present in Ahar IA; Lustrous Red ware appears in Ahar IC. The Iron Age settlement begins with levels containing NORTHERN BLACK POLISHED ware (Ahar IIA), followed by early historic period levels (Ahar IIB–C).

Aharoni, Yohanan (1919–1976)   an Israeli archaeologist, an active excavator whose sites include ARAD, LACHISH and BEERSHEBA.

Ahmose   the first king of the Egyptian 18th DYNASTY and therefore of the NEW KINGDOM. During the reign of Ahmose (*c*.1550–1525 BC) the HYKSOS were expelled from Egypt, and territorial gains were made in NUBIA and Palestine.

Ahrensburgian, *adj.*   relating to an EPIPALAEOLITHIC culture found in north Germany and Holland, in many ways similar to the HAMBURGIAN of the same area, but much later in date (*c*.8500 BC). The north German site of Stellmoor has yielded both Hamburgian and Ahrensburgian levels; the Ahrensburgian phase, dated to the last cold phase of the final GLACIATION, appears to be a temporary reindeer-hunting camp. The tool-kit includes FLINT SCRAPERS, BURINS, TANGED points which were probably used as arrowheads, wooden arrow shafts, and clubs which were used to kill reindeer. See BROMMIAN.

ahu   a rectangular ceremonial platform on EASTER ISLAND and the Society Islands, related to the POLYNESIAN MARAE, and usually built of stone slabs encasing a rubble core. On Easter Island, where *ahu* sometimes supported human statues (MOAI), the earliest appear *c*.AD 600 and the latest date to *c*.AD 1500. In most of eastern Polynesia, the term referred only to a raised platform at the end of a rectangular court, but in the northern Marquesas and Easter Island it denotes the whole ceremonial centre.

Ahualulco   a ceremonial COMPLEX in western Mexico, best known as part of the SHAFT TOMB complex, which is found in association with a distinctive architectural style. This style is characterized by habitation zones dominated by a large multiple-circle complex with BALL COURTS and elite residential architecture. Ahualulco was made up of six circles and one ball court, enclosing about 42 510 sq m. This architectural style was characteristic from about 200 BC until AD 900/1000.

ahuapua'a   a basic unit of land division in the Hawaiian Islands, cross-cutting all major environmental zones from the uplands to the coast, and under the control of a chief. Several have been studied intensively by archaeologists, including HALAWA VALLEY, KAWELA, LAPAKAHI and MAKAHA VALLEY.

Ai   a site in Palestine, excavated by GARSTANG in 1928, by Marquet-Krause in 1933–35 and by Callaway in 1964–72. Ai was occupied during the EARLY BRONZE AGE when its AKROPOLIS included a palace/temple and a rectangular stone tower, part of the fortifications of the 'citadel'; some of this building work may have involved Egyptian craftsmen of the ARCHAIC PERIOD. Ai was destroyed and abandoned at the end of the Early Bronze Age, but was occupied as an unfortified town in the Iron Age.

Aibunar   a Late Neolithic COPPER mine in Bulgaria, located near KARANOVO and AZMAK, and dated by pottery found in the workings to the Karanovo VI period. Eleven galleries have been identified totalling approximately 500 m. The longest gallery was 110 m long at a depth of 20 m. Antler axes and picks were found in the galleries.

'Ain Ghazal   an extremely large settlement on the east bank of the River Jordan occupied from late ACERAMIC NOLITHIC into ceramic Neolithic times, that has been excavated during the 1980s by Gary Rollefson. The excavation revealed a PPNB settlement that grew steadily through time, from 4 ha at c.7250 BC to 9 ha at c.6500 BC and ultimately reaching 12 ha in 6000 BC, making it one of the largest known PPNB sites. The aceramic levels are remarkable for the three caches of plaster human statues, perhaps reflecting an ancestor cult connected with the famous PPNB PLASTERED SKULLS. The lithic changes seen in the terminal aceramic period, designated PPNC, are dated to 6200–5900 BC. This lithic distinction may also capture deeper economic shifts: in PPNB levels goats are thought to be controlled but not domesticated, while in PPNC levels goats, cattle and pigs all appear as domesticates. The subsequent ceramic Neolithic settlement (the Yarmukian) represents seasonal occupations, perhaps by pastoralists connected to farmers in the western Levant.

Ain Hanech   an early PLEISTOCENE site in northern Algeria, yielding PEBBLE tools, particularly spheroids and battered stones, associated with extinct riverine and lacustrine fauna. See ARAMBOURG.

Ain Mallaha   see EYNAN.

Ainu   former HUNTER-GATHERERS occupying Hokkaido and Sakhalin Islands (Japan and (former) USSR). In Hokkaido, they are now settled as farmers with heavy intermarriage with the Japanese. Until recently they were mistakenly identified as a remanent JOMON population or EMISHI, but now they are recognized as a historically formulated ethnic PALAEOASIATIC group first documented in the 14th–16th centuries AD. The Ainu language has no known relatives. See also AMURIAN.

Ajuerado phase   the earliest phase in the pre-village, incipient agriculture sequence in the TEHUACÁN VALLEY, Mexico. Ranging from 7200–7000 BC, subsistence activities during the Ajuerado phase include hunting small animals and gathering wild plants.

Akapana   see TIAHUANACO.

Akashi   the site of fossil HOMO finds near Kobe City, Japan, discovered by Naora Nobuo in 1931. Only the cast of the innominate bone survived the Second World War. Because of their fossilization, the remains were first thought to be PLEISTOCENE in date, but now they are assessed as HOLOCENE. (See also NISHIYAGI.)

Akhenaten   a king of the 18th DYNASTY who reigned c.1353–1337 BC, remarkable among ancient Egyptian monarchs for rejecting the traditional pantheon of gods (especially the cult of AMEN) in favour of a monotheistic worship of the ATEN. Akhenaten, accompanied by his chief wife NEFERTITI, moved the capital of Egypt from THEBES to EL-AMARNA. His memory, together with that of his immediate successors who were associated with the 'Aten heresy', including TUTANKHA-MEN, was reviled by later kings.

Akjoujt   a region of Mauretania, Africa, containing a series of COPPER mines dating back to the 1st millennium BC. Hundreds of copper objects, especially arrowheads, have been found with little or no archaeological context but linked to the mines through chemical composition.

Akkadian(s)   A linguistic term denoting a group of Semitic languages in MESOPOTAMIA, first reflected in CUNEIFORM texts of the mid 3rd millennium BC in the northern part of the Mesopotamian ALLUVIUM, the ancient Akkad. The later languages BABYLONIAN and ASSYRIAN belong to this language group. The term 'Akkadians' is often used to denote people speaking this language during the 3rd millennium, as distinct from SUMERIANS, and ethnic differences are often ascribed to this distinction (see ABU SALABIKH, KISH). In the political history of Mesopotamia, the term is applied to the rule of SARGON'S dynasty (c.2330–2150 BC), with its capital at AGADE in Akkad; by extension the term also describes the material culture (especially CYLINDER SEALS, artistic production and ceramics) of this period.

Ak-Kaya   a group of 14 Middle Palaeolithic sites in the Crimea, Ukraine, which includes Ak-Kaya I–V and ZASKAL'NAYA I–IX. ARTIFACT ASSEMBLAGES from these sites have been assigned to the AK-KAYA CULTURE.

Ak-Kaya Culture   a Middle Palaeolithic culture defined on the basis of ARTIFACT ASSEMBLAGES from the AK-KAYA sites in the Crimea, Ukraine. It is characterized by a high percentage of BIFACIAL FOLIATES, including PRONDNIK knives and BOCKSTEIN knives.

akropolis or **acropolis**   literally 'the high point of a (Greek) city'. It could form a refuge as well as a location for the cults of the city (see TEMENOS). One of the best known is at ATHENS where several highly decorated temples (see PARTHENON, ERECHTHEION) were built. It also attracted dedications (see KOUROS, KORE) from private individuals from all over its territory of Attica.

akroterion   a decorative element found on the roof of a CLASSICAL building, above the apex or the corners of the PEDIMENT. Various forms were used, including PALMETTES, victories and SPHINXES.

Akrotiri   on the CYCLADIC island of THERA or SANTORINI in the Aegean archipelago, the site of a Bronze Age town buried by volcanic ASH in the 16th century BC. The excavations by MARINATOS and Doumas have revealed houses two or even three storeys high, with brilliant polychrome FRESCOES still *in situ* on the walls. It is evident from the finds that the inhabitants of Akrotiri maintained close links with MINOAN Crete.

alabaster   see GYPSUM.

alabastron   a Greek unguent container which should strictly be made of ALABASTER but can be of CLAY.

Alaca Hüyük   a 7 ha prehistoric settlement some 160 km east of Ankara, not far from BOGHAZKÖY in Turkey. The excavations of H. Kocay starting in the 1930s revealed a succession of CHALCOLITHIC, Bronze Age and Iron Age and later (Roman to medieval) settlements. Belonging to the late 2nd millennium is a HITTITE occupation consisting of a walled town with several temples, residential areas and a formal gateway (the 'Sphinx gate'); the excavation revealed an iron foundry within the town. Much of this town, including its monumental aspects, belongs to the Old Hittite period (mid 2nd millennium BC), and is often identified with the Hittite cultic centre Arinna. Of the earlier settlements, the Early Bronze contains the famous 'royal graves', dated to the Early Bronze II (the early-to-mid 3rd millennium BC). These 13 tombs are rectilinear stone- or wood-lined pits, each with one to two inhumations and extremely rich grave goods, including a series of 'standards' (animal figures in bronze inlaid and plated with precious metals), weapons (many of bronze, but also including iron daggers, an early appearance of this metal), vessels in precious metals, bronze human figurines, and much metal and stone jewellery. The cultural origins of this Early Bronze complex are not easily discerned, since many elite goods had an extremely wide currency in western Asia of the time; the animal figure 'standards' are often cited in suggesting a Pontic origin (somewhere around the Black Sea).

Alalakh   see ATCHANA.

Alambra-Mouttes   in eastern Cyprus, the site of an early Middle CYPRIOT settlement of rectangular stone-built houses excavated by Coleman in 1976–82.

Alamgirpur   a small site in Uttar Pradesh northeast of Delhi in northern India, excavated in the late 1950s by Y.D. Sharma, which was inhabited at four separate times. The earliest period is characterized by a ceramic assemblage having extremely strong resemblances to the Mature HARAPPAN, in a village of brick and WATTLE-AND-DAUB architecture. The work at Alamgirpur presented the first evidence of the Harappan ceramic tradition in the Ganges-Yamuna doab (alluvial plain). The presence at Alamgirpur of typically Mature Harappan elements (ceramic forms, TERRACOTTA cakes), within a cultural assemblage that as a whole is still distinguishable from the Mature Harappan of the Sind (Pakistan), has been interpreted either as a regional variant of the Mature Harappan or as a representative of a Late Harappan tradition that perhaps overlapped in time with the Mature Harappan. The first alternative seems preferable. The later occupations at Alamgirpur, separated from the earlier by a weathering surface, belong to the PAINTED GREY WARE tradition, and then to the 3rd–2nd centuries BC and medieval times.

Alashiya   mentioned in Near Eastern texts of the 2nd millennium BC, evidently a source of copper and therefore presumed to be Cyprus. If this is correct, it would appear that Cyprus was an ally of the Egyptian PHARAOH in the 14th century but may subsequently have been incorporated in the HITTITE empire. The texts also record the devastation inflicted by the SEA PEOPLES in c.1200 BC.

Alaska Refugium   a large area comprising interior Alaska that was never GLACIATED during the latter part of the PLEISTOCENE. The refugium was connected to BERINGIA and eastern Siberia, both of which also remained free of glaciers. This huge region allowed unimpeded access for early peoples between Asia and North America.

Albany   a LATER STONE AGE INDUSTRY of the southern and eastern Cape Province in South Africa, sometimes called the OAKHURST Industry, dated to between about 12 000 and 8000 BP, and characterized by few formally-patterned artifacts other than SCRAPERS more than 20 mm long. See LOCKSHOEK.

Albright, William Foxwell (1891–1971)   an American orientalist and linguist whose archaeological work in Palestine included the excavations at BEIT MERSIM.

Alcalà a cemetery in the Algarve, Portugal, of 13 CHAMBERED TOMBS of 'THOLOS' type, with a long passage leading to a circular CORBEL-VAULTED chamber, sometimes with additional side-chambers. The richest, tomb 3, had CALLAIS beads, amber pendants, and COPPER flat axes, daggers and AWLS. Four of the daggers had raised mid-ribs on both sides, once considered evidence for the early use of a two-piece mould, but now thought to have been hammered-up. The tombs were probably built in the 4th millennium BC, but grave-goods indicate their continued use in the 3rd millennium.

Aleria (*Gk* Alalia) a 6th century BC colony in eastern Corsica founded from Phocaea in Turkey. The tombs show close similarities with those in ETRURIA, and contained a considerable amount of Etruscan material. This has been seen by some as evidence for an Etruscan presence on the island.

Alésia an Iron Age OPPIDUM in Côte d'Or, France, site of the last stand by the CELTIC chieftain Vercingetorix against Roman invasion forces of Julius Caesar in 52 BC. The oppidum occupies a steep-sided plateau 97 ha in area, with short stretches of walling, including some of the MURUS GALLICUS type described by Caesar. Excavations undertaken for Napoleon III in 1861–65 to the west of the oppidum uncovered remains of Caesar's siege works. A bronze statue of Vercingetorix was erected at the site in 1865.

Aleutian Tradition a TRADITION found in western Alaska and the adjacent Aleutian Islands, which originated approximately 5000 BP and continued with some modification virtually to the Historic Period. It is characterized by specific stone PROJECTILE POINTS and carved HARPOON heads.

Alexandria a coastal city in Egypt founded by Alexander the Great in 331 BC. Little of the city has been excavated, although the cemeteries lying to the east and west of the settlement have been explored (see HADRA WARE). Important buildings included the tomb of Alexander, the Museum, the Serapeum (the temple of Serapis), the library and the Pharos (lighthouse), one of the SEVEN WONDERS. The cult site of Caesar (the Caesareum), and later of Augustus (the Sebasteum or Augusteum), was marked by two OBELISKS (one of which is Cleopatra's Needle in London).

Alföld see SZAKALHÁT-LEBO.

Al Hiba first tested by KOLDEWEY in 1887, and systematically investigated by Donald Hanson since 1968, al Hiba is the city of Lagash, one of the centres of the ancient MESOPOTAMIAN city-state Lagash. The site, on a former branch of the Euphrates, covers nearly 700 ha in a series of low mounds. It has a sequence of EARLY DYNASTIC levels capped by an E. D. III temple oval (as found at KHAFADJE and 'UBAID). Occupation at the site continued into OLD BABYLONIAN times, though after its absorption into the UR III state, Lagash declined in importance.

alidade a SURVEYING instrument used in conjunction with a PLANE TABLE to map a site topographically or locate features in the field. Although somewhat overtaken by electronic measuring instruments and PHOTOGRAMMETRY, this is still the only instrument that enables maps to be created in the field as work progresses. It consists of a focusing telescope for long sightings mounted on a flat metal base with a straight edge that rests on, but is not attached to, the plane table. The alidade is also equipped with a striding-level to level the scope; a bulls-eye level to level the plane table on which it rests; a vernier scale for measuring vertical angles; stadia and cross hairs for determining distances with measurements taken from a stadia rod; and a compass for determining magnetic bearings.

alignment a setting of standing stones or wooden posts characteristic of the British Isles and northwest France during the Late Neolithic and Bronze Age. Alignments sometimes consist of several parallel lines containing hundreds of stones; the most famous are those of CARNAC in Brittany. Such alignments are normally considered to have had a ritual or religious significance, and some were clearly oriented towards solar or lunar phenomena.

Ali Kosh see DEH LURAN.

Alişar Hüyük a 12 ha site to the southeast of BOGHAZKÖY in northern Cappadocia, central Anatolia, which was occupied from at least the beginning of the Early Bronze Age (perhaps even into the Late CHALCOLITHIC) up to medieval times. The excavation standards of H. van der Osten's work here in the 1920s and 1930s were fairly low, and the STRATIGRAPHIC associations of his vertical sequences are difficult to reconstruct, leaving this early work at Alişar somewhat compromised. The best-known aspect of the site is the early 2nd millennium BC settlement, characterized by a material culture that has strong similarities with those of contemporary Cappadocian sites such as KÜLTEPE; like these contemporary towns it also contains an Old Assyrian KĀRUM, represented by a small archive and scattered texts.

Allahdino a small village site near the Indus delta in the lower Sind in Pakistan that provides a rare glimpse into a small agricultural community of the Mature HARAPPAN civilization. Walter Fairservis's work at the site revealed that most of the artifacts found in urban settings also occur in this rural settlement.

allée couverte sometimes translated as 'gallery grave', one of the two classic types of French MEGALITHIC tomb, the other being the PASSAGE GRAVE. *Allées couvertes* are long rectangular monuments, sometimes with the remains of a covering mound, and are distinguished by the absence of a division between passage and chamber, though some have a small antechamber. Dating from the 3rd millennium BC, they are especially characteristic of Brittany and the Paris basin, those of the latter region often holding the remains of several hundred individuals.

Allerød Interstadial a warm period occurring during the final stages of the last (WEICHSEL) GLACIATION in Europe and starting at *c.*11 800 BP.

alluvial fan a depositional LANDFORM, usually located along valley margins and mountain fronts where tributary streams enter larger valleys or broad lowlands. It is created by the accumulation of ALLUVIUM sedimented as channelized flow becomes unconfined, velocity and depth of flow decrease as waters spread laterally and channels shift position. Fans were, and still are today, prime locations for settlement because they provide a well-drained landscape position in otherwise relatively poorly drained valleys, and they are situated so that upland and FLOODPLAIN resources are both easily accessible.

ALLUVIUM

Archaeological remains tend to be buried more or less intact in alluvial fans as their SEDIMENTS are deposited.

alluvium   a general term for SEDIMENT deposited by rivers, including material at the river bed, margins, and as overbank deposits, which is the primary sediment constituent in FLOODPLAIN, ALLUVIAL FAN, and estuarine depositional environments. The material tends to be organic-rich, producing fertile SOILS suitable for farming.

Almagro Basch, Martín (1911–84)   a Spanish archaeologist, best-known for his work on MEGALITHS, and on the dating and interpretation of Spanish prehistoric CAVE ART, and for his excavation and publication of the northeastern Spanish site of AMPURIAS (Emporion).

Almeria   a dry region of southeast Spain with an important sequence of later prehistoric remains, including the Middle Neolithic Almerian CULTURE, represented by villages such as EL GARCEL, the rich CHALCOLITHIC settlements and tombs such as LOS MILLARES, Gates and ALMIZARAQUE, and the fortified villages of the Argaric Early Bronze Age (see EL ARGAR).

Al Mina   a harbour settlement at the mouth of the River Orontes in Turkey, excavated by WOOLLEY in the 1930s. Exploration confined itself to the town and the associated warehouses. Ten levels (I–X) were identified, dating back to c.700 BC. The earliest (X–VII) contained a significant quantity of imported Greek pottery, especially from Euboea (see LEFKANDI). As a result the site has been interpreted by some as a Euboean settlement and has come to be regarded as one of the key sites for the channelling of eastern ideas and art to the Greek world (see ORIENTALIZING). Others maintain that the earliest levels are part of a PHOENICIAN settlement, and that the presence of Greek pottery merely reflects trading contacts with the Greek world. The next key period (VI–V) covers the 7th century BC. In the 5th century BC, the settlement was replanned with new warehouses. Some contained batches of Greek pottery, transport AMPHORAE and other items of trade. The site seems to have fallen out of use towards the end of the 4th century BC. See also ATCHANA.

Almizaraque   a CHALCOLITHIC settlement and nearby CHAMBERED TOMB in Almeria, Spain. The settlement had a defensive wall and ditch enclosing a number of oval houses with storage pits. Finds included an IVORY 'sandal', ALABASTER idols, decorated pottery and over 100 COPPER objects together with copper-working slag. The nearby PASSAGE GRAVE contained remains of some 50 skeletons, together with CALLAIS beads, V-perforated buttons, copper tools, and POTSHERDS with incised double 'eye' motifs.

Altai Mountains   a mountain range in western Siberia, Russia, and adjacent parts of Kazakhstan, important as a source of raw materials for early METALLURGY in Soviet Central Asia including both TIN and COPPER. Archaeological cultures with a presence in the Altai region and the neighbouring Minusinsk Basin include the Late Neolithic AFANASIEVO culture, the Bronze Age ANDRONOVO and KARASUK cultures, and the nomads who built the frozen tombs at PAZYRYK.

Altaic   a language family within the subdivision of Ural-Altaic including Turkic, Mongolian, Manchu (see MANCHURIA), Tungusic (see TUNGUS), and probably Korean and Japanese. The distribution of these languages in an arc across northern Eurasia argues for considerable continuity of population movement in the past, though the details of these phenomena are currently unknown.

Altamira   a cave in Santander Province, northern Spain, where DE SAUTUOLA discovered PALAEOLITHIC ART on the walls in 1879, though his claims for its antiquity were rejected by the archaeological estab lishment for 20 years. Best known for its ceiling of polychrome bison figures, Altamira contains a wealth of other paintings and engravings, including 'masks' and quadrilateral signs like those of EL CASTILLO. Multiple-line engravings, both on the walls and on PORTABLE ART, have been dated to 13 550 bc. The cave's art probably spans a period from the late SOLUTREAN until its blockage in the mid-MAGDALENIAN. Charcoal in three of the ceiling's bison has yielded radiocarbon dates of 12 380, 11 990 and 11 620 bc.

Altar de Sacrificios   a MAYA site in Guatemala on the western border of the Southern Lowlands. Data indicate the site was invaded during the 9th century AD by a non-CLASSIC Maya group from the Gulf Coast Low lands. Gordon Willey and Ledyard Smith of Harvard University excavated there from the late 1950s to the late 1960s. Evidence for con quest comes from analysis of FINE ORANGE POTTERY found at Altar de Sacrificios, SEIBAL and other sites. The designs on this pottery are distinct from those of the Classic Maya, but local clays, from the Usumacinta River drainage, were used in their manufacture. Such evidence of inva sion helped undermine the traditional view of the Classic Maya as a peaceful, non-combative civilization.

Altithermal   a climatic episode, dated approximately 7500–5500 BP, which created drier and warmer conditions throughout the world. In North America, it is thought by some archaeologists to have forced humans to abandon areas such as the Plains for higher regions.

altitude   the distance an object, land surface or water surface lies above a DATUM plane, usually taken as sea level. Altitude is one of the three dimensions that define the spatial location of artifacts.

Altmühlian   a Middle Palaeolithic industry of central Europe characterized by BLATTSPITZEN, sidescrapers (see SCRAPER) and RETOUCHED BLADES. The Altmühlian dates to the late Middle Palaeolithic, probably the middle of the last GLACIAL.

Alto Salaverry   a Late PRECERAMIC site in the Moche Valley of the north coast of Peru, at which both domestic and ceremonial architecture were excavated by Shelia and Thomas Pozorski. It marks the first appearance of a sunken circular structure, a form that became widely distributed in ceremonial sites of the INITIAL PERIOD.

Altyn-depe   A major site on the Kopet Dagh piedmont in southern Turkmenistan, Altyn contains deposits beginning with NAMAZGA I materials (later 6th millennium BC) and continuing to Namazga V times (late 3rd millennium). Initially a small settlement, the site was enclosed in a wall by the Namazga III period (late 4th millennium), and grew to a size of 25–30 ha during the 3rd millennium (Namazga IV and V periods). V.M. Masson's strategy of extensive horizontal exposure in Namazga V levels has allowed examination of an urban layout: city walls, ceremonial centre, elite quarters and other residential areas, city walls, cemeteries and intra-mural vaulted collec tive burials, and areas of craft production (potting and possible METALLURGY). A massive multi-staged platform has been compared with the MESOPOTAMIAN ZIGGURAT, and a number of artifacts with HARAPPAN materials. Altyn-depe represents the clearest example of

Bronze Age urbanism in Central Asia.

Al-'Ubaid   a site in the far south of MESOPOTAMIA excavated as part of the British work at UR in the early 20th century. 'Ubaid provided the initial material definition of the 'UBAID period (corresponding to the 'Ubaid 3–4 periods in the modern terminology). Although the site provided the first archaeological identification of this culture, the subsequent excavations at Ur and elsewhere provided the stratigraphic basis for its chronological divisions. The site was occupied from 'Ubaid 1 to EARLY DYNASTIC I times, and again during the Early Dynastic III. In addition to the 'Ubaid pottery, the site is best known for the Early Dynastic temple oval, an architectural type also found at KHAFADJE and AL HIBA.

Amapa   a site in Nayarit, Mexico, well known for its metal artifacts. From AD 250–700, Amapa was only a large village. After a period of abandonment, it was reoccupied from AD 900–1200. Metal was introduced to the site at about AD 900. Artifacts at the site suggest western Mexico was more integrated into the MESOAMERICAN culture at this time than previously.

Amarna Letters   Three hundred and seventy nine clay tablets (plus fragments) found in the so-called 'Record Office' at EL-AMARNA in Egypt during the 1880s. The tablets, written in CUNEIFORM script, form part of the diplomatic correspondence between the Egyptian Kings AMENHOTEP III, AKHENATEN, and TUTANKHAMEN, and their vassals and rival powers in the Levant.

Amarna Period   part of the 18th DYNASTY of Egypt during which AKHENATEN and his immediate successors ruled from EL-AMARNA and practised the worship of the god ATEN.

Ambrona   see TORRALBA.

Amekni   a site in the Algerian Sahara dated to 8700 BP and later, with early decorated ceramics but no domestic animals. Several human skeletons are described as Negroid.

Amen   a local god of the town of THEBES in UPPER EGYPT, becoming pre-eminent among the pantheon of Egyptian deities in the NEW KINGDOM as Amen-RE, patron god of the Egyptian Empire.

Amenemhat   see SENWOSRET.

Amenhotep or **Amenophis**   the name of four of the monarchs of Egypt's 18th DYNASTY (early NEW KINGDOM). The reign of Amenhotep III (c.1391–1353 BC) is regarded by many scholars as a 'golden age' of ancient Egypt. Amenhotep IV was later known as AKHENATEN.

Amenophis   see AMENHOTEP.

American Palaeo-Arctic Tradition   a broad TRADITION that includes several COMPLEXES or CULTURES of the North American Arctic and Subarctic dating to c.11 000–6500 bp. These complexes (e.g. DENALI COMPLEX are characterized by the common occurrence of MICROBLADES, BIFACES and BURINS. This tradition was defined by Anderson in 1968.

Amfreville helmet   an Iron Age helmet discovered in 1841 in an old stream bed of the River Seine, Eure, France. A fine example of CELTIC workmanship, the helmet is of bronze decorated with gold leaf and enamel. Dated on stylistic grounds to the 3rd century BC, it is related to Italian models but was probably made by a local North French craftsman.

amino acid racemization a biological dating method that utilizes postmortem changes in indigenous proteins in carbonate shells of molluscs and bones, to estimate the time since death. Protein traces in carbonate fossils consist of amino acids that exist in one of two configurations, referred to as L-isomers and D-isomers. In living organisms, amino acids are molecularly structured in the L-isomer configuration. Upon death, amino acids begin to convert to the D-isomer configuration, a conversion process referred to as racemization. From the zero point at death, D/L ratios begin to increase with time and can be used as relative age indices to construct a CHRONOSTRATIGRAPHY. However, ages are only locally applicable because racemization rates are influenced by the thermal history of the site from which they are collected. Site temperature also causes the effective time range of the dating method to vary with latitude. In tropical areas where reaction rates are relatively rapid, equilibrium is achieved after about 150 000–3000 000 years; in mid-latitudes after about 2 million years; in arctic sites, rates are unmeasurable within the HOLOCENE and equilibrium is not achieved even in 10 million years. Problems with the method include converting D/L ratios to ABSOLUTE AGES because of the difficulties in reconstructing site thermal history, modelling of the racemization reaction, and differing racemization rates among different species. With D/L ratios less than 0.3 and independent age control, the analysis is reliable to about ± 15% to 20%. Certainty decreases with ratios greater than 0.3.

Amino acid racemization is also used to reconstruct palaeotemperatures. If the age of a site is known by other independent methods, the palaeotemperature can be calculated, utilizing similar equations used to determine age, with an uncertainty of about ± 1 °C.

Amorites peoples west of MESOPOTAMIA who are generally believed to have been nomadic. The AKKADIAN designation *amurru*, equivalent to the SUMERIAN term *mar.tu*, specified a lifestyle contrasting with that of urban Mesopotamia. Pressure from Amorite groups was instrumental in the collapse of the UR III kingdom at the end of the 3rd millennium BC, and Amorite dynasties ruled many of the small kingdoms during the subsequent OLD BABYLONIAN PERIOD (*c.*2000–1600 BC), including that of HAMMURABI at BABYLON. Later, the term Amorite referred to a small kingdom in northern Syria, as well as to a language in that area.

amphitheatre a construction formed by two roughly semicircular bands of seating facing inwards towards a central arena. These arenas were used mainly for wild-animal shows and gladiatorial combats throughout the Roman Empire. See COLOSSEUM.

amphora a large jar, typically two-handled, used to store oil, wine or other such liquids.

Ampurias (*Gk* Emporion) a Greek trading port in northeast Spain founded from MARSEILLES in the 6th century BC. The initial settlement was located on an offshore islet. The cemeteries have yielded much imported Greek pottery. See ALMAGRO.

Amratian a phase of the PREDYNASTIC sequence of UPPER EGYPT, also known as NAQADA I, and dated to *c.*4500–4000 BC. The Amratian culture, which seems to have more affinities with the preceding BADARIAN than the following GERZEAN, displayed skill in stone-working, especially in flint, and in the production of painted pottery.

Amri   a prehistoric site in the southern Sind in Pakistan, first explored by Majumdar in the 1920s and then excavated by J-M. Casal in the 1950s, and containing Early HARAPPAN as well as Harappan and post-Harappan levels. The Early Harappan materials provide the definition of the Amri culture of the later 4th millennium BC, whose painted CERAMICS are similar to materials in the Indo-Iranian borderlands to the north. The overlying levels contain increasing amounts of Mature Harappan pottery until the site was clearly contained within the Harappan tradition, followed by Late Harappan materials similar to those at JHUKAR. The main significance of Amri is its contribution to understanding the formation of the Harappan civilization.

AMS   see ACCELERATOR MASS SPECTROMETRY.

Amsadong   a village site of the Korean CHULMUN culture near Seoul, first excavated in 1968 and again in the mid 1970s by a joint university team. Several of the 12 excavated pithouses are now reconstructed as a historical park. Net weights and sinkers indicate river fishing subsistence; QUERNS show plant utilization, but there was no evidence for agriculture despite the site's Neolithic status. It is the type-site of Classic Chulmun pottery and dates to 4490–1510 BC.

Amudian   a brief Palaeolithic BLADE-producing INDUSTRY dating to the Last INTERGLACIAL and found at sites close to the Mediterranean coast such as TABUN, JABRUD, ADLUN and the HAUA FTEAH cave. The Amudian, previously termed the pre-AURIGNACIAN, was named by GARROD after the *Wadi Amud* in Israel, and occurs between the ACHEULIAN and the Middle Palaeolithic. Amud, excavated more recently by M. Suzuki, has yielded the remains of five NEANDERTHALERS. ESR dates point to occupation between 40 000 and 50 000 BP.

'Amuq   a plain in Southern Anatolia, on the Syrian border, northwest of the Orontes River, where soundings were made on multiple sites (Tell Judeideh, Tell Kurdu, Catal Huyuk, Tell Tayinat and several others) by a University of Chicago team. The combined results of these soundings produce a CULTURE HISTORY divided into 22 phases ('Amuq A–V) that covers the 8000 years between the beginning of the ceramic Neolithic and the present. The sequence is a standard for the relative chronology of northwestern Syria and southeastern Anatolia, and reflects some significant interregional ceramic relationships in western Asian prehistory (e.g. HALAF painted pottery in 'Amuq C–D, 'UBAID painted pottery in 'Amuq D–E, Late URUK/ JEMDET NASR in 'Amuq (F–G), KURA-ARAXES/Khirbet Kerak BURNISHED pottery in 'Amuq H–I).

Amurian   a variant of HOMO *sapiens* who inhabited Northeast Asia at the end of the PLEISTOCENE, and who may be the ancestors of the contemporary NATIVE AMERICAN. The present-day AINU of Japan are a remnant Asiatic population of this stock.

Amvrosievka   an Upper Palaeolithic open-air site in southern Ukraine, comprising a massive bed of steppe bison bones (at least 983 individuals) and nearby artifact clusters. The artifacts include MICROBLADES, laterally-grooved bone points, and simple ornaments. Recent studies, building on the earlier excavations of Pidoplichko and BORISKOVSKIJ in 1948–50, have produced a RADIOCARBON date of

15 250 bp. Amvrosievka, along with several other sites in the south Russian Plain such as BOL'SHAYA AKKARZHA and Zolotovka I (Lower Don River), may reflect a regional Upper Palaeolithic practice of killing bison herds, like HOLOCENE tribes of the North American Plains.

amygdaloid, *adj.* almond-shaped. A morphological term used by BORDES to refer to an elongated OVATE or cordiform BIFACE.

An the supreme SUMERIAN god, the provider of life and fertility, and the source of authority; the AKKADIAN equivalent was *Anu.* An literally meant 'sky'. In the hierarchical divine world, An was replaced by other figures (ENLIL, MARDUK), but always remained behind the scenes as the ultimate source of authority. An has a close identification with the city of WARKA.

'Anaeho'omalu a site on the main island of Hawaii, initially in about the 10th century AD an intermittent fishing camp, but by late prehistoric times the site of a permanent fishing settlement centred on a large fishpond. The area also has several lava-tube caves used for burial, and one of the largest PETROGLYPH fields in the Hawaiian Islands, with over 9000 figures.

anaerobic, *adj.* of an environmental state in which free molecular oxygen is not available owing to depletion by SOIL bacteria. This condition is attained in waterlogged or relatively deeply buried situations, leading to the preservation of plant, animal and human remains, and of artifacts fashioned from these materials. Compare AEROBIC.

analogy the argument that if two objects or phenomena are similar in some attributes, they should be similar in others.

Ananino culture an Iron Age culture of the mid 1st millennium BC in the middle Volga basin, Russia. The Ananino culture had close connections with the SCYTHIANS, who occupied the territory to the south.

Anapchi a 7th century AD garden pond in the palace site of the United SILLA Kingdom in Kyongju City, Korea. Excavations in 1975 recovered over 15 000 items including dug-out boats, Buddhist images, pottery and metal vessels, inscribed wooden tablets (see MOKKAN), wooden architectural components, and roof and floor tiles buried in the pond mud. Four palace pavilions have been reconstructed around the relandscaped pond to form a historical park.

Anasazi a Navajo word meaning 'Enemy Ancestors' that was applied by A.V. KIDDER in 1936 to the major prehistoric TRADITION of the northern part of the American Southwest. The Anasazi are believed to be the ancestors of some contemporary PUEBLO Indians. The tradition is broken into eight sequential STAGES. Basketmaker I is a hypothetical, late ARCHAIC pre-agricultural stage; Basketmaker II (AD 1–450) is defined by the appearance of agriculture; and Basketmaker III (AD 450–750) by the appearance of pottery, PITHOUSES, and the BOW-AND-ARROW; the Pueblo I–V stages are characterized by an increasingly complex SUBSISTENCE technology based on the intensive farming of maize, beans and squash, the development of large, multi-room dwellings and sophisticated and regionally diverse pottery techniques and styles. The specific dates are: Pueblo I – AD 750–900; Pueblo II – AD 900–1150; Pueblo III – AD 1150–1300; Pueblo IV – AD 1300–1600; Pueblo V – AD 1600–present. The Anasazi tradition is also broken into regional variants: Chacoan; MESA VERDE; and KAYENTA.

ANATHYROSIS

See CHACO CANYON, PUEBLO BONITO.

anathyrosis a Greek architectural technique, perhaps originating in Egypt, used to match two adjoining blocks or column–drums. Instead of the two touching along a complete face, the centre was hollowed out, thus leaving a point of contact only along the edges.

Anau a TELL site in Turkmenia, 12 km east of Ash-khabad. The work of R. Pumpelly in 1904 on this site produced the first culture historical sequence (late Neolithic to Iron Age) for Central Asia, and at the same time brought an interdisciplinary approach to archaeological investigation (importance of changing climate, interest in development of food production in arid environments, analysis of metals and of fauna) that was not repeated in western Asia until after the Second World War. The cultural sequence is now thoroughly revised and refined, and the breadth of approach was without immediate issue, leaving the Anau excavation largely a historical curiosity. The painted pottery of Anau IA (early 6th millennium BC) fills the gap between the DJEITUN culture and the NAMAZGA sequence (now best seen at sites like Chakmaklik-depe in the Tedjen drainage to the east along the Kopet Dagh mountain range).

Anbangbang a large sandstone ROCKSHELTER in western ARNHEM LAND, North Australia. The earliest levels are undated but are probably PLEISTOCENE. From about 6000 bp the intensity of occupation increased. The uppermost unit, spanning the last 1000 years, is extraordinarily rich in well-preserved organic material.

Andernach see GÖNNERSDORF.

Andersson, Johan Gunnar (1874–1960) a Swedish geologist who was affiliated with the Geological Survey of China as a mining adviser in 1914–25. He is credited with the first discoveries of Neolithic painted pottery sites and of Palaeolithic HOMO *erectus* finds at ZHOUKOUDIAN.

andesite line a line dividing the Pacific region along the point of contact between the Asiatic and Pacific plates through western POLYNESIA. West of the line are varied continental rocks, including andesitic basalts. East of it are coral atolls and volcanic islands of olivine basalts and other basic rocks.

Andronovo culture a Bronze Age culture of western Siberia, Russia, and adjacent parts of Kazakhstan, of considerable duration from before 1500 BC to about 800 BC. Both settlement and burial sites are known, with extensive traces of METALLURGY using the rich mineral resources of this region. A variety of regional groups of the Andronovo culture have been distinguished. Andronovo settlements consist of up to 10 semi-subterranean houses of log-cabin construction, ranging in size from 20 × 30 m to 30 × 60 m. The Andronovo culture is succeeded by the KARASUK culture.

Aneityum a high volcanic island in Vanuatu, Melanesia, investigated by Matthew Spriggs. More than 800 sites document the development of intensive root-crop (*taro*) agriculture from dryland plots 1000 years ago to the construction of large-scale irrigation systems during the last 400 years.

Anghelu Ruju a cemetery in Sardinia of 35 rock-cut CHAMBERED TOMBS of the 3rd millennium BC, first investigated by Taramelli in 1903. They consist of a passage or shaft leading to a chamber which can be round, oval, rectangular or irregular; subsidiary chambers lead off the main chamber. The chamber walls are decorated with carvings of animal horns and BUCRANIA. Grave goods include marble and ALABASTER bracelets, copper tools and weapons, and small female figurines of local stone.

Angkor   the area of the capital of the KHMER state of KAMBUJA, said to have been formed early in the 9th century AD from a group of small neighbouring states. The term is used frequently to refer to the phase of the state's history before the 14th century, when it dominated Cambodia, most of Thailand, southern Laos and south Vietnam. The best known of the hundreds of temples and structures surviving from this period are: Preah Ko and Bakheng (9th–early 10th century), Koh Ker, Pre Rup, Banteay Srei, Khleang and Phimeanakas (10th century), Ta Keo, Baphuon and Phimai (11th century), Wat Phu, *Angkor Wat*, Banteay Samre and Preah Khan (late 11th–12th century), Ta Prohm, Angkor Thom and Bayon (13th century); many of these are famous for their elaborate structure and fine reliefs.

Angles-sur-l'Anglin   a MAGDALENIAN ROCKSHELTER known as the 'Roc aux Sorciers', in the Vienne region of France, where excavations by D. GARROD and S. de Saint-Mathurin led to the discovery in 1952 that the backwall and collapsed ceiling had been sculptured and painted. The bas-reliefs include bison, horses, ibex and four life-size human females from stomach to knee. The occupation layers, containing pigments, grinders, stone picks and PORTABLE ART objects, have been dated by RADIOCARBON to 14 160 bp.

Anglian   see ELSTERIAN.

Anglo-Saxons   the dominant inhabitants of Britain before the Norman conquest. Angles and Saxons were Germanic peoples of Northern Europe who, in the 5th and 6th centuries AD, migrated to the eastern part of what is now England after the end of Roman rule there. This land eventually comprised a series of kingdoms including Northumbria (see YEAVERING), Mercia and Wessex, which later unified into 'England', with its capital at Winchester, in Wessex. The early Saxon period saw the conversion of England to Christianity in the 7th century, which ended the practice of burying weapons and other objects as grave-goods (see SUTTON HOO) with urn cremations. The late Saxon period saw the VIKING invasions of the 9th century (see JORVIK), and ended with the Norman conquest of 1066.

ankh   an Egyptian HIEROGLYPHIC sign, appearing as a 'T' with a loop whose ends join the cross-bar close to the top of the upright stroke. The Egyptian word 'ankh' broadly speaking means 'life', and the sign often appears in Egyptian art with that symbolic connotation.

ankh

23

annealing   a process used in METALLURGY to reduce the brittleness caused by hammering and other working of metals, especially in the case of copper, silver and gold. It involves heating and slowly cooling the metal to increase its ductility. In Andean South America the technique was used especially in the case of copper–silver alloys by the MOCHE culture.

Anshan   see ELAM, MALYAN.

anta   1. a short stub-wall found at the end of, and at right angles to, the long walls of a CLASSICAL temple CELLA. Columns placed between these stub-walls are described as being *in antis*.
2. a Portuguese term for CHAMBERED TOMB. The earliest, in the Alto Alemtejo region of inland central Portugal, have mid 5th millennium THERMOLUMINESCENCE dates: Anta 1 at Poço da Gateira 4510 BC; Anta 2 at Gorginos 4440 BC.

antefix   a CLASSICAL decorative element concealing the outermost end of a tile. They can be made of marble or clay, and show a range of subjects such as a simple PALMETTE, a GORGONEION or a lion's head. They may be placed above the SIMA.

Antequera   an important group of CHAMBERED TOMBS, in Málaga, Spain, each set in a natural hill. Most famous are: a) Cueva de Romeral: a long passage leads to two interconnected CORBEL-VAULTED chambers, one behind the other, in a mound 90 m across. The corbelled vaults are closed at the top by a single MEGALITHIC slab. The main chamber has plastered walls and floor, and measures 5 m in diameter by almost 4 m high.
b) Cueva de la Menga: a bottle-shaped chamber with five huge capstones (largest weighs about 180 tonnes), reached by a short entrance passage.
The tombs probably date to the 4th millennium BC, but no gravegoods are known.

anthracology   the study of human interactions with the plant environment through microscopic identification and statistical treatment of wood charcoal from archaeological sites.

anthropogenic soil   a SOIL that physically, morphologically or chemically has been influenced by human activity. This may include the concentration of phosphorus, organic matter, debris and artifacts, and the physical mixing of differing soil and SEDIMENT components through human activities such as cultivation, deforestation or construction activities.

anthropomorph   1. an object or picture resembling a human form.
2. in prehistoric art, a figure providing visual information recognized by contemporary humans as resembling the human form (*Gk anthropos* man, *morphos* shape, form).

anthropomorphic, *adj.*   1. treating a deity as having a human form or character.
2. attributing human motivation, characteristics or behaviour to animals, inanimate objects or natural phenomena.
3. in ROCK ART, attributing human form to the depiction of a deity.

anthropomorphism   the attribution of human form or character to a deity, or to non-human objects.

anthropomorphous, *adj.*   1. having or suggesting human form and appearance.
2. in prehistoric art, providing visual information recognized by con-

temporary humans as resembling human form.

Antonine Wall the most northerly of the permanent Roman frontiers in Britain which served to secure the Scottish lowlands. It was established during the reign of the emperor Antoninus Pius probably after AD 143. The line of the wall ran from the Firth of Forth in the east to the Clyde in the west and seems to have been constructed by legionaries. The wall was made of turf on a cobbled foundation, and it was protected to the north by a ditch. There were 19 forts along its length in addition to three fortlets. It was probably abandoned in the 150s, and briefly reoccupied c.163.

Anubis an Egyptian deity depicted as a jackal or jackal-headed man. Anubis was the god associated with cemeteries and MUMMIFICATION.

Anyang [An-yang] a Late SHANG site near Anyang City, China, dating to the 13th century BC. Excavated between 1928 and 1937 by LI CHI, the site consists of an oval unwalled area, c.3.75 km × 9.75 km, encompassing: a royal cemetery at XIBEIGANG consisting of 11 SHAFT TOMBS; nearly 2000 small graves and the FU HAO tomb; a temple complex at XIAOTUN of several worship halls and residential buildings; clusters of aristocratic houses; workshops for bronze casting; stone, JADE, bone and shell workshops; and servants' quarters. Some interpret these remains as the Late Shang capital, others as a mortuary complex. The Anyang bronze style with prominent TAOTIE designs suggests preoccupations with death and transformation in ancestor worship rituals, and its ORACLE BONES provide information on the social organization of the Shang state.

Anyathian, *adj.* relating to a putative Lower Palaeolithic INDUSTRY of Upper Burma; original collections are too small and archaeological contexts too vague for reliable dating or assessment.

Anza an Early Neolithic site in Yugoslavian Macedonia (sometimes referred to in the literature as Anzabegovo). The earliest levels at Anza belong to the STARČEVO culture, while the uppermost are of the VINČA culture. Anza lies in a basin called 'Ovče Polje' ('sheep basin') and sheep/goat are the main component of the large faunal assemblage. Early houses resemble those of Bulgarian and Greek sites like KARANOVO and NEA NIKOMEDEIA, rectangular structures with mud-plastered post walls, while later structures have WATTLE-AND-DAUB construction.

Apennine culture a Bronze Age culture of peninsular Italy, originally defined by its dark-BURNISHED pottery with carefully-incised designs. Puglisi argued in 1959 for an economy based on pastoralism, from the high location of many of the sites and the discovery of perforated pottery 'milk boilers', but excavations at the Apennine village of Luni, with long houses cut into the soft rock, have demonstrated mixed farming. Pottery studies support a subdivision into three phases: Apennine, Subapennine and Protovillanovan (see VILLANOVAN), beginning around 1500 BC. West of the Alps the Apennine culture is preceded by a Protoapennine phase (2000–1500 BC), best represented at the site of Tufariello.

Aphaia temple see AEGINA.

Aphrodisias a 500 ha CLASSICAL city on a tributary of the Meander River, southwest Turkey, excavated by ERIM. Most of the extant remains belong to the Roman period and include the AGORA, the ODEUM, the temple of Aphrodite and baths. Many of these public buildings were highly decorated with free-standing statuary which has survived in sufficient quantities to allow study of the Aphrodisian 'school'. The settlement also has a long pre-Classical history: soundings in two of the mounds within the city (the 'AKROPOLIS' and 'Pekmez' mounds) revealed traces of a Late Neolithic occupation (with ceramic parallels to HACILAR VII) and then a sequence of Late CHALCOLITHIC to Late Bronze Age materials that is strongly similar to that at BEYCESULTAN.

Apis   an Egyptian god worshipped at MEMPHIS in the form of a living bull, chosen after the death of its predecessor by virtue of a number of identifying marks. Apis-bulls were interred in the SERAPEUM.

Apis Rock   see NASERA.

apodyterium   the changing-room of a Roman bath-house. Smaller examples may be equipped with niches for storing clothes. See THERMAE.

Apollo 11   a cave in the Huns Mountains of southern Namibia, with MIDDLE and LATER STONE AGE remains, excavated by W.E. Wendt and named after the 1969 moon landing. Of particular interest are several small rock slabs painted with animal figures, which are the oldest dated rock art in Africa, RADIOCARBON dated to 27 500 bp.

apsidal, *adj.*   (of a structure) having one end rounded.

Apulia (*mod.* Puglia)   an area of southeastern Italy. Although containing no Greek colonies, it was strongly influenced by neighbouring Greek cities. In the 5th and 4th centuries BC it produced figure-decorated pottery (see APULIAN POTTERY, GNATHIAN WARE, SOUTH ITALIAN POTTERY).

Apulian pottery   an important type of SOUTH ITALIAN POTTERY, mostly decorated in the RED-FIGURED technique. Production seems to have started in the late 5th century BC and may have been influenced by ATHENIAN POTTERY. One of the early centres seems to have been at TARENTUM. In the middle of the 4th century the scenes became more ornate with additional figures inserted in the field and an increased use of added colours. Plain wares were also produced alongside (see GNATHIAN WARE).

Aqab, Tell   a small prehistoric site in the Khabur region of Syria, just upstream from CHAGAR BAZAR, that provides an unbroken sequence from the Early HALAF into the 'UBAID periods. In addition to defining the presence of Early Halaf occupation, similar to that of ARPACHIYAH to the east, the excavations of T. Davidson and T. Watkins also identified a gradual transition from Halaf to 'Ubaid ceramic styles, where 'Ubaid elements are added to a modified Halaf pottery assemblage until it is fully 'Ubaid in character. Similar to the pottery in the basal levels at Tepe GAWRA, such transitional assemblages can now be identified elsewhere in western Syria and southeastern Turkey. The transitional phase shows that interpretations of the Northern 'Ubaid as population movements and replacements cannot be upheld.

Aqar Quf   the site of the KASSITE city of Dur-Kurigalzu in northern BABYLONIA (near Baghdad, central Iraq). T. Baqir's excavations in the 1940s provided the widest exposure of Kassite period architecture (in this case, dated roughly 1400–1150 BC) yet available. The Iraqi excavation concentrated on the ZIGGURAT and a palace complex, about a kilometre apart. Aqar Quf's ziggurat is one of the best known. The palace complex, built and rebuilt four times, contained wall paintings (preserved only in its last phase), and also provided examples of Kassite period art (e.g. a famous lion head in clay), a small archive, and an ox-hide INGOT of copper belonging to the Aegean world, among other objects. Dur-Kurigalzu is poorly known, apart from these two excavated areas, but seems to have been a substantial settlement, approaching 200 ha in size.

'Aqualithic'   an informal term denoting an early ceramic cultural complex adapted to riverine and lacustrine environments during the North African wet phase between about 10 000 and 8000 BP. The cultural material includes bone HARPOONS, which have a wide distribution from the confluence of the Blue and White Niles to the central Sahara and northern Kenya (see ARAOUANE, TAGALAGAL, TAMAYA MELLET).

aqueduct   a channel for carrying water, often over considerable distances. Aqueducts became an important feature of Roman urban life, providing water for THERMAE and fountains. One of the most impressive surviving examples is the PONT DU GARD. ROME itself was served by numerous aqueducts, the earliest being the Aquae Appia constructed in 312 BC.

Arad   a Palestinian site excavated from 1962–83 by AHARONI and by Amiran. The 'lower city' of the EARLY BRONZE AGE is a substantial settlement of 9 ha, with well-planned fortifications. The excavations at Arad have produced an important corpus of Early Bronze Age pottery, including imports, which has helped to develop chronological links between CANAANITE ceramics and those of ARCHAIC Egypt. The 'upper city' (TELL Arad proper), on a natural hill, is the site of six successive ISRAELITE citadels and includes a sanctuary of the 9th century BC containing a MASSEBAH.

Aramaean   1. a linguistic designation for a west Semitic language.
2. a series of small Iron Age (i.e. after 1200 BC) POLITIES in Syria up to the ASSYRIAN border, which were eventually absorbed into the Assyrian empire. More nomadic and tribally organized Aramaean groups pushed through Assyria and BABYLONIA at the end of the 2nd and beginning of the 1st millennium BC to settle between the Tigris and the Zagros Mountains. The Aramaic language used an alphabetic script, and was increasingly adopted for administrative purposes by the Assyrian, Babylonian and ACHAEMENID empires during the 1st millennium BC. This process introduced the script to peripheral zones of empire, where it was applied to local languages (seen, for example, in the modern Armenian and Georgian alphabets).

Arambourg, Camille (1885–1969)   a French geologist with wide-ranging interests in North African palaeontology and archaeology, whose excavations include the important sites of AIN HANECH and TAMAR HAT in Algeria.

Araouane   a basin of former lakes in western Mali, known particularly for information on lacustrine adaptations in the central Sahara between 9000 and 8000 years ago.

Ara Pacis   a monumental altar by the Tiber in the Campus Martius at ROME dedicated by the Senate on 30 January 9 BC. The altar was contained within a walled precinct which was decorated with a continuous frieze, part of which showed the procession to the altar.

Many scholars have sought to identify the emperor Augustus and members of his family among those present. The earliest remains were found in 1568, but the most extensive exploration of the site leading to a reconstruction of the monument was conducted under Mussolini in 1937–38.

Arapi   the site of a Neolithic–Early Bronze Age settlement mound in Thessaly, Greece, excavated by Milojcic in 1955. The site was first occupied in the ACERAMIC NEOLITHIC and defines the Late Neolithic Arapi culture which is characterized by polychrome decorated pottery.

Aratta   a placename in one of the SUMERIAN epics concerning Enmerkar, an EARLY DYNASTIC ruler of WARKA (Uruk), which deals with an episode of contact with the lord of Aratta, a place to the east, perhaps in eastern Iran. Enmerkar wished to build a temple, for which he required raw materials unavailable in southern MESOPOTAMIA. The epic is frequently cited in connection with long-distance trade in Mesopotamia during the 3rd millennium BC.

Araya   the type-site in Niigata Prefecture, Japan, for a Palaeolithic BURIN technology. The site, dating to 13 200 bp, yielded WEDGE-SHAPED CORES, MICROBLADES and BURIN SPALLS, suggesting the manufacture of composite tools on site. Araya-type burins are known from Mongolia through northern Japan to Alaska.

archaeological geology   the application of geological techniques and methods to the solution of archaeological problems. It differs from GEOARCHAEOLOGY in that the latter is essentially a subfield of archaeology whose explicit focus is the physical CONTEXT of archaeological deposits.

archaeology   the study of the past through the systematic recovery and analysis of MATERIAL CULTURE. The primary aims of the discipline are to recover, describe and classify this material, to describe the form and behaviour of past societies, and finally to understand the reasons for this behaviour. In the Old World the term tends to refer to the body of techniques and theories used in achieving these goals, whereas in the New World archaeology refers also to the subject matter. Archaeology is truly an interdisciplinary subject, and has borrowed many of its major theoretical and methodological concepts and approaches from history and anthropology.

archaeomagnetic dating   a dating method based on the PALAEOMAGNETISM of archaeological materials, such as hearths and stationary kilns. Heating above the Curie point, about 650 °C for haematite, destroys any previous alignment of magnetic particles and as the material cools they realign in accordance with the Earth's magnetic field at that time. Local and regional chronologies are built up by taking series of measurements and can be independently dated.

archaeometry   the use of techniques derived from the hard sciences in the interpretation and analysis of archaeological data.

archaeozoology or **zooarchaeology**   a branch of archaeology involving the analysis of archaeologically-recovered animal remains for information such as physiology, ecology, etc.; for the interpretation of these remains in their association with artifacts and people; and for data on SUBSISTENCE, dietary and butchering patterns, animal domestication and PALAEOENVIRONMENT.

Archaic   (*North American archaeology*) cultures that have a wide-spectrum HUNTING AND GATHERING base, ground stone tools, and increasing sedentism. In many parts of the continent it is used erroneously to refer to the chronological period that follows the PALAEOINDIAN period, from approximately 7000 BP to the time of Christ.

archaic, *adj.* **1.** relating to an early phase of art or a culture. **2.** in Egyptian art, relating to the first two DYNASTIES, *c.*3168–2705 BC. **3.** in Greek art, relating to the period of the emerging city–states from the mid 8th century BC. The traditional end of the period is the Persian attack on Greece in 480 BC although there is a possibility that the archaic style continued for some time after this event. In sculpture the 'archaic smile' refers to the characteristic frozen smile (see KORE and KOUROS).

Archaic Period an era of Egyptian history comprising the 1st and 2nd DYNASTIES (*c.*3000–2649 BC) and Egypt's earliest period as a unified state. The Archaic Period (with the addition of the 3rd dynasty) is sometimes referred to as the *Early Dynastic Period.*

archaistic, *adj.* **1.** (of an artistic style) attempting to evoke an earlier period. **2.** in Greek art (of a phase of HELLENISTIC art, in particular sculpture) seeming to recall ARCHAIC art of the late 6th century BC.

Archanes or **Arkhanes** a major MINOAN centre on the island of Crete. At Turkogeitonia there is a 16th century BC structure which is palatial in character if not in scale. Phourni is an extensive cemetery complex which was in use throughout the Minoan period. Splendid offerings of gold, IVORY and marble have been discovered. Finally, at Anemospilia, Sakellarakis has excavated a shrine which was destroyed, apparently by an earthquake, *c.*1700 BC. A youth, whose skeleton was found in the shrine, is thought to have been a propitiatory sacrifice.

Archéodrome de Beaune a museum of reconstructed buildings and EXPERIMENTAL ARCHAEOLOGY designed for the general public. It was founded in 1978 at a service station on the A6 motorway at Beaune, Côte d'Or, France. Reconstructions include a Palaeolithic encampment based on PINCEVENT, a Neolithic house from Charmoy, and the Roman siege works constructed by Caesar at ALÉSIA.

architrave a horizontal load-bearing block which spans the space between two columns on a CLASSICAL colonnade. See ENTABLATURE.

Arctic Small-Tool Tradition a prehistoric TRADITION (4200–2100 BP) that stretched through the high Arctic, from the Bering Strait in the west to Greenland in the east. It may have originated in the preceding AMERICAN PALAEO-ARCTIC Tradition. Tool assemblages are dominated by uniformly-shaped SCRAPERS and BLADE tools, with some HARPOON heads found in sites in the eastern part of the tradition's distribution. Its economy was based on hunting and fishing.

Arcy-sur-Cure a complex of nine caves near Avalon, northern France, excavated primarily by LEROI-GOURHAN. The best-known site, the Grotte du Renne, has yielded 14 Middle and Upper Palaeolithic levels, including a series of industries apparently transitional between Middle (MOUSTERIAN) and Upper (CHÂTELPERRONIAN) Palaeolithic technology. There is PARIETAL ART in the Grotte du Cheval (engravings) and Grande Grotte (paintings), both dominated by MAMMOTHS.

The Arcy INTERSTADIAL is the name given to a mild climatic phase during the final GLACIATION of Europe (*c.*31 000 BP).

ard   a simple form of plough used to cut a furrow through the soil without turning it over. As a result, it was usually necessary to plough at right angles to the initial direction of ploughing to stir the soil adequately. The earliest ards are known from Near Eastern representations of the 4th millennium BC and from preserved finds in Europe from the 3rd millennium BC. Parallel furrows in subsoil identified as ard marks have been noted at several sites of the 2nd and 3rd millennia BC, including GWITHIAN in Britain and SARNOWO in Poland.

Arene Candide   a large limestone cave on the coast of Liguria, Italy. Deep soundings revealed a rich EPIGRAVETTIAN OCHRE burial with flint knife, BÁTONS DE COMMANDEMENT and a cap decorated with hundreds of seashells. Further ochre burials were found in EPIPALAEOLITHIC levels dated *c.*8400 BC. The cave is also famous for its important stratified sequence of later deposits which provided the key to the Neolithic sequence of Northern Italy, from Early Neolithic IMPRESSED WARE to Middle Neolithic BOCCA QUADRATA and Late Neolithic LAGOZZA.

Argissa   the site of a prehistoric settlement mound in Thessaly, Greece, which was excavated by Milojcic in 1956–58. First occupied in the Palaeolithic period and then more or less continuously throughout the Neolithic and Bronze Age, Argissa has been a key site in reconstructing the Thessalian cultural sequence.

Argos   a site in the Argolid, Greece. The prehistoric settlement was on the Aspis hill and appears to have been extensive in the Middle HELLADIO period but this was not a major MYCENAEAN site. Rich GEO-METRIC graves testify to the rise of Argos as the most powerful city in the Argolid, but in the Peloponnese as a whole Argos was ultimately overshadowed by SPARTA and CORINTH. The most impressive archaeological remains are the HELLENISTIC theatre and the Roman baths. The city's principal sanctuary was the Heraion, north-east of Argos, which is also the site of the Mycenaean settlement and cemetery of Prosymna.

Arikamedu   a port town of the first centuries AD, just south of Pondicherry on the Coromandel Coast in northeastern Tamil Nadu, southern India, which displays evidence of trade with the Roman world. The site, much of which has been eroded away, has been excavated by a number of different archaeologists, including M. WHEELER and J-M. Casal in the 1940s. This work indicated the existence of a late 1st millennium BC settlement containing pottery similar to that of the MEGALITHIC GRAVE complex of south India. Over these levels are large brick buildings and other installations, among which occur sherds of ARRETINE WARE, AMPHORAE, and Roman glass, and other Mediterranean products; this occupation dates to the first few centuries AD. Although no Roman coins were found in these excavations, hoards of 1st–2nd century AD coins are relatively common in southern India. Arikamedu directly illustrates passages in CLASSICAL literature that speak of Roman trade with India.

Ariuşd or **Erosd**   a painted pottery variant in Transylvania of the CUCUTENI-TRIPOLYE culture. Red or orange pottery is painted with elaborate rectilinear and curvilinear patterns in black and white. The site of Ariuşd, a TELL in Transylvania, with seven occupation levels, provided evidence of craft activity, specifically a workshop for pottery manufacture.

Arka an Upper Palaeolithic cave-site located along the Hernád River in northeast Hungary. Artifacts and occasional faunal remains (reindeer, horse and bison) are buried in deposits of LOAM dated to 18 600–17 050 bp. The artifacts include endscrapers (see SCRAPER), BURINS and RETOUCHED BLADES, and are assigned to the GRAVETTIAN. Arka was excavated by VÉRTES in 1960–61.

Arkhanes see ARCHANES.

Arkin the location in LOWER NUBIA of a number of Palaeolithic sites. Arkin 8 is a Late ACHEULIAN campsite with traces of dwellings, while Arkin 5 produced clusters of MOUSTERIAN artifacts.

Arlit a TENERIAN site on the west side of the Air Mountains in Niger, dated to about 5500 BP.

Arnhem Land a region of the Northern Territory of Australia, with a remarkably complete regional sequence which may extend back more than 50 000 years at MALAKUNANJA 2. The region is rich in ROCK ART and it is likely that this too extends back into the PLEISTOCENE. Earlier paintings, in a dynamic style, depict land animals, including some extinct species, and MIMI FIGURES, often with artifacts that were not part of the local tool-kit at European contact. Later X-RAY paintings include depictions of estuarine species. See also ANBANGBANG, LINDNER SITE, NAUWALABILA 1, MALANGANGERR.

Arpachiyah a tiny site near the Tigris in the area of NINEVEH in Iraq. Max MALLOWAN's excavation here in the 1930s revealed a 10-phase architectural sequence of 'UBAID levels (TT1–4) over HALAF levels (TT10–6), with an intermediate transitional phase. The architecture of the Halaf settlements focused on the typical Halafian THOLOS, the first examples of this form to be reported. Mallowan also found pre-TT 10 materials outside his principal sounding, and I. Hijara's investigation in 1976 revealed another six levels containing rectilinear architecture. Mallowan's results provided the basis for dividing Halaf pottery into the three phases still commonly applied to Halaf chronological development (Early: pre-TT 10, Middle: TT 10–7, and Late: TT 6).

Arras an Iron Age BARROW cemetery, type-site of the Arras CULTURE which is restricted to eastern Yorkshire, England, and is known almost exclusively from its burials. The rectangular barrows have a central burial pit with inhumation, often accompanied by weapons. A few contain cart burials, notably three at Arras itself, and others discovered in the 1980s at Wetwang, Garton Station and Kirkburn. The cart burials and barrow form can be paralleled in the Champagne area of northeast France, for example in SOMME-BIONNE, and some have argued that the Arras culture represents immigration or invasion by warriors from that region. The earliest Arras culture graves may belong to the 4th century BC, but the cemeteries appear to have continued in use until the 1st century BC.

Arretine ware a popular type of Roman red-glossed pottery initially produced at Arezzo in Italy especially in the 1st century BC and the 1st century AD. It had a wide distribution in these centuries but it was replaced by other regional red-glossed fabrics. A study of stamps has provided information about the number of workshops. See also TERRA SIGILLATA.

Arslantepe   a site on the Malatya plain in the upper Euphrates drainage (eastern Anatolia) that was occupied from CHALCOLITHIC to late Roman times. The best-known monuments of the site belong to the Syro-Hittite world (very early 1st millennium BC) and include a fortification wall entered through a 'Lion gate' in the tradition of HITTITE and MYCENAEAN architecture; just as important, however, are the far earlier settlements that were interacting with MESOPOTAMIA during the Late URUK period (mid 4th millennium BC). Excavations began here with L. Delaporte's work in the 1930s and continued with that of C. Schaeffer in the 1940s, focused on the Bronze Age and Iron Age occupations. Since the early 1960s an Italian team has conducted more methodical work on the earlier levels. Apart from the Syro-Hittite remains, the site's most important contribution lies in the Early Bronze Age period VIA of the Italian sequence. These levels reveal a Late Uruk element (e.g. BEVELLED RIM BOWLS) in the otherwise local ceramics, and a complex of buildings which contain BULLAE (envelopes) sealed with local STAMP SEALS or in some cases with Late Uruk CYLINDER SEALS. This combination of features has been interpreted as reflecting a local consequence of the Late Uruk expansion, the adoption of Mesopotamian redistribution centres as a new administrative form; but this innovation does not appear to have had significant local consequences.

Artenac   a cave-site near Angoulême, Charente, France, destroyed by quarrying in the 1960s, and type-site of the CHALCOLITHIC Artenacien CULTURE, which includes copper beads, finely-flaked flint daggers, and fine pottery decorated with bands of wavy lines, triangles or dot-filled lozenges, and *anses nasiformes* or beaked handles. Artenacien material is found on defended promontory settlements, in simple MEGALITHIC tombs and in burial caves over an area stretching from Aquitaine to the western edge of the Paris basin, and is dated to between 3000 and 2000 BC.

articulation   the joint between rigid parts of the body. Studies of faunal remains from archaeological contexts frequently include attempts to rearticulate, or join, skeletal parts. These studies provide information on TAPHONOMIC processes at work at the site, indicative of the integrity of the site. These studies also provide insights for SITE STRUCTURAL analysis at the site. Methods of butchering, size and composition of herds and estimates of the number of individuals represented at the site are other types of information gained from articulating skeletal remains.

artifact   any movable object that has been used, modified or manufactured by humans. See MATERIAL CULTURE, TOOL.

aryballos   a round container which seems to have been used by the Greeks for perfumed oil. It has a narrow neck with two small handles. In art they are often shown attached to the wrists of athletes by means of a thong. Many examples of the shape were made at CORINTH (see CORINTHIAN POTTERY) and some have been found in the GIGLIO ISLAND shipwreck.

as   a small Roman bronze coin, 4 being the equivalent of a SESTERTIUS and 16 a DENARIUS.

Asana   a seasonally-occupied, open-air PRECERAMIC site located at an altitude of 3430 m in the western slopes of the Andes in southern Peru. Excavations by Mark Aldenderfer have revealed domestic structures, circular to ovoid in plan, with prepared white–clay floors, set between large boulders. Dating to as early as 7870 bc, these may represent the earliest domestic structures in the Andean region. In addition, a ceremonial COMPLEX dating to 2660 bc has been identified at the site. The complex includes a prepared clay floor, clay-lined fire basins, surface hearths, and two possible altars.

ash   **1**. unconsolidated detrital volcanic material less than 4 mm in diameter deposited as a result of volcanic eruption. Ash falls can quickly bury and preserve archaeological sites, create STRATIGRAPHIC separation of occupation surfaces, and in some instances in effect create archaeological sites by falling on occupied areas, causing death or evacuation, and effectively 'freezing' intact and undisturbed evidence of activities and structures. See TEPHRA.
2. soft and solid residual remains of burned organic material, including human or animal cremation.

Ashdod   a Palestinian site. A CANAANITE city of the LATE BRONZE AGE which seems to have been destroyed by the SEA PEOPLES, it became one of the cities of the PHILISTINE Pentapolis.

Asherah   see ASTARTE.

Ashkelon   a Palestinian site, sporadically excavated since 1815, especially by GARSTANG in 1920–21. The LATE BRONZE AGE levels produced objects of Egyptian and CYPRIOT origin, while the Iron Age is represented by the PHILISTINE city. Much archaeological material of the Roman Period has also been found at Ashkelon.

ashlar   masonry consisting of rectangular cut blocks of stone laid horizontally in regular courses.

ash mound   a distinctive site type of the central Deccan in southern India, the remains of Neolithic cattle pens, dated to the 3rd millennium BC. Excavations of these sites in Karnataka show that they consisted of a double palisade of palm trunks, of which the inner enclosed the cattle, and the outer the herders' dwellings. The accumulation of dung inside the inner palisade fuelled the fires that seem to have been a regular (and perhaps intentional) event at these sites, thereby producing the salient characteristic of this site type.

Asia   a Late PRECERAMIC site on the south central coast of Peru. It covers some 30 ha, and comprises a series of mounds that may have served as residential structures. Burials from the site indicate social distinctions based on equal access to resources, especially cloth; some individuals showed evidence of TREPHINATION.

Asiab   an early 7th millennium BC site in the Kermanshah district of the Zagros Mountains in western Iran; excavations here reveal a small community living in circular semi–subterranean structures, and relying heavily on goats. Although not morphologically domesticated, the age structure of the goats suggests herding.

askos   a spouted vessel, used to pour oil or other liquids. The name comes from the Greek for a wineskin, which the askos sometimes resembles.

Asmar, Tell   The ancient city of Eshnunna, excavated as part of FRANKFORT's Diyala project in the 1920s and 1930s, Tell Asmar (on the lower Diyala River in eastern central Iraq) was inhabited from URUK to early OLD BABYLONIAN times. The excavations revealed an EARLY DYNASTIC I to AKKADIAN sequence at the Abu Temple, exposed an extensive residential district of later Early Dynastic and Akkadian date, and found a major industrial installation (in the 'Northern Palace', probably textile production) of the same date; the work also recovered monumental architecture of the early Old Babylonian period. A large cache of statuary from the Early Dynastic II Abu Temple, human figures in poses of supplication and awe, are some of the best-known examples of this genre. Together with the work at KHAFADJE and elsewhere in the lower Diyala, the excavations at Tell Asmar permitted the initial archaeological definition of the Early Dynastic and Akkadian periods. During the early 2nd millennium, just prior to the regional ascendency of HAMMURABI, Tell Asmar was the centre of the regionally-important kingdom of Eshnunna.

aspect see MIDWESTERN TAXONOMIC SYSTEM.

Aspero a Late PRECERAMIC site (4360 to 3950 bp) on the north central coast of Peru. Covering some 12 ha, it is one of the largest Preceramic settlements known in Andean South America, and represents the emergence of complex social organization. At least six PLATFORM MOUNDS and other structures were built along a natural hillslope through successive filling of small rooms. The largest mound, Huaca de los Idolos, measures 30 m by 50 m and is 10 m high. Built in stages, each level comprises a series of rooms which were filled in with quarried rock held in mesh bags, and the next level superimposed. Dedicatory caches were buried as well, including small wooden artifacts, textiles, plant material, clay figurines and feathers. Subsistence was based primarily on maritime resources, with some cultigens playing a minor role; agriculture was devoted mostly to the production of industrial resources, such as cotton and gourds.

Asprochaliko a Palaeolithic rockshelter located on the Louros River in northwestern Greece. Artifacts are buried in a deep sequence of cave deposits; faunal remains (mostly deer and caprines) are rare. The lowermost cultural layers contain a MOUSTERIAN industry that includes sidescrapers (see SCRAPER) and points. Assemblages with similar but smaller tools ('Micro-Mousterian') occur in overlying levels. The upper cultural layers contain an Upper Palaeolithic industry with BACKED BLADES dated to c.26 000 bp.

assemblage a collection of artifacts that can be considered a single analytical unit. The size of an individual assemblage varies considerably. For example, an assemblage may represent artifacts used in a particular activity or the remains of a particular CULTURE found at a SITE.

Assur 1. an Assyrian god. Originally the principal deity of the city of ASSUR, eventually holding a place comparable to that of MARDUK at BABYLON, Assur became the more 'national' god of the NEO-ASSYRIAN empire. Here the god Assur provided the symbolic focus of a universalizing elite ideology that transcended the various boundaries within the empire; the adjective 'Assyrian' came to denote 'holy', and wars undertaken in Assur's name had ideological as well as more concrete value.
2. the ancient centre of ASSYRIA, set on a promontory overlooking the Tigris River in northeastern Iraq, where the excavations by W. Andrae exposed a wealth of 2nd and 1st millennium BC public and residential architecture. Much of the public architecture was built or largely reconstructed by SHAMSHI-ADAD I (1813–1781 BC), including the ZIGGURAT of ENLIL, the temple of ASSUR (see 1. above), and the

inner city walls. Later MIDDLE and NEO-ASSYRIAN kings persistently renovated these buildings and added further substantial construction, providing the city with three ziggurats and at least 38 temples within the 140 ha contained by the city walls. Besides this religious architecture, the city contained at least two palaces. The 'old palace' was built in the early 2nd millennium and used through the Middle Assryian period, but was subsequently adapted as a mausoleum of the 9th century (SARCOPHAGI of the kings AŠŠURNAṢIRPAL II and Shamshi-Adad V occur here). The 'new palace' was constructed by Tukulti-Ninurta I (1243–1207 BC) who also built KAR-TUKULTI-NINURTA just outside Assur. In the temple of ISHTAR, a deep sounding documented a sequence of temples on this site that begins (on virgin soil) in the mid 3rd millennium BC. The terminology Assur H to Assur A refers to this sequence; the architecture of Assur G, belonging to the AKKADIAN period, is the earliest with an adequately-known floor plan. The latest substantial occupation of the site occurred in PARTHIAN times. The German work also recovered large numbers of Middle Assyrian tablets that provide important information about this time.

Aššurnaṣirpal II (883–859 BC)   one of the great NEO-ASSYRIAN kings, who greatly extended ASSYRIAN domination westward toward the Mediterranean, warring with such Syrian kingdoms as Bit-Adini, and taking tribute from the PHOENICIANS. He founded the new capital at KALHU, which was built and populated by people deported from conquered lands to the west and north; to inaugurate the city, he held a feast for some 52 000 guests from regions of the Assyrian empire and from neighbouring states, in addition to the 17 500 people from Kalhu itself. His son and successor, Shalmaneser III (858–824 BC), further expanded the empire in all directions.

Assyria   the northeastern part of MESOPOTAMIA in historic times, with its focus on the city of ASSUR (on the Tigris River in the Mesopotamian piedmont), as distinct from BABYLONIA on the Mesopotamian ALLUVIUM to the south. Assyria was the setting of major episodes of empire building, beginning with SHAMSHI-ADAD (1813–1781 BC), and followed by the MIDDLE ASSYRIAN and NEO-ASSYRIAN expansionary states of the later 2nd and earlier 1st millennia BC.

Astarte   the goddess of love and war, a ubiquitous female deity of the ancient Near East. She was worshipped by the CANAANITES and PHOENICIANS; her cult was adopted by the PHILISTINES and by the ASSYRIANS and BABYLONIANS who knew her as ISHTAR.

Asturian   a MACROLITHIC INDUSTRY of the MESOLITHIC period of Northern Spain. Discovered in 1914 by the Conde de la Vega del Sella, it is known almost exclusively from *concheros* (SHELL MOUNDS) at cave mouths in the coastal area (see LA RIERA). The Asturian follows the AZILIAN, though it is not clear how the two are connected. Poor in cultural materials, it is characterized by a long, pointed unifacial QUARTZITE pick. Dates span the 9th and 8th millennia bp.

Asuka   a region of Nara Prefecture, Japan, which was the focus of early Buddhist culture in the 6th–7th centuries AD. It is the location of the earliest temple built in Japan, the Asuka-dera of 588 (which is still extant but not architecturally continuous), the Kawahara-dera (which has been excavated and reconstructed in plan), and several contemporaneous palace sites, including FUJIWARA. Asuka was the seat of the RITSURYO government of Japan until the capital was removed to HEIJO. The region is now protected as a Historical District.

Aswan   a modern town at the southern boundary of UPPER EGYPT. Archaeological remains in this region include granite quarries, rock-cut tombs of the OLD and MIDDLE KINGDOM, ELEPHANTINE, PHILAE and, since its re-erection during the NUBIAN RESCUE CAMPAIGN, the TEMPLE of KALAB-SHA.

Ataki I   an Upper Palaeolithic open-air site on the Dnestr River in western Ukraine. Four occupation HORIZONS are buried in slope deposits overlying ALLUVIUM of the second TERRACE; the second and third horizons have yielded RADIOCARBON dates of 15 375–16 600 bp. The principal excavations were undertaken by Chernysh in 1965.

Atchana, Tell   the ancient *Alalakh*; WOOLLEY'S excavations in the 1930s and 1940s at this site on the northern bend of the Orontes River (northwest Syria) defined 17 phases of Middle and Late Bronze Age occupation. The lasting significance of his work here rests not so much on the exposure of residential, palatial and cultic architecture and the accompanying material culture, as on his recovery of two archives dated respectively to the 18th/17th (Alalakh VII) and the 15th (Alalakh IV) centuries BC. These two sets of text throw considerable light on the political affairs of their times (the important Syrian kingdom of Yamkhad and a MITANNI client-state respectively), and on the progressive HURRIAN influence on Syrian societies. Woolley also explored AL MINA (literally 'port') at the mouth of the Orontes, where he exposed 10 levels dated between the 8th and 3rd centuries BC, which contained warehouses filled with Greek materials. Several kilometres upstream, he examined a settlement (Sabouni) which contained Bronze Age and 1st millennium habitation, also indicating strong interregional connections (MYCENAEAN and CYPRIOT painted pottery, as well as later Greek materials).

Aten   an Egyptian deity represented by the sun's disc. During the reign of AKHENATEN the Aten was elevated as the sole god of the monotheistic state religion promulgated by that king.

Aterian   a Middle Palaeolithic stone INDUSTRY with BIFACIAL FOLIATE POINTS and/or TANGED tools, and much use of the LEVALLOIS TECHNIQUE, found in North Africa from the Atlantic coast to the Nile from before 100 000 to about 50 000 years ago.

Aterian Point.

Athabascans   NATIVE AMERICANS who speak languages belonging to the Athabascan or Dene language family. The Northern Athabascans comprise a variety of individual contemporary tribes who live mostly in Alaska and the Yukon. The Southern Athabascans, comprising

Apache and Navajo, now live in the American Southwest, and are thought to have diverged from the northern group sometime around AD 500.

Athenian pottery   pottery that was produced at ATHENS over a long period. In the Late GEOMETRIC period monumental KRATERS and AMPHORAE, with scenes of mourning (see EKPHORA, PROTHESIS) and heroic events, were used to mark the tombs of members of the social elites. Athens is best known for its figure-decorated pottery (see BLACK-FIGURED, RED-FIGURED, SIX'S TECHNIQUE, WHITE-GROUND) produced during the ARCHAIC and CLASSICAL periods. Its products were widely exported and have been found throughout the regions bordering the Mediterranean and the Black Sea. Many examples have been found in tombs in CAMPANIA, ETRURIA (see CERVETERI, TARQUINIA, VULCI) and at SPINA. Alongside these decorated wares were produced the plain wares (see BLACK-GLOSSED). In the HELLENISTIC period Athens continued to export pottery (see MEGARIAN BOWLS, WEST SLOPE WARE).

Athens   a Greek city which, as a result of being perceived as a centre of democracy, has received considerable archaeological attention. The main monuments include the local sanctuary on the AKROPOLIS where there were several different cults. The main one was that of Athena (see PARTHENON). The political and commercial centre, the AGORA, has been excavated by the American School. The German excavations have revealed some of the cemeteries in the KERAMEIKOS. Although many of the monuments relate to the 5th century BC city, there are numerous Roman traces. The emperor Hadrian helped to finish the massive *Olympieion* (the temple of Olympian Zeus) and had an arch erected to mark the boundary between the City of Theseus and the City of Hadrian. See ATHENIAN POTTERY.

Athribis (*Arabic* Tell Atrib)   an Egyptian site in the central southern Nile DELTA. Little now remains, or has been recovered archaeologically, of this important ancient Egyptian city. The excavations by Rowe in 1938 and the current work of the Polish Mission have uncovered a good deal of the Graeco–Roman city, but earlier periods at Athribis are only attested archaeologically by objects discovered by SEBBAKH–diggers.

Atlanthropus   a genus used by ARAMBOURG for HOMO *erectus* fossils from TERNIFINE.

Atlantic Bronze Age   a regional TRADITION of the Late Bronze Age represented in western Iberia, western France and the British Isles, best known for its metalwork, including the distinctive CARP'S TONGUE SWORD.

Atlantic climatic period   a POSTGLACIAL climatic and vegetational period of temperate Europe between *c*.5500 and 3000 BC defined on the basis of POLLEN ANALYSIS by Blytt and Sernander. The Atlantic period is traditionally characterized by warmth and dampness in northern Europe, with mean annual temperatures approximately 2 °C warmer than today, the result of polar air circulation having been displaced northward (compare SUB-BOREAL CLIMATIC PERIOD).

atlatl   a particular form of projectile technology, consisting of a throwing stick used as an extension of the arm to propel the pointed dart shaft through the air. The atlatl was introduced to the North American continent at the end of the PALAEOINDIAN period. It is associated with ARCHAIC stage cultures, although EXPERIMENTAL

ARCHAEOLOGY has shown the feasibility of firing earlier Palaeoindian points with the atlatl technology. It was superseded by the BOW-AND-ARROW. See PROJECTILE POINT, SPEARPOINT, SPEARTHROWER.

Atlitian an Upper Palaeolithic INDUSTRY, including BLADES, SCRAPERS and BURINS, which has only been found at a few sites in the Levant region. The best-known Atlitian site is EL-WAD.

atomic absorption spectrometry a technique used to determine quantitatively the chemical composition of artifactual metals, minerals and rocks to identify raw material sources, relate artifacts made of the same material, or trace material trade. A dissolved sample of material is atomized in a flame. A cathode lamp made from the element to be analysed is shown through the flame where atoms of the element in the atomized sample absorb light of the same wavelength produced by the lamp in proportion to the concentration of the element in the sample. After passing through the flame, the light intensity is measured with a photomultiplier and compared to the light intensity before passing through the sample to determine the amount of absorption.

atrium an open central court in a Roman or Etruscan house. An IMPLUVIUM may be placed in the centre for rain water.

Attic-Kephala the term proposed by Renfrew for the FINAL NEOLITHIC phase on sites such as ATHENS and THORIKOS in Attica and KEPHALA on Kea.

attribute 1. a characteristic element of a particular CULTURE or group. 2. a specific element of an individual ARTIFACT, such as a pottery rim, or PROJECTILE POINT base.

Atwater, Caleb (1778–1867) an American antiquary whose essay in 1820 on the mounds of the American Midwest established him as one of the most important pioneers of American archaeology. Atwater meticulously described and measured many mounds around his Ohio home. He argued that they had been made by Hindus who had emigrated to Mexico from India. See DAVIS, HAVEN, SQUIER, THOMAS.

Aubrey, John (1626–97) a Wiltshire antiquary sometimes called the first English archaeologist, who made the first detailed SURVEYS of surviving field monuments including STONEHENGE and AVEBURY, which he correctly recognized as places of prehistoric ritual but erroneously attributed to the Druids. In the 1660s Aubrey produced plans and descriptions of Avebury and Stonehenge for Charles II, in the course of his researches discovering the circle of holes within the ditch of Stonehenge now known as the Aubrey Holes.

auger a tool used to collect SEDIMENT and SOIL samples below the ground surface without hand excavation. The operation of an auger is based on rotation of a shaft with a spiral cutting surface. There are different types of augers ranging from economical hand-operated ones to large truck-mounted rigs. The twisting motion of the auger as it penetrates tends to mix samples making them of limited use for analytical investigations. See CORE.

aula the entrance hall in a Roman house.

Au Lac the pre-Chinese conquest Vietnamese state in the Red River valley of the 3rd century BC, once thought to be legendary, but now linked to the DONG SON period in the region. The capital is thought to have been at the site of CO LOA.

Aulnat an Iron Age settlement site in Puy-de-Dôme, France, established in the 3rd century BC, with evidence of industrial activities including the working of gold, silver, bronze, coral, glass, bone and textiles. Gold and silver coins were among the products. Imported Mediterranean luxury goods indicate that this became an important site, but it was abandoned in the 1st century BC soon after the Roman conquest.

Aunjetitz culture   see ÚNETICE.

aureus   a Roman gold coin. Under Augustus there were 42 to the Roman pound (327.45 g). Compare DENARIUS.

Aurignacian   an Upper Palaeolithic industry which developed in the Near East and spread westwards, arriving in Spain by 39 000 bp (see SERIÑA, EL CASTILLO) and by at least 34 000 bp in France (see ABRI PATAUD) where it succeeded the CHÂTELPERRONIAN and preceded the GRAVETTIAN. The tool-kit is characterized by the presence of many BURINS, and also contains long BLADES, *carinated* (steep-ended) SCRAPERS, and split-based bone POINTS. The name is derived from the Aurignac ROCKSHELTER in the French Pyrenees, first excavated by E. LARTET.

aurochs (*Bos primigenius*)   the wild ancestor of domestic cattle, found throughout prehistory in western Eurasia, generally inhabiting open woodland. It had a dark coat, stood up to 1.8 m at the shoulder, and weighed up to one tonne. It became extinct through hunting, and by interbreeding with domesticated cattle, the last individual dying in Poland in AD 1627.

Australian Core Tool and Scraper Tradition   a stone ARTIFACT INDUSTRY first defined at MUNGO by Rhys Jones and Harry Allen and characterized by CHOPPING TOOLS, HORSEHOOF CORES and steep-edged FLAKE SCRAPERS. ASSEMBLAGES of this type date to the Late PLEISTOCENE and HOLOCENE, and some items survive into Late Holocene AUSTRALIAN SMALL TOOL TRADITION assemblages. Moreover, some Pleistocene sites, such as DEVIL'S LAIR and UPPER SWAN, do not fit this characterization. Previous attempts at classification of Australian assemblages are now subsumed into the pan-continental Australian Core Tool and Scraper Tradition, and terms such as Tartangan, GAMBIERAN and KARTAN are now rarely used. Consequently, use of this term masks regional and temporal variability. As more detailed regional studies are conducted, the concept is likely to be substantially modified.

Australian Small Tool Tradition   a term applied to mid-to-late HOLOCENE stone ARTIFACT ASSEMBLAGES on the Australian mainland, but absent from TASMANIA. The Small Tool Tradition dates from about 5000 years ago and comprises a number of elements including a range of hafted tools such as BONDI POINTS, geometric MICROLITHS, TULAS, ELOUERAS, and unifacial and bifacial points, as well as BLADE technology. The distribution of these types varies in space and time. All except Bondi points and geometric microliths were in use at the time of European contact.

Australopithecus   a genus of small-brained, bipedal, fossil HOMINID. The most ancient australopithecine is *A. afarensis* known from 3.75–3 million year-old deposits in East Africa (see HADAR, LAETOLI, 'LUCY'). Five million year-old fragments from Lothagam in northern Kenya may also be australopithecine. *A. africanus* (see DART, TAUNG) lived about 3–2 million years ago and is best known from

STERKFONTEIN and MAKAPANSGAT in South Africa. *A. afarensis* and *A. africanus* are sometimes called 'gracile' australopithecines because they were small and lightly built. The gracile australopithecines are often regarded as direct human ancestors.

More massive 'robust' australopithecines appear later in time than the gracile ones and are known from many sites in Kenya and Tanzania (*A. boisei*) (see OLDUVAI, ZINJANTHROPUS) as well as in South Africa (*A. robustus/Paranthropus*) (see KROMDRAAI, SWARTKRANS). They date to between 2 and 1 million years old and are contemporary with HOMO *habilis* and *H. erectus*.

(a)

(b)

Australopithecus (a) *A. africanus* (b) *A. robustus*.

Austronesian the major language family spoken throughout island Southeast Asia, MELANESIA (except for most of Papua New Guinea), MICRONESIA and POLYNESIA. Austronesian speakers are commonly thought to have spread through Southeast Asia about 5000 years ago, and LAPITA is regarded as the archaeological signature of their expansion into the Pacific.

Auvernier a lake dwelling on the northern edge of Lake Neuchâtel, Switzerland, with Neolithic and Late Bronze Age occupation. The Neolithic levels include Early Neolithic CORTAILLOD, Middle Neolithic HORGEN and Late Neolithic CORDED WARE material. The rich Late Bronze Age material belongs to the HALLSTATT A2-B phase, *c*.1100–750 BC, and includes the remains of a metal workshop.

Avaris the capital of the HYKSOS in Egypt, possibly to be identified with the site of TELL ED-DABA.

Avdeevo an Upper Palaeolithic open-air site on the Rogozna River (Sejm tributary) near Kursk in European Russia. The single occupation HORIZON is buried in ALLUVIUM of the first TERRACE, and has yielded RADIOCARBON dates ranging between 11 950 and 22 700 bp. Woolly MAMMOTH dominates the large faunal assemblage. A complex arrangement of pits and hearths appears to reflect the presence of several former structures. The artifacts, which include SHOULDERED POINTS and animal and VENUS FIGURINES, are assigned to the KOSTENKI-WILLENDORF CULTURE or EASTERN GRAVETTIAN. Avdeevo was excavated in 1946–49 by Gvozdover, Voevodskij, and ROGACHEV; investigations were resumed by Gvozdover in the 1970s.

Avebury a major Neolithic ritual complex in Wiltshire, England, comprising: a) WEST KENNET long BARROW *c*.3500 BC; b) WINDMILL HILL CAUSEWAYED CAMP *c*.3350 BC; c) Avebury HENGE monument *c*.2600 BC, over 400 m in diameter, surrounded by a deep ditch with outer bank and a setting of stones along its inner edge. Further stone settings stand within the monument, and an avenue of stones leads to the smaller circle known as the Sanctuary (a second avenue recorded in the 16th century has since been destroyed); d) SILBURY HILL *c*.2600 BC. Recent investigations have revealed further earth and timber enclosures dating from the end of the Neolithic period at West Kennet Farm, and the Avebury area also has several Bronze Age barrow cemeteries, demonstrating its continued importance in the post-Neolithic period.

Avebury, John Lubbock, Lord (1834–1913) an English antiquary and author of *Prehistoric Times* (1865), which advanced archaeology as the 'link between geology and history' and helped bring it to the reading public. Avebury, in this book, was the first to use the terms PALAEOLITHIC and NEOLITHIC.

Aveline's Hole a cave-site in the Mendip Hills, Somerset, England, which has yielded a CRESWELLIAN EPIPALAEOLITHIC INDUSTRY and a MAGDALENIAN-style HARPOON.

Awdaghast or **Tegdaoust** an 11th century AD trading centre in southern Mauretania, Africa, initially controlled by Sanhaja nomads and later part of the GHANA empire.

awl a piercing implement made of bone, antler, wood, metal or stone, often found in prehistoric tool-kits.

axial-chambered tomb see SEVERN-COTSWOLD.

Axum the capital of an Ethiopian kingdom of the 1st to 7th centuries AD. Sporadically excavated since 1906, the most impressive monuments at the site are monolithic granite grave-markers, roughly-dressed or elaborately-carved, the largest being over 30 m tall.

Ayia Irini a site on the CYCLADIC island of Kea in the Aegean that was excavated by CASKEY in 1960–76. The site, on a promontory, appears to have been occupied more or less continuously throughout the Bronze Age. In the 2nd millennium BC Ayia Irini was a fortified town and maintained close economic links with MINOAN Crete. Among the most remarkable finds were the large, in some cases almost life-size, female TERRACOTTA figures from the Temple.

Ayia Triadha the site of a MINOAN town on the island of Crete, built around a magnificent NEOPALATIAL VILLA. The sophisticated design and opulent decoration of the villa and the presence of an archive of LINEAR A tablets have led to the suggestion that Ayia Triadha may have superseded PHAISTOS as the administrative centre of southern Crete.

Ayios Epiktitos-Vrysi   the site of a Neolithic II (later 5th millennium BC) settlement in northern Cyprus, which was excavated by Peltenburg in 1969–73. A perimeter wall and ditch protected the settlement which consisted of semi-subterranean houses built of stone and PISÉ.

Aylesford   an Iron Age cemetery in Kent, England, discovered by Sir Arthur EVANS in 1890 and associated with the BELGIC peoples of southern England encountered by the Romans. Together with the major cemetery of Swarling (discovered in 1924), Aylesford became the type-site of the late Iron Age Aylesford-Swarling culture dated to between 75 BC and the Roman conquest of AD 43. The characteristic burial rite is cremation, sometimes in an elaborate bronze-bound bucket, within a flat grave, associated with wheel-turned pottery and, in richer examples, imported Roman wine AMPHORAE.

Aynan   see EYNAN.

Azelik   a town in Niger, Africa, with evidence of copper SMELTING by the middle of the 1st millennium BC or perhaps earlier. Like AKJOUJT, this provides evidence of a brief 'Copper Age' in this part of Africa before the adoption of iron.

Azilian   the final Palaeolithic/initial Mesolithic INDUSTRY of south-west Europe, first identified by PIETTE in 1887 at LE MAS D'AZIL where it filled the hiatus between the Palaeolithic and the Neolithic. It comprises MICROLITHIC tools, notably the *Azilian point* (a double-pointed BACKED BLADE), flat perforated and barbed HARPOONS of red deer antler, and small schist pebbles bearing red dots or stripes: the pebbles are known from France, northern Spain, Italy and Switzerland, but Le Mas d'Azil itself yielded over 1000 harpoons and more than 75 per cent of the *c*.2000 pebbles known. Dates for the Azilian fall primarily between 9000 and 8000 bc.

Azmak   a Neolithic TELL site located near Stara Zagora in south-central Bulgaria. The Early Neolithic levels at Azmak are contemporaneous with those at KARANOVO I and have provided important evidence on subsistence and settlement layout. Later levels of the 8 m-high mound correspond to Karanovo V and VI and belong to the GUMELNIŢA culture. The Karanovo VI layer at Azmak contained two large multiroomed structures.

Aztec, *adj.*   relating to the last great native MESOAMERICAN empire, defeated by CORTES in 1521. The Aztecs were originally a group of CHICHIMECS who moved east and south into the VALLEY OF MEXICO. They eventually settled at the site of TENOCHTITLÁN, having been given a sign by their tribal deity. The Aztecs were a fierce tribe who gained dominance in the area through their warring and political alliances (see also TRIPLE ALLIANCE), ultimately expanding their empire throughout much of Mesoamerica. The Aztecs had a complicated system of trade and redistribution that extended throughout Mesoamerica and beyond its frontiers (see POCHTECA). The city of Tenochtitlán and the Valley of Mexico were supported by this system of trade, tribute, and intensive agricultural production within the valley itself.

Azykh Cave   a Palaeolithic site in Azerbajdzhan. The cave is situated at an elevation of 800 m in the Lesser Caucasus Mountains. The lower levels (X–VII) reportedly contain a pebble-tool industry without parallel in the region, associated with some isolated faunal remains; its age is unknown. Above these layers rest two levels (VI–V) containing assemblages with large BIFACES and sidescrapers (see SCRAPER) assigned to the ACHEULIAN and associated with Middle PLEISTOCENE fauna (e.g. *Bison schoetensacki*). A level (III) containing a Middle Palaeolithic assemblage (dominated by sidescrapers) and remains of Merck's rhinoceros, CAVE BEAR and others overlies the Lower Palaeolithic industries; it is thought to date to the Late Pleistocene. Azykh Cave was discovered and investigated by Gusejnov during 1960–73.

B

Ba [Pa] see ZHOU, DIAN.

Baal the most important male deity of the CANAANITES, identified by the HYKSOS with the Egyptian deity SETH.

Baalbek (*Gk* Heliopolis) an important Roman religious centre in modern Lebanon. A major building was the monumental temple of Jupiter-Hadad.

Babadan A a Palaeolithic site in Miyagi Prefecture, Japan, with lithics, including CHOPPERS, dated between 50 000–70 000 bp. Unlike at SOZUDAI, the tools are of convincing human manufacture, giving support to the existence of an Early Palaeolithic in Japan.

Babylon the ancient capital of MESOPOTAMIA, and perhaps the most famous archaeological site in Iraq. Babylon was periodically the political centre of southern Mesopotamia, especially during OLD BABYLONIAN and NEO-BABYLONIAN times when it was the seat of empires created by HAMMURABI and NEBUCHADNEZZAR respectively. At other times during the 2nd and 1st millennia, the city remained the focus of population and of traditional political feelings in southern Mesopotamia, and served as the regional capital of invading empires (NEO-ASSYRIAN, ACHAEMENID; Alexander the Great died in the city). The site was inhabited at least by the EARLY DYNASTIC III and continued in use until medieval times. KOLDEWEY'S work at the turn of the century, and that of others more recently, focused on the 1st millennium BC city, which covered some 850 ha and contained such famous monuments as the ISHTAR Gate, the ZIGGURAT *Etemenanki* (the 'tower of Babel'), and the palace of Nebuchadnezzar (which contains a structure Koldewey identified as the 'hanging gardens'). Earlier occupation has been uncovered only in the 'Merkes' section of the city, where excavation reached an Old Babylonian residential district beneath KASSITE period levels. See SEVEN WONDERS.

Babylonia the region comprising the whole of the southern ALLUVIUM of MESOPOTAMIA from the ascendency of HAMMURABI early in the 2nd millennium BC. It was roughly equivalent to the 3rd millennium designations SUMER and AKKAD combined. Although the name derives from the city of BABYLON, the region was not necessarily integrated and ruled from that centre, as this was a relatively infrequent circumstance (occurring notably under Hammurabi himself, and under the NEO-BABYLONIAN dynasty of NEBUCHADNEZZAR II).

Bacho Kiro a Palaeolithic cave-site located in the Balkan Mountains of central Bulgaria. Artifacts and faunal remains (e.g. horse, AUROCHS, CAVE BEAR) are buried in clay and rubble deposits. The two lowest layers contain Middle Palaeolithic tools (primarily sidescrapers – see SCRAPER), and are stratigraphically correlated with the end of the Early GLACIAL and the early cold maximum of the LAST GLACIAL. Overlying layers contain early Upper Palaeolithic artifacts (e.g. endscrapers, RETOUCHED BLADES) dated to an early INTERSTADIAL of the Last Glacial (RADIOCARBON date of › 43 000 bp), which represent the oldest Upper Palaeolithic industry ('Bachokirian') in Europe. AURIGNACIAN assemblages occur in the upper levels. Bacho Kiro was excavated by GARROD in the 1930s, and Kozłowski and others in the 1970s.

backed blade a BLADE with one long edge deliberately blunted by steep RETOUCH. Some smaller backed blades and backed *bladelets* may have been used as arrow tips; others were apparently used as knives. Backed blades are frequently encountered in GRAVETTIAN assemblages.

Bacsonian a term characterizing a stone INDUSTRY, dating to *c*.8000–2500 BC, found in a series of cave-sites on the northern fringe of the Red River valley in north Vietnam, related to the HOABINHIAN, (see fig.) developing EDGE-GRINDING in later phases, when pottery was also in use. The type-site of the industry is Bac Son.

Bactrian Bronze Age a CULTURE, initially identified from materials looted from graves in northwestern Afghanistan and sold on the antiquities market, that produced a range of materials (pottery, SEALS and other metal work, ornamented stone vessels, stone statuettes and other materials) which are strongly represented in Baluchistan and the margins of the Indus (SIBRI), and also appear across the Iranian plateau as far west as SUSA. V.I. Sarianidi's work on the DASHLY sites and that of Askarov at SAPALLI-DEPE provide the archaeological context of this important culture area.

Badarian the earliest phase of the PREDYNASTIC sequence of UPPER EGYPT, dating to *c*.5000–4500 BC. The Badarians probably practised a semisedentary economy; their most technologically accomplished product is a polished thin-walled pottery. A small number of copper objects, possibly imports, are found at Badarian sites.

Baden culture an ENEOLITHIC culture of east-central Europe, centred on Hungary and Czechoslovakia but also reaching into the northern Balkans and southern Poland. The Baden culture is also frequently referred to as the Radial-Decorated Pottery culture, on the basis of the incised lines on its vessels which radiate upward from the base. The chronology of the Baden culture is divided into three phases. The early phase (*c*.2750–2450 bc) is essentially equivalent to the Boleráz group of the Hungarian Plain, while the 'classic' and late phases (*c*.2600–2200 bc) saw the broader distribution of this culture. Baden settlements are generally dispersed sites with relatively thin deposits, which contrast with the stratified sites that characterize the preceding cultures of southeastern Europe. The appearance of evidence for wheeled vehicles, such as the wagon model from BUDAKALASZ, cups and vessels presumably associated with milk handling, large numbers of spindle whorls, and the shift to a dispersed settlement pattern are viewed as elements of the SECONDARY PRODUCTS REVOLUTION proposed by Sherratt.

Bader, Otto Nikolaevich (1903–80) a Russian prehistoric archaeologist who investigated sites from many periods ranging from the Palaeolithic to the Iron Age. He excavated several important Palaeolithic sites, including KAPOVAYA CAVE and SUNGIR', as well as many sites dating to the Mesolithic and Bronze Age.

Bahrain tumulus fields densely packed fields of TUMULI in Bahrain and at several places on the adjacent mainland that are constructed as single or multiroom chambers over which desert soils are heaped. The initial construction and use of these monuments belong to the Bronze Age BARBAR CULTURE, though numbers of them were reused at later times. Also associated with these tumuli fields are densely packed complexes of CIST burials.

Băile Herculane a ROCKSHELTER site in southwest Romania with Early MESOLITHIC occupation levels which have provided information on the surrounding vegetation (Alpine forest-steppe, with juniper and willow predominant), subsistence (forest, steppe and riverine species), and the chipped stone industry (small blunted BLADES, DENTICULATED blades and SCRAPERS), In addition, there is a later occupation of the ENEOLITHIC SALCUȚA and COȚOFENI cultures.

Baker's Hole, Northfleet an English Lower Palaeolithic working site in Kent which appears to have been a factory specializing in the production of large LEVALLOIS FLAKES. Unfortunately the site was destroyed by quarrying before it could be properly excavated.

baktun a unit in the CLASSIC MAYA LONG COUNT, equalling 144 000 days, or about 400 years. See TUN.

Balakot a coastal site west of Karachi in Pakistan, where the excavations of George Dales revealed a settlement of the 4th millennium BC beneath Mature HARAPPAN levels. During the earlier period, the Balakotian, ceramic connections are northward into Baluchistan and have little connection with later developments at the site. The two periods of occupation contrast in subsistence patterns, with a Balakotian focus on cattle and a Harappan focus on sheep/goats and on maritime resources including a shell bangle workshop.

Balawat A 60 ha walled town with a 3 ha citadel near the Upper Zab River east of Mosul, northern Iraq, the ASSYRIAN town Imgur-Enlil, refounded by the king AŠŠURNAṢIRPAL II (883–859 BC) as a 'country retreat'. The 'work' (by tunnelling) of H. Rassam in the 1880s recovered the objects for which the place is best known, the two Balawat bronze doors (actually bronze REPOUSSÉ strips covering wood), which narrate and illustrate campaigns of Aššurnaṣirpal II and of his successor Shalmaneser III (858–824 BC). MALLOWAN'S brief work here in the 1950s focused on the Temple of Mamu, and recovered a third bronze door. Although certainly the best known and the most complete, the Balawat doors represent a common NEO-ASSYRIAN decorative practice, traces of which have been observed in most excavated Assyrian cities.

Ballana and Qustul two cemeteries on opposite sides of the Nile in LOWER NUBIA, excavated by EMERY and Kirwan from 1931–34. The large TUMULI contained the royal burials (including small numbers of sacrificed retainers) of the X-GROUP.

Ballana culture see X-GROUP.

Ballawinne   see WARGATA MINA.

ball game   a game played in MESOAMERICA with a rubber ball, possibly with a wooden core. While there is a certain amount of variation in the game throughout Mesoamerica, *ball courts* are a major functional class of formal architecture at Mesoamerican centres. There are historical accounts of the ball game from the time of the Spanish conquest, and the game appears to have originated during OLMEC times. See also HOHOKAM.

Balma de Montbolo   see MONTBOLO.

balneum   a small Roman bath-house perhaps attached to a private house. Compare THERMAE.

Balof 1   a limestone sinkhole on New Ireland in the BISMARCK ARCHIPELAGO, MELANESIA. Two shelters have been excavated, with basal dates of *c.*7000 bp at Balof 1 and *c.*14 000 bp at Balof 2. In the lower levels of both sites, OBSIDIAN from TALASEA occurs. Obsidian from LOU ISLAND appears about 3000 bp.

Bambandyanalo   a rocky hill which forms the eastern boundary of the K2 site in the northern Transvaal, South Africa. It has given its name to a FACIES of Phase A of the southern branch of the LEOPARD'S KOPJE tradition of the southern African Iron Age, which dates to the 11th–12th centuries AD. The name is sometimes applied to the K2 site.

Bambata   1. a cave in the Matobo Hills of southwestern Zimbabwe, containing a long stratified sequence spanning the Upper PLEISTOCENE and HOLOCENE, as well as interesting rock paintings.
2. thin-walled, elaborately-stamped pottery from the upper levels of cave and rockshelter sites in Botswana, South Africa and Zimbabwe, associated with dates from the 1st century BC–9th century AD. Some researchers suggest that it is the consequence of STONE AGE people imitating contemporary Iron Age pottery, while others consider that it is an Early Iron Age ware.
3. a MIDDLE STONE AGE industry of Zimbabwe and southern Zambia, with a minimum age between 45 000–30 000 BP, characterized by unifacial points, SCRAPERS and occasional bifacial points.

Banawali   a large prehistoric site in Haryana (northern India), where excavations in the 1970s revealed three periods of occupation that span roughly the millennium between 2500 and 1500 BC. The earliest settlement contains pottery similar to that at KALIBANGAN during the Early HARAPPAN period. The second period is Mature Harappan in character, as shown by its typical urban form (two separately-walled areas, with residential blocks on regular streets), pottery and small finds, though echoes of the Early Harappan pottery are still present. In the third period, the pottery is comparable to the Late Harappan wares of the eastern Punjab that are variously called Bara ware, Late Siswal ware or OCHRE COLOURED POTTERY.

Ban Chiang   a prehistoric settlement in the Songkhram valley, northern KHORAT, Thailand, occupied between *c.*3600 BC and AD 300, a period spanning the transition from late Neolithic to the use of bronze and then iron. Bronze was in use before 2000 BC, and was worked on the site after about 1500 BC. Iron appeared between 800 and 400 BC, first in bimetallic (bronze and iron) implements; later tools were made entirely of iron, and bronze remained in use for ornaments. Woven cloth was in use by at least 2000 BC, and silk occurs in graves with iron. The best-known CERAMICS from the site, the elaborately-painted red-on-buff ware, were made towards the end of the settlement's history, in the last three centuries BC. The carved ceramic rollers, possibly associated with a local textile-printing industry, were even later. Despite evidence for relatively far-ranging trade ties, the ceramic tradition appears to have been very localized. Extensive disturbance of the site and difficult stratigraphy have given rise to some debate concerning the accuracy of dating; dates given above are more conservative than those in initial reports.

Ban Chiang Red-on-buff ware.

Ban Chiang Hian   a large (approximately 38 ha) double-moated late prehistoric/protohistoric settlement (see MOATED SITES) in the middle Chi valley, KHORAT, Thailand, possibly settled by 1600 BC (bronze appears in basal layers) and still occupied in the mid 1st millennium AD. A sharp break in pottery styles c.500 300 BC accompanied the introduction of iron and of water buffalo; by this time the settlement was large and formed the centre of a cluster of smaller settlements, including Non Noi and Ban Kho Noi.

band   a type of social organization. It is most often associated with HUNTERS-AND-GATHERERS, and comprises small groups of people, with little or no social ranking, and a sexual division of labour. See TRIBE, CHIEFDOM, STATE.

Bandkeramik   see LINEAR POTTERY CULTURE.

Ban Don Ta Phet   a late prehistoric burial site near U THONG, western-central Thailand, c.400–200 BC, which provides evidence for long-range trade linking sea and land routes. Grave furnishings include etched stone and other beads from India, a two-headed nephrite pendant from southern Vietnam, and bronze containers from north Vietnam (see DONG-SON). Local goods include iron tools distantly related to those of the Malay Peninsula, and high-tin cast bronze bowls with incised decorations. Similar bowls have been found in peninsular Malaysia and as far west as TAXILA in Pakistan.

Bandung microliths   a mid-HOLOCENE OBSIDIAN industry of the Bandung Plateau, west Java, characterized by small backed FLAKES and other tools broadly similar to those of the TOALIAN in Sulawesi and the obsidians from TIANKO PANJANG and KERINCI in Sumatra.

Ban Kao   a pair of sites (the Bang and Lue sites) in west-central Thailand on a tributary of the Khwae Noi, which served as occupation and burial sites, and which have yielded large numbers of POLISHED STONE ADZES and a mass of pottery, including tripod pottery common to a number of sites in peninsular Thailand and Malaysia.

Although corrected RADIOCARBON dates for the sites range from c.3000–1500 BC, no bronze has been found.

Ban Kao Tripod pot.

Ban Nadi   a small prehistoric settlement located about 30 km south of BAN CHIANG, in KHORAT, Thailand, occupied from c.1500 BC to c.AD 200 300. After 500 BC the settlement was the site of a local centre of tin-bronze production and trade, specializing in jewellery, axes and PROJECTILE POINTS. From c.100 BC to AD 200 iron was also SMELTED and forged, to produce hoes, knives, spearheads and bangles. The site's bronze workshop (with clay furnaces) began to cast lead-bronze bells, bowls and bracelets at this time.

banner stone   a ground and polished stone artifact that may have served either as an ATLATL weight or as a ceremonial object. The term is most often used in the American Midwest and East.

Banpo [Pan-p'o]   a Neolithic village site, dating to 3000–4000 BC, near Xian City, China. Excavated from 1954 to 1957 by the Institute of Archaeology, it became the type-site for the YANGSHAO phase of the Early Neolithic in the central LOESS highlands. The site covers 5–6 ha, including pit-houses and storage pits enclosed by a deep village ditch, examples of which are now openly exposed to view as a site museum. Kilns and cemetery remains occurred outside the ditched area, and remains of millet, pig and dog show it was part of the northern agricultural regime (see CISHAN).

Banshan [Pan-shan]   one of five Neolithic cemeteries in the Ban-shan Hills of Gansu Province, China. ANDERSSON, the alleged discoverer of the Chinese Neolithic, obtained many splendid painted burial jars from here in the early 1920s and removed them to Sweden.

Ban Tha Kae   a key prehistoric site just north of LOPBURI in the Chao Phraya valley, central Thailand. The site, near the copper sources of Khao Wong Prachan and the copper-processing site of NON PA WAI, has a long sequence, as yet poorly dated, ranging from late Neolithic through bronze and iron-production, parallel to KHORAT sites.

Bantu   a group of languages within the Niger-Congo language family, traditionally spoken by black people in much of southern and central Africa, and linked to the spread of the IRON AGE in southern Africa.

Banyan Valley Cave   see SPIRIT CAVE.

bar and dot notation   a MESOAMERICAN counting system in which a bar counts for five, a dot for one. The earliest example of the bar and dot system is on STELA 2 at CHIAPA DE CORZO, with a date of 36 BC. The system was in use throughout many parts of Mesoamerica, and is most closely associated with MAYA and ZAPOTEC writing systems.

baray a Khmer term referring to the large rectangular water reservoirs associated with the ANGKOR period.

Barbar a site in northern Bahrain in the Persian Gulf consisting of a sequence of square temples built on an oval platform, dating from the late 3rd millennium to the mid 2nd millennium BC. The site gives its name to an archaeological CULTURE, defined by pottery types, SEALS and other materials contained in the lower levels of the QAL'AT AL BAHRAIN, Barbar itself, the BAHRAIN TUMULUS FIELDS and other sites; this complex dates to the second half of the 3rd and earlier part of the 2nd millennia BC. Sites of this type are distributed along the southern coast of the Persian Gulf from Failaka (near the MESOPOTAMIAN delta) to Qatar, with materials occasionally occurring in southeastern Arabia and on the Indus coast (see PERSIAN GULF TRADE).

barbotine a term used in CERAMICS to describe rough plastic relief on the surface of pottery.

Barca a Bronze Age fortified settlement of the OTOMANI culture in eastern Slovakia near Kosice. The most striking feature of the Barca settlement is its large houses. Twenty-three were found in the surviving portion of the enclosure, aligned in rows of 4 to 7 and separated by intervals of 40 to 60 cm. Between these rows of houses were 'streets' about 2.5 m wide. Most are three-room structures, many with HEARTHS, although some have only one or two rooms.

bar hammer technique see SOFT HAMMER TECHNIQUE.

Barkaer two parallel rectangular Neolithic timber structures in Jutland, Denmark; approximately 8.5 m long, they are subdivided by 21 and 28 wickerwork partitions respectively. Originally interpreted as houses (an early form of terrace!) they are now thought to be the timber frameworks of funerary long mounds built on the site of an earlier settlement *c*.4000 BC.

Barnenez one of the earliest NEOLITHIC CHAMBERED TOMBS of western Europe, this sub-rectangular dry-stone CAIRN in Finistère, France, contains 11 chambers side by side reached by long, narrow, irregular passages. Excavations suggested the mound was built in two phases, an initial mound with five chambers (four dry-stone, one MEGALITHIC) being subsequently enlarged by an extension with six more (five dry-stone, one megalithic). The megalithic chamber of the first phase (chamber H) contained carved ORTHOSTATS including three axe motifs. RADIOCARBON dates suggest that the initial mound was built *c*.4500 BC, with the extension following some 300 years later.

barrow see TUMULUS.

Barumini the site in Sardinia of a monument called Su Nuraxi, the most famous of the Bronze Age NURAGHI, consisting of a central round tower of massive basalt blocks and later outworks. The central tower was built *c*.1800 BC and was originally some 17 m high with three tall CORBEL-VAULTED chambers one above the other. The outworks – four round towers around the base of the central tower, and a perimeter wall with smaller towers enclosing a village – were built over a thousand years later, in the 8th century BC, possibly in response to the Carthaginian threat.

Base Ring   Late CYPRIOT pottery which has a dark, lustrous SLIP and relief decoration. Base Ring juglets or *bilbils* resemble inverted poppy-heads and may have contained opium.

Base Ring Juglet.

basilica   a long, rectangular Roman building with an internal colonnade. They are often found in the vicinity of a FORUM and seem to have been used for judicial hearings and other civic functions. The term later came to be applied to church buildings which adopted this type of open-plan layout.

Basin of Mexico   a closed basin surrounded by mountains, 2400 m above sea level. Cultural remains in the basin date as early as 19 000 BC at the site of Tlapacoya, which later became a large PRECLASSIC village. Tlatilco, whose earliest material dates to 15 000 BC, was also an important Preclassic site in the basin, well known for its spectacular burials. The Basin of Mexico contains the current capital of Mexico, Mexico City, as well as the remains of the AZTEC capital of TENOCHTITLÁN, and the cities of CUICUILCO and TEOTIHUACÁN. At the time of the Spanish conquest in 1521, the entire basin was intensively cultivated in order to support the resident population.

In addition to dry farming SWIDDEN AGRICULTURE, irrigation techniques and CHINAMPAS were employed. The southern portion of the basin is better suited for agriculture, and was occupied earlier and more intensively than the northern part.

Archaeological research in the Basin of Mexico has focused primarily on the later stages of Teotihuacán and the Aztec period. Within the basin, there were two periods of florescence: the first from *c*.100 BC to AD 650 with the rise of Cucuilco and then Teotihuacán; and the second from AD 1200 to 1520, with the appearance of the city-state of Azcapotzalco, and the subsequent rise to power of the Aztecs.

Basketmaker   see ANASAZI.

Basse-Yutz   a pair of bronze wine flagons with coral and enamel inlay discovered in 1927 in an uncertain context in Moselle, France, probably originally from a CELTIC chieftain's grave. The flagons combine a vessel shape copied from Italian models with Celtic-style decorative elements, including ZOOMORPHIC handles and lids. They are dated on stylistic grounds to *c*.400 BC.

Bastam   a large (21 ha) URARTIAN fortified settlement, just northwest of Lake Urmia in northwestern Iran, which represents one of the few thoroughly-excavated Urartian sites. W. Kleiss's work exposed an administrative town set along a ridge, divided into upper and lower sections. The architecture of the citadel is dominated by monumental buildings ('palaces') with pillared halls; the administrative centre yielded several Urartian texts and a large number of sealed BULLAE (envelopes), reflecting monitored storage and flows of goods. The careful stratigraphic excavation permitted a detailed chronological ordering of Urartian and immediately post-Urartian pottery; this aspect of the German work is one of the most enduring contributions to Urartian studies in recent times.

Batalimo   a site in the southern Central African Republic with large quantities of FLAKES, sidescrapers (see SCRAPER), flaked axes, and elaborately-decorated dark brown or black pottery. It is described as a Neolithic site dated to ad 380. However, it may date from the Iron Age.

Batán Grande   a large urban site located in the Lambayeque region of the far north coast of Peru, pertaining to the MIDDLE HORIZON and LATE INTERMEDIATE PERIOD, the centre of Sicán culture. Excavations by Izumi Shimada indicate that it was an important locus of metallurgy.

Batavia   a Dutch East Indiaman, wrecked off Western Australia in AD 1629. Significant finds included military and navigation equipment and a complete sandstone portico intended for the fort at Batavia in the Dutch East Indies.

Bat Cave   a series of adjacent stratified ROCKSHELTERS, located in New Mexico, USA, which provided controversial evidence for early agriculture in the New World. The earliest evidence of humans in the cave is between 10 000 and 9 000 BP. Up to 2800 BP, the site was used only occasionally by hunting groups. Between 2800 and 2200 BP large pits and hearths were constructed, and a more regular use of the site is indicated. The pits contained cultigens (maize and squash). The maize is primitive but similar to maize found in later PUEBLO sites. Beans were apparently not used at the site until later. CERAMIC levels are dated between 1800 and 800 BP.

Bath (*Lat.* Aquae Sulis)   a Roman spa town in England. The waters were sacred to the Celtic Sulis who was identified with the CLASSICAL goddess Minerva. Excavations have revealed a temple built in the CORINTHIAN ORDER which lay in a precinct adjoining the extensive baths.

bâton de commandement   an Upper Palaeolithic artifact, occasionally encountered in AURIGNACIAN assemblages but more typically found in MAGDALENIAN tool-kits. It consists of a decorated cylinder of antler with a hole through the thickest part. The baton may be decorated with intricate engraving. Its function is unknown, although it is generally interpreted as a shaft-straightener. Today it is more usually called a *bâton percé* (perforated baton).

Battersea Shield   a bronze shield with glass inlays dredged from the River Thames, London, England, in 1857. The shield is sub-rectangular in shape with rounded ends and slight waisting in the centre. It would originally have been fixed to a wooden backing. The main face is decorated with three cast bronze discs with central bosses and tendril ornament. Stylistic criteria suggest a date in the early 1st century AD. The shield may have been deposited in the river as a votive offering.

bâton de commandement

battleship curve   a graph, shaped like the profile of an early 20th century battleship, that represents changes through time in the frequency of a particular ATTRIBUTE from increasing to decreasing popularity.

Batungan   two cave-sites, at Masbate, central Philippines, yielding flaked stone tools and pottery. A small amount of it is decorated with stamped patterns similar to pottery of Yuan-Shan in Taiwan, and there is a possible connection with KALANAY (Sulawesi) and LAPITA ware. The date is *c*.900 BC or earlier.

Baturong Caves   rockshelter sites, in Sabah, north Borneo, including Hagop Bilo, yielding a stone industry characterized by long BLADE-like knives, dating *c*.17 000–12 000 BP, succeeding the TINKAYU industry and preceding that of the MADAI CAVES.

be   an administrative unit in the emerging YAMATO state organization of the 5th–6th centuries AD in Japan. Craftspeople and palace service personnel were assigned to *be* groupings and their products and labour collected for court use.

beaker   a decorated, handleless drinking vessel, characteristic of the European Late Neolithic Early Bronze Age. See BELL BEAKER.

Beazley, Sir John Davidson (1885–1970)   a British scholar who is best known for his work in identifying the 'hands' of the painters and potters of ATHENIAN POTTERY (see also BLACK-FIGURED, RED-FIGURED). These identifications supplemented the names of craftsmen which appear on the pottery. He named these anonymous people either after the museum in which one of the pieces was located (e.g. 'the painter of London E105'), a former owner (e.g. 'the Ready painter'), or a mannerism of the style (e.g. 'Elbows Out').

bec   a Palaeolithic FLAKE tool RETOUCHED on one edge to form a point, used for boring.

bed   the smallest formally-recognized division of SEDIMENT or rock within a STRATIGRAPHIC series. It is greater than 1 cm thick and distinguished from overlying and underlying beds by well-defined divisional planes, or bedding planes. Excavations at archaeological sites and contextual interpretation are often conducted at the scale where recognition of individual beds, or even finer stratigraphic intervals, is significant.

beehive tomb   see THOLOS.

Beersheba   a Palestinian site, the traditional southern boundary of the Land of Israel. It was substantially occupied only in the ISRAELITE Period when massive fortifications surrounded a carefully-planned city that included an impressive water-supply system, large storehouses and a building described as a 'Governor's Palace'.

behavioural archaeology   the study of the laws pertaining to the relationship between MATERIAL CULTURE and human behaviour, and the impact of human and natural agencies on material culture between its original use in the past and its subsequent discovery by archaeologists.

Behbet el-Hagar   a site in the Nile DELTA, Egypt, the main cult centre of the goddess ISIS during the LATE PERIOD. Behbet el-Hagar now largely consists of a mass of fallen granite blocks from the TEMPLE, the construction of which was probably initiated by Nektanebo I (380–362 BC) and continued, in particular, by PTOLEMIES II and III (285–221 BC).

Beidha   a NATUFIAN and PPNB site in the highlands of southern Jordan, where Diana Kirkbride's excavations in 1958–67 produced a sequence of PPNB architecture that documents a shift from roughly circular (earlier) to agglomerated rectilinear (later) constructions. Subsistence at Beidha included probably domesticated goat as well as other wild species; and barley and emmer, though not yet morphologically domesticates, seem to have been cultivated. The material culture includes small vessels and figurines of unfired clay and a wide range of exotic materials (including a little Anatolian OBSIDIAN) in addition to the chipped stone, ground stone and bone industries. Excavations also uncovered 43 burials, including examples with detached skulls.

Beikthano   a protohistoric and early historic settlement and Buddhist religious site in central Burma, possibly associated with the state centred on ŚRI KSETRA during the early-mid 1st millennium AD.

Beit Mersim   a Palestinian site excavated in 1924–32 by ALBRIGHT and Fisher. The TELL of Beit Mersim is important for its carefully-excavated strata, especially of the MIDDLE BRONZE AGE, the pottery of which formed a basis for the ceramic chronology of Palestine.

Belgae   the name given by Roman authors (notably Caesar) to the peoples of northeastern Gaul (modern northeastern France and Belgium) and southeastern Britain in the 1st century BC/AD. The continental Belgae were divided into 27 different branches. Most of these were CELTIC, but the easternmost seem to have been purely Germanic. The Belgic confederation is thought to have come into being around 100 BC, and survived until conquered by Caesar in 57 BC. An important Belgic site excavated in recent years is the sanctuary at Gournay-sur-Aronde in Oise, France, dedicated to gods of war, death and fertility, with offerings of weapons and animal sacrifices. The Belgic peoples of Britain carried the same tribal names as their continental neighbours and may have been formed by an immigrant aristocracy. They are associated with the burials of the AYLESFORD–Swarling culture.

Bel'kachi   a stratified Neolithic site in the Lena basin of Siberia. The Early Neolithic levels at Bel'kachi I have produced sand-tempered pottery with net or mat impressions, dated by RADIOCARBON to about 4000 BC. Overlying these deposits are layers of a 'developed' Neolithic which has been termed the 'Bel'kachinsk culture', whose pottery has distinctive cord-wrapped paddle impressions. The upper levels at Bel'kachi I have check-stamped pottery, often tempered with animal hair. Bel'kachinsk stone tools and pottery are widespread in Siberia and have some analogues in North America.

Bell Beaker   a type of pottery vessel found throughout large areas of western and central Europe in the Final Neolithic or CHALCOLITHIC period c.2500–1800 BC. The name derives from the characteristic vessel form, which resembles an inverted bell, with globular body and flaring rim. Bell Beakers were objects of value and were highly decorated in a variety of regionally and chronologically specific styles, two of the most important early types being the Maritime Beaker of Iberia and the All-Over Ornamented Beaker of the Lower Rhineland. A range of special artifacts is often associated with Beakers in grave assemblages, including archer's WRISTGUARDS of polished stone, V-perforated buttons and copper-TANGED daggers.

Bell Beaker

Bellows Beach   one of the earliest sites in Hawaii, on Oahu, dating to AD 600–1000. The ASSEMBLAGE of one-piece pearlshell FISH-HOOKS, ADZES and a shell grater, with bones of pig, dog and rat is a typical Early Eastern POLYNESIAN one and resembles the material from the HALAWA dune site.

Belverde   a Bronze Age ritual complex in Tuscany, Italy, consisting of ritual deposits among crevices and beneath overhangs among massive tumbled boulders. This unique site, nestling below a steep cliff, has yielded large numbers of bronze objects and items of pottery, including vessels containing carbonized foodstuffs. Basins and steps were carved on the tops of a few of the larger boulders. The plateau above the cliff is occupied by a fortified site, probably of the Late Bronze Age or Iron Age.

Belzoni, Giovanni Battista (1778–1823)   an Italian theatrical strong-man who excavated for Egyptian antiquities, chiefly on behalf of Salt, the British Consul in Egypt. His best-known discovery is the tomb of Seti I, in the VALLEY OF THE KINGS.

bench   1. an erosional TERRACE LANDFORM consisting of an alluvial cut surface on bedrock confined to a valley.
2. an erosional Landform consisting of a wave-cut surface, level to gently seaward-sloping, formed in coastal areas as a sea-cliff retreats

from wave action. This type of bench is often referred to as a wave-cut platform.

Benfica a locality near Luanda on the Angolan coast with numerous SHELL MIDDENS, mostly associated with the 16th century AD village of Benfica, but also comprising older stone artifact assemblages and Early Iron Age pottery dated to the 2nd century AD.

Beni Hassan a site in UPPER EGYPT, best known for its 39 rock-cut tombs of the MIDDLE KINGDOM, some belonging to the NOMARCHS of the region. Painted scenes on the walls of some of these tombs provide much information on daily life and military activity during the period. Two kilometres to the south is the ROCK-TEMPLE constructed by HATCHEPSUT called the Speos Artemidos.

Benin a southern Nigerian city which flourished from before the arrival of Europeans in the late 15th century AD, best known for its 4000–7000 CIRE PERDUE 'bronzes', most of which are brasses, in the form of near life-size human heads and plaques, a tradition which continued until the 19th century AD. Suggestions that the origins of the Benin brass-casting tradition may be traced to IFE are disputed.

Bennett, Wendell Clark (1905–53) an American archaeologist who undertook several major field projects in Andean South America, principally in Peru and Bolivia. In 1932 he worked in Bolivia, establishing a chronological sequence for the site of TIAHUANACO, and identifying the CHIRIPA culture. In 1936–38 he worked on the north coast and highlands of Peru, where he confirmed TELLO's assertion that CHAVÍN was the earliest complex civilization. He was one of the principal organizers of the Virú Valley survey of 1946–47. In 1950 he mapped and tested the site of HUARI, for the purpose of establishing a chronological sequence for the site.

Berdyzh an Upper Palaeolithic open-air site on the Sozh River (Dnepr tributary) in Belarus. The main HORIZON is buried in slope deposits overlying ALLUVIUM of the second TERRACE, and has yielded RADIOCARBON dates of 23 430 and 15 000 bp. The faunal remains are predominantly woolly MAMMOTH, and as many as three former MAMMOTH-BONE HOUSES may be present.

Berekhat Ram an ACHEULIAN open-air site in the northern Golan Heights, Israel, which was discovered during agricultural work and excavated by N. Goren-Inbar in 1980–81. The site has yielded many waste FLAKES but comparatively few tools, including eight BIFACES, LEVALLOIS flakes and sidescrapers – see SCRAPER. A pebble may have been modified to enhance its natural resemblance to a female figurine.

Berelekh the northernmost Palaeolithic site in the world, located at a latitude of 71° N near the mouth of the Indigirka River in northeastern Siberia. The site contains a bed of over 8000 mammal bones, primarily woolly MAMMOTH, which apparently accumulated under natural conditions c.14 000–12 000 years ago, and an overlying Upper Palaeolithic HORIZON dating to 13 400–10 600 bp. The bone bed was studied by Vereshchagin, and the archaeological horizon by Mochanov, who assigned it to the DYUKTAI CULTURE.

Berenice the name of several HELLENISTIC foundations named after the various women of that name married to different PTOLEMIES. These cities include:

1. (*mod.* Benghazi) the harbour town on the coast of Cyrenaica, Libya, replacing the settlement at Euhesperides dug by the British.

2. a port on the Egyptian coast of the Red Sea founded by Ptolemy II. It was linked to Coptos on the Nile by a camel route. In the 1st and 2nd centuries AD it was an important port linking the Nile valley, and ultimately the eastern Mediterranean, with Arabia, India and eastern Africa.

3. Pella in Jordan, said to have been called by this name.

Beringia   a land mass located in the present-day Bering and Chukchi Seas, formed by the drop in sea levels as a result of the formation of continental glaciers at the end of the PLEISTOCENE. This allowed humans to enter the New World, by a route called the Bering Land Bridge.

Bernal García, Ignacio (1910–92)   an eminent Mexican archaeologist, a pupil of CASO, best known for his work at MONTE ALBÁN, DAINZÚ and other Oaxacan sites, and for excavations and restorations at TEOTIHUACÁN.

Bernam-Sungkai   a district of peninsular Malaysia, including Slim River, known for its metal age (*c.*300 BC?) stone slab graves, perhaps contemporary with those of PASEMAH.

Bersu, Gerhard (1889–1964)   a German archaeologist, Director of the Römisch-Germanischen Kommission at Frankfurt until removed by the Nazis in the 1930s. Bersu then emigrated to Britain, introducing continental methods of excavation including area excavation of settlement sites. These he put to good use in the now classic excavations at the Iron Age farmstead of LITTLE WOODBURY in 1938–39. During the Second World War, Bersu excavated Iron Age houses on the Isle of Man during his internment there as a German citizen.

beta ray backscattering   a technique used to determine quantitatively the chemical composition of surface layers of materials such as the content of glass, GLAZES, and SLIPS. A sample is bombarded by a beam of electrons generated from a weak radioactive beta source producing backscattered electrons. The concentration of an element known to be present can be estimated based on the percentage of backscattering, which is dependent on the atomic number of the elements of the artifact surface layers.

Bethel   a Palestinian site, excavated sporadically in the 1930s–1960s by ALBRIGHT and Kelso. Occupied noncontinuously from the CHALCOLITHIC, the strongly-fortified settlement of the MIDDLE BRONZE AGE included a fine stone sanctuary found to contain animal bones and ceramic cult-vessels, while ASTARTE-plaques were common. Following its conquest by the ISRAELITES Bethel became a comparative backwater, although it was a relatively large city in the Roman and BYZANTINE periods.

Beth-Shan   a Palestinian site, the CLASSICAL Scythopolis, occupied virtually continuously from the CHALCOLITHIC to the mediaeval period, and excavated sporadically by the University of Pennsylvania Museum from 1921–33. Beth-Shan is best known for its successive strata of Late Bronze Age–Iron Age temples, which contained a large amount of NEW KINGDOM Egyptian material including STELAE and architectural elements. A monastery of the 6th century AD at Beth-Shan contains fine MOSAIC floors.

Beth-Shemesh   a Palestinian site, excavated by Mackenzie in 1911–12 and by Grant in 1928–33. Probably founded in the MIDDLE BRONZE AGE, possibly as a HYKSOS fortified settlement, and later a significant Late Bronze Age and PHILISTINE town.

Betovo a Middle Palaeolithic open-air site on the Desna River near Bryansk in European Russia. Artifacts and faunal remains are buried in a humic sand bed, although their age is unclear, the predominance of arctic species among the fauna (e.g. snow lemming) indicates a cold interval (early LAST GLACIAL?). The artifacts include many DENTICULATES. Betovo was dug by Tarasov in the 1970s and 1980s.

bevelled rim bowl a pottery form typical of the URUK culture in MESOPOTAMIA and surrounding regions. The bowls were mass-produced by pressing a coarse slab of clay into an open mould and then trimming the excess clay at the top of the mould to produce the characteristic rim. Found in huge numbers, often in temples or other 'public' buildings, the vessels are usually regarded as instruments for apportioning rations to institutional personnel; other ideas include vessels for cultic offerings, making bread and processing milk.

bevelled rim bowl

Beycesultan a 15 ha prehistoric site on the upper Meander River in southwestern Anatolia excavated by S. Lloyd in the 1950s, which provides a key stratigraphic sequence of 40 levels that run from the Late CHALCOLITHIC to the terminal Bronze Age. In addition to the pottery chronology (essentially equivalent to the Chalcolithic levels at HACILAR), Beycesultan provides early examples of MEGARON (porch and hall) architectures, possibly first in the Late Chalcolithic level XXIV, and then certainly in EARLY BRONZE III levels (X–VIII). The Late Chalcolithic level XXXIV also contained a small hoard of copper tools, a particularly early concentration of metals. The MIDDLE BRONZE AGE walled town included the 'burnt palace', built of brick and timber walls and focused on pillared courtyards, which covered over half a hectare. Other massive 'public' architecture was also present on the opposite side of the town. The Late Bronze Age occupation of the site was on a reduced scale, though still presenting large blocks of residential buildings (and still using the megaron form); the last occupation seems to have ended around 1000 BC.

Bhimbetka a rock ridge 45 km southeast of Bhopal in Madhya Pradesh, central India, which presents a large series of ROCKSHELTERS that contain stratified Palaeolithic to historic period deposits and an extremely rich corpus of ROCK ART. Excavations at several shelters (especially shelter IIIF-24) reveal a succession of ACHEULIAN (HAND-AXES, CLEAVERS, a high LEVALLOIS index), Middle Palaeolithic (disappearance of BIFACES, increased BLADE frequency), Upper Palaeolithic (tendency toward bladelet production), and MESOLITHIC industries.

The Mesolithic, the most frequently represented period at the rock-shelters, is characterized by a bladelet industry and by grinding equipment; this lithic assemblage continues into levels in which occur copper tools and CHALCOLITHIC pottery. RADIOCARBON determinations date the Mesolithic industry to 6000–1000 BC. The rock art belongs to the Mesolithic period and later into historic periods. The art, painted in a wide range of colours, presents a diverse array of human and animal figures which are either displayed individually or set in scenes of hunting, warfare or ceremony; some of the later art shows horse and elephant riders. As with most rock art, the chief means of dating are stylistic analysis and observation of superposition (relative patination being not particularly pertinent here); V.S. WAKANKAR's proposed stylistic periodization for the entire Indian subcontinent is often cited in connection with the Bhimbetka corpus, but this system has uncertain validity. In 1990, PETROGLYPHS were found in one shelter.

bi   a disc-shaped JADE with a large central hole, used in early China to symbolize Heaven. It was worn suspended from the belt by court nobles in the HAN Dynasty.

Bibracte   an Iron Age OPPIDUM mentioned by Caesar as the capital of the Aedui and now identified with Mony Beuvray, Nièvre, France. Excavations in the 19th and early 20th century by Bulliot and DÉCHELETTE found it to be the classic example of early urban development in France. The oppidum was divided into residential and industrial quarters by a regular system of streets, with houses based on Roman models. The site was replaced in the later 1st century BC by the new town of Augustodunum (Autun), 27 km away.

biface, handaxe or ***coup-de-poing***   a bifacially-worked implement, usually a CORE TOOL, which forms the type-fossil for the ACHEULIAN (see fig.) but which is also found in certain MOUSTERIAN assemblages (see fig.). Biface technology developed from African PEBBLE-tool IN-DUSTRIES, spreading to Europe, India and southwest Asia with clear variation in appearance and workmanship. Bifaces range in shape from triangular or pear-shaped to oval, and in length from approximately 8 to 20 cm. They are believed to be multi-purpose tools. See also BOUT COUPÉ, FICRON, OVATE, CORDATE.

bifacial foliate   an artifact class comprising a variety of leaf-shaped

bifacial foliate

stone tools characterized by complete or nearly complete flaking on both sides. See also BLATTSPITZEN, WILLOW-LEAF, LAUREL-LEAF.

Big Game Hunting Tradition   a North American cultural TRADITION, characterized by the hunting of MEGAFAUNA, such as MAMMOTH and bison. This tradition was particularly widespread in the PALAEOINDIAN period, but was replaced in many areas of the continent by the ensuing ARCHAIC, except for areas like the Plains where it continued until European contact.

Big Horn Medicine Wheel   a MEDICINE WHEEL located in the Big Horn Mountains of Wyoming, USA, that consists of a central D-shaped stone cairn, from which radiate 28 spokes made of individual stones. The outer circumference of the 'wheel' is surrounded by six smaller cairns. It has been suggested that the site was astronomically aligned.

Bilzingsleben   a Lower Palaeolithic open-air lakeshore site located near the confluence of the Wipper and Wirbelbach rivers in eastern Germany. Artifacts are buried in spring deposits dated by the URANIUM/thorium method to *c.*230 000 bp; occupation extends back to *c.*350 000 BP; associated faunal remains include typical Middle PLEISTOCENE forms (e.g. macaque). The artifacts include CHOPPING TOOLS, DENTICULATES and SCRAPERS and provide evidence of a Lower Palaeolithic INDUSTRY without HANDAXES in central Europe. Human skeletal remains, reflecting a mixture of HOMO *erectus* and *H. sapiens* traits, were also found, as well as some incised lines on bones which may be non-functional.

Birch Creek   the location of a series of stratified ROCKSHELTERS in central Idaho, USA, with occupation ranging from approximately 8500 BP to the Historic Period. The sites are important for the construction of CULTURE HISTORY in this section of the Rocky Mountains and for understanding the prehistory of the Shoshonean, a widespread linguistic group of the American West.

Bird, Junius Bouton (1907–82)   an American archaeologist who conducted field research primarily in South America. He excavated the site of FELL'S CAVE in Tierra del Fuego, establishing the presence of a PALAEOINDIAN occupation in South America. He worked in the Atacama region of northern Chile, and also, as part of the Virú Valley survey, excavated the site of HUACA PRIETA on the north coast of Peru, establishing the existence of the PRECERAMIC Period. He was especially interested in textile technology, and devoted much of his boundless energy to the study of textiles.

Bir Kiseiba   an area in the eastern Sahara of southern Egypt with early CERAMICS and cattle bones dated to *c.*9500 BP (see NABTA PLAYA).

Birrigai   a ROCKSHELTER in the southeastern highlands of the Australian Capital Territory, demonstrating occupation of this region at the LAST GLACIAL MAXIMUM. Intermittent occupation began *c.*21 000 bp, increasing in intensity from *c.*3000 bp.

Bir Tarfawi   a small oasis in southwestern Egypt with ACHEULIAN and Middle Palaeolithic sites. The latter date between perhaps 175 000–90 000 BP and are associated with considerable evidence for meat- and plant-food processing and probably hunting.

birth-house   see MAMMISI.

Bisitun   a site located east of Kermanshah on the pass through the mountains towards Hamadan in western Iran, that is the setting for the famous trilingual CUNEIFORM inscription of the ACHAEMENID king

Darius I, providing an account of his accession to the throne (by usurpation); the text accompanies a carved depiction of the king's triumph. The repetition of the text in the Old Persian, BABYLONIAN and ELAMITE languages allowed RAWLINSON to initiate successful decipherment of cuneiform scripts. Monumental inscriptions and reliefs of other periods also appear at Bisitun, including a PARTHIAN relief which echoes that of Darius. Bisitun is also the location of a Palaeolithic cave site excavated by Carleton Coon in the 1940s.

Biskupin   a Late Bronze Age/Early Iron Age fortified site in northwest Poland, excavated in 1933–39 by Józef KOSTRZEWSKI. Located on a peninsula, Biskupin is surrounded by a wooden-crib rampart which enclosed a settled area of 2 ha. Streets paved with logs separated rows of houses. Excavations at Biskupin yielded many preserved artifacts of wood, cloth and bone. The main occupation at Biskupin is dated to the HALLSTATT D period, with the settlement being either abandoned or destroyed c.400 BC. The settlement at Biskupin has been reconstructed as an archaeological park open to the public.

Bismarck Archipelago   islands off the HUON PENINSULA, Papua New Guinea, which since 1985 have been the subject of an intensive research programme, instigated by Jim Allen, to investigate the origins of the LAPITA cultural complex. The excavated sites fall into two broad groups: PLEISTOCENE ROCKSHELTERS and Lapita sites. The research has shown that occupation of the Bismarcks and exploitation of marine resources go back more than 30 000 years, and that OBSIDIAN from TALASEA was being transported 20 000 years ago. Evidence has also been presented for faunal introductions to the Bismarcks by humans: *phalanger* (possum) in the Late Pleistocene, and two species of rat and a wallaby in the mid-HOLOCENE. See BALOF, ELOAUA ISLAND, LOU, MATENBEK, MATENKUPKUM, WATOM.

black-and-red ware   a series of CHALCOLITHIC and Iron Age pottery wares in India. They are black on the interior surface and rim, and red on the exterior surface. Depending on the cultural contexts in which the ware appears, black-and-red pottery may bear painted decoration (e.g. at AHAR, KAYATHA, RANJPUR), while the specific characteristics of fabric, form and surface treatment of other black-and-red wares are highly variable through the Gangetic drainage (e.g. HASTINAPURA, KAUSAMBI, RAJGHAT, CHIRAND), the northern Deccan (e.g. INAMGAON, NEVASA) and further south (e.g. PIKLIHAL, MEGALITHIC GRAVES). This formal and temporal variability leaves the term with only a broad descriptive significance.

black-figured, *adj.*   (of pottery) characterized by figures or decorative elements that appear in black against the lighter clay background with the detail incised. The technique was also occasionally used on funerary plaques, and was first employed at CORINTH in the 7th century BC (see CORINTHIAN POTTERY), but it is often associated with ATHENS where it appeared in the late 7th century and was common well into the 5th century. However, it was not confined to these two centres (see CHALCIDIAN WARE, PONTIC WARE). Compare RED-FIGURED.

black-glazed   see BLACK-GLOSSED.

black-glossed or black-glazed, *adj.*   (of pottery) characterized by a technique used to decorate plain wares giving them an appearance of a black sheen. Black-glossed wares were made alongside the figure-decorated wares (see BLACK-FIGURED, RED-FIGURED), but their popularity continued well into the HELLENISTIC period (see WEST SLOPE WARE). One of the most important centres of production was at ATHENS, from the 6th to the 2nd centuries BC (see ATHENIAN POTTERY), although it was also made at several centres throughout Italy and Sicily. From the middle of the 5th century BC, shapes were frequently ornamented with STAMPED DECORATION, and from the 4th century BC ROULETTING became common on open shapes.

Blackwater Draw   an important site, actually a series of individual localities, in eastern New Mexico, USA, that is famous for the early investigations on CLOVIS and FOLSOM conducted there since the early 1930s. The surrounding area was once a series of glacial lakes and ponds, and the remains of camel, horse, bison and MAMMOTH have been found, as well as extensive PALAEOINDIAN remains, which include not just Clovis and Folsom, but also AGATE BASIN, CODY and FREDERICK.

blade   a long, flat and narrow FLAKE with parallel sides struck from a prepared CORE, usually by indirect PERCUSSION involving the use of a punch placed between the hammer and the STRIKING PLATFORM. Traditionally, blades are defined as measuring at least twice as long as they are wide, with shorter narrower blades being classed as *bladelets*; however, different authorities use different length:breadth ratios. Blades were occasionally manufactured during the Middle Palaeolithic, but Upper Palaeolithic INDUSTRIES show a great increase in blade production and the development of specialized blade tools. See BACKED BLADE, BURIN, SCRAPER.

bladelet   see BLADE.

blank   see CORE.

Blattspitzen   a category of stone artifact, characterized by complete or nearly complete flaking of both sides and pointed at one or both ends. Blattspitzen are found in some late Middle and early Upper Palaeolithic industries of Central and Eastern Europe.

Blegen, Carl William (1887–1971)   an American archaeologist who excavated at KORAKOU, PROSYMNA and PYLOS in Greece, but who is perhaps best remembered for his extensive excavations at TROY.

blow-out   an erosional LANDFORM consisting of a local trough, basin or hollow in SAND-dominated material, caused by wind erosion as a local area is destabilized and becomes susceptible to deflation. The term often includes the resulting down-current accumulation of material that forms a blow-out DUNE. Blow-outs cause disturbance of original archaeological CONTEXT, as coarser artifactual material settles in the hollow as a residual accumulation and finer material is winnowed out. Simultaneously, burial of artifactual material by the hollow fill may occur downwind.

blow sand   see COVER SAND.

Bluefish Caves   three small caves in the OLD CROW Basin of the northern Yukon, Canada, which may constitute the oldest archaeological site in North America. Discovered in 1975, they have been investigated by Cinq-Mars and Morlan since 1978. They contain excellently preserved deposits invaluable in reconstructing the environment during the late GLACIAL period. A small quantity of artifacts is buried in shallow LOESS and rubble deposits, associated with remains of woolly MAMMOTH, Dall sheep, reindeer and other vertebrates. Sixteen RADIOCARBON dates on various bone fragments span 25 000–12 000 bp, but their relationship to the artifacts is problematic. There seems to be definite evidence for human occupation in deposits from at least 13 000–10 000 bp, including a WEDGE-SHAPED MICROCORE, MICROBLADES and BURINS that are similar to tools manufactured in Siberia at the same time, and animal bones that may have been cut with a stone BLADE. In the lower levels (down to 20 000 bp) DEBITAGE FLAKES, cut and butchered animal bone, and the very large numbers of animal bones are also suggestive of human occupation.

bluestone   a type of stone, bluish-grey in dry weather, used in the construction of the second phase of STONEHENGE. The main material is spotted dolerite, but the Stonehenge bluestones also include unspotted dolerite, rhyolite and volcanic. The source has been traced to the Preseli Hills of South Wales, 215 km away, from where the 80 or so bluestones, each weighing around four tonnes, are thought by some scholars to have been brought specially to Stonehenge, using river and sea transport as far as possible.

Bluff Cave   see NUNAMIRA.

Boat Axe culture   a subgroup of Scandinavia's SINGLE GRAVE/CORDED WARE cultures, characterized by a thin stone battleaxe whose shape resembles an upturned boat.

Bocca Quadrata or **Square Mouth**   a Middle Neolithic culture of Northern Italy characterized by pottery vessels with a rounded body ending in a square mouth. Decoration consists mainly of incised geometric motifs. It is especially common in the Po plain and Liguria *c.*5400–3800 BC, and is present at the ARENE CANDIDE cave and the lake dwelling of Molino Casarotto.

Bockstein   the collective name of a series of neighbouring open and cave-sites in the Lone Valley, Württemberg, Germany, which have yielded artifacts and faunal remains from the Middle and Upper Palaeolithic, and which have been excavated principally by Wetzel and Bosinski. The Bocksteinloch, a small cave, and the Bocksteinschmiede, the open area in front of the cave, are perhaps the best-known sites, and have produced over 200 MICOQUIAN-style CHERT BIFACES dated by STRATIGRAPHY to the end of the last INTERGLACIAL. The later material includes Bockstein knives.

Bodrokeresztúr   an ENEOLITHIC culture of the Hungarian Plain which succeeds the TISZAPOLGÁR Culture *c.*3300 bc and is followed in turn by the BADEN Culture, contemporaneous with CUCUTÉNI-TRIPOLYE to its east. Bodrokeresztúr grave-goods resemble those of Tiszapolgár, with undecorated globular pots on pedestals, massive copper shaft-hole 'axe-adzes', and virtually no figurines. Settlement pottery, however, is different, with the use of stab-and-drag (also known as 'Furchenstich') ornament in chequerboard and hatched patterns filled with white incrustation. Domestic cattle predominate in faunal samples.

bog   a soft waterlogged area that supports a spongy vegetation community, including sedges, mosses, rushes and grasses, and is maintained by either relatively large amounts of rainfall, geomorphic setting, impedance to throughflow of groundwater, or a combination of these. Bog environments are usually ANAEROBIC and conducive to the preservation of organic remains; they are good sources of PALAEOENVIRONMENTAL information. PEAT bogs are also a potential source of fuel. See also FEN.

Boghazköy   the ancient Hattusha, the HITTITE capital in the Halys River drainage of north central Anatolia, which has been the subject of long-term German research since the beginning of the 20th century. The Hittite city sprawls over a slope that is marked by several hills, the most important of which are Büyükkale and Büyükkaya; the walls of the city enclose about 180 ha. The area was first occupied in CHALCOLITHIC times (at Yarikkaya, about 3 km from the city), followed by EARLY BRONZE AGE occupation (at Büyükkaya). The settlement at the town itself began by the end of the Early and into the MIDDLE BRONZE AGE on and near Büyükkale; during the Middle Bronze Age the place was a KÁRUM involved in the Old ASSYRIAN CAPPADOCIAN TRADE. Although it was the royal seat of the Old Hittite period, relatively little of this occupation has been recovered (also on and near Büyükkale). By the time of the Hittite Empire (third quarter of the 2nd millennium BC), the city consisted of a walled citadel (at Büyükkale) composed of large administrative buildings containing several extremely valuable archives, a separately-walled inner town (about 80 ha) containing the massive Temple I along with residential areas to the northwest of Büyükkale, and a walled outer city (roughly 100 ha) upslope and south of Büyükkale with four excavated temples and several residential districts also enclosed by a wall (covering about 100 ha). The walls of the latter part of town contain the famous 'Sphinx' and 'Lion' Gates which are so often compared to the gate at MYCENAE. After the destruction of Hattusha and the collapse of the Hittite empire in around 1200 BC, the place was reoccupied by a far smaller settlement (at Büyükkale) down to the mid 1st millennium BC.

Bohai [Po-hai]   1. the bay at the northern end of the Yellow Sea separating the China mainland from the Korean peninsula. The coastal area of Bohai Bay includes the southern end of the DONGBEI region of China, containing the HONGSHAN, XINLE and XIAJIADIAN cultures.
2. a historic state succeeding KOGURYO in the Manchurian region, AD 698–926; it is spelled 'Parhae' in Korean.

Bohunice   a Middle Palaeolithic open-air site located at the edge of Brno in Moravia, Czechoslovakia. Artifacts and occasional faunal remains are buried in LOESS deposits that date (on the basis of STRATIGRAPHIC correlation) to the early cold maximum of the LAST GLACIAL. The assemblage includes sidescrapers (see SCRAPER), DENTICULATES, BURINS and LAUREL-LEAF POINTS, and has been used to define a distinct late Middle Palaeolithic industry (i.e. BOHUNICIAN).

Bohunician, *adj.*   of a Middle Palaeolithic INDUSTRY of Moravia, Czechoslovakia, characterized by endscrapers and sidescrapers (see SCRAPER) and some BIFACIAL FOLIATES. The industry occurs in the late Middle Palaeolithic (during the middle of the LAST GLACIAL), and may be transitional to the Upper Palaeolithic. The Bohunician was defined by Valoch in 1976.

Boian culture   a Late Neolithic culture of the lower Danube basin (eastern Bulgaria and Romania), *c.*4100–3700 bc, generally discussed as part of a complex of cultures, including the MARITSA and VADASTRA, contemporaneous with layer V at KARANOVO. Boian fine pottery is characterized by narrow channelling, and in its later stages by graphite painted decoration which subsequently became the distinctive feature of the succeeding GUMELNIŢA culture. Notable sites of the Boian culture include Radovanu and the eponymous site of Boian A in southeastern Romania, with dates between 4200 and 3700 bc.

Boker Tachtit a stratified open-air Palaeolithic site in the central Negev, Israel, excavated in 1975–80 as part of Anthony Marks' Negev project. It has an industry transitional between the Middle and Upper Palaeolithic that differs from that found further north in the Levant. In the Boker Tachtit industry, dated to at least 43 000 BC, a LEVALLOIS technique produced both POINTS and BLADES while opposed-platform blade CORES are also present; typologically, the assemblages differ markedly from the local MOUSTERIAN industry.

Boleráz see BADEN CULTURE.

Bølling Interstadial a warm period occurring during the final stages of the last (WEICHSEL) GLACIATION in Europe and starting at *c.*13 300 BP.

Bol'shaya Akkarzha an Upper Palaeolithic open-air site near the Black Sea coast outside Odessa in southwest Ukraine. An assemblage of stone artifacts (age unknown) is associated with thousands of steppe bison bone fragments (see also AMVROSIEVKA). The site was excavated by BORSIKOWSKIJ in 1954 and 1961.

Bonampak a CLASSIC Lowland MAYA site in Chiapas, Mexico. The site is significant for its beautiful wall paintings, some of which depict a battle or raid. This graphic illustration of Maya warfare was important evidence suggesting that the traditional view of non-violent Maya civilization was inaccurate. These murals also provide detailed information about other aspects of Maya life, including dress, music and rituals.

Bondaian a regional variant of the AUSTRALIAN SMALL-TOOL TRADITION in eastern New South Wales, characterized by BONDI POINTS and other MICROLITHIC implements.

Bondi point an asymmetric BACKED BLADE, characteristic of the AUSTRALIAN SMALL-TOOL TRADITION, distributed widely in southern parts of the continent, but absent in much of the tropical north.

bone dating dating methods applied to collagen and mineral components of human and animal bones. ABSOLUTE AGES with margins of uncertainty can be obtained by RADIOCARBON DATING, URANIUM SERIES DATING methods, and in some cases, AMINO ACID RACEMIZATION. RELATIVE AGES can be obtained by Amino Acid Racemization, NITROGEN DATING and FLUORINE DATING methods. In *bone collagen dating*, protein collagen is extracted from bone and dated by Radiocarbon. The collagen is selected for dating because it is less likely to be contaminated with modern carbon in the soil environment than the total organic carbon or apatite carbonate fraction.

Bonfire Shelter a bison KILL-SITE in Texas, USA, unusual because it has a long, albeit discontinuous, sequence of use (approximately 10 000 BC–AD 600) in an area that was not a primary bison habitat. The site is located in a ROCKSHELTER into which bison may have been driven from above, although new excavations of a portion of the site suggest that the earliest levels may have been associated with an animal trap, rather than a jump.

boomerang a curved throwing stick, one form of which can be made to return to the thrower. Returning and non-returning boomerangs are widely used by Australian Aborigines for hunting, fighting and as toys. The oldest Australian examples from WYRIE SWAMP are 10 000 years old. Although often thought of as uniquely Australian, they are known from other parts of the world. Archaeological examples have been found in MESOLITHIC Holland and Egypt, while a curved piece of MAMMOTH tusk from OBLAZOWA, southern Poland, dating to 23 000 bp, is the oldest-known boomerang-like artifact. See also LITTLE SALT SPRING.

Boomplaas   a cave in the southern Cape Province of South Africa, which contains a 5 m deep stratified deposit spanning the last 80 000 years, with successive MIDDLE and LATER STONE AGE industries excavated by H.J. Deacon in the 1970s. The excellent preservation and careful excavation of the large and small mammal remains, pollen, charcoal, sediments and artifacts have provided a unique record of environmental and cultural changes in the southern Cape.

Boqueirão   see PEDRA FURADA.

bora ground or **bora ring**   a group of Australian circular earthen structures, commonly linked by a pathway, used for ceremonies in north-central New South Wales and southeast Queensland. Similar features are also known from Victoria.

Border Cave   a South African cave on the KwaZulu-Swaziland border. Its stratified 2 m deep deposit contains MIDDLE STONE AGE assemblages dating from before 130 000 years ago, EARLY LATER STONE AGE assemblages dating to between 45 000–33 000 BP, and, in the uppermost layers, recent Iron Age material. Although some human remains are of doubtful provenance, an adult mandible from deposits RADIOCARBON dated to more than 49 000 bp, as well as a partial cranium and an infant skeleton thought to be c.100 000 years old, confirm the presence of anatomically modern HOMO *sapiens* in southern Africa during the early Upper PLEISTOCENE. The infant skeleton is the only definite burial attributed to the Middle Stone Age in southern Africa.

Bordes, François (1919–81)   a French prehistoric archaeologist best known for his pioneering study of the SEDIMENTS of the River Seine, and for his classification of the MOUSTERIAN of southwest France by means of the *système Bordes*, which involved the consideration of tool-type percentages plotted on CUMULATIVE GRAPHS and various technological and TYPOLOGICAL ratios. Bordes excavated at the Palaeolithic sites of COMBE-GRENAL and PECH DE L'AZÉ, and was an expert flint-knapper.

Bordj Mellala   an Algerian early Neolithic site dating to c.7000 BP, associated with geometric MICROLITHS as well as numerous ostrich eggshell beads and decorated water containers. Refitting of the stone artifacts has led to the recognition of specialized activity areas within the site.

Boreal climatic period   one of five POSTGLACIAL climatic and vegetation periods distinguished by Blytt and Sernander on the basis of POLLEN ANALYSIS, dated roughly to c.7600–5500 BC. The Boreal period in northern Europe represents the first real establishment of European woodlands, and sea levels rose rapidly as the ice-sheets melted, separating Britain, Ireland and the Danish islands from the European continent.

boreal forest or **taiga**   a group of related vegetation communities dominated by coniferous trees that exists in higher latitudes of the northern hemisphere but generally south of TUNDRA. Climatic conditions that favour such communities are severe winters and short growing seasons; in some areas they are growing on PERMAFROST. During GLACIAL episodes of the QUATERNARY the location of the boreal forest shifted southward. Boreal forests supported animals now extinct, such as the MASTODON, that were potential food sources.

bored stone   a roundish stone with a hole bored through its middle, found in a variety of sizes on sites throughout southern and central Africa dating to the last 40 000 years. Some were impaled as weights on digging sticks used to uproot plant tubers, a practice which is depicted in rock paintings as well as recorded ethnographically in southern Africa and Ethiopia.

Boriskowskij, Pavel Iossifovitch (1911–91)   an eminent Russian Palaeolithic specialist, pupil of EFIMENKO, best known for his excavations at AMVROSIEVKA, BOL'SHAYA AKKARZHA, KOSTENKI and PUSHKARI. He was especially notable for addressing the social aspects of the Middle/Upper Palaeolithic transition, from a MARXIST perspective, in the early 1930s.

Borobudur   a great stone STUPA near Magelang in central Java, thought to be the largest in the world, and famous for its reliefs illustrating Buddhist literature, built in the late 8th–early 9th centuries AD by the rulers of MATARAM. The structure comprises six square terraces surmounted by three round terraces and a large bell-shaped stupa. The scenes in the reliefs fall into three zones: the lowest, on the hidden base, illustrate the 'world of desire' (*kamadhatu*); above this is the 'world of form' (*rupadhatu*); then comes the 'world of formlessness' (*arupadhatu*).

Bosumpra   a cave in central Ghana with a LATER STONE AGE industry associated with charred oil-bearing seeds, which suggest a transition from the use of wild *Canarium* to the domestic oil palm, *Eleis*.

Bosutswe   see TOUTSWE.

bothros   a pit in Greek archaeology, typically used for storage purposes or rubbish disposal.

Bouar   a 130 × 30 km area in the Central African Republic with hundreds of MEGALITHS, consisting of standing stones on oval TUMULI, which may be burial grounds. Initial construction is thought to have taken place in the 6th–5th millennia BC, with later re-utilization.

Boucher de Perthes, Jacques (1788–1868)   a French customs official and amateur antiquary who first recognized the true antiquity of humankind in France by correctly identifying Lower Palaeolithic BIFACES from the River Somme gravels as the tools of 'antediluvian (pre-flood) man' found in association with the bones of extinct animals. After gaining support from Joseph Prestwich and John Evans in 1859, Boucher de Perthes' theories were slowly accepted by the French and British scientific establishments.

Bougon   an important cemetery of MEGALITHIC tombs at Deux-Sèvres, France, comprising eight chambers in five mounds labelled A–F (D is a field boundary). RADIOCARBON dates indicate that the oldest of the chambers (E1 and F0) date to the mid 5th millennium BC, and hence are among the oldest CHAMBERED TOMBS in Europe. The cemetery was greatly aggrandized in later centuries with the construction of the large mounds A, C and F. Many of the mounds are multi-phase, but the scarcity of associated material has made it very difficult to establish the precise chronology of the sequence. Pottery ranges from possible Early Neolithic sherds beneath one of the mounds, to material of the Late Neolithic or Early Bronze Age.

boulder the size subdivision of GRAVEL CLASTS larger than 256 mm in diameter, according to the Wentworth–Udden classification system. In the past, 'boulder' has carried the connotation of having been transported from a distance, and being somewhat rounded, although these inferences are not necessarily accurate.

bouleuterion a meeting place for the council (*boule*) in a Greek city normally adjacent to the AGORA. The buildings are usually square and contain a room which served as a debating chamber. Seats were normally placed around three sides, either in straight rows, or in curved tiers as found in theatres. At ATHENS, the bouleuterion contained seating for 500.

boundary the zone of vertical change from one SOIL HORIZON to another. Boundaries are described in terms of the vertical distance over which the change occurs, such as abrupt, clear or gradual, and the horizontal character of the boundary, such as whether it is smooth, wavy or irregular. Compare CONTACT.

Boussargues an enclosed village site in Hérault, France, with APSIDAL houses surrounded by a wall with projecting circular huts or towers, all built of dry-stone work. The circular huts had CORBEL-VAULTED roofs. Within the apsidal houses, pottery of the CHALCOLITHIC FONTBOUISSE culture (*c.*2500 BC) has been found. Finds of carbonized acorns and other nuts indicate that forest resources probably played an important part in the economy. The settlement is one of a number of enclosed Fontbouisse villages known in the area.

bout coupé, *adj.* ('cut-end') a term used by some British archaeologists to describe a well-made cordiform or sub-triangular refined BIFACE recovered from northwest Europe, usually encountered as an isolated and undated find, but believed to be a diagnostic MOUSTERIAN tool.

bout coupé Biface.

bow-and-arrow   an offensive weapon for firing small projectiles over great distances that is especially useful in the characterization of some North American cultures. The technology was introduced to North America as early as the PRE-DORSET in the Central Arctic, and quickly spread throughout many other regions as a distinct HORIZON. It is best recognized by small PROJECTILE POINTS.

Boxgrove   an ACHEULIAN site in West Sussex, England, which is as yet only partially excavated by Roberts, but which has yielded an important and extensive *in situ* BIFACE manufacturing floor, with lithic tools and DÉBITAGE, and associated faunal material.

Boyne Valley tombs   a major cemetery of MEGALITHIC tombs in a bend of the River Boyne, Meath, Ireland, comprising three large tombs (Dowth, KNOWTH and NEWGRANGE) together with several smaller mounds. The tombs consist of circular mounds containing one or more PASSAGE GRAVES. Knowth and Newgrange are famous for the complex MEGALITHIC ART which decorates the stones of their chambers and passages and of the kerbs which surround their covering mounds.

BP, *abbrev. for*   before present, by convention meaning before AD 1950; therefore, to convert a date from BP to BC (before Christ) it is necessary to subtract 1950 years. The use of lower case letters (*bp* or *bc*) indicates a RADIOCARBON date which has not been CALIBRATED, and is therefore likely to appear younger than it should.

brachycephalic   see CEPHALIC.

Bradshaw figures   small red finely-painted human figures in animated scenes common in the Kimberley region of Western Australia, and named after Joseph Bradshaw who 'discovered' them in the late 19th century. They are clearly of some antiquity because some artifacts depicted did not exist in recent Kimberley culture. Contemporary Aboriginal people attribute them to spirits, and they often underlie polychrome WANDJINA paintings. They resemble the MIMI figures of ARNHEM LAND.

Brak, Tell   a 40 ha site in the Khabur triangle of northeastern Syria known largely from the excavations by MALLOWAN in the 1930s, which revealed occupation at the site from 'UBAID to the mid 2nd millennium BC. Among Mallowan's more notable discoveries is a sequence of Late URUK to JEMDET NASR temples (the 'Eye Temple', named after the recurrent eye motif within this building) beneath the palace of the AKKADIAN king NARAM-SIN (2254–2218 BC) and another of UR III construction; domestic architecture of the latter periods was also uncovered. In later levels, Mallowan found a MITANNI palace and temple. David and Joan Oates reopened investigation of Tell Brak during the late 1970s and 1980s, greatly refining the late 4th-mid 2nd millennium chronology of the site, and providing important new details about the Late Uruk and the early 2nd millennium BC occupations. The emerging Late Uruk evidence indicates a massive presence of southern MESOPOTAMIAN forms (a numerical tablet, many SEALS and sealings, much of the pottery, brick morphology), and the site was clearly involved in the Late Uruk expansion. The recent work has also revealed a massive Old ASSYRIAN building and traces of a city wall belonging to this time, perhaps a reflection of SHAMSHI-ADAD's empire building in the late 19th century BC.

Branč   an Early Bronze Age inhumation cemetery in southwestern Slovakia, belonging to the so-called NITRA group (contemporaneous with the ÚŇETICE culture further to the west). Susan Shennan's analysis of the approximately 300 burials produced clear evidence for social differentiation. A number of the female graves, including those of several children, were especially richly furnished, leading her to conclude that the females either achieved wealth by marriage or had it ascribed at birth. Several smaller cemeteries in this region suggest similar patterns.

Brandberg   a mountain massif in the Namib desert of central Namibia with STONE AGE and IRON AGE material, particularly well known for its rock paintings, of which some 43 000 were documented by Harald Pager. One of the most celebrated of all rock paintings is the so-called 'White Lady of the Brandberg', made famous by the Abbé BREUIL's romantic interpretation of it as a white woman with Mediterranean features. It seems, however, that Breuil was misled by natural marks on the rock and that the figure represents a male SAN or Herero.

Brassempouy   a cave-site in the Landes, southwest France, where excavations by PIETTE in the 1890s and by Delporte in the 1980s have revealed occupation from the MOUSTERIAN to the AZILIAN. The Grotte du Pape is best known for its series of IVORY 'VENUS FIGURINES' and small ivory human head, generally attributed to the GRAVETTIAN, but ascribed by BREUIL to an early AURIGNACIAN or even CHÂTELPERRONIAN layer. The nearby Galerie des Hyènes contains Aurignacian material, together with a little MAGDALENIAN.

Brauron   the TEMENOS of the goddess Artemis Brauronia in Attica, Greece, where young Athenian girls attended ceremonies dressed as bears. Excavations have revealed remains of a temple of the DORIC ORDER, as well as a STOA which included several dining-rooms (see SYMPOSIUM).

breccia   a rock consisting mostly of angular rock fragments larger than SAND size and cemented together. Uncemented counterparts, such as are found in some cave deposits or at the base of cliffs, are more accurately described as angular BOULDER or COBBLE GRAVELS, or DIAMICTON. Production of relatively large angular rock fragments is associated with cold climatic conditions where frost-related processes are intense. Caves that experienced human occupation may have archaeological deposits incorporated into or interstratified with deposits with abundant angular rock fragments.

Breitenbach   an Upper Palaeolithic open-air site located on the El-ster River in eastern Germany. Artifacts and faunal remains (e.g. woolly MAMMOTH, reindeer) are contained in a buried soil probably dating to an INTERSTADIAL preceding the LAST GLACIAL MAXIMUM. The artifacts include endscrapers (see SCRAPER), BURINS and several bone points, and are assigned to the AURIGNACIAN.

Breuil, Abbé Henri Edouard Prosper (1877–1961)   a French priest and prehistorian, particularly noted for his TYPOLOGICAL classification of Palaeolithic artifacts and for his recording and 'sympathetic magic' interpretation of PALAEOLITHIC ART.

bridging argument   an argument linking the materials in the archaeological record with interpretations about cultural systems (see also ACTUALISTIC STUDY, WARRANTING ARGUMENT). It allows the pre-diction of specific sets of phenomena based on prior generalizations (see DEDUCTION).

bristlecone pine the most useful tree species *(Pinus aristata)* in DENDROCHRONOLOGY studies. It is found in the Sierra Nevada of California at higher elevations. With a life span of up to at least 4600 years, the bristlecone pine provides continuous tree-ring records for dating purposes and PALAEOENVIRONMENTAL reconstruction.

Broad Spectrum Revolution the concept of a subsistence shift in western Asia, from a relatively narrow to a wider array of foodstuffs, including small mammals, invertebrates, aquatic resources and a diversity of plants. In an attempt to explain the origins of food production, several commentators (notably Kent Flannery) have suggested that late PLEISTOCENE foraging communities in western Asia were able, through this shift, to live in larger and more sedentary communities, which could act as a buffer against environmental change. This 'broad spectrum revolution' (e.g. in the KEBARAN COMPLEX and the NATUFIAN in the Levantine sequence) would establish economic, demographic and social conditions conducive to experimentation with domesticable plants and animals, and so stands as a prelude to the 'Neolithic revolution'. Although the Broad Spectrum Revolution is still widely cited, more recent studies indicate that generalized foraging was a common pattern through much of the Upper Pleistocene in western Asia (and especially the Levant), and that the discontinuity in subsistence patterns implicit in the idea is overstated.

broch a circular dry-stone defensive tower found in coastal parts of northern and western Scotland and the islands. Up to 10 m tall with several stages of curving galleries within the thickness of the outer wall, brochs also had stone-built internal room divisions covered probably by a lean-to roof, leaving the central area open to the sky. Some, such as Gurness on Orkney, stood at the centre of a settlement of dry-stone houses within an outer defensive ditch. The origins of the broch lie in the mid 1st millennium BC, but most were probably built in the 2nd and 1st centuries BC/AD.

Broederstroom an extensive Early IRON AGE site in the central Transvaal, South Africa, consisting of a series of villages built between the 5th and 7th centuries AD. The excavation of Negroid human skeletal remains, collapsed circular huts, grain bins, iron-working debris, the bones of domestic sheep, goats and cattle as well as hunted animals, provides an unusually detailed picture of southern African Early Iron Age village life.

Broighter a gold boat model, part of a hoard discovered in Co. Londonderry, Ireland, by a ploughman in 1891, which also included a gold collar, twisted TORCS, necklaces and a hanging bowl. The boat, only 18.5 cm long, has oars, benches for the rowers and a mast. It may be LA TÈNE D, late 1st century BC.

Broken Hill a mine near Kabwe in central Zambia, now quarried away, which has yielded remains including a superbly preserved cranium thought to be at least 110 000 years old. This is often described as 'Rhodesian Man', HOMO *sapiens rhodesiensis*, an extinct subspecies intermediate between *H. erectus* and *H. sapiens*. However, recent researchers place less emphasis on formal subspecies names for archaic *H. sapiens* from Africa.

Brommian a culture of Denmark, South Sweden, North Germany and Poland, dating to the ALLERØD and DRYAS III phases, and named after the Zealand lakeside reindeer-hunting camp of Bromme (c.10 000 bc). Of uncertain origin, and possibly derived from the MAGDALENIAN, it resembles the HAMBURGIAN, and may be the origin of the SWIDERIAN and AHRENSBURGIAN. It is characterized by the Lyngby point and Lyngby reindeer-antler 'axe' or club.

Bronocice   a Middle Neolithic hilltop site in southern Poland, with occupations of the FUNNEL BEAKER culture and a BADEN-like culture. The site at Bronocice, covering over 50 ha, is extraordinarily large compared with contemporaneous sites in the same region. Notable among the Funnel Beaker finds is a pot with incised decoration believed to depict a wheeled vehicle.

bronze   an alloy of COPPER, usually made by the addition of TIN and sometimes including small amounts of other metals, used in the production of weapons, implements, art works and decorations. The BRONZE AGE cultural period takes its name from the proliferation during that time of items manufactured from bronze.

Bronze Age   the period of antiquity in the Old World in which BRONZE became the primary material for tools and weapons. One of the elements of THOMSEN'S THREE AGE SYSTEM, the Bronze Age in Europe conventionally spans the period from 2000 to about 700 BC. The fact that tin and copper normally do not occur naturally in proximity resulted in a significant rise in trade, which was one of the factors in the progressive differentiation of access to status, power and wealth.

In *East Asia*   the period of bronze use on the China mainland coincided with the stratification of society and state development in the SHANG and ZHOU periods of the 2nd–1st millennia BC (see CHINESE DYNASTIES). On the Korean peninsula, the Bronze Age commenced about 700 BC but was derived from a northern source (see TUNGUS). Iron was introduced from China c.400 BC, so that the Late Bronze Age and the Early Iron Age of Korea are contemporaneous (see KOREAN PERIODIZATION). Both bronze and iron were transferred to the Japanese islands from the Korean peninsula c.300 BC at the same time as wet-rice agriculture. Thus the Neolithic, Bronze Age and Iron Age were all encompassed by the YAYOI culture in Japan (see JAPANESE PERIODIZATION).

bronze mirrors   smooth-faced BRONZE discs with cast decoration on the back. Appearing in East Asia in the late 2nd millennium BC, they became a major toilette item of the HAN-dynasty elite in China; but in Korea and Japan, they fulfilled ritual or ceremonial functions, whether imported from China or manufactured locally. Korean mirrors of the Bronze Age are noted for their fine-lined geometric decoration, while some local Japanese mirrors of the KOFUN period bear CHOKKOMON designs. (See fig.)

Brørup   see CHELFORD.

Brynzeny I   a cave-site in Moldova, located on a tributary of the Prut River, containing Palaeolithic, Mesolithic and younger artifacts. The lowest horizon is assigned to the early Upper Palaeolithic on typological grounds by the excavator, but no RADIOCARBON dates are available. A carved and decorated woolly MAMMOTH tusk represents a rare PALAEOLITHIC ART object from this region. The site was discovered and excavated by Ketraru in 1963–65.

Brześć Kujawski   a multi-period site in north-central Poland first excavated by Konrad JAŻDŻEWSKI in 1933–39, with later excavations by Chmielewski in 1952 and by R. Grygiel and P. Bogucki in

1976–1984. Over a dozen archaeological cultures are represented at Brześć Kujawski, with major settlements of the Early Neolithic LINEAR POTTERY and LENGYEL cultures and later during the LA TÈNE period of the Iron Age. Brześć Kujawski is best known for the trapezoidal LONGHOUSES and rich burials of the Lengyel occupation, which have also been found recently at the nearby site of OSŁONKI.

Bubanj-Hum   an ENEOLITHIC regional group in Serbia, centred on the sites of Bubanj and Hum near Niš in the Morava valley. The Bubanj-Hum group succeeded the VINČA Culture in this region and appears to have lasted through several long phases. Phase 1A is the most distinctive, with graphite painted wares and BURNISHED ware. Phase IB is contemporaneous with BADEN in north Serbia and Hungary, while II is related to COȚOFENI and SALCUȚA in Bulgaria. The deposits at Bubanj itself have provided one of the more complete stratigraphic sequences for the central Balkans during this period.

Bubastis   the CLASSICAL name for the Egyptian site of TELL Basta, situated in the southeastern Nile DELTA. Most of the construction of the major surviving monuments of the site, excavated by NAVILLE in 1887–89, was initiated by kings of the 22nd DYNASTY, who came from Bubastis.

bucchero   a type of pottery produced in ETRURIA, especially in the ARCHAIC PERIOD. It was fired with a restricted supply of oxygen to give an even, black appearance through the fabric. It was BURNISHED before firing, which resulted in a lustrous appearance. Decorative motifs, often consisting of semicircles or fans, were incised or impressed.

Buchau or **Wasserburg Buchau**   a Late Bronze Age settlement in southern Germany excavated by Reinerth in the 1930s. It is located on an island in the moor surrounding the Federsee and has traces of two occupations. The first had 38 rectangular post structures, 37 of which were single-room buildings 4 m by 5 m while one was a larger two-roomed building. The second settlement had nine complexes of large multi-roomed houses, along with assorted outbuildings. Both settlements were surrounded by a palisade. Buchau provides some of the rare settlement data for the URNFIELD period in central Europe.

bucranium   an ox-skull normally carved in relief and forming part of the decorative scheme of buildings in the Roman world. A second context for their use was funerary (see CINERARIUM, SARCOPHAGUS). They are often associated with garlands.

Buda Industry   a Lower Palaeolithic INDUSTRY of Hungary characterized by the production of CHOPPING TOOLS on pebbles and FLAKE tools. The industry was defined by VÉRTES in 1965 and is best represented at the Middle PLEISTOCENE site of VÉRTESSZÖLLÖS.

Budakalász   a cemetery of the BADEN culture near Budapest in Hungary. It is known especially for the model of a four-wheeled wagon found in one of the graves, one of the first definite chronological markers of the use of a wheeled vehicle. Other finds at Budakalász include burials of paired cattle, which S. Piggott has suggested implies the use of cattle for traction.

Buddhagupta stone   one of several SANSKRIT language inscriptions of c.5th century AD found on the west coast of peninsular Malaysia, connected with a Buddhist traders' cult apparently unique to maritime Southeast Asia; related inscriptions have been found in west Kalimantan (Borneo) and Brunei.

Bug-Dniester culture a complex of sites in the valleys of the Bug and Dniester rivers in Ukraine, in which pottery manufacture appears to have developed within a hunter-gatherer economic context about 5500–5000 bc. Short-lived sites on river terraces were located in the larger valleys. Bug-Dniester economy was based on red deer, wild pigs and cattle, roe deer, birds, shellfish and fish, with traces of plant gathering. CRIŠS and LINEAR POTTERY sherds suggest that the Bug-Dniester culture was in contact with neighbouring early agricultural groups, but evidence of farming is scanty.

Buhaya see KATURUKA.

Buhen a site in LOWER NUBIA, excavated mainly by EMERY from 1957–65. Buhen was occupied during the OLD KINGDOM, an early example of Egyptian expansion into Nubia, and was an important fortress during the MIDDLE and NEW KINGDOM.

Bukit Tengku Lembu a rockshelter site in peninsular Malaysia, with remains related to the BAN KAO Neolithic (see GUA KECHIL) and some later blackware pottery of uncertain origin, but which may be Indo-Roman ROULETTED WARE like that found at SEMBIRAN and BUNI.

Bükk culture a regional late variant of the LINEAR POTTERY culture, centred on the Bükk mountains of northeastern Hungary, often in cave-sites. Bükk pottery is very finely made, with multiple parallel lines in spiral and curvilinear patterns. SHERDS of Bükk pottery sometimes appear at distant sites, such as OLSZANICA in southern Poland.

bulb of percussion a convex swelling found on the ventral or inside surface of a struck FLAKE (see figure) just below the point of impact. A small concave scar, the bulbar scar, is often found on the bulb of percussion.

bulla 1. a hollow ball of clay, characteristic of the writing systems of early MESOPOTAMIA, that contains TOKENS and bears a seal impression and/or numerical notations on its outer surface; such objects appear in Late URUK contexts.

bulla

2. a clay sealing used to monitor flows of goods, to mark ownership and so forth. In the literature about western Asian civilizations these objects are commonly called *sealings*.

3. a round amulet worn on the chest. Etruscan examples are normally made of bronze and can be decorated in relief. In Roman society a gold bulla was worn by children of the social elite to signify free birth; it later came to be worn by the children of freedmen. When the child came of age, the bulla was placed in the household shrine or lararium. A fine example was found in the House of Menander at POMPEII.

Buni a port and burial site in west Java, of the first centuries AD, yielding crucibles and other remains of a bronze-working industry and Indo-Roman ROULETTED WARE similar to that of SEMBIRAN on Bali; it was an important early Indonesian port on the spice trade route.

Buret' an Upper Palaeolithic open-air site on the Angara River in south-central Siberia. The cultural layer is buried in slope deposits on a low TERRACE; it overlies a buried soil and is believed to date to *c*.20 000 bp. The features, which include traces of former structures, and the artifacts, which include human and animal figurines, are similar to the nearby site of MAL'TA. Buret' was discovered and excavated by OKLADNIKOV during 1936–40.

burial the deliberate disposal of the dead. *Primary* burials are those in which the dead body has been laid down only once; *secondary* burials are those involving the deliberate movement and relocation of the body as part of the burial ritual; a *flexed* burial occurs when the body is coiled into a foetal position; an *extended* burial occurs when the body is stretched out, with the arms at its side.

Archaeologists have traditionally assumed that the burial STATUS of the dead reflected their social status while alive, but recent POST-PROCESSUAL critiques suggest that this assumption is no longer valid in all cases. See PRIMARY/SECONDARY CREMATION/INHUMATION.

Burial Mound Period a term used in eastern North America for that period when CULTURES were characterized by the construction of BURIAL MOUNDS. See ADENA, HOPEWELL, TEMPLE MOUND PERIOD.

burial mounds earthen mounds deliberately constructed over BURIALS. They are most often interpreted as marks of STATUS or rank. Bodies were either interred on earthen platforms within log frames, or cremated and the remains placed in scooped-out basins. See also TUMULUS, TOUMBA, SOROS.

buried soil SOIL covered by younger natural or ANTHROPOGENIC deposits with a vertical separation between the buried and modern soil or land surface; the buried soil is referred to as a PALAEOSOL. Buried soils represent former land surfaces with spatial, temporal and environmental significance, and form the basis for reconstructing former LANDSCAPES.

burin a characteristic Upper Palaeolithic BLADE tool with a sharp transverse chisel-like working-edge formed by the removal of a sliver of stone called a burin SPALL. Traditionally regarded as engraving tools used to work bone, IVORY, antler, soft stone and wood, recent USEWEAR ANALYSIS suggests that burins may have been multi-purpose artifacts. By convention, the spall removal is indicated in drawings by a small arrow.

burnish a polish applied to the surface of an object such as pottery or bronze to enhance its appearance or for decorative purposes. On a pot, burnishing is carried out, usually with a wooden or bone tool, between drying and firing, and makes the vessel more watertight.

burin

Burrill Lake   a large sandstone rockshelter on the south coast of
New South Wales, Australia, excavated in 1967–68 by Ron Lampert.
First occupied about 20 000 years ago, the older levels are
characterized by SCRAPERS and FLAKE tools of the AUSTRALIAN CORE
TOOL AND SCRAPER TRADITION. From c.5000 years ago a range of small
tools were added to the assemblage.

Burrup Peninsula   an area of the northwest coast of Western
Australia rich in archaeological remains. Over 10 000 engravings have
been recorded on boulders, with very high concentrations at some
sites. The subjects range from geometric figures to detailed
representations of humans and animals, and include CLELAND HILLS
faces. There are many open sites including quarries and artifact
scatters, as well as SHELL MIDDENS ranging from 6700 bp to 200 bp.
There are also many stone features including fish traps, standing
stones and an enigmatic series of dry-stone walls and terraces.

Burzahom   a site lying at 1800 m in Kashmir. It was initially tested
in 1939 by de Terra & Patterson, and then excavated in 1960–71 by
T. Khazanchi, who defined four phases of occupation. In the earliest
phase, the settlement is characterized by pit dwellings up to 4 m
deep, wider at the top than the bottom, and surrounded by POST-
HOLES to support a perishable superstructure, along with large storage
pits; the material inventory includes a BURNISHED handmade pottery
with basal mat impressions, a rich bone industry, and a ground stone
and chipped stone industry distinctive of this region of south Asia.
The second occupation marks an architectural shift to above-ground
MUD-BRICK structures, though the basic material culture continues
much as before. In the third phase a MEGALITHIC circle was constructed, while the pottery shifts to a coarse red ware; the last period
is early historic. The chronology of the site is poorly known, but
seems to cover the 3rd and early 2nd millennia BC.

Bush Barrow   an Early Bronze Age burial-mound in the
Normanton Down cemetery (England), located approximately 1 km
south of STONEHENGE. The barrow was opened by William
Cunnington in 1808 and found to contain the remains of a single individual accompanied by rich grave-goods including a gold belt-
fastener and lozenge-shaped breastplate, a stone macehead with bone

handle mounts, two bronze daggers and a low-flanged axe. The burial was probably that of a powerful Early Bronze Age chieftain buried around 2000 BC.

Bushmen see SAN.

Butana seven large sites in eastern Sudan containing 2 m of deposit dating between 5500–4500 BP, with ceramics, stone artifacts and wild animal remains, which have given their name to a cultural group within the KASSALA phase (see GASH).

Butmir culture a Late Neolithic culture of Bosnia, known from the type-site near Sarajevo and other settlements, including OBRE. Butmir ceramics are often elaborately decorated with incised geometrical and curvilinear patterns.

Butser an experimental farm and open-air museum on the South Downs, Hampshire, England, the scene of scientific investigations into Iron Age plant cultivation and animal husbandry. Reconstructions of round-houses, granaries and storage pits of Iron Age type have also been made in order to test hypotheses about constructional details.

Byblos a site in Lebanon, on a promontory overlooking the Mediterranean, excavated by MONTET in 1921–24 and by Dunand, chiefly in 1925–38. Occupied in the Neolithic and CHALCOLITHIC, it was a densely-packed, strongly-fortified city, containing a series of religious structures including the 'OBELISK TEMPLE', in the EARLY to MIDDLE BRONZE AGE. Byblos' importance stemmed from being a major trading centre, especially for the supply of raw materials to Egypt; it was ruled in the Middle Bronze Age by a line of princes whose 'court-style' in artistic taste was based on Egyptian models. Byblos' role as a trading centre later declined with the rise of TYRE and SIDON.

Býči Skála a prehistoric cave site located northeast of Brno in the Moravian KARST zone, Czechoslovakia. Artifacts and faunal remains (e.g. CAVE BEAR, reindeer) are buried in LOAM deposits. The artifacts in the lowest cultural layer comprise a mixture of Middle and Upper Palaeolithic types (e.g. sidescrapers – see SCRAPER – and BURINS), and their age and affiliation are unclear. Late Upper Palaeolithic and late prehistoric remains occur in the upper levels. Excavations in the late 19th century found about 40 inhumation burials, as well as cremated bones, of the HALLSTATT period of the Early Iron Age. Three of the graves seem to be of particularly high-status individuals, with wagons with iron tyres. Numerous bronze objects, including buckets, kettles and bowls, a bull figurine with iron inlays, a bronze helmet, and many pins, FIBULAE, and about 100 bracelets were found in the cave's deposits.

Bygholm a hoard from Jutland, Denmark, of four copper flat axes, a copper dagger and three copper spiral rings, found together with a TRB C vessel and dated to c.4000 BC. These are among the earliest metal objects to be found in Denmark.

Bylany a large settlement of the LINEAR POTTERY and STROKE-ORNAMENTED POTTERY cultures in Bohemia near Prague, excavated by B. Soudský. Bylany is an archetypal Linear Pottery site, situated on LOESS on the lower slope of a stream valley. Numerous rectangular LONGHOUSES were found, and detailed CERAMIC analysis has led to the identification of over 20 phases of settlement, each with 5–6 (rarely more than 10) houses. Soudský proposed a model of Linear Pottery cyclical shifting settlement, but recent work at other sites has led some to argue for occupations of longer duration.

Byzantium   (*adj.* Byzantine) later Constantinopolis, a Greek colony founded in the 7th century BC on the European side of the Hellespont in Turkey. The city was destroyed after it stood against the emperor Septimius Severus in *c.*AD 195 and was refounded in AD 324 by the emperor Constantine; it was officially inaugurated in AD 330. One of the most magnificent buildings was the church of S. Sofia, later turned into a mosque. In the Hippodrome (see CIRCUS) the bronze serpent column from the Plataean monument at DELPHI may still be seen along with two OBELISKS.

Byzovaya   an Upper Palaeolithic open-air site on the Pechora River in European Russia, and the northernmost Palaeolithic locality in Europe (65° N). Artifacts and faunal remains (predominantly woolly MAMMOTH) are buried in fluvial deposits comprising the second/third terrace. The occupation probably antedates the LAST GLACIAL MAXIMUM (i.e. over 25 000 bp). Byzovaya was excavated in the 1960s by Kanivets.

C

Caballo Muerto   a complex of monumental constructions pertaining to the INITIAL PERIOD and EARLY HORIZON, located in the Moche Valley on the north coast of Peru. The site covers some two square kilometres and comprises 17 mounds. The most complex construction at the site is the Huaca de los Reyes, a multi-level, U-shaped complex, roughly 240 m square, decorated with relief friezes painted yellow, white and red. An individual entering the complex from the east and moving toward the pyramid at the west end would pass through a series of structures, stairways, pillared halls and courtyard, rising to successively higher levels. This complex is considered to be an especially elaborate example of religious architecture pertaining to the late Initial Period.

Cabalwanian industry   a stone INDUSTRY based largely upon FLAKES, recognized from surface collections made to the west of the CAGAYAN VALLEY in Luzon, north Philippines. Once thought to be Lower Palaeolithic, it is now thought to date to the early HOLOCENE and to represent a development parallel to the HOABINHIAN.

Cabenge   an area of southwest Sulawesi yielding late PLIOCENE fauna. The stone tools found in apparent association with the bones are probably earlier than the TOALIAN tools of the same area, comprising a range of large CORE tools fitting into the CHOPPER/ CHOPPING TOOL tradition, but may not be old enough to be associated with HOMO *erectus*.

Cacaxtla   a Late CLASSIC site in central Mexico. Spectacular murals at the site portray dignitaries in MAYA dress, and suggest that the Maya were not only influenced by Central Mexico, but also exerted their own influence in this area.

Caere   see CERVETERI.

Caeretan ware   a type of ARCHAIC pottery found in ETRURIA and once thought to have been made at CERVETERI. It was decorated in a BLACK-FIGURED style and showed the influence of Greek craftsmen.

Caesarea   a coastal site in Israel, the capital of the Roman province of Judaea. Sporadically excavated by many archaeologists, this substantial port is largely the result of an energetic building programme initiated in 22 BC by Herod the Great, although Caesarea also contains important remains of the BYZANTINE and Mediaeval (Crusader) periods.

Cagayan Valley   a region of northern Luzon, Philippines, yielding early and middle PLEISTOCENE faunal remains. The stone tools once thought to have been in association with them are thought now to date to the early HOLOCENE. See CABALWANIAN.

Cahokia   a large site located a few miles east of St. Louis, Missouri, USA, that was occupied from approximately AD 700–1500. Earliest occupation was associated with the WOODLAND stage, and this was followed by MISSISSIPPIAN stage groups in about AD 900. During this period, Cahokia developed into a large and complex regional economic and ceremonial centre of a once densely populated area now called the American Bottoms, and possibly even reached the STATE level of social organization. The most striking features of the Cahokia site, which at its peak occupation covered nearly 16 sq.km, are the numerous earthen mounds, possibly originally totalling more than 120. Mounds were either PLATFORM, BURIAL, or ridge-top mounds (shaped like an old-fashioned ridge tent). The largest of these is Monk's mound, a platform mound, which was built in the period AD 900–1200. It covers 6 ha and rises in four terraces to a height of over 35 m. It was surmounted by a large building, probably a ceremonial centre and the home of the major ruler. Excavations at mound 72 unearthed nearly 300 burials, mostly of young women. These are thought to have been sacrificial burials, presumably related to the burial of a male ruler in the same mound. Nearby Woodhenge comprises the remains of a circle of upright logs, thought to have served as some form of calendar or as a celestial observatory. Cahokia derives its name from that of a local Indian group.

Cahuachi   a large ceremonial site, the principal centre of the NASCA culture of Peru. The site comprises some 40 ADOBE mounds and pyramids, and extensive cemeteries, but little habitation refuse. Excavations by Helaine Silverman suggest that it was an empty ceremonial centre, occupied only during religious ceremonies. The site was mostly built in Early Nasca times (phases 2–4), but probably continued to serve as a locus of ritual offerings through Late Nasca times (phases 5–8) and the MIDDLE HORIZON.

Cai Beo   a coastal site in north Vietnam, with a sequence covering the transition from late HOABINHIAN stone tools to EDGE-GRINDING (c.5000 BC at Da But) to Neolithic POLISHED STONE ADZES c.4500 BC. Parallel sites nearby include Quynh Van and Bao Tro.

cairn   a mound of stones. The most common examples are clearance cairns created when stones were cleared from a field in preparation for cultivation, and funerary cairns covering graves or burial chambers.

Cairo   the modern capital of Egypt and major centre of Islamic civilization since its foundation by the Fatimid DYNASTY in AD 969.

Cajamarquilla an urban site near Lima, on the central coast of Peru, a centre of the Lima culture of the EARLY INTERMEDIATE PERIOD. The nearby cemetery, Nievería, has produced many HUARI-related artifacts, suggesting intensive interaction with, if not control by, Huari.

Čaka a Late Bronze Age URNFIELD cemetery in Slovakia. One of the high-status burials at Čaka yielded a sheet-bronze breastplate, one of the oldest examples of body armour in Europe, dated to the 13th century BC.

caldarium the hottest room in a Roman bath-house. A plunge-bath was attached, which made it a very humid room. See THERMAE.

calendar round a 52-year cycle devised by the MAYA. It is a combination of two cycles, and includes all variations of days and numbers of the 260-day almanac (TZOLKIN) and the 365-day year. See also LONG COUNT.

calendric systems MAYA calendar systems, depending on astronomic calculations and the use of the LONG COUNT. The Maya believed in a cyclical history in which events (including disasters) literally repeated themselves. Calendric systems were used not only in timing agricultural activities, but also to calculate the occurrence of important events in order to prepare for them.

calibration the adjustment of data by means of some systematic change to exclude extraneous or error-producing information. For example, to achieve a result in calendar years in RADIOCARBON DATING, application of a correction factor is necessitated by the discovery, from ISOTOPIC and radiocarbon dating analysis in DENDROCHRONOLOGY of tree rings, that atmospheric production rate of ^{14}C has not been constant through time, but rather variable. RADIOCARBON ages are originally reported in uncalibrated radiocarbon years that assume no atmospheric ^{14}C flux. Radiocarbon years are adjusted, or calibrated, to calendar years by taking this flux into account.

Calico Mountains an open-air site located on former Lake Manix in the Mojave Desert of southeastern California (USA). lithic debris (fragments, FLAKES and BLADES) thought to represent artifacts is buried in fan deposits recently dated by the URANIUM-thorium method to c.200 000 BP. If accurately interpreted as a human site, Calico Mountains would constitute the earliest settlement in the New World (i.e. Lower Palaeolithic); however, the lithic debris is not widely accepted as of human manufacture. The site was investigated by Simpson, LEAKEY and others.

Calixtlahuaca a site in the Toluca Valley in the state of Mexico that has a ceramic sequence from TEOTIHUACÁN times to the AZTEC conquest period. There is also some evidence of occupation during the PRECLASSIC. It was occupied by the Matlatzincas, a NAHUA group, enemies of the Aztecs, from AD 1200–1472. The Matlatzincas were conquered by the Aztecs in the subsequent period (AD 1474–1510). The site is best known for the Temple of QUETZALCÓATL in his form as the wind god, Ehecatl. This temple is a circular structure, that went through three construction periods. The archaeologist José García Payón directed most of the excavations carried out at the site in the 1930s.

callais   an attractive greenish stone more properly known as either turquoise or variscite depending on the variety, used for the manufacture of beads and pendants found in Neolithic CHAMBERED TOMBS in Brittany and Iberia, in the SEPULCROS DE FOSA of eastern Spain, and in CHASSÉEN settlement sites of southern France. Neolithic variscite mines have been discovered at Gava near Barcelona; other sources are known in Brittany.

Callanish   a Neolithic STONE CIRCLE on the island of Lewis, Outer Hebrides, Scotland, consisting of 13 tall thin stones of local gneiss, the tallest 4.75 m high. To one side within the circle is a round mound containing a small PASSAGE GRAVE. Rows of stones lead away from the circle to the W, NNE, ENE and S, the last of these double and forming an avenue. There are a number of other stone circles nearby.

Całowanie   an Upper Palaeolithic open-air site located on the Vistula River in eastern Poland. ARTIFACTS are buried in stream and DUNE deposits. Two lower cultural layers are dated to c.11 500 BP and contain BACKED BLADELETS, while the overlying layers are dated to c.11 000–10 000 BP and contain TANGED points.

Camden, William (1551–1623)   a Tudor antiquary and historian who travelled extensively in Britain looking at antiquities. He was the author of the first general account of British antiquities, the *Britannia* (1586), which was revised and reissued in several editions for over 200 years, and which helped awaken public interest in what he called 'the back-looking curiosity'.

cameo glass   a Roman glass object made up of two or more layers of different coloured glass bonded together. Normally a lighter colour forms the top surface, through which the engraver cuts to reveal the darker base. The overall impression would be similar to the result of cutting cameos from onyx. An important example of this technique is the Portland Vase in the British Museum, although it was also used on decorative plaques in the House of Fabius Rufus at POMPEII as well as on finger-rings.

Campania   an agriculturally rich area of Italy adjoining the Bay of Naples. It was the location of one of the earliest Greek colonies at CUMAE and it was also under the influence of the Etruscans (see ETRURIA). See CAMPANIAN POTTERY, HERCULANEUM, OPLONTIS, POMPEII.

Campanian pottery   a type of SOUTH ITALIAN POTTERY. Production seems to have started before the middle of the 4th century BC, perhaps under the influence of SICILIAN POTTERY. There seem to have been three main centres of production: two at Capua and one at CUMAE. Late in its production it seems to draw inspiration from APULIAN POTTERY.

Canaanites   an ethnic group identified with the sophisticated urban civilization of the Levant during the Bronze Age (see HAZOR, JERICHO, LACHISH, BEIT MERSIM). The Canaanites were dislodged from much of their territory by the ISRAELITES and PHILISTINES, but much of their culture persisted among the PHOENICIANS.

candi   a late 1st millennium–early 2nd millennium AD funerary temple of Java which combined imported Hindu or Buddhist religion with local ancestor veneration cults.

Can Hasan III   an ACERAMIC NEOLITHIC site in southern central Anatolia, where David French's excavations revealed a small settlement (somewhat less than a hectare) having a densely agglomerated complex of rooms and courtyards, with access seemingly through the roof in the Anatolian Neolithic manner (see ÇATAL HÜYÜK). French assigns this settlement to the middle of the 7th millennium bc. The significance of Can Hasan lies in its subsistence evidence: in addition to the wild animals (cattle and sheep/goat probably being herded), the site contains a wide variety of crop species (bread wheat, club wheat, emmer, einkorn, 2-rowed hulled and possibly naked barley, lentils and vetch).

canopic jars   containers used by the Egyptians for the preservation of the internal organs removed during MUMMIFICATION. Canopic jars of the NEW KINGDOM often have lids in the form of the heads of the protective deities, the four sons of HORUS: Imset (human-headed, containing the liver), Hapy (baboon-headed, the lungs), Qebhsenuef (falcon-headed, the intestines), and Duamutef (jackal-headed, the stomach).

cantharus   see KANTHAROS.

Cape Coastal Ware   a STONE AGE pottery style found in coastal sites from southern Namibia to the eastern Cape Province of South Africa, after c.1600 BP. It is characterized by pointed-based pots, and is generally connected with the historically known KHOIKHOIN people.

Capeletti   see DAMOUS EL-AHMER.

capital   the top part of a CLASSICAL column comprising: in the DORIC ORDER, an ECHINUS and ABACUS; in the IONIC ORDER, VOLUTES, echinus and abacus; and in the CORINTHIAN ORDER, acanthus leaves.

Cappadocian trade   the regular trade between a large number of ASSYRIAN family commercial firms of the 2nd millennium BC and areas to the west in Anatolia, particularly the regions of Cappadocia. The trade was organized as a series of foreign colonies (see KĀRUM, KANISH) attached to local towns but existing as largely self-regulating communities. The Cappadocian trade dealt largely with tin and textiles shipped via ASSUR from further east and south in exchange for Anatolian copper (though the latter is not well attested). The rich CUNEIFORM sources from Kanish, BOGHAZKÖY, ALIŠAR and elsewhere make this the best documented trading system of ancient MESOPOTAMIA, but Assur of the early 2nd millennium may not be representative of other times and places in western Asian history.

Capsian   an EPIPALAEOLITHIC BLADE and BURIN stone industry from northern Algeria and Tunisia, dating between the 10th and 6th millennia BP.

Capsian Neolithic   a stone industry associated with pointed-base pottery from the Atlas Mountains of Algeria and the northern Sahara, dating from c.6200–5300 BP. It is assumed to have affinities with the earlier CAPSIAN (see DAMOUS EL AHMAR, HASSI MOUILAH).

capstone   see DOLMEN, CORBEL-VAULTED.

Carchemish   a city on the middle Euphrates, established no later than the mid 3rd millennium BC. It was an important political centre during the 2nd and first half of the 1st millennium BC, though often in clientage to stronger regional powers (HITTITES, NEO-ASSYRIANS), according to the fairly rich textual sources. The archaeological excavations there began in the 1870s and continued sporadically until 1920, when the newly drawn Turkish-Syrian border divided the site in two. Although these excavations produced Early Bronze, Late

Bronze and Early Iron Age materials, only the latter are published in any detail. During this period (the so-called Syro-Hittite), the city was separated into citadel, inner town and outer town, covering about 150 ha in all. The best-known archaeological aspects of the city are the Syro-Hittite sculptures and inscriptions. A series of HALAF-period round dwellings and pottery kilns were discovered at Yunus, on the outskirts of the city, and are frequently used to illustrate Halaf architecture.

Cardial ware   the earliest Neolithic pottery type of the west Mediterranean and parts of Atlantic Europe. The vessels are often of fine quality and are sometimes decorated with the edge of a *Cardium* (cockle) shell, from which the pottery takes its name, though other types of impressed decoration are also common (hence the alternative term IMPRESSED WARE). Cardial ware is dated to between *c*.6000 BC and 5300 BC, and is followed in some regions by an EPICARDIAL phase *c*.5300–4600 BC.

cardo   the main street in a Roman town or camp usually laid out on a north–south axis. The FORUM was placed at the intersection with the DECUMANUS maximus. The rectangular blocks between the streets are described as INSULAE.

carination   a break in the profile of a pot which forms a keel or ridge, usually marking the junction of the body with the neck.

Carnac   a complex of Neolithic ritual monuments around the Gulf of Morbihan, Brittany, France, including single standing stones (notably the *Grand Menhir Brisé*, now fallen and broken in four pieces), long mounds with several closed burial chambers (such as Er Grah and Le Manio), classic PASSAGE GRAVES with MEGALITHIC ART (La Table des Marchands and Kercado), and massive ALIGNMENTS of standing stones. The most famous of these are the Le Menec alignments, consisting of 11 parallel lines of stones over 1 km long. Of the Carnac burial mounds the TUMULUS de Saint-Michel is the most impressive, over 110 m long and 10 m high, with a chamber which contained a number of fine polished stone axes including several of JADEITE. The Tumulus de Saint-Michel together with the *Grand Menhir Brisé* and the long mounds belong to the 5th or early 4th millennium BC; the passage graves to the 4th or 3rd millennium, and the alignments to the mid 3rd millennium BC.

Carnarvon   see CARTER.

Carnarvon Gorge   an area in south central Queensland, Australia, outstanding for its stencilled ROCK ART. Stencils include a range of artifacts and natural items and complex composite designs. Engravings and a few paintings also occur, while CATHEDRAL CAVE, one of the largest sites, also has occupation deposits.

carp's tongue sword   a Late Bronze Age sword type, a characteristic product of the ATLANTIC BRONZE AGE, with a blade narrowing to an elongated, parallel-sided tip, in an attempt to combine the qualities of a slashing and a stabbing weapon. For illustration, see page 417.

Carrowmore   a cemetery of MEGALITHIC tombs in Sligo, Ireland, consisting of circular boulder kerbs with central boulder-built chambers. Some consider this to be an early form of CHAMBERED TOMB, but despite the absence of pottery from some tombs, the associated RADIOCARBON date of *c*.4500 BC, which would make these the earliest chambered tombs of Ireland and among the oldest any-where in western Europe, must be regarded with caution. A date in the late 5th or early 4th millennium BC is nonetheless likely.

carrying capacity the optimal population size that can be supported by a particular environment, a key concept in DEMOGRAPHY and PALAEOECONOMY. Stress between a population's size and the environment's ability to support it is cited in many studies as a fundamental cause of cultural change. However, some archaeologists consider the concept of carrying capacity to be essentially irrelevant for studies of human behaviour, because of the human ability to raise artificially the carrying capacity of a given area through changes in technology and subsistence practices.

Cartailhac, Emile (1845–1921) a French prehistorian who was a dominant figure in the development of the discipline, but who is best known for his initial vehement rejection of ALTAMIRA's authenticity, followed by a published *Mea Culpa*, after which he became CAVE ART's fervent champion.

Carter, Howard (1874–1939) an English artist and Egyptologist. His best-known archaeological work was financed by the Earl of Carnarvon, especially the discovery in 1922, and subsequent examination, of the tomb of TUTANKHAMEN.

Carthage a PHOENICIAN colony in modern Tunisia, traditionally founded in 814 BC. Excavations have revealed traces of the *tophet* (sanctuary) of the goddess Tanit which may date back to the 8th century BC. Recent excavations have uncovered traces of the circular harbour with ship-sheds. Despite the destruction of the city by ROME in 146 BC, a colony was established of which the AMPHITHEATRE and AQUEDUCT remain.

cartonnage a material composed of layers of linen or PAPYRUS cemented by plaster or glue and moulded to the required shape before drying and painting. Cartonnage was often used as a substitute for wood in the funerary equipment of LATE PERIOD Egypt.

cartouche an Egyptian HIEROGLYPHIC device consisting of a loop formed by a double thickness of rope with the end tied to form a straight line at the base of an elongated oval. Two of the names borne by the king, the throne-name and the birth-name, were each enclosed in a cartouche. See fig. overleaf.

carved tree or **dendroglyph** a tree with designs, usually geometric, cut into the bark or heartwood. Such trees have a limited distribution in eastern and central New South Wales and south east Queensland, Australia, and were commonly associated with ceremonial activities such as burial or initiation. Carved trees also occur in the Chatham Islands. See MORIORI.

caryatids columns in the form of standing women. Some of the earliest were used in treasuries at DELPHI in the 6th century BC. Six such figures formed a porch on the ERECHTHEION. Each seems to have held an OINOCHOE and a PHIALE, vessels used for pouring a LIBATION to the gods. Lord ELGIN removed one of them and it is now in the British Museum. Copies were made in the Roman period for Hadrian's VILLA at Tivoli.

Casamance see MEGALITHIC MONUMENT.

Casas Grandes a site located beyond the northern frontier of MESOAMERICA, about 160 km south of the United States border.

cartouche

Charles DiPeso, who excavated the site in the 1960s and 1970s, believed it was established by Mesoamerican merchant priests. Casas Grandes was built of ADOBE, and included workshops, ceremonial structures, integrated apartments and an underground drainage system. Although the interpretation is debated, at its height Casas Grandes is thought to have been a trading outpost between Mesoamerica and the American Southwest. The city was destroyed in AD 1340 by the indigenous population. The site is also called Paquimé.

Cascioărele an ENEOLITHIC settlement of the GUMELNIŢA culture in southern Romania, about 60 km south of Bucharest. The settlement is on an island in Lake Catalui about 100 m in diameter. Sixteen one-room post houses occupy the interior of the settlement, widely spaced with varied orientations. Most houses contained a square hearth, evidence of weaving and food-processing equipment. Among the artifacts are a beam of red-deer antler interpreted as an ARD, one of the earliest in southeast Europe, and an elaborate model of a house or shrine.

Caskey, John (1908–81) an American archaeologist who was Director of the American School of Classical Studies at Athens from 1948–59, and who excavated at LERNA and AYIA IRINI on Kea.

Caso Andrade, Alfonso (1896–1970) a Mexican archaeologist who began his career in 1927, working first in the VALLEY OF OAXACA at MONTE ALBÁN. He also studied the Mesoamerican CALENDRIC SYSTEMS, and later worked on genealogies of the MIXTEC.

Cass ny Hawin a small Mesolithic settlement site on the Isle of Man, off the western coast of Britain, excavated by Woodman (1982–83). The site has yielded an unspecialized group of stone tools including MICROLITHS, but no faunal remains.

Castelluccio   A 3rd millennium BC cemetery of several hundred simple rock-cut tombs cut into limestone cliffs of the Cava della Signora, a narrow valley in eastern Sicily. Most consist only of a single chamber, circular or oval in plan, although some have a small ante-chamber. Two of the tombs had blocking stones with carved spirals. The burial rite was collective inhumation, accompanied by pottery, occasional copper objects, and curious bossed bone plaques, perhaps originally ornamental belt fasteners.

Castelnovian   see CHÂTEAUNEUF-LES-MARTIGUES.

Castillo   see EL CASTILLO.

Castor Ware   see NENE VALLEY WARE.

castro   a fortified camp of the Portuguese Iron Age (see VILA NOVA DE SÃO PEDRO).

catacomb   an underground set of galleries and rooms used as a cemetery. An extensive series have been explored outside ROME, although others are known. The Rome series have been an important source for early Christian art and iconography.

Catacomb Grave Culture   the second in the series of KURGAN (following YAMNAYA, preceding SRUBNAYA) cultures of the south Russian and Ukrainian steppes between the Dniepr and the lower Volga, dated primarily to the early part of the Bronze Age between *c.*2000 and 1500 bc. The graves of this culture are not true CATACOMBS in the Roman sense, but rather are burials in which the skeleton and grave-goods were placed in a niche in the side wall of a shallow shaft. The filled-in shaft was then covered over by a BARROW.

Çatal Hüyük   the most celebrated Neolithic site of western Asia along with JERICHO. Located on the Konya Plain in southern central Anatolia and excavated by J. Mellaart in the 1960s, it covers 21 ha, the largest site of its time. The 14 excavated buildings date to between the later 7th and mid 6th millennium BC. The architecture consists of tightly packed rooms, with access through the roof; the walls of many rooms are decorated with exuberant murals, and some (identified as shrines) also have BUCRANIA fixed to the wall or on benches. The dead were buried beneath the floors of houses, often in collective graves; some differentiation of wealth is evident. The community seems to have practised irrigation farming, and had access to a wide variety of exotic raw materials. In terms of wider developmental trends in western Asia, Çatal Hüyük appears to be both precocious and without issue; the reasons for the appearance of such a large town at this time and place excite considerable speculation, mostly concerning the control of the OBSIDIAN trade.

Catastrophe Theory   a mathematical MODEL that investigates how a small change in one variable can have major effects on other related variables. The model has applications in understanding the collapse of complex social systems as a result of apparently small factors.

catena   a sequence of SOILS formed within the same parent material in a local area, under normal conditions of weathering and erosion, that have differing characteristics due to variation in LANDSCAPE position. Systematic changes in soil characteristics with relief and drainage allow interpretation of former landscapes of which archaeological sites may be components.

Cathedral Cave   one of the richest art sites in CARNARVON GORGE,

Australia, with sporadic evidence of occupation from about 3500 bp including stone and bone ARTIFACTS, together with well-preserved seeds from cycads. These are palm- or fern-like plants, which produce seeds high in food value but which must be processed to remove toxins. In some parts of Australia, cycad use is associated with ceremonial gatherings. The site was first occupied about 3500 bp and it has been suggested that large ceremonies and cycad processing are thus a recent phenomenon associated with the AUSTRALIAN SMALL TOOL TRADITION. Compare CHEETUP.

Catherwood, Frederick (1799–1854)   an English architect, one of the first great explorers of MESOAMERICA, who, with his American companion, JOHN LLOYD STEPHENS, explored the MAYA lowlands in 1841 and 1843. Catherwood's accurate and beautiful drawings of these expeditions provided insights into a relatively unknown culture, and are still useful for their details of Maya GLYPHS.

cation ratio dating   a developing dating technique used to date GEOMORPHIC surfaces and ARTIFACTS, that is based on the premise that the ratio of Calcium and Potassium/Titanium in rock varnish decreases exponentially with age. Whether it actually does so is controversial. CALIBRATION to absolute ages for a region is accomplished by determining cation ratios associated with surfaces dated by independent means. See DESERT VARNISH.

Caton-Thompson, Gertrude (1888–1985)   a British archaeologist and student of Sir Flinders PETRIE, best known for her work in Egypt (see FAIYUM, EL-HAMMAMIYA, OASES) and for her 1929 excavation at GREAT ZIMBABWE which corrected myths by showing that it was of African construction. She also worked in the northern Transvaal and the Arabian peninsula.

Caune de l'Arago   see TAUTAVEL.

causewayed camp   a Neolithic enclosure with one or more circuits of ditch interrupted by numerous causeways. An embankment or palisade stood within the ditch. The number of causeways and the location of the sites argue against a defensive purpose, and they have been interpreted as tribal meeting places or ritual centres; the latter explanation gains support from the presence of human remains in the ditches. Causewayed camps date mainly to the 4th millennium BC and are found throughout southern and eastern England: see WINDMILL HILL, CRICKLEY HILL, HAMBLEDON HILL, HEMBURY, MAIDEN CASTLE, ABINGDON.

cavea   the tiered seating in a Roman theatre or AMPHITHEATRE.

cave art   see PALAEOLITHIC ART.

Cave Bay Cave   a rockshelter on Hunter Island off northwest TASMANIA, Australia. Excavations by Sandra Bowdler revealed three separate occupation episodes *c.*23 000 bp, 7000 bp and from 2500 bp. Faunal remains demonstrate a shift from a PLEISTOCENE land-based economy, while the site was part of the mainland, to a marine economy in the early HOLOCENE as the sea approached present levels. After abandonment in the mid-Holocene, this and other sites on the island show seasonal specialized use over the last 2000 years.

cave bear (*Ursus spelaeus*)   an extinct species of bear which lived from about 300 000 to 10 000 years ago. It was restricted to central latitudes of Europe, from southern England to the northern Mediterranean, and eastwards to the Black Sea. Cave bears were up to 2.7 m long and weighed up to 300–400 kg, twice the weight of modern European brown bears (*Ursus arctos*). They had a relatively large head with a characteristic domed forehead, and relatively short, stocky legs. Studies of their tooth structure, as well as of the mineral content of their bones, indicate that their diet was almost exclusively vegetarian. Large numbers of cave bear fossils are found in certain caves, a result of animals occasionally dying during their winter hibernation.

Cave of Hearths a cave near the MAKAPANSGAT AUSTRALOPITHECINE site in the northern Transvaal, South Africa, with a long record of human habitation from ACHEULIAN to Iron Age times. A mandible fragment found with the Acheulian material is described as early or archaic HOMO *sapiens* or *H. sapiens rhodesiensis* (see BROKEN HILL). Some of the Acheulian layers probably contain hearths, but comprise mainly burnt bat guano, which may have been ignited naturally or accidentally.

Cayla de Mailhac a hilltop defended settlement in Aude, France, occupied during the Late Bronze Age and Iron Age. It was destroyed in the 1st century BC, probably by the Romans. The large URNFIELD cemetery associated with the earlier phases of occupation of the settlement is divided into three stages – Le Moulin, Grand Bassin I and Grand Bassin II – which together span the 9th to 5th centuries BC (Late Bronze IIIb to Iron Age II). They form the type-series for the chronology of this period in the Languedoc region of southern France. The latest phase, Grand Bassin II, is marked by the appearance of Greek and ETRUSCAN imports.

Çayönü a 3 ha prehistoric site on the River Tigris drainage in the Diyarbakir district of Turkey excavated by Robert Braidwood. Its occupation dates to roughly 7300–6500 BC. The sequence of stone architecture at the site shows considerable sophistication, and includes at different times elaborate foundations and *terrazzo* floors (a decorative technique of coloured stones laid as patterns in cement and then polished). The material culture of the community encompassed various uses of unfired clay (figurines, geometrics (see TOKENS), basketry lining), hammered native copper, and rich lithic and bone industries. The community cultivated wheat and legumes, which increased in importance through time, and shifted from mostly hunted cattle, deer, sheep, goat and pigs to (probably) mostly herded sheep, goat and pig by the end of the occupation.

Ceahlău-Cetăţica an Upper Palaeolithic open-air site located along a small tributary of the Siret River in eastern Romania. Artifacts and faunal remains (which include woolly MAMMOTH and reindeer) are buried in LOESS deposits on a medium terrace. The lowermost levels contain small assemblages with BIFACIAL FOLIATES, sidescrapers and endscrapers (see SCRAPER) and are assigned to the early Upper Palaeolithic (not clearly attributable to either the AURIGNACIAN or the SZELETIAN). The upper levels contain BACKED BLADES, and are assigned to the GRAVETTIAN.

Cederberg a range of the Cape Fold Mountains north of Cape Town, South Africa, particularly known for its rock paintings, which date from LATER STONE AGE to historical times. Depictions of humans, hand prints, animals (especially elephant and sheep), geometric designs and historical scenes are interpreted by some scholars as related to the trance hallucinations of shamans.

celadon a type of STONEWARE, with a revolutionary GLAZE containing calcium and feldspar, produced in quantity in China in the 9th–14th centuries AD (see CHINESE DYNASTIES). The glaze is most often dark greenish-blue from reduced firing, but some oxidized yellowish-brown glazes are also included. The northern Yaozhou and the southern Longquan kilns are best known. Celadon became the first trade CERAMICS to be exported from China in quantity (see SINAN) to many destinations in East and Southeast Asia, and the Koreans continued to develop the celadon tradition in the Koryo period (see KOREAN PERIODIZATION, WANDO; compare YUE ware).

cella the largest room in a CLASSICAL temple, which sometimes contained the cult-statue. To its rear was the ADYTON.

celt see SHOE-LAST ADZE.

Celts a protohistoric people of central and western Europe, often equated with the Iron Age in the region, and described by CLASSICAL writers as ferocious warriors. In artistic depictions, such as the 'dying Gaul', Celtic men have wavy hair and moustaches, and wear TORCS. The Celts invaded Italy and sacked ROME in the early 4th century BC, and later invaded Greece and Anatolia, but in later centuries the Romans gradually took over all their territories except for Scotland and Ireland.

cenote a natural well or sinkhole created when bedrock has collapsed, exposing the water table. One of the most famous is the Sacred Cenote at CHICHÉN ITZÁ, 60 m in diameter with walls 26 m above the water level. The MAYA offered rituals and sacrifices at the Sacred Cenote.

Central Cattle Pattern a homestead organization associated with most speakers of Eastern BANTU languages in the southern African Iron Age, who exchange cattle for wives. It is characterized by a central area of stock byres, storage facilities controlled by a central political authority, high-status burials, and a men's court, which is surrounded by circular houses and privately owned grain bins.

central place theory a MODEL developed by geographers, which argues that sites are distributed evenly over a region, and that settlements are spatially organized in a hierarchy of importance, dependent on their control of resources.

centuriation a Roman technique for dividing up agricultural land into equal areas often of 200 *iugera* (approximately 50 ha). It was particularly common at colonies where each member of the foundation would be assigned an equal share. Centuriation may be noted by AERIAL PHOTOGRAPHY where it shows as a grid pattern.

cephalic index a measure for the shape of the cranial vault, derived by Anders Retzius in 1842. The measure is the ratio of the maximum breadth divided by the maximum width of the skull. Retzius used the cephalic index to divide European populations into three types: *dolichocephalic* (long, narrow); *mesocephalic* (intermediate); and *brachycephalic* (short, broad).

ceque one of a series of imaginary lines radiating outward from the INCA city of CUZCO, Peru. A total of 41 ceques extended from the Temple of the Sun to the edges of the surrounding valley. Along each ceque were located a series of *huacas* (shrines) at which offerings were made on successive days. The combination of *huacas* and ceques served to mark 328 days in the Inca calendar. According to research by Anthony Aveni and Tom Zuidema, some of the ceques may have had astronomical significance.

ceramic petrology the study of the composition, material sources and construction technology of pottery. Mineral constituents of CERAMICS that may help identify a material source are identified by one or more methods. Pottery can be broken down into particles with HEAVY MINERAL ANALYSIS conducted on the residue. More commonly, a PETROLOGICAL ANALYSIS is undertaken in which a THIN SECTION is made and mineral constituents are identified on the basis of their optical properties. Thin sections oriented perpendicular to vessel walls may reveal internal structures as well as mineral additives (TEMPER), that provide clues to construction technology and techniques. If a CLAY source can be identified, the distribution of ceramics made from that source should hold clues to trade and economic systems.

ceramics baked clay or pottery, often used for containers. The plasticity and additive technology of ceramics make this medium one of the most culturally sensitive of all prehistoric artifacts, that have been extensively used by archaeologists as time-markers, as well as for the information they can provide on social organization.

ceremonial centre a predominant form of urban centre in MESOAMERICA, especially among the OLMEC and MAYA cultures. Ceremonial centres are typically composed of monumental religious architecture, administrative buildings, BALL COURTS and elite residential compounds. The majority of the population associated with a ceremonial centre inhabited the surrounding countryside, and occupied the centre only during religious and other special events.

Cerén, Joya de a MAYA 'POMPEII' in El Salvador, just west of San Salvador, discovered in 1976. Excavations by Payson Sheets have revealed that the village was buried under ASH by a volcanic eruption in *c*.AD 600. The remarkable preservation has yielded wooden objects such as digging sticks and pestles inside houses, part of the oldest painted CODEX yet found, dishes of food left on hearths, and rows of maize in a cornfield.

Cernavodă a Late Neolithic and ENEOLITHIC site complex in southeast Romania. The best known is a cemetery of the HAMANGIA culture with over 300 inhumations. Many of the graves contained ANTHROPOMORPHOUS figurines, including several with more facial and body detail than previous Balkan figurines. Nearby is a later settlement with several metres of deposits, which is the type-site for the Cernavodă culture at the transition from the Eneolithic to the Early Bronze Age. Cernavodă shell-tempered, fluted pottery represents a break from that of the preceding GUMELNIŢA culture.

Cernica a Late Neolithic cemetery near Bucharest, Romania, with 115 burials of the HAMANGIA culture. Among the grave-goods were COPPER beads made of malachite or a similar ore which had been cold-hammered but not heated. Other grave-goods included pottery, polished stone tools, and bracelets of SPONDYLUS shell.

Cerny an Early Neolithic culture of the Paris basin and middle Loire, France, characterized by round-based vessels with impressed decoration or applied cordons. Cerny (*c*.4400–4000 BC) follows the Villeneuve-St-Germain group in the Paris basin Neolithic sequence, and precedes the CHASSÉEN.

CERRO SECHÍN

Cerro Sechín a monumental site in the Casma Valley of the north central coast of Peru. A square central mound, measuring 53 m square and 4 m high, is faced with bas-relief stone carvings depicting warriors, captives, weapons and disarticulated human body parts. The dating of the site is unclear; some researchers consider it to date to the EARLY HORIZON, and suggest that it may commemorate the conquest of this region by a group from the highlands. Others argue for a date in the INITIAL PERIOD.

Cerveteri (*Lat.* Caere) a walled city in south ETRURIA. It is best known for its cemeteries, such as that at Banditaccia just to the north. A wide range of tombs have been found including some under TUMULI and others cut into the TUFF. One of the more elaborate is the Tomb of the Reliefs which is an underground room laid out like a TRICLINIUM with drinking vessels, armour and other items cut in relief. The tombs have been an important source for ATHENIAN POTTERY. Cerveteri was served by the port of Pyrgi, where three gold plaques have been found providing parallel texts in Etruscan and PHOENICIAN. See also CAERETAN WARE.

Cevdar see CHEVDAR.

C-group a population of LOWER NUBIA broadly contemporary, and sharing cultural traits, with the KERMA culture of UPPER NUBIA (*c.*2200–1500 BC). The C-group, like the PAN-GRAVE people, seem to have been primarily cattle-herders. Their most distinctive material product is hand-made black pottery with incised geometric designs. Links with the preceding A-group are uncertain. Elaborate buildings and the importation of luxury items from Egypt in late C-group times suggest that STATE formation was underway.

chacmool an ANTHROPOMORPHOUS altar common at CHICHÉN ITZA and TULA but also found at other MESOAMERICAN centres. Reclining human figures, whose hands, resting on the stomach, provided an altar on which offerings were placed, these sculptures are associated with temple entrances. Their name, meaning 'red paw' or 'great paw' in the Yucatec language, was first given to them by Augustus Le Plongeon in the 19th century.

chacmool

Chaco Canyon   a wide canyon in north-Central New Mexico, USA. It is the location of some of the most visually impressive and important sites of the American Southwest. Chaco Canyon reached its zenith in the period approximately AD 1000–1150. The cluster of sites may have served as a ceremonial and/or trading centre for subsidiary sites, called Chacoan outliers, found throughout the northern Southwest. Many of these sites are connected to Chaco Canyon by roads up to 96 km long, some of which were merely depressions running along the surface while others were well constructed with stone edgings. See ANASAZI, FAJADA BUTTE, PUEBLO BONITO, WETHERILL.

Chaeronea   see CHAIRONEIA.

Chagar Bazar   a large (10 ha) prehistoric TELL site in the Khabur triangle in northeastern Syria. Max MALLOWAN's excavations during the 1930s occurred in separate parts of the mound. A deep sounding exposed 10 HALAF levels, the lowest of which also contained SAMARRAN painted and 'AMUQ B-related sherds. NEUTRON ACTIVATION ANALYSIS of the later Halaf pottery at Chagar Bazar indicates that most of it was locally produced and distributed to smaller settlements to the north, an indication of economic specialization and possibly of socio-political complexity within the region. Elsewhere on the mound, Mallowan's work revealed five levels belonging to the 3rd and 2nd millennia BC. The uppermost of these levels contains a large building, possibly a palace, that contained a small archive dated to SHAMSHI-ADAD I (1813–1781 BC).

Chaironeia or **Chaeronea**   a large Neolithic settlement mound in Boeotia, Greece, which is the source of distinctive red-on-cream Middle Neolithic pottery. A stone lion in the village of Chaironeia guards the tomb of the Thebans who were killed in the battle of 338 BC.

Chaiya   a city on the east coast of peninsular Thailand with two early historic sites: Wat Wiang, a moated settlement occupied in the late 1st–early 2nd millennium AD and source of inscriptions associating the town with Grahi, ŚRIVIJAYA and TAMBRALINGA; and Ban Phum Rieng, a site closer to the shore which has yielded finds linking it to the nearby port of LAEM PHO.

Chalandriani   the site of a large Early CYCLADIC cemetery on the island of Syros in the Aegean, which was excavated by TSOUNTAS. The fortified settlement on the precipitous hill of Kastri is also Early Cycladic but appears to be later in date and to have been occupied by settlers from Anatolia.

Chalcatzingo   a large OLMEC community in Morelos, Mexico, known primarily for its carvings on boulders and other rock faces. The community was probably an important point on a trade route. The site was discovered by Eulalia Guzmán in 1934.

chalcedony   a group of water-bearing silica minerals characterized by very fine grained (cryptocrystalline) QUARTZ, colloidal silica, a small amount of water and submicroscopic pores. Chalcedony is transparent to opaque and is found in a wide range of colours. 'Chalcedony' is reserved for those specimens that are fairly uniform in colour, whereas *agate* is used for specimens characterized by colour bands or concentric rings. Some of the banded varieties are called *onyx*. In the archaeological record, chalcedony was used for beads, jewellery, SEALS, and was worked into stone tools by flaking and chipping.

CHALCIDIAN WARE

Chalcidian ware a type of ARCHAIC BLACK-FIGURED pottery mostly found in ETRURIA and in the Chalcidian colony of Rhegium (*mod.* Reggio) situated on the 'toe' of Italy. The name is derived from the local style of lettering of the inscriptions which form part of the scheme of decoration. Recent CLAY analyses have been unable to identify the place of manufacture.

Chalcolithic a term for the Copper Age. See ENEOLITHIC.

Chaldeans a seminomadic ethnic group, associated with UR and Abraham in popular and Biblical belief, which moved into southern MESOPOTAMIA early in the 1st millennium BC from the west; this movement, along with that of ARAMAEANS, contributed to the political and economic upheavals in ASSYRIA and BABYLONIA of that time. Unlike the Aramaeans, the Chaldeans became largely sedentary, though still organized as tribal descent groups, in southern Babylonia. These groups strongly resisted the Assyrian occupation of Babylonia in the 8th–7th centuries BC. Although the rulers of the NEO-BABYLONIAN empire are often referred to as the 'Chaldean dynasty', these kings (e.g. NEBUCHADNEZZAR II) are not known to be Chaldeans.

Cham an ethno-linguistic group belonging to the AUSTRONESIAN family, once controlling the central coast of modern Vietnam, and forming the state of CHAMPA.

chamber(ed) tomb a tomb, either stone-built and covered by an earth mound or rock-cut, generally used for multiple inhumations.

'Cham forts' see 'MOI FORTS'.

Champa an early, loosely structured state formed by the Cham people on the central coast of modern Vietnam, comprising several distinct geographical foci: Amaravati, Vijaya, Kauthara and Pandurangga. First mentioned by the Chinese, as Lin-yi, in the 3rd century AD, it was one of the earliest INDIANIZED states in Southeast Asia. It remained an important sea trading state until its progressive absorption by Vietnam after the 13th century. Major sites include: Vo Canh (earliest SANSKRIT inscription in Southeast Asia, from the 3rd century AD?); Po Nagar (centre of Kauthara); and, in Amaravati, Mi Son, Dong Duong, and Tra Kieu (all major ceremonial centres).

Champ Durand a Neolithic enclosure in Vendée, France, consisting of three concentric rock-cut ditches with numerous entrance gaps. Rubble in the ditches probably came from a dry-stone rampart on their inner edge. Associated material is of Late Neolithic type, and includes PEU-RICHARDIEN decorated pottery which allows the site to be dated to *c.*3300–3000 BC.

Champollion, Jean François (1778–1867) a French philologist instrumental in the decipherment of Egyptian HIEROGLYPHS, initially through his work on the ROSETTA STONE.

Chancay a culture of the LATE INTERMEDIATE PERIOD on the north central coast of Peru. It is characterized by a distinctive ceramic style found in the Chancay and Chillón Valleys as well as to the north and south. A typical form is an elongated jar, with a face painted on a small neck; CERAMICS are not highly polished, and are typically painted in black geometric designs on an off-white SLIP. Numerous large cemeteries pertaining to this culture yield evidence of social stratification. One of several distinctive coastal cultures at this time, it was conquered by the INCA empire. (See also CHIMÚ.)

Chancelade or **Raymonden**   two MAGDALENIAN rockshelters in the Dordogne, France, which included hearths, HARPOONS, MOBILIARY ART and the tightly flexed OCHRE-covered burial of an adult male. The Chancelade man, found in 1888, was a HOMO *sapiens sapiens*, but skeletal analysis suggests that he would have been dissimilar in appearance to CRO-MAGNON man, being shorter and having a different facial shape.

Chan Chan   an urban site covering over six square kilometres, the capital of the CHIMÚ POLITY of the LATE INTERMEDIATE PERIOD, located in the Moche Valley on the north coast of Peru. Investigations by Michael E. Moseley, Carol Mackey, Kent Day and others indicate that the site comprises some nine large rectangular compounds each of which may have served as the administrative headquarters, ceremonial centre and subsequent mausoleum of each of the successive Chimú rulers. The presence of extensive secondary architecture suggests a resident population in excess of 10 000 persons. The lack of contemporaneous sites indicates that nearly the entire population of the Moche valley may have lived at the site.

Chang'an [Ch'ang-an]   the name of both the Early HAN and Tang capitals (see CHINESE DYNASTIES) of China. These two walled cities of the same name are located adjacent to each other in Shaanxi Province, the latter incorporating modern Xian City. The gridded street layout and gated walled enclosure of Tang-period Chang'an, with the royal palace positioned for the first time in the north, became the model for urban development in the 7th century AD Korean states and Japan (see SILLA, HEIJO, PUYO, FUJIWARA).

Changjiang [Ch'ang-chiang]   literally 'long river', the Chinese name for the Yangtze River, heartland of the wet-rice agricultural regime (see HEMUDU).

Chanhu-daro   a group of three mounds covering nearly 20 ha (but originally larger) in the southern Sind (southern Pakistan). Chanhu-daro was excavated first by N.G. Majumdar and then by Ernest Mackay in the 1930s. Mackay's work revealed a Mature HARAPPAN city beneath ill-defined Late Harappan (JHUKAR) levels. Chanhu-daro's contribution to Harappan archaeology rests largely on the recovery of craftsmen's workshops (especially stone beads). Although it represents one of the few investigated Late Harappan sites in the Sind, Mackay's failure to excavate it by natural stratigraphic units leaves considerable confusion about the nature of the period.

Chania or **Khania**   the site of ancient Kydonia, in the west of Crete, that was evidently a MINOAN administrative centre and should be the site of a palace, but the excavations at Kastelli in the old town have uncovered only a fraction of the Bronze Age settlement. Nevertheless LINEAR A tablets have been discovered, together with STIRRUP JARS which have inscriptions in LINEAR B.

Chansen   a moderate-sized protohistoric and early historic settlement north of LOPBURI in the Chao Phraya valley, central Thailand. Evidence of trade with India dates to the first two centuries AD, and of trade with 'FUNAN' sites in the Mekong delta to the 5th and 6th centuries. Phase 5 of occupation (*c.*AD 600–800) is related to the state of DVARAVATI.

Charama   a post-ACHEULIAN and pre-BAMBATA early Upper PLEISTOCENE STONE AGE INDUSTRY of Zambia and Zimbabwe, characterized by light-duty FLAKE tools, especially SCRAPERS, small picks, and disc CORES.

Charavines   the LAKE DWELLING of Les Baigneurs, on the southern side of Lake Paladru, Isère, France, now under water. The well-preserved remains of timber houses and organic materials, excavated since 1972, have allowed a remarkably detailed picture of the settlement's history to be established through DENDROCHRONOLOGY of the structural timbers. The first village, of six or seven rectangular houses, was established in about 2740 BC. Repaired after 9 years, these houses were then abandoned at the end of 20 years. Fifty-seven years later the village was rebuilt, and occupied for a further 20 years before final abandonment. Notable among the many organic remains recovered are finely flaked flint daggers with handles of coiled willow.

charcoal   see ANTHRACOLOGY.

Charentian   a major MOUSTERIAN variant rich in sidescrapers (see SCRAPER) identified by BORDES in southwest France. The Charentian TRADITION may be subdivided into the LA FERRASSIE type, which has few transverse scrapers but a frequent use of the LEVALLOISIAN technique, and the QUINA type with many transverse scrapers but little Levallois material. See LA QUINA, LA FERRASSIE.

chasing   see REPOUSSÉ.

Chassey   a promontory settlement, in Côte-d'Or, France, type-site of the Middle Neolithic Chasséen culture found throughout much of eastern and southern France c.4500–3500 BC. The principal pottery forms are round-based bowls with sharp CARINATION, often of very fine fabric; and cubic or cylindrical objects with saucer-like tops and incised decoration of cross-hatched and dot-filled triangles known as 'VASE-SUPPORTS' or 'incense-burners'. The latter term is probably nearer the true function of these enigmatic pieces. Chasséen material is found at promontory settlements in eastern and northeastern France, at the large open sites of the Toulouse area including VILLENEUVE-TOLOSANE and ST MICHEL-DU-TOUCH, and in MEGALITHIC tombs of western France.

Châteauneuf-les-Martigues   a rockshelter in the southern Rhône valley, Bouches-du-Rhône, France, with Mesolithic and Neolithic occupation. The earliest layers (9 to 7) contain geometric MICROLITHS and other material of the late Mesolithic *Castelnovian* culture. This is followed c.5000 BC by Early Neolithic layers with CARDIAL WARE pottery and bones of domestic sheep. Early RADIOCARBON dates from the site which suggested the appearance of Neolithic features before 6000 BC have now been discounted.

Châtelperronian   the earliest Upper Palaeolithic French FLAKE IN-DUSTRY named after the cave site of Châtelperron, Allier, central France, and characterized by the presence of curved BACKED BLADES (Châtelperron points or knives), flakes, endscrapers and BURINS. It is generally accepted that the Châtelperronian represents a local development evolving c.36 000 bp from the final MOUSTERIAN of southwest France. The Châtelperronian is occasionally termed the Lower PERI-GORDIAN.

chattel art   see MOBILIARY ART

Chavín   a large town and temple complex located in the north central highlands of Peru, pertaining to the EARLY HORIZON. Investigations by Julio C. TELLO, Luis G. Lumbreras and Richard Burger indicate that the Old Temple complex (*c.*900–400 bc) was built originally to a U-shaped plan, arranged around a sunken circular courtyard. Deep inside the original structure is found a monolithic stone carving, the Lanzón, on which is depicted an ANTHROPOMORPHOUS being with a fanged feline mouth and snakes for hair. It is one of the few large Chavín stone carvings still in its original location.

Later the complex was modifed, with the New Temple (*c.*400–200 bc) incorporating the old, and forming a new U-shaped layout surrounding a large sunken rectangular court. One of the stone carvings associated with the New Temple was the Raimondi STELA, on which was carved a human figure, with an elaborate headdress, holding a staff in each hand. This may be one of the earliest representations of the Staff Deity, which is seen in the art of later civilizations, especially TIAHUANACO and HUARI.

Chavín probably functioned as a pilgrimage centre. (See also PACHACAMAC.) The art style of Chavín, together with new technological innovations in textile art and METALLURGY, are found widely distributed through the northern highlands and the north, central and south coast of Peru. It is the spread of the Chavín style that originally gave definition to the Early Horizon, although at present its distribution is less extensive than originally thought. Work by Richard Burger indicates that many 'Chavinoid' sites actually pre-date the construction of Chavín. (See also CUPISNIQUE, PARACAS.)

Cheddar See GOUGH'S CAVE.

chedi a Thai term for STUPA.

Cheetup a granite rockshelter in southwest Western Australia. The shallow deposits date to the Late PLEISTOCENE. A feature similar to pits described ethnographically for leaching the highly toxic seeds from cycad plants, and containing well-preserved cycad seeds, has a minimum date of 13 200 bp. Compare CATHEDRAL CAVE.

Chelford a PLEISTOCENE site in Cheshire, England, which has given its name to the Chelford INTERSTADIAL, a warm phase during the Early DEVENSIAN COLD STAGE and dated to *c.*61 000 BP, which is accepted as the equivalent of the Continental Brørup Interstadial.

Chellean an outdated classificatory term used for the first primitive stage of BIFACE manufacture believed to precede the ACHEULIAN, and named after the type-site of Chelles in the Somme Valley, France. It is now generally accepted that Chellean implements should correctly be classified as early Acheulian. The term Chelleo-Acheulian, which was once applied to African EARLIER STONE AGE biface ASSEMBLAGES, has also been replaced by the term Acheulian. See also ABBEVILLIAN.

chemical analysis a general term for the quantitative or qualitative determination of the chemical composition of material utilizing a range of physical and chemical analytical techniques. Chemical analyses have been applied to nearly the full range of artifactual materials, SOIL and SEDIMENT recovered from archaeological CONTEXTS to solve problems of material characterization, CORRELATION, material source identification, manufacturing technology, and artifact composition.

Chenjiawo [Ch'en-chia-wo] see LANTIAN.

Chenla see ZHENLA.

Cheops see KHUFU.

CHEPHREN

Chephren   see KHAFRE.

chert   **1.** a member of the CHALCEDONY group of water-bearing silica minerals characterized by its opaqueness. 'Chert' is used to refer to such material where it occurs as STRATA or massive deposits, but it can also occur as NODULES. FLINT is often distinguished from chert by its dark or black colour, although mineralogically they form a continuum, with chert having less water and being slightly coarser-grained. The hardness of chert, its interlocking fine grains, and ability to fracture concoidally producing razor-sharp edges made it a principal raw material used in tool manufacture. **2.** a sedimentary silicious rock mostly consisting of chert, the mineral.

Chesowanja   a central Kenyan site with faunal remains and OLDOWAN stone tools associated with small clay CLASTS, which some interpret as early evidence that HOMINIDS were using and controlling FIRE 1.42 million years ago. However, because it has been shown that erosion of naturally burnt clay areas can result in fragments like those at Chesowanja, some researchers consider the case for the controlled use of fire at Chesowanja unproven.

Chevdar or **Cevdar**   an early Neolithic TELL site located on the Topolnitsa River in Bulgaria. In one of the earliest uses of flotation in European archaeology, soil samples from floors and ovens at Chevdar yielded considerable information on plant use by the earliest Neolithic communities of the Balkans. The faunal sample consisted primarily of sheep and goat, with fewer cattle, pigs and some wild animals. The subsistence data from Chevdar, as at KAZANLUK, have been interpreted as reflecting both an arable component, based on a rotational system of cultivation, and a mobile pastoral component.

Chiapa de Corzo   a site in west-central Chiapas, Mexico, which not only has some of the earliest evidence of occupation in Chiapas, but has also been occupied almost continuously from the Early PRECLASSIC (1500–1000 BC) through the Spanish conquest and into modern times. Its primary importance lies in its well-stratified deposits, the chronology that has been developed subsequently, and the ability to tie this chronology to the remainder of MESOAMERICA. It has been excavated by a number of scholars working with the New World Archaeological Foundation. See BAR AND DOT NOTATION.

Chibuene   a trading settlement on the Mozambique coast, first occupied in the 8th century AD, which developed into an important link in the trade between the East African coast and interior sites such as MAPUNGUBWE and GREAT ZIMBABWE in the first half of the 2nd millennium AD.

Chichén Itzá   a MAYA CEREMONIAL CENTRE in central Yucatán, Mexico, one of the best-known sites in MESOAMERICA, whose ceramic evidence indicates occupation from the Late PRECLASSIC to the Late POSTCLASSIC. The features at this site include El Castillo, a square-based, stepped PYRAMID, approximately 25 m high; the Sacred CENOTE, a natural well 60 m in diameter, with sides 26 m above the water surface, into which human and other sacrifices were thrown; El Caracol ('snail' in Spanish), a name referring to the building's spiral stairway: El Caracol was probably an observatory, and is the only round structure at Chichén Itzá. The centre also contains the Temple of the Warriors, which at one time was attributed to 'TOLTECS' during their occupation of the city. Many Mesoamericanists now reject the Toltec invasion theory, and see Chichén Itzá as having dual, complementary styles of architecture, with the 'Toltec' buildings perhaps built by the Putun or Chontal non-Classic Maya from southwest Yucatán.

Chichimec   a general term applied specifically to peoples moving south into the Basin of Mexico from the north between AD 1175–1425. The term is used more generally to refer to 'barbarian' cultures on the northern frontier of MESOAMERICA. The Chichimec were typically portrayed as fierce warring peoples, new to Mesoamerican civilization and culture. Perhaps the most famous descendants of the Chichimec were the AZTECS. Chichimec is also a linguistic group. See also GRAN CHICHIMECA.

chiefdom   a type of social organization characterized by a degree of social ranking and larger population aggregates. They are led by individual chiefs who control access to resources and have specific political and economic powers.

Chifumbaze   an Early IRON AGE complex distributed over an enormous area of eastern and southeastern Africa, dating from about 2500 years ago to at least the 11th century AD. Sites contain the first evidence in eastern and southeastern Africa for settled village life and METALLURGY, and, in southeastern Africa, for the manufacture of pottery. The complex is generally divided into an Eastern Stream or UREWE tradition and a Western Stream or KALUNDU tradition (see CHONDWE, GOKOMERE, KAPWIRIMBWE, KWALE, MATOLA, NKOPE).

Childe, Vere Gordon   (1892–1957)   one of the leading archaeologists of the 20th century. Born in Australia, he emigrated to Britain where he spent the whole of his professional life. Never a prolific excavator (SKARA BRAE being a rare exception), he is most famous for his massive syntheses of PREHISTORY. Early work on European languages and ethnicity, published as *The Aryans* in 1926, broadened into a general survey of European prehistory in the Neolithic and Bronze Age, *The Dawn of European Civilization* (which, revised and corrected, ran through six editions between 1925 and 1957), and *The Danube in Prehistory* published in 1929. For Childe, the succession of cultures at the VINČA TELL near Belgrade formed the key to the chronology of southeast Europe. He subsequently widened his interests to include the early farming communities and civilizations of the Near East with *The Most Ancient East*, 1928, and *Man Makes Himself*, 1936. In 1927 he became the first Professor of Prehistoric Archaeology at the University of Edinburgh, moving in 1946 to be Director of the newly established Institute of Archaeology in London. Widely respected for his knowledge of European languages and prehistory, he has also had a profound influence on later generations of archaeologists through his writings on the nature of archaeological concepts and entities, including the idea of the CULTURE, still a major building block of European prehistory. The theoretical underpinnings to his work are strongly MARXIST.

Chimú   a large urban society located on the north coast of Peru during the LATE INTERMEDIATE PERIOD. The Chimú capital was at CHAN CHAN, in the MOCHE Valley, and Chimú control extended from the central coast of Peru nearly to Ecuador; it was the largest POLITY conquered by the INCA. The Chimú first began to expand in the 13th or 14th century AD, and controlled several valleys to the north and south. A second expansion, accomplished in the mid 15th century, brought the Chimú to their maximum extent; this later expansion may have been related to the fact that the Inca were also beginning to expand at this time. The Chimú built many impressive hydraulic constructions, and brought large tracts of land under cultivation. One canal may have served to connect the Chicama and Moche valleys, but there is some dispute over whether or not the canal actually functioned, and over the reasons for its abandonment. The Chimú were conquered by the Inca Empire after a bloody struggle, and the Chimú political apparatus was gradually dismantled.

China Lake   an area containing a group of prehistoric open-air sites on the margins of the Mojave Desert in southern California, USA. At one locality, artifacts (two FLAKES) and MAMMOTH remains were found on the surface of lake deposits, associated with an ancient soil. Although a URANIUM SERIES date of 42 350 bp was obtained on a mammoth tooth, the surface CONTEXT precludes reliable dating of the artifacts, and the site is not widely accepted as evidence of settlement prior to 12 000 BP in North America.

chinampa   an intensive agricultural technique used in the BASIN OF MEXICO, and often referred to as 'floating gardens'. Agricultural production takes advantage of the standing water, ALLUVIUM, and mouldering vegetation in swampy or marshy areas.

To start a new chinampa, long rectangular mats of floating plants were grown in open, deeper ponds, and then dragged to a new location and secured with cypress stakes. A number of such mats were stacked on top of each other. The resulting chinampa was about 10 m by 110 m, and raised above the water level. Canals were dug on three or four sides of the chinampa, which were laid out in a grid. The lake mud from constructing the canals was then piled on the vegetation. Seedlings started elsewhere were then transplanted to the chinampa. Special canoe–latrines carried human waste from TENOCHTITLÁN to the chinampas, providing a rich fertilizer.

The farmland created was extremely efficient because it existed where previously no agricultural produce could be grown. The chinampa grew staple root, vegetable, grain and fruit crops. A household would support itself using several chinampas, which were kept in production all year round. In 1519, 10 000 ha of chinampa reportedly supported about 100 000 people.

Chinchorro   a site on the coast of northern Chile, at which the earliest-known intentionally mummified humans have been found. Dating to c.7000 bp, the bodies were eviscerated, skinned, covered with clay and frequently painted in red pigments. Clay masks were placed on the faces.

Chindadn point   a small teardrop-shaped BIFACIAL type of point found in early prehistoric sites of central Alaska, dating to c.12 000–10 000 bp. First discovered by Cook at HEALY LAKE, they have also been found at WALKER ROAD and are diagnostic of the NENANA COMPLEX.

Chinese dynasties   the traditional subdivisions of Chinese history based on DYNASTIES, each comprising a series of emperors, usually blood relatives, who succeeded each other on the throne. A change in dynasty meant a change of family holding power. Chinese dynasties did not necessarily encompass the whole country, but often merely parts of it (e.g. in the THREE KINGDOMS). In chronological order, the dynasties are: XIA [Hsia] (17th century BC); SHANG (16th–11th centuries BC); ZHOU [Chou] (1027–221 BC); QIN [Ch'in] (221–207 BC); HAN (206 BC–AD 220); Three Kingdoms/Six Dynasties (AD 220–280); Western Jin [Chin] (265–316); Eastern Jin [Chin] (317–420); Northern and Southern (420–581); Sui (581–618); Tang [T'ang] (618–907); Five Dynasties (907–960); Song [Sung] (960–1279); Liao (916–1125); Jin [Chin] (1115–1234); Yuan (1271–1368); Ming (1368–1644); Qing [Ch'ing] (1644–1911); Republic of China (1912–1949); People's Republic of China (1949–present). (See NEOLITHIC, BRONZE AGE, IRON AGE.)

Chinhan see SAMHAN.

Chiot pottery pottery produced in the ARCHAIC period on the Greek island of Chios, although some have suggested that it was also made at NAUCRATIS. The pots, often chalices, were decorated with a cream SLIP and decorated on the exterior with figured scenes either in outline or in silhouette. In the GLAZED interior, floral patterns such as PALMETTES were often added in red.

Chirand a site on the ALLUVIAL plain of the lower Ganges River in Bihar in northeastern India, where excavations during the 1960s and 1970s revealed five periods of occupation. The last two of these are early 1st millennium AD and mediaeval respectively; the first three are Neolithic (Chirand I), CHALCOLITHIC (Chirand IIA–B) and NORTHERN BLACK POLISHED WARE (Chirand III). Chirand I, dating to the earlier 2nd millennium BC (and perhaps extending into the 3rd), is a village of plastered bamboo, a BLADE lithic industry, handmade red and grey BURNISHED pottery, and a subsistence based on the cultivation of rice and other cereals, fishing and hunting. Chirand II, which is divided into two phases belonging to the later 2nd and earlier 1st millennium BC respectively, is largely a continuation of the Neolithic culture though a black-and-red ware now occurs; copper artifacts first appear in Chirand IIA levels and iron in Chirand IIB. In Chirand III, beginning around 500 BC, NBPW replaces the black-and-red ware, and MUD-BRICK architecture appears (baked brick by the end of the period); with this development, this part of the Gangetic drainage was culturally united with upstream regions in the second great episode of urbanization and state formation in northern India.

Chiripa a culture pertaining to the EARLY INTERMEDIATE PERIOD on the Bolivian altiplano. The site that gives its name to the culture was first occupied in the EARLY HORIZON; in the Early Intermediate Period a large ceremonial component was built, including a series of 16 structures symmetrically arranged around a rectangular sunken plaza. The Chiripa culture is roughly contemporaneous with the PUCARA culture of the Peruvian altiplano, and precedes the TIAHUANACO culture.

chocolate flint a variety of high-quality flint from the HOLY CROSS MOUNTAINS in central Poland, used by prehistoric peoples from the Mesolithic to Early Bronze Age. It occurs in round flat nodules and in slabs no more than 10 cm thick. Chocolate flint is very homogeneous and has excellent flaking qualities. It was usually mined from shallow pits about 2.5 m deep. Four chocolate flint mines have been investigated, at Tomaszów, Wierzbica-Zele, Polany and Polany-Kolonie.

Choga Mami   a 3 ha site near Mandali, to the east of the Tigris in central Iraq, where Joan Oates' excavations have revealed a SAMARRAN settlement with HALAF materials in certain contexts, under 'Transitional' levels (later occupations had been eroded away). In addition to exposures of architecture that complement those found at Tell es-SAWWAN, Oates' work revealed a Samarran period irrigation canal, the first direct confirmation of water works in this culture. The 'Transitional' pottery shows both Samarran and 'UBAID 1 characteristics, and is similar to the newly defined 'Ubaid 0 pottery at 'OUELI (and especially the earliest levels at the latter site). The question remains open, however, whether this pottery at Choga Mami represents a chronological or geographical transitional style.

Choga Zanbil   a walled city of nearly 100 ha, founded on the Karun River near SUSA in lowland Khuzistan, western Iran, in the 13th century BC by a king of ELAM. R. Ghirshman's extensive excavations exposed a walled ZIGGURAT compound, numerous other temples, and three large buildings, at least one of which was a funerary cult centre. Choga Zanbil provides a particularly clear example of a planned religious centre that is relatively unobscured by later occupation (down to the 6th century BC).

Choisy-au-Bac   a lowland settlement site at the confluence of the rivers Oise and Aisne, in France, occupied without break from Late Bronze IIIb to HALLSTATT D. Three principal phases of occupation have been recognized, with rectangular houses, some 5 m × 7 m in size. In the second phase, the settlement was defended by a ditch and rampart. Among the remains of the first and second phases was bronze-working debris, while iron-working furnaces were found in the third phase.

Chojnice–Pienki Culture   a late Mesolithic cultural group of the Vistula and Oder drainages in Poland, overlapping spatially and chronologically with the JANISŁAWICE culture during the late BOREAL and ATLANTIC CLIMATIC PERIODS. The Chojnice-Pienki culture is viewed as having been derived from the preceding KOMORNICA culture, with the addition of trapeze-shaped PROJECTILE POINTS.

chokkomon   a design of shattered spirals engraved on a variety of artifacts of KOFUN-period Japan. Its symbolism is unknown.

Chokurcha   two Middle Palaeolithic cave-sites in the Crimea, Ukraine. At Chokurcha I, three occupation levels were identified in shallow LOAM and rubble deposits; associated faunal remains are predominantly of woolly MAMMOTH, steppe bison and wild ass. The artifacts were lost during the Second World War, but apparently included both sidescrapers (see SCRAPER) and BIFACIAL FOLIATES. At Chokurcha II, a single occupation horizon was found. The faunal remains are dominated by wild ass; the tools include many sidescrapers. Recently, some specimens of figurative MOBILIARY ART, otherwise unknown in the Middle Palaeolithic, were reported. Chokurcha I was excavated by Ernst from 1928–40. Chokurcha II was discovered and investigated by Bader in 1974; recent excavation has been conducted by Stolbunov.

Cholula   an urban MESOAMERICAN centre in Pueblo, Mexico, which was important first during the PRECLASSIC, and, after a hiatus, became a major centre again during the POSTCLASSIC. Archaeological research at the site focused on the huge TEMPLE MOUND there, which under-

chokkomon Bronze mirror; Haniwa shield; stone panel.

went four periods of modification, until it covered 16 ha and reached a height of 55 m. It is the largest single Precolumbian structure in the New World.

Cholula is close to the BASIN OF MEXICO and, after the fall of TEOTIHUACÁN, may have exerted authority over the southern part of the basin. Its greatest period of expansion and influence was during the late Postclassic. Cholula POLYCHROME POTTERY is among the most beautiful in Mesoamerica.

Chondwe an Early Iron Age group of the CHIFUMBAZE complex in central Zambia, dating to the middle of the 1st millennium AD.

Chontal see CHICHÉN ITZÁ, COZUMEL.

chopper/chopping tool a simple Lower Palaeolithic CORE tool with a sharp cutting edge formed either by the removal of FLAKES from one side of the implement (chopper) or by BIFACIAL flake-removal to create a transverse edge (chopping tool). Chopper and flake industries have been found in Africa (OLDOWAN), Europe (see e.g. CLACTONIAN) and the Near East, but are particularly associated with East and South Asia, where the earliest sites such as ZHOUKOUDIAN are regarded as forming an Asian Chopper/Chopping

Tool Tradition, considered by MOVIUS to be more primitive than the HANDAXE tradition of Europe. They appear in assemblages labelled PACITANIAN and NGANDONG in Java, CABENGE in Sulawesi, and CABALWANIAN in the Philippines. Recent work has thrown doubt on earlier assumptions. It now appears that the Asian tools may be late PLEISTOCENE or HOLOCENE in date, forming part of a broader 'pebble-and-flake' industry containing a range of tool types, brought into the region by HOMO *sapiens* rather than by the earlier *Homo erectus* (see HOABHINIAN).

Choris   see NORTON.

Chosen   the Japanese name for pre-modern Korea; see also CHOSON.

Choson   an early POLITY on the northwestern Korean peninsula mentioned in the HAN-dynasty chronicles of China. Extant from at least 197–108 BC, it was conquered by the Han and incorporated into the LELANG COMMANDERY.

Chou   see ZHOU.

chous   1. a Greek measure equal to 12 KOTYLAI. This varied from city to city, but at ATHENS it was the equivalent of 3.2 litres.
2. a type of OINOCHOE made at Athens which may have served as a measure. The mouth normally had three points to the spout ('trefoil'). A miniature version is often decorated with scenes of children playing.

chous

Christy, Henry (1810–65)   an English businessman and banker who was also an ethnologist (especially in Mexico) and was the partner of LARTET in his pioneering excavations in the Palaeolithic sites of southern France in the 1860s.

chromatography   a qualitative method of chemical analysis used to separate and identify substances in a complex mixture; in archaeology it is used to identify and distinguish *amber* from different sources. Substances are separated by passing the solution through a selectively absorbing medium where they migrate at different rates. The result is a STRATIFICATION of constituent layers on the absorbing medium, or a chromatogram, with identification based on the location and colour of the resulting layers.

chronology   the order or sequence of events with respect to time and determination of ages. Chronologies can be based on RELATIVE DATING, where events or materials are related to one another but not to absolute ages. Relative chronologies can be established based on STRATIGRAPHY and CORRELATION, ARTIFACT TYPOLOGIES, or CROSS-

DATING; or chronologies can be based on ABSOLUTE DATING, where events or materials are assigned ages in years.

chronometric dating dating methods that report results as absolute ages. In chronometric studies, it is typical to report results with a measure of uncertainty, usually a standard deviation. DENDROCHRONOLOGY has the possibility of providing the most precise age estimates, although it is applicable only locally. Other chronometric dating techniques include RADIOCARBON DATING, POTASSIUM-ARGON DATING, URANIUM SERIES DATING, THERMOLUMINESCENCE DATING, and in some cases, AMINO-ACID RACEMIZATION.

chryselephantine, *adj.* (of luxury Greek statues) combining IVORY and gold. Two of the most famous in CLASSICAL antiquity were the cult-statues of Athena and Zeus in the PARTHENON and at OLYMPIA respectively, dating to the 5th century BC. Examples of chryselephantine statues have been found from ARCHAIC deposits at DELPHI. The workshop for the statue at Olympia, created by the sculptor Pheidias, has been discovered.

Chubu a modern district in central Honshu Island, Japan, often used in archaeological writings, comprising Niigata, Toyama, Ishikawa, Fukui, Gifu, Nagano, Yamanashi, Aichi and Shizuoka Prefectures. (See JOMON, IDOJIRI.)

Chulmun a type of Neolithic textured-surface pottery (the term Chulmun means 'comb-patterned') giving its name to the POST-GLACIAL horticultural/hunter-gatherer culture of the Korean peninsula. The Chulmun period, spanning the 7th–2nd millennia BC, probably saw the beginnings of millet cultivation at its end (see KOREAN PERIODIZATION). Chulmun pottery was succeeded by MUMUN pottery and the introduction of rice *c.*1500 BC. Regional styles of Chulmun pottery include Classic Chulmun typified by the AMSADONG site, which has incised herringbone patterns on conical pots, the decoration receding from base to rim through time. Other important Chulmun culture sites are TONGSAMDONG and OSAN-RI. (Compare JOMON, DAPENGENG, SHENGWEN, XINLE.) The PALAEOASIATIC peoples of the Chulmun period were probably succeeded by TUNGUS-speakers.

chultun an underground storage chamber. The term is most commonly used in the context of lowland MAYA settlements. Today, bell-shaped chultuns are dug and plastered and serve as water reservoirs during the dry season in the northern part of the Yucatán. A chultun at the prehistoric site of KABÁH has been renovated as a water reservoir, and chultuns are thought to have served this purpose during prehistoric times as well. They also provide excellent storage facilities for *ramon nuts*, a highly nutritious food still relied on by the modern Maya. The ability to store ramon nuts for extended periods of time would imply less dependence on maize production, since they are plentiful and are cultivated in trees located around the residence. A lower dependence on maize production in turn suggests a higher CARRYING CAPACITY, thus suggesting higher population estimates for the area than previously thought. Finally, cultivation and harvesting of ramon nuts could be carried out by women and children, thus freeing the men in households to build and maintain CEREMONIAL CENTRES.

Ciempozuelos a group of BEAKER burials discovered in 1894, notable for their fine pottery and characteristic of the second Beaker phase on the central Meseta, in Spain. The graves were simple pit burials with 12 pottery vessels, a copper dagger and a copper awl. The pottery was heavily incrusted with white paste, and highly decorated bowls were prominent alongside the typical Bell Beakers.

Cimmerians a horse-riding group, with a probable origin in the steppes north of the Black Sea, who moved across the Caucasus mountains and severely disrupted first the URARTIAN state and then the ASSYRIAN northwestern and western marches of the NEO-ASSYRIAN empire in the 8th century BC. The Cimmerians seem to have occupied the region of northern Anatolia near the Black Sea, and exerted considerable pressure on Anatolian states, destroying PHRYGIA shortly after 700 BC and warring with the Lydians (see SARDIS), until the Assyrian king Assurbanipal (668–627 BC) defeated them in Cilicia, southwest Anatolia.

cinerarium a container for cremated remains, often placed in the niches of a COLUMBARIUM. At ROME they are frequently in the shape of a small box made of marble. A small panel may be inscribed with the name of the deceased. Cineraria may be decorated with simple patterns often consisting of garlands.

circus a long enclosure for chariot-racing in the Roman world. A central barrier divided the space into two tracks. Seating for the spectators was on banks, sometimes tiered, on the outside. The earliest example at ROME was the Circus Maximus which measures some 600 m long, and 150 m wide. In the Greek world the circus is normally called a *hippodrome* (see BYZANTIUM). See also STADIUM.

cire perdue see LOST WAX.

Cishan [Tz'u-shan] a site in Hebei Province, China, belonging to the earliest Neolithic millet agricultural regime of the north. Pithouses, storage pits and burials have been excavated. Artifacts include QUERNS with knobbed legs; serrated ground-stone sickles; tripod vessels, hailed as one of the earliest 'Chinese' cultural elements to appear (see DING); and bone and stone fishing and hunting implements. A case has been made here for the world's first domestication of the chicken, from the Common Jungle Fowl. Pig, dog and millet were also domesticated, in contrast to the southern agricultural regime known from HEMUDU. Cishan is dated to the early 6th millennium BC. (See also PEILIGANG.)

cist grave a grave, the sides of which are typically formed of stone slabs set on edge, but may be constructed of rubble or brick, and which is covered by stone slabs. From the Greek *kiste*, a box.

Clactonian a British Lower Palaeolithic FLAKE tool INDUSTRY named after the site of *Clacton-on-Sea*, Essex, and characterized by the presence of thick flakes, CHOPPERS and flake CORES, the use of the HARD HAMMER flaking technique and the absence of BIFACES. The Clactonian is dated to the HOXNIAN INTERGLACIAL, and is therefore contemporary with, or slightly earlier than, the Early ACHEULIAN in Britain, but is generally accepted as a distinct industry. A yew spear point, 36.7 cm long, recovered from Clacton represents the only surviving wooden artifact from Lower Palaeolithic Britain.

Clairvaux-les-lacs a series of Neolithic village sites which occupied the shores of Lake Clairvaux, Jura, France, from 3700–2400 BC. The earliest of these, La Motte-aux-Magnins, consisted of 12 buildings on a small island near the northern edge of the lake. Access would only have been possible by skin boat or dug-out canoe. Among the wealth of organic remains recovered were fishing floats of tree bark and pottery with remains of carbonized food. Some of the pottery, which belonged to the Burgundian Middle Neolithic group, had been decorated with bands of tree bark cut into lozenge shapes.

Clarke, David Leonard (1937–76)   a British archaeologist, noted for his outstanding contributions to theoretical archaeology. His work has much in common with NEW ARCHAEOLOGY, although his ideas developed essentially independently from that school of thought. In *Analytical Archaeology* in 1968, Clarke argued that archaeology must become a science by developing an explicitly archaeological theory based on GENERAL SYSTEMS THEORY.

classical, *adj.*   **1.** relating to the Greek and Roman civilizations, hence classical sculpture, art, period, etc.
2. relating to a period of Greek art dating to the 5th and 4th centuries BC. It traditionally starts after the Persian invasion of Greece in 480 BC (see ARCHAIC). The 4th century phase is sometimes known as the Late Classical period.

Classic period   a phase from AD 250 to AD 650–900, that represents the general period of large populations and elaborate social organization throughout MESOAMERICAN culture. The end of the period varies from region to region. The concept of the Classic period in Mesoamerica refers generally to the peak of artistic and religious endeavours in Precolumbian society. This term is partly an historical expression of archaeological reconstructions; recent research at many Mesoamerican sites negates some of the traditional assumptions associated with the term.

clast   an individual grain that is a constituent of a SEDIMENT body. Archaeological debris, once culturally deposited, consists of clasts in an otherwise natural sediment body and is subject to the same processes and factors as the rest of the deposit.

clay   **1.** a size term for SEDIMENT or SOIL particles that are less than 0.004 or 0.002 mm in diameter depending upon the classification system used. As a particle size term, the definition of clay-size particles is independent of mineral composition or other properties other than size. Compare SAND.
2. an abbreviated term for clay minerals, the finely crystalline water-bearing alumino-silicate minerals belonging to the phyllosilicate mineral group. Clay-size particles consisting all or in part of clay minerals are a chief constituent in CERAMICS.
3. a TEXTURE term used in describing sediment and soils, defined, depending on the classification system used, as containing a certain percentage of clay-size particles relative to sand- and SILT-size particle content.
4. a descriptive term for a sediment body (deposit) composed primarily of clay-size particles that is typically soft and plastic when moist. Material collected from this type of deposit is used in making pottery, tiles, bricks and cement.

Clazomenae   see EAST GREEK POTTERY.

cleaver   a BIFACIAL stone artifact typically found in ACHEULIAN ASSEMBLAGES dating to the Lower and Middle PLEISTOCENE. It is similar to a HANDAXE but has a broad axe-like cutting edge instead of a pointed end. See fig. overleaf.

cleaver Examples from W. Europe and Africa.

Cleland Hills a PETROGLYPH site in central Australia. Most of the heavily weathered pecked engravings are tracks or circles characteristic of PANARAMITEE ART. Sixteen small engravings seem to portray human faces and these are paralleled only in the Pilbara region of Western Australia, notably on the BURRUP PENINSULA.

Cleopatra's Needle see ALEXANDRIA.

Cliff Palace a major site in MESA VERDE, Colorado, USA, this ANASAZI PUEBLO is located in a large cliff overhang. The site is a multi-storey pueblo, with over 200 rooms and 23 KIVAS. The site was abandoned with the rest of Mesa Verde at the end of the 13th century AD and was discovered by WETHERILL in 1888.

clinker-built, *adj.* (of a ship) built by a North European ship-building technique in which the hull is formed first of overlapping planks caulked together and the internal frame only added later. The Halsnoy boat *c.*350 BC is the earliest known clinker-built vessel; later examples include the SUTTON HOO ship of *c.*6th century AD and the famous Viking ships of Oseberg and Gokstad of the 8th–9th centuries AD. Clinker-construction remained in use in some parts of Northern Europe into the 20th century.

cloisonné, *adj.* relating to a technique used in the manufacture of jewellery whereby strips of metal are attached to an item so as to form cells, or *cloisons*, which are then enamelled or inlaid.

Clovis 1. the earliest FLUTED POINT type of the PALAEOINDIAN period. The point is characterized by its symmetry, careful flaking and the removal of a small flute from its face. The date range for Clovis points is approximately 11 500 to 11 000 BP. The classic Clovis sites lie west of the Mississippi, USA, but increasing numbers of Clovis sites are being found in the eastern portion of the continent.

Although this point type was first found at the DENT site in Colorado, it was not formally recognized as a new type until excavations were conducted at BLACKWATER DRAW locality 1.
2. a COMPLEX that forms part of the LLANO TRADITION, found mainly in the southern and central Plains of North America, although increasing numbers of Clovis-type points are now being recovered in the eastern half of the continent, forcing a reassessment of the complex and what it represents in terms of prehistoric social organization. The complex also comprises MAMMOTH bones, and associated artifacts such as distinctive stone knives, smooth IVORY and bone cylinders, bone points and bone foreshafts. The complex shows similarities in particular stone tool types, ivory artifacts and the use of red OCHRE to Upper Palaeolithic complexes in Asia and eastern Europe.

Clovis Point.

Cmielów   a settlement of the FUNNEL BEAKER CULTURE located on the eastern slopes of the HOLY CROSS MOUNTAINS in central Poland. Cmielów appears to have served as a 'production settlement' at which 'banded' FLINT, extracted from nearby mines such as the ones at KRZEMIONKI, was reduced into CORES and semi-finished axes. Excavations at Cmielów also produced evidence for COPPER METALLURGY and a large sample of faunal and botanical remains.

Coalescent Tradition   see PLAINS VILLAGE INDIAN.

cobble   a size subdivision of GRAVEL that ranges between 64 mm and 256 mm in diameter, according to the Wentworth-Udden classification system. Cobble gravel was commonly employed as building stone.

Cochise Culture   see PICOSA.

codex (*pl.* codices)   a hand-drawn manuscript recording historic, tribute, or religious information. In MESOAMERICA the manuscripts were of bark or animal skin, lightly covered with plaster. HIEROGLYPHIC writing and pictures were then inscribed on the manuscript.

Cody   see PLANO, BLACKWATER DRAW.

Coedès, George (1886–1969)   a French epigrapher who was a leading authority in southeast Asian studies, best known for discovering the Indonesian empire of SRIVIJAYA in 1918, and for his books *The Indianized States of Southeast Asia* (1944) and *Les Inscriptions du Cambodge* (8 vols, 1942–66).

Cognitive Archaeology   see STRUCTURAL ARCHAEOLOGY.

coinage   a standardized series of metal tokens, their specific weights representing particular values, and usually stamped with designs and inscriptions. They were used in many parts of the ancient world for everyday exchange.

Greek coinage first appears in the ARCHAIC foundation deposit of the Artemision at EPHESUS. Much early coinage was struck in silver, though the weight of the different coins changed from city to city (see OBOL, DRACHMA). Many of them bear the device of the city; for example, the owl of ATHENS, or the turtle of AEGINA. See also MINA, STATER, TALENT.

Roman coinage was struck at ROME and at various points throughout the empire. Different materials were used: gold (AUREUS), silver (DENARIUS), and BRONZE (AS, SESTERTIUS). Although Rome was the main mint, even quite minor cities could strike coins; these often show the head of the emperor and a relevant motif, such as a deity, for the city. See also RADIATE.

Colchester (*Lat.* Camulodunum) a Roman colony in England, established on the site of the Iron Age capital and mint. In AD 49 the emperor Claudius founded Colonia Claudia Victricensis, and tombstones of veterans have been found. One of the most impressive buildings was the temple (now forming the foundations of Colchester castle) which an inscription shows was dedicated to Claudius. The colony was extensively damaged during Boudicca's revolt in AD 60, but was rebuilt. The city was walled towards the end of the 2nd century, and remains may be seen of the main west gate (Balkerne Gate). To the west of the city over 30 kilns have been found, whose wares were widely distributed (see SAMIAN WARE). See also WHEELER.

Collared urn the most important and widespread type of cinerary urn of the British Bronze Age. Developed probably from Neolithic vessels of the PETERBOROUGH WARE tradition, the first Collared urns appear around 2000 BC. They remained in use for some 600 years, commonly holding cremated remains beneath a burial mound. The Collared urn is characterized by a heavy overhanging rim or collar, usually bevelled internally; incised decoration is found on both collar and bevel. In addition to the Collared urn, several other varieties of Bronze Age cinerary urn are known, including the Cordoned urn, the Trevisker urn, the Bucket-shaped urn and the Wessex biconical urn.

collective tomb a tomb which is used for multiple, usually successive, interments.

Colless Creek a rockshelter with a rich artifact assemblage in northwest Queensland, Australia. Occupation substantially pre-dates 17 350 bp and the site may have been used for at least 30 000 years.

colluvium an unlithified deposit resulting from mass wasting processes where gravity plays a significant role. Colluvium includes the relatively thin veneer of material in transport down HILLSLOPES, material behind barriers to downslope movement, and potentially thick deposits found at the base of hillslopes and cliffs as fans and wedges. Major processes leading to accumulation of colluvial deposits are SOIL erosion, SOLIFLUXION, various debris flows, and debris and rock slides and falls. Archaeological deposits may be buried in colluvium along valley margins, or mixed and displaced by colluvial processes. Human activities that lead to erosion are also likely to enhance some colluvial processes by destabilizing the LANDSCAPE.

Co Loa a large settlement site on the Red River in north Vietnam, belonging to the DONG SON period and thought to have been the capital of the early Vietnamese state of AU LAC. The site has two sets of moats and three sets of ramparts, the outermost enclosing an area of some 600 ha The main find from the site is the 72 kg bronze drum containing over 100 bronze ploughshares.

Cologne (*Lat.* Colonia Claudia Ara Augusta Agrippinensium) a Roman colony in Germany founded in AD 50 in honour of Agrippina, wife of the emperor Claudius. It became the base for the Rhine fleet as well as an important commercial centre. Its cemeteries have yielded large quantities of glass which was produced locally. Fine MOSAICS have been found including one of the god Dionysos and another of Greek philosophers.

Colosseum an especially ornate form of AMPHITHEATRE at ROME. The outside is decorated in the three main architectural orders: DORIC, IONIC and CORINTHIAN. Construction seems to have started under the emperor Vespasian (AD 69–79) and it was finally dedicated under Titus in AD 80. It may have held around 50 000 spectators.

Colossi of Memnon a pair of massive seated statues of AMENHOTEP III, one of the few remnants still standing of that king's MORTUARY TEMPLE at THEBES (EGYPT)-WEST BANK.

columbarium 1. a dove-cot in the Roman world.
2. an underground burial chamber in the Roman world. Its walls were covered in small niches, hence the name, into which were placed CINERARIA. Inscriptions at ROME suggest that they were normally the place of burial for slaves and freedmen.

Columnata a major, if enigmatic, site in the Atlas Mountains of northern Algeria with good preservation, including several human burials of Mechtoid type dated between 8300–7300 BP (see MECHTA AFALOU).

Combe Capelle a rockshelter in Dordogne, France, which has yielded CHÂTELPERRONIAN, AURIGNACIAN, GRAVETTIAN and SOLUTREAN industries and, in 1909, an early burial of a short, robust male HOMO *sapiens sapiens* whose stratigraphic position remains uncertain.

Combe-Grenal a well-stratified southwest French cave and rock-shelter, excavated by BORDES in 1953–65 and best known for its 55 distinct MOUSTERIAN levels which have been dated to the early WÜRM GLACIATION. The site has played an important part in the interpretation of the Mousterian variants of southwest France. Its nine ACHEULIAN levels are dominated by reindeer, while some Mousterian layers display a more temperate forest fauna.

comitium a building often sited near the FORUM in a Roman town and used for voting and for other political assemblies.

commandery a military establishment in HAN-dynasty China for governing 'barbarian' or newly conquered areas. It contrasts with 'principality', the established regional administrative unit governed through a local elite. See LELANG.

compartmented seal the typical SEAL form of the Bronze Age in western Central Asia and northern Afghanistan (with a focus in the BACTRIAN BRONZE AGE), and usually made of metal. They are often round, but may also be square, cruciform, star-shaped or scalloped. The seals' motifs are comparably geometric (most often cruciform or radiating 'petals' or lines) but may be naturalistic (eagles, scorpions, goats, mythical animals, etc.). Many of the seals are open work, composed simply of the frame and the motif cast in metal, with the remaining space within the frame left hollow.

compartmented seal

complex   a collection of TRAITS and artifacts that make up a separate class or taxon. The complex may or may not be equivalent to an ancient people. Very often the term is used to designate classes whose origins are unclear.

compluvium   the central opening in the roof over the middle of the ATRIUM in a Roman house. The IMPLUVIUM was placed underneath it.

component   a STRATIGRAPHIC layer within a site that belongs to a single CULTURE, and is interpreted as the remains of a single people deposited in a relatively short time period. Similar components in a region are grouped into the same culture or PHASE.

composite soil   a SOIL PROFILE that imposes its characteristics upon more than one parent material. Each parent material may have been affected by earlier PEDOGENESIS and have preserved features of older soil profiles. Recognition of composite soils, although not always straightforward, is important because of STRATIGRAPHIC, temporal and archaeological contextual implications. Synonymous with composite soil are 'welded soil', 'superimposed soil', and 'polypedomorphic soil'.

Conchopata   a MIDDLE HORIZON site in the Ayacucho region of Peru, at which two major offering-deposits of HUARI CERAMICS have been found. The offerings comprise large quantities of smashed pottery, buried in unstructured pits. The first, excavated by Julio C. TELLO, is characterized by large open urns on which are painted an elaborate iconography similar to that of the Gateway of the Sun at TIAHUANACO. These depictions of the Staff Deity suggested to early researchers that Huari iconography was derived from the site of Tiahuanaco. The second offering-deposit includes a series of elaborately painted face-neck jars, which may represent Huari rulers.

concretion   the rounded to irregular segregation of mineral matter in a SOIL that exhibits concentric internal fabric formed by periodic deposition of minerals from solution, usually around a central nucleus that may consist of archaeological debris. Because concretions form under certain conditions, mineralogical, ISOTOPIC and RADIOMETRIC characteristics of concretions are aids to environmental reconstruction and to determining the age of those conditions. Compare NODULE.

cone mosaic   a typical decoration of building façades in the 'public' architecture of the URUK period of southern MESOPOTAMIA and surrounding regions. It was made of cones with coloured ends which were pressed flat into plaster and brickwork to form MOSAICS of geometric patterns. The best examples of this technique are found in several buildings within the EANNA precinct at WARKA.

cone mosaic

conjoining or **refitting**   the rejoining or fitting together of struck stone FLAKES to recreate the original CORE, or the refitting of waste flakes to finished or unfinished tools. The technique is used to study the dispersal of implements and DÉBITAGE at ancient working sites, and to gain an understanding of the KNAPPING process.

consistency   a SOIL property defined by the forces of cohesion and adhesion, or by resistance to deformation or rupture. It is one of the properties routinely noted in describing and interpreting soils. Consistency can vary greatly with both soil-water and CLAY content.

Constantinopolis   see BYZANTIUM.

contact   the interface of surfaces between two vertically or laterally successive STRATIGRAPHIC units. Description and interpretation of contacts is significant in working out the geological history of an area, and in making inter- and intraregional CORRELATIONS. Contacts may be conformable, where depositional conditions were not significantly altered or interrupted between adjacent units. An UNCONFORMITY occurs where a surface of nondeposition or EROSION separates adjacent units. Both types are likely to be expressed in the field and can be described as abrupt, gradational, or intercalated. Numerous sedimentary, palaeontological and structural criteria are used to distinguish the two contact types. Compare BOUNDARY.

contamination   extraneous material that is not a part of the natural ASSEMBLAGE. Depending on the nature of the archaeological sample, contamination can be caused by post-depositional additions, intrusions or alterations. In DATING methods, contamination is the inclusion of any extraneous substance that can cause an erroneous age determination.

context   the situation or circumstances in which a particular item or group of items is found, or in which a particular event or group or series of events occurs. For example, the context of archaeological debris can refer to the physical or cultural associations of the debris, and their interrelationships; it can also refer to, and be defined by, what physically and culturally preceded and followed the use, manufacture, discard and transformations of the debris.

COOBOOL CREEK

Coobool Creek part of the MURRAY BLACK COLLECTION of Australian Aboriginal skeletal remains, comprising over 100 individuals collected from the Wakool River, southern New South Wales. The collection resembles the KOW SWAMP material, and Brown's analysis suggests that artificial cranial deformation is a component of variation in PLEISTOCENE Aboriginal crania.

Cook, James (1728–79) an English navigator who conducted three voyages of exploration in the Pacific between 1769 and 1779. The accounts of the peoples of Australia, POLYNESIA and MELANESIA in his journals are key sources of information about those societies at the time of European contact.

copal a MAYA term for an incense made of pine resin. The incense was used extensively during ceremonies throughout MESOAMERICA, and continues to be used today in religious contexts.

Copán a site in Honduras, thought to be one of the intellectual and artistic centres of MAYA culture. It was the largest Lowland Maya city during the Late CLASSIC, and is well known for its sculpture and the dynastic sequence recorded in HIEROGLYPHIC writings at the site, featuring the ruler '18 Rabbit' and his son. The first archaeological expedition to Copán was made by Colonel Juan Galindo for the Guatemalan government in 1834. Many other archaeologists and institutions have subsequently carried out work at the site.

Coppa Nevigata a small mounded prehistoric settlement near a former lagoon at the northern edge of the Tavoliere plain, Puglie, Italy. At the base of the mound was an Early Neolithic layer rich in cockle shells associated with CARDIAL WARE pottery but no domestic animal remains or QUERNSTONES. The flint industry in this earliest layer, known as the Sipontian, is found only at this site and is probably a specialized tool-kit for the opening of cockle-shells. An early RADIOCARBON date suggesting an occupation before 6000 BC should be regarded with caution, but the site may well date from the 6th millennium BC.

copper a ductile, malleable metallic element used in the manufacture of functional and decorative artifacts that occurs as nodules of native copper or as a constituent in copper ORES such as MALACHITE. Copper was obtained from ores by SMELTING; it could be cold worked or cast, and was used to make BRONZE alloys.

Copper Age see ENEOLITHIC.

copper hoard a hoard of COPPER artifacts, many of which occur in the Ganges-Yamuna *doab* (alluvial plain) and in the area south of the lower Ganges, the former occasionally associated with OCHRE COLOURED POTTERY. The hoards, which include flat axes, ANTHROPOMORPHOUS axes, barbed HARPOONS, and sword blades, have in the past been cited as evidence of the Vedic arrival (see SANSKRIT) but this correlation seems specious. Other copper hoards, with different artifact typologies, also occur elsewhere in India and Pakistan.

coprolite preserved or fossilized faeces (excrement) of humans or animals. Preserved in arid or waterlogged environments, coprolites provide dietary and PALAEOENVIRONMENTAL information. Remains in human faeces are an indication of what was consumed by the individual. Remains in animal faeces not only indicate diet, but reflect to some degree what the surrounding regional environment was like. See COPROLOGY.

copper hoard

coprology   the study of preserved or fossilized faeces (excrement) of humans or animals. See COPROLITE.

corbelled vault   a simple system of roofing whereby successive courses of masonry are laid, each overlapping the previous one, until they meet in the centre and the vault can be closed by a capstone, in some cases a MEGALITHIC slab. The technique was often used in the Neolithic CHAMBERED TOMBS of Western Europe, especially those of dry-stone construction, and in MYCENAEAN THOLOS tombs (see fig.) and Sardinian NURAGHI.

corbel-vaulted, *adj.*   characterized by a CORBELLED VAULT.

cordate, *adj.*   a morphological term used to describe a refined heart-shaped (*cordiform*) BIFACE with a flat profile, characteristic of the MOUSTERIAN of western Europe.

Corded Ware Culture   a Late Neolithic culture of central Europe, widely distributed in various related variants from European Russia to Holland during the second half of the 3rd millennium bc. The Corded Ware culture takes its name from the characteristic cord-marked decoration on its pottery, although it should be noted that cord marking occurs in other central European Neolithic cultures such as FUNNEL BEAKER and GLOBULAR AMPHORA as well. The Corded Ware culture is often believed to represent a wave or series of waves of migrants from the steppe region of southern Russia into Europe, possibly pastoralist INDO-EUROPEAN speakers. On the other hand, the Czech archaeologist Neustupny has argued that the economy of the Corded Ware culture was based on agriculture, suggesting that these were sedentary communities. The difficulty is that the Corded Ware culture is known primarily from burials, often under mounds. In southern Scandinavia, the Corded Ware culture is known as the SINGLE GRAVE culture, while local variants such as RZUCZEWO and ZŁOTA reflect specific social and economic developments within the broader Corded Ware complex.

Cordilleran   See LAURENTIDE.

core   1. *n.* intact solid cylinders of SOIL or SEDIMENT collected with a coring device and used to obtain undisturbed samples. Cores are used to evaluate the geological context of archaeological material and surrounding environments; to evaluate vertical and horizontal limits of cultural debris, MIDDEN, and structures; to sample lake or BOG sediments for POLLEN and macrobotanical remains for palaeoenvironmental reconstruction; and for STRATIGRAPHIC and CORRELATION purposes (see DEEP SEA CORES). Unlike an AUGER, the core is undisturbed; sediment contacts, soil boundaries, and structures are intact and can be described accurately.
2. *n.* a sampling tool consisting of a hollow cylindrical barrel used to collect a core sample. Continuous cores can be obtained by returning repeatedly to the same hole and withdrawing increments the length of the core barrel. Coring devices range from hand-operated to truck-mounted rigs.
3. *n.* (also called **blank** or **nucleus**) the original piece of stone which is worked during KNAPPING. The core either may be itself shaped by the removal of waste FLAKES to create a core tool such as a BIFACE or CHOPPER, or may simply be the raw material for the manufacture of flakes which are then further RETOUCHED to make flake tools. A prepared-core knapping technique involves the planned working of the core before removing a flake or BLADE. See DISCOIDAL NUCLEUS TECHNIQUE, LEVALLOIS TECHNIQUE.
4. *vb* to collect a core.

core-formed glass   a form of glass created by twisting melted glass round a core. Different colours may be used to give a striped effect. It is a technique used in the eastern Mediterranean especially in the CLASSICAL and HELLENISTIC periods.

Coricancha   the 'enclosure of gold' in CUZCO, Peru, this was the most sacred religious site of the INCA empire. The enclosure included temples dedicated to the worship of the sun, stars, rainbow, thunder and (possibly) the moon. Ritual offerings of maize beer were made into subterranean AQUEDUCTS under the enclosure. According to early Spanish reports, the walls were covered with sheets of gold; life-size models of llamas and maize plants of gold and silver were found here. The Coricancha was plundered at the time of the Spanish Conquest, and the gold artifacts melted down.

Corinth   (*Gk* Korinthos, *Lat.* Colonia Laus Julia Corinthiensis)   a city located where the Peloponnese meets the isthmus which links it to the Greek mainland. The site was important as it also controlled the short overland crossing from the Saronic Gulf to the Corinthian Gulf through the ports of Kenchreai and Lechaion respectively. The city was a major centre in the ARCHAIC period and CORINTHIAN POTTERY was widely exported. In 146 BC the city was destroyed by the Roman general Mummius, and the site seems to have been virtually vacated until the foundation of a Roman colony in 44 BC. Remains of this Roman city, the FORUM, surrounding administrative buildings, theatre and THERMAE, have been uncovered by recent excavations by the American School. See also PERACHORA.

Corinthian order a scheme of architecture closely related to the IONIC ORDER. It differs in the type of CAPITAL which is formed by a mass of acanthus leaves out of which spring small VOLUTES. All four sides were similar, unlike Ionic capitals. The earliest-known Corinthian capital was used in the interior of the temple of Apollo at Bassae, along with the Ionic order; on the exterior the temple is of the DORIC ORDER. The order became more popular during the HELLENISTIC period and was widely used in the Roman Empire.

Corinthian order Capital.

Corinthian pottery a widely distributed fabric made at CORINTH and found throughout the Mediterranean. Production was mainly during the ARCHAIC period, although it continued into the CLASSICAL. A range of shapes were made, from small perfumed-oil containers (see ARYBALLOS, ALABASTRON) to AMPHORAE and KRATERS. PAYNE devised a chronological scheme which was divided into different phases: Protocorinthian, Transitional, Early, Middle and Late Corinthian.

cornice the uppermost part of the ENTABLATURE located above the TRIGLYPHS and METOPES in the DORIC ORDER, or above the frieze in the IONIC ORDER.

correlation the demonstration of equivalency of STRATIGRAPHIC units. Because there are multiple classes of stratigraphic units, equivalency can be expressed in lithological, palaeontological, cultural or chronological terms. In any case, the basis for equivalency should be clearly stated.

There are many methods of correlation and normally multiple methods are used together. Correlation of units defined by objective lithological criteria (lithostratigraphic units, see STRATIGRAPHY) can be done by tracing lateral continuity, lithological identity, and position

115

in a stratigraphic sequence, identifying structural relationships to UN-CONFORMITIES, faults, and folds, intrusions, and by other methods. Equivalency of biostratigraphic units (see STRATIGRAPHY) is demonstrated by identifying similar characteristics of fossil content and fossil ASSEMBLAGES. Correlation of chronostratigraphic units can be based on palaeontological criteria and correlation, ABSOLUTE DATING methods, RELATIVE DATING methods, CROSS-DATING methods, and position relative to the GLACIAL–INTERGLACIAL cycle as determined by physical and biological attributes.

corrugation a decorative technique on pottery, whereby the individual circular coils making up the walls of the vessel are left unsmoothed on the exterior, thus forming a distinctive overlapping surface. Corrugation also improves a vessel's conductivity of heat.

Cortaillod a Neolithic village site on the shore of Lake Neuchâtel, representing the second phase of Neolithic occupation of Switzerland, following the EGOLZWIL phase shortly before 4000 BC. Although the Cortaillod villages had domestic livestock and may have practised cereal cultivation, wild plant and animal resources continued to play an important part in the diet. In eastern Switzerland, the Cortaillod was replaced by the PFYN culture shortly after 4000 BC; in western Switzerland it was replaced by the HORGEN assemblage in around 3300 BC.

Cortés, Hernán or **Hernando Cortez** (*c*.1485–1547) the Spanish conqueror of the AZTEC empire and founder of the colony of New Spain. Cortés landed near Yucatán in April 1519. After capturing Tabasco and founding the city of Veracruz, he began a forced march to the interior of Mexico and TENOCHTITLÁN. Cortés gained the support of a number of enemies of the Aztec empire. This support, and the advice and aid of a captured princess (Doña Marina, or Malinche), allowed him to take Moctezuma, the Aztec ruler, hostage, and rule the city. In 1520 the Spanish were driven from Tenochtitlán, but it was finally conquered and destroyed in 1521 when Cortés defeated Moctezuma's successor, Cuauhtémoc. Subsequently, Cortés was appointed governor of Mexico, completing the conquest of the surrounding area, and building the colonial capital. He later led a number of other expeditions through Mexico, not always with success. His later years were spent primarily in Spain.

Cortes de Navarra an URNFIELD settlement in the Ebro valley, Navarre, Spain, consisting of stone-built rectangular houses grouped together in terraces. The occupation falls at the Late Bronze Age/Early Iron Age transition, 8th/7th century BC. The settlement was excavated primarily by MALUQUER DE MOTES.

cortex a tough, dull-white, powdery and porous covering or crust found over the outer surface of newly exposed FLINT NODULES and tabular flint. The cortex is usually discarded during the KNAPPING process.

Coţofeni culture a late ENEOLITHIC culture of the eastern Balkans, centred on southern Romania. The Coţofeni culture succeeded the CERNAVODĂ culture and the KRIVODOL group in the lower Danube basin during the late 3rd millennium bc. Its CERAMICS are reminiscent of the contemporaneous BADEN culture to the northwest with handled mugs and pitchers, and of the BUBANJ-HUM IB phase of Serbia. Coţofeni settlements are generally small and short-lived.

Cougnac a decorated Palaeolithic cave-site in the Quercy region of

France, discovered in 1952. Best known for its paintings of MEGA-LOCEROS and ibex, its art has been assigned on stylistic grounds to the SOLUTREAN period. Charcoal from a black painted dot recently produced a RADIOCARBON date of 12 350 bc (early MAGDALENIAN), while a reindeer bone gave a date of 13 050 bc.

coup-de-poing   see BIFACE.

court cairn   a type of Neolithic CHAMBERED TOMB common in Ireland, in which the burial mound encloses a courtyard in front of the passage leading to the burial chamber. The design may be considered a development from the horned CAIRN in which the horns have grown to completely enclose the space in front of the tomb.

cover sand or **blow sand**   a sheet of SAND deposited by the wind. Cover sand may be found on TERRACES within outwash plains of GLACIAL meltwater streams and the adjacent uplands where it may be interstratified with LOESS. Sand beaches can be the source for cover sand deposited in coastal areas. Deposition can effect rapid burial of archaeological deposits. If deposition is thick and rapid enough, artifact associations are likely to be preserved intact. See DUNE.

Coveta del Or   a cave-site on the Mediterranean coast of Valencia, Spain, with Early Neolithic CARDIAL WARE pottery, bones of domestic animals, and remains of cultivated wheat, with RADIOCARBON dates of c.4500 bc.

Coxcatlán phase   the occupation phase from c.5500–4500 BC in Mexico's TEHUACÁN VALLEY, during which maize first appeared. Wild and semi-domesticated plants continued to make up a large part of the diet. In addition to collecting wild plants and producing some gardens, the society also hunted small game.

Cozumel   an island off the east coast of the Yucatán peninsula, Mexico, that was both an important trade port and a place of pilgrimage to honour the cult of Ix Chel, MAYA goddess of women, childbirth and the moon. The island was first occupied by the Maya at about the time of Christ, but began its climb to prominence from AD 800–1000. During its peak (AD 1400), Putun, or Chontal, Maya traders (a Maya-speaking group of the Gulf Coast Lowlands, not part of the Classic Maya culture) used it to store goods; long causeways from the coast led to large inland storage platforms.

crannog   an artificial island in a lake or marsh forming the foundation for a small settlement. Crannogs are found in northern Britain and Ireland and date from the Late Bronze Age to early Christian period.

cremation   see PRIMARY CREMATION, SECONDARY CREMATION.

crescent   see SEGMENT.

Creswellian   British Late Upper Palaeolithic industry named after the sites of *Creswell Crags* in the Peak District of Derbyshire, and found at caves as far south as the Mendips in Somerset, the Gower Peninsula in Wales, and Devon. The assemblage includes a variety of BACKED BLADES including points and trapeze shapes. The industry is associated with cold fauna and dates to the end of the DEVENSIAN COLD STAGE (c.20 000–10 000 BP).

Crickley Hill   a Neolithic CAUSEWAYED CAMP and Iron Age HILLFORT in Gloucestershire, England. The causewayed camp was replaced in the Late Neolithic period by a defended enclosure with houses and streets within. This met its end in violence, as shown by the scatter of leaf-shaped flint arrowheads along the rampart, fanning out into the interior of the enclosure from the gates. A rectangular timber shrine was erected later in the Neolithic in the centre of the earlier causewayed camp, and was succeeded by a long mound and STONE CIRCLE. The site was reoccupied in the 7th century BC when an Iron Age promontory fort was constructed. This had two phases of construction, the first around 700 BC, with timber-laced rampart and rectangular long houses, the second, destroyed in the 5th century, with round houses and a massive curving hornwork to defend the entrance passage.

Criş culture   an Early Neolithic culture of Romania and Moldova, part of the vast complex of Balkan Early Neolithic cultures that includes KARANOVO I, KREMIKOVCI, STARČEVO, and KÖRÖS. As is the case with Starčevo and Körös sites, Criş settlements do not appear to be TELLS but rather flat open habitations. An important aspect of the Criş culture is the apparent contact that it had with forager populations of the BUG-DNIESTER culture to its east.

CRM   see CULTURAL RESOURCE MANAGEMENT.

Cro-Magnon   a French rockshelter in LES EYZIES, Dordogne, which in 1868 yielded AURIGNACIAN artifacts and associated HOMO *sapiens sapiens* burials, including four adults and various fragmented bones and infant remains. The bones indicate tall and muscular people with a long skull, high forehead and broad face. Compare CHANCELADE. The finds gave their name to the modern form of *Homo*.

cromlech   1. (*Brittany*) a STONE CIRCLE.
2. (*Wales*) the general term for any MEGALITHIC tomb.
The word is a traditional CELTIC term.

cross-beds   a SEDIMENTARY structure in which fine STRATA or LAMINAE between bedding planes (e.g. within a BED) are inclined relative to the bounding bedding planes. Cross-bedding forms in granular material as the result of migration of DUNES and sandwaves within a current more or less at right angles to the prevailing current and are larger in scale than CROSS-LAMINAE. The type, size, constituents and orientation of cross-bedding are the result of prevailing hydrological or AEOLIAN conditions. Orientation of cross-bedding gives information on prevailing palaeocurrent direction, which can be used to reconstruct past depositional environments that may have related archaeological deposits.

cross-dating   a correlation dating technique that can yield a relative or absolute age or chronology. Cross-dating is assignment of an age to an artifact at a location, based on the age of a TYPOLOGICALLY similar, or diagnostic, artifact, determined by some dating method or established chronology, at another location. If in the latter case the artifact is from a CONTEXT dated by some CHRONOMETRIC DATING method, then an absolute age estimate can be applied to the artifact in the former case. Also, associated material found in the same context can be assigned the same age. The method is typically interregional and is necessarily based on assumptions of rates of typological evolution and diffusion. Ideal artifacts are those with a short but well-dated life-span with a wide geographic range. The method is always subject to some error because the assumption of diffusion implies a DIACHRONIC nature.

cross-laminae   a SEDIMENTARY structure in which LAMINAE are deposited at an inclined angle to the main depositional surface (bedding plane). Cross-laminae form in granular material as the result of migration of ripples within the current more or less at right angles to the prevailing current, and are smaller in scale than CROSS-BEDS. The type, size, constituents and orientation of cross-laminae are the result of prevailing hydrological or AEOLIAN conditions, and can be used to reconstruct prevailing palaeocurrent direction and past depositional environments.

Crow Creek   a habitation site in South Dakota, USA, that belongs to the Initial Coalescent Period of the PLAINS VILLAGE INDIANS. Recovered at the site were over 500 human skeletons, the remains of individuals who were massacred and later mutilated. The bodies were then buried *en masse* at the bottom of the settlement's fortification ditch. The conflict may have been over territory or access to scarce resources, since many of the skeletons showed signs of malnutrition. Burial sites of this magnitude are rare on the Plains, and thus Crow Creek gave archaeologists an invaluable opportunity to examine ancient DEMOGRAPHY and disease patterns.

Crvena Stijena   a prehistoric cave-site located near the Adriatic coast in Montenegro. Palaeolithic artifacts and faunal remains (including red deer, bison and marmot) are buried in LOAM and GRAVEL deposits dating to the LAST GLACIAL. The lower layers contained a Middle Palaeolithic industry dominated by SCRAPERS while overlying layers yielded Upper Palaeolithic assemblages often assigned to the AURIGNACIAN. Above several levels of Mesolithic occupation was a layer with IMPRESSED WARE pottery, from which the animal bones suggest that a hunting and gathering economy continued after the introduction of pottery. Later levels include one of the DANILO culture of the late Neolithic, and an uppermost layer with HALLSTATT A–B metalwork.

cryoturbation   the disturbing or mixing of SEDIMENT or SOIL material by frost action, and the freezing of the active layer of PERMAFROST late in the melt-season. Advance of the freezing front leads to expansion and heave, and growth of ice lenses disrupts the soil mass. Among the results of cryoturbation are complex INVOLUTIONS which signify former cold climatic conditions. Frost activity in caves tends to produce angular CLASTS that accumulate in greater concentrations during colder climatic episodes. In STRATIFIED cave deposits these rubble zones are often indicative of more severe climatic episodes.

cryptoportico   an underground corridor, usually in the substructure of a large Roman building complex.

cubiculum   1. the bedchamber in a Roman house.
2. a chamber in a CATACOMB where groups of people perhaps gathered for rites linked to the dead.

Cucuteni-Tripolye   one of the major ENEOLITHIC cultures of southeastern Europe, distributed throughout a broad region in southwestern Ukraine (where it is known as the *Tripolye* culture), Moldova and northeastern Romania (where it is known as the *Cucuteni* culture), named after the eponymous sites of Cucuteni in the Siret valley of Romania and Tripolye near Kiev in Ukraine. The chronology of this culture is complicated by differing Soviet and Romanian sequences, which have each been finely subdivided, spanning the late 4th and early 3rd millennia bc. Romanian archaeologists recognize the existence of a 'pre-Cucuteni' culture whose antecedents appear to lie in the late Neolithic BOIAN culture of central Romania. Cucuteni-Tripolye settlements have benefited from the excavation of large contiguous areas, which have often revealed large village plans as at KOLOMIISHCHINA and VLADIMIROVKA. House sites are indicated by PLOSHCHADKI, fired clay and timber platforms. Cucuteni-Tripolye sites in Ukraine often occur on high promontories, as at POLIVANOV YAR, while many in Romania are surrounded by elaborate defensive ditch systems. Cucuteni-Tripolye trichrome (red-black-white) painted pottery reflects a high level of technological skill in its decoration and firing.

Cuello a small MAYA settlement in northern Belize, excavated by N. Hammond (from 1975). It is the earliest-known ancient Maya site and has shed considerable light on the emergence of Lowland Maya culture and its rise towards civilization. The site has 14 major phases of construction, beginning in the Middle PRECLASSIC c.1200 BC (the 'Swasey' phase, known only at this site) and ending c.AD 300 in the early CLASSIC.

Cueva Morin a northern Spanish Palaeolithic cave-site in Santander, best known for its seven MOUSTERIAN levels, some with fragments of living floors and associated tools including FLAKE CLEAVERS; a lower PERIGORDIAN layer dated to 36 350 bp; and its AURIGNACIAN levels including dwelling structures and burials. The site was most recently investigated by Freeman and González Echegaray in 1966–69, and was one of the first Spanish sites to be dug by the scientific method of controlled horizontal excavation.

Cuicuilco a ceremonial site containing the earliest monumental and ceremonial architecture found in the BASIN OF MEXICO. These monumental constructions date to 600–200 BC, when Cuicuilco was the major centre in the valley. From 200 BC to AD 300, outside influences began mitigating Cuicuilco's effect in the valley, and in c.AD 300 or 400, the volcano Xitle erupted, covering much of the area in lava and forming the *Pedregal*, or volcanic desert. Ironically, the principal deity at Cuicuilco was a fire god, known in AZTEC times as Xiuhtecuhtli (Huehueteotl).

In 1922, Byron Cummings and Manuel GAMIO recognized that a 'hill' on the *Pedregal* was not a natural formation. Subsequent excavation uncovered a large TEMPLE-MOUND. The site is famous for this massive circular PYRAMID, a truncated cone with stepped sides and ramps. It is over 100 m in diameter at the base and approximately 20 m high, and shows at least three phases of construction.

Cuiry-lès-Chaudardes an Early Neolithic village site of the Paris Basin LINEAR POTTERY culture, Aisne, France, occupied c.4800 BC. The village consisted of a number of timber longhouses, between 10 m and 39 m in length and 5 m to 7 m broad, represented today only by POSTHOLES. The remains of the settlement cover 7 ha but the houses were rebuilt from time to time and only a few of them would have been in use at any given moment. Alongside the houses were pits from which clay had been dug to seal the house walls. These pits were later used for rubbish disposal and have yielded a variety of remains including bones of domestic animals (principally cattle), POTSHERDS decorated in the typical Bandkeramik style, grindstones for the preparation of flour, and flint tools and waste FLAKES.

Cu Lao Rua   a site near Saigon in southern Vietnam occupied during the transition from late Neolithic (shouldered POLISHED STONE ADZES) to early Bronze period, overlapping with HANG GON.

cult temple   a term used to distinguish a TEMPLE erected to serve the cult of a particular deity (who was regarded as dwelling therein) from a MORTUARY TEMPLE.

cultural resource management   the legally mandated protection of archaeological SITES located on public lands in the USA, that are threatened by destruction through development, energy exploration and other such activities. The most extensive laws have been enacted to protect sites on federal lands, but states and even some cities have enacted similar legislation.

culture   1. non-genetically determined human behaviour.
2. the constellation of beliefs, behaviours and customs peculiar to a specific people.
3. in archaeology, the constellation of specific elements of MATERIAL CULTURE, thought to represent a particular people. This term is most often used in the Old World.

culture areas   major anthropological subdivisions of the North American continent, which are individually characterized by relatively uniform environments and relatively similar CULTURES. The culture area concept was devised at the end of the 19th century, as a means of organizing museum data. Although it was conceived for ETHNO-GRAPHIC displays, the divisions have been used extensively by archaeologists also, on the assumption that the culture areas had a considerable time depth. Examples include the Southwest, the Plains and the Northwest Coast.

culture history   the organization of the archaeological record into a basic sequence of events in time and space. Culture history is based on INDUCTION and the NORMATIVE view of culture. Explanations for changes in culture-historical sequences include DIFFUSION and migration, and have been criticized by PROCESSUAL ARCHAEOLOGISTS for not being explanations at all, but merely descriptions of behaviour. Culture history remains the primary goal of most archaeological work in many areas, despite the addition of processual studies to the discipline.

Cumae   (*Gk* Kyme) a Greek colony in CAMPANIA dating to the mid 8th century BC. Tombs have yielded some of the earliest Greek pottery in Italy. On the AKROPOLIS, temples of Apollo and Jupiter were located. See CAMPANIAN POTTERY.

cumulative graph   a statistical method used by archaeologists to compare ASSEMBLAGES on the basis of ARTIFACT TYPOLOGY. BORDES used the method to subdivide the MOUSTERIAN INDUSTRIES of southwest France, noting the presence, absence and percentage-value of well-defined tool types and plotting his results as a cumulative percentage frequency graph (or 'ogive').

cuneiform   the characteristic wedge-shaped writing of western Asia, used for over 3000 years, cuneiform was produced by impressing sharpened reeds into clay tablets. The writing system emerged during the 4th millennium BC in southern MESOPOTAMIA as a system of accountancy (see TOKENS) during the URUK period, and by the end of the 4th millennium BC (the JEMDET NASR period) was being used to record lexical lists (occupations, place names). Royal inscriptions appeared by the mid 3rd millennium, and recording of literary works began soon after that (represented by texts from ABU SALABIKH in southern Mesopotamia and from EBLA in northern Syria). Cuneiform continued in use until the end of the 1st millennium BC, and was used to represent many different languages of ancient western Asia in addition to SUMERIAN and AKKADIAN (for example, ELAMITE, HITTITE, URARTIAN, PERSIAN).

cuneiform Tablet.

cup-and-ring mark   a common motif in the ROCK ART of Great Britain, consisting of a roughly circular central hollow surrounded by one or more concentric rings. These and other motifs are found on the backs of stones in the MEGALITHIC CHAMBERED TOMBS of the BOYNE VALLEY, and can therefore be dated to the Neolithic period (4th or 3rd millennium BC). Important concentrations of cup-and-ring marks are found in Scotland and northern England.

cup-and-ring marks.

Cupisnique the style of pottery pertaining to the north coast of Peru during the EARLY HORIZON. This style is typified by blackware jars with globular bodies, stirrup spouts, and relief decoration; the iconography depicted is closely related to the styles of CHAVIN.

Curacchiaghiu a rockshelter in Corsica, France, with Mesolithic and Neolithic occupation levels. RADIOCARBON samples from this site and from Strette in the north of the island show that the colonization of Corsica can be dated to before 6500 BC. The Early Neolithic levels of Curacchiaghiu, dated to c.5600 BC, contain pottery with punch-impressed decoration which may be a local development of the CARDIAL WARE found at contemporary sites on the Corsican coast.

curation an activity in which artifacts are reused, reworked and transported, to the extent that their initial locations of manufacture and use are no longer known.

curia **1.** the meeting place at ROME for the Senate, located near the COMITIUM in the FORUM. The structure built by Caesar, for which work commenced in 44 BC, consisted of a hall 25.2 m long and 17.6 m wide. Seating consisted of marble benches across the width of the room.
2. the meeting place for assemblies, especially the ruling bodies of Roman towns and colonies. Like their counterpart at ROME, they were usually placed adjacent to the FORUM.

cursus a Neolithic ritual monument consisting of two parallel banks with external ditches. They are usually straight, but with occasional changes of axis, and can be several kilometres long. The longest of all is the Dorset cursus which extends for 8 km with banks 91 m apart and has been dated to 2500 BC. Cursus monuments are restricted to southern and eastern England.

Cuzco or **Cusco** the capital of the INCA Empire, located in the south highlands of Peru. The name means 'navel' in Quechua, as it was the point at which the four quarters of the empire articulated, the symbolic navel of the world. Cuzco was founded in c.AD 1200 by Manco Capac, the progenitor of the Inca dynasty, and rebuilt by Pachacuti at the time of the Inca expansion. The site was built in the form of a puma, and divided into upper (*hanan*) and lower (*urin*) halves. A U-shaped central plaza, the Aucaypata, was flanked by public buildings, and contained an USNU platform. The walls of many of the principal buildings were made of stones that were carefully cut, and fitted together without the use of mortar. The site was primarily a ceremonial and political centre rather than a population centre. (See also TAWANTINSUYU, CORICANCHA.)

Cycladic, *adj.* relating to and defining the Bronze Age culture of the Cyclades, the islands of the central southern Aegean. The Cycladic period is divided into three phases: Early (c.3000–2000 BC), Middle (c.2000–1550 BC) and Late (c.1550–1050 BC), and there is a further tripartite subdivision of each of these phases. Renfrew has proposed, as an alternative to the traditional Early Cycladic subdivisions, a culture sequence: GROTTA-PELOS, KEROS-SYROS, and PHYLAKOPI I.

Cyclopean a style of masonry most typically used in MYCENAEAN fortifications. Large irregular blocks of stone, their surfaces roughly hammer-dressed, were laid uncoursed and the interstices between the blocks were filled with smaller rocks and stones. Later Greeks supposed that the walls had been built by the giant Cyclopes.

cylinder hammer technique   see SOFT HAMMER TECHNIQUE.

cylinder seal   a cylinder on which a scene, design and/or inscription is carved. This was the standard SEAL form of the MESOPOTAMIAN civilization, beginning with the URUK period, and was used by rolling it across the clay surface to be sealed (tablets, jar stoppers, door locks and so forth), thus producing the impression (single or repeated) of the seal's design. Dating is based on changes in the design carved on the seal, and in the seal's size and proportion, while the seals' iconographic content can provide a rich source of social information. Compare STAMP SEAL.

cylinder seal Impression.

Cypriot, *adj.*   denoting the Bronze Age culture of Cyprus. The Early Cypriot period (*c.*2500–1900 BC) is known primarily from cemeteries, such as PHILIA and VOUNOUS, rather than settlements. Middle Cypriot (*c.*1900–1650 BC) sites include ALAMBRA and EPISKOPI. This is a period of regional diversity and the construction of fortresses suggests internal unrest. In the Late Cypriot period (*c.*1650–1050 BC) the main settlements were on the south and east coasts, at ENKOMI, KITION, HALA SULTAN TEKKE, KALAVASOS and MARONI. Trade between Cyprus, Egypt and the Near East increased as the demand for Cypriot COPPER intensified. It is thought that the SEA PEOPLES may have been responsible for the destruction of a number of sites *c.*1200 BC and subsequently it seems that MYCENAEAN Greeks settled on Cyprus, but the impressive architecture of Enkomi and Kition suggests that the 12th century was a period of considerable prosperity.

Cypro-Minoan, *adj.*   relating to and defining the SYLLABIC script which was in use on Cyprus from the 15th century BC. The script recalls MINOAN LINEAR A and may have been introduced from Crete by merchants. Cypro-Minoan inscriptions appear on baked clay tablets, bronze votives, IVORIES and SEALS, but the script has never been deciphered. It was apparently revived in the 8th century BC and used to write Greek until the 3rd century BC.

Cyrene   a Greek colony in Libya founded from THERA in the late 7th century BC. Imported Greek pottery of the ARCHAIC period has been found in the extramural sanctuary of Demeter. Excavations have revealed part of the Roman city.

Cyrus II   the first great ACHAEMENID king. Cyrus began his rule (around 559 BC) as a client of the MEDIAN state to the north. From his home in Fars in southwestern Iran, Cyrus managed first to defeat the Medes, and then to expand both westward through the mountains into Anatolia (defeating Croesus of Lydia in western Anatolia; see SARDIS) and eastward across the Iranian plateau and into Central Asia. Having largely encircled the NEO-BABYLONIAN empire, he then invaded and conquered BABYLON itself in 539 BC. Cyrus died from wounds received while campaigning against a SCYTHIAN group (the Massagetae) in Transcaucasia in 530 BC. Later Achaemenid kings extended Cyrus' empire into Egypt (Cambyses, 529–522 BC), western India (Darius, 521–486 BC), and Macedonia (Darius); the famous attempts to occupy Greece (Xerxes 485–465 BC) failed.

D

Dabban   an early BLADE and BURIN stone INDUSTRY of Cyrenaica, Libya, with dates ranging from 40 000–14 000 years ago (see HAUA FTEAH).

Dacia   an early state on the territory of present-day Romania, which flourished during the final centuries BC. Dacian towns are characterized by monumental architecture, as well as by religious precincts, such as the sanctuary at SARMIZEGETHUSA. Dacia was absorbed by the Roman Empire under TRAJAN in AD 106, and abandoned in AD 270.

daga   puddled clay used to plaster walls and floors of houses in sub-Saharan African Iron Age settlements.

Dahshur   an Egyptian royal NECROPOLIS, best regarded as a southern extension of SAQQARA. The major monuments at the site are the PYRAMIDS of SNEFRU of the OLD KINGDOM; and AMENEMHAT II, SENWOSRET III, and Amenemhat III of the MIDDLE KINGDOM. The subsidiary tombs of the Princesses Khnemet and Iti near the pyramid of Amenemhat II produced the 'Dahshur Treasure' of jewellery and accoutrements, as did, to a lesser extent, the tombs of the royal ladies associated with the pyramids of Senwosret III and Amenemhat III. The main excavators at Dahshur have been de Morgan in 1894–95, Fakhry in 1951–55, and, currently, the German Archaeological Institute.

Daima   a large mound in northeastern Nigeria, which, together with neighbouring sites, provides evidence for permanent settlements of wood-walled, clay-floored houses, hunting and fishing, as well as domestic cattle and goats, extending back to the late 2nd millennium BC. Iron appeared between the 1st and 6th centuries AD. Several centuries later Daima became part of a wide-ranging trade network, which may be linked to the rise of Kanem in the late 1st millennium AD.

Daimabad   a site on a tributary of the Godavari River in Maharashta, western India, that has been the object of three separate investigations during the 1950s (M. Deshpande) and 1970s (S.R. Rao and S. Sali). This work revealed a stratigraphic sequence of five phases during the 3rd and 2nd millennia BC. The basal levels represent a food-producing community (including barley, rice, lentils), characterized by a coarse grey ware along with some painted pottery. The succeeding phase marks a major shift in material culture with reported HARAPPAN and Harappan-derived red wares; and the next phase represents yet another shift, to include a white-painted grey ware. Above these levels are two later phases of occupation, characterized by MALWA and JORWE wares respectively. While the architecture of the earlier levels is fragmentary, that of the later two phases is clearer, including platforming in a possible cultic complex, and domestic structures. By the last phase of occupation, SUBSISTENCE included cultivation of sorghum and millet. Daimabad is perhaps best known for the chance find of a COPPER HOARD, tentatively assigned to the Jorwe phase; the hoard consists of three large figures of animals on wheels (rhinoceros, elephant and buffalo) and another of a chariot.

Dainzú   a large archaeological site in central Oaxaca, Mexico, dating to c.300 BC (MONTE ALBÁN I), of which only a small portion has been excavated. It is especially known for the bas-relief carvings that are similar to the DANZANTES at Monte Albán. Those at Dainzú also include figures of ball players. The site was discovered and excavated during the 1960s by Ignacio BERNAL.

Dalles, the   a section of the Columbia River along the Oregon and Washington borders, USA, that is the locality of a number of important archaeological sites, presumably because of the high salmon productivity of that section of the Columbia. The Five Mile Rapids site has a sequence that goes back to approximately 10 000 BC, and other sites show similar antiquity. Later periods are also well represented. The tool assemblages and faunal remains are indicative of a heavy reliance on salmon, although other fauna are also present.

Dalton   1. a PROJECTILE POINT class with much internal variation, some of which is due to reuse and resharpening. It spans the transition from PALAEOINDIAN to ARCHAIC in much of midwestern and eastern North America.
2. a COMPLEX associated with the Dalton point form.

Damb Sada'at   see QUETTA.

Dambwa   an Early IRON AGE group of the CHIFUMBAZE complex, dating to between the 5th and 8th centuries AD, distributed in the Zambezi Valley and in northwestern Zimbabwe (see KUMADZULO).

Damous el Ahmar   an Algerian cave with a CAPSIAN NEOLITHIC industry and two human skeletons of the mechtoid type (see MECHTA AFALOU). OCHRE staining of the skulls and associated tools and food remains indicate funerary rites.

Danangombe or **Dhlo Dhlo**   the 17th–19th century AD capital of the Torwa state in southwestern Zimbabwe. Although smaller than its predecessor KHAMI, architectural principles are similar and include profusely decorated stone walling.

Danebury   an Iron Age HILLFORT in Hampshire, England, excavated by Barry Cunliffe. In the earliest phase, the 6th century BC, the defences consisted of a single bank and ditch with two entrances. In the early 4th century a second line of ramparts was added outside the first, and the entrances were strengthened by outworks. Within the interior were traces of storage pits, rectangular four-post granary structures and round houses arranged along metalled streets. Occupation appears to have declined during the following centuries and by the 1st century BC the hillfort was probably used only as a refuge in times of danger.

Danger Cave a deeply stratified cave site, located in extreme western Utah, USA, that has a basal occupation dated to 11 500–11 000 BP. The assemblage has possible SAN DIEGUITO affiliations. The site's latest occupations date to after 2000 BP. The excellent preservation in the cave allowed a detailed reconstruction of ARCHAIC lifestyles. The evidence from the site was instrumental in the definition of the DESERT TRADITION.

Daniel, Glyn Edmund (1914–86) a British prehistorian whose early work concentrated on the MEGALITHS of Europe. He is perhaps best known for developing the study of the history of archaeology as a legitimate scholarly enquiry and for popularizing the discipline through numerous books and television programmes.

Danilo culture a Neolithic culture of the Dalmatian coast of Croatia and adjacent parts of Bosnia known from both cave and open sites, dated to between 4700 and 3900 bc. The Danilo culture appears to have developed from the IMPRESSED WARE cultures of the Mediterranean zone. Its fine wares are characterized by incised geometrical shapes, often decorated with red and white post-firing incrustation. Other Danilo fine ware, sometimes called RIPOLI ware, appears to have come from the Italian peninsula.

Danubian cultures a cultural tradition defined by CHILDE in his study of the Neolithic and ENEOLITHIC cultures of the Danube Basin, now outdated. Danubian I is essentially equivalent to the LINEAR POTTERY culture; Danubian II to the STROKE-ORNAMENTED POTTERY, LENGYEL, TISZA, and RÖSSEN cultures; late Lengyel groups like BRZEŚĆ KUJAWSKI and JORDANÓW are attributed to Danubian III. Childe's Danubian sequence had an additional three phases that covered the Eneolithic and Early Bronze Ages, but these never came into common use.

Danzantes (*Sp.* 'dancers') stone slabs at MONTE ALBÁN, Mexico, carved with figures in dynamic poses once thought to resemble dancers. The figures are now considered to represent captives, some of them possibly dead, as indicated by their closed eyes. Some of the carved stones are incorporated into the building of the Danzantes (structure L). Guillermo Dupaise uncovered some of the Danzantes in the early 19th century.

Dapengeng [Ta-p'en-keng] a Neolithic site near Taipei City, Taiwan, giving its name to a POSTGLACIAL culture of the 6th–5th millennia BC typified by textured pottery, extensive use of plant cordage for decorating pottery vessels (see SHENGWEN), making fish nets, etc. (Compare JOMON, CHULMUN.)

Dar es-Soltan a Moroccan site with a long sequence spanning a final ATERIAN industry at the base, followed by IBEROMAURUSIAN and topped by CAPSIAN NEOLITHIC material.

Dart, Raymond Arthur (1893–1988) a professor of anatomy at the University of the Witwatersrand in South Africa, who discovered the first AUSTRALOPITHECINE fossil in 1924 (see TAUNG). Initially scorned by other scientists, Dart was eventually vindicated. In 1955 he suggested that the faunal remains at MAKAPANSGAT were used by australopithecines as bone, tooth and horn tools, which he called the

Osteodontokeratic Culture. This idea has not stood the test of time, but it served to stimulate studies of TAPHONOMY.

Dashly an oasis in southern Bactria in northwestern Afghanistan, that contains a large number of Bronze Age, ACHAEMENID and CLASSICAL sites, the first of which are extremely important. V.I. Sarianidi's work in the 1970s, which focused on the two sites Dashly 1 and Dashly 3, defined the BACTRIAN BRONZE AGE (late 3rd and early 2nd millennia BC). These settlements are focused on large roughly square fortresses with circular towers placed at regular intervals along their sides. Other major architecture (at Dashly 3) includes a 'palace' comparable in many respects to that at SAPALLI-DEPE, and a circular double-walled building, with a complex of rooms in its interior and square towers set into its outer wall, thought to be a temple. Dashly 3 also contained residential areas, a concentration of pottery kilns, and (in a late level over the 'palace') a metal-working area.

dating see ABSOLUTE DATING, RELATIVE DATING.

datum or **datum point** a point used as a reference for vertical and horizontal measurement. A site GRID, excavation units, and artifactual finds are laid out or measured with reference to a site datum, preferably linked to a national standard, usually taken as sea level.

Davis, Edwin Hamilton, (1811–88) an American antiquary who collaborated with E.G. SQUIER in the description and analysis of Ohio mounds and earthen enclosures. See ATWATER, HAVEN, THOMAS.

Dawenkou [Ta-wen-k'ou] a middle Neolithic site in Shandong Province, China, type-site of the Dawenkou culture of the eastern seaboard (*c*.4500–2700 BC), which is distinguished by elaborately shaped pottery deriving from the QINGLIANGANG tradition and increasingly rich burials. It is parallel to the YANGSHAO culture of the northern LOESS lands. (Compare HONGSHAN.)

Daxi [Ta-hsi] see HEMUDU.

Dazaifu a special administrative centre of the RITSURYO state of 8th century AD Japan, located in Fukuoka Prefecture. It served as a bureaucratic gateway from Kyushu to the continent, regulating diplomatic relations with SILLA and the TANG Court (see CHINESE DYNASTIES). Several building foundations have been identified through excavation and are marked out on the present surface as a Historical Site.

Dead Sea Scrolls see QUMRAN.

Debert a CLOVIS site located in Nova Scotia, Canada, and dated to approximately 11 000–10 000 BP. There is evidence of separate concentrations of hearths and artifacts. Caribou and other animals were hunted. The site was located less than 100 km from the southern edge of the glacial wall of the VALDERS ADVANCE.

débitage the waste FLAKES and small chips produced when KNAPPING a stone implement. Some waste flakes, such as Palaeolithic BIFACE trimming flakes or Mesolithic TRANCHET AXE sharpening flakes, have a characteristic appearance and indicate the tools that were made or sharpened at a site even when the tools themselves are absent.

Déchelette, Joseph (1862–1914) one of the greatest French archaeologists, author of the comprehensive multi-volume *Manuel d'archéologie préhistorique, celtique et gallo-romaine* (Vols I and II, 1908–15). This was intended as a definitive synthesis of all the information then available on the prehistoric and Roman archaeology of

Europe, especially France and adjacent areas. Only two volumes (prehistory and protohistory) had been prepared when Déchelette was killed in action in the first days of the First World War, but the great project was subsequently completed by Albert Grenier.

decumanus   the main street in a Roman town or camp usually laid out on an east–west axis. The main street was called the *decumanus maximus*, and met the CARDO at the FORUM.

deduction   reasoning whereby specific outcomes can be predicted from general propositions. An example might be concluding that the aeroplanes made in a particular country are untrustworthy because the country's overall manufacturing capabilities are questionable. This deduction could then be tested with specific data. See INDUCTION.

deductive-nomological, *adj.*   relating to a form of scientific reasoning, in which a general law is established, ramifications of that law are deduced, and these ramifications are used to explain a specific set of data. See POSITIVISM, NEW ARCHAEOLOGY.

deep sea cores   CORES collected from ocean floor locations that supply a more or less continuous depositional record throughout the QUATERNARY. The continuous records, in contrast to discontinuous continental records, form a potential basis for worldwide STRATIGRAPHIC CORRELATION based on ISOTOPIC palaeontological and MAGNETIC characteristics; they can help provide a chronology for early humans and they contain a wealth of palaeoclimatic information. Changes in ocean temperature and salinity are estimated from relative abundance of marine fossil species, fossil assemblage composition, and morphological variations. Changes in *Foraminifera* assemblages (see OXYGEN ISOTOPE ANALYSIS) identified with depth in the core are compared statistically with the ecology of living species to identify these parameters.

Ages for cores are obtained by URANIUM SERIES DATING, RADIOCARBON DATING, PALAEOMAGNETISM, and palaeontological extinctions. Not all methods can be applied to all cores, and there is significant interpolation between determined ages, with the assumption of uniform SEDIMENTATION rates.

Deh Luran   a small plain in lowland Khuzistan, western Iran, that was the setting for the important work of Frank Hole and Kent Flannery on the origins of food production. Their excavations at Tepe Ali Kosh, Tepe Sabz, Choga Sefid and other sites produced a cultural sequence that begins around 8000 bc (?) and runs through the URUK period into historic times. In the early phases of the sequence (the Bus Mordeh, Ali Kosh and Mohammad Jaffar phases, down to about 6200 bc) can be traced the transformation of morphologically wild but herded goats and sheep into domesticated forms; domesticated cereals are present throughout, but increase in importance through time. At the same time, the settlement at Ali Kosh becomes increasingly sedentary and grows in size, and pottery appears in the Mohammad Jaffar phase.

Deir el-Bahri   a locality within THEBES (EGYPT)-WEST BANK, the site of the MORTUARY TEMPLE of Nebhepetre Montuhotep (*c.*2033–1982 BC) of the MIDDLE KINGDOM and that of HATCHEPSUT built over 500 years later. Both buildings are remarkable for their construction on a series of terraces rising towards the cliffs of the Theban mountain of which Deir el-Bahri is a natural 'bay'. The temple of Hatchepsut contains a number of important reliefs, including those showing the transport of an OBELISK and an expedition to the Land of PUNT.

Deir el-Medina　a locality within THEBES (EGYPT)-WEST BANK, the site of the village (70 houses) of the workmen who constructed the tombs in the VALLEY OF THE KINGS during the NEW KINGDOM. Deir el-Medina was excavated by Bruyere in 1922–51, and produced a large number of written documents, chiefly OSTRAKA, due to the atypically high level of literacy among the workers who lived there. The evidence of economic and social life provided by this documentation has made Deir el-Medina one of the best-known communities of the ancient Near East.

Delos　the island birthplace of Apollo and Artemis, and an important sanctuary which contained a colossal marble KOUROS and the 5th century BC temple of Apollo. Elsewhere there was a sanctuary of Artemis with a temple in the IONIC ORDER. In the HELLENISTIC period the island became an important port and there are traces of houses, many of which contained portrait sculpture. The processional way was flanked by lions, one of which now stands outside the Arsenal at Venice.

Delphi　an important PANHELLENIC sanctuary in Greece associated with the cult of Apollo. Inside the sanctuary were numerous THESAUROI. Victors in the associated Pythian games set up dedications, one of which was the bronze charioteer. A further dedication, set up after the Persian wars by the Greeks, was the Plataean monument consisting of twined snakes supporting a cauldron (see BYZANTIUM).

Delta　the greater part of LOWER EGYPT, comprising the fan-like alluvial plain formed by the branches of the River Nile, which begin to diverge immediately to the north of CAIRO. Archaeological sites in the Delta (e.g. TANIS, BUBASTIS) tend to be less well preserved than their UPPER EGYPTIAN counterparts because of their less arid natural setting.

demography　the study of populations, in particular their size and composition. Its value in archaeology lies in providing information on the vital relationship between the subsistence economy, the environment and individual populations. The absolute size of a prehistoric population is extremely difficult to estimate; because of this, relative estimates based on such factors as changes in the numbers of settlements, sites and houses through time are often preferred. The study of human skeletons can give further clues as to the age and sex composition of a population, as well as to the prevalence of particular diseases or dietary patterns. See CARRYING CAPACITY.

demotic　(*Gk* 'of the people') the cursive script that succeeded the HIERATIC, from the 7th century BC to the 5th century AD, as the script used in Egyptian documents. Demotic was probably a more faithful written form of vernacular speech than hieratic, the use of which was continued for religious texts.

Denali Complex　a prehistoric culture or complex in central Alaska dating to *c.*10 500–7000 bp. It is characterized by WEDGE-SHAPED MICROCORES, MICROBLADES, BURINS and BIFACIAL POINTS. The Denali Complex appears closely related to the Siberian DYUKTAI CULTURE, and was defined by West in 1967.

denarius　a Roman silver coin, probably first struck in the late 3rd century BC. A wide range of designs were shown, and under the republic they often bore an image of the moneyer's ancestor. Under Augustus there were 84 denarii to the Roman pound (327 45 g).

Dendera a site in UPPER EGYPT, its principal feature being the well-preserved TEMPLE of the goddess Hathor. The present temple and its subsidiary buildings (including two MAMMISI) are almost all the work of the PTOLEMIES and Roman emperors up to the reign of TRAJAN. On the desert edge behind the temple is an important cemetery of MASTABA tombs of the OLD KINGDOM to First INTERMEDIATE PERIOD.

Dendra or **Dhendra** the site of a Bronze Age cemetery in the Argolid, Greece. Greek and Swedish excavations have revealed a Middle HELLADIC TUMULUS, an intact MYCENAEAN THOLOS tomb of the 15th–14th centuries BC, and rich CHAMBER TOMBS, one of which produced a bronze suit of armour. The associated settlement may be the Mycenaean citadel of Midea which was fortified in the 13th century BC.

dendrochronology a biological dating method based on tree-ring sequences used to date timbers and other logs from archaeological structures and sites. Each year, trees add a ring of growth and the age of living trees is determined by counting their growth rings. Climatic conditions affect the growth of trees as expressed by the width of these rings; during dry years ring width is relatively thin, and during moist years it is relatively thick. Hence, trees of the same species and similar age in an area affected by similar climatic conditions will exhibit similar sequences of ring widths. By finding older and younger trees that overlap in age, a relative chronology can be constructed to which the tree-ring pattern of timber finds can be compared. Absolute ages can be obtained by overlapping tree-ring sequences up to living trees. The longest (oldest) sequence to date is based on the BRISTLECONE PINE for western America and extends back 9000 years. A sequence that is not linked to living trees is referred to as a FLOATING CHRONOLOGY and is only useful for relative chronologies in the region from which they are derived. RADIOCARBON DATING can provide approximate ages for the floating chronologies.

Tree-ring series are also used to identify and date palaeoclimatic changes. Statistical models that relate tree-ring width and growth rate of living trees to historic climatic parameters affecting tree growth are then applied to prehistoric changes in ring width to infer past climatic conditions.

dendroglyph see CARVED TREE.

dendrogram a strip chart recording the analysis of tree-ring widths for a sample or samples which is compared to a master CHRONOLOGY in DENDROCHRONOLOGY studies.

Dene see ATHABASCAN.

Denekamp Interstadial a warm period occurring during the Middle PLENIGLACIAL phase of the last (WEICHSEL) GLACIATION in Europe at c.30 000 BP.

Denisova Cave a Palaeolithic site on the Anuj River in the Altai region of Siberia. At least 16 cultural layers have been identified in a sequence of sandy LOAM and CLAY deposits; associated faunal remains have not been studied, and only preliminary results are available concerning artifacts. The uppermost 5–6 layers are assigned to the Upper Palaeolithic and contain SCRAPERS, BURINS and some typical Middle

Palaeolithic tools. The lower layers contain Middle Palaeolithic assemblages (e.g. scrapers and DENTICULATES). Presumably, most or all of the cultural layers date to the LAST GLACIAL. Denisova Cave appears to be one of the most important sites for the study of the Middle/Upper Palaeolithic transition in northern Asia. It was discovered and excavated by Ovodov from 1977–84.

Dent a PALAEOINDIAN site in northern Colorado, USA, where the first CLOVIS points were found in 1932, although they were not recognized as being a new point type by their excavators. The site also provided the first unequivocal evidence for the association of stone PROJECTILE POINTS and MAMMOTH remains. A RADIOCARBON date of approximately 11 200 BP was later obtained from site material.

denticulate 1. a FLAKE or BLADE tool with a series of notches removed from one edge to give a tooth-like working edge.
2. the name given by BORDES to one of the southwestern French MOUSTERIAN variants, whose tool-kit contains few SCRAPERS but a high proportion of notched and denticulate pieces.

depas or **depas amphikypellon** the Homeric term which SCHLIEMANN used to describe the two-handled cups which he found in EARLY BRONZE AGE contexts at TROY.

depositional environment the sum total of SEDIMENTARY and biological conditions, factors and processes that characterize an area and result in a deposit or series of deposits that reflect those circumstances. Archaeological debris is deposited within a depositional system and is subject to the circumstances of that system during its evolution. Conversely, understanding a depositional environment implies knowledge about factors and processes that may have influenced occupation and subsequent transformations of the archaeological record. See LITHOFACIES, LITHOFACIES ANALYSIS.

Dereivka a Late Neolithic settlement and cemetery site in Ukraine, located on a tributary of the Dnieper River. Dereivka is a site of the SREDNI STOG culture. The settlement component covers about 3000 sq m, with several traces of dwellings as well as hearths and other features. The faunal sample from these deposits was dominated by horse bones, probably of domesticated animals. Antler artifacts believed to be cheekpieces imply that the Dereivka horses were used for riding.

Desert Tradition/Culture the concept of an adaptation of combined hunting and gathering and incipient food production in marginal environments, representing a relatively static adaptation up to modern times. The concept, devised by J. Jennings at DANGER CAVE (which, it was later realized, had been a lakeshore settlement, not a desert camp), originally referred to prehistoric societies in the Great Basin and southwestern United States showing an initial dependence on agriculture. It was then extended to groups from Canada to Guatemala. Nineteenth century Indian groups in the Great Basin were considered modern analogues. The Desert Tradition, dating from about 9000 BP to European contact, is characterized by a nomadic, wide-spectrum hunting and gathering economy; its material culture includes grinding stones, basketry, a variety of smaller PROJECTILE POINTS than those associated with large game hunting, and an absence of CERAMICS.

desert varnish a chemical crust of bacterial origin, consisting of oxides, that is deposited on exposed rock, artifact and PETROGLYPH surfaces. A type of rock varnish, desert varnish can be used in CATION RATIO DATING. It may also have incorporated organic matter that can provide an age by ACCELERATOR MASS SPECTROMETER RADIO-CARBON DATING.

Developed Oldowan (A, B, C)   a series of EARLIER STONE AGE industries of the OLDOWAN Industrial Complex recognized at OLDUVAI GORGE and other African sites, dating from about 1.6 to almost 0.6 million years ago, but differing from the classic Oldowan Industry in the types of stone artifacts present.

Devensian   see WEICHSEL.

Deverel–Rimbury   a Bronze Age culture of southern Britain, known both from burial mounds with inurned cremations and from settlement sites such as the small farmsteads of Itford Hill and New Barn Down (Sussex) and from the enclosure at South Lodge (Wiltshire). The characteristic pottery form is the simple coarse Bucket urn. Deverel-Rimbury sites are found throughout southern and eastern England in the period 1400–1200 BC (Middle Bronze Age), but the origins can now be traced back several centuries to the Early Bronze Age.

Devil's Lair   a limestone cave in Western Australia, excavated by Charles Dortch and Duncan Merrilees, with one of the longest occupation sequences in Australia, including well-defined hearths and occupation floors and a rich faunal assemblage. The cave was occupied intermittently from about 30 000 bp to the early HOLOCENE. Stone artifacts include a range of small RETOUCHED FLAKES and ADZE flakes of CHERT or QUARTZ and limestone artifacts. Bone tools – mostly POINTS – were found, as well as several bone beads made from *macropod* (kangaroo/wallaby) fibulae. Three enigmatic limestone plaques with possibly engraved lines were also recovered.

Devil's Tower   see GIBRALTAR.

Devon Downs   a limestone shelter on the Lower Murray River, South Australia, with six metres of rich deposits spanning the last 6000 years, where Hale and Tindale conducted the first scientific excavation in Australia in 1929. This provided the basis for Tindale's pioneering attempt to establish an Australian culture sequence.

Dhang Rial   a mound near Wun Rok in southern Sudan with a two phase IRON AGE sequence beginning about AD 500, overlying a ceramic LATER STONE AGE occupation.

Dhar Tichitt   an area of southern Mauretania, Africa, which has produced evidence of grain domestication in the 2nd millennium BC from plant impressions in pottery.

Dhendra   see DENDRA.

Dhimini   a prehistoric settlement mound in Thessaly, Greece. In the Late Neolithic period an elaborate system of fortifications was erected to protect a large MEGARON, presumably the residence of the ruler. The elegant bichrome pottery in use at this time characterizes the Dhimini culture. Two THOLOS tombs date from the MYCENAEAN period.

Dhlo Dhlo   see DANANGOMBE.

diachronic, *adj.*   **1.** relating to development through time, as compared with SYNCHRONOUS.

2. (applied to bounding surfaces, or rock units with one or more bounding surfaces) not synchronous, but rather of different ages in different locations, or time-transgressive. See also ISOCHRONOUS.

diamicton or **diamict**   a SEDIMENT or SOIL TEXTURE comprising larger than SAND-size CLASTS in and supported by a MATRIX of sand, SILT and CLAY, regardless of origin. Many GLACIAL debris-flow and colluvial deposits are accurately described as diamictions. The term was defined to avoid confusion with the misuse of the genetic term 'TILL' and its derivatives. It is now recognized that much of the material traditionally called 'till' was actually deposited by post-depositional mass movements that redeposited original till material.

Dian [Tien]   a regionally distinctive Bronze Age culture centred on Lake Dian in Yunnan Province, China, dating to the late 1st millennium BC. Bronze drums resembling those from the Southeast Asian DONG SON culture reveal southward connections, while trade was active with the southern ZHOU states Shu and Ba to the north and with the HAN Dynasty thereafter. (See CHINESE DYNASTIES.)

diaphysis   the shaft of a long bone. Compare EPIPHYSIS.

diatomites   SEDIMENTS formed mainly from the silicate exo-skeletons of DIATOMS found in lakes, for example in the Sahara and East Africa, during moist periods of the last two million years. RADIOCARBON dating of calcium carbonate concretions on the surface of diatomites to provide terminal dates for when the lakes were at their capacity is considered problematic.

diatoms   single-celled algae which grow in marine or fresh water and secrete silicious skeletons that are morphologically distinct by species. Diatom skeletons are sampled at different depth-intervals from DEEP SEA CORES or lake CORES for identification and analyses of ISOTOPIC composition, fossil assemblage composition and morphological changes, in order to determine alterations in PALAEOENVIRONMENTAL factors. See DIATOMITES.

Didyma   the extramural sanctuary of MILETUS, Turkey, probably dating back to the 8th century BC. During the ARCHAIC period the sanctuary attracted a number of wealthy dedications, some of which were removed during the PERSIAN sack after the Ionian revolt. The reconstructed HELLENISTIC temple included a NAISKOS inside the ADYTON.

Die Kelders   a cave on the southern Cape coast of South Africa with a 7 m deposit containing MIDDLE STONE AGE remains separated from a SHELL MIDDEN, which accumulated in the first five centuries AD, by thick sterile sands. The shell midden documents the first well-described discovery of domesticated sheep in a southern Africa LATER STONE AGE context, and also contains some of the earliest Later Stone Age pottery in southern Africa.

Dieng   a complex of Hindu temples built by the rulers of MATARAM in the late 8th and 9th centuries AD around the volcanic hot springs of the mountains of north-central Java. Most were probably CANDI.

differential fluxgate gradiometer   see MAGNETOMETER.

diffusion   a process whereby ideas, objects or cultural TRAITS are transferred from one CULTURE or society to another. It is an important explanatory concept in CULTURE HISTORY.

Dilmun   see PERSIAN GULF TRADE.

Dimolit   a Neolithic open settlement site in northern Luzon, north Philippines, occupied from c.2500 BC, with links in pottery to later phases at MUSANG CAVE and early material at Arku Cave, both of which have yielded items paralleled in Taiwanese Neolithic sites.

ding [ting]   a legged tripod first occurring in the Chinese Neolithic in ceramic (see CISHAN) then in the SHANG period in bronze. The category includes tripods and quadrapods. Bronze *ding* often bear TAOTIE designs.

Dingcun [Ting-ts'un]   a Middle Palaeolithic site group in Shanxi Province, China, which yielded human fossil remains and large FLAKE tools including CHOPPERS and prismatic points, with some stone balls. It is the type-site of the Dingcun culture in the Fen River area.

dingo   an Australian dog, one of the few pre-European placental mammals in Australia and a HOLOCENE introduction. The earliest secure dates are all between 3500 and 3000 bp at Wombah, New South Wales, Madura Cave and FROMMS LANDING; it is not found in TASMANIA. Its origins are unknown but it seems to resemble most closely Indian mid-Holocene dogs. See also THYLACINE.

dinos   a Greek round-bottomed cauldron which would have been placed on a stand or tripod. Several bronze examples have survived, and clay ones are decorated in the BLACK-FIGURED and RED-FIGURED techniques. They were probably intended for the mixing of wine, and were part of the equipment for the SYMPOSIUM.

Diouwar   see FABOURA.

Diprotodon   a giant marsupial, a rhinoceros-sized wombat-like animal, the largest of the extinct Australian species of PLEISTOCENE MEGAFAUNA.

direct historical approach   a technique developed in the 1930s by W.D. STRONG and others for extending knowledge of the HISTORIC PERIOD into the PREHISTORIC PERIOD. The technique consists of identifying the Historic Period occupants of a site through documentary evidence. The site, including its prehistoric COMPONENTS, is then excavated and cultural continuity is established between the two periods. This allows the use of ANALOGY, and more importantly HOMOLOGY, in the study of prehistoric CULTURES at the site and elsewhere in the surrounding region.

Diring   a prehistoric open-air site on the Lena River in northeast Siberia. A series of late Neolithic burials assigned to the Ymyakhtakh Culture were found on a high terrace in 1982. Subsequent investigation uncovered an assemblage of QUARTZITE CORES, PEBBLE TOOLS, and FLAKES in deeply buried ALLUVIUM. The alluvium has been dated by PALAEOMAGNETISM and TL to a minimum age of 1.8 million years, although this is controversial. The older remains were discovered and investigated by Mochanov in 1982–87.

discoidal nucleus technique   an efficient prepared CORE KNAPPING technique which became relatively common during the Middle Palaeolithic. The core is worked in a manner similar to that used in the LEVALLOIS TECHNIQUE, with flaking continued until the core is too small to use.

disconformity   a type of UNCONFORMITY separating essentially parallel STRATA that can represent a significant period of non-deposition. Recognition is important for correct interpretation of archaeological site STRATIGRAPHY.

Dissignac   a Neolithic burial mound in Loire-Atlantique, France, containing two PASSAGE GRAVES side by side. Remains of a settlement beneath the mound yielded MICROLITHS, Early Neolithic pottery and a PALAEOSOL with pollen of cultivated cereals dated by RADIOCARBON to *c*.4000 BC.

distal, *adj.*   remote from the point of origin. For example, distal ALLUVIAL FAN means the toe of the fan where it merges with a valley floor, well removed from the apex of the fan and adjacent mountain front, valley wall or ESCARPMENT; the finger is at the distal end of the human arm, furthest from its point of attachment to the body. Compare PROXIMAL.

distance-decay function   a mathematical MODEL that expresses the inverse ratio between the quantity of a particular substance and the distance from its source. It is especially useful in formulating models of prehistoric trade and EXCHANGE.

distributional archaeology   an approach that emphasizes the collection and analysis of high-resolution spatial and attribute data of ARTIFACTS and FEATURES in order to address archaeological issues. The emphasis is on the individual pieces of archaeological deposits rather than on the unit of an archaeological site.

Diuktai   see DYUKTAI CULTURE.

Divostin   a Neolithic site in Serbia, with occupations of the STARČEVO (Divostin I) and VINČA (Divostin II) cultures. Divostin I features consisted of many large pits and several surface structures. Divostin II features included a number of post structures and fired clay floors, including seven Late Vinča house plans.

Djebel   see JEBEL.

Djeitun   a half-hectare site in southern Turkmenia where excavations revealed a 6th (and even the late 7th) millennium BC Neolithic culture, characterized by square MUD-BRICK architecture, a hand-made pottery only a little of which is painted, and food production based on barley, wheat, sheep, goat and cattle, together with foraging. The settlements of this culture are generally small (0.5–2 ha), and are situated along the Kopet Dagh, including sites at Togolok, Cagalli and Chopan, as well as at Djeitun itself. This archaeological culture marks the earliest Neolithic of Central Asia, and may have been a centre of domestication for bread wheat.

Djenne   see JENNE-JENO.

Djetis   see JETIS.

Djoser   an Egyptian king of the 3rd DYNASTY, during the OLD KINGDOM. His STEP PYRAMID at SAQQARA (attributed to the architect Imhotep) represents a major technological advance on the earlier royal MASTABA tombs.

Dnepr-Donets culture   a prehistoric culture of the middle and lower Dnepr basin in Ukraine, contemporaneous with the CUCUTENI A culture of Romania and the TRIPOLYE B1 culture of western Ukraine, but with a mixed subsistence strategy in which hunted and gathered resources appear to have played a dominant role. Dolukhanov characterizes the Dnepr-Donets culture as a 'CERAMIC MESOLITHIC' group and views the presence of domestic cattle bones as due to trade.

Dobranichevka   an Upper Palaeolithic open-air site on the Supoj River (Dnepr tributary) in central Ukraine. The occupation is apparently buried in slope deposits comprising the upper FACIES of the second terrace; it yielded a single AMS RADIOCARBON date of

12 700 bp. The faunal remains are dominated by woolly MAMMOTH, and the excavators uncovered a total of four MAMMOTH-BONE HOUSES with associated pits, hearths, and debris concentrations. In this respect, Dobranichevka is very similar to MEZHIRICH and MEZIN.

Dodona   the oracle of the god Zeus in northern Greece. Excavations in the TEMENOS have uncovered many bronze dedications including tripods. Remains include a theatre and HELLENISTIC STADIUM.

Doian   see EIBIAN.

Doigahama   an early-to-middle YAYOI cemetery site in Yamaguchi Prefecture, Japan, first excavated by T. Kanaseki in 1953. His analysis of the skeletal remains, which distinguishes a physical type different from the PALAEOASIATIC JOMON, supports the hypothesis of substantial migration from the mainland during Yayoi into western Japan.

Dölauer Heide   a Neolithic hilltop settlement of the FUNNEL BEAKER culture in southeastern Germany. Fortifications, consisting of up to five bank-and-ditch systems in places, enclose a hilltop area of 25 ha. Traces of a palisade were also identified in places. On the spurs of the hilltop, outside the fortification, are a number of BARROWS.

dolichocephalic   see CEPHALIC INDEX.

dolium   a Roman large coarse-ware container. They could be sunk into the ground and were probably used for storing olive oil and wine. Some have been found set into the hulls of shipwrecks, making the ships an early version of 'supertankers'.

dolmen   1. a traditional French term for a MEGALITHIC tomb consisting of ORTHOSTATS and capstone, probably derived from the Cornish *tolmên*, a natural feature in which boulders support a 'capstone' to form a kind of chamber.
2. (*East Asia*) a MEGALITHIC stone burial feature in western China (Tibet, Sichuan, Gansu) and the coastal areas of the Yellow Sea basin (the Shandong peninsula in China, the Korean peninsula, and northwestern Kyushu in Japan). Mainly dated to the 1st millennium BC, these dolmens occur in three forms: raised table, low table and unsupported capstone. Polished stone implements are the characteristic grave-goods. (See BRONZE AGE.)

Dolní Věstonice   an Upper Palaeolithic open-air site located along the Dyje River in Moravia, Czechoslovakia. Artifacts and faunal remains (such as woolly MAMMOTH (predominant), horse, reindeer) are buried in LOESS deposits. The main cultural layer is dated by RADIOCARBON and stratigraphic correlation to the beginning of the LAST GLACIAL MAXIMUM (25 000 BP). Multiple HEARTHS and traces of a large former structure are present. The assemblage contains BURINS, SCRAPERS and BACKED BLADES, and is assigned to the EASTERN GRAVETTIAN. Among the many art objects are hundreds of animal and human figurines of fired loess, including a VENUS FIGURINE. Dolní Věstonice was excavated by ABSOLON and others. A number of human remains have also been uncovered, including a triple burial.

Domica   a 5 km long KARST cave in eastern Slovakia, continued on the Hungarian side as the Aggtelek cave. The stratified deposits in the Domica/Aggtelek cave have provided considerable information on the development of the LINEAR POTTERY culture in the upper Tisza basin in southeastern Slovakia and northeastern Hungary, particularly the BÜKK group.

Donau   see GÜNZ GLACIATION.

DONGBEI

Dongbei [Tung-pei]   the northeastern region of present-day China, including the Manchurian basin and BOHAI Bay, composed of Liaoning, Heilongjiang and Jilin Provinces. This region is often treated separately from the archaeology of the North China Plain, and includes the easternmost extension of the NORTHERN ZONE.

Dong Dau   a site in north Vietnam which has given its name to the early bronze period which succeeded PHUNG NGUYEN in *c*.1500 BC and gave way to the GO MUN phase in *c*.1200 BC. Technology and forms of bronze items were very similar to those of General Period B in KHORAT.

Dong Son   a site just to the south of the Red River valley in north Vietnam. It gave its name to the early Iron period in the region, which appears to have developed out of the GO MUN between *c*.600 and 400 BC. Although iron was used for tools, the Dong Son culture is best known for its bronze working, especially for the very large decorated cast-bronze drums, bronze SITULAE (buckets), bells, tools and weapons from elaborate boat burials. Objects from the graves include bronze jewellery, glass beads from South Asia or other parts of Southeast Asia, Chinese items including some HAN coins, mirrors, weapons and bronze vessels. The drums of the period (classed as Heger I) were traded in large numbers west and south into the mainland of Southeast Asia, northwest into DIAN in Yunnan, and by sea to the Malay peninsula, Sumatra, Java, Bali and numerous islands bordering the Java and Banda Seas. The patterns on these drums were incorporated into the design repertoire of much of island Southeast Asia. The major sites include Chao Can (8 boat burials, *c*.600–200 BC), Viet Khe (opulent boat burials with up to 100 artifacts each, including Chinese imports, *c*.600–200 BC), Lang Ca (314 burials), and CO LOA (possibly the capital of the early state of AU LAC, *c*.3rd century BC). The end of the period overlaps with that of early Chinese conquest, just before 100 BC.

Don Noi   a large stone-working site near chalcedony quarries in west-central Thailand, perhaps dating to the 3rd millennium BC. The implements produced include both flaked ADZES and utilized FLAKES. It is unclear whether this type of industry, which appears at other sites from north-west to peninsular Thailand, was a transitional one, linking the HOABINHIAN with the Neolithic POLISHED STONE ADZE tradition or whether it was one of several contemporary traditions perhaps related to different ethnic groups.

Dorak   a site just south of the Sea of Marmora in northwestern Anatolia, famous for the report of two looted 'royal tombs' of the Yortan culture. In the 1950s, J. Mellaart was shown the materials from the two tombs and allowed to draw and describe, but not to photograph, these objects. According to Mellaart's description, the preservation in the two cist tombs was excellent, allowing recovery of textiles, as well as an extremely rich array of objects in precious metal, stone and other materials (including turquoise, amber, lapis lazuli), vessels and weapons of gold, silver, electrum, bronze and iron. The Dorak materials vanished immediately after Mellaart's report, causing a considerable controversy, and leaving the status and even the actual existence of the Dorak tombs in doubt.

Dorian   a Greek dialect spoken in the Peloponnese, the southern Aegean islands and on the southwest coast of Asia Minor. It seems likely that it was introduced into southern Greece late in the 2nd millennium BC, but the tradition that a Dorian invasion brought about the collapse of the MYCENAEAN civilization has been discredited.

Doric order   a scheme of architecture widely used in the mainland of Greece and the Greek colonies in the western Mediterranean. The columns have no base. The CAPITAL is formed by a distinctive ECHINUS and ABACUS. The ENTABLATURE comprises a plain ARCHITRAVE, and above that alternating TRIGLYPHS and METOPES. See PARTHENON.

Dörpfeld, Wilhelm (1853–1940)   a German archaeologist who trained as an architect and excavated first at OLYMPIA, and then at TROY as SCHLIEMANN's assistant and later, in 1893–94, as his successor. Subsequently he undertook excavations on LEUKAS which he identified as the Homeric Ithaca, home of Odysseus.

Dorset   a prehistoric ESKIMO culture of the eastern Arctic that originated about 1000 BC and lasted until AD 1000 when it was replaced by the THULE culture. The Dorset culture was dependent on the hunting of sea-mammals, although caribou were taken with the spear. It is noted for the development of beautiful carvings in wood, bone and IVORY of human and animal forms, some realistic, others supernatural.

Dosariyah   a small surface site near the coast in the eastern province of Saudi Arabia, perhaps the best representative of the 'UBAID interaction with the Persian Gulf. In addition to the 'Ubaid 3–4 pottery and chipped stone, the site contains a fauna that consists largely of sheep/goat, cattle and gazelle, the first two of which are probably domesticates.

Dos Pilas   the largest MAYA city in the Petexbatun region of Guatemala during the Late CLASSIC. It grew increasingly bellicose, and by AD 700 had absorbed several neighbouring sites such as Aguateca.

Intensification of warfare (as shown by fortifications in the Terminal Classic) may ultimately have caused the collapse of the Petexbatun POLITIES. The tomb of a Late Classic ruler with a spectacular headdress ('Ruler 2', AD 698–725) was recently discovered by A. Demarest at the base of a TEMPLE-MOUND.

dotaku   a type of bronze bell peculiar to YAYOI-period Japan. Cast from melted down continental bronzes, the bells were originally functional with clappers, but became progressively ceremonialized and heavily decorated. Mainly limited to the SETOUCHI and TOKAI regions, they were buried in isolated caches on hilltops, and they are thought to have played a role in agricultural fertility rituals.

double axe   a cutting tool which has two blades and consequently does not have to be sharpened as often as a single axe. In MINOAN Crete the double axe was one of the most common religious symbols. Votive double axes, sometimes set between HORNS OF CONSECRATION, were frequently dedicated in shrines and sanctuaries. The cult status of double axes may have derived from their use as a sacrificial implement.

Douglass, Andrew Ellicott (1867–1962)   an American astronomer who devised the DENDROCHRONOLOGY dating method as early as 1901. In 1929 he published the first continuous tree-ring sequence for the southwestern United States. It extended far enough back from modern times to be useful in dating southwestern PUEBLO villages.

acroterium

mutule

cornice

triglyph

metope

abacus

echinus

anathyrosis

capital

pediment

entablature

anta

Doric order Portico.

Dowris a large hoard of over 200 BRONZES, from Co. Offaly, Ireland including 44 spearheads, 43 axes, 24 trumpets, and 44 bells or rattles. The hoard is dated to the 8th century BC and has given its name to the Dowris phase of the Irish Late Bronze Age.

Drachenloch a Swiss Alpine cave site at 2245 m altitude, best known for its supposed evidence for a Middle Palaeolithic CAVE BEAR cult, including what was thought to be a stone cist containing bear skulls and piles of long bones of bears arranged along the cave walls.

TAPHONOMIC studies have shown that all these features were almost certainly produced naturally by rockfalls and hibernating bears. Compare LES FURTINS.

drachma a unit of silver coinage in the Greek world. It was equivalent to six OBOLS. At ATHENS they were decorated with the motifs of Athena's head and her owl; thus they acquired the name 'owls'. At Athens they weighed 4.31 g and on Aegina 6.30 g. They could be issued in multiples of a drachma, for example the *didrachm* (= 2 drachmas), the *tetradrachm* (= 4) or the *dekadrachm* (= 10). See STATER.

Dragendorff, Hans (1870–1941) a German scholar who devised a classification scheme for shapes of TERRA SIGILLATA, published in 1895–96.

Drakensberg a South African mountain range forming the southern and eastern boundary with Lesotho, particularly known for its remarkable abundance of LATER STONE AGE rock paintings, especially those of eland. Some of these are interpreted by certain scholars in terms of the trance hallucinations of shamans.

Drakhmani see ELATEIA.

drift a collective term for any or all debris of all TEXTURES transported and deposited by or from GLACIAL ice and meltwater derived from the ice.

dromos the entrance passage of MINOAN-MYCENAEAN THOLOS and CHAMBER TOMBS.

Dry Creek a multi-component open-air site on the Nenana River in the northern foothills of the Alaska Range, southcentral Alaska, USA. Three cultural layers are buried in deposits of LOESS and wind-blown SAND on the margin of an ancient TERRACE. The lowest layer contains a small assemblage with a bifacial point and poorly preserved remains of sheep and *wapiti* (red deer). It is dated to 11 120 bp and assigned to the NENANA COMPLEX. The middle cultural layer contains a large MICROBLADE assemblage assigned to the DENALI COMPLEX, dated to 10 690 bp and associated with remains of steppe bison and sheep. A small assemblage with SIDE-NOTCHED POINTS, classified as NORTHERN ARCHAIC and dated to 4670–3430 bp, was recovered from the upper layer. Dry Creek represents the most important early prehistoric site in Alaska; it was excavated by Powers in 1973–77.

Dryas a series of cold climatic phases in northwest Europe, named after a TUNDRA plant, when the climate of the North Atlantic returned to almost full GLACIAL conditions. Dryas I started *c.*16 000 or 14 000 BP Dryas II *(Older Dryas)* was *c.*12 300–11 800 bp and Dryas III *(Younger Dryas)* from *c.*11 000–10 000 bp.

Dubois, Eugène (1858–1941) a Dutch physician and palaeoanthropologist who discovered the HOMINID remains at TRINIL, Java, in 1891.

Dudeşti culture a middle Neolithic culture of southeastern Romania, contemporaneous with the VADASTRA immediately to the west, VINČA A/B (Vinča-Tordos) in Yugoslavia, and KARANOVO III (VESELINOVO) in Bulgaria. Dudeşti pottery reflects the widespread shift in the Balkans during the late 5th millennium bc to the use of dark BURNISHED pottery.

Dufaure see DURUTHY.

Duff, Roger (1912–78) a New Zealand archaeologist best known for his fundamental work *The Moa-hunter Period of Maori Culture*. He also excavated the WAIRAU BAR site and developed a TYPOLOGY for stone ADZES of POLYNESIA and Southeast Asia.

Dumuzi   a shepherd god, in SUMERIAN myth, who was the husband of INANNA, the union of pastoralist and agricultural production. A series of poems describe their courtship and wedding, followed by the death of Dumuzi by drowning. Inanna eventually succeeds in rescuing Dumuzi from death, but only at the cost of her own life; ENKI arranges affairs so that each lives for half the year. Dumuzi appears as Tammuz in later western Asian myth.

Dundo   a town in the Luemba Valley of northeastern Angola, where alluvial deposits of the Congo River have yielded a STONE AGE sequence, mostly from secondary contexts, as well as fossil pollen assemblages.

dune   a depositional LANDFORM made by mounds of SAND deposited by the action of wind. Migration of active dunes can bury archaeological deposits. Relict dunes provide information for PALAEOENVIRONMENTAL reconstruction, such as general climatic conditions and prevailing palaeowind direction. Dunes are most commonly associated with deserts but also form in coastal areas and on sandy valley surfaces. Multiple dune forms are possible depending on prevailing wind conditions, vegetation and the supply of sand. See also COVER SAND.

Dunhuang [Tun-huang]   the site of the Mogao grottoes in northwestern China containing Buddhist sculptures and FRESCOES. The 492 surveyed caves stretch over 1.5 km of cliff face, all dating from the 5th–14th centuries AD (see CHINESE DYNASTIES). The artificially excavated grottoes follow two types of Indian cave temples: one with an ante-room and/or a corridor leading into the main chamber; the other with many niches or small rooms leading off the main chamber. Brightly painted frescoes cover more than 45 000 sq m of wall and ceiling space, and more than 2000 sculptures are constructed in high relief with clay-surfaced straw-covered wooden frames. Manuscripts and paintings obtained in 1905 by Aurel STEIN from caches at Dunhuang were brought to the British Museum.

Dur-Kurigalzu   see AQAR QUF.

Durrington Walls   a major Neolithic HENGE monument in Wiltshire, England, with bank and ditch enclosing an oval area of 12 ha. Within the enclosure, excavations by G. Wainwright revealed POST-HOLES of a large circular timber structure over 38 m across and a smaller one approximately 27 m across, which may have been houses or shrines. Among the pottery, Late Neolithic GROOVED WARE is conspicuous. RADIOCARBON tests date the henge to c.2600 BC.

Dürrnberg bei Hallein   an Iron Age salt-mining centre in the Salzach valley south of Salzburg in Austria. In the 5th century bc, Dürnberg eclipsed the large salt-mining complex at HALLSTATT, 40 km to the east, by reason of its position on the Salzach and the greater availability of land for agriculture and grazing on the floodplain. The remains of miners' settlements and graves have been found. Wealthy burials are common, and artifacts link Dürnberg with many other parts of central Europe and the Mediterranean area.

Duruthy   a major rockshelter in the Landes, southwest France, excavated primarily by R. Arambourou from 1958 until the 1980s. It was occupied from at least the early MAGDALENIAN to the AZILIAN, and also contained some CHALCOLITHIC burials. The middle Magdalenian layers have been dated to the 14th millennium bp, and the late Magdalenian to the 12th millennium, when the site was a winter settlement for people exploiting reindeer and bovids. Very similar data have recently emerged from excavations by L. Straus at the nearby shelter of *Dufaure*. Duruthy's Magdalenian contains a wealth of PORTABLE ART, including fine carvings of horses, and a series of engraved carnivore canines.

Duvanli a 5th century BC TUMULUS cemetery in Thrace (modern Bulgaria). The graves included imported ATHENIAN POTTERY, both RED-FIGURED and BLACK-GLOSSED, and several items of Greek GOLD-FIGURED silver plate.

Dvaravati an early MON state in central Thailand, for which few records have survived. It was mentioned in Chinese records of the 7th century AD and probably survived until the 11th century when the region came under Khmer influence. The capital may have been located at NAKHON PATHOM, and such settlements as LOPBURI, U THONG and CHANSEN may have been attached to it. The term is applied to a style of Buddhist art heavily influenced by that of north India's Gupta dynasty (4th–5th centuries AD) and to a lively indigenous style of TERRACOTTA modelling and STUCCO relief sculpture.

Dvuglazka Cave a Palaeolithic and Mesolithic site on the Tolchei River (Yenisei tributary) in south–central Siberia. Artifacts and faunal remains are buried in a sequence of LOAM and rubble. The uppermost cultural layer contains a Mesolithic assemblage. A small quantity of Upper Palaeolithic artifacts was found, associated with remains of sheep and other mammals (including woolly MAMMOTH) in an underlying cultural layer. The lower levels contain a sequence of small assemblages assigned to the Middle Palaeolithic and associated with remains of horse, woolly rhinoceros, steppe bison, and sheep. The fauna appears to reflect a warm and dry climate (prior to the LAST GLACIAL?). The artifacts include LEVALLOIS CORES, many DENTICULATES, and some SCRAPERS. Dvuglazka represents the northernmost Middle Palaeolithic locality in Asia; it was discovered and excavated by Abramova in 1974–79.

dynasty nominally a line of hereditary rulers. The dynasties of Mesopotamia were distinguished by their places of origin, such as those of UR. In China (see CHINESE DYNASTIES), the dynasties often encompassed only regions rather than the whole country.

The dynastic divisions conventionally used to refer to periods of Egyptian history also include rulers seemingly not of the main royal line (e.g. at the end of the 18th Dynasty), but the term is nonetheless a useful point of reference. The divisions are shown in the table overleaf.

Dyuktai Cave an upper Palaeolithic site on the Dyuktai River (Aldan tributary) in northeast Siberia. Five cultural layers are buried in sandy LOAM and rubble deposits; among the faunal remains are woolly MAMMOTH, steppe bison, reindeer and elk. RADIOCARBON estimates from the cultural layers range between 14 000 and 12 100 bp. The artifact assemblages are similar and contain WEDGE-SHAPED MICRO-CORES, MICROBLADES, BURINS and bifacial points; they are assigned to the DYUKTAI CULTURE. Dyuktai Cave was discovered and excavated by Mochanov in 1967–70 and 1980–82.

Egyptian dynasties (with approximate dates BC)

Archaic Period

Dynasty	1	3000–2840	Dynasty	2	2840–2700

Old Kingdom

Dynasty	3	2700–2600	Dynasty	4	2600–2500
Dynasty	5	2500–2350	Dynasty	6	2350–2190
Dynasty	7/8	2190–2160			

First Intermediate Period

Dynasty	9	2160–2106		
Dynasty	10	(Middle Egypt)		2106–2010
Dynasty	11	(Thebes)		2106–2023

Middle Kingdom

Dynasty	11	(Unification)			2023–1963
Dynasty	12	1963–1786	Dynasty	13	1786–1633

Second Intermediate Period

Dynasty	14	(W. Delta, contemp. Dynasties 13/15)	1786–1633
Dynasty	15	(Major Hyksos)	1648–1540
Dynasty	16	(Minor Hyksos, contemp. Dynasty 15)	1648–1540

New Kingdom

Dynasty	17	1633–1550	Dynasty	18	1550–1295
Dynasty	19	1295–1186			

Third Intermediate Period (*Dynasties 22–24 Libyan, 25 Nubian*)

Dynasty	20	1186–1070	Dynasty	21	1070–945
Dynasty	22	945–715	Dynasty	23	818–715
Dynasty	24	727–715	Dynasty	25	715–664

Late Period (*Dynasties 27 and 31 Persian*)

Dynasty	26	664–525	Dynasty	27	525–404
Dynasty	28	404–399	Dynasty	29	399–380
Dynasty	30	380–343	Dynasty	31	343–332

Dyuktai Culture an upper Palaeolithic culture of northeast Siberia dating to *c*.20 000–10 000 BP and possibly earlier. Diagnostic artifacts include WEDGE-SHAPED MICROCORES, MICROBLADES, BURINS and bifacial points. Dyuktai assemblages have been found at DYUKTAI CAVE and a number of open-air sites in the Lena Basin, as well as open-air sites in western BERINGIA (e.g. USHKI LAKE). The Dyuktai Culture appears closely related to the DENALI COMPLEX of Alaska and may be ancestral to the earliest lithic technologies, in particular the bifacially flaked points, of North America. It was defined by Mochanov in 1969.

Dzhruchula a Middle Palaeolithic cave on the Dzhruchula River in the southern foothills of the Greater Caucasus, altitude 600 m, in Georgia. Two main cultural layers were distinguished in a sequence of LOAM and rubble. Faunal remains associated with the lower layer are predominantly of CAVE BEAR; those associated with the upper layer are chiefly of herbivores (e.g. red deer). The age of the occupations is unknown, but they apparently occurred under mild climatic conditions. Tools from both layers are primarily SCRAPERS and points; the upper assemblage reflects heavy emphasis on LEVALLOIS TECHNIQUE and BLADES. Dzhruchula was discovered and excavated by Tushabramishvili from 1957–66.

Dzibilchaltún   a large ceremonial MAYA site in northwest Yucatán, Mexico, where about 8400 structures have been mapped in an area of 19 sq km. The supporting hinterland is estimated at 90 sq km. The site is important for its almost continuous occupation from 500 BC to the present. Ninety percent of the mapped structures were occupied during the late CLASSIC and Early POSTCLASSIC, from AD 600–1000. The maximum population occurred in the later part of this period. From AD 1000–1200, the population dropped to less than 10% of its former size.

The archaeological work of E. Wyllys Andrews IV and George Brainerd, begun in 1941 at this site, was interrupted by the Second World War. In 1956 and 1965 Andrews returned to resume work at the site.

Dzierzysław   an Upper Palaeolithic open-air site located in Upper Silesia, Poland. Displaced artifacts are buried in LOESS and slope deposits. The cultural layer contains an assemblage (e.g. SCRAPERS, LAUREL-LEAF POINTS) assigned to the SZELETIAN, which probably dates to the middle of the LAST GLACIAL.

E

Ea   see ENKI.

Eanna sounding   a deep test excavation in the Eanna precinct at WARKA which has a special place for studying the origins of writing and the state in southern MESOPOTAMIA. The 18-level sequence represents the 'UBAID (XVIII–XV), Early URUK (XIV–IX), Middle Uruk (VIII–VI), Late Uruk (V–IV), JEMDET NASR (III), and EARLY DYNASTIC (II–I) periods. The principal architectural exposures in the Eanna precinct belong to levels V–III, where a number of monumental buildings form a single complex whose function is usually assumed to be religious, but which also served a more broadly administrative purpose. The latter aspect is clearly visible in the presence in these levels of CYLINDER SEALS, sealings and written texts, all typical administrative artifacts of Mesopotamian civilization here appearing for the first time. Economic texts first appear in Uruk IV, first with numbers only (IVb) and then with numbers together with words (IVa), and non-economic texts appear in Uruk III levels. Taken together with the rich small finds (especially of the Uruk III levels), the evidence from Warka indicates large economic organizations probably founded on religious and/or economic power over certain aspects of community life.

Earlier Stone Age   the first stage of STONE AGE technology in sub-Saharan Africa, dating from perhaps more than 2.5 million to *c*.150 000 years ago (see MIDDLE AWASH). The earliest collections are considered representative of the OLDOWAN Industrial Complex, which was succeeded by the ACHEULIAN Industrial Complex between *c*.1.5 million and 150 000 years ago.

Early Bronze Age   a period in the Levant beginning shortly before the ARCHAIC PERIOD in Egypt, and dated to *c*.3200–1950 BC. It was an era of increasing urbanization typified in its latest phase (Early Bronze Age III) by walled towns. The period seems to have been brought to an end by the incursions of the AMORITES.

Early Dynastic Period 1. the chronological block between the JEMDET NASR and AKKADIAN periods in southern MESOPOTAMIA; the conventional date of the period is 2900–2330 BC, although CALIBRATED RADIOCARBON dates for the previous periods suggest a slightly earlier beginning, and recent reconsiderations of later political chronologies may alter the date of its end. The Early Dynastic period is divided into four phases (E.D. I, II, IIIa and IIIb, the last also called 'proto-imperial') on the basis of changes in pottery, SEALS and other aspects of the material culture. This archaeological definition was first achieved during the 1930s through work in the lower Diyala River (Tell ASMAR, Tell KHAFADJE); but more recent work further south in Mesopotamia (ABU SALABIKH) has revealed regional differences that question the suitability of the Diyala results elsewhere in the region. Considerable development of the CUNEIFORM writing system occurred during this period, and for the first time contemporary royal inscriptions and more detailed economic texts are available for study; the period corresponds to most of the pre-Akkadian section of the SUMERIAN KING LISTS. This period thus represents the earliest conjunction of archaeological and written evidence for the social and political history of southern Mesopotamia.

2. (*Egypt*) see ARCHAIC PERIOD.

Early Horizon (900–0 BC) the period during which the CHAVÍN culture, in Andean South America, flourished and culturally integrated the northern highlands and coast of Peru. After the collapse of Chavin, regional differentiation of culture areas increased, culminating in the complex cultures of the EARLY INTERMEDIATE PERIOD.

Early Intermediate Period (AD 1–600) a period of development of distinctive regional cultures, in Andean South America, especially in the central Andean region. Two of the better-known cultures are the MOCHE and NASCA civilizations, although numerous, less-studied (and artistically less-spectacular) cultures pertain to other regions of the coast and highlands. Out of this background emerged the first round of imperial expansions, in the MIDDLE HORIZON.

Early Later Stone Age (ELSA) an informal MICROLITHIC late PLEISTOCENE STONE AGE industry known from a few sites in South Africa. At BORDER CAVE it is characterized by minute backed pieces, bone points, ostrich eggshell beads, and incised bone and wood.

Early Man shelter a site in southeast Cape York peninsula, Australia, excavated by Andrée Rosenfeld. The lowest deposits date to about 13 000 bp and cover weathered and patinated PANARAMITEE-style engravings. The stone tool sequence is similar to MUSHROOM ROCK, while faunal remains, predominantly rock wallabies, and bone tools are preserved from deposits between 6000 and 3000 years old.

earth lodges structures, of varying shape and size and made of wood with an earthen covering, that served both habitation and ceremonial functions. The term is especially applied to structures found in some CULTURES of the American Midwest and East regions. Archaeologically, earth lodges are represented by hard-packed floors and/or POSTHOLES that are the remains of wall and roof supports.

Easter Island   the easternmost inhabited island of POLYNESIA, 3700 km from South America and 2200 km from Pitcairn Island. Now called Rapa Nui, it was christened by the Dutch commander Roggeveen, who found it on Easter Sunday 1722 and spent a few hours ashore observing the natives' way of life. After sporadic archaeological study in the late 19th and early 20th centuries, important work was done by Thor Heyerdahl's 1955 expedition, which first brought MULLOY here. The 166 sq km island is one huge stone-age site, with hundreds of MEGALITHIC statues (MOAI) and platforms (AHU, and see VINAPU), house foundations, ROCK ART, OBSIDIAN sources, and stone-quarries in volcanic craters (see RANO RARAKU, PUNA PAU). RADIOCARBON dates suggest a colonization by Polynesians in the first centuries AD. The island's extreme isolation led to unique cultural developments, notably the moai and the RONGORONGO 'script'. Relentless deforestation for timber and land-clearance caused soil erosion, devastated the economy, and ended statue-transportation. Food shortages and probable population pressure led to a period of strife after *c*.AD 1600, when the MATAA were manufactured and the moai toppled, and which the birdman cult at ORONGO was designed to overcome through the choosing of an annual leader.

Eastern Anatolian Bronze Age   see KURA-ARAXES CULTURE.

Eastern Gravettian   an Upper Palaeolithic industry or culture widely distributed across central and eastern Europe during the LAST GLACIAL MAXIMUM (*c*.30 000–20 000 BP). The assemblages contain SHOULDERED POINTS and BACKED BLADES, and sometimes VENUS FIGURINES; many sites have yielded evidence of MAMMOTH BONE HOUSES. Compare GRAVETTIAN.

Eastern Stream   see CHIFUMBAZE.

East Greek pottery   pottery that was produced in numerous centres during the ARCHAIC PERIOD along the west coast of Turkey and the offshore Greek islands. Important centres include Chios (see CHIOT POTTERY), Samos, EPHESUS, MILETUS (see FIKELLURA WARE), Clazomenae and Rhodes, many of which have been recognized only as a result of chemical analysis. Related to this pottery production were painted clay SARCOPHAGI at Clazomenae.

East Turkana   see KOOBI FORA.

Ebbsfleet   see PETERBOROUGH.

Ebla   a 56 ha site in northern Syria, some 70 km south of Aleppo. Now known as Tell Mardikh, it was the ancient Ebla, and Italian excavations since the 1960s have led to the discovery of a large 3rd millennium archive, making the site one of the most important to be worked in the past generation. The multiple soundings in the site provide a sequence of six major periods, spanning the late 4th to late 1st millennia BC. The most significant discovery at the site, the archive of some 15 000 texts and fragments within a palace complex (Palace G), belongs to the phase Mardikh IIB1 and is controversially dated to *c*.2400–2250 BC. These documents have generated considerable interpretative dispute, but in general reveal an unexpectedly rich and thriving urban state in Syria, interacting with neighbours to north and east. Contemporary with the late EARLY DYNASTIC city-states and early AKKADIAN rulers in southern MESOPOTAMIA, the political and social aspects of Ebla show some similarities with the northern parts of the latter area (see KISH, ABU SALABIKH), but were nonetheless distinct.

Eburran an East African OBSIDIAN industry, characterized by large BACKED BLADES, SEGMENTS, SCRAPERS and BURINS, formerly known as the 'Kenya Capsian'. It is restricted to a small area near Lake Nakuru in southern Kenya and dates to between 13 000 and 9000 BP and later.

echinus found at the top of CLASSICAL column-shafts forming part of the CAPITAL. In the DORIC ORDER it is the convex, cushion-shaped section located immediately below the ABACUS. In the IONIC ORDER it is placed between the VOLUTES of the capital and is frequently decorated with an egg-and-dart pattern.

ecofact faunal or floral material found in a site.

ed-Daba, Tell a site in the eastern Nile DELTA, Egypt. The probable location of the city of AVARIS, Tell ed-Daba, with its clear signs of Palestinian MIDDLE BRONZE AGE occupation, has been excavated by Bietak since 1969.

Edfu a site in UPPER EGYPT. Earlier religious buildings at Edfu were all but swept away by the TEMPLE of the god HORUS, which was constructed under PTOLEMAIC kings between 237 and 57 BC, and which is the most complete surviving example of an ancient Egyptian temple. To the west are tombs of the OLD and MIDDLE KINGDOM, and the TELL of the ancient town, which seems to have had continuous occupation from at least as early as the Old Kingdom until the uppermost Graeco-Roman levels. Edfu has chiefly been excavated by the French Oriental Institute in 1914–33 and by a Franco–Polish mission in 1937–39.

edge-ground stone tools 1. a tool category occurring in several sites in northern Australia and New Guinea in PLEISTOCENE contexts. Pleistocene ground-edge hatchets were first reported at Nawamoyn and MALANGANGERR in the 1960s; FLAKES with ground facets have been reported from other Pleistocene sites in ARNHEM LAND, the Kimberley, southeast Cape York and the NEW GUINEA HIGHLANDS, while a complete hatchet from Sandy Creek 1, southeast Cape York, confirms that this technology was present in the region before 32 000 bp. Elsewhere in Australia, edge-ground tools do not appear before the late HOLOCENE and are absent from TASMANIA.
2. flaked stone tools, sharpened by grinding or polishing the cutting surface only, that are found in the BACSONIAN and HOABHINIAN of Southeast Asia. This may represent a transitional stage between flaked tools and the fully POLISHED STONE ADZES of the Southeast Asian Neolithic.

Eemian Interglacial the last INTERGLACIAL in North Europe, following the SAALIAN and preceding the WEICHSEL GLACIATION, and spanning from c.125 000 to 115 000 BP. Its Alpine equivalent is RISS-WÜRM, in North America the SANGAMON, and in Britain the Ipswichian, whose type-site is Bobbit's Hole, Ipswich.

Effigy mound culture a Late WOODLAND culture in the Upper Mississippi Valley, USA, characterized by BURIAL MOUNDS built in the shape of various animals, often birds.

Efimenko, Pyotr Petrovich (1884–1969) a Soviet archaeologist who was instrumental in the development of Palaeolithic archaeology during the period after 1930. Efimenko denounced traditional West

European concerns with STRATIGRAPHY and TYPOLOGY, and advocated study of 'sociological issues' from a MARXIST theoretical perspective. He excavated at KOSTENKI, reporting the first discovery of a Palaeolithic LONGHOUSE (1931–36 excavations), which he linked to the social organization of its occupants. In 1938, Efimenko published a major synthesis of Palaeolithic prehistory entitled *Primeval Society*.

Egolzwil   a village site on the shore of the former Lake Wauwil, Luzern, representative of the earliest phase of the Neolithic in western Switzerland. The earliest settlement is Egolzwil 3, with cereals and domestic animals and simple round-based pottery, dated to the late 5th or early 4th millennium BC.

Egtved   a Middle Bronze Age burial in an oak tree trunk coffin under a circular TUMULUS in Jutland, Denmark. Exceptional conditions of preservation had allowed the survival of clothing including a woollen tunic and corded knee-length skirt. There were bronze bracelets on the wrists and a bronze belt-disc with a central spike. Though the body had decomposed it could be identified as that of a young woman approximately 20 years old. The coffin also contained cremated remains of a 9 year-old child.

Egyptian dynasties   see DYNASTY.

Ehringsdorf   a Middle PLEISTOCENE open-air site located near Weimar in eastern Germany. Artifacts and faunal remains (e.g. *Elephas antiquus, Dicerorhinus mercki*) are buried in spring deposits dated (by URANIUM SERIES) to *c*.225 000 bp. The artifacts, which include SCRAPERS, points and BIFACES, are typical of the Middle Palaeolithic, despite their age. Associated human skeletal remains are classified as NEANDERTHALS.

Eibian   an East African MICROLITHIC LATER STONE AGE industry formerly known as the 'Doian', characterized by PRESSURE-FLAKED small points and other tools. It is thought to date to the late or terminal PLEISTOCENE.

Eilsleben   a fortified settlement of the LINEAR POTTERY CULTURE in eastern Germany near Magdeburg. As was the case at KÖLN-LINDENTHAL, the settled area at Eilsleben was surrounded by a rampart and ditch system which became progressively more elaborate over the duration of the settlement.

Ein Gev I   an open air KEBARAN site on Lake Kinneret in the Jordan valley, Israel, which contains semi-subterranean pit structures, about 6 m across and spaced roughly 20 m apart; the tightly flexed burial of a woman was also found in the settlement. Along with the Kebaran lithic assemblage, some of whose BLADES display SICKLE SHEEN, the material culture includes a series of mortars, pestles and a few grinding stones. Together with the wild fauna (mostly gazelle), these materials are usually taken to represent an intensifying interest in wild cereals as an early step toward food production.

Ein Mallaha   see EYNAN.

Ekain   a MAGDALENIAN cave-site in the Basque country of northern Spain, where cave art was discovered in 1969. It contains about 50 figures, mostly paintings, including a fine panel of horses. Excavation has revealed material of the AURIGNACIAN and early Magdalenian (16 500–15 400 bp), but the art can be assigned to the later Magdalenian, dating to 12 050 bp, through stylistic analogy with an engraved stone from that layer. The occupants in this period were heavily dependent on ibex.

ekphora   a funerary procession in the Greek world, that might include a cortege with chariots and mourners. Ekphorai are commonly depicted on the ceramic monumental funerary markers at ATHENS in the 8th century BC. See also PROTHESIS.

el-Ajjul, Tell   a Palestinian site excavated by PETRIE in 1930–34, and including two cemeteries of the transitional EARLY to MIDDLE BRONZE AGE, one of which was remarkable for the large number of graves found to contain COPPER daggers. The Middle Bronze Age at Tell el-Ajjul is notable for its substantial palaces and for the quantity of gold jewellery and SEALS (including SCARABS) recovered from the excavations, the latter being an indication of Egyptian influence from the MIDDLE KINGDOM to the NEW KINGDOM.

Elam   an early state located in south-west Iran, an extension of the southern plain of Mesopotamia. With its centres in SUSA in the Khuzistan lowlands and in Anshan in the Fars uplands of southwestern Iran (see Tal-i MALYAN), Elam represents a civilization that looked towards both Mesopotamia and the Iranian plateau, a duality that was often expressed as an oscillation in material culture and political forms between the two. Because it was influenced at its inception by URUK-period Mesopotamia (see ACROPOLE OF SUSA, PROTO-ELAMITE), and repeatedly invaded or occupied by later Mesopotamian states, its political history is one of endemic antagonism toward its neighbours to the west, and Elam in its turn often raided southern Mesopotamia. The Elamite cultural tradition came to an end largely as a consequence of absorption into the world empires of the mid 1st millennium BC; though Susa was a principal seat of the ACHAEMENID rulers, who continued to use Elamite in some public inscriptions, the area lost much of its distinctiveness at this time.

el-Amarna   a city founded on a virgin site in northern UPPER EGYPT, that became the capital of Egypt during the AMARNA PERIOD. Constructed over a relatively short period (including the use of TALATAT), the central area of the city, containing the 'Great Temple' of ATEN and the 'Great Place', was subsequently robbed of its stone masonry. The functions of some of the public buildings at el-Amarna are open to debate, but it is clear that the new city was intended to serve as the religious and administrative centre of the state (see also AMARNA LETTERS), with suburbs, villas and a workers' village on the outskirts of the central area. In the cliffs behind the city are rock-out tombs of the officials of King AKHENATEN. The site has chiefly been excavated by PETRIE (1891–92), Borchardt (1911–14) and the Egypt Exploration Fund/Society (1901–07, 1921–36, 1977–present).

Elands Bay   a cave on the southwestern coast of the Cape Province of South Africa, excavated in the 1970s and 1980s by John Parkington. The basal layers of its 3 m deep stratified deposit contain early MIDDLE STONE AGE material which may be as old as late Middle PLEISTOCENE. This is separated from LATER STONE AGE material by a break in the sequence. The faunal remains document the effects of the rise in sea level at the end of the Pleistocene, which transformed the setting of the cave from an inland riverine to a coastal estuarine situation.

Elandsfontein   an open archaeological and possibly also carnivore site originally near a waterhole, covering about 300 ha between shifting sand dunes in the southwestern Cape Province of South Africa. It contains rich collections of fossil animal bones, as well as stone artifacts and pottery. The fragmented 'Saldanha' cranium of an archaic HOMO *sapiens* was found here on an exposed surface in 1953, and is considered to be of late Middle PLEISTOCENE age.

El Argar　a rich Early Bronze Age settlement site in ALMERIA, Spain, excavated by Louis SIRET, and the type-site of the Argaric culture. Fortified Argaric villages with rectangular houses are known throughout Almeria. Burial was in stone cists or jars below the floors of the houses. At El Argar itself 950 such burials were found. The richest Argaric burials contain gold and silver diadems, and daggers and swords of copper and bronze.

Elateia (formerly **Drakhmani**)　the site of a prehistoric settlement mound in Pthiotis, Greece, which was excavated by Weinberg in 1959. Elateia has the most complete stratified sequence of Central Greek Neolithic pottery deposits.

el-Bersheh　a site of rock-cut tombs of Egypt's MIDDLE KINGDOM, some belonging to the NOMARCHS of that period. El-Bersheh was chiefly explored by the Egypt Exploration Fund in 1891–93.

El Beyed　a late ACHEULIAN site in Mauretania, Africa, rich in HANDAXES, large LEVALLOIS CORES and quantities of angular BLADES.

El Castillo　a major cave-site discovered in 1903 by H. Alcalde del Rio in a conical hill in Santander Province (northern Spain). The 20 m stratigraphy at the entrance spans the entire Palaeolithic period, and has been investigated by H. Obermaier (1910–15) and by V. Cabrera (since 1980). Its earliest AURIGNACIAN material has been dated by RADIOCARBON (AMS) to *c*.38 700 bp. The Middle Palaeolithic economy was based on horse and bovid hunting, but the Upper Palaeolithic saw a shift to a specialized exploitation of deer. The cave contains engravings and paintings from different phases of the later Upper Palaeolithic (*c*.20 000 to 10 000 BC) including 155 animal figures, 50 red hand stencils, and numerous quadrilateral forms. Charcoal in two polychrome bison figures has produced radiocarbon dates of 11 110 and 10 960 bc. The hill (Monte Castillo) also houses other decorated Palaeolithic caves: Las Chimeneas, Las Monedas and La Pasiega, the latter containing 440 animal figures.

electromagnetic surveying　a geophysical SURVEYING technique designed to locate archaeological FEATURES and SEDIMENT or SOIL textural discontinuities. The technique is based on the induction of an electric current flow in near-surface materials and the measurement of electrical conductivity of the current. The electric current is conducted primarily by water in pores in the soil, so the conductivity is a function of porosity, water content and water chemistry. Porosity, water retention and ion absorption in turn are affected by particle size, so that contrasting TEXTURES, such as pit fill *versus* surrounding MATRIX, will produce an anomalous reading. Electromagnetic survey is conducted with either a PULSED INDUCTION METER or a SOIL CONDUCTIVITY METER, neither of which is as accurate as a RESISTIVITY METER or PROTON MAGNETOMETER. See also RESISTIVITY SURVEYING.

electron probe microanalysis　a physical technique of chemical analysis used to determine the chemical composition of stone, CERAMICS, pigments, glass, metal, surface applications and stains. A highly focused electron beam bombards a point on a polished sample surface, exciting electrons which emit secondary X-rays. The wavelengths of these secondary X-rays are characteristic of the elements that emitted them, and the concentrations of elements can be calculated from the intensities of the energy spectrum.

electron spin resonance dating (ESR) a radiogenic dating method that utilizes residual effects of changing energy levels of electrons under conditions of natural irradiation of alpha, beta and gamma rays. The method is applicable to teeth, bone, heat-treated CHERT and FLINT, CERAMICS, archaeological SEDIMENTS, shells, spring TRAVERTINE and SPELEOTHEMS. When minerals form, all electrons are in their ground state. With irradiation, the energy level of electrons can be increased temporarily, but then they return to positive charged sites near the ground state. However, some electrons are trapped in naturally occurring charge-deficit sites which can be detected by ESR spectrometry. The number of trapped electrons is a function of the amount of natural radiation and the duration of that irradiation. The age of a sample can be calculated by determining the number of trapped electrons at a given site and the dose rate of natural radiation. There are numerous factors that affect these values and they must be taken into account. The main factors that limit the effective age range of the dating technique are sample saturation and thermal stability for the upper limit, which may range up to two to three million years; and the dose rate, mineral sensitivity to radiation, and sensitivity of the ESR spectrometer for the lower limit, which can be as low as several hundred years.

Principal sources of error are post-depositional physical or chemical changes, errors in chemical analyses and reproducibility of signal intensity, and systematic errors. Because of the multiplicity of factors that may contribute to error, precision is difficult to estimate and varies with the type of sample. Precision of replicate analyses is of the order of 10 to 20% for the types of samples examined.

electronic distance measuring devices (EDM) SURVEYING and mapping instruments that utilize sophisticated electronics and infrared or laser beams in measuring and calculating distances, locating points and determining angles. Often computer compatible, an EDM is far more accurate, time efficient, and expensive than conventional surveying instruments such as a TRANSIT or THEODOLITE.

Elephantine an island in the ASWAN region, Egypt, regarded as Egypt's southern border during the OLD and MIDDLE KINGDOM. The town, on the southern tip of the island, has been excavated by the German Archaeological Institute since 1969; the TELL-like settlement debris seems to indicate continual occupation from the ARCHAIC PERIOD to the Graeco-Roman Period.

Eleusis the site of a major Greek sanctuary in Attica, dedicated to the goddess Demeter, in whose honour the Mysteries were celebrated. The CLASSICAL Telesterion, or temple of Demeter, was constructed on the site of a MYCENAEAN MEGARON which may have been a shrine. The Romans were generous benefactors, especially Hadrian and Marcus Aurelius who built the PROPYLAEA.

el-Fara, Tell (north) a Palestinian site chiefly excavated by de Vaux from 1946–60. The CHALCOLITHIC settlement was composed of circular, semi-subterranean dwellings, while the Early Bronze Age occupation seems to have been abandoned, perhaps due to incursions by the AMORITES. The site was resettled in the MIDDLE BRONZE AGE and later became an ISRAELITE town.

el-Fara, Tell (south)   a Palestinian site, excavated by PETRIE in 1928–29. The first settlement seems to have been the HYKSOS fortifications. The most impressive excavated remains of the Late Bronze Age are of a large building called 'The Residency', while the site was occupied by the PHILISTINES in the Iron Age.

El Garcel   a hilltop settlement in ALMERIA, Spain, of round or oval WATTLE-AND-DAUB houses with underground storage pits and simple round- or pointed-based pottery vessels. Dated to the Middle Neolithic (5th millennium BC), it is the principal site of the Almerian culture, which includes a number of similar hilltop villages which may originally have been defended.

Elgin, Lord   (1766–1841)   a British diplomat whose removal of some of the sculpture from the PARTHENON, in part with the permission of the Turkish authorities, has been the source of much controversy. The acquisition of the sculptures by the British Museum generated a renewed interest in CLASSICAL art and in Hellenism. Elgin's collection should not be seen in isolation. It was part of a wider taste among the social elites of Europe to acquire Classical art to decorate their homes as well as to fill national museums.

El Guettar   a site in Tunisia rich in animal fossils and associated with a MOUSTERIAN-type industry of over 50% SCRAPERS, probably contemporary with the ATERIAN. The excavator claims the presence of a conical 'shrine' 75 cm high and 1.3 m across, filled with stone tools and bones, and constructed of limestone and flint spheroids.

el-Hammamiya   a site in UPPER EGYPT remarkable for its stratified settlement sequence from the BADARIAN to the GERZEAN, excavated by CATON-THOMPSON in 1924.

el-Hesy, Tell   a Palestinian site, chiefly of the MIDDLE BRONZE AGE–Iron Age, important as the site where PETRIE carried out his pioneering work on the STRATIGRAPHIC aspects of TELL sites.

El Inga   an Early PRECERAMIC site in highland Ecuador at which FLUTED stemmed FISHTAIL POINTS were located. Though not well dated in absolute terms, it is clearly a PALAEOINDIAN site, and is probably roughly contemporaneous with FELL'S CAVE, and thus one of the earliest reliably dated sites in South America.

El Juyo   a well-stratified Upper Palaeolithic cave-site near Santander, northern Spain, which is best known for its faunal evidence indicating intensive red deer hunting, probably by driving rather than stalking, during the SOLUTREAN and MAGDALENIAN phases. The Lower Magdalenian living floors have been dated to 14 440 bp. The most recent excavations, by González Echegaray and Freeman, began in 1978, and revealed a possible 'sanctuary' with a block resembling a human face.

El-Kab   a site in UPPER EGYPT on the eastern bank of the Nile, chiefly explored by a Belgian Mission since 1967. The most substantial archaeological remains at El-Kab are the massive MUD-BRICK enclosure walls of the town, whose dilapidated contents include the TEMPLE (NEW KINGDOM and LATE PERIOD) of the patron goddess of Upper Egypt, Nekhbet. In the cliffs behind the town are rock-cut tombs, the most important being of the 18th DYNASTY. El-Kab is also the type-site of the El-Kabian, a MICROLITHIC EPIPALAEOLITHIC industry, dated to c.6000 BC.

el Khiam a prehistoric site in the Judaean hills of Palestine, which gives its name to a point type characteristic of the PPNA lithic industry. The point is made of a truncated and symmetrically notched BLADELET whose tip is usually formed by marginal RETOUCH.

el-Lahun or **Kahun** an Egyptian site at the entrance to the FAIYUM, chiefly of the MIDDLE KINGDOM, excavated by PETRIE in 1887–88 and 1913. The major archaeological features of el-Lahun are the PYRAMID of SENWOSRET II, the subsidiary burial of Princess Sat-Hathor-Iunet with its rich grave-goods, the adjoining town for functionaries connected with the pyramid, and the numerous HIERATIC PAPYRI recovered from the site.

Ellerbek see ERTEBØLLE.

Elmali a town in Lycia in Turkey where painted tombs which combine both Anatolian and Greek style and iconography have been found. One tomb shows a warrior mounting a chariot and a SYMPOSIUM scene.

elm decline an episode in the POLLEN history of northwest Europe c.4000 BC marked by a significant decline in the quantity of elm pollen. Once thought the result of the activities of early farming communities, it is now attributed to disease, beetles of the kind which carry Dutch elm disease having been found in a 4th millennium context at Hampstead Heath, London.

Elmenteitan 1. a stone industry of the PASTORAL NEOLITHIC complex of early East African herders, restricted to the west side of the central Kenyan Rift Valley. It dates from about the 12th century BC to well into the 1st millennium AD, and is characterized by large double-edged OBSIDIAN BLADES, plain pottery bowls and shallow stone bowls, as well as cremation of the dead (see NJORO RIVER CAVE).
2. a Pastoral Neolithic and Iron Age pottery tradition associated with Elmenteitan stone artifacts, confined to the west side of the Kenyan Rift Valley.

El Mirador a Late PRECLASSIC site in northern Petén, Guatemala, near the Mexican border. It is one of the earliest urban centres in the Maya Lowlands, with an architectural complex perhaps larger than that of TIKAL. Its Tigre PYRAMID consists of more than 380 000 cubic metres of mud and stone, larger than many of Tikal's monuments combined. Ian Graham was the first to report on the site in the 1960s. It was joined by a causeway to nearby NAKBE, a site it rapidly eclipsed c.2300 bp, perhaps owing to a better water supply and a more defendable position.

Eloaua Island an island in the Mussau group of MELANESIA, with the two oldest LAPITA sites found in the BISMARCK ARCHIPELAGO, dated to 3450–2350 BP. One of these, ECA, is waterlogged and has extraordinary preservation of house posts and plant remains. As well as Lapita pottery, there is evidence for shell artifact manufacture and marine-oriented subsistence. OBSIDIAN from both TALASEA and LOU occurs, with the proportion of Lou obsidian increasing over time.

elouera a triangular-sectioned backed FLAKE resembling an orange segment, with use-polish from working bark and softwood along the straight edge. An element of the AUSTRALIAN SMALL TOOL TRADITION, its distribution is restricted to eastern Australia.

elouera

El Paraiso   a large ceremonial site located in the Chillón Valley of the central coast of Peru, pertaining to the Late PRECERAMIC and the INITIAL PERIOD. It comprises a central group of six or seven mounds arranged in a U-shaped configuration. In all, the site covers some 60 ha, and includes more than a dozen mounds. There is some question as to whether or not the U-shaped configuration was intentional; however, the predominance of such configurations in ensuing periods suggests that its presence in the Late Preceramic was not fortuitous. El Paraiso is the earliest of a series of large U-shaped ceremonial sites found on the central coast during the Initial Period. subsistence at the site was based on fishing, wild plants and cultivated plants. The growth of the site may have been related to increased cotton production in the region.

El Riego phase   the occupation phase from *c.*7000 to 5500 BC in Mexico's TEHUACÁN VALLEY, when the society remains one of hunter-gatherers, but three plants show evidence of some domestication. These are squash (*Cucurbita mixta*), chili peppers and avocados. They make up only a small part of the diet, however. The population in the valley at this time is estimated at three households, or 12 to 24 people.

ELSA   see EARLY LATER STONE AGE.

Elsloo   a settlement and cemetery of the LINEAR POTTERY culture in Limburg, the Netherlands, excavated by P.J.R. Modderman. The 80 houses at Elsloo could be organized into six main chronological phases, with between 11 and 17 houses in use at any one time. The cemetery is the largest Linear Pottery burial ground known, with 113 graves, 37 of which were cremations. In the inhumation burials, the bones generally were poorly preserved in the decalcified LOESS, but the grave-goods have provided important information on the Linear

155

Pottery social order. Elsloo, together with the neighbouring settlements of SITTARD, Stein and Geleen, has been the basis for discussions of variability in Linear Pottery houses, flint tools and pottery.

Elster(ian) a North European Middle PLEISTOCENE cold stage including at least one GLACIAL advance; it started *c*.450–400 000 BP and ended with the HOLSTEINIAN INTERGLACIAL, *c*.300 000 BP. The British equivalent is the Anglian cold stage (formerly known as the 'Lowestoft' glaciation); its type-site is Corton in Suffolk. The Alpine equivalent is the MINDEL glaciation, and the North American equivalent is the Kansas.

El Tajín or **Tajín** a CEREMONIAL CENTRE in north-central Veracrúz, Mexico, occupied from about AD 100 to 1200. The site shows influences from many other cultures, TEOTIHUACÁN, MAYA and 'TOLTEC', and there are also indications that the site influenced Teotihuacán, at least. The primary archaeologist at the site was José García Payón.

Els Tudons a stone-built NAVETA ('little boat') in Menorca, Spain, a communal tomb shaped like an upturned boat with rounded prow and squared stern. The entrance in the centre of a concave façade leads through an antechamber to a double-decker tomb, with the lower storey separated from the upper by a ceiling of massive stone slabs serving also as the floor of the upper chamber. Navetas were built and used in the TALAYOTIC period of the Bronze Age *c*.1500–800 BC.

eluvial horizon a SOIL HORIZON defined by its loss of soil material in solution or suspension by PEDOGENESIS. The most common eluvial horizon is the E horizon. Eluviation and leaching are the general processes by which material is removed. Compare ILLUVIAL HORIZON.

el-Wad a well-stratified prehistoric cave-site on MOUNT CARMEL, Israel, where GARROD in 1929–33 recovered an industry apparently transitional between the Middle and Upper Palaeolithic, and which includes MOUSTERIAN tool types and EMIRAN points. This is followed by AURIGNACIAN-like Upper Palaeolithic levels, ATLITIAN layers, and NATUFIAN occupation levels including over 60 burials. Compare ES-SKHUL, TABUN.

el-Yehudiyeh, Tell (*Arabic* 'Mound of the Jews') a site in the southeastern Nile DELTA, Egypt, its major feature being a rectangular enclosure of approximately 25 ha surrounded by a GLACIS, called the 'HYKSOS Camp'. Northeast of the enclosure is the site of the Jewish temple and town founded by the priest Onias in the reign of PTOLEMY VI.

emblema a small disc, often of silver, normally decorated with a scene or motif in relief. They were used to decorate the interior of bowls, to which they were attached by solder. Many appear to be HELLENISTIC in date.

emblem glyph a MAYA GLYPH (see figure) identifying a place or POLITY. Emblem glyphs were first recognized in Maya HIEROGLYPHIC writing by Heinrich Berlin in 1958. See fig. on opposite page.

Emery, Walter Bryan (1903–71) an English Egyptologist, best known for his work in THEBES (EGYPT)–WEST BANK, NUBIA (especially BUHEN and BALLANA AND QUSTUL) and SAQQARA (particularly the tombs of the ARCHAIC PERIOD).

Emiran a brief early Upper Palaeolithic industry found in the

emblem glyph Copán.

Levant region and named after the Emireh cave at the northern end of the Sea of Galilee, Israel. Emiran tool-kits include BACKED BLADES and may contain MOUSTERIAN artifact-types; this has led to suggestions that the Emiran represents a transitional industry on the Middle and Upper Palaeolithic boundary, although the possibility of contamination from an earlier archaeological occupation layer exists.

Emishi an early historical name for the farming populace of the TOHOKU region of Japan who lived outside the RITSURYO state's territorial administration. Also called Ezo and mistakenly identified with the later AINU.

Emporion see AMPURIAS.

endogamy the practice of marrying someone *within* one's own social unit, such as the clan or tribe. The opposite of EXOGAMY.

endscraper see SCRAPER.

Eneolithic or **Aeneolithic** a term used widely to refer to a period (primarily in the 4th and 3rd millennia bc) in many parts of the Near East and Europe (especially southeastern Europe), when COPPER METALLURGY was in the process of being adopted by cultures which were otherwise essentially 'Neolithic' in character. The Eneolithic is also sometimes called the *Chalcolithic* (particularly in the Near East) and the *Copper Age*. North and west of the Carpathians, chronological nomenclature rarely includes this term, instead moving directly from the 'Late Neolithic' to the 'Early Bronze Age'.

Engaruka an IRON AGE site in northern Tanzania with remains of an elaborate and extensive irrigation system built mainly after the 14th century AD.

Enki or **Ea** the third (with AN and ENLIL) of the great SUMERIAN gods, associated with sweet water and purification. (Ea was his AKKADIAN name.) This god organized the world and created humanity, often interceding with the other gods on behalf of humanity. His prominent characteristics were cunning and moderate counsel, and in many myths he takes the role of trickster. Enki had a close association with the city of ERIDU, the first created city of Sumer.

Enkomi the site of a major CYPRIOT settlement in eastern Cyprus. Excavations at Enkomi began in 1890 and continued until 1974. The site, which was first occupied in the 17th century BC, profited from the COPPER trade. The ores were brought from the mines in the interior, SMELTED in the town and then exported. By the 14th century, Enkomi was clearly one of the most powerful and prosperous settlements on Cyprus and may have been ALASHIYA, the ancient capital. *Circa* 1200 BC, however, the site was destroyed, possibly by the SEA

PEOPLES. Subsequently, massive CYCLOPEAN fortifications were constructed and the town was rebuilt on a grid plan. There is fine ASHLAR architecture, in particular the sanctuary of the Horned God. Eventually, *c*.1050 BC, Enkomi was abandoned in favour of SALAMIS.

Enlène   see VOLP CAVES.

Enlil   the chief god in the SUMERIAN pantheon, who replaced his father AN in this role. He represents the ambivalent force of the wind and storms, bringing both life and destruction. In the latter aspect, Enlil was responsible for the great FLOOD that almost destroyed humanity, having become annoyed with all the noise that the mortals made. Enlil's seat was in NIPPUR, which formed the ideological centre of Sumer.

en-Nasbeh, Tell   a Palestinian site, probably the biblical Mizpah, excavated by Bade from 1926–35. It was a major settlement of the early Iron Age, comprising an ISRAELITE town defended by a massive wall and well-preserved gateway. Tell en-Nasbeh has produced an important corpus of Israelite pottery from the TELL and its adjacent tombs.

Ensérune   an OPPIDUM in Hérault, France, founded in the 6th century BC, replanned in the 4th century as a carefully ordered town of stone buildings arranged along roadways. A stone-built rampart enclosed both the town and a cemetery area to its west. This consisted of inurned burials, sometimes in imported Italian vessels. A further major reconstruction was undertaken in *c*.200 BC, when the cemetery was built over and a local script, based on Greek but hitherto undeciphered, came into use.

entablature   the horizontal element of a CLASSICAL building between the column CAPITALS and the PEDIMENT or roof. In the DORIC ORDER it comprises the ARCHITRAVE above which were placed the alternating TRIGLYPHS and METOPES. In the IONIC ORDER a continuous frieze was placed above the architrave.

entasis   a Greek architectural technique of exaggerating the curvature of a column shaft of buildings of the DORIC ORDER to give the optical illusion of straight sides.

Entremont   an OPPIDUM in Bouches-du-Rhône, France, of roughly triangular plan with a drystone defensive wall of the 3rd century BC punctuated by projecting rectangular towers. Within the oppidum, dry-stone houses are arranged along a grid-plan street layout. A shrine near the centre of the settlement had human skulls nailed to the wall including one with a javelin in it; there were also sculptures depicting piles of human heads. Entremont had close trade contacts with the Greek colony of MARSEILLES (Massalia), but was destroyed in the Roman conquest of Provence in *c*.125 BC.

environmental archaeology   a subfield of archaeology where the aim is to identify processes, factors and conditions of past biological and physical environmental systems and how they relate to cultural systems. It has been enveloped in the last decade by the broader contextual archaeology which aims at determining the dynamic interrelationships between environment and culture by focusing on and evaluating CONTEXT.

eolian   see AEOLIAN.

eolith   a naturally shaped or fractured stone believed by early antiquarians to be the oldest known artifact type, dating to the pre-

Palaeolithic era. It is now accepted that eoliths are not human-made. See HARRISON.

Epano Englianos   see PYLOS.

Ephesus   a major port on the west coast of Turkey. British excavations in 1869 located the temple of Artemis (*Artemision*), and subsequent work by the Austrians has uncovered many of the important public buildings. The ARCHAIC temple in the IONIC ORDER provides a TERMINUS ANTE QUEM for the use of coinage as a hoard of electrum coins was found in the foundation deposit. The temple, one of the SEVEN WONDERS, was burnt in 356 BC and Alexander the Great initiated its reconstruction. The bases of the columns were decorated with reliefs. Several GYMNASIA have been uncovered including that of Publius Vedius Antoninus dedicated to Artemis and the emperor Antoninus Pius. The theatre, which belongs to the HELLENISTIC period, could have seated some 24 000 people. Nearby the Celsus Library, constructed in AD 110, has been reconstructed; it also served as a tomb. The public administrative buildings have been excavated in the vicinity of the so-called State AGORA.

Epicardial   an Early Neolithic pottery style of *c*.5300–4600 BC, developed from and succeeding the CARDIAL style in southern France. Decoration using the edge of a *Cardium* shell is replaced by incised decoration as the dominant mode, with great diversity of regional and local variants.

Epidauros   a Greek sanctuary of the healing god Asklepios in the Peloponnese. One of the best-preserved monuments is the theatre, which would have seated some 14 000 people. In addition to the temple, there were numerous buildings associated with the cult, including a STADIUM.

Epigravettian   a term given to the late GLACIAL industries of Italy, and divided into early (20–16 000 bp), evolved (16–14 000 bp) and final phases; the latter lasts until *c*.8000 bp, evolving into the MESOLITHIC, and is followed by the SAUVETERRIAN and CASTELNOVIAN in the 7th millennium.

Epipalaeolithic   a term used for the final Upper PALAEOLITHIC industries occurring at the end of the final GLACIATION which appear to merge technologically into the MESOLITHIC. See AHRENSBURGIAN, HAMBURGIAN, AZILIAN. The term Epipalaeolithic is occasionally used instead of Mesolithic, but in the Levant it denotes the period from *c*.20 000 to 10 000 BP (see KEBARAN).

epiphysis   the articulating end of a long bone. Compare DIAPHYSIS.

Epi-Pietersburg   a southern African HOWIESONS POORT-like MIDDLE STONE AGE industry which succeeds the PIETERSBURG. At BORDER CAVE it is associated with RADIOCARBON dates in excess of 49 000 years and is considered to date to some 80 000 years ago.

Episkopi-Phaneromeni   the site of a Middle-Late CYPRIOT settlement in southern Cyprus, occupied *c*.1600–1500 BC, and a Middle Cypriot CHAMBER TOMB cemetery excavated by Carpenter in 1975–78.

epistemology   that element of scientific reasoning that evaluates the veracity of what is known.

ER 1470   see KOOBI FORA.

Érd   a Middle Palaeolithic open-air site located near Budapest in central Hungary. Artifacts and faunal remains are buried in LOESS deposited in limestone hollows that may have served as carnivore dens. CAVE BEAR predominates heavily among the faunal remains, which in general suggest human occupation prior to the LAST GLACIAL. The tools are chiefly composed of SCRAPERS. Érd was excavated by Gábori–Csánk in 1963–64.

Erebuni   see KARMIR-BLUR.

Erechtheion   a temple on the Athenian AKROPOLIS to the north of the PARTHENON serving the cult of Erechtheus, a legendary king of ATHENS. It was built in the IONIC ORDER, construction starting in 421 BC. It housed several different cults, in addition to that of Erechtheus, and contained the old cult-statue of Athena. The CARYATID porch projected over the ruined foundations of an earlier temple perhaps to allow continuity of the cult on the site.

Erevan Cave   a Middle Palaeolithic site on the Razdan River in Erevan, Armenia. Artifacts were found at most levels in a sequence of LOAM and rubble; associated faunal remains include rhinoceros, horse, elk and red deer. The age of the occupations is unknown, but they apparently occurred during cool climatic conditions. The artifacts include many sidescrapers (see SCRAPER). Erevan Cave was excavated by Eritsyan in the late 1960s.

Eridu or **Abu Shahrain**   the TELL-site at Abu Shahrain that has been identified as ancient Eridu, the oldest city in southern MESOPOTAMIA, according to SUMERIAN mythology. The excavations by F. Safar and S. Lloyd in the 1940s revealed a long sequence of 'UBAID period occupation and provided the ceramic definition of the 'Ubaid 1 (Eridu) phase. Eridu is best known for the sequence of 'Ubaid and URUK period temples, which documents the development of the tripartite arrangement of monumental architecture typical of these periods. This sequence begins with a small room fitted with an altar (levels XVII–XVI), after which occur increasingly large multi-roomed buildings set on platforms. In this sequence, levels XI–VIII belong to the 'Ubaid 3, and levels VII–VI to the 'Ubaid 4 period; the subsequent levels (V–I) belong to the Uruk period. The usual identification of the buildings at Eridu as temples (and the comparable structures at WARKA, GAWRA and elsewhere) has recently been challenged by several French scholars, who interpret the large tripartite buildings on platforms as elite residences or, more plausibly, as audience halls, thus giving very different social implications to this architectural tradition. Other aspects of the 'Ubaid levels at Eridu include a large cemetery ('Ubaid 4 in date) and exposures of often flimsy residential architecture (in the 'Hut Sounding'). By the end of the 'Ubaid period, the Eridu settlement covered roughly 12 ha, making it one of the largest known 'Ubaid towns. Architecture of the 3rd millennium is present nearer the surface, including an EARLY DYNASTIC palace (one of the few excavated so far) and a ZIGGURAT of the UR III period.

Erim, Kenan (1921–90)   a Turkish archaeologist who first worked in Sicily. His extensive excavations at APHRODISIAS started in 1961, and it is fitting that he was buried there.

Erimi-Bamboula   a deeply stratified site of the 4th millennium BC in southern Cyprus. It was excavated by Dikaios in 1973 and is the type-site for the CHALCOLITHIC I Erimi culture which is characterized by Red-on-White pottery. The settlement consisted of circular huts built of WATTLE AND DAUB on stone foundations. The dead were buried INTRAMURALLY.

Er Lannic an islet in the Morbihan, France, with remains of two Neolithic STONE CIRCLES, now partly submerged by the rise in sea level. Associated material comprises stone-built cists or hearths, polished stone axes and much pottery, including 162 decorated vase-supports. These may be remains of a cemetery which preceded the stone circles.

Erligang [Erh-li-kang] see ZHENGZHOU, SHANG.

Erlitou [Erh-li-t'ou] a site in Henan Province, China, where HANGTU foundations for two palace compounds have been excavated. Some assign the remains to the legendary XIA Dynasty, though they are included in pre-dynastic SHANG by others (see CHINESE DYNASTIES). The four bronze JUE vessels discovered there are the earliest examples of the Shang bronze-casting tradition in piece-moulds. It is the type-site for the Erlitou culture of the HUANGHE corridor in the early 2nd millennium BC.

Erosd see ARIUŞD.

erosion a group of processes involving the physical breakdown or chemical solution, removal, and transportation of materials by the actions of water, wind and ice. Erosion is capable of disrupting the CONTEXT of archaeological deposits by total or partial site destruction, burial or redistribution. Some erosional processes are accelerated by the activites of people on the LANDSCAPE, such as cultivation and deforestation. Some forms of erosion that can have significant impact on the archaeological record are:
  (a) SOIL erosion – accelerated downslope removal of soil material by various processes; more effective during heavier rainstorms, and on ground with little vegetation cover; main processes are:
      (i) rainsplash erosion or raindrop erosion – direct dislodgement of material by raindrop impact and secondary displacement of larger CLASTS by undermining
      (ii) sheetwash or sheetflood erosion – removal and downslope transportation of soil material by the action of a thin sheet of water; incorporates material displaced by rainsplash erosion as well as effecting its own erosion through forces operating at the base of the sheetflow
      (iii) rill erosion – development of small channels only centimetres wide and deep at the base of sheet flows as they become locally concentrated.
  (b) GULLY erosion – in stream valleys or on HILLSLOPES, gullies lengthen by upvalley migration.
  (c) wind erosion – removal of material by the wind; most effective where winds are strong, vegetation is sparse and soil moisture is lacking; main types are:
      (i) deflation – loose material winnowed, picked up and carried by the wind as the wind's driving force overcomes the forces binding the particles; may create localized SAND BLOWS or scour broad areas.
      (ii) abrasion – loosening and removal of material by the impact of material already picked up by the wind.

Ertebølle culture the final MESOLITHIC coastal KITCHEN MIDDEN culture of Scandinavia and the western Baltic, (equivalent to the north German *Ellerbek*) named after the type-site, a coastal SHELL MOUND in Jutland, Denmark, which is dated to c.3900–3250 BC. The assemblages contain introduced Neolithic artifacts, pottery and polished stone axes, while remaining Mesolithic in character although with relatively few MICROLITHS.

escarpment or **scarp** a LANDFORM consisting of a steep slope marking an abrupt change in altitude between two adjacent land surfaces. Escarpments mark geomorphic discontinuities that are usually accompanied by STRATIGRAPHIC and PEDOLOGICAL discontinuities as well. Vegetation can vary greatly on either side of an escarpment, and large-scale cliffs can be barriers to migration.

Eshnunna see ASMAR.

Esh Shaheinab the type-site for the KHARTOUM NEOLITHIC in the Sudan, containing bones of domestic stock dated by one of the first RADIOCARBON dates to 5300 bp.

Eskimo the aboriginal inhabitants of the Arctic regions of North America, characterized by great uniformity in culture, language and physical stock. Internal divisions of the Eskimo are based either on geographical location or on particular adaptive TRAITS. The term 'Eskimo' is a derogatory Algonkin word that means 'eater of raw flesh'. The Eskimo call themselves INUIT.

Esna a site in UPPER EGYPT, chiefly known for the surviving HYPOSTYLE HALL of the TEMPLE to the ram-headed god Khnum, started at least as early as the joint reigns of PTOLEMIES VI and VIII (170–164 BC), but decorated mainly by Roman emperors of the 1st–3rd centuries AD. The MIDDLE KINGDOM to early NEW KINGDOM cemetery at Esna was excavated by GARSTANG in 1905–06.

ESR see ELECTRON SPIN RESONANCE.

Es–Skhul a cave in the Israeli MOUNT CARMEL complex which has yielded NATUFIAN, Upper Palaeolithic and LEVALLOISO-MOUSTERIAN occupation levels, and the remains of at least seven adults and three children dated to *c*.100 000 BP by ESR. Once thought to be NEANDERTHALERS, they are now seen as morphologically modern, perhaps ancestral to European CRO-MAGNONS. Compare TABUN, QAFZEH.

Estaquería a MIDDLE HORIZON site in the Nasca Valley of the south coast of Peru. The site includes a large rectangular area in which there originally stood 12 rows of 20 upright posts, some over 50 cm in diameter. Excavated in 1926 by Alfred KROEBER, it also includes a rectilinear ADOBE compound, and it is surrounded by large cemeteries. The site may have served a ceremonial function.

etched carnelian beads South Asian carnelian beads with a decoration obtained by heating them, after a design in an alkali or metallic oxide paste has been painted on the surface; the paste design then stands out as a white or black pattern against the dull red of the stone. Developed by the Mature HARAPPAN period, the technique continues into modern times, and such beads may be widely traded, as the Harappan examples from Iranian and MESOPOTAMIAN sites illustrate.

ethnoarchaeology the study of human behaviour, and of the MATERIAL CULTURE of living societies, in order to see how materials enter the archaeological record, and hence to provide hypotheses explaining the production, use and disposal patterns of ancient material culture. Ethnoarchaeological studies, one type of ACTUALISTIC STUDY, gained importance under the NEW ARCHAEOLOGY as the need for WARRANTING ARGUMENTS in interpreting the archaeological record was stressed. It is a tool to develop MIDDLE RANGE THEORY, linking human behaviour with the archaeological record. See also TAPHONOMY.

ethnographic parallel   a contemporary culture or particular behaviour that, by the process of ANALOGY and HOMOLOGY, is thought to be similar to archaeologically recognizable behaviour and so can provide insights on the latter.

ethnography   the description and analysis of individual contemporary cultures, using anthropological techniques such as participant observation (whereby the anthropologist lives in the society being studied) and a reliance on informants (individuals from whom specialized cultural knowledge is sought). Ethnography has provided many data of use to the archaeologist through reliance on ANALOGY and HOMOLOGY. See ETHNOLOGY.

ethnology   the use of ETHNOGRAPHIC data in a comparative analysis to understand how CULTURES work and why they change.

ethology   the study of animal behaviour, which provides hypotheses for explaining human behaviour. See PALAEOECONOMY.

Etiolles   an extensive MAGDALENIAN open-air site lying close to the River Seine, 30 km south of Paris, France. Excavated by Y. Taborin, it has 26 recognized *in situ* domestic units from successive occupations, including HEARTHS and FLINT KNAPPING areas. Dating to 12 000 bp, the site is remarkable for the extreme abundance of its flint and DÉBITAGE.

Etowah   a large TEMPLE MOUND site in Georgia, USA. It comprises three individual mounds, the largest of which is over 20 m high, and is surpassed in volume only by CAHOKIA. It was perhaps a centre for the SOUTHERN CULT. See MISSISSIPPIAN.

Etruria   the area to the north of ROME bounded by the rivers Tiber and Arno and the Tyrrhenian Sea. The inhabitants of the area, the Etruscans, colonized areas as far away as ALERIA, the Po Valley (see SPINA) and parts of CAMPANIA. The area is rich in mineral resources which led to a wide range of metal products including gold, iron and bronze. The dead were buried in extensive cemeteries either in underground tombs or under TUMULI (see CERVETERI). They were accompanied by a wide range of funerary goods, and the tombs themselves are an important source for ATHENIAN POTTERY. The walls of the tombs, especially at TARQUINIA, were decorated with a wide range of painted figured scenes. See also ETRUSCAN POTTERY.

Etruscan pottery   pottery produced at various centres in ETRURIA, especially during the ARCHAIC and CLASSICAL periods. Although plain wares were particularly common (see BUCCHERO, IMPASTO), figure-decorated pottery was also produced (see CAERETAN WARE, PONTIC WARE).

eustasy   changes in sea-level on a worldwide basis. The main factors that influence sea-level are global ice volumes, plate tectonics, changes in ocean volumes and dimensions, and movement of mantle material. During the GLACIAL-INTERGLACIAL cycles of the QUATERNARY, sea levels fell as oceans were depleted of water and ice sheets grew, and rose as glaciers melted returning the stored water to the ocean basins. Continental configurations were changed both by alternating exposure of land, making human and animal occupation and migration possible altering coastal environments, and by flooding of land, subjecting any cultural remains to submarine erosional and depositional processes. Compare ISOSTASY.

eustatic, *adj.*   pertaining to vertical changes in worldwide sea level. See EUSTASY.

Eutresis   a settlement site in Boeotia, Greece, which was excavated by Goldman in 1924–27 and by CASKEY in 1958. Eutresis was first occupied in the later Neolithic period and appears to have been inhabited continuously until the 13th century BC, when it was extensively fortified. Subsequently abandoned, the site was reoccupied in the CLASSICAL and HELLENISTIC periods. Eutresis is especially important because of its sequence of Early HELLADIC levels and is the type-site for the Early Helladic I Eutresis culture.

Evans, Sir Arthur (1851–1941)   a British scholar and archaeologist whose major contribution to Greek archaeology was his excavation of the MINOAN palace at KNOSSOS from 1899 onwards. It was Evans who first identified this early Cretan civilization and named it after the legendary King Minos.

Evans, Clifford (1920–81)   an American pioneer of Amazonian archaeology, together with his wife and partner, Betty Meggers. Affiliated with the Smithsonian Institution since 1951, Evans and Meggers conducted research in Ecuador, Venezuela, British Guiana and Brazil, and provided the chronology and cultural definitions of prehistoric cultures of the northern Amazonian region.

evolution   a theory of biology developed by Charles Darwin, whereby an organism's degree of adaptation to the environment determines its chances of surviving, and thus successfully creating offspring and passing on its genes to the next generation. The MODEL was first used by anthropology in the 19th century to explain the progressive and unilinear development of human societies from 'savagery' to 'civilization'; however, it was later rejected at the end of that century, largely as a result of work by Franz Boas and other anthropologists, because of its explicitly racist overtones. The work of Leslie WHITE and Julian STEWARD succeeded in reintroducing evolutionary models to anthropology and archaeology, and neo-evolutionary thought remains one of the major principles of NEW or PROCESSUAL ARCHAEOLOGY.

excavation   the systematic recovery of archaeological data through the exposure of buried SITES and artifacts. Excavation is destructive to any site, and is thus accompanied by a comprehensive recording of all material found and its three-dimensional locations. As much material and information as possible must be recovered from any 'dig'. A full record of all the techniques employed in the excavation itself must also be made, so that future archaeologists will be able to evaluate the results of the work accurately. Excavation is also costly. For both these reasons, it should be used only as a last resort. Excavation can be either partial, in which only a sample of the site is investigated, or total. Samples are chosen either intuitively, in which case excavators investigate those areas they feel will be most productive, or statistically, in which case the sample is drawn using various statistical techniques in order to ensure that it is representative. An important goal of excavation is a full understanding of a site's STRATIGRAPHY, which refers to the vertical layering of a site. These

LAYERS, or levels, can be defined naturally (e.g. SOIL changes), cultur-ally (e.g. different occupation levels) or arbitrarily (e.g. 10 cm levels). See SURVEY.

exchange   a system which facilitates the transfer of goods and services between societies and/or individuals. Exchange systems can vary in size and complexity from individual, one-off bartering to complex market economies employing standardized currencies.

exogamy   the practice of marrying someone *outside* one's own social unit, such as the clan or tribe. The opposite of ENDOGAMY.

experimental archaeology   the controlled replication of ancient technologies and behaviour, in order to provide hypotheses that can be tested by actual archaeological data. Experiments can range in size from the reproduction of ancient TOOLS in order to learn about their processes of manufacture and use, to the construction of whole villages and ancient SUBSISTENCE practices in long-term experiments.

extramural   See INTRAMURAL.

Eyasi   a locality in northern Tanzania with fauna, including extinct mammal species, artifacts and archaic HOMO *sapiens* remains. It was formerly thought to be of the late PLEISTOCENE age, but is now con-sidered to date to the late Middle Pleistocene.

Eynan, Ain Mallaha or **Ein Mallaha**   an extensive NATUFIAN open-air fishing settlement next to Lake Huleh in the Jordan valley, Israel. Jean Perrot's excavations (1955–79) revealed three successive occupations, which contained perhaps 50 semi-subterranean stone-lined circular structures, 3–9 m in diameter, and often containing internal HEARTHS and storage bins. Large storage pits and burials lie outside the structures: one 10th millennium bc burial contained an old woman (?) with a puppy, but the best-known burial is that of a male and female found with their legs removed in an elaborately paved and walled round tomb. There is some evidence for collective burial after decomposition. In addition to its lithic industries Eynan also has a rich bone tool industry, bone and stone artwork, and stone vessels.

Ezero   an ENEOLITHIC and Early Bronze Age cultural complex of the lower Danube basin and the Black Sea coast of Bulgaria, named after the TELL site at Ezero in central Bulgaria. The Ezero sequence provides the most detailed chronology for southeastern Europe from the end of the Eneolithic into the Early Bronze Age. Early and Mid-dle Ezero are contemporaneous with BADEN in central Europe, and the intensification of sheep/goat husbandry at Ezero is taken as sup-port for the SECONDARY PRODUCTS REVOLUTION. The Early Bronze Age level at Ezero is fortified with a stone wall.

Ezo   see EMISHI.

F

Faboura a vast accumulation of *Arca senelis* bivalve shells covering over 7 ha and up to 8 m high, southeast of Joal in Senegal, dated to between 1900–1300 BP and linked to the local Manding people.

fabricator a stone or bone used in the manufacture of other tools. The term is usually applied to MESOLITHIC *plano-convex* (i.e. one side flat, one rounded) slug-shaped stone tools used in RETOUCH.

facies a part that is distinguished from the whole of a recognized unit on some basis of appearance or composition. Originally developed for geological applications, such as LITHOFACIES and bio-facies, the facies concept has been widely applied, including PEDO-LOGY (SOIL facies) and archaeology (to a CULTURE or INDUSTRY).

faience a material used in ancient Egypt, the Near East and the Aegean for GLAZED figurines and jewellery. It consists of a body of quartz sand, soda and lime, covered by a soda-lime glaze which is usually coloured green or greenish-blue but can be polychrome.

Faiyum a fertile depression in the Egyptian Sahara, watered by an arm of the River Nile. Important during the Neolithic (see FAIYUM 'A'), but largely undeveloped by the ancient Egyptians except during the MIDDLE KINGDOM (see HAWARA, QASR ES-SAGHA) and during the Graeco-Roman Period (see KARANIS).

Faiyum 'A' the earliest-known phase of the PREDYNASTIC sequence of LOWER EGYPT, represented by the (possibly seasonal) settlement sites in the northern FAIYUM explored by Gardner and CATON-THOMPSON in 1924–26. Although agriculturalists, the population of Faiyum 'A' were largely dependent on the hunting of large mammals such as elephant and hippopotamus.

Fajada Butte a geological feature in CHACO CANYON, New Mexico, USA, on which is located the 'sun-dagger'. This comprises two vertical slabs of rock, through which, at the summer and winter solstices, sunlight falls onto carved spiral designs. The site has been interpreted by some as a solar observatory, but others question this function.

false colour infrared photography a photographic technique, utilizing film sensitive to infrared wavelengths, that achieves greater resolution of certain features than conventional photography because the wavelengths are unaffected by atmospheric haze and the photographic images are not represented by true colours. Differences in water absorption qualities of photographed features are also enhanced; contrasts between SOIL and SEDIMENT of different TEXTURES, different vegetation, and the difference between vegetation and soil are sharp.

False colour infrared photography can be used for on- and off-site soil and geomorphic mapping to help construct the geological CON-TEXT of sites. Archaeological FEATURES of contrasting texture and earthworks may also be expressed.

false-necked amphora see STIRRUP JAR.

Fat'janovo culture or **Fatyanovo culture**   a regional culture on the northeastern edge of the broader CORDED WARE complex, named after the cemetery of Fat'janovo near Yaroslavl on the upper Volga in central Russia. Fat'janovo graves are shallow shafts with no burial mounds. Vessels buried with the dead include spherical AMPHORAE with cord decoration, and Fat'janovo 'battleaxes' have distinctive drooping blades. The Fat'janovo culture appears to have been long-lived, lasting into the early part of the Bronze Age.

faunal analysis   see ARCHAEOZOOLOGY.

Fauresmith,   an outdated term for final ACHEULIAN collections from the southern African interior, characterized by small well-finished pointed HANDAXES.

feature   a nonportable element of a larger SITE. Examples include fire-hearths, interior walls and ACTIVITY AREAS.

Federmesser   a small BACKED BLADE, very similar to the AZILIAN POINT, that characterizes the Final GLACIAL industries of the North European Plain in the 10th/9th millennia bc, and the CRESWELLIAN culture of Britain.

Fell's Cave   an Early PRECERAMIC (PALAEOINDIAN) site (9050 and 8770 bc) in Chile, near the southern tip of South America, at which FLUTED stemmed FISHTAIL POINTS were found by Junius BIRD. The tools were found in a sealed deposit, associated with extinct late PLEISTOCENE fauna. (See EL INGA).

fen   a wetlands community, characterized by alkaline conditions, that grows in zones between fresh water and land, such as along lake margins, and rapidly evolves during a transition of infilling and shallowing. As with other types of BOG, fens are locations where preservation of organic material is good, thus providing an excellent source of PALAEOENVIRONMENTAL and artifactual information.

Fengate   a complex of farmsteads in England, associated with small square fields and droveways or tracks on the edge of the Cambridgeshire Fens, dating from the Middle Neolithic to the end of the Middle Bronze Age. Occupation resumed in the Early Iron Age with a new layout of fields and a larger settlement, the Cat's Water village, with remains of over 50 buildings of which about 10 would have been in use at once.

Fengbitou [Feng-pi-t'ou]   a site on the southwestern coast of Taiwan which gives its name to the Fengbitou Neolithic culture of western Taiwan, dated to 2400–1800 BC.

Ferrières-les-Verreries   a Late Neolithic DOLMEN in Hérault, France, type-site of the Ferrières culture (*c.*3200–2800 BC), characterized by pottery decorated with incised lines and geometric motifs.

fibula   a pin with a catch used from the Bronze Age to the ANGLO-SAXON period. Fibulae may be highly decorated and are normally made of bronze although examples are known in precious metal. They seem to have been used for fastening clothing.

ficron   a morphological term generally used to describe a long pointed BIFACE with slightly concave sides and a well-made tip. BORDES specifically used the term to denote a roughly worked pointed biface, the probable forerunner of the MICOQUIAN biface form.

Fikellura ware   a style of ARCHAIC EAST GREEK POTTERY using a

BLACK-FIGURED technique. The name is derived from the Fikellura cemetery on Rhodes where many examples of the fabric have been found. The fabric had at one time been attributed to Samos and Rhodes on stylistic grounds, but recent CLAY analyses have demonstrated that the source was in fact MILETUS.

filigree a technique used in the manufacture of jewellery whereby wire, usually gold or electrum, more rarely silver, is soldered onto metalwork.

Filimoshki a PLEISTOCENE open-air locality on the Zeya River (Amur tributary) in far eastern Siberia, that yielded flaked QUARTZITE cobbles of possible human manufacture. The modified cobbles were recovered from ALLUVIUM of the second TERRACE in 1961 by OKLADNIKOV, who classified them as Lower Palaeolithic tools. However, their age and status as artifacts remain problematic.

Filitosa a fortified promontory settlement in Corsica, France, dominated by a Bronze Age *torre* or tower, the Corsican equivalent of the Sardinian NURAGHE. The origins of the Corsican torri lie at the CHALCOLITHIC or Early Bronze Age *c.*2500–2000 BC. The Filitosa example is a circular dry-stone tower standing within a walled enclosure with oval houses. It dates probably from the middle of the 2nd millennium and incorporates in its construction a number of re-used STATUES-MENHIRS of men armed with bronze swords and daggers.

Final Neolithic a transitional phase in which there is some use of COPPER or BRONZE but stone is still predominant. See also ENEOLITHIC.

fine orange pottery a Late CLASSIC pottery type from the lowland MAYA area of MESOAMERICA, found at sites under the influence of TEOTIHUACÁN. The TEMPERless pottery comes from the region of the Usumacinta drainage near the Gulf Coast. The appearance of the pottery at such sites as ALTAR DE SACRIFICIOS and SEIBAL suggests a foreign influence in these centres during Late Classic times.

Fiorelli, Giuseppe (1823–96) one of the early directors of the excavations at POMPEII in 1860–75. The previous haphazard diggings, essentially in search of treasure and *objets d'art* to be placed on display in royal palaces, were replaced by a systematic strategy. He devised a scheme for dividing the city up into regions. He also developed a technique for taking plaster casts of the hollows in the hardened ASH and cinders, thus gaining impressions of the dead and other organic material such as that used in furniture.

fire see SWARTKRANS, CHESOWANJA.

fire hardening the exposure of a wooden tool to fire in order to dry out the wood but not to char it, which makes the tool harder and therefore more efficient. See LEHRINGEN.

Fishbourne the site of a substantial palace near Chichester (*Lat.* Noviomagus Regnensium) in England, excavated in the 1960s by the Sussex Archaeological Society under Barry Cunliffe. It started as a coastal depot with granaries to serve the Roman invasion. This was replaced by a residential structure with a bath-house, followed in *c.*AD 75 by the extensive building, covering some 4 ha. The building was decorated with MOSAICS, STUCCO mouldings and painted wall plaster. The central square was laid out as a formal garden.

fish-hooks (*Pacific***)** artifacts of two basic types: *bait* hooks, for angling; and *lure* hooks, for towing behind a moving canoe. They may be made of shell, bone, stone, tortoise shell or wood. They are extremely varied in form, especially in Eastern POLYNESIA, and act as temporal and cultural markers in the region.

fishtail point   the most distinctive artifact of a stone tool tradition of South America, dating to *c.*11 000 to 8000 bc. The points are FLUTED and stemmed, having a roughly fish-like outline. The complex shows technical similarities to the CLOVIS tradition of North America, and thus represents the PALAEOINDIAN period in South America.

0   5 cm

fishtail point

fission track dating   a radiogenic dating method based on the natural and spontaneous nuclear fission of Uranium 238 and its physical product, linear atomic displacements (tracks) created along the trajectory of released energized fission fragments. Knowing the rate of fission, which is a constant, the uranium content of the material, and the number of fission tracks by counting, one can determine the age of the material. The method is most widely used to date TEPHRA BEDS and OBSIDIAN, with the tracks in glass and accessory zircon being counted. Archaeological samples such as pottery and obsidian must have been heated to anneal any previous tracks that would date the constituent mineral but not ARTIFACT. Accuracy, minimum age determinations and datable materials all depend on ^{238}U concentrations.

Five Mile Rapids site   see DALLES.

Flag Fen   a Late Bronze Age settlement of long rectangular timber houses on an artificial timber platform in the Cambridgeshire fens, England. The timbers had been laid on the mud of the fen bottom in about half a metre of water. The island was reached by a timber trackway from the mainland at FENGATE. The settlement, excavated by F. Pryor, was occupied *c.*1000–700 BC, and associated artifacts include flint tools, a bronze dagger, a bracelet of Kimmeridge shale, pottery, and wooden items.

flake   a sliver of stone removed from a CORE during KNAPPING, either as a planned artifact or as a waste by-product. See fig. overleaf. Flakes may be RETOUCHED to make a *flake tool*, or may be used in an unmodified state. Waste flakes are those discarded during the manufacture of a tool. See BLADE, BULB OF PERCUSSION, DÉBITAGE.

flint   a member of the CHALCEDONY group of water-bearing silica

striking platform

point of percussion

bulb of percussion

bulbar scar

fissures

rings *or* waves

flake

minerals characterized by its opaqueness and dark colour, the result of included organic matter. Flint normally occurs in nodules. Its ability to fracture conchoidally made it ideal for fashioning stone implements with sharp edges. The best-known flint is from the chalk in England and Northern Europe. See CHERT, GRIMES GRAVES, KRZEMIONKI, SPIENNES, CHOCOLATE FLINT.

floating chronology   a chronometrically dated chronology that is not anchored to precise time from the present, usually used in reference to DENDROCHRONOLOGY and VARVE chronologies.

flood   a universal deluge, notions of which occur not only in the Old Testament but also in SUMERIAN and AKKADIAN texts. The SUMERIAN KING LISTS make the distinction between ante-diluvian and post-diluvian rulers. WOOLLEY's deep soundings at UR exposed a level of major flooding, and similar levels have been observed at KISH and Shuruppak to the north; such deposits reflect the shifting of river courses in southern MESOPOTAMIA.

floodplain   a depositional LANDFORM comprising that portion of a river valley subject to flooding. As flood waters recede, the suspended SEDIMENT load is deposited as ALLUVIUM and causes slow vertical accretion. Floodplains are usually an amalgam of secondary features including individual flood basins that may support swamps and marshes, abandoned channels, secondary flood channels, tributary stream courses, and NATURAL LEVEES. With a variety of secondary landforms, floodplains can be a diverse and rich resource base. Because of the intermittent addition of organic nutrient-rich alluvium, floodplains were and are prime agricultural land. Aggradation also may cause burial and preservation of archaeological deposits in many of these subenvironments. Conversely, stream channel migration may erode large tracts of floodplain and any archaeological deposits buried below or resting upon the floodplain.

Florisbad   a spring deposit in the central Orange Free State, South Africa, which has yielded archaic HOMO *sapiens* remains thought to date to the late Middle PLEISTOCENE, as well as MIDDLE STONE AGE remains.

fluorine dating a RELATIVE DATING technique applied to bone. Bone absorbs fluorine from groundwaters at a rate that is proportional to the time since burial, if groundwater migration rates remain constant. Fluorine concentrations are determined by CHEMICAL ANALYSIS.

fluted point a point belonging to the early part of the PALAEOINDIAN period characterized by extreme symmetry, careful flaking and the removal of a long, parallel and shallow FLAKE, or flute, from one or both sides of the point. The technology is peculiar to the New World, and is associated with the CLOVIS and FOLSOM point styles.

fluxgate gradiometer see MAGNETOMETER.

focus see MIDWESTERN TAXONOMIC SYSTEM

fogou see SOUTERRAIN.

Folsom **1.** a PALAEOINDIAN, FLUTED POINT type that differs from CLOVIS mainly in the length of its flute, which extends over most of the point's side. The date range for the point type is approximately 11 000–10 200 BP.

2. a COMPLEX associated with the point type, characterized by a concentration on the hunting of now extinct bison, as well as a specific LITHIC ASSEMBLAGE. The most representative Folsom complex site is LINDENMEIER.

3. the type-site in New Mexico, USA, where 19 points were found associated with the remains of 23 extinct bison, close to a relict marsh.

Folsom Point.

Fontanalba see MONT BÉGO.

Fontbouisse a CHALCOLITHIC settlement in Gard, France, of drystone houses with APSIDAL ends, type-site of the Fontbouisse culture (c.2800–2200 BC) also represented at the villages of Cambous and La Conquette, and the enclosed sites of BOUSSARGUES and LÉBOUS. Burial was in simple MEGALITHIC tombs or natural caves in the vicinity of the settlements, though INTRAMURAL burials of very young children are known. Fontbouisse pottery is characterized by complex incised and channelled decoration, and the region's earliest COPPER objects are sometimes found.

Fontbrégoua a cave site in Var, southern France, with a 10 m sequence of EPIPALAEOLITHIC and Neolithic occupation. The earliest levels c.8000 BC have yielded evidence of hunting and gathering including carbonized hazelnuts and plant remains. The Early Neolithic levels have domestic livestock and pottery and span the CARDIAL and EPICARDIAL phases. Above are deposits with Middle Neolithic

CHASSÉEN, Late Neolithic and BELL BEAKER remains. Pits of human bones bearing cutmarks, found amid pits of butchered animal bones, have been claimed as evidence of Neolithic cannibalism.

Font-de-Gaume   a cave near LES EYZIES, Dordogne, France, where Palaeolithic paintings were discovered by PEYRONY in 1901. About 230 figures are known, dominated by 82 bison, and including some polychrome work. The art is attributed to the MAGDALENIAN (*c.*14 000–10 000 BC).

Fontéchevade   a French cave-site in the Charente region, principally excavated by Germaine Henri-Martin in 1937–54. It is dated to the RISS GLACIATION, and has yielded a Lower Palaeolithic TAYACIAN industry similar to that recovered from CLACTON with many CHOPPING TOOLS. Human skeletal remains from the cave have been classed as a form of PRE- or early NEANDERTHALER. The upper levels have produced Middle and Upper Palaeolithic material.

Ford, James Alfred   (1911–68)   an American archaeologist who specialized in southeastern North America and made fundamental contributions to the technique of SERIATION. Ford further argued that archaeological TYPES were imposed on the data by the classifier, and this led to a series of famous debates with Albert SPAULDING, who championed the view that types were 'discovered'.

formation processes or **site formation processes**   the sum total of processes, natural and cultural, acting individually or in concert, that result in the archaeological record as it exists today. An understanding of formation processes must precede any archaeological inference because of the transformations that may have altered the original cultural and natural depositional record.

Formative Period   1. a cultural STAGE, used in North America, that is defined by the presence of agriculture and villages. Normally, the Formative is also often accompanied by pottery, weaving, stone-carving and ceremonial architecture.
2. In MESOAMERICA, another term for the PRECLASSIC period, used in highland sequences.
3. In Andean South America, the period including both the INITIAL PERIOD and EARLY HORIZON (*c.*1800–1 BC), beginning with the introduction of CERAMIC technology. Elsewhere in South America, it also begins with the introduction of ceramics; this occurred *c.*7600 bp in Amazonia (see TAPERINHA), and *c.*5200 bp in northwest Colombia.

Fort Ancient   a series of cultures or societies located along the Ohio River and its tributaries, USA, which date to between AD 900–1600. The ASPECT is characterized by an increasing dependence on agriculture. PLATFORM and BURIAL MOUNDS, and palisaded houses are known. Fort Ancient has heavy MISSISSIPPIAN influence.

Fort Harrouard   a promontory fort in Eure-et-Loir, France, with occupation from the Middle Neolithic to the end of the Gallo-Roman period. Neolithic occupation is divided into two phases: CHASSÉEN with decorated VASE-SUPPORTS and TERRACOTTA female figurines, followed by ARTENACIEN. Evidence of METALLURGY has been recovered in the Middle and Late Bronze Age levels, including crucibles, moulds, and a stone-filled pit interpreted as the remains of a bronze-working furnace.

Fort Rock Cave   an early site in Oregon, USA, containing charcoal dated to over 13 000 BP in association with a MANO and METATE, PROJECTILE POINTS and other stone artifacts. The validity of this association has been questioned. The occupation level above this basal component is dated to over 10 000 BP.

forum   an open space in the heart of a Roman city or colony. It served a variety of functions as it was surrounded by administrative buildings (see CURIA, COMITIUM) and religious structures as well as by shops and sometimes libraries. At ROME there were several fora. The main area was the *Forum Romanum*, which included temples of Saturn, Castor and Concordia, triumphal arches and various administrative buildings. The *Forum Augustum*, some 100 m in length, served as a precinct to the temple of Mars Ultor built in the CORINTHIAN ORDER. The *Forum Traiani* contained Greek and Latin libraries as well as TRAJAN'S COLUMN. Compare AGORA.

fossil beach or **raised beach**   a LANDFORM representing a former beach that has been elevated relative to sea or lake level since the time it was active. Vertical displacement may be caused by isostatic crustal changes or eustatic sea level fluctuations, both common processes during the QUATERNARY. Lake levels may be influenced by changes in desiccation and precipitation. The age of archaeological deposits associated with fossil beaches can be no older than the age of beach activity; archaeological SURVEYS should be planned accordingly. See ISOSTASY, EUSTASY.

Franchthi Cave   a prehistoric site located on the Peloponnesian coast in southern Greece. The lowest cultural layers contain late Upper PALAEOLITHIC artifacts (e.g. small BACKED BLADES, GEOMETRIC MICROLITHS) associated with the remains of wild ass, red deer, fish, and other vertebrates; these layers are dated by RADIOCARBON to *c.*22 000–10 300 BP. The upper layers contain a lengthy sequence of MESOLITHIC and Neolithic occupations, the former including dozens of burials and some possible cremations.

Frankfort, Henri (1897–1954)   a Dutch archaeologist and intellectual historian, who worked in Egypt (ABYDOS, AMARNA, Armant) and in Iraq, where he led the University of Chicago's Diyala project that provided important information on EARLY DYNASTIC MESOPOTAMIA. While he published important studies on pottery and on CYLINDER SEALS, Frankfort's later comparative work, on kingship, religious attitudes and art in western Asia and Egypt, is perhaps more enduring.

Fraser Cave   see KUTIKINA.

Frederick   see PLANO, BLACKWATER DRAW.

Fremont   a TRADITION, with great internal variation, found throughout much of present day Utah, USA, between AD 400 and 1350. The tradition has some similarities to the ANASAZI in pottery types and PITHOUSE architecture. Maize, beans and squash were grown, although hunting and gathering remained an important component of their diet. Possible origins for Fremont include Anasazi immigration, movement from the Plains to the east, and a DIFFUSION of TRAITS from the MOGOLLON.

Frere, John (1740–1807)   a British antiquary who first recognized the true nature of PALAEOLITHIC artifacts, recovered from undisturbed PLEISTOCENE deposits in the Hoxne brickpit in association with the bones of extinct animals. Although Frere's work was published, his interpretation of the finds was largely ignored, because it contradicted the accepted Creation date of 4004 BC. See also PENGELLY.

fresco a decorative technique used on plastered surfaces. In true or *buon fresco* the pigment is applied before the plaster has dried; whereas the term *fresco secco* implies that the surface of the plaster is dry.

frigidarium the cold room in a Roman bath-house. A cold plunge-bath or a basin was provided. The frigidarium was located close to the APODYTERIUM and would have been one of the first rooms to be used by the bathers. See THERMAE.

Fromms Landing limestone shelters in the Lower Murray Valley, Australia, excavated by John Mulvaney. The deposits span the last 5000 years and parallel the sequence from nearby DEVON DOWNS. They include one of the earliest securely dated finds of DINGO.

frying pan the term used to describe the shallow circular vessels which are especially characteristic of the CYCLADIC GROTTA-PELOS and KEROS-SYROS cultures. Made of clay, or occasionally of stone, the frying pans often have complex designs stamped or incised on their underside and were evidently not used for cooking. However, their precise function remains obscure – suggestions include mirrors, drums and lids.

Fuchsberg a Neolithic pottery style, characterized by rich incised decoration, occupying the transition between the Danish Early and Middle Neolithic *c*.3400 BC. Fuchsberg pottery is a prominent element at the Neolithic enclosures of SARUP and TOFTUM.

Fudodo a Middle JOMON site in Toyama Prefecture, Japan, where a large oval pit-building, 8 m × 17 m with 16 POSTHOLES for massive pillars and four stone-lined hearths, has been excavated. The structure has been interpreted as a communal gathering- or work-place for winter tasks in the snow-laden HOKURIKU region.

Fu Hao a consort of a Late SHANG king whose tomb near Anyang City, China contained over 400 bronze ritual vessels plus other grave-goods. Her name is known from inscriptions on the bronzes and ORACLE BONES. The Fu Hao tomb was the only royal burial among the SHAFT TOMBS at ANYANG to have survived intact.

Fujinoki a late 7th century AD round MOUNDED TOMB in Nara Prefecture, Japan, whose stone SARCOPHAGUS yielded an eclectic but spectacular collection of horse trappings and gilt-bronze ornaments of different periods of manufacture. Some, such as the gilt-bronze shoes, are too large to be anything but ceremonial. The peninsular style of the goods indicates close relationships between the YAMATO and PAEKCHE elite.

Fujiwara a site in the ASUKA district of Nara Prefecture, Japan, comprising the first urban capital built on the Chinese CHANG'AN model. Constructed in AD 694 under the late YAMATO state, it was abandoned after only 20 years when the capital was moved to HEIJO. Fujiwara is now excavated year-round by the Nara National Cultural Properties Research Institute and is documented to have covered 2 km east–west × 3 km north–south with the palace in the north.

Fukui a Late Palaeolithic cave-site in Nagasaki Prefecture, Japan, yielding Incipient JOMON pottery together with OBSIDIAN MICROLITHS. Dated by RADIOCARBON to 12 700 bp, it is the earliest occurrence in the world of CERAMIC vessels (see also KAMIKUROIWA).

fulcrum the curved, raised structure at one end of a Roman banqueting couch which could be used as an arm rest. The edges of the fulcrum were frequently decorated with mounts, sometimes in bronze, ivory or bone.

Funan   the Chinese name for an early state located in the lower Mekong region of Cambodia and south Vietnam, first recorded as a trading partner of China in the 3rd century AD, and, according to Chinese records, conquered by the KHMER state of Chenla in the 7th century. The indigenous name has been lost, but is assumed to have included the Khmer word *bnam*, 'hill'. Its main centres may have been OC ÈO and ANGKOR Borei.

funerary cones   Egyptian solid pottery cones, averaging 25–30 cm long. Their dates range from the MIDDLE KINGDOM to the LATE PERIOD, but the vast majority are of the NEW KINGDOM. Rows of these cones were set into the façade of private tombs, with their outward-facing bases stamped before firing with the name and titles of the tomb-owner. Known examples come almost exclusively from THEBES (EGYPT) – WEST BANK.

Funnel(neck) Beaker   a vessel with globular body and out-turned rim, characteristic of the Early and Middle Neolithic culture of northern Europe. See TRB CULTURE.

Fuyu   see PUYO.

Füzesabony culture   the third phase of the tripartite division of the early part of the Hungarian Bronze Age defined by Moszolics on the basis of the sequence of the TÓSZEG TELL (see also HATVAN and NAGYRÉV). The Füzesabony culture is considered by many as the equivalent, with the same sort of settlements and material culture, of the OTOMANI culture of Transylvania. Notable Füzesabony finds include antler cheekpieces for horse-bits, found at a number of sites.

fynbos   a term used for the vegetation of a major domain of the Cape Floristic Kingdom of the southwestern and southern Cape Province of South Africa. It is characterized by unusually high species richness but is treeless and somewhat grassless. It is dominated by shrubs up to 3 m tall, and seems to have been attractive to HUNTER-GATHERERS for long periods, especially during the last 125 000 years.

G

Gagarino   an Upper Palaeolithic open-air site on the Don River in European Russia. The occupation horizon is buried in slope deposits comprising the upper FACIES of the second TERRACE. The artifact assemblage, which includes SHOULDERED POINTS and VENUS FIGURINES, may be assigned to the KOSTENKI-WILLENDORF CULTURE or EASTERN GRAVETTIAN; RADIOCARBON estimates of 21 800 and 30 000 bp are broadly consistent with this dating. An oval depression with central hearth and two associated pits apparently marks the location of a former structure. The latter, found in 1927, represents the first such discovery in European Russia; its superstructure may have originally been composed of the bones of woolly MAMMOTH, subsequently lost to weathering and erosion. Gagarino was discovered in 1926 by

Zamyatnin, who conducted excavations from 1927 to 1929; further excavations were undertaken by Tarasov (1961–69).

Galgenberg   see KREMS.

Galilee skull   see TURVILLE-PETRE.

Galindo   a MIDDLE HORIZON site in the Moche Valley of the north coast of Peru. The valley was largely abandoned by the MOCHE culture at this time. The site is in a strategic location near the valley neck, and is fortified. Excavations by Garth Bawden suggest that it was the centre of a small local POLITY; he finds no evidence that it was under the control of the HUARI Empire, which was expanding at the time. Other researchers disagree, suggesting that Huari concentrated the remaining local population at the site after its conquest of the Moche region.

gallery grave   see ALLÉE COUVERTE.

Gallery Hill   a PETROGLYPH site in the Pilbara region of Western Australia. The earlier abraded linear motifs include tracks, circles, kangaroos, emus and sometimes human figures. The later pecked engravings show a much wider range of subjects including mammals, reptiles, artifacts and ANTHROPOMORPHS, in dramatic compositions. Seed-grinding patches are also associated with the art.

Gallinazo   the ceramic style and culture in a portion of the north coast of Peru at the end of the EARLY HORIZON and beginning of the EARLY INTERMEDIATE PERIOD, c.200 bc–ad 200. Related to the contemporaneous Recuay style of the highlands, it is the precursor of the MOCHE style, and is found from the Virú Valley to the Moche Valley.

Gambieran   a distinctive local industry of large carefully RETOUCHED FLAKE tools made of FLINT, confined to coastal southeast South Australia and southwest Victoria. Finds of Gambieran material in dated contexts at KOONGINE and WYRIE SWAMP confirm an Early HOLOCENE age.

Gamble's Cave   a cave in the central Kenyan Rift Valley, which contains a well-represented EBURRAN industry, followed by ELMENTEITAN assemblages. Several skeletons from the Eburran layers were described as Caucasoid, but they are now considered Negroid.

Gamio, Manuel   (1883–1960) a Mexican archaeologist, one of the first in MESOAMERICA to excavate using metric STRATIGRAPHY, beginning in 1910. Gamio also set up a CERAMIC sequence for the VALLEY OF MEXICO. He began an integrated study of the TEOTIHUACÁN Valley in 1917 that extended from modern to prehistoric times, and incorporated ethnographic, historical and archaeological data. Gamio's systematic approaches set a standard among other Mesoamerican archaeologists for the investigation of Mesoamerican prehistory.

Gandhara grave culture complex   a culture of the 2nd and 1st millennia BC found in the valleys of northern Pakistan, notably in Swat, that contain a large number of cemeteries composed usually of pit graves, roofed with stone and containing one or two inhumations; cremation burials appear in some graves, the ashes often held in containers of various kinds. The grave-goods found with the bodies are mostly a distinctive red or grey plain BURNISHED pottery. Metal is present mostly as copper pins, while iron also occurs (including some horse bits); at least one horse burial is also recorded. The periodization and chronology of this grave complex is debated: some have placed the complex between the 11th and 3rd centuries BC; others prefer a shorter duration, between the 11th and 8th centuries BC.

Ganj Dareh   a site in the Kermanshah area of the Zagros Mountains, western Iran, where Philip Smith's excavations provide a long sequence of five phases that begins perhaps in the mid 9th (phase E) and runs to the early 7th (phase A) millennium bc. The earliest phase E contains only a series of pits and scattered ASH lenses and debris on weathered surfaces; goats dominate the fauna, and have an age structure consistent with hunting. In the subsequent phases of occupation, MUD-BRICK and WATTLE-AND-DAUB rectilinear structures appear, in which occur a wide range of unfired clay objects (bins, very large vessels as well as small ones, rims of stone mortars, ovens, figurines and geometrics – see TOKENS). The fauna of these settlements is still focused on morphologically wild goats, which now have age patterns consistent with herding and whose hoofprints are occasionally found on mud bricks.

Garagay   an INITIAL PERIOD site near Lima, on the central coast of Peru. The site includes a large U-shaped temple complex, and painted friezes depicting a monstrous human head. The art style is similar to other ceremonial sites on the central coast prior to the expansion of CHAVÍN influence.

Gargas   a cave in the Hautes-Pyrénées, France, first known for its richness in Ice Age fauna, where PALAEOLITHIC ART was discovered on the walls in 1906. Together with a few paintings and 148 engravings of animals, there are about 230 red or black hand stencils which often have 'missing' fingers. Sometimes seen as ritual mutilation or the result of disease, they are most probably a kind of sign-language using bent fingers. The cave was occupied from at least the Middle Palaeolithic onwards, and the animal engravings have been attributed to the GRAVETTIAN through comparison with stratified portable engravings.

Garrod, Dorothy Annie Elizabeth (1892–1968)   a British archaeologist notable for her work on the Palaeolithic of England and GIBRALTAR, and for her extensive work at MOUNT CARMEL (Israel) between 1929 and 1934, where she and Dorothy Bate revealed a long sequence of Lower Palaeolithic to EPIPALAEOLITHIC cultures in the TABUN, EL WAD and ES SKHUL caves. She also excavated in southern Kurdistan, Bulgaria, France (ANGLES SUR L'ANGLIN) and southern Lebanon (ADLUN). In 1939 she became Disney Professor of Archaeology at Cambridge University, the first woman professor at Oxford or Cambridge.

Garstang, John (1876–1956)   an English archaeologist who excavated extensively in Egypt (e.g. BENI HASSAN, ESNA, ABYDOS), the Sudan (MEROE), Palestine (e.g. JERICHO), Syria (Sakje-Geuzi), and Turkey (MERSIN).

Gash   a group of 35 sites in the Atbara region of Sudan with evidence of a food-producing economy post-dating the BUTANA sites. The main site of Mahal Teglinos contains 3 m of deposit, including human burials indicating a social hierarchy.

Gaudo   a CHALCOLITHIC cemetery in Campania, Italy, of 3rd millennium BC rock-cut tombs, type-site of the Campanian Gaudo group. This is a variant of the Central Italian RINALDONE, and is characterized by collective burial in rock-cut tombs, highly BURNISHED pottery and occasional metalwork, including copper daggers and awls and silver beads.

Gavrinis a Neolithic rectangular CAIRN on a small island in the Gulf of Morbihan, France, containing one of the most richly decorated MEGALITHIC PASSAGE GRAVES. The upper surface of the capstone of the chamber – invisible once the cairn was in place – has carvings of an axe or plough and two long-horned bovids; it is part of a carved MENHIR which was broken up and re-used in the tomb. Twenty-nine of the ORTHOSTATS of passage and chamber carry rich non-representational decoration of meanders, zigzags and chevrons. There are RADIOCARBON dates of *c*.3400 BC.

Gawra, Tepe a TELL-site, located east of the River Tigris near KHORSABAD, Iraq, which was occupied from the 6th to the 2nd millennia BC. The STRATIGRAPHIC sequence of 20 levels produced by E. Speiser and A. Tobler in their excavation during the 1930s established one of the basic reference points for the archaeology of northern Iraq. The lowest levels reveal a transition between HALAF and 'UBAID pottery styles (see Tell AQAB), followed by a long-lasting 'Ubaid settlement. One of the best-known features here is the temple complex of the penultimate 'Ubaid level (Gawra XIII), which shows striking resemblances to the 'Ubaid temples at ERIDU and WARKA. The next set of levels form the 'Gawran' period, of the 4th millennium BC, containing (in Gawra XI–A) the famous round house as well as a sequence of temples. The later levels (Gawra VII–I) belong to the 3rd and 2nd millennia BC, terminating in a thin MITANNI settlement.

Gaza a Palestinian site and the southernmost city of the PHILISTINE Pentapolis, which is now probably beneath the modern town of Gaza. The most impressive archaeological remains at Gaza are the MOSAICS of the Synagogue (probably of the 6th century AD) and the 'Great Mosque' which was originally a Crusader cathedral of the 12th century AD.

***ge* [ko]** a dagger-axe made first in bronze in the Chinese SHANG Dynasty, then in iron from the ZHOU Dynasty onwards (see CHINESE DYNASTIES). Early versions are TANGED for hafting; later ones have a perforated projection extending at right angles to the blade for binding onto a haft. They might derive from JADE prototypes. Often mis-translated as 'HALBERD', *ge* are, however, not thrusting but chopping implements.

Gebel Barkal a mountain in UPPER NUBIA, explored chiefly by REISNER in 1916, and by the University of Rome from 1973 to the present. It was a centre for the worship of AMEN during the Egyptian occupation in the NEW KINGDOM, and later. The TEMPLE built by RAMESSES II was extended by NAPATAN and MEROITIC rulers, who also built palaces there. A series of nearby PYRAMIDS seems to be related to the Meroitic Period.

Gedi an early Swahili coastal town situated on a tidal inlet south of Malindi in Kenya, which enjoyed prosperity from about AD 1300 until the 16th century, as a result of trade stimulated by the exploitation of Zimbabwean gold (see GREAT ZIMBABWE, KILWA), and which has been subjected to intensive archaeological investigation.

Geissenklösterle a cave in Baden-Württemberg, southwest Germany, discovered in 1957, where excavations by J. Hahn in 1974–83 revealed possible Middle Palaeolithic, AURIGNACIAN (36–34 000 bp), GRAVETTIAN (23 000 bp), MAGDALENIAN and

MESOLITHIC material. The Aurignacian levels yielded a series of IVORY figurines and an ivory bas-relief of a human, of 32–30 000 bp.

Gela a Greek colony in southern Sicily traditionally founded in 688 BC from Rhodes and Crete. It in turn went on to found AGRIGENTO. In the early 5th century BC much of its population was moved to SYRACUSE and it was refounded in 466 BC. It was again largely abandoned in 404 BC, and a new colony was established in the late 4th century. The remarkable defensive walls at Capo Soprano which have stone bases and MUD-BRICK upper parts belong to this later colony.

Gelidonya a cape on the dangerous southern coast of Turkey, which is the site of a Bronze Age shipwreck excavated by Bass in 1960. The cargo included COPPER and TIN INGOTS, BRONZE tools, and pottery which indicates that the ship went down in the 13th century BC.

gelifluction the mass movement processes, both flows and slides that take place in susceptible materials resulting from ice melt and thaw in the PERIGLACIAL environment. Gelifluction is a slightly more specific process than SOLIFLUCTION although the terms are often used interchangeably. As with other colluvial processes, gelifluction can cause destruction or redistribution of archaeological deposits.

general systems theory a theory that human society can be likened to a system composed of interdependent parts or subsystems, such that change in one subsystem affects all others. The theory is very similar to the Functionalism of 1930s British anthropology, but differs in its use of terms drawn from cybernetics and engineering (the disciplines in which general systems theory was developed), in its acknowledgement of the DIACHRONIC nature of society, and in its attempt to quantify the degree of change throughout the system. See David CLARKE.

geoarchaeology an ecological approach to archaeological deposits that has as its goal the understanding of the physical CONTEXT of archaeological remains. Geoarchaeology is concerned with geomorphic, STRATIGRAPHIC, and temporal context, site formation, post-depositional transformations of archaeological deposits, and data recovery, all with emphasis on the interrelationships among cultural and land systems. Compare ARCHAEOLOGICAL GEOLOGY.

geochronology the study of earth history with respect to the timing and sequencing of geological events to which archaeological events can be correlated. Geochronology can involve both ABSOLUTE DATING and RELATIVE DATING methods. See STRATIGRAPHY.

geoglyphs see NASCA LINES.

Geographical Society Cave a Palaeolithic site near Nakhodka in eastern Siberia. Artifacts are buried in clay and rubble deposits in a limestone cave. Associated faunal remains include woolly MAMMOTH, woolly rhinoceros, hyaena, bear and others; a RADIOCARBON date of 32 570 bp was obtained on one of the bones. The artifacts are confined to a small assemblage of pebble CORES, FLAKES and a scraping tool. It is assigned to the early Upper Palaeolithic on the basis of estimated age rather than typological characteristics. The site was investigated by OKLADNIKOV in the 1960s.

Geoksjur an oasis east of the Tedjen River (southern Turkmenia), which contains a series of prehistoric sites. Geoksjur 1, the largest at 12 ha, contains a sequence of 10 levels spanning the later 5th and 4th millennia BC, and corresponding to the first three periods of the standard NAMAZGA sequence. Settlement in the Geoksjur oasis was tied to a former course of the Tedjen, and disappeared when the river shifted further west. The oasis gives its name to a style of painted pottery of the Namazga III period (late 4th millennium BC), characterized by densely packed repeated geometrical motifs, which appears as far away as SHARH-I SOKHTA in eastern Iran and the QUETTA region of the Indo–Iranian borderlands.

Geoksjur Painted pottery.

geology   the study of physical, chemical and biological processes and products as they apply to the origin, history and structure of the Earth. Many of the specialized branches of geology make technical, methodological and theoretical contributions to the field of archaeology, because the Earth's surface is the platform on which all human activity has been conducted. Among the branches contributing greatly are STRATIGRAPHY, GEOMORPHOLOGY, sedimentology, PEDOLOGY, GEOPHYSICS and GEOCHRONOLOGY. See also ARCHAEOLOGICAL GEOLOGY.

Geometric   the term used for the pottery made in Greece *c.*900–700 BC and, by extension, for the period as a whole.

geometric pottery   the impressed pottery of southeastern China existing from *c.*2000 BC to the 3rd century AD, characterizing the protohistoric WUCHENG, HUSHU and Maqiao cultures of that region.

geomorphology   a branch of GEOLOGY concerned with LANDSCAPES, their evolution, and the processes operating within Earth's surface systems. Cultural remains are a part of these systems, having been deposited on, and in part resulting from, interactions with, landscapes of the past. Thus an understanding of the geomorphology of places where cultural debris was excavated is fundamental to archaeological inference.

geophysics   a subfield of both GEOLOGY and physics concerned with the structure, composition and development of the earth from a physical perspective. Many of the archaeological SURVEYING techniques designed to identify FEATURES without EXCAVATION utilize instruments that measure physical properties of surface materials, such as RESISTIVITY SURVEYING and ELECTROMAGNETIC SURVEYING. Some dating techniques, most notably PALAEOMAGNETISM, are based on geophysical properties of the earth.

geosol   a fundamental unit in pedostratigraphic classification consisting of a SEDIMENT or rock body characterized by one or more SOIL HORIZONS. A geosol is a formally recognized SOIL or PALAEOSOL that has a significant distribution. Recognition of geosols aids in the

CORRELATION of archaeological materials associated with them. See also STRATIGRAPHY.

Gergovia an Iron Age OPPIDUM, capital of the Arverni, occupying a steep-sided plateau of 150 ha overlooking modern Clermont-Ferrand, Puy-de-Dôme, France. The Gallic chief Vercingetorix took refuge here in 52 BC and resisted all attempts by Julius Caesar to capture the oppidum. Ditches of Caesar's siege camps have been found and excavated. Vercingetorix later withdrew to ALÉSIA, where he was ultimately forced to surrender.

Gerzean a PREDYNASTIC culture of UPPER EGYPT, sometimes referred to as NAQADA II, dated to between c.4000–3500 and 3000 BC and which was the successor of the AMRATIAN. The most important of the Gerzean sites so far discovered are Naqada and HIERAKONPOLIS. The Gerzean displays an increasing craft-specialization, including metal-working, and ample evidence of contacts with southwestern Asia; presumably fundamental political developments also occurred in this period, culminating in Egypt's becoming a unified state.

Getae the inhabitants of the Wallachian plain of Romania during the later part of the Iron Age. Sometimes referred to in the literature as *Geto-Dacians* or *Thraco-Getians* because of their position between the THRACIANS and DACIA, the Getae were conquered by Rome in AD 106.

Gezer a Palestinian site, chiefly excavated by Macalister in 1902–09 and the Hebrew Union College in 1964–73. Occupied from the CHALCOLITHIC to the BYZANTINE Periods, Gezer was an undefended town in the EARLY BRONZE AGE, and reached its greatest importance in the MIDDLE BRONZE AGE III when it was fortified with a wall and towers and, later, a GLACIS. An important part of the site is the 'High Place', a structure containing a row of 10 standing-stones of probable cultic purpose (see MASSEBAH). Gezer may have been destroyed by TUTHMOSIS III, but was rebuilt in LATE BRONZE AGE II, and probably destroyed again by Merenptah. The PHILISTINE Period is well attested at Gezer, but the town seems to have declined in importance under the ISRAELITES, the only substantial building of this period so far excavated being a SOLOMONIC Gate.

Ghana the first of the West African empires on the border of southern Mauretania and Mali, dating from at least the 8th century to the end of the 11th century AD. It may have arisen as a result of agricultural people organizing themselves to withstand depredation by Saharan nomads. The economy was based on trade in gold, IVORY and salt.

Ghassulian the major CHALCOLITHIC phase in Palestine, dated to the 4th millennium BC, best known from the sites of TELEILAT GHASSUL and NAHAL MISHMAR. Besides the early exploitation of COPPER, the Ghassulian is also notable for its well-made pottery and for being the last period of large-scale use of stone tools in Palestine.

Ghirshman, Roman (1895–1979) a Ukrainian/French scholar, one of the most energetic developers of the archaeology of Iran and Afghanistan. After working at TELLO (in southern Iraq) with de Genouillac, he undertook seminal excavations at the prehistoric sites of GIYAN and SIALK in western Iran, and then worked at a number of later historic period sites in eastern Iran and Afghanistan. After the Second World War and until 1963, Ghirshman directed the French excavations at SUSA, and also excavated at CHOGA ZANBIL and at other sites near Susa.

Gi   a pan locality in northwestern Botswana with rich MIDDLE STONE AGE remains, including an open living site, as well as LATER STONE AGE remains, including a MICROLITHIC INDUSTRY associated with pits interpreted as game traps.

Giant's Grave (*It*. Tomba di Giganti)   the name given to the CHAMBERED TOMBS of Sardinia consisting of an elongated CAIRN covering a long burial chamber of CYCLOPEAN construction with CORBELLED roof. In some examples there is a horned façade. The *tombe di giganti* belong to the Bronze Age NURAGHIC culture of the 2nd millennium BC.

Gibraltar   a promontory at the southern tip of Spain best known for its prehistoric cave sites, which have yielded NEANDERTHAL remains (including the first ever found in Europe in 1848) and Middle and Upper Palaeolithic stone artifacts. Devil's Tower rockshelter, which yielded a stratified Neanderthal child's skull, was excavated by GARROD in 1925–26. Gorham's Cave was excavated by John Waechter in 1948–54.

Giglio Island   an island lying off the coast of ETRURIA which is the location of a possible ARCHAIC Etruscan shipwreck. Although damaged by looters, the cargo consisted of AMPHORAE carrying olives, INGOTS and perfumed-oil contained in CORINTHIAN and Etruscan ARYBALLOI.

Gilf el Kebir   a high plateau of Nubian sandstone in the Sahara Desert, southwest Egypt, discovered by Ball and Prince Kemal el-Din in 1928 and since investigated by a variety of workers. The site has yielded surface-scatters of Late ACHEULIAN artifacts, including a few BIFACES, but is best known for its Neolithic material, also recovered in the form of surface-scatters, which includes stone tools made of a local sandstone, grinding stones, bone, ostrich eggshell and pottery decorated with impressed and incised designs, and for its prehistoric rock engravings in the southern part of the Gilf.

Gilgamesh   a famous figure of early 3rd millennium BC MESOPOTAMIA, who belongs to both myth and history. The historical Gilgamesh remains shadowy: he is named as ruler of WARKA in the SUMERIAN KING LIST and in myths about him; and some of his contemporaries (such as Enmebaragesi of KISH) named in the myths are also known from their own inscriptions. Moreover, the Gilgamesh epic cycle seems to reflect the emergence of new kinds of (secular and military) political authority in EARLY DYNASTIC southern Mesopotamia, and in the hands of such commentators as T. Jacobsen are seen to represent a real historical process. The more mythical aspects of the Gilgamesh epic cycle address social and individual psychological confrontations of fate, social honour, friendship and death.

Gilimanuk   a settlement and burial complex in west Bali of the early centuries AD, yielding extended burials, jar burials and stone SARCOPHAGI, with bronze, iron, and both imported and locally manufactured glass and stone beads.

Girsu   see TELLO.

Gishi Wajinden   see WEIZHI.

Giyan, Tepe   a prehistoric site near Nehevand in Luristan (western Iran), where excavations by G. Contenau and R. GHIRSHMAN in the 1930s provided the cultural sequence that until recently was standard for Luristan. The five-phase sequence (Giyan I–V) begins in the mid 5th millennium BC and continues into the Iron Age, containing a series of painted pottery styles, including the Iron Age 'genre Luristan' painted pottery. Although Giyan still counts in discussions of the prehistory of western Iran, the more recent work at GODIN Tepe, Baba Jan and elsewhere have supplanted it as the anchor of regional prehistory.

Giza   the site of the PYRAMID-COMPLEXES of the Egyptian Kings KHUFU, KHAFRE and MENKAURE. The other monuments of greatest importance at the site are the Great SPHINX and its TEMPLE, and the tomb of HETEPHERES.

Gla   a MYCENAEAN citadel on a rocky outcrop in what was formerly Lake Copais in Boeotia, Greece. Early in the 13th century BC Gla was massively fortified, the walls encompassing an area of 235 000 sq m. On the summit of the outcrop an L-shaped structure was built which may have had an administrative function but is not a conventional Mycenaean palace. Other structures appear to have been granaries, and it is suggested that Gla may have been fortified by the communities living around Copais, possibly under the leadership of ORCHOMENOS, when the Mycenaeans drained the lake. The citadel was burnt and abandoned late in the 13th century BC.

glacial   1. *n.* a cold climatic episode characterized in northern latitudes by the presence and growth of widespread glacial ice and cold climate processes, deposits, flora and fauna. 'Glacial' has been used as a geologic–climatic unit and as a basis for correlation of deposits. Compare INTERGLACIAL, STADIAL. See STRATIGRAPHY, QUATERNARY.
2. *adj.* referring to cold climatic conditions.
3. *adj.* referring to or derived from a glacier.

glaciation   a large-scale process whereby the land is subject to EROSION and deposition by continental and alpine glacier ice. Glaciation occurred repeatedly during the QUATERNARY as glaciers expanded and contracted, modifying LANDSCAPES and affecting ice-marginal environments and the level of ocean basins.

glacis   sloping ramparts with a smooth plastered surface, used to fortify several sites in the Near East during the MIDDLE BRONZE AGE (e.g. JERICHO, LACHISH, EL-YEHUDIYEH), and associated by some scholars with the HYKSOS.

Glasinac   a mountain valley near Sarajevo in Bosnia, in which several thousand TUMULI with over 10 000 cremation burials of the Late Bronze and Early Iron Ages (contemporaneous with the HALLSTATT period in central Europe) were found. The metal artifacts and pottery in these tumuli show connections with Greece, Italy and the Danube basin.

Glastonbury   an Iron Age LAKE VILLAGE in Somerset, England, excavated by Bulleid and Gray in 1894–1914. The village consisted of some 90 circular structures within a stockaded enclosure, standing on an artificial timber and brushwood platform within the fenlands of the SOMERSET LEVELS. The circular buildings, some dwellings, others workshops or animal sheds, had thick clay floors and clay-built hearths. The settlement dates from the 3rd/2nd to the middle of the 1st century BC and yielded numerous organic remains including wooden bowls and basins, basketry, and the wickerwork of the original house walls.

GLAZE

glaze   a type of SLIP of powdered glass applied to a pot or other object to produce a glassy appearance when fired, and to make porous materials impermeable.

gley horizon   a SOIL HORIZON characterized by grey, blue or olive colours due to excessive moisture under ANAEROBIC conditions. Gley horizons and gley soils occur where the water table is high or where a hardpan or relatively impermeable horizon prevents downward passage of water through the SOIL PROFILE. Gley horizons and gley soils are conducive to the preservation of plant, animal and human remains.

gleying   the process whereby iron in SOILS and SEDIMENTS is bacterially reduced under ANAEROBIC conditions. Such conditions are favoured in perennially moist environments where drainage is poor or the water table is high, such as lakes, BOGS, FENS, swamps, poorly drained depressions and FLOODPLAINS. Gleying results in grey, blue and green soil colours and the formation of GLEY HORIZONS.

Glob, Peter Vilhelm (1911–85)   a Danish archaeologist, Director General of Museums and Antiquities in Denmark, famous for his popularizing work on the bog bodies of TOLLUND and GRAUBALLE, published as *The Bog People*, and for its sequel *The Mound People*, describing the Bronze Age clothing and other remains from EGTVED, Muldbjerg and Borum Eshøj.

Globular Amphora culture   a late Neolithic culture of the Vistula, Oder and Bug drainages in north-central Europe, whose characteristic vessel form is a bulbous pot with a narrow neck and small handles for hanging. Cord-marked decoration is common. The origin of the Globular Amphora culture is hazy, with most linking it to the late FUNNEL BEAKER culture. It is contemporaneous with the CORDED WARE/SINGLE GRAVE complex, between 2600 and 2200 bc. Single burial in stone CISTS is common, and axes made from the banded flint of the HOLY CROSS MOUNTAINS are frequent grave-goods.

Glozel   an assemblage of pottery, clay tablets, bricks, TERRACOTTAS and glass, found in Allier, France, by Emile Fradin in 1924, that has been claimed as evidence for an indigenous literate French civilization prior to contact with Greeks and Romans. The clay tablets carry inscriptions in a hitherto undeciphered script. The find, still credited in some quarters, is now widely held to be a fraud, but scientific argument still rages about the date of the individual objects, with THERMOLUMINESCENCE indicating 700 BC–AD 100, whereas this is ruled out on ARCHAEOMAGNETIC grounds.

glyph   a symbol in a writing system. In the MESOAMERICAN system, a glyph may represent an idea, word, sound, syllable or some combination of these.

glyph Maya name glyph.

184

Gnathian ware a pottery fabric made in the 4th and 3rd centuries BC in southern Italy. It seems to have been produced initially in APULIA, although other workshops were located in CAMPANIA, LUCANIA and Sicily. The pots are decorated in a BLACK-GLOSSED technique and over-painted in white, yellow and red. The scheme of decoration is either a pattern or simple figures. Unlike other SOUTH ITALIAN POTTERY the fabric was widely exported and is especially common in North Africa.

Gniezno an early mediaeval stronghold in western Poland and the principal town of the Polanie tribe. Settlement began at Gniezno in the 8th century AD, and by the end of the 10th century the town had become one of the key centres of the early Polish state.

Gobedra a northern Ethiopian rockshelter with a stratigraphic sequence covering the last 12 000 years. Of particular interest are seeds of cultivated finger millet (*Eleusine coracana*) found in a layer tentatively dated to between 7000–5000 years ago. If correctly associated with these dates, the remains would be the earliest-known evidence for an indigenous African crop.

Gobi core see WEDGE-SHAPED MICROCORE.

Godin Tepe a prehistoric site in the Kangavar valley of Luristan, western Iran; the work of Cuyler Young here and at Seh Gabi Tepe provides a cultural sequence, running from the early 5th millennium BC to the late Iron Age, which provides the basic framework for the culture history of this section of the Zagros Mountains. Perhaps the most significant contribution of the site to wider problems of western Asian archaeology is the period Godin V, in which Late URUK materials (pottery, SEAL styles, tablets) are concentrated, along with local materials, within the 'oval enclosure' in the centre of the town. Godin V is prominent in the Late Uruk phenomenon, and presents a situation different from those at HABUBA KABIRA and ARSLANTEPE. Analysis of a stain on an AMPHORA has revealed the world's earliest wine, *c*.3500 BC.

Gogoshiis Qabe or **Gure Makeke** a rockshelter in southern Somalia, with a continuous MIDDLE through LATER STONE AGE sequence, including a series of early HOLOCENE burials. Some of these were associated with lesser kudu horn cores and possibly represent the earliest unequivocal evidence for the intentional placement of grave-goods with a corpse in East Africa.

Gokomere an Early IRON AGE site in southeastern Zimbabwe, occupied between the 5th and 7th centuries AD, which has given its name to an Early Iron Age group (see CHIFUMBAZE). Finds include pottery, copper and iron fragments, an Indian Ocean shell and the remains of large cattle byres.

Golasecca an Iron Age cemetery, type-site of the Golasecca culture of Lombardy, Italy. This is characterized by cemeteries of cremation burials in urns, sometimes accompanied by wheeled vehicles, as at Ca' Morta. The burial rite and metalwork reflect influences from the HALLSTATT sphere north of the Alps. The earliest graves of the Golasecca culture date to *c*.900 BC; it becomes absorbed into the CELTIC world in the 3rd century BC.

gold-figured, *adj.* denoting a technique used to decorate Greek silver plate with gold foil. Some of the more important examples of the technique, which include cups, a PHIALE and a KANTHAROS, have been found at DUVANLI and SEMIBRATNY. They show complex figured scenes such as chariot-races. Detail is incised in the gold foil. The decoration evokes the RED-FIGURED technique used particularly on ATHENIAN POTTERY. See also SILVER-FIGURED.

gold-glass *adj.* denoting a technique by which gold foil is either attached to the surface of a glass vessel or sandwiched between two layers of glass. The foil is cut to provide the decoration, which may be quite complex. The earliest examples seem to date from the 3rd century BC, although the term is often applied to vessels made at ROME in the 3rd and 4th centuries AD which are frequently decorated with Christian themes.

Goljamo Delčevo or **Golyamo Delchevo** a TELL site of the CUCUTENI-TRIPOLYE culture in northeast Bulgaria, notable for its system of rectangular fortifications including palisades and a bank and ditch, within which was a series of densely packed structures separated by narrow passages. A cemetery with 30 graves was located nearby.

Gombe Point a site overlooking the Congo River in Kinshasa, Zaire, where the first stratigraphic succession of stone industries in central Africa was described. However, the absence of distinct archaeological horizons and lack of consecutive order in the dates suggest to recent researchers that the archaeological deposit is mixed.

Gomolava a double TELL site on the Sava river in Serbia, with stratified deposits from the Late Neolithic to the Middle Ages. The Neolithic occupation is 1.3 m thick and belongs primarily to the VINČA CULTURE, with two habitation levels. The earlier, Vinča B period, has pits, presumed pit-dwellings, and above-ground houses. The later, from the Vinča C period, has multi-roomed houses. Among the botanical remains was flax, probably domesticated. The Vinča C horizon also contained a cemetery with 26 burials.

Go Mun a site in north Vietnam which has given its name to the phase of the bronze period in the region which succeeded DONG DAU in *c.*1200 BC and ended in *c.*600 BC. As in General Period B in KHORAT, a broad range of bronze tools, weapons and ornaments supplemented the persisting tradition of POLISHED STONE ADZES.

Gongwangling [Kung-wang-ling] see LANTIAN.

Gönnersdorf an extensive Upper Palaeolithic open-air site on the right bank of the Rhine, northwest Germany, excavated by Gerhard Bosinski in 1968–76. It is best known for *c.*400 MAGDALENIAN engraved schist plaques, some of which depict stylized females with prominent buttocks, while others depict a variety of animals. A RADIOCARBON date of 12 600 bp has been obtained for the Late Magdalenian occupation. The site was preserved by a thick pumice layer from a volcanic eruption during the ALLERØD. Its fauna is dominated by horses. Habitation structures include a number of tents, paved with schist plaques. Seashells from the Paris Basin and the Mediterranean were present. Similar finds were made at Andernach on the left bank, opposite.

Gontsy an Upper Palaeolithic open-air site on the Udaj River (a tributary of the Sula, which empties into the Dnepr) in Ukraine. Gontsy represents one of the earliest Palaeolithic discoveries in eastern Europe in 1871–73. The remains are buried in slope deposits overlying ALLUVIUM of the second TERRACE. A single RADIOCARBON date of 13 400 bp is reported. The faunal assemblage is dominated by woolly MAMMOTH, and a MAMMOTH BONE HOUSE with associated pits, hearths and debris concentrations is present. The site was excavated by GORODTSOV in 1911 16 and Pidoplichko in 1935; more recent investigations have been conducted by Sergin in 1977–80.

Gonur-depe   a large site (perhaps 50 ha) with a central fortress and surrounding residential and craft areas, set in the Murghab delta in southeastern Turkmenia and excavated by V.I. Sarianidi in the 1970s and 1980s. The material culture defines the Gonur phase of the regional chronology, intermediate between the KELLELI and TOGOLOK phases, and showing strong continuity with both; the phase may be dated to the late 3rd–early 2nd millennia. Characteristic elements of the material inventory are the Murghab seal-amulets whose rich iconography has been compared with both MESOPOTAMIAN and Late HARAPPAN styles.

Gonvillars   a cave-site in Haute-Sâone, France, with a stratified sequence of Neolithic deposits. Shortly after 5000 BC a Bandkeramik group (see LINEAR POTTERY CULTURE) established an encampment at the mouth of the cave. The pottery which they used is very similar to that of the Paris basin Bandkeramik. Hunting was important – this may have been a temporary hunting camp – but the inhabitants also had domestic sheep and dog, and cultivated cereals. They were followed shortly before 4000 BC by RÖSSEN groups, who occupied the cave for approximately 500 years.

Goodwin, Astley John Hilary (1900–59)   the first and, for a long time, the only qualified archaeologist employed in sub-Saharan Africa. His 1929 synthesis, written with C. VAN RIET LOWE, *The Stone Age cultures of South Africa*, set out the classification of the southern African Stone Age into EARLIER, MIDDLE and LATER STONE AGE stages, which are still used today.

Gordion (*Lat.* Gordium)   the PHRYGIAN capital in the 8th century BC, situated 90 km southwest of Ankara in central Anatolia, on the Sakarya River. The work of R. Young in 1950–74 and his successors revealed the 8 ha citadel within whose walls were a series of large MEGARON structures set around a courtyard; the halls of these megara had galleries along three sides, supported by wooden pillars. Smaller megara set in rows along streets lay on terraces behind this complex. Young also investigated a series of burial mounds, including the great royal tomb, perhaps of an ancestor of Midas, which was richly supplied with grave-goods (including inscriptions on beeswax in the Phrygian script). Several deep soundings have revealed a sequence of levels from the late EARLY BRONZE AGE to the post-HITTITE period, when construction of the early Phrygian citadel complex began. Gordion was sacked by the CIMMERIANS, and though occupation at the site continued into Roman times, it had lost much of its political importance. Skeletal material from the main TUMULUS has been the subject of the facial reconstruction of 'King Midas'.

gorget   a flat, regularly shaped artifact made from stone or other suitable material that was worn as an ornament over the chest. It is especially common in prehistoric cultures of the American Southeast and Midwest.

gorgoneion   the mask of the gorgon. This mythical monster, whose glance could turn people to stone, was beheaded by the hero

Perseus. The mask became a symbol to ward off evil, and one forms the centre of the PEDIMENT on the ARCHAIC temple of Artemis on Corfu. Its use may have been to instil a feeling of awe in those entering the TEMENOS. The motif was widely used on ATHENIAN POTTERY especially during the late Archaic period, as well as on Roman CINERARIA.

Gorman, Chester F. (1938–81) an American prehistorian known for his work on early METALLURGY and horticulture in Thailand, particularly at SPIRIT CAVE in 1965/6 and at BAN CHIANG in 1974/5.

Gorodtsov, Vasili Alekseevich (1860–1945) a Russian archaeologist who established the presence of, and developed a chronology for, the Bronze Age in Russia. Gorodtsov also produced several syntheses of Russian prehistory, and emphasized formal TYPOLOGY. He excavated at the Palaeolithic sites of GONTSY, IL'SKAYA I and TIMONOVKA.

Gorodtsov Culture an early Upper Palaeolithic culture defined on the basis of several assemblages from the KOSTENKI-BORSHCHEVO sites on the Don River in European Russia, which appear to date to c.30 000–25 000 bp. The assemblages contain many endscrapers (see SCRAPER) and typical Middle Palaeolithic tools (e.g. sidescrapers), and a rich inventory of bone tools (e.g. needles, AWLS).

Gough's Cave a cave in Cheddar Gorge, Somerset, England, which has yielded Upper Palaeolithic (CRESWELLIAN) flint, bone and antler artifacts, animal bones (horse and red deer) which show clear cut-marks indicating butchery, and human bones which may provide evidence, in the form of deliberate cut-marks, for prehistoric cannibalism. The site has been excavated by a number of different workers from 1927 onwards.

Gournia the site of a MINOAN town on the island of Crete, which was excavated by Boyd-Hawes in 1901–04. The town, which dates from the NEOPALATIAL period, c.1600–1450 BC, is dominated by the 'Palace' which imitates the major Minoan palaces in detail if not in scale, and must have been the residence of the local governor.

Gozlu Kule see TARSUS.

Gradesnitsa a Late Neolithic village site of the GUMELNIŢA culture in northwest Bulgaria. Similar in size and layout to other Gumelniţa sites such as POLYANITSA, with closely packed houses arranged along narrow alleyways, Gradesnitsa is known especially for a 'ritual assemblage' which includes an inscribed clay tablet similar to the ones found at TĂRTĂRIA, but dated slightly earlier.

gradiometer a geophysical instrument, used in conducting SURVEYS, that measures the gradient in a magnetic or gravitational field. It is used to identify shallowly buried cultural FEATURES and structures. See DIFFERENTIAL FLUXGATE GRADIOMETER, FLUXGATE GRADIOMETER.

Gradistea Muncelului see SARMIZEGETHUSA.

graffiti writing applied to walls or other objects. Commercial graffiti were scratched or sometimes painted on the underside of Greek pottery. They sometimes refer to lists of pottery vessels in a consignment, the size of batches, prices and perhaps the names of traders. Other graffiti consist of personal names and should be understood as owners' marks. Graffiti can provide important information about language; for example, in the Roman colony at CORINTH the public inscriptions tend to be in Latin, whereas the graffiti on pottery are usually in Greek.

Graig Lwyd a Neolithic stone quarry and axe factory in Gwynedd, Wales, at the eastern end of Penmaenmawr Mountain, source of the Group VII axes. The material has been identified as augite granophyre. The factory remained in use from *c*.4000 BC to 2500 BC.

grain size analysis see PARTICLE SIZE ANALYSIS.

Gran Chichimeca the region to the north of MESOAMERICA where the CHICHIMECS lived prior to their movement south. Originally referring to the area outside the Mesoamerican culture sphere, the term is now also used to refer to the area beyond the geographical sphere of Mesoamerica, including areas as far north as the southwestern United States.

Grand Menhir Brisé see CARNAC.

Grand Pressigny a complex of flint quarries, the largest in Europe, extending over several square kilometres on plateaux and valley slopes overlooking the rivers Creuse and Claise, (Indre-et-Loire, France). The flint is of exceptionally high quality and honey-coloured in appearance. In many places the flint is not far below the surface, and extraction probably took the form of surface workings and shallow pits. A number of working areas have been found on the valley floors. Grand Pressigny flint was used primarily for the production of impressive BLADES, up to 40 cm in length; the distinctive blade CORES are known as LIVRES DE BEURRE, after the shape of the local 19th century butter slabs. Grand Pressigny flint was widely traded, and material of similar appearance is found in BEAKER graves in the southern Netherlands, but only petrographic analysis will demonstrate whether this is really from the Grand Pressigny source. The exploitation of Grand Pressigny flint was a final Neolithic and CHALCOLITHIC phenomenon in *c*.2800 to 2400 BC.

granulation a technique used in the manufacture of jewellery whereby grains of gold or electrum, more rarely silver, are soldered onto metalwork.

grattoir see SCRAPER.

Grauballe Man a prehistoric body found preserved in a PEAT bog in Jutland, Denmark, in 1952. He had had his throat cut, possibly after being knocked unconscious. Stomach contents showed that his last meal had been a gruel with 63 varieties of seed, including spelt, rye, clover, buttercup and black nightshade. There is a RADIOCARBON date of *c*.ad 310.

Grave Creek Mound the largest conical earth mound in the New World, located in northern West Virginia, USA. The mound is about 19 m high, with a basal diameter of 73 m. The mound's base was surrounded by a moat approximately 1.5 m deep and 10 m wide. The mound was the centre of a complex of smaller mounds and earthworks. It was constructed during the 3rd and 2nd centuries BC, as a mortuary mound over a high status burial. It belongs to the ADENA culture.

gravel 1. a general size-term for material greater than two mm in diameter. Gravel is subdivided into granule, PEBBLE, COBBLE and BOULDER gravel.
2. a sedimentary deposit consisting largely of gravel-size CLASTS.

Gravettian   an Upper Palaeolithic INDUSTRY named after the site of *La Gravette*, Dordogne, France. It appears to have developed in central Europe and expanded east and westwards. In France the Gravettian, also known as the Upper PERIGORDIAN, is found stratified above the AURIGNACIAN and below the SOLUTREAN, and dated *c.*28 000–20 000 BP. The tool-kit contains BACKED BLADES, SCRAPERS, characteristic backed points, and, in some phases, NOAILLES BURINS. See also EASTERN GRAVETTIAN.

Gravisca   one of the ports of TARQUINIA in ETRURIA. Recent excavations have brought to light the remains of the harbour facilities and found large quantities of Greek pottery. A stone anchor dedicated by a Sostratos to 'Aeginetan Apollo' is evidence for Greek merchants.

gravity model   a MODEL that suggests that the degree of interaction between CULTURES is directly proportional to their proximity to each other.

Graziosi, Paolo (1906–88)   an Italian prehistorian best known for his excavations and ROCK-ART studies in Italy and North Africa. He discovered the art at LEVANZO, and published a major volume *L'Arte dell'Antica Eta della Pietra* (1956).

Greater Peten   a major architectural style of the CLASSIC MAYA lowlands. Typical of this style is the use of polychrome painted STUCCO on wall surfaces. The motifs are often repeated in a variety of combinations. See also PUUC and RIO BEC-CHENES.

Great Langdale   a Neolithic axe-factory in Cumbria, England, consisting of a number of extraction sites where high-quality stone (epidotized intermediate TUFF, the Group VI material of the British polished axe classification) was quarried in surface workings or shallow pits. The site is high in the Lake District hills, but was connected to lower-lying sites such as Ehenside Tarn where the final stages of pecking and polishing were completed. The most prominent feature today is the massive scree down the hillside at Pike of Stickle which contains many axe rough-outs and waste FLAKES. This was the most productive of all the Neolithic axe factories, with products traded widely throughout Britain from *c.*4000 BC for over 1000 years.

Great Serpent Mound   a huge ritual earthen mound in Ohio, USA, which has the form of a curved serpent almost 390 m long, 6 m wide and 1.5 m high. The serpent holds either an egg or a frog in its jaw. A nearby BURIAL MOUND belongs to the ADENA COMPLEX, to which the serpent mound itself is dated by association.

Great Wall   a monument bordering the northern LOESS area of China, ostensibly built to protect agriculturalists from the incursions of steppe nomads in the mid 1st millennium BC (see XIONGNU). The existing wall, over 2000 km in length, is actually composed of a series of walls built by individual ZHOU-period states; it was linked together and extended by the First Emperor of QIN. It stretches from the BOHAI Bay in the west to the Tarim Basin in the east; the portion now seen by tourists near Beijing is a Ming (see CHINESE DYNASTIES) reconstruction.

Great Zimbabwe   a Late IRON AGE town with impressive stone walling in southeastern Zimbabwe, the most elaborate to which the term *dzimbahwe* (see ZIMBABWE) is applied. After an Early Iron Age occupation between AD 500 and 900, not associated with building in stone, Shona speakers occupied Zimbabwe Hill from about AD 1000 and later began building stone walls. Between about AD 1270 and 1450, Great Zimbabwe was the capital of a vast Shona empire that stretched from the Zambezi River to the northern Transvaal of South Africa and eastern Botswana. In contrast to most other societies of southern Africa at this time, social organization was based on class distinction between commoners and a ruling class. The kings accumulated wealth and prestige by controlling trade between the southern African interior and the East African coast. Archaeologically, this culture is recognized as the Zimbabwe Tradition (formerly Ruins Tradition) and is divided into MAPUNGUBWE, Zimbabwe and KHAMI phases.

Some people still cling to the outdated idea that Great Zimbabwe was built by outsiders such as PHOENICIAN traders. However, the archaeological evidence as well as historical accounts from early Portuguese traders indicate that the pottery, houses and buildings are African and are the work of the ancestors of the Shona people of modern Zimbabwe (see CATON THOMPSON).

Grebeniki culture   a Late MESOLITHIC culture of the area between the Carpathians and the Dniester valley in Ukraine in about 6000 BC, succeeded by the BUG-DNIESTER complex's foraging adaptation in about 5500 BC.

greenstone   a green-coloured, slightly metamorphosed basic igneous rock, the colour of which is due to the minerals chlorite, hornblende or epidote. The term has been adopted without differentiation for rocks including SERPENTINE, olivine, JADE, JADEITE, and NEPHRITE that were used for fine axes, figurines, and ceremonial objects.

In southeastern Australia, greenstone EDGE-GROUND hatchets were widely traded during the Late HOLOCENE. MOUNT WILLIAM is the best-known source. Greenstone was also important in NEW ZEALAND, where it was worked into a range of wood-working tools and ornaments, usually by splitting, sawing and grinding rather than flaking.

greyware   CERAMIC ware found at MONTE ALBÁN and the VALLEY OF OAXACA, Mexico. Both common household ware and specialized ceramics are made from greyware. Specialized ceramics were of a polished greyware, and are found in high frequencies in this area. In latter periods in the Oaxaca sequence, after the collapse of Monte Albán, MIXTEC greyware was distributed throughout the Valley of Oaxaca in much the same way as were the ZAPOTEC peoples immediately after the Spanish conquest. This correlation between the distribution of Mixtec ceramics and Zapotec households is used to suggest the merging of the two cultures, probably during Monte Albán V in the period AD 1250–1521.

grid   a systematic array of perpendicular lines used as a frame of locational reference on an archaeological site. Elements of the grid are usually assigned some value of distance and direction with reference to a local or regional DATUM. Excavation units, recovered debris, and other field observations are recorded and sometimes planned with reference to the grid. Grids are usually aligned with respect to the primary compass directions, but it is often advantageous to align them with respect either to the expected site structure, or to the primary depositional slope of the LANDFORM the site is situated upon.

Grimaldi   a cave and rockshelter complex on the Italian Riviera close to the French border, which has produced Middle and Upper

Palaeolithic material, most notably AURIGNACIAN and GRAVETTIAN assemblages, which have been termed Grimaldian industries. The caves have also yielded a series of 17 elaborate HOMO *sapiens sapiens* burials, including grave-goods and evidence for partial burning of the bodies; their date remains uncertain, but they are usually assigned to the Gravettian. A series of small VENUS FIGURINES, of equally uncertain date, were also found. See also GROTTE DES ENFANTS.

Grimes Graves a Neolithic flint mine in Norfolk, England, with traces of over 360 shafts surviving as shallow depressions over an area of 7 ha. The high-quality flint was in three bands within the chalk, known as *floorstone, wallstone* and *topstone*. The best quality flint was the tabular floorstone. With the aid of antler picks, hour-glass shafts up to 12 m deep were dug in the chalk, with galleries radiating from their base. Despite the large number of shafts which were dug, exploitation was probably a small-scale, possibly seasonal, occupation, with only one or two shafts in use at any one time. The site appears to have continued in use from soon after 3000 BC to the Early Bronze Age.

Grimston see HANGING GRIMSTON.

gród (*pl.* grody) early mediaeval fortified enclosures of east-central Europe. Most numerous in Poland, such strongholds also occur in eastern Germany (where they are known as *Burgwalle* or *Herrenburgen*) and Czechoslovakia (where they are called *hradiste*), as well as eastward into Russia and the Baltic states. They are characterized by earthen ramparts, often with wooden reinforcement. Some of the largest became the nuclei of urban centres, such as GNIEZNO and MIKULČICE.

Gródek Nadbużny a Neolithic settlement of the FUNNEL BEAKER culture in southeast Poland, excavated in 1954–57. Structural remains at Gródek Nadbużny are characterized by PLOSHCHADKI. A wide variety of flint types were used, and there is evidence of COPPER METALLURGY.

Groitzsch a group of Upper Palaeolithic open-air sites located on the Mulde River (an Elbe tributary) in eastern Germany. Artifacts are buried in sand overlying a GLACIAL MORAINE; the cultural layer probably dates to the end of the PLEISTOCENE. Traces of two former structures with paved floors were excavated. Artifacts include end-scrapers (see SCRAPER) and BURINS, and are assigned to the MAGDALENIAN.

groma a four-armed Roman instrument used for surveying. Plumb lines were attached to each of the arms, and the groma allowed accurate alignments to be made. This was particularly useful for laying out the grid-pattern of forts and towns, for the construction of roads, and for CENTURIATION.

Grooved Ware a pottery style of the British Late Neolithic, also known as Rinyo-Clacton ware after the sites of Rinyo in Orkney and Clacton in Essex. The typical form is the flat-based straight-walled vessel decorated with elaborate surface grooving. The pottery is found in settlement sites and CHAMBERED TOMBS, but appears to have had some special significance as it is found in especially high frequencies at major ritual sites such as HENGES.

Grotta dell'Uzzo a cave-site near the northwestern tip of Sicily, with a stratified sequence of Mesolithic and Early Neolithic deposits.

Grooved Ware

In the Mesolithic layers (dated to between 8000 BC and 6500 BC), six inhumation burials were discovered. Early Neolithic levels with CARDIAL IMPRESSED WARE, bones of domestic sheep, goat and pig, and traces of wheat and barley follow probably around 6000 BC, making this one of the earliest Neolithic sites in the central Mediterranean. The Early Neolithic is followed by Middle Neolithic layers with STENTINELLO and painted Masseria La Quercia ware, and finally by dark-faced wares of Late Neolithic Diana style.

Grotta Guattari a cave in the Monte Circeo, 100 km southeast of Rome, Italy, where the skull and jawbone of a 45 year-old NEANDERTHAL man were found in 1939, allegedly inside a ring of stones. This was interpreted by A. Blanc and others as evidence of ritual and cannibalism, since the hole at the skull's base had been widened. Recent TAPHONOMIC studies suggest strongly that the cave was a hyena den, the stone-ring was natural, and there are no human-made traces on the Neanderthal bones. Dates from AUROCHS teeth (ESR) and calcite (URANIUM/thorium) indicate that the bones were deposited between 57 000 and 51 000 BP.

Grotta-Pelos or **Pelos-Lakkoudes** a cultural phase, named after archaeological sites in the Cyclades, which in Renfrew's classification of the CYCLADIC culture sequence, corresponds to Early Cycladic I (c.3200–2700 BC) in the traditional chronology.

Grotte des Enfants a cave in the GRIMALDI complex which has produced Upper Palaeolithic material including an adult male CRO-MAGNON HOMO *sapiens sapiens* burial lying above the double inhumation of a young man and an older woman; the latter were first thought to have Negroid characteristics, but are now seen as Cro-Magnon.

Grotte Vaufrey a cave in Dordogne, France, where excavations by J-P. Rigaud in 1969–82 revealed a 4 m stratigraphy from MINDEL/RISS to early WÜRM, including a very early (pre-Würm) occurrence of the MOUSTERIAN. Dating of SPELEOTHEMS by URANIUM SERIES analysis, and of burnt flints by THERMOLUMINESCENCE indicate a span from 246 000 to 74 000 BP. The cave seems to have had a series of repeated short occupations.

Gua Cha a rockshelter in peninsular Malaysia utilized between *c*.10 000/8000 and 2000 BP, largely for burials. Stone tools span the transition from HOABINHIAN to Neolithic, the latter associated with remains similar to BAN KAO. A similar sequence is found at Kota Tongkat.

Gua Kechil   one of a number of rockshelter sites in peninsular Malaysia yielding remains related to the BAN KAO Neolithic. Other sites include GUA CHA, Gua Musang, Gua Berhala, Gua Bintong, Gua Kajang, Gua Kelawak and BUKIT TENGKU LEMBU, and open sites like JENDERAM HILIR.

Gubs Shelter No. 1   a Palaeolithic rockshelter on the Gubs River (Kuban' tributary) in the northern Caucasus of European Russia. A Middle Palaeolithic assemblage was found in the lower portion of a sequence of LOAM and rubble deposits; the tools are primarily side-scrapers (see SCRAPER). Two Upper Palaeolithic cultural layers overlie this assemblage. The lower layer contains a high number of end-scrapers; the upper layer yielded a very different assemblage composed largely of BACKED BLADES. Faunal remains were sparse, but indicate cold climatic conditions; the entire sequence is thought to date to the LAST GLACIAL. The shelter was discovered and excavated by Autlev in 1961–63; further excavation was conducted by Amirkhanov in 1975–76.

Gudea   a ruler of LAGASH during the post-AKKADIAN period (*c*.2125 BC), best known for the numerous inscribed statues of him found at TELLO, which are among the best-known objects of SUMERIAN art. The inscriptions boast of great power and extensive trading connections, though in the circumstances of the post-Akkadian period these claims are surely exaggerated.

Gudenus Cave   a prehistoric cave-site located on the River Danube west of Vienna, Austria. Artifacts and faunal remains (e.g. CAVE BEAR, woolly MAMMOTH and reindeer) are buried in stream (?) and cave deposits. The lowest cultural layer contains Middle Palaeolithic artifacts, including sidescrapers (see SCRAPER) and BIFACES. A small Upper Palaeolithic assemblage (MAGDALENIAN), including an animal figurine, was recovered from an overlying level. Neolithic and later remains occur in the uppermost layer.

Guilá Naquitz   a PRECERAMIC site in the eastern VALLEY OF OAXACA, Mexico, dating from 8750–6670 BC. The site was discovered in 1964, and excavations were begun in 1966 by Kent Flannery. The small rockshelter was completely excavated by an interdisciplinary team, with research centred on the question of the origins of agriculture, and modelling a system of foraging and incipient cultivation. Guilá Naquitz represents one of the most thoroughly researched preceramic sites in MESOAMERICA, and is part of a larger study of the preceramic settlement system in the Valley of Oaxaca.

Guitarrero Cave   a site in the Callejón de Huaylas region of northern Peru, whose occupation began in the PRECERAMIC period and continued through later CERAMIC periods. Excavations by Thomas Lynch suggest that the site was a wet-season camp occupied by hunter-gatherers whose subsistence strategy was one of TRANSHUMANCE. The earliest domesticated beans known at present in South America, dating from *c*.8000 BC, were found here.

gully   an erosional LANDFORM consisting of a trench greater than several centimetres deep and wide, characterized by steep vertical sidewalls and headwall. They form in existing valleys or on HILLSLOPES. EROSION of gullies can remove large quantities of unlithified SEDIMENT and can rapidly destroy archaeological deposits. Occurrences of settlement in deep gullies that provide shelter, particularly from winds, have been documented.

Gumanye   a Late IRON AGE site in southern Zimbabwe which has given its name to a FACIES of the KUTAMA tradition, which is associated with a northward spread of people from the Transvaal at the beginning of the Late Iron Age in about AD 1000, and the appearance of Shona people at GREAT ZIMBABWE in the 11th century. Gumanye sites are mainly small villages on defendable hilltops.

Gumban A   see NDERIT WARE.

Gumelniţa culture   a Late NEOLITHIC/ENEOLITHIC culture of the eastern Balkans, *c.*3800–3000 bc, roughly contemporary with VINČA D and Layer VI at KARANOVO. Many Gumelniţa settlements, such as POLYANITSA, are characterized by closely packed rectangular structures separated by narrow passages, the whole complex surrounded by a square earthwork; while others, such as CASCIOĂRELE have somewhat more dispersed layouts. CERAMICS of the Gumelniţa culture are often decorated with graphite designs, reflecting a sophisticated control of firing conditions. There is considerable evidence for emergent social differentiation in the Gumelniţa culture, particularly as indicated by the finds from the cemetery at VARNA.

Gundestrup   a large silver cauldron discovered in a PEAT bog in Jutland, Denmark, in 1891. The vessel consists of 12 separate plates of sheet silver, a round plate and two tubular fragments, which were found dismantled, stacked within the curved base. The plates of the cauldron are decorated with scenes in raised relief, representing ritual or mythological events. The figures on the outer face were originally covered in thin gold-leaf, with inlaid eyes of red or blue glass. Attempts have been made to interpret the scenes in the light of later Scandinavian mythology, but recent studies suggest that the cauldron was manufactured not in northern Europe but in THRACE, probably in the later 2nd century BC.

Günz glaciation   the first major Alpine GLACIAL advance which started *c.*590 000 years ago, marking the onset of the PLEISTOCENE phase which lasted until the end of the MINDEL GLACIATION. The preceding Basal Pleistocene or Donau phase was a long period of alternating colder and warmer climates.

Gupta dynasty   see DVARAVATI.

Gura Baciului   an Early Neolithic site of the CRIŞ culture in Transylvania, contemporaneous with other early farming settlements in southeastern Europe such as KARANOVO I, SESKLO, and ANZA. OBSIDIAN from sources nearby in Hungary forms a major component of the lithic assemblage.

Gure Makeke   see GOGSHIIS QABE.

Gutians   a people of the 3rd millennium BC whose original home was somewhere in the Zagros Mountains east of MESOPOTAMIA, perhaps Luristan. They are best known for their contribution to the fall of the AKKADIAN empire, when groups of Gutians invaded southern Mesopotamia. The Gutian, or post-Akkadian, period in Mesopotamian political history is one of extreme fragmentation, when Akkadian, SUMERIAN and Gutian dynasties ruled petty city-states; GUDEA of LAGASH (see TELLO) is the best known of these rulers. The period lasted for as little as 40 years, before Ur-Nammu (2112–2095 BC) founded a dynasty at UR and began the political re-integration of the region under the Ur III state.

guttae   peg-like features which appear on the underside of MUTULES and TRIGLYPHS on CLASSICAL buildings of the DORIC ORDER.

Gvardzhilas-Klde   an Upper Palaeolithic cave-site on the Chernula River (Kvirila tributary) on the south slope of the Greater Caucasus (altitude 600 m) in Georgia. At least two cultural layers have been defined in a sequence of rubble, CLAY and LOAM deposits. The faunal remains are chiefly of goat and woodland bison. The artifacts include many BACKED BLADES and GRAVETTIAN POINTS, and many non-stone items (e.g. needles, HARPOONS); the age of the industry is unknown. Gvardzhilas-Klde was discovered and excavated by Krukovskij in 1916, and investigated in 1953 by Kalandadze and Tushabramishvili.

Gwisho   a series of mounds beside hot springs in western Zambia, which contain evidence of LATER STONE AGE ZAMBIAN WILTON occupation from about 5000–3500 years ago, of particular interest because organic remains were preserved in the waterlogged deposits. About 35 poorly preserved KHOISAN skeletons were recovered from graves.

Gwithian   a small Middle Bronze Age farming settlement in Cornwall, England, with sub-rectangular houses and associated fields. The spread of broken pottery over fields suggests the practice of manuring, and marks in the field corners indicate that wooden spades may have been in use to help make good use of land which was beyond the reach of the ARD.

gymnasium   a sports-ground in a Greek city which contained a PALAESTRA. They were also centres of education.

gypsum   a hydrated calcium sulphate mineral found in evaporite deposits, desert SOILS, and as a primary or secondary mineral in limestone, shale, marl and CLAY. Gypsum is usually white or colourless, but can be grey, yellow, brown, blue or red. Combined with sand, water and organic fibres, gypsum was used in the manufacture of plaster-like mixtures used as cements, coatings of architectural surfaces, and in making casts, moulds and sculpture. The dense, fine-crystalline variety is ALABASTER.

H

Ha'amonga-a-Maui   a massive TRILITHON of coral at Hahake, Tongatapu, that is unique in the Pacific. The lintel rests in slots on the top of the uprights; according to tradition the monument was built in about AD 1200 by a member of the Tui Tonga dynasty. See also MU'A.

Habuba Kabira   a fortified site on the great bend in the middle Euphrates in Syria, which is the best known of several Late URUK period settlements at this location. The large walled town of Habuba Kabira South seems to have been built as a planned community which existed for about 50 years. Virtually everything about it – architecture, pottery, SEALS, numerical tablets – is southern MESOPOTAMIAN in character. The town was part of a series of closely connected settlements on this part of the Euphrates, including Tell Qannas (the 'AKROPOLIS' of the settlement) and the nearby Jebel Aruda, perhaps a cultic centre; the settlement complex at Habuba Kabira-Tell Qannas covered at least 20 ha, perhaps even 40 ha. The discovery of these settlements in the 1970s caused considerable discussion of Late Uruk state formation, expansionism and trade colonies.

Hacilar   an important site, situated in a valley on the northern side of the Taurus Mountains in southwestern Turkey and excavated by James Mellaart in the 1950s, which presents two distinct aspects. The bulk of the settlement is a small area (under one hectare) with occupation spanning the late Neolithic and early CHALCOLITHIC periods (roughly 5600–4500 BC), providing an important chronological anchor for this part of western Asia. The community inhabited rectangular houses, built as single rooms with internal divisions of space, set close together. Below these levels, and separated by an occupational gap, are seven ACERAMIC NEOLITHIC levels dated to the earlier 7th millennium; these levels provide evidence of morphologically domesticated barley and emmer, while the animals are not yet morphologically changed.

Hadar   a locality in northeastern Ethiopia, which has proved to be one of the most abundant sources of HOMINID fossils in Africa for the period from about 3.5 to 2.5 million years ago (see 'LUCY').

Haddenham   a Neolithic long BARROW in Cambridgeshire, England, on an old land surface later covered by FEN PEAT, thus preserving the original barrow in waterlogged conditions where the timber structures could survive. Many of the features usually found in MEGALITHIC chambered long mounds such as WEST KENNET were here represented by massive timberwork: a curved façade either side of the entrance; a passage; and a burial chamber containing remains of several individuals. So enormous were some of the pieces of timber that the structure has been dubbed 'megaxylic' (from Greek *megas* 'large' and *xylon* 'wood'). The great importance of the site is that it shows the kind of wooden structures which may originally have existed within many of the non-megalithic long mounds of northern Europe.

Hadra ware   a type of HELLENISTIC pottery first recognized in the Hadra cemetery at ALEXANDRIA. A common shape was the HYDRIA which was used as a burial container, often inscribed with the name of the deceased, and sometimes the date, painted or incised on the shoulder. Recent CLAY analysis has shown that the fabric was also produced on Crete.

Hadrian's Wall   in North Britain, served as the main permanent northern boundary of the Roman Empire, except for short periods when the ANTONINE WALL was occupied. It was the idea of the emperor Hadrian and it lay to the north of the earlier Stanegate line (see VINDOLANDA). The wall ran from Wallsend on the Tyne to Bowness-on-Solway. However, further fortlets on the east and west coasts to the south of the wall were designed to stop infiltration. Work started in AD 122, mainly done by legionaries. In the east a stone wall was constructed, whereas in the western sector turf was used initially, although this was later replaced by a stone wall built to a narrower gauge. The wall was secured by milecastles with two turrets in between; a later plan brought the main forts onto the line of the wall.

Hafit   a mountain ridge near Buraymi in southeastern Arabia on which are a number of CAIRNS containing a JEMDET NASR-type of painted pottery, other MESOPOTAMIAN CERAMIC forms, bead types belonging to the same cultural configuration, as well as more locally derived materials. These early 3rd millennium burials provide the earliest local material evidence for Mesopotamian interaction with ancient Magan (see PERSIAN GULF TRADE). Although poorly related to contemporary settlement, these burials provide the name for the earliest Bronze Age cultural period in southeastern Arabia. Similarly constructed tombs and occasional pottery finds extend through the piedmont of southeastern Arabia.

Hagia Triada   see AYIA TRIADHA.

Haguenau   an important cemetery of Bronze Age and Iron Age burial-mounds in the Forêt de Haguenau, Bas-Rhin, France, overlooking the Rhine. The richest of the mounds date to the Middle Bronze Age (c.1500–1350 BC), when this part of France came under the influence of the TUMULUS culture of southern Germany, as shown by the metal types including heavy PALSTAVES, and the distinctive pottery with geometric excised decoration, originally filled with coloured paste.

Haithabu or **Hedeby**   a trading town on the Schlei estuary at the southern end of the Jutland peninsula in northwest Germany. Haithabu was settled during the 7th century AD and over the next 200 years developed as a major commercial centre of the southeast Baltic region. Many years of excavations have revealed evidence not only of trade but also of local industrial activities.

haji   the unglazed earthenware of KOFUN-period and early historic Japan, derived from the YAYOI tradition but influenced by SUE-ware shapes from the late 5th century AD. (Compare SATSUMON.)

Hajjar bin Humeid   a small site (under 5 ha) in the Wadi Beihan of Yemen, which was until recently the only stratified sequence of pre-Islamic occupation in southwestern Arabia. G. van Beek distinguishes 19 STRATA (lettered S–A) in a small test-pit. In addition to exposing an architectural sequence (walls and parts of houses in most levels), the excavation produced a well-controlled CERAMIC sequence from the beginning of the 1st millennium BC to the middle of the 1st millennium AD. This sequence thus corresponds to the emergence and florescence of the SOUTH ARABIAN CIVILIZATION.

Hajji Mohammad   a small site near WARKA, where German soundings in the 1930s ceramically defined the 'UBAID 2 (Hajji Mohammad) period in southern MESOPOTAMIA. The German work also revealed WATTLE AND DAUB domestic architecture of the same date.

Halaf, Tell   a large TELL-site on the River Khabur in northeastern Syria, near the Turkish border, where the investigations by M. von Oppenheim between 1899 and 1929 focused on the 1st millennium BC settlement, the ancient Guzana. It was the seat of an ARAMAEAN kingdom and then a provincial capital of the NEOASSYRIAN empire (and the area to which many Samarians were deported in the 8th century); the Assyrian archives provide valuable details of imperial administrative affairs of the time. The foundation trenches of the Aramaean palace have dug into earlier levels that contained a previously unknown style of painted pottery, now called *Halaf ware* and subsequently identified at Tell ARPACHIYAH and elsewhere. Oppenheim identified another early CERAMIC style at the site (his *Altmonochrom*, corresponding to the 'Dark Faced BURNISHED' ware of the 'AMUQ B), which perhaps represents a pre-Halaf occupation.

Halaf culture complex a range of items of material culture named after the initial discovery of its painted pottery style at Tell HALAF. The Halaf culture complex is chronologically divided into three phases (Early, Middle and Late) dating roughly to the late 6th and early 5th millennia BC. The Early Halaf is found in the Khabur triangle, while the Middle and Late Halaf have an extremely wide distribution, from Cilicia in the west to the Diyala River in the east, covering an arc against and within the inner Tauros–Zagros mountain chain; the pottery also occurs further afield to the north, as at TILK-ITEPE and some Transcaucasian sites. Halaf settlements tend to be uniformly small (generally under 4 ha), classically composed of THOLOS dwellings (a round chamber with a rectilinear entrance passage). The painted pottery is decorated with geometric, floral and some naturalistic motifs (especially BUCRANIA); the Late Halaf pottery includes a polychrome painted ware. Subsistence activities focused on dry farming (of wheat and barley) and animal herds (sheep, goat, cattle, pig). Well-known Halaf sites include Tell AQAB, ARPACHIYAH, and YARIM TEPE 2.

Hala Sultan Tekke the site of a major Late CYPRIOT town in southern Cyprus, which is being excavated by Åström. A fine harbour and the COPPER trade presumably account for the wealth and cosmopolitan tastes of the inhabitants, who acquired items from the Aegean, Anatolia, Syria and Egypt. The site was eventually abandoned in the 11th century BC, possibly because an earthquake had destroyed the harbour.

Halawa Valley the site on Molokai, Hawaii, of intensive archaeological research into settlement patterns. On the coast is one of the earliest settlements in Hawaii dating to *c.*AD 650 with an assemblage similar to BELLOWS BEACH. From *c.*AD 1200 settlement shifted inland as dependence on irrigation agriculture of *taro* (a root crop) increased. The pattern of taro cultivation along the valley bottom with settlements along the sides and mouth is typical of wet windward valleys in the Hawaiian Islands. Compare KAWELA, LAPAKAHI, MAKAHA VALLEY.

halberd a weapon with a pointed or V-shaped blade mounted with its long axis at right angles to the handle, yet with its flat surface in the same plane as the shaft. Halberd blades are very common among Bronze Age finds from temperate Europe.

half-life the time required for half the nuclei in a given sample of a specific radioactive ISOTOPE to decay to another isotope. The half-life value is different for each isotope, but in all cases is a critical component in the calculation of ages by RADIOMETRIC DATING methods. Also, it is the half-life that in effect determines the general age range over which a radiometric dating method is potentially useful.

Halicarnassus a Greek city on the west coast of Turkey. It became the capital of the *satrap* (Persian governor) Mausolus and it was here that his funerary monument, the Mausoleum (one of the SEVEN WONDERS), was constructed. This was decorated with sculpted friezes as well as portrait sculpture; some fragments may be seen in the British Museum.

Hallstatt **1.** a cultural tradition of the late Bronze Age and early Iron Age between *c.*1200 and 600 bc in continental temperate Europe, named by Paul REINECKE after the cemetery and salt-mining site of Hallstatt in Austria. The beginning of the Hallstatt tradition (phases A and B) is equivalent to the URNFIELD period of the late Bronze Age. The Iron Age begins with Hallstatt C, while a final phase, D, marks the transition to the subsequent LA TÈNE period. Within the Hallstatt tradition are a number of regional cultures, such as the LUSATIAN culture. The Hallstatt period is characterized by the emergence of centres of production and trade, such as at STIČNA in Slovenia, the HEUNEBURG and HOHENASPERG in southern Germany, and Hallstatt itself in Austria. Elsewhere, there were fortified settlements such as SENFTENBERG in eastern Germany and BISKUPIN in Poland. The late Hallstatt period saw the emergence of a strongly differentiated social order, in which control of trade with the Mediterranean world played a major role.

2. a site on the western side of Lake Hallstatt in the Austrian Alps, overlooking the modern town. Along an Alpine valley was a cemetery with over 2 000 graves, both cremations and inhumations, containing vast quantities of grave-goods both imported and of local manufacture. Swords with amber and IVORY pommels reflect participation in an exchange network that reached from Africa to the Baltic. Further up the valley are the traces of prehistoric salt workings, in which miners' clothing and tools are often found preserved in ancient galleries.

Hallur a prehistoric site in southern India, excavated by Nagaraja Rao in the 1960s, and containing a stratigraphic sequence important to regional chronology and development. Rao defined three periods at the site (Hallur IA–B, II), which date to the 2nd and early 1st millennia BC. The architecture, at least in Hallur IB, comprises circular structures of bamboo and daub (similar to those elsewhere in the region, e.g. TEKKALAKOTA). Copper tools (mostly axes, and also a fish hook) are present in Hallur IB, while iron appears in Hallur II. This evidence stands at the beginning of the region's MEGALITHIC GRAVE culture, when iron becomes fairly common. The initial occupation contains bones of cattle, sheep and goat, all of which appear in the subsequent occupations. Hallur IB, however, also contains a small amount of horse bone. This suggestion of horse riding is amplified by ROCK ART in the region which depicts horse riders. As at similarly dated sites (e.g. Tekkalakota), Hallur IB presents evidence for cultivation of millets.

Hal Saflieni a rock-cut HYPOGEUM in Malta, consisting of a system of intercommunicating underground chambers. These originally contained the remains of several thousand individuals. The earliest chambers, dating probably to the 5th millennium BC, are those of the upper level. As these became full, two further series of chambers were cut at lower levels. Also to this later phase (3rd millennium BC) belong finely cut chambers with decoration, two in relief, two in red

OCHRE, the designs consisting of running spirals and chequers. These chambers may have been imitations of above-ground MEGALITHIC temples, of the type which originally stood over the hypogeum itself, or may be better seen at TARXIEN.

Hamada, Kosaku   (1881–1938) a Japanese art historian and archaeologist who established the first formal course in archaeology in Japan in 1913. Co-founding the Far Eastern Archaeological Society in 1925, he encouraged scholarly interchange between Japan and China.

Hamangia   a Late Neolithic culture of the Black Sea coastal plain of Romania and Bulgaria, contemporaneous with the early stages of the BOIAN and MARITSA cultures further inland. Hamangia open settlements do not form TELLS, but rather appear to have single thick occupation layers. Burials of the Hamangia culture occur in cemeteries set apart from the settlements, as at CERNAVODĂ and CERNICA. The Hamangia culture was rather short-lived (about 4000–3700 bc) and was succeeded by the GUMELNIŢA culture.

Hambledon Hill   a Neolithic CAUSEWAYED CAMP and Iron Age HILLFORT in Dorset, England, excavated by R. Mercer. The causewayed camp yielded disarticulated human remains and may have been used for the exposure of corpses. A long BARROW stood nearby on the same hilltop. On another part of the hill was a palisaded settlement enclosure (the Stepleton Enclosure) which was destroyed by fire, possibly due to hostile attack. In addition to the enclosures, two series of large Neolithic dykes were also built across the arms of the promontory. The hilltop was reoccupied in the 1st millennium BC when it became the site of an impressive Iron Age hillfort, with two parallel banks and ditches enclosing traces of at least 200 hut circles.

Hamburgian   a Late Upper Palaeolithic reindeer-hunting culture found in north Germany and Holland and contemporary with the Late MAGDALENIAN of France. The Hamburgian is in many ways similar to the AHRENSBURGIAN which follows it in the same area. The typical assemblages include HARPOONS, TANGED points, endscrapers (see SCRAPERS), a few MICROBURINS and specialized borers known as *Zinken*. The neighbouring north German sites of Stellmoor and Meiendorf, excavated by A. Rust, are Hamburgian seasonal reindeer-hunting camps, preserved by waterlogged conditions and dating to 13 000–11 750 BP. They have both yielded the skeletons of young reindeer apparently deposited in a lake either as an offering or as a method of refrigeration. See also BROMMIAN.

hammerstone   a hard stone used as a hammer during the KNAPPING of flint and other stone. See HARD HAMMER TECHNIQUE.

Hammurabi   (1792–1750 BC) one of the best known of the ancient MESOPOTAMIAN kings. He was the sixth king of the AMORITE DYNASTY at BABYLON. Under the earlier rulers in this line, Babylon was a petty kingdom. Hammurabi changed this status by forming a series of alliances successively to deal with competing kingdoms, thereby managing to conquer Babylonia and the middle Euphrates, including MARI. Although his inscriptions claim conquests into ASSYRIA, Hammurabi's effective control stopped at the frontier; unlike other southern Mesopotamian empire builders, Hammurabi never attempted invasion of ELAM, although he did fight defensive wars with Elamite forces. The collapse of Hammurabi's kingdom began soon after his death.

Han   1. a term used for unrelated ethnic groups in China and Korea. In China it implies 'pure' Chinese as distinct from minority groups, and in Korea it refers to the inhabitants of the SAMHAN in the PROTO-THREE KINGDOMS period.
2. a historical period or DYNASTY in China (206 BC–AD 220), with the WANGMAN interregnum (AD 9–25) separating the Early (Western) and Late (Eastern) Han periods. As the first centralized state in China following unification by QIN in 221 BC, the Han Court instituted iron and salt monopolies, extended territorial administration through the COMMANDERY system (see LELANG), opened commerce to the West via the SILK ROUTE, and began the tradition of court histories (see HOUHANSHU). Aristocratic burials of the period are very rich (MANCHENG, MAWANGDUI), but most tombs have only LEAD-GLAZED WARE.

handaxe   see BIFACE.

Hane   an Early Eastern POLYNESIAN DUNE site at the mouth of the Hane Valley on Ua Huka Island, Marquesas, which documents settlement of the Marquesas from about AD 300 up to European contact.

Hang Gon   a prehistoric bronze-working site near Saigon in southern Vietnam, overlapping in period with CU LAO RUA. Iron period urnfield remains of the late 1st millennium BC relate later phases of occupation to SA HUYNH.

Hanging Grimston   a long BARROW on the Yorkshire Wolds, England, which gave its name to the Grimston-Lyles Hill pottery style of the British Earlier Neolithic of the 4th millennium BC. The characteristic vessel shape is the round-based CARINATED bowl with everted rim.

hangtu [hang-t'u]   the Chinese technique of pounded-earth construction of walls and foundation platforms for buildings; first developed in the terminal Neolithic (LONGSHAN) period and subsequently used for monumental architecture. (See ERLITOU, QISHAN, XIAOTUN. Compare PISÉ.)

haniwa   the unglazed earthenware funerary sculptures of KOFUN-period Japan, erected on MOUNDED TOMB surfaces either to outline and protect the burial precincts or as sumptuary display. See fig. at CHOKKOMON.

Harappa   one of the great cities of the Mature HARAPPAN civilization, located in the Punjab region of Pakistan, and excavated by M.S. Vats in the 1920s and 1930s, by M. WHEELER in the 1940s and more recently by G. Dales. Although the Mature Harappan occupation is the best explored aspect of the city, both Early Harappan (the 'pre-defence' levels) and Late Harappan ('Cemetery H' and related habitation levels) are also documented. The Mature Harappan city, covering about 80 ha, presents the standard Harappan form of a citadel with monumental architecture, and with a larger zone of residential architecture to the east; the excavations at MOHENJO-DARO provide a clearer picture of Harappan urbanism.

Harappan civilization   one of the great civilizations of antiquity, located in Pakistan and north-west India. A development of the 3rd millennium BC in the greater Indus valley, and named after the site of HARAPPA, the civilization represents one of world archaeology's great traditions. It is divided into three phases – Early, Mature (or Urban) and Late (or Post-Urban). The Harappan tradition emerged from a series of cultural provinces in the Punjab, Sind and neighbouring Baluchistan regions of the northwestern Indian subcontinent (see AMRI, KOT DIJI, KALIBANGAN) early in the 3rd millennium. Around 2600–2500 BC the Mature Harappan abruptly coalesced from these antecedents. The Mature Harappan is typified by urban centres and massive 'public' architecture, the use of characteristic 'administrative' devices (a still undeciphered writing system, square SEALS, and metrical standards, especially for weight), technological sophistication, and wide contacts with surrounding regions (from Central Asia to southeastern Arabia and southern MESOPOTAMIA). Covering an enormous area (some 800 000 sq km), many aspects of the material culture (in architecture, pottery, metal and bead forms, seals) are present throughout the Harappan region, though significant regional variation does exist (see ALAMGIRPUR, MITATHAL, RANJPUR). Around 2000–1900 BC, this urban expression of the Harappan tradition collapsed, leaving regional Late Harappan cultures in villages and small towns whose continuity with the Mature Harappan is evident principally in pottery, but which had lost many of the artifacts that were central to Mature Harappan society (especially seals and writing). Late Harappan cultures existed through most of the 2nd millennium BC.

Harare   see KUTAMA.

hard hammer technique   the use of a HAMMERSTONE to remove FLAKES during the KNAPPING of flint and other stone. Hard hammer flakes are short and deep with a prominent BULB OF PERCUSSION. Compare SOFT HAMMER TECHNIQUE.

hard water effect   a potential source of CONTAMINATION and error in RADIOCARBON DATING. Hard water is water enriched in dissolved salts of calcium and magnesium which may derive from older or dead carbon in some reservoirs. $^{14}C/^{12}C$ ratios of aquatic plants and organic and inorganic carbonate precipitates will reflect the reservoir ratio. If old or dead carbon is present, the resultant radiocarbon ages will be too old. Typically these reservoirs are in areas of limestone terrain or other carbonate rocks where carbonate dissolution leads to the introduction through groundwater of old or dead carbon. Other factors affecting reservoir $^{14}C/^{12}C$ ratios include exchange with the atmosphere, introduction of HUMUS, the amount of soil carbonate, and temperature and precipitation. If the hard water effect is suspected and corrections are not made, ages should be reported as maximums only.

Hargeisan   a stone industry of northern Somalia characterized by the production of large BLADES from prismatic CORES, which precedes the appearance of MICROLITHIC assemblages.

Harifian   a hunting/gathering culture in the Negev and Sinai, whose members lived in seasonal encampments with permanent architecture. These communities represent a specialized desert adaptation with a Late NATUFIAN-derived lithic industry which was largely contemporary with the PPNA communities further north in the Levant. The characteristic tool type of the Harifian is the Harif point, which is an obliquely truncated BLADELET with a pointed base formed by the MICROBURIN technique and steep RETOUCH. The designation was defined by Antony Marks' work in the Negev.

Harmal, Tell   a tiny administrative centre (1.7 ha in area) belonging to the kingdom of Eshnunna (see Tell ASMAR) during the OLD BABYLONIAN period, lying just outside Baghdad in central Iraq. T. Baqir excavated a large proportion of the site in the 1950s, revealing a walled settlement with administrative, cultic and residential buildings. Despite its small size, it contained a large number of literary and 'scholarly' texts in addition to administrative archives; a pair of life-size lion figures in TERRACOTTA found here are famous examples of Old Babylonian art.

harpoon   technically, a spear-like implement with a detachable head which is used in hunting or fishing. However, archaeologists use the term to refer to all barbed bone or antler points. Harpoons are particularly associated with the MAGDALENIAN and the Mesolithic of Europe.

Harrison, Benjamin (1837–1921)   an English grocer and amateur archaeologist who collected hundreds of Palaeolithic stone tools from north Kent, and who excavated at the OLDBURY rockshelter site. Harrison is best remembered for his strong belief in EOLITHS as genuine stone tools.

Hasanlu   a prehistoric site in the Urmia basin, south of Lake Urmia (northwest Iran), which was the focus of a large project conducted by Robert Dyson from the 1950s to the 1970s. In addition to Hasanlu itself, the project excavated at Pisdeli, Hajji Firuz, Dalma, Dinkha and others, to produce a 10-phase chronological sequence that begins in the late 7th millennium BC and continues (with breaks) into Islamic times. The project has also shed considerable light on early CERAMIC NEOLITHIC adaptations (the Hajji Firuz phase, late 7th to mid 6th millennia BC), on the chronology and origins of the Iron Age in western Iran, on early 1st millennium BC upland communities under pressure from ASSYRIAN imperial expansion (Hasanlu IV, from which the famous gold bowl derives), and on regional interactions during other periods (e.g. the Dalma pottery of the 5th millennium, Dinkha pottery of the 2nd millennium BC).

Hascherkeller   a Late Bronze Age/Early Iron Age site of the HALLSTATT period in Bavaria, Germany, near the city of Landshut on the Isar River. Settlement remains consisted of three farmsteads enclosed by earthworks, within which was evidence for the manufacture of pottery and for bronze casting. Hascherkeller has been interpreted as typical of the rural farmsteads that dotted central Europe in the first part of the last millennium BC, prior to the emergence of centres of production and commerce such as HALLSTATT, STIČNA and the HEUNEBURG.

Hassi Mouilah   an important Algerian CAPSIAN NEOLITHIC site, dated to c.5300 BP. Finds include many pointed-base pots with overall impressed decoration, PROJECTILE POINTS, and geometric MICROLITHS, as well as ostrich eggshell and amazonite beads.

Hassuna, Tell   a prehistoric site on the Tigris near the confluence of the Upper Zab, in northern Iraq, where the excavations by S. Lloyd and F. Safar in the 1940s defined a sequence of a previously unknown pre-SAMARRAN culture in northern MESOPOTAMIA, now named after the site. The 17 levels defined fall into four cultural phases. At the bottom (level Ia) is an ephemeral occupation, perhaps by a semi-sedentary community whose material culture is similar to that at UMM DABAGHIYAH. Following this phase are three architectural levels (Ib–c, II) now identified as 'Archaic Hassuna', and then three levels (III–V) of 'Standard Hassuna.' The subsequent occupations consisted of five HALAF levels (VI–X) and three 'UBAID levels (XI–XIII); two much later occupations (levels XIV–XV) cap the mound. In this sequence, Samarran painted wares occur in levels III through VIII, indicating a considerable chronological overlapping of Hassuna, Samarran and Halaf CERAMIC styles. Lloyd and Safar's excavations provided the type-site for the HASSUNA CULTURE COMPLEX, and defined its two developmental phases; these are still used today.

Hassuna culture complex   a late Neolithic culture that is roughly and uncertainly dated to the 6th millennium BC, and has its distribution in the Jezirah of northern Iraq, running from the Tigris River in the area of the Upper Zab toward the Khabur triangle; it seems to be derived from the earlier Neolithic found at such sites as UMM DABAGHIYAH and the basal level of HASSUNA. The culture complex, best known from the sites Hassuna and YARIM TEPE 1, is divided into two phases, the 'Archaic' and 'Standard' Hassuna, according to changes in the painted and incised decoration of the pottery. The architecture of these settlements forms complexes of small rooms set around open spaces. Subsistence was focused on the cultivation of a variety of wheats and barley, and on herding sheep, goat and cattle; the material culture incorporates a variety of exotic materials, including copper, turquoise and carnelian beads. Although once considered representative of early agricultural colonization in northern MESOPOTAMIA, a number of earlier sites are now known.

Hastinapura   a site of some 30 ha on the upper Ganges in northern India, where B.B. Lal's excavations revealed a cultural sequence from the 2nd millennium BC to mediaeval times, though with major breaks. The earliest evidence of occupation is a few OCHRE COLOURED POTTERY SHERDS beneath a PALAEOSOL, over which are levels of fragmentary WATTLE AND DAUB and MUD-BRICK architecture, together with PAINTED GREY WARE as well as a variety of other wares. These people cultivated rice and kept a wide variety of animals, including horse, and also used IRON as well as COPPER. Following major flooding and erosion, the site was reoccupied by people using NORTHERN BLACK POLISHED WARE in a community of brick architecture laid out on regular drained streets, who habitually used iron and employed coinage. The later levels belong to the late 1st millennium BC and to mediaeval times. Lal's work at Hastinapura provided the first good stratigraphic context for Painted Grey Ware, which marks the trend toward urbanism and the early Indian kingdoms, in the Gangetic region, fully expressed in the Northern Black Polished Ware horizon.

Hatchepsut   an Egyptian queen, reigning in c.1479–1457 BC, during the 18th DYNASTY. Her reign is a rare example of a woman assuming the monarchy in ancient Egypt. The best-known monuments of Hatchepsut are the 'Red Chapel' at KARNAK and her MORTUARY TEMPLE at DEIR EL-BAHRI.

Hatnub (*Egyptian* 'House of Gold')   a site in UPPER EGYPT, 18 km southeast of EL-AMARNA, the location of ALABASTER quarries worked from at least as early as the OLD KINGDOM until the MIDDLE KINGDOM. Hatnub has provided inscriptional material left by expeditions sent to the quarry, in the form of loose STELAE and GRAFFITI on the quarry walls.

Hattusha see BOGHAZKÖY.

Hatvan culture the second culture in the tripartite sequence of the Hungarian Early Bronze Age defined by Moszolics on the basis of the stratigraphy at TÓSZEG, where the Hatvan culture occurs between NAGYRÉV and FÜZESABONY. Cremation burial in pits was practised. Hatvan settlements are also known, characterized by fortifications and long post structures. The Hatvan culture is believed to have originated in eastern Hungary and spread westward.

Haua Fteah a very large cave in northern Libya, excavated by MCBURNEY, and containing the most complete sequence of Upper PLEISTOCENE and HOLOCENE stone industries known from North Africa. The lowest layers are as yet unexcavated and the earliest industry so far described is the Libyan AMUDIAN (pre-AURIGNACIAN) BLADE industry. It was succeeded at least 60 000 years ago by the LEVALLOISO-MOUSTERIAN, which was in turn replaced about 40 000 years ago by the DABBAN industry. This continued until about 18–16 000 years ago, when it was followed by the Eastern ORANIAN, and later by LIBYCO-CAPSIAN material. Pottery as well as domestic sheep and/or goats are present by about 7000 years ago.

Haven, Samuel Foster (1806–81) an American antiquary whose monograph *Archaeology of the United States* (1856) did much to debunk many of the wilder speculations on North American PRE-HISTORY, in particular the origins of the Midwestern mounds. See ATWATER, DAVIS, SQUIER, THOMAS.

Hawara a site in Egypt of the second PYRAMID of King AMENEMHAT III dated to *c.*1844–1797 BC, possibly a later and more elaborate replacement for that at DAHSHUR. The particularly large MORTUARY TEMPLE attached to the pyramid seems to have been identified by some Greek and Roman authors as the 'Egyptian labyrinth' of legend.

Hayonim Cave a well-stratified prehistoric site in western Galilee, Israel, which has been excavated by a variety of workers since 1965. The earliest occupation level in the cave yielded MOUSTERIAN artifacts and bones. This was followed by an AURIGNACIAN layer with flint and bone tools, KEBARAN deposits and finally several NATUFIAN layers including 16 graves and six structures.

Hazleton a Neolithic chambered long BARROW of Severn-Cotswold type in Gloucestershire, England, with two MEGALITHIC chambers reached by passages entered from near the middle of the long sides. Careful excavation allowed the construction sequence of the mound to be studied, consisting of a number of dry-stone cells filled with rubble. Remains of around 40 persons were found in the burial chambers. RADIOCARBON dates indicated a short period of construction and use in *c.*4700 BC.

Hazor a Palestinian site, the most important CANAANITE town excavated so far, explored by YADIN in 1955–58 and 1968. The central part of Hazor, a natural spur termed the 'upper city', was occupied in the EARLY BRONZE AGE. In the MIDDLE BRONZE AGE the 'upper city' was defended by a substantial (8 m thick) brick wall, while a GLACIS seems to have enclosed an area of approximately 80 ha to the north termed the 'lower city'. Canaanite Hazor flourished from the 18th century BC, but was destroyed by the ISRAELITES in the late 13th century BC. The 'upper city' was later fortified by SOLOMON and Ahab, prior to its sacking by the ASSYRIANS in 732 BC.

Head-Smashed-In   a KILL-SITE in southern Alberta, Canada, in which bison were killed by stampeding them *en masse* over a cliff. The site has evidence of almost continuous use going back to about 3700 BC.

Healy Lake   a prehistoric open-air site in the Tanana Valley, central Alaska, USA. Four cultural layers have been defined in shallow LOESS deposits. The lowest layer appears to date to *c.*11 000–10 000 bp and contains CHINDADN POINTS and MICROBLADES. It was investigated by Cook and McKennon in 1962–67.

hearth   the fire site, a FEATURE of many domestic habitation sites. The hearth is often centrally located, and has a variety of shapes and sizes. The burnt earthen rims of some hearths provide suitable oxidized material for ARCHAEOMAGNETIC DATING.

Heathery Burn   a cave-site, in Co. Durham, England, with remains of Late Bronze Age occupation. Discovered during quarrying in the late 19th century, the cave held an extensive deposit of pottery, animal bones and bronzes, sealed under STALAGMITE. The finds included horse-riding equipment and evidence of metalworking. The cave may have been used as a hunting shelter by local chieftains in the 8th century BC.

Heavenly Horse tomb   a 5th century AD MOUNDED TOMB of the SILLA Kingdom in Kyongju City, Korea. A mound of pebbles covered with a layer of earth, 57 m in diameter, enclosed and protected from robbers an internal WOODEN-CHAMBER containing the lacquered wooden coffin of a male dressed in a gold crown and a girdle decorated with curved beads (see MAGATAMA). Grave-goods included horse trappings, glass cups, LACQUER ware and ox horns. The tomb's intact interior has been restored as a display area for a site museum within the mound.

heavy mineral analysis   heavy minerals are those of relatively high SPECIFIC GRAVITY, such as garnet, tourmaline, epidote and zircon, that usually occur as accessory detrital mineral grains in SEDIMENTARY deposits. The heavy minerals in pottery TEMPER and matrix, or any other material produced from a sedimentary deposit, can be examined to help identify the geological PROVENANCE or source of the material. Different sources within a region may be characterized by contrasting heavy mineral suites. Heavy minerals are separated from the light minerals of lesser specific gravity by pouring the sample into a column of heavy liquid with relatively high density. The most commonly used is bromoform with a specific gravity of 2.85. The heavy minerals sink and are siphoned off whereas the lighter minerals will float on the heavy liquid. The heavy mineral fraction is then identified and counted using low-power microscopy and compared to heavy mineral analyses from potential sources. Although the analysis is routine, the heavy liquids utilized are generally toxic and extreme care must be taken.

Hedeby   see HAITHABU.

heiau   a Hawaiian stone temple, equivalent to the MARAE of Eastern POLYNESIA. Most are complex arrangements of walls, terraces and platforms. See also AHU.

Heidelberg jaw   see MAUER JAW.

Heijo   the site of the 8th century AD palace and capital of the RITSURYO state in Nara Prefecture, Japan, also known as the Nara

Palace and Capital. Excavated continuously since 1952, the palace site was bought in 1961 and established as a historical site and museum. Plans of excavated palace buildings are reproduced in surface landscaping, and samples of buildings and the palace wall have been reconstructed. Occupied from 710–784 (see JAPANESE PERIODIZATION), the 4.3 km × 4.8 km capital followed the Chinese gridded-city plan as established at CHANG'AN (see also FUJIWARA). The discovery at Heijo of inked MOKKAN has added a documentary perspective to the information given in the 8th century court histories, the KOJIKI and NIHON SHOKI.

hei tiki   a MAORI neck pendant of stylized human form, often of GREENSTONE.

Heliopolis   a once-important ancient Egyptian city, major cult centre of the god RE. Little remains of it apart from the still-standing OBELISK of King SENWOSRET I. It is now a northern suburb of Cairo.

Helladic   the Bronze Age culture of central and southern Greece. The chronological system devised by WACE and BLEGEN has three main divisions: Early (*c.*3000–2000 BC), Middle (*c.*2000–1550 BC) and Late (*c.*1550–1050 BC), each of which is further subdivided into three phases designated by Roman numerals. Late Helladic is the period of the MYCENAEAN civilization.

hellenistic, *adj.*   relating to a period of time dating from the death of Alexander the Great (323 BC) to the establishment of the Roman Empire in the 1st century BC. The hellenistic world consisted of the kingdoms carved out from the former Persian empire as well as the Greek mainland. The term *hellenistic art* can be applied to post-CLASSICAL material outside this geographical area, such as in ETRURIA or southern Italy. See also ARCHAISTIC.

Hell Gap   1. a deeply stratified site in eastern Wyoming, USA, which provides virtually a complete PALAEOINDIAN sequence for the Plains of North America. The site was occupied from about 11 200 BP to 8000 BP.

2. a PLANO TRADITION COMPLEX dated 10 000–9500 BP.

3. a PROJECTILE POINT TYPE belonging to the Plano tradition.

Hembury   a Neolithic CAUSEWAYED CAMP in Devon, England, partly overlain by a later Iron Age HILLFORT. POST-HOLES of a circular Neolithic house were found beneath the Iron Age west gate. The causewayed camp yielded WINDMILL HILL pottery and RADIOCARBON dates indicating occupation in *c.*4200–3900 BC.

Hemudu [Ho-mu-tu]   an Early Neolithic site in Zhejiang Province, China. Located on the coast of Hangzhou Bay, it has wet-preserved wooden raised-stilt architecture and abundant plant and animal remains, notably thick deposits of rice grain, husks and straw. It is the type-site of the southern rice-growing regime in contrast to the northern millet regime represented at CISHAN. Marshland species are well represented, indicating broad-spectrum collecting and aquatic domesticate experimentation. Dog, pig and water buffalo were the main domesticated animals. It is dated to the late 6th and early 5th millennia BC, and is succeeded by the QINGLIANGANG culture in the early Neolithic; and by the Daxi, Qujialing and LIANGZHU cultures in the middle Neolithic (*c.*3800–2800 BC).

henge   a prehistoric ritual enclosure, usually circular or nearly so, consisting of bank and ditch with one or two opposing entrances.

The bank is usually outside the ditch, and excavations at major henges such as DURRINGTON WALLS and Mount Pleasant have shown that substantial circular timber buildings once stood in the interior. Henges are especially common in the lowland south and east of England, but are also found further west and north where they sometimes enclose a STONE CIRCLE.

Hengelo Interstadial   a Continental Middle PLENIGLACIAL INTERSTADIAL occurring during the final GLACIATION between the Moershooft and DENEKAMP interstadials and starting at *c*.39 000 BP.

Hengistbury Head   a promontory jutting into the Solent estuary in Dorset, England, with an Upper Palaeolithic (CRESWELLIAN) open-air site which has yielded a well-defined scatter of flint artifacts proved by CONJOINING to belong to one ASSEMBLAGE; THERMOLUMINESCENCE dates around 12 500 bp have been obtained. A nearby Mesolithic site has evidence for on-site flint-KNAPPING. The site rose to prominence in the Iron Age, *c*.100 BC, as a trading centre with connections to continental Europe. Roman wine AMPHORAE and luxury goods were among the imports. The entrepôt fell into decline in the mid 1st century BC.

heqin [ho-ch'in]   the system of reverse tribute employed by the HAN DYNASTY court in China for pacifying surrounding populations. As a reward for voluntary submission of tribute and acknowledgement of Han hegemony, lavish gifts of precious goods were bestowed on embassies from regions such as YAYOI Japan or the XIONGNU.

Herculaneum (*Gk* Herakleion)   a small coastal town in CAMPANIA in Italy, buried under volcanic mud after the eruption of Vesuvius in AD 79. It probably started as an ARCHAIC Greek foundation. First attempts at exploration were made in the 18th century through tunnels around the theatre, but systematic excavations were conducted only in the 19th century and then again from the 1920s. Some of the houses have yielded important finds, such as the VILLA of the PAPYRI containing important portraits as well as a library including works of Epicurus. The mud has allowed many timber items such as furniture to survive.

herm   a low stone shaft on the top of which may be carved a portrait or the head of a deity. On some examples two heads are carved back-to-back (*janiform*). Although herms are found in the Greek world, for example in the AGORA of CLASSICAL ATHENS, they were particularly popular as decorative elements in the gardens of Roman houses.

Hermopolis Magna (*Arabic* el-Ashmunein)   a site in northern UPPER EGYPT, with its NECROPOLIS at TUNA EL-GEBEL. Hermopolis Magna has chiefly been excavated by Roeder in 1929–39, and by the British Museum in 1980–90. The site is a substantial TELL, largely composed of the remains of the buildings erected within the sacred enclosure of this important city. The fragmentary stone structures on the *tell*, the earliest of which date to the MIDDLE KINGDOM, are mostly the remains of various phases of building at the great TEMPLE of THOTH. The most important standing building is the remains of a Roman BASILICA.

Herodium   a Palestinian site, chiefly excavated in 1962–67 by Corbo. An impressive fortress constructed by Herod the Great (37–4

BC), it consisted of a circular fortified palace on the summit of a conical hill. Herodium also served as the site of Herod's tomb, and was a stronghold for Jewish rebels in the revolts against Roman rule.

Hetepheres   a queen of the Egyptian OLD KINGDOM, the wife of SNEFRU and mother of KHUFU. Her unmarked tomb, within her son's PYRAMID-COMPLEX at GIZA, was discovered by REISNER in 1925. This seems to have been a reburial of the funerary equipment (but without Hetepheres' MUMMY) from her original tomb, the location of which is unknown.

Heuneburg   an Early Iron Age fortified site of the HALLSTATT period in Baden-Württemberg, Germany, which flourished c.600–500 BC. The fortifications at the Heuneburg enclosed an area of 3 ha by headwaters of the River Danube. In most phases, they were built from rubble-filled timber cribs, but in Period IV they were built on a Mediterranean-style plan from MUD-BRICKS on a stone foundation. The settlement deposits at the Heuneburg contain considerable evidence for local manufacturing activity and trade with the Mediterranean. Imported objects include coral, fine pottery and Greek AMPHORAE from Massalia (modern MARSEILLES) presumed to have contained wine.

Hierakonpolis   a site in southern UPPER EGYPT, a major settlement of the PREDYNASTIC and ARCHAIC PERIOD. The town-enclosure at Hierakonpolis (the 'Kom el-Ahmar') was excavated by Quibell and Green in 1897–99, particularly a series of successive shrines, the earliest of which dates to the early Archaic/late Predynastic, as does a famous cache of votive objects, mainly of Kings NARMER and 'Scorpion'. Hierakonpolis has also been explored by Fairservis and Hoffman in 1969–88.

hieratic, (Gk 'sacred')   a cursive form of HIEROGLYPHIC script, developed for everyday use in hand-written documents, and used in varying forms throughout Egyptian history until replaced for widespread nonreligious use by DEMOTIC.

hieroglyphic (Gk 'sacred carved writing')   a pictorial script employed by the ancient Egyptians from the beginning of the 3rd millennium BC until the end of the 4th century AD. It was primarily used for religious purposes and on public monuments, surviving in these contexts even after it had been superseded in more vernacular contexts by the cursive scripts HIERATIC and DEMOTIC which evolved from it. Pioneering work in the decipherment of hieroglyphic texts was carried out by CHAMPOLLION.

Higgs, Eric Sidney (1908–76)   a British archaeologist who conducted innovative work on the origins of agriculture. Higgs pioneered the technique of SITE CATCHMENT ANALYSIS and also initiated a school of archaeological thought called PALAEOECONOMY.

High Lodge   a British Palaeolithic site in Suffolk. The original interpretation, based on ARTIFACT TYPOLOGY, was that it had yielded three separate INDUSTRIES: a slightly worn ACHEULIAN OVATE BIFACE industry, a rather crude FLAKE industry, and a MOUSTERIAN industry with finely made tools but no prepared-CORE flaking technique. Recent excavation suggests that High Lodge may be c.450 000–500 000 years old, and that the entire ASSEMBLAGE may be similar to material from CLACTON and SWANSCOMBE.

Hili 8   one of a number of scattered small settlements in the

Buraymi district of southeastern Arabia. It provides the key architectural and CERAMIC sequence for the Bronze Age of the region (*c*.3000–1800 BC). Here S. Cleuziou exposed a MUD-BRICK tower (a typical architectural form in settlements of the period) that underwent a sequence of rebuilding. These excavations also provided important evidence for the emergence of Arabian oasis farming and water management, a component of which was domesticated sorghum *(Sorgo bicolor)* from the beginning of the sequence; this occurrence of domesticated sorghum is among the earliest known, and may point to a non-African centre of its domestication. As part of the project, several UMM AN-NAR-type tombs were also excavated, one of which contained the remains of around 100 individuals together with many ceramics, stone vessels and other small finds.

hillfort any hilltop fortress, though the term now most commonly refers to sites of the Late Bronze Age or Iron Age. The earliest hillforts of *c*.1000 BC were followed in the 7th and 6th centuries BC by sites with increasingly elaborate fortifications, including timber-framed ramparts and long, heavily defended entrance corridors. These gave way to massive multiple-dump ramparts and intricate entrances with outworks in the 3rd and 2nd centuries BC, a form which sees its fullest expression at MAIDEN CASTLE. In upland Britain, earth and timber defences were replaced by dry-stone walling. Some hillforts may have been permanent settlements, but many were merely temporary refuges. See also CRICKLEY, DANEBURY, HAMBLEDON, MONTLASSOIS.

hillslope a nearly ubiquitous sloping LANDFORM that ascends to higher GEOMORPHIC surfaces and descends to lower geomorphic surfaces. Hillslopes are the products of both erosional and depositional processes and are inherently unstable, thus presenting a potentially complex CONTEXT for archaeological deposits. Hillslopes can be segmented into the following geomorphic components, listed in descending order, all of which need not be present to form a hillslope:

   (a) *summit* – more or less level upland position at a drainage divide.

   (b) *shoulder* – convex surface immediately below the summit where erosional processes dominate.

   (c) *backslope* – more or less linear slope segment where both erosional and depositional processes occur; the backslope may have an associated thin surface veneer of material in transit downslope.

   (d) *footslope* – concave segment where depositional processes dominate.

   (e) *toeslope* – slightly concave, flattening segment where depositional processes dominate. The toeslope may represent all or part of a valley ALLUVIAL surface.

Footslopes and toeslopes are areas where archaeological deposits may be buried and preserved, and where cultural debris eroded from upslope may be redeposited. The shoulder and backslope are areas where archaeological deposits may be eroded. Material in these positions may be *in situ*, or temporarily redeposited while in transport downslope. The summit is subject to AEOLIAN deposition which may bury cultural deposits, and localized sheetflood EROSION and deposition which may differentially redistribute cultural debris locally.

Himiko   see YAMATAI.

hinge fracture   a fracture which occurs by error during FLINT KNAP-PING, producing a characteristic FLAKE with a smooth, almost rounded end. It is either caused by a misdirected hammer blow allowing the fracture force to escape to the outside of the CORE, or is a direct result of the conchoidal nature of the stone itself.

Hippodamian planning   the rectangular type of town layout which was practised, though not exclusively, by Hippodamos of MILETUS in the 5th century BC. Miletus, a harbour city in western Turkey, received a new layout after its destruction by the Persians in 494 BC, consisting of some 400 blocks. Public buildings and spaces were fitted into this grid, sometimes requiring multiples of the basic blocks. Hippodamos is said to have planned the PIRAEUS. See also PRIENE.

hippodrome   see CIRCUS.

hiri   an ethnographically documented Papuan coastal exchange system linking the Motu of the Port Moresby area with the Elema and Naman of the Papuan Gulf, through exchange of clay pots for sago and of shell valuables for canoe logs. Like the MAILU system, the *hiri* seems to have operated for about the last 400–500 years and is archaeologically documented from sites such as Popo and MOTUPORE.

Hisarlik/Troy   a tiny site (about 2 ha in area), first excavated by J. von Hahn in 1864, and then, famously, by H. SCHLIEMANN in (1871–90), by W. DÖRPFELD in the 1890s and by C. BLEGEN in the 1930s; it has a far greater historical importance than would be expected from its size. Set on a plain overlooking the southern entrance to the Dardanelles in northwestern Anatolia, it contains a series of walled Bronze Age settlements (Troy I–VII, with subphases), as well as later CLASSICAL period occupation on its surface; in absolute dates the Bronze Age settlement began in the late 4th millennium and continued to the 12th century BC. This sequence defines a key reference for comparative chronologies, especially for pottery, but also for metal types and architectural forms. In the occupation history of the site, Troy II and VII are most widely discussed. The famous 'treasure of Priam' (a hoard of objects in precious metals and semi-precious stones) came from one of the Troy II (EARLY BRONZE AGE II) levels. Troy II was a small fortified town whose interior at one point (Troy IIc) was dominated by a large MEGARON complex (courtyard, storerooms and ancillary buildings in addition to the three megara themselves); at other times Troy II was composed of regular blocks of rooms separated by streets. Troy VIIa, on the other hand, is the best candidate for the Troy of the *Iliad*, though considerable controversy surrounds this issue. At this time, the area enclosed by the town walls was filled with small houses densely packed together, most of which contained large storage jars sunk into floors; finds of MYCENAEAN painted pottery reflect contact with that world. The settlement ended in massive fires.

Hissar, Tepe   an important site in the Damghan plain of north-eastern Iran, excavated by Erich Schmidt in the 1930s and re-examined by Robert Dyson in the 1970s. Schmidt defined eight occupational phases at the site (Hissar I–III, with subdivisions), which may be dated to between the late 5th and early 2nd millennia BC. Evidence from Hissar II (later 4th to early 3rd millennia BC) suggests that this community was involved in the PROTO-ELAMITE phenomenon, manifested in a number of pottery forms, SEALS and tablet blanks. The material culture at the end of the sequence (Hissar IIIC) marks the appearance of a BURNISHED grey ware that figures prominently in discussions of Indo-Aryan movements and the origins of the western Iranian Iron Age.

historic period   any period in the past that can be studied by using contemporary written documents. See PREHISTORIC PERIOD, PROTOHISTORIC PERIOD.

Hittites   a people of obscure origin who settled in Anatolia and the Levant in the later 3rd millennium BC, like other speakers of INDO-EUROPEAN languages such as the Luwians. The Hittites settled in the area of BOGHAZKÖY by the beginning of the 2nd millennium. Their subsequent history, down to around 1200 BC, is one of cycles of integration and expansion followed by collapse, a process that is reflected in the division of Hittite political history into Old Kingdom (perhaps 1700–1600 BC) and Empire (roughly 1450–1200 BC). In the latter period, the Hittites were major players in the military and diplomatic struggle for Syro–Palestinian client states, usually in opposition to the Egyptians, as reflected in the AMARNA archives. The Hittite state collapsed during the regional upheavals at the end of the LATE BRONZE AGE, notably the movements of the SEA PEOPLES and pressures from Anatolian groups from the north. During the Iron Age, some petty states in northern Syria continued certain aspects of the Hittite cultural tradition (variously named Neo-Hittite, Syro–Hittite, Neo-Luwian), before being swept away by ASSYRIAN empire building.

Hjortspring   a boat or war canoe, deposited as a ritual offering in a bog at Als, Denmark, in c.200 BC. The boat, the earliest known CLINKER-BUILT vessel, was 19 m long and was powered by oars with no mast. It was part of a larger offering consisting of hundreds of spears, swords and shields, as well as chain mail and domestic items. The Hjortspring hoard may have been an offering of war booty in thanksgiving for victory.

Hluboke Mašůky   a fortified Neolithic settlement of the LENGYEL culture in southern Moravia. The fortifications consisted of a ditch about 1 km in circumference and 1.8 to 2.8 m deep, reinforced by a two-row palisade through which four gates opened into the interior of the ramparts.

Hoabinhian   a loosely related group of early-to-mid-HOLOCENE stone tool INDUSTRIES (a 'techno-complex') of mainland and parts of maritime Southeast Asia, first identified in cave sites of Hoa Binh province in north Vietnam, bordering the Red River valley. Dates range from c.10 000 BC to 2000 BC, depending upon the area. Many of the occupation sites of this period are thought to have been lost with the flooding of SUNDALAND during the POST-GLACIAL sea-level rise. Three broad phases have been recognized in the Vietnamese and related sites: the 'archaic', characterized by massive unifacially worked pebble tools; the 'intermediate', recognized by the reduction in size of pebble tools and the appearance of BIFACIAL working and occasional EDGE-GRINDING (see also BACSONIAN); and 'late', characterized by smaller SCRAPERS, knives, grinding stones, piercers, rare sawn and polished stone tools, shell artifacts, and, towards the end, pottery. The relative crudeness of tools in earlier phases may have been due to greater reliance upon bamboo, wood and rattan than upon stone. Debate continues concerning when during this sequence the transition occurred from broad-spectrum hunting and gathering to horticulture and then rice agriculture (see SPIRIT CAVE).

0   10 cm

Hoabinhian Stone tools. Top left: edge-ground Bacsonian axe. Top right: a sumatralith.

Hochdorf an Iron Age TUMULUS located near Stuttgart in Baden-Württemberg, Germany, dated to the final quarter of the 6th century bc (late HALLSTATT period). Discovered in 1978, the Hochdorf tumulus was about 30 m high and surrounded by a stone wall. It contained a burial chamber built of alternating layers of planks and stones. The occupant of the burial chamber was a tall (1.83 m) high-status male, between 30 and 40 years old. His grave-goods were extraordinarily rich, many the products of Mediterranean workshops, and include a Greek bronze cauldron with reclining lions on its rim, gold-covered shoes, and a bronze couch.

Hoëdic a Mesolithic cemetery and settlement on a small island off the southern coast of Brittany, France. The cemetery consists of burials in shallow depressions in the bedrock, beneath the base of the settlement MIDDEN. Nine graves (two double, one triple) contain remains of 14 individuals, in four graves accompanied by red-deer antlers. Nearby was a circular paved area which may have been used in funerary rituals. Though formally Mesolithic, Hoëdic has also yielded remains of domestic sheep, probably adopted from early farming groups on the Atlantic coast of France further to the south. There is a single RADIOCARBON date of 4625 bc. See also TÉVIEC.

Hohenasperg an Iron Age fortified site of the 6th century bc dated to the HALLSTATT D period. The Hohenasperg is one of a number of early Iron Age commercial centres that includes the HEUNEBURG and MONT LASSOIS. As was the case at other such commercial centres, finds at the Hohenasperg and the nearby TUMULUS at Kleinaspergle include many luxury items of Greek origin.

Hohlenstein–Stadel a cave in Baden-Württemberg, southwest Germany, containing occupation of the MOUSTERIAN, AURIGNACIAN, MAGDALENIAN (14th millennium bp) and Mesolithic. In the Aurignacian levels, a 28 cm IVORY statuette of an ANTHROPOMORPH with a feline head has been found, dating to 31 750 bp.

Hohokam a prehistoric TRADITION located in southern Arizona, USA, which may be culturally antecedent to the contemporary Pima and Papago Indians. The term comes from a Pima Indian word that means 'all used up'. Both indigenous and external origins for Hohokam have been proposed. The tradition is divided into the *Pioneer* (AD 150–550), *Colonial* (AD 550–900), *Sedentary* (AD 900–1100), *Classic* (AD 1100–1450), and *Post-Classic* (AD 1450–1700 *Periods*). The tradition is characterized by changes in house and pottery styles, and the early use of irrigation agriculture. Main crops were maize, beans and squash, with a variety of lesser plants. The Hohokam also built 'BALL-COURTS' – oval depressions about 60 m long – which are very similar to those used by the MAYA. Their function amongst the Hohokam is not clear, however, and they may have served as ceremonial dance courts, rather than for a ball-game itself. The Sedentary Period is marked by a strong MESOAMERICAN influence in the form of PLATFORM MOUNDS, cotton fabric, COPPER bells and other items. See SNAKETOWN.

hokei shukobo literally 'square-moated burial precincts' of YAYOI- and KOFUN-period Japan. Within each precinct, measuring 6–25 m per side, occur coffin or pit burials of adults, and jar burials of children – giving rise to their interpretation as family burial grounds. Variations without moats or with round shapes are also known.

Hokule'a an experimental replica of a POLYNESIAN double-hulled canoe built by Ben Finney and sailed from Maui in the Hawaiian Islands to Tahiti and back in 1976 by traditional navigation methods. The voyage has thrown considerable light on ancient Polynesian voyaging.

Hokuriku a pre-modern administrative district of Japan (see RITSURYO) along the northern Japan Sea coast of Honshu Island, Japan – often used in archaeological writings; it consists of modern Niigata, Toyama, Ishikawa and Fukui Prefectures. See FUDODO.

Holmes, William Henry (1846–1933) an American archaeologist who did much to debunk many of the wilder claims about the antiquity of humans in North America, and whose 1903 monograph on CERAMICS laid the foundations for the subsequent CULTURE HISTORY of the eastern United States.

Holocene 1. a chronostratigraphic unit (see STRATIGRAPHY), either the latest stage of the PLEISTOCENE Series or the latest series of the QUATERNARY System, the hierarchical usage varying regionally. In either case, the Holocene was never formally defined, but is accepted to replace the term 'Recent'. The Holocene stage (series) encompasses all deposits younger than the top of either the WISCONSINIAN STAGE of the Pleistocene Series in North America and the WÜRM/WEICHSEL in Europe. The Holocene follows the last Pleistocene GLACIATION and is typically characterized by INTERGLACIAL conditions and processes. Its lower boundary is generally assigned an age of 10 000 bp, although clearly the transition from GLACIAL to interglacial conditions was globally time-transgressive and differed in character regionally. Many technological, economic and social advances took place during the Holocene, evidence of which is preserved in the archaeological record in Holocene deposits.

2. a geochronological unit (see STRATIGRAPHY), either the latest age of the Pleistocene Epoch or the latest epoch of the Quaternary Period, the hierarchical usage varying regionally. The lower boundary is generally assigned an age of 10 000 bp.

Holsteinian Interglacial a North European Middle PLEISTOCENE warm phase occurring between the ELSTERIAN and SAALIAN cold stages, starting *c*.300 000 BP and ending *c*.200 000 BP. The Alpine equivalent is the MINDEL-RISS, the American the Yarmouth, and the British the Hoxnian, after its type-site at Hoxne, Suffolk (see FRERE).

Holy Cross Mountains a range of low mountains in central Poland, important in prehistory both as sources of flint (including CHOCOLATE FLINT) during the Mesolithic, Neolithic and Early Bronze Age and as a centre for iron metallurgy during the Iron Age, at sites like SŁUPIA STARA.

hominid an abbreviated or popular form of Hominidae, the family to which humans (HOMO) and AUSTRALOPITHECINES belong.

Homo the HOMINID genus to which humans belong. There was a steady increase in the number of hominid species between about 5 and 2 million years ago. Hominids reached their greatest diversity *c*.2 million years ago with as many as five species present (see AUSTRALOPITHECUS), including the oldest species of the genus *Homo*, *H. habilis* ('handy man'). It was small and lightly built like gracile australopithecines, but had a larger brain and is generally credited with being the OLDOWAN toolmaker. *H. habilis* fossils have been found at East and South African sites dating to between 2.2 and 1.6 million years ago (see KOOBI FORA, OLDUVAI GORGE). Some researchers suggest that there were two species of 'habilines'.

Human fossils dating to between 1.6 and 0.5 million years ago are attributed to *H. erectus* ('upright man'). This species had a larger brain (approximately 900–1225 cc) and was bigger than *H. habilis*, with a muscular, stocky build, and a heavy face with thick browridges. *H. erectus* is considered to have made ACHEULIAN stone artifacts. It is thought that *H. erectus* populations spread out of Africa about 1 million years ago, which led to the establishment of regional populations throughout Eurasia. These gradually evolved into archaic *H. sapiens* by 500 000 years ago.

In Europe and western Asia, the archaic *H. sapiens* form dating to between *c*.100 000 and 33 000 years ago is called *H. sapiens neanderthalensis* or *H. neanderthalensis*. NEANDERTHALERS, named after the Neanderthal site near Düsseldorf, Germany, made Middle Palaeolithic stone artifacts. They had a large brain, massive browridges, a receding chin and a heavy muscular build. Debate still rages about how they were replaced by anatomically modern *H. sapiens*, whether they are at least partly ancestral to modern humans or represent an evolutionary dead-end. The oldest-known anatomically modern *H. sapiens* fossils come from sites in Africa and the Near East (see BORDER CAVE, KLASIES RIVER MOUTH, QAFZEH) and date between 130 000 and 80 000 years ago. Some researchers suggest that modern people spread from Africa to other parts of the world (the 'Eve' or 'out of Africa' hypothesis – but see JINNIUSHAN, MABA).

Homolka   a Late Neolithic fortified site in Bohemia of the RIVNAČ culture. The hilltop settlement of Homolka was enclosed by two, apparently successive, palisade systems, within which were a number of small rectangular huts. Some of the huts appear to have been burnt, and despite the fortifications the duration of the Neolithic settlement at Homolka is thought to have been brief.

homology   a specific form of reasoning by ANALOGY, whereby two temporally separate phenomena are similar to each other because of their historical and/or genetic connection to each other.

Honam   the district of South Korea comprising North and South Cholla Provinces in the southwestern peninsula. This name is used in categorizing regional archaeological finds.

Hongshan [Hung-shan]   a site in Liaoning Province, China, giving its name to a precocious northeastern Neolithic culture of surprising complexity. Outstripping the YANGSHAO and early DAWENKOU cultures of north and central China, the Hongshan has elaborate JADE ornaments of different animals (totems?), substantial temple sites of stone enclosures and altars, and female figurines and mask representations. It is dated to c.3500–3000 BC. The recently discovered site of Niuheliang has life-size female statues in painted clay, high-status burials and many fine jade ornaments: this 'goddess temple' was probably a ceremonial centre.

Hopewell   a WOODLAND STAGE COMPLEX dated to approximately 100 BC to AD 500, and centred in southern Ohio, USA, but which spread beyond this core area throughout much of the American Midwest. Hopewell BURIAL MOUNDS were often constructed in groups that were enclosed by earthworks. Some earthworks represented effigies. Yellowstone OBSIDIAN, distinctive platform pipes, and mica sheets carved into mythical animals are also characteristic of the phase. Hopewell seems to represent some form of Interaction Sphere based on the exchange of raw and finished materials, such that Hopewell TRAITS were adopted by existing cultures. Although the cultivation of maize, beans and squash was practised, Hopewell sites seem to have relied heavily on hunting and gathering.

Horgen   a Swiss Middle/Late Neolithic culture, dated c.3400–2800 BC, that follows PFYN and, in western regions, the CORTAILLOD, but sees a decline in the use of COPPER. Its type-site is a settlement site on Lake Neuchâtel.

horizon   any ARTIFACT or element of cultural behaviour found in numerous cultural units over a relatively wide area, that was introduced to those cultures in a relatively brief period of time, and which is thus indicative of a rapid dissemination of ideas. An example is the spread of the BOW-AND-ARROW technology through prehistoric North America. Horizons, like the horizon style concept used in South American archaeology from which it was derived, allow the archaeologist to link together separate cultural units for the purposes of reconstructing CULTURE HISTORY. See also SOIL HORIZON.

horns of consecration or **sacral horns**   one of the most common MINOAN religious symbols, being most plausibly interpreted as the horns of a sacrificed bull. In pictorial representations, horns of consecration often crown the façade of a shrine or sanctuary, presumably to indicate the sanctity of the structure concerned.

horreum   a Roman granary. The floors were usually raised to allow air circulation and prevent the entry of rodents. Horrea were an integral part of Roman military encampments. Extensive examples remain at OSTIA.

horsehoof core   a steep-edged, usually large, single platform CORE with stacked step fractures, considered characteristic of the AUSTRALIAN CORE TOOL AND SCRAPER TRADITION, but also found in more recent contexts. Although often thought to be CHOPPING TOOLS for wood-working, they are clearly worked-out cores associated with the exploitation of particular raw materials.

0   4 cm

horsehoof core

Horus   an Egyptian deity depicted as a falcon or falcon-headed man. The son of OSIRIS and ISIS, Horus was particularly associated with kingship and worshipped in local manifestations, e.g. at EDFU.

Hoshino   a deeply stratified Palaeolithic site in Tochigi Prefecture, Japan, that provides the stone tool chronology for the KANTO region. The lower eight cultural STRATA producing lithics lie under a volcanic pumice layer dated by RADIOCARBON and FISSION TRACK to 40–50 000 bp. This is considerably older than the majority of Japanese Palaeolithic sites and lends support to those who believe the archipelago was occupied in the Middle PLEISTOCENE. (See NISHIYAGI, BABADAN A, NAKAMINE.)

Hottentot   see KHOIKHOIN.

Houhanshu   the *'Chronicles of Later Han'* compiled in AD 398–445 from the WEIZHI. They contain the court histories of the Later HAN DYNASTY as well as ethnographic accounts of peoples in the peripheral regions of East Asia (see YAMATAI).

Howiesons Poort   a MIDDLE STONE AGE INDUSTRY of southern Africa, characterized by the production of small BLADES, standardized backed artifacts such as SEGMENTS, and, in some collections, both unifacial and BIFACIAL points in addition to typical Middle Stone Age

FLAKE-blade forms. It is linked to RADIOCARBON dates greater than 40 000 BP and a date *c*.80 000–60 000 BP enjoys some support (see EPIPIETERSBURG, KLASIES RIVER MOUTH).

Hoxnian   see HOLSTEINIAN.

hradiste   see GRÓD.

Huaca de la Luna   see MOCHE.

Huaca de los Reyes   see CABALLO MUERTO.

Huaca del Sol   see MOCHE.

Huaca La Florida   a large U-shaped monumental site near Lima, on the central coast of Peru, pertaining to the early INITIAL PERIOD (*c*.1700 bc), with construction beginning perhaps as early as the Late PRECERAMIC. The site includes a central platform over 17 m high, flanked by long narrow wings, 3–4 m high and 500 m long; the site exceeds 1 000 000 cu m of artificial fill, according to Thomas Patterson. The site was probably used for only a few centuries and then abandoned.

Huacaloma   an INITIAL PERIOD and EARLY HORIZON site in the Cajamarca region of the north highlands of Peru. In the Early Huacaloma period, a rectangular structure with a central hearth is found, reminiscent of structures at KOTOSH. In the Late Huacaloma period, the early buildings were buried and others built over them. At the contemporaneous site of Layzón, a series of six platforms were built up the side of a hill. The ceremonial architecture reached its climax in the Layzón Period, of the late Early Horizon and early EARLY INTERMEDIATE PERIOD.

Huaca Prieta   a Late PRECERAMIC site (*c*.2300 bc) in the Chicama Valley on the north coast of Peru. Excavations by Junius B. BIRD revealed elaborate twined textiles made of cotton, depicting images of birds and other designs. The site represented a sedentary occupation by preceramic people, whose subsistence was based primarily on fishing and some domesticated squash and beans. Most agriculture was devoted to the production of industrial plants such as gourds and cotton.

Huai Yai   a prehistoric site near LOPBURI in central Thailand, which, together with the adjacent site of Huai Yai Reservoir, was a centre of COPPER and BRONZE production during the 2nd and 1st millennia BC, respectively. Huai Yai was, at the same time, a centre of production of POLISHED STONE ADZES and stone bracelets, indicating a substantial period of overlap in use of stone and copper tools.

Huanghe [Huang-ho]   the Chinese name for the Yellow River of northern China. The Huanghe corridor connects the North China Plain in the east with the Wei River valley in the west (see ERLITOU).

Huánuco Pampa   an INCA city located in the north central highlands of Peru. It covers some two square kilometres, and is arranged around a central plaza measuring 550 by 350 metres. The site includes functionally specialized sectors including high-status residence, large-scale food preparation, a military garrison, and a compound with restricted access in which probably lived the Chosen Women. Hundreds of storage buildings, with a storage capacity totalling 37 000 cubic metres, were built along the hillside above the site. Excavations by Craig Morris suggest that the site had no large permanent population, but rather was occupied by people brought in temporarily to render their labour service to the empire.

HUARI

Huari or **Wari**   **1.** an empire pertaining to the first half of the MIDDLE HORIZON in *c*.ad 650–800 in Peru. Huari iconography shares some symbols, especially the Staff Deity, with the contemporaneous TIAHUANACO culture of Bolivia and adjacent regions. Huari styles of architecture and artifacts are found throughout most of highland and coastal Peru. Because of their stylistic similarity to Tiahuanaco stone carving, Huari artifacts were initially termed 'Tiahuanacoid' or 'Coast Tiahuanaco.' Eventually the site of Huari was identified as the source of the style, first through excavations by Julio C. TELLO, and later by investigations by John H. Rowe, Donald Collier and Gordon R. Willey.

Large planned complexes of rectilinear architecture probably served as Huari provincial administrative centres, indicating imperial control of the highlands. While Huari artifacts are found widely distributed on the coast of Peru, no administrative centres have been identified yet, so the nature of the Huari presence remains unclear. Offering-deposits of intentionally smashed CERAMICS have been found both in the highlands and on the coast. The expansion of the empire followed a period of climatic deterioration and widespread political upheaval at the end of the EARLY INTERMEDIATE PERIOD. The causes of its collapse are unknown. See CONCHOPATA, GALINDO, JINCAMOCCO, PACHECO, PIKILLACTA, TIAHUANACO, MARCA HUAMACHUCO.
2. the capital of the Huari Empire, a large urban site located in Ayacucho, Peru. The architectural core of the site covers 3 square kilometres, and the total extent of the occupation may have been as much as 10 square kilometres. The site had a large resident population numbering probably in the tens of thousands. In addition to diagnostic planned rectilinear architecture, there are tombs and ceremonial structures of cut stone. The site was occupied since the Early Intermediate Period, Huarpa times, but did not coalesce into a large political centre until the middle horizon. It was abandoned at the time the empire collapsed.

Huaricoto   a ceremonial site in the Callejón de Huaylas region of the north highlands of Peru, pertaining to the Late PRECERAMIC, INITIAL PERIOD and EARLY HORIZON. The site, excavated by Richard Burger and Lucy Salazar-Burger, includes a small artificial mound comprising 13 superimposed constructions. Offerings were burned in HEARTHS in ritual chambers, and periodically the structures were ritually interred, in a manner similar to other sites pertaining to the KOTOSH Religious Tradition of the Late Preceramic and Initial Periods.

Huashan   a site in southwest China, near the Vietnamese border, which has the world's biggest ROCK ART panel. A limestone cliff along the Zuojiang River has over 1800 red paintings covering an area 200 m wide and 40 m high. They comprise mainly ANTHROPOMORPHS together with a few ZOOMORPHS and motifs interpreted as bronze drums (see DONG SON) and ring handled swords. These motifs, together with RADIOCARBON dates of stalactites, place the art between 2370 and 2115 years ago, the period between the Early Warring States (see ZHOU) and the Eastern HAN Dynasty.

Huasteca   a subarea on the northern frontier of MESOAMERICA in northern Tamaulipas, Mexico, and the Texas coast of the United States. This area was occupied by hunter-gatherers who served as a buffer between the high cultures of Mesoamerica and the southeastern United States. The area is named after the Huasteca Maya who occupied the area at the time of Spanish contact, but these people did not show elements of the Mesoamerican MAYA culture. The area has an archaeological sequence extending from the Early PRECLASSIC to the AZTEC conquest and Spanish contact.

Huelva   a large hoard of bronzes from Andalusia, Spain, dating to the 8th century BC, including Central European types and CARP'S TONGUE SWORDS of the ATLANTIC BRONZE AGE.

human evolution   see HOMO.

humus   1. decayed organic compounds in the SOIL that impart brown and black colours, particularly to the A horizon. Humus does not include the living soil biomass, undecayed plant and animal parts and tissues or their partial decomposition products. It is a source of nutrients for plant and crop growth. See SOIL HORIZON.
2. organic material and leaf litter on the forest floor.

Hunam-ri [Hunamni]   a MUMUN pottery site in Kyonggido Province, Korea, at which one of the 19 excavated pit houses yielded carbonized rice, foxtail millet, barley, sorghum and soybeans – thought to be the earliest agricultural remains on the peninsula, dated by RADIOCARBON to between 3280 and 2520 bp (see KOREAN PERIODIZATION).

hunebed   (literally 'Hun's grave') a traditional name for MEGALITHIC tombs of the Neolithic of northern Germany and the northern Netherlands, comprising an elongated rectangular central burial chamber, usually with a short entrance passage in the middle of one side and surrounded by a kerb of large stones. They are associated with TRB C material (TIEFSTICHKERAMIK phase) of the 4th millennium BC. Some believe that the name is derived from the Old German 'hune' meaning 'huge', for they are often 50 m or more in length.

hunter–gatherer   a type of society in which SUBSISTENCE is based on the hunting of wild animals and the gathering of wild plants. It is most commonly associated with a BAND level of social organization. Over the past 3 000 000 years of human EVOLUTION, hunting and gathering has been the single most practised form of economy, although currently there is probably not one true hunter and gatherer society anywhere in the world, as a result of pressure from industrialized and agricultural societies.

Huon Peninsula   part of the northeast coast of Papua New Guinea, containing uplifted coral-reef formations spanning much of the PLEISTOCENE. WAISTED AXES have been found in stratified contexts sealed beneath volcanic ASHES dating to c.40 000 bp.

Hureidah   a site near the modern town of Hureidah, on the Wadi 'Amd in the Hadramaut region of Yemen (southwestern Arabia), where G. CATON THOMPSON excavated a temple of the god Sin, together with a small group of tombs and a farmstead, in 1937; this work was the first systematic excavation in SOUTH ARABIA. The rectangular temple, of dressed stone blocks on a plastered rubble platform, shows several episodes of modification; although usually assigned a 7th–6th century BC date, the evidence for this is tenuous.

Hurrian(s)   a non-Semitic, non-Sumerian language whose speakers appeared in northern MESOPOTAMIA during the later 3rd millennium BC. These people seem to have come from the mountainous regions to the north, perhaps from the Caucasus, and some scholars suggest a connection with the KURA-ARAXES culture. Hurrian speakers established a number of small kingdoms in northern Mesopotamia, Syria, and southwestern Anatolia; during the 2nd millennium people with Hurrian names represented large proportions of the populations in some of these areas. By the mid 2nd millennium, the elites in many of the Hurrian states such as that of MITANNI bore INDO-EUROPEAN (Indo-Aryan) names and/or titles e.g. *mariyanna*.

Hushu   a site in Jiangsu Province, China, giving its name to the Hushu culture in the area around Nanjing City. The culture is characterized by GEOMETRIC POTTERY and bronze implements, tools and vessels. It is contemporaneous with the SHANG and early ZHOU bronze cultures (see CHINESE DYNASTIES).

Huxley's Line   the biogeographical divide between Bali and Lombok, and Borneo and Sulawesi, which then runs west of the Philippines, marking the eastern boundary of the east Asian faunal zone. The placental mammal fauna progressively diminishes in variety as one moves east into WALLACEA. It also marks the eastern edge of the SUNDA shelf, and therefore the edge of the Asian landmass exposed at periods of low sea level during the PLEISTOCENE. On present evidence, it also seems to mark the limit of the spread of HOMINIDS before the emergence of anatomically modern humans.

hydria   a Greek jar used to carry or store water. A hydria should have two horizontal loop handles on the body and a single vertical handle from the rim to the shoulder.

hydria

Hyksos   the foreign rulers who seized control of a substantial area of Northern Egypt during the Second INTERMEDIATE PERIOD. They were probably derived from the Palestinian immigrants who infiltrated the Eastern DELTA during the MIDDLE KINGDOM, eventually becoming powerful enough to form the 15th DYNASTY. Their capital in Egypt was the Delta city of AVARIS, from where they were ultimately expelled by AHMOSE.

hypocaust   the Roman means of heating buildings. The floor was supported on low pillars of tile. Hot air from a furnace would be drawn into this space and up through vertical flues built into the walls. Hypocausts are found in both houses and THERMAE.

hypogeum   a rock-cut CHAMBER TOMB, often used for a series of inhumations.

hypostyle hall   part of an Egyptian TEMPLE, situated between the sanctuary and the open court behind the PYLON, whose name refers to the densely packed columns contained between screen-walls at its front and rear.

hypothetico–deductive reasoning   a form of scientific reasoning, in which a hypothesis is set up, predictions are deduced from the hypothesis, and these predictions are tested for their accuracy against empirical data. See POSITIVISM, NEW ARCHAEOLOGY.

Hyrax Hill   a site on the shores of Lake Nakuru in central Kenya with LATER STONE AGE material, a PASTORAL NEOLITHIC settlement of at least 500 square metres associated with a cemetery containing 19 stone-covered flexed burials, and IRON AGE remains, including a series of so-called SIRIKWA HOLES.

I

Iberomaurusian, Mouillian or **Oranian**   a stone INDUSTRY characterized by small BACKED BLADELETS, and widespread in north African coastal areas from south of Rabat in Morocco as far east as Tunis, from at least 22 000 to 10 000 years ago (see TAMAR HAT, TAFORALT).

Iblis, Tal-i   a prehistoric mound in the Kirman district of Iran, discovered by Aurel STEIN in the 1930s and excavated by Joseph Caldwell in the 1960s. Caldwell's work reveals a long (but interrupted) sequence from the early 4th to 1st millennium bc (uncorrected RADIOCARBON dating). The importance of the site rests on the documentation of early copper SMELTING operations within the context of a village architectural sequence; METALLURGICAL activity seems particularly important in the mid 4th millennium, but extends into the early 3rd, when some CERAMIC evidence indicates contacts with the PROTO-ELAMITE world to the west.

ice age   a general term for periods characterized by the expansion of continental and alpine glaciers. It is often used to refer to the last GLACIATION of the QUATERNARY.

ice-free corridor   an area of land between the Cordilleran and LAURENTIDE GLACIAL systems of North America, which was never glaciated. The corridor ran down the East Slope of the Rockies and provided access to the continental interior for early humans entering the New World at the end of the PLEISTOCENE. Some geologists argue that the corridor may have been open since 55 000 BP.

ice wedge   a vertical, narrow and deep wedge-shaped vein of ground ice that penetrates the SOIL or SEDIMENT mass with only minor disruption of the mass on either side of the wedge. Ice wedges form where there is PERMAFROST in the PERIGLACIAL environment. Casts of fossil ice wedges are one of the few true indicators of former permafrost conditions.

idiographic, *adj.* pertaining to individual, idiosyncratic or unique events. Idiographic explanation, which is the opposite of NOMOTHETIC explanation, is concerned with the specific histories of people, and was considered to be unscientific by NEW ARCHAEOLOGY.

Idojiri a group of over 50 site localities in Nagano Prefecture, Japan, which is representative of the dense mountain settlement of the Middle JOMON period in the CHUBU region. Abundant stone QUERNS and starchy biscuit remains indicate the processing of plant foods in a possible horticultural exploitation pattern.

Ife an important town in southern Nigeria which has yielded a remarkable series of near life-size TERRACOTTA and 'bronze' (actually brass) representations of human heads in a naturalistic style, dating from AD 1100–1450, and thought to be derived, perhaps indirectly, from the earlier NOK tradition.

Igbo Laja see OWO.

Igbo Ukwu a remarkable southeastern Nigerian site, apparently dating to the 9th century AD, which indicates that the centralization of social authority and the concentration of wealth seen in later times were already taking place at the end of the 1st millennium AD. The finds include a shrine full of ritual 'bronze' (brass) vessels and regalia, a disposal pit with quantities of 'bronze' and copper items as well as pottery, and a burial of an important person. The CIRE PERDUE 'bronzes' are unique, being exceptionally delicate and intricate, and unlike those from BENIN and IFE.

Ignateva Cave or **Yamazy-Tash** a prehistoric cave-site located along a tributary of the Belaya River in the southern Urals of European Russia. The lower cultural layer contains artifacts (e.g. MICROLITHS) and faunal remains (e.g. CAVE BEAR, reindeer), and is assigned to the late Upper Palaeolithic. During the early 1980s, numerous schematic cave paintings (extinct animals, human females and abstract signs) were reported from Ignateva Cave, which may be Palaeolithic. The upper cultural layer contains Iron Age remains.

'Ili'ili'opae one of the largest HEIAU in the Hawaiian Islands, on Molokai.

Illahun see EL-LAHUN.

Illinoian see SAALIAN.

illuvial horizon a SOIL HORIZON defined by accumulation, or illuviation, of material derived from one or more overlying soil horizons either by deposition of fine particles from suspension, precipitation from solution, or by both. The most common illuvial horizon is the B horizon. Compare ELUVIAL HORIZON.

Illyria an area described by CLASSICAL writers as lying to the west of the Vardar and Morava valleys to the south of the Roman province of PANNONIA and west of MOESIA, extending to the Adriatic Sea and the eastern edge of the Alps. The inhabitants of Illyria during the last centuries BC, the Illyrians, resisted Greek influence but later were absorbed into the Roman Empire.

Ilsenhöhle see RANIS CAVE.

Il'skaya I a Middle Palaeolithic open-air site on the Il' River (Kuban' tributary) in the northern Caucasus, European Russia. As many as 12 occupation horizons are buried in slope deposits overlying ALLUVIUM of the third TERRACE. The faunal remains are dominated by steppe bison; although the age of the occupations is unclear, the large body-size of some of the carnivores suggests a cold interval (early LAST GLACIAL?). Sidescrapers (see SCRAPER) predominate among the tools. The site was excavated by Zamyatnin in 1926/28, GORODTSOV in 1936–37 and Praslov in 1963 and 1967–69.

Imgur-Enlil   see BALAWAT.

impasto   a type of early pottery made in ETRURIA especially during the VILLANOVAN PERIOD. It was made from unrefined clay and fired to a dark brown or black colour. Common shapes include biconical urns and hut models which were used for cremations.

impluvium   a water tank placed in the centre of the ATRIUM under the COMPLUVIUM in a Roman house.

Impressed Ware   the earliest Neolithic pottery of Mediterranean Europe, with decoration impressed into the clay using wooden sticks, combs, finger nails or seashells. The most characteristic Early Neolithic Impressed Ware is that decorated with the edge of a cockle (*Cardium*) shell, and known as CARDIAL WARE.

Inamgaon   an important site in Pune, excavated by the Deccan College during the 1960s and 1970s, which provides a detailed view of the 2nd millennium MALWA and JORWE cultures of the northern Deccan (Maharastra, western central India). The Malwa phase at the site contains large rectangular domestic structures of WATTLE AND DAUB, often with internal divisions, and with circular platforms, storage bins and jars. The community cultivated, possibly with some irrigation, wheat, barley, sorghum and various legumes, kept cattle, sheep, goat and pig, and also hunted and fished. The Jorwe community lived in structures similar to those built earlier, though now some differences in size of structure are apparent, perhaps reflecting some social differentiation. Subsistence also continued much in accordance with earlier patterns, now definitely with irrigation. At Inamgaon by late Jorwe times, the settlement was smaller, and constructed of small round wattle-and-daub huts.

Inanna   the 'queen of heaven', a SUMERIAN deity, roughly equivalent to the AKKADIAN Ishtar, the daughter of NANNA/Sin; she was the goddess both of love and of war, as well as of the storehouse and rain, and was closely associated with WARKA.

Inca or **Inka**   an extensive empire occupying most of Andean South America at the time of the Spanish conquest in AD 1532. Its expansion began in the mid 15th century when Pachacuti defeated the Chankas, the traditional enemy of the Inca, and began to conquer regions beyond CUZCO, the capital city. Most of the extent of the empire was conquered by his son Topa Inca Yupanqui. The empire was torn by a bloody war of succession between the brothers Atahuallpa and Huascar. The war ended at about the time that Francisco PIZARRO arrived in Peru; he took Atahuallpa captive in Cajamarca and ended Inca rule.

The Inca incorporated regions into their empire through a combination of diplomacy and military conquest. Lands and animals in subject regions were divided into three parts: one for the Inca, one for the cult of the sun god, and the rest for the people of the region. Tribute, *mita*, was collected in the form of labour, provided in rotation by each household. Normal *mita* requirements included working the lands of the Inca and the Sun, and producing textiles. Some villages provided special services, such as serving as litter-bearers of the Inca, or as *chaski*, the runners who carried messages along the Inca road system, *capac ñan*, that tied together the far-flung empire. The Inca left local religious beliefs intact, but decreed that the worship of the sun god be added to local religions. When possible, the Inca also left local political control intact, and ruled through alliance with local rulers; where this was not possible, local systems were reorganized, and sometimes Inca rulers were installed. Particularly hostile groups were moved to new locations; these *mitmag* settlements were sometimes placed in friendly regions to diffuse conflict. *Mitmag* were also used to exploit natural and agricultural resources of particular interest to the Inca. A special class of retainers, *yanakuna*, was created by the Inca to serve as lower-level bureaucrats and as personal servants to the royal Inca nobility.

Anyone directly related, within five generations or less, to the Inca ruler was considered to be Inca. Non-Incas could also be raised to the status of Inca-by-privilege by the emperor. The Inca dynasty was begun by Manco Capac, the legendary founder of Cuzco; Atahuallpa was the 13th ruler of the dynasty. The Inca were said to be direct descendants of Inti, the sun god, and his sister-wife, Quilla, the moon god.

Inca Pirca   an INCA site in highland Ecuador, which has a unique oval platform, 37 × 12 m in extent and 3 to 4 m high, faced with cut stone. On the summit was a gable-roofed building which was divided lengthwise into two rooms. Although the structure has been called a castle or guardhouse, it more likely had a religious function.

index fossil   a fossil that has a widespread geographical range but is temporally restricted to a brief period of existence. These fossils are useful in biostratigraphic classification of rock or SEDIMENT units (see STRATIGRAPHY). The concept is used for cultural ARTIFACTS referred to as 'diagnostic'. Artifacts that share the attributes of index fossils are useful in the CROSS-DATING and CORRELATION of deposits that contain them, and construction of chronologies. See TYPE.

Indianization   the process by which Southeast Asian states of the 1st millennium AD borrowed, adapted and assimilated aspects of South Asian political, religious and literary culture; it should not be confused with colonization or wholesale copying, since the end result was distinctively Southeast Asian.

Indian Knoll   an ARCHAIC site in Kentucky, USA, comprising a SHELL MOUND and the possible remains of living floors. Most significantly, the remains of over 1100 burials were also found, many of them accompanied by exotic grave-goods, suggestive of some degree of social ranking.

Indo-European   a large language group that includes most of the modern European languages (e.g. Romance, Germanic, Slavic, Baltic, Greek, Albanian) except Basque, Finnish and Hungarian; modern Indo-Iranian (e.g. Persian, Hindi) and other tongues (e.g. Armenian); and also numerous dead languages (e.g. HITTITE, Tocharian, PHRYGIAN). Various attempts have been made to explain this pattern of languages as a result of migrations or invasions in prehistoric and early historic times. The most widely accepted solution places the Proto-Indo-European homeland in the southern Russian steppes in the broad zone north of the Black and Caspian Seas during the 5th millennium BC, but the problem of identifying language groups from archaeological remains makes it difficult to assess the conflicting hypotheses.

induction the process of reasoning whereby general propositions are derived from an analysis of individual events. An example might be concluding that a country's total manufacturing ability was poor based on its inability to produce efficient cars. Compare DEDUCTION.

Indus civilization see HARAPPAN.

industry a frequently repeated ASSEMBLAGE of restricted content, such as stone tools only. Industry is occasionally used as a synonym for assemblage.

infrared absorption spectrometry a physical technique used to determine mineralogy or chemical composition of ARTIFACTS and organic substances, particularly amber. A sample is bombarded by infrared radiation which causes the atoms in the sample to vibrate at frequencies characteristic of the atom species present. That part of the radiation spectrum vibrating at the same frequencies is absorbed; the amount of transmitted radiation at each wavelength is detected, forming the basis for identification.

Ingaladdi a rockshelter in Australia's Northern Territory. The upper deposits, from 3000 bp, contain TULAS and points from the AUSTRALIAN SMALL TOOL TRADITION. The lower layers, mainly rock rubble, contained FLAKE SCRAPERS, small HORSEHOOF CORES and engraved sandstone fragments, and accumulated between 7000 and 5000 bp.

Ingombe Ilede an IRON AGE site in southern Zambia, occupied in the 14th and 15th centuries AD by people who traded extensively with the East African coast as well as the interior. A series of elaborate graves contained metal bangles, woven cotton cloth, marine gastropod shells, gold beads, large quantities of imported glass beads, bundles of copper wire, bars and cross-shaped INGOTS, as well as iron hoes and gongs.

ingot a quantity of a resource (usually metal) of standardized form and weight, used as currency and for trade: e.g. the Bronze Age Mediterranean had copper ingots in the form of an oxhide and weighing approximately 30 kg. See KAŞ.

inhumation see BURIAL, PRIMARY, SECONDARY.

Initial Period the period 1800–900 BC in Andean South America, during which CERAMICS were introduced, and agriculture and animal husbandry formed the subsistence base for most cultures. Monumental ceremonial architecture became widely distributed on the coast of Peru, where centres followed a U-shaped plan on the central coast, and a linear plan with PLATFORM MOUNDS and sunken circular courts in the north. In the north highlands of Peru the KOTOSH Religious Tradition was widespread. A period of cultural heterogeneity, the Initial Period ended with the abandonment of many of the coastal centres, and the beginning of the CHAVIN cult.

Inka see INCA.

insula (*Lat.* island). The term is normally applied to a block within the grid-pattern of a Roman city. See CARDO, DECUMANUS.

intaglio 1. *n.* a gem-stone in which the decoration is cut into the surface.
2. *adj.* relating to a technique by which the decoration is cut into the

surface. The technique is widely used on gems as well as on glass
vessels.

'Intercultural' style carved chlorite   the name given to a group
of vessels and other objects that appear in western Asia during the
3rd millennium BC, which are made of chlorite, STEATITE, SERPENTINE
and other soft stones, and which share a rich iconography. Such
objects are distributed from the middle Euphrates to central Asia, the
Indus and southeastern Arabia, though most come from southern and
western Iran, southern MESOPOTAMIA and the western Persian Gulf.
The discovery of a production centre at Tepe YAHYA provoked considerable interest in this style, especially with respect to inter-regional
exchange and shared beliefs in western Asia of the mid and later 3rd
millennium.

'Intercultural' style carved chlorite Vessels.

interglacial   1. *n.* a relatively warm climatic episode, between GLACIAL
episodes, characterized by little or no glacial ice, warm climate processes,
deposits, flora and fauna, and increased soil-forming processes in some
areas. In reference to the QUATERNARY, interglacials were considerably
briefer than glacials. Compare INTERSTADIAL. See STRATIGRAPHY.
2. *adj.* referring to relatively warm climatic conditions.
3. *adj.* referring to or derived from nonglacial processes and conditions.

Intermediate Period   one of three particular periods of Egyptian
history when the central cohesion of the state collapsed, resulting in the
country being ruled by a number of regional potentates (i.e. between OLD
KINGDOM / MIDDLE KINGDOM / NEW KINGDOM / LATE PERIOD).

interstadial   1. *n.* a relatively brief and warmer climatic episode
within a longer, cooler GLACIAL episode. An interstadial is usually
characterized by some degree of glacier recession, climatic amelioration with attendant changes in flora and fauna, and increased expression of PEDOGENESIS. However, the expression of an interstadial is
likely to be more variable regionally than an INTERGLACIAL.
2. *adj.* referring to relatively brief and warmer climatic conditions
within a glacial episode.

intramural *adj.*   (of graves) located within the confines of a settlement, as opposed to those outside, which are *extramural*.

Inuit   the name which the Eskimo call themselves. It means 'The
People'.

involution   a structure formed by contortion of saturated SEDIMENT or SOIL material resulting from seasonal freezing accompanied by high pore-water pressures. Soil involutions are most commonly found associated with the active layer of PERMAFROST, but can form where permafrost is not present and are not diagnostic. Churning action that creates involutions may also cause disturbance or mixing of any archaeological deposits that are present in affected areas. Involutions may also be confused with archaeological FEATURES. See CRYOTURBATION.

Inyanga   a highland region in eastern Zimbabwe, with evidence of STONE AGE, Early IRON AGE (see GOKOMERE) and, particularly, Late Iron Age occupation. In the 17th and 18th centuries AD, Barwe/ Tonga people built substantial fortified stone-walled settlements covering some 8000 square kilometres.

Iolkos   see VOLOS.

Ionic order   a scheme of architecture usually found in the cities of western Turkey as well as in the islands of the eastern Aegean. The CAPITAL is formed by two sets of VOLUTES, between which there is an ECHINUS decorated with an egg-and-dart pattern. The columns rest on elaborately carved, often horizontally fluted, bases. The ENTABLATURE allowed for a continuous frieze, which could be decorated in relief. Ionic columns could be used as internal columns for a STOA as they tended to be taller. See ERECHTHEION.

Ionic order Capital.

Ipiutak   see NORTON.

Ipswichian   see EEMIAN.

iron   a ductile, malleable, magnetic metallic element, used in the manufacture of functional and decorative artifacts that commonly occurs in oxide form, such as *haematite*. Iron METALLURGY characterized the cultural period termed the Iron Age.

Iron Age   the third stage in THOMSEN'S THREE-AGE SYSTEM, a period of antiquity in the Old World in which IRON METALLURGY superseded the use of BRONZE for tools and weapons. In *Europe*, the earliest iron appears around 1100 bc, but conventionally the transition from the Bronze Age to the Iron Age is placed in the early part of the 1st millennium bc. In temperate Europe, this is during the second half of the HALLSTATT period. The Iron Age continues through the LA TÈNE period in central and western Europe. The appearance of the Romans ends the Iron Age in western Europe, while beyond the Roman frontier, the Iron Age continues until the so-called migration period in the 4th to 6th centuries AD.

In *East Asia*, iron came into use in China *c*.500 BC in the middle ZHOU period. It was introduced to the Korean peninsula *c*.400 BC, making the Late Bronze Age in Korea contemporaneous with the Early Iron Age, and the Late Iron Age contemporaneous with the PROTO-THREE KINGDOMS period (see KOREAN PERIODIZATION). Both bronze and iron were first used by the YAYOI peoples in Japan (see JAPANESE PERIODIZATION).

Iron SMELTING apparently spread from western Asia to north *Africa* by the 8th century BC. It may have been introduced to sub-Saharan Africa from PHOENICIAN or Greek colonies on the north African coast, or via the Nile Valley (see MEROE), or by other routes. The earliest-known evidence for iron smelting in sub-Saharan Africa is thought to date to about 400 BC at TARUGA in Nigeria and to about 500 BC at Buhaya in Tanzania. The sub-Saharan African Iron Age is also linked to the spread of Negroid BANTU-speaking peoples from west to southern Africa, which they reached in the first few centuries AD. Iron Age people were farmers who lived in settled village communities and brought not only knowledge of metal working, but also pottery as well as domestic plants and animals.

The southern African Iron Age is divided into the Early Iron Age, dating from about AD 200 until AD 1000, and the Late Iron Age, dating from AD 1000 until the 19th century. The date of AD 1000 is an arbitrary division. The Early Iron Age includes the first metal-using agriculturalists and their immediate descendants (see CHIFUMBAZE). The period from the late 1st millennium AD, as well as the Late Iron Age, saw the development of wealthy states with stratified societies in many parts of sub-Saharan Africa (see GHANA, GREAT ZIMBABWE, MALI, MAPUNGUBWE, SONGHAY).

Isaac, Glynn Llywelyn   (1937–85) a palaeoanthropologist who played a pivotal role in the post-1960s florescence of knowledge about early PLEISTOCENE culture in East Africa. His work at OLORGESAILIE is regarded as a classic and he is particularly credited with developing new approaches to the interpretation of very early archaeological remains.

Isbister   a Neolithic CHAMBERED TOMB on the island of South Ronaldsay, Orkney, Scotland, consisting of a passage leading to a main chamber of long rectangular plan with four irregular oval side chambers. Remains of some 342 people were found within the chambers, mostly as disarticulated bones. There was some evidence of sorting, with long bones and skulls placed in different parts of the tomb. RADIOCARBON dates indicate construction in *c*.3150 BC.

Ischia (*Gk* Pithekoussai) an island off CAMPANIA, southern Italy. Some MYCENAEAN pottery has been found, but the island is best known for the Euboean colony which was founded in the 8th century BC before CUMAE. Evidence for IRON SMELTING has been discovered, perhaps reflecting the exploitation of the mineral resources of ETRURIA and Elba.

Isernia or **La Pineta** a well-stratified Lower Palaeolithic open-air site in the Volturno Valley, central Italy, which is not yet fully excavated, but which has produced many disarticulated animal bones associated with thousands of stone tools including limestone CHOPPERS and chopping tools and flint FLAKES. POTASSIUM ARGON dates place the campsites at *c.*730 000 BP, and the fauna (bison, rhinoceros, etc.) indicates a steppe environment.

Ishango a STONE AGE MIDDEN accumulation at Lake Edward in eastern Zaire, dated to about 20 000 BP. It has a long occupation sequence containing faunal remains, a stone artifact industry with some backed MICROLITHS, and an abundant bone industry.

Ishtar see INANNA, ASTARTE.

Isin a city on the palaeo-Euphrates near NIPPUR. The mound of Isin covers about 150 ha. Although investigated early in the 20th century, systematic excavation began in the mid-1970s with B. Hrouda's work, which has addressed primarily 2nd and 1st millennium BC levels. Earlier occupation is also apparent in late 4th and 3rd millennium sherds from disturbed contexts, and in 'UBAID sherds recovered from surface contexts; very recently the German team excavated a building of EARLY DYNASTIC I date. Isin takes its importance from its political history, as the seat of a major kingdom of the OLD BABYLONIAN period and as the origin of the dynasty (the Isin II, 1157–1026 BC) that ruled BABYLONIA after the KASSITE period.

Isin/Larsa period see OLD BABYLONIAN PERIOD.

Isis an Egyptian anthropoid goddess, the wife of OSIRIS and mother of HORUS. The most important cult centres at which she was worshipped as the principal deity are PHILAE and BEHBET EL-HAGAR. During the Roman Period the cult of Isis became popular in parts of the Roman Empire outside Egypt, including a substantial temple to the goddess in ROME itself.

Isle Royale an island in northwest Lake Superior, North America, that is the location of 10 sunken ships, ranging in age from the mid-1800s to the present. The cold fresh water of the lake has preserved the wrecks to a degree unknown in salt water, and has thus provided UNDERWATER ARCHAEOLOGY with almost unprecedented opportunities for research. See PADRE ISLAND SHIPWRECKS.

isochronous, *adj.* formed during the same span of time, for example, one SEDIMENT unit having upper and lower boundaries that are SYNCHRONOUS with a second sediment unit would be isochronous with the second unit. See also DIACHRONIC.

isostasy a process by which the distribution of mass within the Earth's crust is balanced by large-scale topography. Changes in crustal mass that affect ISOSTATIC equilibrium can occur through stripping by EROSION, loading of GLACIAL ice, loading of SEDIMENTS derived from erosion into basins, and tectonic changes. In response, equilibrium in part is restored by vertical movements of crustal blocks. During the QUATERNARY, crustal loading by continental glaciers caused crustal depression beneath the ice and crustal forebulge beyond the ice margin. As mass decreased with melting of the ice and was transferred to ocean basins, crustal readjustments caused uplift in some areas and downwarping in others. In coastal areas, isostatic crustal adjustments, always in interaction with EUSTASY, had considerable impact on land exposure or submergence, with attendant archaeological implications for settlement, migration and changing environmental resources. In some regions, isostatic and EUSTATIC sea level changes resulted in flights of FOSSIL BEACH ridges.

isostatic, *adj.* pertaining to changes in altitude of the earth's crust in response to shifts in the crustal mass as compensation for loading and unloading of the crust. Isostatic adjustments have considerable impact on the preservation and location of archaeological sites along coastal areas and lakes, and on strategies for identifying them. See ISOSTASY.

isotope atoms of the same element that have different atomic masses due to different numbers of neutrons in the nuclei, but that have similar chemical properties. Many isotopes are naturally unstable, or radioactive, because of the composition of the nuclei, and tend to change spontaneously to stable configurations, or stable isotopes. This process forms the basis for RADIOMETRIC DATING.

isotopic replacement a chemical process, a source of CONTAMINATION in RADIOMETRIC DATING, whereby an ISOTOPE within a sample used for dating is exchanged with an isotope of the same element that is a different age. For example, the ^{14}C isotope in carbonate material, such as shell or bone, may be replaced during recrystallization by 'younger', 'older', or 'dead' carbon isotopes dissolved in surrounding groundwater; the sample will yield an inaccurate age.

Israelites a Semitic people, apparently of nomadic origin, whose emergence in the Levant is identified with a shift of settlement at the start of the Iron Age (*c.*1200 BC), when a new pattern of small villages dispersed in upland regions replaced the urban life of the Bronze Age. Explanations for this process range from the nomadic invasion thesis (derived from Biblical accounts in Exodus) to settlement of indigenous populations of nomads and brigands, to social revolution by the urban lower classes at the end of the Bronze Age. The Israelites' conquest of areas occupied by the CANAANITES brought them into an ultimately successful conflict with the PHILISTINES. The major building works carried out under the united kingdom belong to the reign of SOLOMON. The northern kingdom of Israel (see SAMARIA) was conquered by the ASSYRIANS in the late 8th century BC, while the southern kingdom of Judah was reduced by the BABYLONIANS in the early 6th century BC. See also JERUSALEM.

Istállóskö an Upper Palaeolithic cave-site located in the Bükk Mountains of northeastern Hungary. Artifacts and faunal remains (e.g. reindeer, red deer and steppe bison) are buried in LOESS and rubble. The lower cultural layer contains an AURIGNACIAN assemblage which includes numerous split-base bone points, but few stone tools (e.g. BURINS). This layer yielded a RADIOCARBON date of 42 350 bp, and apparently represents one of the oldest Aurignacian occupations in Europe. The upper cultural layer contains a younger Aurignacian assemblage (*c.*31 000 bp) including a bone 'flute', burins, endscrapers (see SCRAPER) and bone points. Istállóskö was excavated by Hillebrand in 1913–25, VÉRTES in 1947–51 and others.

Isturitz a cave-system in the Pyrénées-Atlantiques, southwest France, comprising three superimposed tunnels. The uppermost, Isturitz, excavated by E. Passemard in 1912–22 and by R. de Saint-Périer in 1928–50, is enormously rich in occupation material from the MOUSTERIAN to the late MAGDALENIAN, and in PORTABLE ART from the later Upper Palaeolithic. It also houses some deep wall-engravings of animals. Below it is *Oxocelhaya* (or Haristoy) which contains some PARIETAL ART. The lowest tunnel, *Erberua*, is protected by the underground river which was first breached in 1973. It houses paintings and engravings on its walls, and intact Magdalenian HEARTHS on its floor.

Itazuke the type-site in Fukuoka Prefecture, Japan, for Early YAYOI pottery. Itazuke is also important for its extensive early Yayoi-period paddyfield remains of canals, embankments, etc., which for a long time were evidence of the first agriculture in Japan (compare TORO). Recent excavations at Itazuke, Nabatake and Magarita sites document the beginnings of rice-growing in the previous JOMON period (compare TORIHAMA).

ivory the enlarged teeth of certain mammals utilized as a resource. The most important sources were the tusks of elephants and MAMMOTHS (upper incisor teeth) and of walruses (upper canines). It formed a highly prized resource in prehistory, used for carving, engraving and the manufacture of tools from the early Upper Palaeolithic onwards.

Iwajuku the first Palaeolithic site discovered in Japan, in 1949. Layers I and II are assessed to be 20 000 and 15 000 years old, respectively. They contained elongate BLADES, SCRAPERS and CHOPPERS in I and thin, small blades in II. Iwajuku 0, below I, has yielded crude 'tools', estimated over 50 000 years old, that are similar to those at SOZUDAI with the same problems of manufacture recognition.

Iwo Eleru a rockshelter in the now forested area of southwestern Nigeria, with the longest dated sequence of MICROLITHIC artifacts known from West Africa. The oldest layers date to about 12 000 years ago and include a burial of the oldest Nigerian skeleton yet uncovered, which is considered to have Negroid features. Layers postdating 5000 years ago may contain evidence for the beginning of agriculture in the forests of West Africa.

Ix Chel see COZUMEL.

Iximché a highland MAYA site in Guatemala with strong Mexican influence. Its easily defensible position on a hill surrounded by ravines is typical of the POSTCLASSIC PERIOD. In one burial, dating to less than 100 years before the Spanish conquest, was found the largest cache of gold items in the Maya area, excluding that dredged from the Sacred CENOTE at CHICHÉN ITZÁ. At the time when it was conquered by Pedro de Alvarado in 1524, Iximché was the capital of the Cakchiquel Maya. Various archaeologists have worked at Iximché, including Jorge F. Guillemín, supported by the Guatemalan government, and Robert Wauchope, who analysed the CERAMICS from the site.

Izmir a city on the west coast of Turkey. The earliest settlement dates to the 3rd millennium BC. The ARCHAIC city lay at modern Bayrakli where a temple of Athena has been found. The Roman state AGORA, including a BASILICA, has been uncovered. In the HELLENISTIC period the city seems to have been a centre for the production of TERRACOTTA figurines.

J

Jabrud or **Yabrud**   a group of three prehistoric ROCKSHELTER sites in Syria excavated by A. Rust, producing Palaeolithic, NATUFIAN and Neolithic occupation levels and giving its name to the Palaeolithic Jabrudian INDUSTRY. Typical Jabrudian tool kits contain SCRAPERS made on thick FLAKES with unfaceted STRIKING PLATFORMS associated with Upper Palaeolithic-style BLADES, and often yield many BIFACES. The Jabrudian dates to c.150 000 BP, and is a kind of final ACHEULIAN.

jacal   see ADOBE.

jade   a reddish-brown, green or whitish hard, semi-precious stone (NEPHRITE, JADEITE) used in East Asia from the Neolithic period onwards (see HONGSHAN, LIANGZHU) for ornamental and ritual objects (see BI, ZONG, MAGATAMA). It cannot be cut or flaked but must be worked through abrasion. See MANCHENG.

jadeite   a stone carved by MESOAMERICANS into ornaments and statuary. The OLMEC are widely known for their jadeite carvings, which include masks and WERE-JAGUARS. Jadeite and jadeite objects were traded throughout Mesoamerica, from Olmec times to the Spanish Conquest. Known sources of jadeite include the Balsas Valley in Guerrero and the Motagua River Valley in Guatemala, but a number of sources have not yet been identified. Jadeite had ritual significance, symbolizing water. Mesoamerican nobles were buried with a piece of jadeite in their mouths, representing their heart. Mesoamerican jadeite is often, erroneously, called JADE, which does not exist in the region: it varies from colourless to white, green, and greenish-blue; emerald to light green stones are considered the most precious. See also GREENSTONE.

Jaguar Cave   1. a cave in Tennessee, USA, containing aboriginal footprints in wet clay. A RADIOCARBON date on associated torch charcoal of approximately 4700 BP is the earliest evidence of a visit to a deep cave in North America.
2. a cave-site in Idaho, USA, dating to the 9th and 10th millennia BC, which is important for its very early evidence of the dog.

Jamestown   the site of the first permanent English settlement in America, founded in Tidewater, Virginia in AD 1607. Archaeological excavations at the site added immensely to the existing historical documentation on early colonial life. See MARTIN'S HUNDRED.

Janisławice   a single MESOLITHIC burial with numerous grave-goods from central Poland, dated to the ATLANTIC climatic period, c.6000–4000 BC. Janisławice is the type-site of the Janisławice culture, the late Mesolithic group inhabiting the GLACIAL outwash of east-central Europe. Assemblages of the Janisławice culture typically contain raw materials from distant sources, especially CHOCOLATE FLINT.

Jankovich   a prehistoric cave-site located near the River Danube in north-central Hungary. Artifacts and faunal remains are buried in rubble and 'cave earth' deposits. The lower cultural layer yielded a Middle Palaeolithic assemblage ('Jankovichian'), containing BIFACIAL FOLIATES and sidescrapers (see SCRAPER) and associated primarily with remains of CAVE BEAR. The overlying cultural layer contains an Upper Palaeolithic assemblage (probably GRAVETTIAN) associated primarily with remains of reindeer. Neolithic and Bronze Age artifacts were found in the uppermost level and floor of the cave. Jankovich was excavated by Hillebrand in 1913–25, VÉRTES in 1956 and others.

Japanese periodization the artificial classification of prehistoric and historic eras used by archaeologists and historians for Japan. The major chronological divisions after the Palaeolithic are: JOMON (10 000–300 BC); YAYOI (300 BC–AD 300); KOFUN (300–710); Nara (710–794); Heian (794–1183); Mediaeval (= Kamakura, Muromachi, Momoyama, 1183–1603); Feudal (Edo/Tokugawa, 1603–1868); Meiji (1868–1914); Taisho (1914–25); Showa (1925–88); Heisei (1989–present). (See NEOLITHIC; BRONZE AGE; IRON AGE.)

Jarlshof a settlement in the Shetland Islands, Scotland, named after a house in a Walter Scott novel. Preserved by wind-blown sand, it was uncovered by violent storms in the 19th century AD. Early 2nd millennium BC houses of SKARA BRAE type were followed by Bronze Age occupation, and then Iron Age structures – SOUTERRAINS, WHEEL-HOUSES and a BROCH. There was a VIKING farmstead in the 9th century AD, and a medieval fortified farm.

Jarmo a small ACERAMIC NEOLITHIC to CERAMIC NEOLITHIC village site in the Zagros foothills of northwestern Iraq that was a central focus of Robert Braidwood's interdisciplinary project on the beginnings of domestication in the 1950s. Although now superseded by subsequent work, the Jarmo project largely defined the task of explaining the origins of food production. The site dates to the later 7th millennium BC, and exhibits many of the characteristics now recorded in other prehistoric localities of the 'hilly flanks' of the Zagros.

Jastorf culture an Iron Age culture of the southern Baltic region during the late HALLSTATT period, extending from Lower Saxony through Pomerania, representing some of the earliest IRON METALLURGY of the North European Plain.

Java Man remains of HOMO *erectus* (once *Pithecanthropus erectus*) found in 1891 by DUBOIS at TRINIL in Java, probably dating to *c.*1 million to 500 000 BP, less robust than the *H. erectus* of JETIS (MOJOKERTO child). See SANGIRAN.

Jażdżewski, Konrad (1908–85) a leading figure in Polish archaeology during the mid 20th century. After the Second World War he served as director of the Museum of Archaeology and Ethnography in Łódź. He excavated sites from many different periods, including BRZEŚĆ KUJAWSKI (NEOLITHIC) and ŁĘG PIEKARSKI (Iron Age).

Jebel Irhoud a site in Morocco containing fossils of HOMO *sapiens neanderthalensis*-type together with LEVALLOISO-MOUSTERIAN artifacts. ESR dates range from over 80 000 to perhaps 150 000 BP.

Jebel Moya a mountain in the southern Gezira of Sudan with many graves. Occupation at about 4000 BP has pottery like that of the NUBIAN C GROUP. Later occupation has MEROITIC traits.

Jebel Uweinat a mountain on the frontier where Sudan, Libya and

Egypt meet. It is rich in ROCK ART depicting domestic animals and was a focal point for Neolithic herders around 6200 BP.

Jefferson, Thomas (1743–1826) an early President of the United States of America, famous in archaeology for what amounts to the first scientific and controlled excavation in the discipline. In 1784, Jefferson excavated a BURIAL MOUND on his Virginia estate, in order to recover specific information on its construction and use.

Jelling one of the most remarkable groups of monuments in Denmark, including the two largest BARROWS in that country – 78 m across and 11 m high, traditionally seen as the resting places of the last pagan monarchs, Gorm (died *c.*AD 950) and his queen Thyra. They may have been buried together in one mound, since the other had no burial chamber. Between them stands a Romanesque church, with two very fine RUNE-stones outside, one of which bears the oldest crucifixion scene in Denmark. There are also 50 stones forming a boat-shaped outline.

Jemdet Nasr a site near KISH in the northern end of the MESOPOTAMIAN alluvial plain, where Stephen Langdon's excavations in the 1920s revealed a style of painted pottery which now defines the Jemdet Nasr period in the southern Mesopotamian sequence. This period (equivalent to the URUK III of the EANNA SOUNDING sequence) is dated to the last few centuries of the 4th millennium and represents a basic continuation of the preceding Late Uruk period, with some important developments, most notably in the application of writing to lists (professions, places, objects). The site of Jemdet Nasr itself was occupied from Late Uruk to EARLY DYNASTIC I times; a substantial building of Jemdet Nasr date may represent the earliest-discovered palace in southern Mesopotamia.

Jenderam Hilir an open site in peninsular Malaysia in the Dengkil region, with tripod pottery of the BAN KAO Neolithic.

Jenne-jeno or **Djenne** a now-abandoned section of the modern town of Jenne in Mali. It was occupied from the 3rd century BC, with the growth of urban settlement in the late 1st millennium AD, when it became part of a wider social network of at least 400 other sites, based on far-flung river trade.

Jenness, Diamond (1886–1969) a pioneering Canadian ethnologist and archaeologist, who established much of the groundwork for understanding the archaeology of the Arctic. In 1925 Jenness first described the DORSET culture, which pre-dated the THULE culture.

Jericho (*Arabic* Tell es-Sultan) a 4 ha site in the Jordan Valley, Israel, chiefly excavated by GARSTANG in 1930–36 and KENYON in 1952–58, with a long and virtually uninterrupted sequence from the NATUFIAN period to the LATE BRONZE AGE. Kenyon's work provided information on the origins of food production (with botanical and faunal evidence of early domesticates) and the subsequent developments towards urban life in Palestine. The site is famous for its Neolithic settlement: during the PREPOTTERY NEOLITHIC 'A' phase, there were stone fortifications including a large tower against the inner face of the town wall. The most notable feature of PPNB Jericho are the PLASTERED SKULLS. During the MIDDLE BRONZE AGE Jericho was defended by a GLACIS, but little archaeological evidence has survived of the Late Bronze Age to corroborate the Biblical account of its destruction by Joshua and the ISRAELITES; in any case, any falling walls were more probably caused by one of the area's frequent earthquakes.

Jerusalem a city in the Judaean hills, Israel, which was occupied for thousands of years and which has been excavated virtually continuously since the 1860s. Comparatively little remains of ancient Jerusalem, chiefly because of the repeated destructions suffered by the city (e.g. that of Titus in 70 AD) and later BYZANTINE and Islamic overbuilding. The first major construction at Jerusalem seems to have been the stone fortifications of the LATE BRONZE AGE. Jerusalem was captured by the ISRAELITES under David in *c*.996 BC and extended to the north by SOLOMON, who built a temple and palace in an area later overbuilt by the Herodian temple platform, and by Hezekiah, whose water tunnel is still visible. Jerusalem was patronized by the Byzantine emperors because of its Christian associations and by Islamic caliphs as a holy city. Most of the walls to be seen at Jerusalem are the work of Suleiman the Magnificent (1538–41 AD) on top of Herodian and Roman foundations, while the octagonal 'Dome of the Rock' (685–692 AD) is the most striking of the Islamic buildings in Jerusalem.

Jerzmanowice see NIETOPERZOWA CAVE.

Jerzmanowician an early Upper Palaeolithic INDUSTRY of Poland characterized by BIFACIAL FOLIATES, RETOUCHED BLADES, and DENTICULATES. The Jerzmanowician was defined by Chmielewski in 1961 on the basis of artifacts from NIETOPERZOWA CAVE.

jet lignitic fossil wood that is dense, hard and black. An ability to accept a strong polish and workability made it desirable in jewellery manufacture. Jet is found in geologically young shales and other fine-grained rocks.

Jetis or **Djetis** a geological formation (bed) along the Brantas River in east Java which has yielded remains of early PLEISTOCENE (pre-TRINIL) fauna apparently adapted to open forest environment, and HOMO *erectus* remains referred to as the MOJOKERTO child; date *c*.1.5 million years BP and before.

Jevišovice a stratified Late Neolithic site in Moravia of the FUNNEL BEAKER and BADEN cultures. Although excavated in the early part of the 20th century, Jevišovice continues to provide the basic chronological yardstick for the Late Neolithic and ENEOLITHIC in this part of the Carpathian Basin.

Jhukar a site in the Sind, Pakistan, excavated by N.G. Majumdar in the 1920s, that gives its name to the Late HARAPPAN culture of the region, also represented at AMRI and CHANHU-DARO. The Jhukar is characterized by considerable continuity with the Mature Harappan in its pottery but a loss of many other typical Harappan elements (notably writing, SEALS, urbanism). At the same time, several metal forms appear that relate to northeastern Iran and Central Asia (see SIBRI).

Jincamocco a MIDDLE HORIZON site located in the central highlands of Peru. The site comprises a large rectangular enclosure of HUARI-style architecture, measuring 128 by 256 metres, and an additional 12 ha of rectilinear architecture. Excavations by Katharina Schreiber indicate that the site functioned as a regional administrative centre of the Huari Empire (AD 650–800), and that the empire extensively reorganized the region in which it was located in order to provide centralized political control, and to increase local production of maize.

Jingdezhen [Ching-te-chen]   a city in Jiangxi Province, China, forming the focus of an ancient kiln works centre. Porcelains were produced here from the end of the Tang dynasty (late 10th century AD) until 1911. Before the 14th century, the Song and Yuan courts (see CHINESE DYNASTIES) were supplied with the best products from the larger kilns; then imperial kilns were built for the direct supply of the Ming court. The type of kiln used was the sloping *long* kiln until the Qing Dynasty, when an egg-shaped kiln was invented. Documents of the 13th century count 300 kilns in production. (Compare STONEWARE, YUE, CELADON.)

Jinniushan [Chin-niu-shan]   a site in Liaoning Province, China, dating to the Early and Late Palaeolithic. The lithics in the lower strata including SCRAPERS and bipolar FLAKES, resemble those from ZHOUKOUDIAN Locality 1, and the upper levels have yielded HOMO *sapiens* remains. These fossils have transitional characteristics between *H. erectus* and modern Asians and comprise primary evidence for refuting the 'Eve hypothesis' of population replacement by incoming *H. sapiens sapiens*. See also MABA.

Jomon   the POSTGLACIAL period of hunting and gathering in Japan (10 000–300 BC), divided into six phases: Incipient (10 000–7500 BC), Earliest (7500–5000), Early (5000–3500), Middle (3500–2500/2000), Late (2500/2000–1000), and Final (1000–300). The period coincides with the existence of Jomon pottery (see FUKUI Cave), succeeded by YAYOI pottery in 300 BC (see JAPANESE PERIODIZATION). It is characterized by marine resource utilization and settled village living from Early Jomon; the development of widespread trading networks and ritual development in Middle Jomon in the CHUBU and KANTO regions; collapse of settlement in these regions in Late Jomon; and the development of deep-sea fishing communities in TOHOKU in Final Jomon. Also, during the last millennium BC, rice agriculture was adopted by north Kyushu Jomon groups, setting the stage for the Yayoi expansion (see ITAZUKE). To what extent horticulture was practised in other Jomon phases and areas is uncertain (but see TORIHAMA). (See also FUDODO, IDOJIRI, OYU, KAMIKUROIWA, KAMEGAOKA, KASORI, OMORI.) The PALAEOASIATIC Jomon peoples have been incorrectly identified with the modern AINU, also of PALAEOASIATIC stock. The term Jomon means 'cord marked'.

Jones-Miller   a HELL GAP COMPLEX site located in northeast Colorado, USA. The site is a KILL and/or butchering SITE. A POSTHOLE and associated artifacts at the site have been interpreted as the remains of a 'medicine post' similar to those used by some historic Plains tribes as locations for offerings to ensure a successful kill.

Jordanów or **Jordanów Śląski**   a cemetery of a late phase of the LENGYEL culture in Silesia in southwestern Poland, excavated by Seger at the beginning of the 20th century when the locality was known as Jordansmühl. (Jordanów, and the regional group of the Lengyel culture named after it, are often mistakenly called 'Jordanova' in some literature.) Of particular importance are the Jordanów copper ornaments, which include binocular spirals and beads resembling those from BRZEŚĆ KUJAWSKI and OSŁONKI. These copper ornaments are among the earliest-known from north of the Carpathians.

Jorvik   see YORK.

Jorwe   a small single-period site, where excavations by H.D. Sankalia provided the initial definition of the material culture of Maharashtra, western central India, during the second half of the 2nd millennium BC. Together with the evidence of additional excavated sites, the Jorwe culture is characterized by a fine black-on-red ware decorated with painted registers of geometric motifs, a rich copper tool INDUSTRY in addition to equipment in stone, the cultivation of barley, wheat and various legumes, the keeping of cattle, buffalo, sheep and goat, as well as hunting.

Judds Cavern   see WARGATA MINA.

jue [chueh]   a bronze wine vessel characteristic of the SHANG bronze tradition of China (see CHINESE DYNASTIES), and used for heating wine in ancestral rituals.

Juxtlahuaca Cave   a cave-site in Guerrero, Mexico, known for its polychrome cave paintings in the OLMEC style. Dating to *c*.3000 years ago, these paintings are some of the oldest documented in the New World, and are located nearly a mile inside the mountain.

K

K2   a Late Iron Age site in the northern Transvaal, South Africa, which accumulated to a depth of more than 6 m during the 11th–12th centuries AD. K2 has given its name to the southern FACIES of the initial phase of the LEOPARD'S KOPJE Complex. It dominated the Limpopo Valley, developed specialized craftsmen in bone and IVORY working, and traded these products locally and with the East African coast, in exchange for items such as glass beads. More than 70 human skeletons were previously described as of KHOISAN physical type, but are now considered Negroid. At about AD 1200, the centre of the state moved to the nearby MAPUNGUBWE Hill (see BAMBANDYANALO).

Kabáh   a MAYA Late CLASSIC centre in west-central Yucatán, Mexico, that peaked from the 8th to the 10th century AD and was then virtually abandoned. A paved causeway (*sacbe*) runs from the arch at Kabáh to the PUUC city of UXMAL. Although it was one of the larger cities of the region, little is known of Kabáh beyond its ceremonial architecture. Its most famous construction is the Kodz Pop, a range-type building whose façade is covered with long-nosed masks. The site was first explored by various archaeologists through the Peabody Museum, Harvard University.

Kabambian   an Iron Age group which succeeds the KISALIAN in southeastern Zaire from the 14th–18th centuries AD. Its development is linked to the growth of inter-regional trade in *croisettes* (cross-shaped COPPER INGOTS) as well as the expansion of long-distance trade with the East African coast.

Kabwe   see BROKEN HILL.

Kadero   a KHARTOUM NEOLITHIC site in the Nile Valley, some 3 ha in extent, with high percentages of domestic stock. Some of the numerous human burials were richly furnished with stone mace heads, palettes, necklaces of carnelian beads, IVORY bracelets, pottery and quantities of OCHRE.

Kadesh (TELL Nebi Mend) a site on the River Orontes in Syria, excavated by Pézard in 1921–22 and by Parr in the 1970s. Kadesh, being in a strategic position, was a relatively important city during the LATE BRONZE AGE, and was the site of the inconclusive battle between RAMESSES II and the HITTITES in c.1275 BC.

Kafiavana a rockshelter in the NEW GUINEA HIGHLANDS, excavated by Peter White. The deposits span the last 11 000 years and contain amorphous stone artifacts, bone tools, and a rich faunal assemblage. Marine-shell ornaments and ground axe-ADZES appear c.9000 bp, and pig remains occur from about 6500 bp.

Kahun see EL-LAHUN.

kaizuka literally 'SHELL MIDDEN' in Japanese; a characteristic feature of the JOMON and early YAYOI periods.

Kakovatos the site of a MYCENAEAN settlement in Messenia, Greece, which DÖRPFELD erroneously identified as the Homeric PYLOS. The three THOLOS tombs which he excavated do, however, suggest that this was a regional centre.

Kalabsha the original site in Egypt of an unfinished Graeco–Roman temple dedicated to the Nubian god Mandulis, and re-erected at ASWAN during the NUBIAN RESCUE CAMPAIGN.

Kalambo an Early Iron Age group of the CHIFUMBAZE complex in northern Zambia, which takes its name from a large 4th century AD village site at KALAMBO FALLS.

Kalambo Falls a Zambian site near the southeastern corner of Lake Tanganyika, excavated in the 1950s by J. Desmond Clark. Deposits of ancient lakes have preserved traces of occupation spanning the STONE and IRON AGES. The earliest remains recovered are late ACHEULIAN, dating to the late Middle PLEISTOCENE, but older material may lie below the modern water table. The late Acheulian layers are of particular interest, since many contain plant remains and worked wood (see KALAMBO, KAPOSWA).

Kalanay a cave-site in Masbate, central Philippines, with metal period jar burials of the late 1st millennium BC or later, which has given its name to a pottery complex or 'CULTURE' thought to date to c.400 BC to AD 1500, and exhibiting some similarities with the SA-HUYNH pottery of coastal Vietnam.

Kalasasaya see TIAHUANACO.

Kalavasos a site in southern Cyprus that has, since 1976, been the focus of a series of excavations directed by Todd. At *Tenta* there is an ACERAMIC NEOLITHIC I (7th millennium BC) settlement surrounded by an enclosure wall. The houses were circular two-storey structures built of stone and MUD-BRICK. Human figures were painted in red OCHRE on the wall of one house. *Ayious*, a CHALCOLITHIC (early 4th millennium BC) site, consists of a warren-like arrangement of pits, some of which were connected by tunnels. Their function is obscure but may have involved specialized processing activities. *Ayios Dhimitrios*, occupied c.1325–1225 BC, is one of the most extensive Late CYPRIOT towns. A large ASHLAR structure is thought to have served as an administrative centre and a spectacularly rich CHAMBER TOMB has recently been discovered.

Kalhu an imperial ASSYRIAN city on the River Tigris, south of NINE-VEH, Iraq, best known for the extensive excavations on the citadel (*Nimrud*) and arsenal ('Fort Shalmaneser') conducted by LAYARD, MAL-LOWAN and others. The oldest discovered materials at the site are NINEVITE 5 pottery sherds at Nimrud, and Middle Assyrian texts and materials establish the existence of a town in the later 2nd millennium BC. It was established as the imperial seat by AŠŠURNAṢIRPAL II (883–859 BC), and later Assyrian kings also built extensively in the city; Sargon II (721–705 BC) moved the imperial seat to KHORSABAD, and after this time Kalhu was a provincial capital. The rectangular city wall enclosed about 360 ha, with Nimrud and 'Fort Shalmaneser' set in corners of the wall and separated from the rest of the city as walled compounds containing a massive temple, palace and other administrative buildings. The excavations of the Assyrian city produced a large amount of monumental art, important administra-tive archives, an important corpus of carved IVORIES, an example of a folding ivory 'book' with beeswax-coated leaves on which is written a CUNEIFORM text, and many other small objects. Recent Iraqi work revealed at Nimrud an intact royal grave of Sargon's time, containing two women and a spectacular array of gold jewellery, glass and other objects within a vaulted CHAMBER TOMB. Later post-Assyrian occupa-tion, on a reduced scale, continued until the HELLENISTIC period.

Kalibangan a major site on the extinct Ghaggar/Hakra River in northern Rajastan, India, containing both Early and Mature HARAPPAN settlements. The Mature Harappan settlement lies in two separate walled sections, covering some 15 ha, in the familiar Harappan urban form. The Early Harappan levels (spanning the first half of the 3rd millennium BC) occur below the Mature Harappan citadel. The pottery of this earlier walled place, though showing some similarities with the KOT DIJI style, is characteristic of this region. As in other regional expressions of Early Harappan, some formal antecedents to Mature Harappan CERAMICS occur. Similar pottery occurs further east in Haryana, India. Kalibangan is also well known for the plough scars discovered outside the settlement, and dated to this Early Harappan phase.

Kalomo a Late Iron Age tradition of southern Zambia, dating from the end of the 9th century until the 13th century AD. Houses were arranged around open areas apparently used as cattle byres, and many Kalomo villages were occupied repeatedly.

Kalumpang a Neolithic site in west central Sulawesi which, together with the related site *Minanga Sipakko*, has produced undated late Neolithic assemblages including POLISHED STONE ADZES, ground slate PROJECTILE POINTS, possible stone reaping knives and pottery, some aspects of which have been related to Taiwanese Neolithic and to LAPITA wares of Oceania.

Kalundu a southern Zambian site which has given its name to an Early Iron Age tradition of the CHIFUMBAZE COMPLEX, dating from the early 5th–9th centuries AD, also synonymous with the Western Stream of this complex.

Kamabai a rockshelter in the Guinea Highlands of Sierra Leone with three cultural horizons dated between 4500 and 600 BP, showing a sequence from the LATER STONE AGE through the 'Guinea Neolithic' to the Iron Age.

Kamares a MINOAN cave sanctuary on the slopes of Mount Ida in Crete. The finds from the cave included Middle Minoan (*c*.2000–1550 BC) pottery with white, red, crimson and orange decoration on a dark ground, which became known as *Kamares ware*.

Kambuja the KHMER state centred on Cambodia, the pre-14th century phase of which is often referred to as ANGKOR. The name is borrowed from SANSKRIT.

Kamegaoka a waterlogged Final JOMON site in Aomori Prefecture, Japan, which has yielded abundant wooden vessels painted with LACQUER, basketry, stone and bone personal ornaments, CERAMIC figurines and engraved plaques, etc. The Final Jomon assemblage of sophisticated ritual and finely made objects spread throughout TOHOKU is often assigned to the 'Kamegaoka culture' but is also known as the 'Obora culture'.

Kamennaya Mogila a MESOLITHIC or ACERAMIC NEOLITHIC site in southern Ukraine, near the coast of the Sea of Azov. Claims have been made for the occurrence of very early domesticated cattle and sheep/goat at Kamennaya Mogila, but these have been disputed on grounds of uncertain dating. Situated on a river floodplain, the settlement resembles those of the BUG-DNIESTER culture (e.g. at SOROKI).

Kamid al Loz, Tell a 6 ha site in the Biqa' valley of Lebanon, investigated by German groups between the 1960s and 1980s, that represents the seat of a petty state during the LATE BRONZE AGE, the Kumidi mentioned in the AMARNA archive. The archaeological work traces a settlement history from the late Neolithic to BYZANTINE times. Through most of this sequence, Kamid al Loz was an unfortified village. The exposed MIDDLE BRONZE AGE and Late Bronze Age levels, in contrast, indicate a walled town within which were significant palace and temple constructions as well as domestic architecture. Kumidi lay on both the north–south route through the Biqa' valley and on the route connecting the Damascus basin with the Mediterranean, a setting that helps explain its strategic importance in periods of competing regional powers during the Bronze Age.

Kamikuroiwa an Incipient JOMON rockshelter site in Ehime Prefecture, Japan, which has yielded early CERAMICS (10 700 bp) as at FUKUI. Small cobbles bearing incised drawings of female features from Kamikuroiwa are the earliest PORTABLE ART recovered in Japan.

Kamilamba the earliest-known Iron Age tradition in the Upemba Depression of southeastern Zaire, dated to about the 6th–8th centuries AD, named after the Kamilamba site where an Iron Age layer succeeds LATER STONE AGE material.

Kaminaljuyú a MAYA centre in the southern highlands of Guatemala, best known for the strong TEOTIHUACÁN influence during the Early CLASSIC. Evidence for this influence lies in ceremonial and ritual objects, and in locally produced items with Teotihuacán form and decoration. The relationship between Teotihuacán and Kaminaljuyú was probably commercial and religious. Contacts between Central Mexico and Teotihuacán were directed through Kaminaljuyú.

Kaminaljuyú controlled the OBSIDIAN production on the Pacific slopes. During the Late Classic, Kaminaljuyú shows less evidence of Mexican influence, probably owing to the collapse of Teotihuacán.

Kamoa the first site in central Africa in which ACHEULIAN material was identified, thus extending the known antiquity of human occupation in this region to the EARLIER STONE AGE. It is located on the banks of the Kamoa River in southeastern Zaire and contains a succession of industries from Earlier to LATER STONE AGE.

Kampong Sungai Mas see SRIVIJAYA.

Kampong Sungei Lang the site, near Klang, in peninsular Malaysia, of a metal age 'boat burial', the grave-goods of which include two DONG SON bronze drums, MUTISALAH beads and iron implements (see TULANG MAWAS), dated *c*.300 BC. Related sites include TEMBELING, Kuala Trengganu (burial with two drums and beads), Kampong Pencu (bronze bell with Dong Son-style decoration), and Klang (bronze drum, three bells, iron hoard). It is probably contemporary with the BERNAM-SUNGKAI slab graves.

Kaneaki a HEIAU in the MAKAHA VALLEY, Molokai, Hawaii, now reconstructed. One of the few *heiau* ever excavated, it has been shown to have six construction phases beginning about AD 1460.

Kanem see DAIMA.

Kangaroo Island an island off the South Australian coast which, although uninhabited at European contact, is rich in KARTAN sites attesting to previous Aboriginal occupation. Kartan surface sites on Kangaroo Island are thought to be late PLEISTOCENE and were replaced by an amorphous small tool industry known from Seton Cave. The most recent work at Cape du Couedic, however, where Kartan material has been found associated with a wider range of artifacts and dated to around 7000 bp, has cast doubt on this interpretation.

Kanish see KÜLTEPE.

Kansai an early mediaeval administrative district of west-central Japan (see JAPANESE PERIODIZATION) corresponding roughly to the modern KINKI district; often used in discussions of Japanese archaeology.

Kansas see ELSTERIAN.

Kansyore Ware a distinctive type of mainly comb-stamped pottery associated with pre-Iron Age sites of the first millennium BC in the Lake Victoria basin of East Africa.

Kantarawichai a large late prehistoric/early historic moated settlement (see MOATED SITES) lying between NON CHAI and BAN CHIANG HIAN in the Chi valley, KHORAT, Thailand. Buddhist remains of the mid 1st millennium AD are similar to those of DVARAVATI sites.

kantharos or **cantharus** a type of CLASSICAL drinking cup with two vertical handles which can project above the rim. Early examples are often stemmed, although in the 5th century BC a stemless version was produced. In the 4th and 3rd centuries BC it became one of the most popular types of drinking vessel in the Greek world.

Kanto a modern administrative district of eastern Honshu Island, Japan – often used in archaeological writings – comprising Tokyo Metropolitan District and Kanagawa, Saitama, Gunma, Tochigi, Ibaragi and Chiba Prefectures. (See HOSHINO.)

Kaposwa a late HOLOCENE MICROLITHIC LATER STONE AGE industry represented at KALAMBO FALLS in northern Zambia.

Kapovaya or **Shul'gantash** a cave located on the upper Belaya River in the southern Ural Mountains, European Russia, containing rare examples of east European PALAEOLITHIC CAVE ART. Approximately 40 naturalistic and stylized paintings (monochrome and poly-chrome) of extinct mammals (woolly MAMMOTH, woolly rhinoceros) are preserved on the walls and ceiling of the cave; many abstract designs (e.g. geometric figures) are also present. A cultural layer (comprising stone artifacts, ornaments, former hearths, and faunal remains (primarily mammoth)), was excavated within the cave, and is assigned to the Upper Palaeolithic. Kapovaya was investigated during the 1960s and 1970s by BADER and during the 1980s by Shchelinskij.

Kapwirimbwe   an Early Iron Age village east of Lusaka in Zambia, occupied in the 5th century AD, which has given its name to a tradition of the CHIFUMBAZE complex. A late phase of the Kapwirimbwe tradition is represented at the Twickenham Road site in Lusaka, which dates between the 9th and 11th centuries AD.

Kara–Bom   a Palaeolithic open-air site located near the confluence of the Semisart and Kaerlyk rivers in the Altai region of Siberia. Artifacts and isolated faunal remains (including woolly rhinoceros) are buried in LOAM, CLAY, and rubble deposits overlying bedrock (?). Among the artifacts are LEVALLOIS CORES, RETOUCHED BLADES, DENTICULATES and endscrapers (see SCRAPER). The assemblage is thought to date to the early Upper Palaeolithic on typological grounds, but this is unconfirmed by RADIOMETRIC estimates or STRATIGRAPHIC correlation. Kara-Bom was discovered and excavated by OKLADNIKOV in 1980.

Karako   a YAYOI-period site in Nara Prefecture, Japan, which serves as the type-site for the western Yayoi pottery chronology. The first excavation in 1938 revealed a series of storage pits; recent excavations have recovered a double moat around the presumed village site, and a fragment of a bronze bell (see DOTAKU) casting mould indicates craft production on site.

Karanis   the Classical name for the site of Kom Aushim, situated in the northeastern FAIYUM, Egypt. Excavations by archaeologists from Michigan University in 1924–35 yielded over 5000 PAPYRI and OSTRAKA, which are a major source of evidence for the economy and administration of Roman Egypt during the 2nd–4th centuries AD.

Karanovo   a stratified TELL site in eastern Bulgaria which has provided the basic chronological sequence for the Neolithic and much of the ENEOLITHIC of the eastern Balkans. The 12 m of deposits at Karanovo contain seven major phases of occupation. Karanovo I gives its name to the earliest Neolithic occupations north of Greece, and forms part of the complex of cultures that include STARČEVO, CRIŞ and KÖRÖS. Karanovo II continues this tradition. Karanovo III is an occupation of the Middle Neolithic VESELINOVO culture, while levels IV and V are contemporaneous with the Late Neolithic VINČA culture of the western Balkans. The very thick Karanovo VI level represents perhaps several centuries of occupation by the Eneolithic GUMELNIŢA culture. The final level, VII, is a very early stage of the Bronze Age.

Karari   an EARLIER STONE AGE industry of the OLDOWAN industrial Complex found in the upper layers of the KOOBI FORA formation on the east side of Lake Turkana in northern Kenya, dating to about 1.5–1.25 million years ago. It is characterized by more artifact types than in the underlying KBS industry, as well as the appearance of BIFACES.

Karasuk culture   a Bronze Age culture of the central Asian steppe of Kazakhstan and Russian Siberia, which developed from the ANDRONOVO culture. The typical Karasuk artifact is a short knife or dagger, bent at the point where the handle joins the blade. Remains of Karasuk bridles mark the beginning of horse riding on the Siberian steppe.

Karatepe   an 8th century BC Neo-HITTITE fortified palace on Ceyhan River in the Adana plain, southwestern Anatolia, whose architecture was documented by H. Bossert. Of particular importance are the reliefs and inscriptions on the two monumental gateways, which carry the bilingual PHOENICIAN–Luwian HIEROGLYPHIC texts that were instrumental in the decipherment of the Luwian writing system.

Karbuna   a hoard of the CUCUTENI-TRIPOLYE culture found in Moldova between the Prut and Dniester rivers. Eight hundred and fifty-two stone, bone, shell and copper artifacts were found in a 34 cm-high decorated vessel. Of the 444 copper items, 87% were beads, while the remainder were bracelets, discs, plaques, pendants and two axe-adzes. Among the shell ornaments were several made from SPONDYLUS.

Karkarichinkat (Nord and Sud)   two mounds in the TILEMSI Valley of Mali, Africa, occupied by herder-fishers between *c*.3900 and 3300 BP.

Karmir-blur   an URARTIAN town near modern Erevan (Armenia), comprising a citadel and walled residential area that together cover some 40 ha. B.B. Piotrovsky's excavations reveal the citadel to be a strongly fortified dense array of storerooms (especially for cereals, wine and weapons) beneath residential suites. The lower town consisted of blocks of buildings which vary in size and complexity. Karmir-blur was occupied largely in the 7th century BC (though some pre-Urartian graves do occur, and the place was also used in HELLENISTIC times), and seems to have replaced the 8th century complex at Erebuni as the Urartian seat near Erevan. Erebuni has a similar division between citadel and town, though differing in architectural detail, and is famous for its wall paintings that clearly show the NEO-ASSYRIAN inspiration for much of the Urartian elite art. The Erebuni citadel was also the site of an ACHAEMENID administrative centre.

Karnak   a vast complex of religious buildings in the northern part of the Egyptian city of THEBES. The central part of the site is the TEMPLE enclosure of the god AMEN, containing his main temple together with a series of subsidiary religious structures, the whole complex covering an area of approximately 120 ha. From the NEW KINGDOM this was the most important religious establishment in the Egyptian Empire with considerable economic and political power, but Karnak (called in Egyptian 'the Most Select of Places') was the site of a temple from at least as early as the MIDDLE KINGDOM. To the south of the Amen enclosure is the smaller complex of the goddess Mut, consort of Amen, while to the north is that of the god Montu, the predecessor of Amen as pre-eminent deity at Thebes. A processional route runs south from Karnak to the LUXOR temple.

Karolta 1   a PETROGLYPH site in northwest South Australia with PANARAMITEE-style engravings. Controversial CATION RATIO dates have been obtained from 24 motifs ranging from 31 600 to 1400 bp. If confirmed, these dates would indicate both the early occupation of the arid zone and the long continuity of this style of art.

karst a terrain with a unique set of LANDFORMS and drainage patterns characterized by formation and enlargement of cavities resulting largely from chemical weathering and EROSION, primarily by the solution process, in regions of carbonate and evaporite rocks. Caves, collapse features, sinkholes (dolines), deranged and disrupted surface drainage, springs and an active subterranean drainage system are some of the more common characteristics of karst topography.

Kartan a variant of the AUSTRALIAN CORE TOOL AND SCRAPER TRADITION found on KANGAROO ISLAND and in neighbouring areas of mainland South Australia, and comprising HORSEHOOF CORES, unifacial pebble CHOPPERS, large steep-edged FLAKE SCRAPERS and WAISTED AXES, but very few flakes or flake tools. Recent research on Kangaroo Island suggests that KARTAN sites, previously thought to be PLEISTOCENE in age, may be the result of specialized exploitation of particular raw materials rather than a distinct industry.

Kar-Tukulti-Ninurta a city near ASSUR that was a new foundation by the MIDDLE ASSYRIAN king Tukulti-Ninurta I (1243–1207 BC) as a cultic and royal residential centre, and that provides a good illustration of the Assyrian habit of founding new royal seats. The settlement forms a walled square enclosing about 60 ha, which is divided into two sections by a canal running through the middle; the western of these sections contains a large palace complex, a temple of Assur, and domestic architecture, while the eastern section remained unbuilt.

kārum 1. an AKKADIAN term denoting the 'harbour' of a city, usually set apart from the rest of the community, in which trade occurs; in this sense, the *kārum* may be a harbour proper (as at UR) or simply a section of the town in which commercial exchange takes place (as at Kanish; see KÜLTEPE). 2. an Akkadian term for the organization of merchants residing in the physical *kārum*, where the merchant community is largely self-governing (though with specified legal, economic and social obligations to the larger community); the best-known example of this organization comes from the Old ASSYRIAN trading colony at Kanish in Cappadocia.

Kaş the site of a Bronze Age shipwreck off Cape Uluburun, just east of Kaş on the southern coast of Turkey, which has been excavated by Bass and Pulak since 1984. Items recovered from the ship, which was presumably en route to the Aegean when it sank in the 14th century BC, include copper, tin and glass INGOTS, bronze tools and weapons, Near Eastern, Egyptian and Aegean jewellery, and CYPRIOT, CANAANITE and MYCENAEAN pottery.

Kasori a Middle/Late JOMON SHELL MIDDEN site in Chiba Prefecture, Japan, now a historical park. At least 47 pit-houses have been excavated in a circular village plan with shell deposits around its rim. It is the type-site for Kasori-type Jomon CERAMICS and representative of plaza-type Jomon village sites.

Kassala a cultural phase from the eastern Sudan comprising the BUTANA, GASH and MOKRAM Groups.

Kassites a mountain people of the Zagros, with a distinctive language and culture, who began infiltrating MESOPOTAMIA in the early 2nd millennium BC. After the sack of BABYLON by the HITTITE king Mursili I (*c.*1620–1595 BC), a Kassite dynasty established itself in Babylonia and by the mid 15th century controlled all of the region.

Lasting until around 1160 BC, the Kassite rule represents the longest episode of political integration in the history of southern Mesopotamia (though interrupted by the invasion of the MIDDLE ASSYRIAN king Tukulti-Ninurta I in 1225 BC). Although it maintained political stability, brought economic prosperity, and encouraged artistic and literary achievement in Babylonia, the Kassite period is relatively little studied and therefore comparatively unknown. Important sites of the Kassite period include AQAR QUF, WARKA and, especially for the texts, NIPPUR.

Kastri 1. a site on the island of Kythera, off the southern coast of mainland Greece, that was excavated by Coldstream and Huxley in 1963–65. Originally an Early HELLADIC settlement, Kastri was colonized *c.*2500 BC by MINOANS, apparently from the west of Crete. As trade between Crete and Laconia intensified in the 2nd millennium Kastri prospered but the collapse of the Minoan palace economy led to the abandonment of the site.
2. a site on the island of Syros; see CHALANDRIANI.

Kastritsa an Upper Palaeolithic cave-site located on Lake Ioannina in northwestern Greece. A series of occupation levels dating between *c.*22 000–11 000 bp are buried in SILT, SAND, and rubble; the faunal remains are heavily dominated by red deer, together with AUROCHS and steppe ass. The Upper Palaeolithic artifacts include BACKED BLADES, SHOULDERED POINTS, bone points, and decorated pebbles. Traces of a structure partially surrounding a former HEARTH were encountered near the entrance of the cave. Kastritsa was investigated by HIGGS and others in the 1960s.

Katotan see KATOTO.

Katoto an Iron Age cemetery with collective graves in southeastern Zaire, probably dating to the 13th century AD, which has given its name to an Iron Age tradition contemporaneous with the KISALIAN.

katun a period of time in the CLASSIC MAYA LONG COUNT equalling 7200 days, or about 20 years. The celebration of katuns was a major ritual of kingship in the Classic period. The katun is the chronological unit comprising the SHORT COUNT.

Katuruka an Early Iron Age site in the Buhaya region of northeastern Tanzania, with evidence of sophisticated iron-SMELTING technology dating to the last few centuries BC and associated with UREWE pottery. This is the oldest-known evidence for iron-working in central and southern Africa.

Kauri Point a PA in Tauranga, North Island, that was the site of one of the first major systematic excavations in NEW ZEALAND. First occupied about 500 years ago, it had three phases of fortification interspersed with periods of undefended settlement. The nearby swamp has excellent preservation of artifacts, including a remarkable series of wooden combs.

Kausambi a site on the Yamuna River near its confluence with the Ganges in Uttar Pradesh, northern India, that was subject to intensive investigation in the 1940s to 1960s by G.R. Sharma, providing important evidence of the origins and development of the Gangetic Iron Age urban civilization. The earliest documented levels of the site, Kausambi I, contain a pottery related to the OCHRE COLOURED POTTERY horizon and dated to the middle of the 2nd millennium BC. These are followed by levels of the Kausambi II period, which contain black-and-red, red, grey and black wares, that relate to the cultural province of the lower Ganges to the east; iron objects appear at this time, dated roughly to the second quarter of the 1st millennium BC. The first defensive walls of the settlement were constructed during this period. The following Kausambi III period is characterized by NORTHERN BLACK POLISHED WARE, beginning perhaps around 500 BC. The palace complex of the town was first built in the early part of this phase, and the city walls enclosed as much as 250 ha. These levels are followed by those belonging to the early 1st millennium AD.

Kawahara-dera   see ASUKA.

Kawakiu Bay   a site in western Molokai, Hawaiian Islands, with large MIDDEN deposits and stone structures indicating the presence of a permanent fishing community. The site has been dated by OBSIDIAN HYDRATION to AD 1750.

Kawela   a dry leeward valley in south Molokai, Hawaiian Islands. The pre-European settlement pattern is well preserved, and most features date to the last one or two centuries before European contact. Agriculture was largely limited to some irrigation cultivation of root-crops (sweet potato and *taro*) and large fishponds were the main focus of production. See HALAWA VALLEY, LAPAKAHI, MAKAHA VALLEY.

Kaya   the name of a confederation of small POLITIES on the southern Korean coast in the 4th and early 5th centuries AD (see KOREAN PERIODIZATION). Kaya was flanked on the west by the state of PAEKCHE and on the east by SILLA. Kaya remains consist mainly of CIST burials or MOUNDED TOMBS containing multiple cist burials and grey STONEWARE, the first to be produced in Korea and which stimulated SUE ware production in Japan.

Kayatha   a site on the Malwa plateau of central India, where excavations have defined a sequence of three CHALCOLITHIC cultures, as well as Iron Age and early historic levels. At the base of the Chalcolithic sequence, dated to the second half of the 3rd millennium BC (and therefore contemporaneous with the Mature HARAPPAN to the north), is a culture complex characterized by Kayatha ware (violet-painted brown slipped) as well as incised and red-painted buff wares. The community inhabited small huts, and used both lithic and copper equipment. The second phase marks the appearance of pottery similar to that of the Banas culture, typified by a white painted black-and-red ware (see AHAR), and dated to the early 2nd millennium. The last Chalcolithic phase, dated to the second quarter of the 2nd millennium, belongs to the MALWA culture as seen at NAVDATOLI.

Kayenta   a regional variant of the ANASAZI TRADITION, located in northeast Arizona, USA, and most clearly defined during the PUEBLO II stage. Kayenta is recognized by specific pottery types and architectural construction techniques.

Kazanluk or **Kazanlik**   a large Neolithic, Eneolithic and Early Bronze Age TELL in the Valley of Roses in southern Bulgaria with a six-metre stratigraphy. The bottom two metres are of the Early Neolithic KARANOVO I culture, above which was a VESELINOVO (Karanovo III) layer, a Karanovo V–VI occupation enclosed by a stone wall, and an Early Bronze Age occupation. As at CHEVDAR, careful sieving produced a large sample of faunal and botanical remains, indicating a subsistence strategy based on emmer wheat and sheep/goat in the Early Neolithic settlement.

KBS **1.** an EARLIER STONE AGE industry of the OLDOWAN industrial complex found in the lower layers of the KOOBI FORA formation on the east side of Lake Turkana in northern Kenya, dating to about 1.8 million years ago.
2. a TUFF layer at the Koobi Fora site. The dating of this layer was formerly controversial, but is now well established at 1.8 million years ago.
3. a site at Koobi Fora. from which stone artifacts and animal bones are an important source of information on early HOMINID behaviour.

Kebaran a culture discovered by TURVILLE-PETRE in 1931 during his excavations in *Kebara Cave*, MOUNT CARMEL, Israel. It forms the earliest Levantine EPIPALAEOLITHIC (*c.*20 000–14 500 BP) which comes after the local Upper Palaeolithic, and was followed by the *Geometric Kebaran* complex (14 500–12 500 BP) and then the NATUFIAN. The Kebaran was produced by nomadic hunter-gatherers with an increasing reliance on wild cereals, and marks an early step towards sedentism, domestication and food production (see EIN GEV I). Its flint industry is characterized by BLADELETS and MICROLITHS modified to form backed and pointed pieces, and groundstone tools such as mortars and pestles.

Kebaran sites vary from small seasonal occupations to large lowland winter base-camps such as *Ohalo II*, a site on the shore of the Sea of Galilee and occupied *c.*19 000 BP, which had a heavy dependence on fish and plants including the oldest grains of wild barley and wheat ever found.

Kebara Cave was occupied from the Middle Palaeolithic to the Epipalaeolithic, and contains NEANDERTHAL burials dated to *c.*60 000 BP. Upper Palaeolithic skeletons are known from Ohalo II and Ein Gev I.

Kehe [K'o-ho] an early Palaeolithic site in Shanxi Province, China, belonging to the heavy tool tradition with LANTIAN and DINGCUN, as opposed to ZHOUKOUDIAN with mainly FLAKE tools.

Keilor a site near Melbourne, Victoria, Australia, where a fully modern cranium was found in 1940 in ALLUVIAL SEDIMENTS and dated to *c.*13 000 bp. Artifacts have been found throughout the sequence. The earliest levels are estimated to have a minimum date of 36 000 BP.

Kelleli a group of Bronze Age sites in the lower Murghab delta (southeastern Turkmenistan), whose material culture defines the Kelleli phase of the regional chronology, tentatively dated to the third quarter of the 3rd millennium BC; Kelleli settlements are generally very small (up to about 6 ha).

Kellia a site on the desert fringe of the western Nile DELTA, Egypt. Excavated since 1964 by a Franco-Swiss mission, Kellia is an extensive Coptic monastic settlement with continuous occupation from the 4th–8th centuries AD. The pottery recovered from the excavations at Kellia comprises one of the most important CERAMIC ASSEMBLAGES of the Late Roman Period from Egypt.

Kel'taminar or **Kel'teminar** a culture complex, found in Khoresmia and the Kyzyl Kum southeast of the Aral Sea in Kazakhstan, Uzbekistan and Turkmenia defining a pottery-using, foraging/herding adaptation that appears to be a response to the HOLOCENE wet phase when more surface water was available in this desertic landscape. In some areas, these groups also worked copper and turquoise, presumably for exchange with agricultural neighbours to the south (reflected in stylistic echos of NAMAZGA II–III in Kel'teminar pottery). The culture complex is poorly dated, but seems to belong in the 5th–3rd millennia BC, spanning the Mesolithic to the early Bronze Age. Most sites comprise unstratified surface remains and are difficult to date: some (eg. Djanbas 4) have evidence of reed and wood structures. The culture is thought to have played a role in the subsequent development of the SRUBNAYA and ANDRONOVO cultures.

kendi   a spouted water container in use in maritime Southeast Asia during the late 1st and early 2nd millennia AD.

Kenniff Cave   a sandstone shelter in south central Queensland, Australia, with stencilled art and over three metres of occupation deposits going back 19 000 years. Excavated in 1962 by John Mulvaney, this site provided the first evidence of PLEISTOCENE occupation of Australia, and established the foundations of the two-phase sequence in current use throughout the continent.

Kent's Cavern   a British prehistoric cave-site on the south Devon coast, first excavated by Father MacEnery in 1825 and since invest-igated by Goodwin-Austen, PENGELLY, and at least 12 other workers. MacEnery's recognition of PALAEOLITHIC ARTIFACTS and associated fauna *in situ* beneath a stalagmite floor was one of the first indications of the true age of British stone tools. The site has yielded Upper Palaeolithic (including CRESWELLIAN BLADE tools and bone artifacts), Middle Palaeolithic BIFACES, and rather crude Lower Palaeolithic implements including bifaces and a CHOPPER. The upper layers have produced some Mesolithic, Neolithic and more recent material.

Kenya Capsian   SEE EBURRAN.

Kenyon, Dame Kathleen Mary (1906–78)   a British archaeologist who worked extensively in Britain up to the early 1950s, but is best known for her work at JERICHO in 1952–58 and JERUSALEM in 1961–67. The work at Jericho firmly established the existence of an ACERAMIC NEOLITHIC (PPNA/B) and an EPIPALAEOLITHIC subsistence focused on wild cereals (NATUFIAN).

Kephala   the site of a FINAL NEOLITHIC settlement and CIST GRAVE cemetery on the Cycladic island of Kea, excavated by CASKEY and Coleman in 1961–66. The close links between Kephala and sites in Attica, such as ATHENS and THORIKOS, have led to the recognition of an Attica–Kephala culture.

Kerameikos   one of the main cemetery areas of ATHENS and the location for some of the pottery workshops. German excavations have revealed extensive remains of the cemeteries outside the Dipylon and Sacred Gates. Some are private although a multiple burial for the Spartans killed at the end of the 5th century BC has been located. Many of the tombs were marked by STELAI with relief decoration, and through inscriptions it has been possible to identify family plots.

Kerinci   a highland area of west-central Sumatra, which has produced prehistoric surface finds ranging from OBSIDIAN MICROLITHS similar to TIANKO PANJANG of the mid-HOLOCENE to DONG SON bronze remains of the last centuries BC.

Kerma   a Sudanese site, a major centre of the Kingdom of KUSH, excavated by REISNER in 1913–16. The only substantial surviving building associated with the settlement is a massive MUD-BRICK structure, the 'Western Deffufa', a castle containing a series of apartments. To the east is a large cemetery of TUMULUS graves, including the royal NECROPOLIS of the kings of Kush, probably dating to the Second INTERMEDIATE PERIOD (c.1633 1550 BC). These tumuli, the most impressive of which are as large as 90 m in diameter, were elaborately built with internal mud-brick reinforcing walls; in addition to the main burial chamber some of the larger tombs also contained sacrificial human interments (over 300 in one case).

Kerma Ware distinctive handmade pottery with very thin walls and a black-and-red lustrous finish, found in a range of elegant shapes; a product of the KERMA culture.

Kernonen a burial mound of the Armorican EARLY BRONZE AGE Tumulus Culture c.2000–2500 BC, in Finistère, France. The circular stone CAIRN covered a rectangular dry-stone chamber containing the remains of a single individual accompanied by exquisitely flaked flint barbed-and-TANGED arrowheads, originally held in a quiver, amber beads, four bronze axes, and three fine bronze daggers with wooden hilts decorated with thousands of tiny gold nails.

kernos a composite Greek cult vessel, made of clay or stone, used for the offering of first fruits.

Keros–Syros a cultural phase, named after two islands in the Cyclades, which in Renfrew's classification of the CYCLADIC culture sequence, corresponds to Early Cycladic II (c.2700–2300 BC) in the traditional chronology.

Kesslerloch a Swiss MAGDALENIAN reindeer-hunting cave-site, first excavated by K. Merk in 1874, and occupied during a cold phase of the final GLACIATION, with reindeer bones representing about 80% of the recovered fauna. The site is best known for its bonework including HARPOONS and SPEARTHROWERS, and art objects including a famous engraving of a rutting reindeer. The stone tool-kit includes many borers.

Ketrosy a Middle Palaeolithic open-air site on the Dnestr River in western Ukraine. The occupation horizon is buried in ALLUVIAL and slope deposits on a low TERRACE, and is thought to date to an INTERSTADIAL preceding the early cold maximum of the LAST GLACIAL. Faunal remains include woolly MAMMOTH and steppe bison. Sidescrapers (see SCRAPER) and DENTICULATES predominate among the tools. Ketrosy was discovered and excavated by Anisyutkin during 1972–79.

keyhole tombs MOUNDED TOMBS of KOFUN-period Japan, with a ground plan shaped like an old-fashioned keyhole. They are assumed to be the tombs of the rulers and highest-ranking elite. The symbolism of the shape is unknown and generally unrepresented in other East Asian mounded tomb traditions. In the 4th–5th centuries AD, two sizes are found, their lengths averaging approximately 100 and 200 m (compare OJIN, NINTOKU).

Khafadje a site on the lower Diyala River in eastern central Iraq, and excavated as part of FRANKFORT's Diyala project in the 1920s and 1930s. Khafadje has a stratified CERAMIC sequence from JEMDET NASR to late EARLY DYNASTIC times which, together with the results from Tell ASMAR, provided the yardstick for the archaeological periodization of 3rd millennium BC southern MESOPOTAMIA. The excavation exposed a long succession of Sin temples (Jemdet Nasr to Early Dynastic III), a three-phase Temple Oval (E.D. II–III), and an extensive residential district which contained a large number of burials beneath floors.

Khafre or **Chephren**   an Egyptian king of the 4th DYNASTY (during the OLD KINGDOM), and owner of the second PYRAMID-COMPLEX to be built at GIZA; this includes the still-impressive Valley Temple and the Great SPHINX, whose features are presumably a portrait of Khafre.

Khami   **1.** a capital of the Torwa state in southwestern Zimbabwe, built in the 15th century AD after the decline of GREAT ZIMBABWE, and occupied until the mid 17th century, when the capital moved to DANANGOMBE. The site has distinctive architecture consisting of house platforms and low walls often decorated with ornate herringbone and chequered stone arrangements. Imported goods and considerable quantities of gold found by early treasure hunters indicate that trade with the East African coast was important.
2. the third phase of the ZIMBABWE tradition, which continued to the early 19th century AD.
3. a MICROLITHIC LATER STONE AGE INDUSTRY of the last 8000 years from the Matobo Hills of southwestern Zimbabwe, also known as the MATOPO Industry.

Khania   see CHANIA.

Khartoum Neolithic   a Sudanese INDUSTRY dating to *c*.5200 BP and characterized by domestic stock, pottery and a distinctive ADZE or 'gouge' (see ESH SHAHEINAB, KADERO).

Kheit Qasim   three adjacent sites (I, II and III) in the Jebel Hamrin area of eastern central Iraq (on the upper Diyala drainage and the edge of the Zagros foothills), which have been excavated by J-F. Forest as part of recent rescue work. Kheit Qasim I is a large EARLY DYNASTIC cemetery of brick tombs with multiple inhumations. This funerary tradition, unusual for southern MESOPOTAMIA, is duplicated at another Hamrin site of similar date (Tell Ahmad al-Hattu), and may reflect a connection with communities in the Zagros. Kheit Qasim II is a contemporary village settlement; a larger fortified Early Dynastic I settlement occurs nearby at Abu Qasim. Kheit Qasim III is a small 'UBAID period site, the excavation of which revealed an elaborate dwelling with a tripartite floor plan focused on a large 'T' shaped central hall; perhaps derived from SAMARRAN house forms (e.g. at Tell es-SAWWAN), this is duplicated at other sites in the Hamrin (e.g. Tell ABADA, Tell Madhur), and is thought to have housed extended families as the basic social and economic units of 'Ubaid society.

Khirbet Kerak   (also called TELL Beth Yerah) a Palestinian site on the southwestern shore of the Sea of Galilee. It was settled from the EARLY to MIDDLE BRONZE AGE and again in the HELLENISTIC to BYZANTINE Periods. It is the type-site for 'Khirbet Kerak Ware', a class of Early Bronze Age BURNISHED pottery vessels with incised or ribbed decoration, probably of Anatolian origin.

Khirokitia   the site of a prehistoric settlement in southern Cyprus, which was excavated by Dikaios in 1936–46 and by Le Brun in 1977–81. Khirokitia was first occupied in the ACERAMIC NEOLITHIC I phase (7th millennium BC), abandoned and then reoccupied in Neolithic II (later 5th millennium BC). The settlement, which was surrounded by a massive enclosure wall, consists of circular houses built of stone and MUD-BRICK. The roofs were apparently flat, not domed as was once believed. The dead were buried INTRAMURALLY.

Khmer an ethno-linguistic group once occupying Cambodia, southern Vietnam and adjacent parts of Thailand, and, at the height of the power of the state of ANGKOR, dominating most of Thailand and southern Laos. They were linguistically related to the MON.

Khoikhoin, Khoi, Khoikhoi or **Khoekhoe** a STONE AGE pastoral people with pottery, cattle, sheep and goats, who lived in the western parts of southern Africa during the last 2000 years, known to European colonial inhabitants as 'Hottentots'. It is possible that the Khoikhoin obtained their stock from BANTU-speakers in northern Botswana, from where they migrated to the southwestern Cape (see CAPE COASTAL WARE, KHOISAN).

Khoisan a collective term for KHOIKHOIN and SAN peoples from southern Africa since they share the same genetic ancestry. Morphologically, they are small, light-skinned people with tufted black head hair, sparse body hair, and short, broad noses.

Khok Charoen a prehistoric cemetery in the upper Pa Sak valley, central Thailand, which has yielded POLISHED STONE ADZES and stone ornaments but to date no metal, despite THERMOLUMINESCENCE dates of about 1000 BC.

Khok Phanom Di a large prehistoric settlement located on the old coastline of south-central Thailand. Although RADIOCARBON dates place occupation between *c*.2000 and 1400 BC, no metal has been recovered from the site, which is best known for its rich pottery-making (and probably exporting) tradition and for burials which indicate sharply defined social stratification. Other, as yet undated, sites near the coast in central Thailand, such as Khok Phlap and Khok Rakaa, at which BRONZE working occurred and where assemblages parallel those of General Period B in KHORAT, may overlap in date with this site.

Khorat an extensive low plateau in northeast Thailand, drained by two river systems, where rice agriculture appears to have begun before the 4th millennium BC. Hundreds of sites have been mapped in the region, only a few of which have been excavated. Pre-modern developments have tentatively been divided into four broad periods.

General Period A (*c*.3600–2000 BC) refers to the period of initial settlement of known early sites, most of which are in the northern (Songkhram) basin (see BAN CHIANG, PHU WIANG, NON NOK THA). The period is characterized by subsistence based upon rice cultivation and rearing of pigs and dogs, supplemented by broad-spectrum hunting and gathering; use of POLISHED STONE ADZES and stone and shell jewellery indicates a degree of regional trade, as well as incipient social ranking.

General Period B (*c*.2000–800/400 BC) covers the period of transition to the use of tin-bronze, dispersed small-scale production of bronze using metals imported from mining and processing sites in the mountains bordering the plateau (PHU LON, NON PA WAI), the presence of cattle, and increases in population, number of settlements and degree of social ranking. Many of the sites in the north were occupied by this period (see BAN NADI), and some of those in the southern Chi-Mun basin (BAN CHIANG HIAN) as well.

General Period C (*c*.800/400 BC–AD 300/500) was when iron replaced bronze in tools and weapons, water buffalo became

Khorat Bronze axes.

prominent, and wet-rice cultivation appears to have been established, as settlement spread down from low terraces into the floodplains. Rapid population growth occurred, and clusters of small villages formed about larger settlements, suggesting that small political units were developing, particularly in the Chi-Mun basin (see NON CHAI, KANTARAWICHAI, MUANG FA DAET, NON DUA, PHIMAI, MUANG SIMA).

General Period D (c.AD 300/500–1300) occurred when larger settlements of the previous period expanded and those of the Chi-Mun basin acquired encircling moats (see MOATED SITES). The period is that of formation of small states, later absorbed into larger ones, long-distance trade relations and a degree of INDIANIZATION.

Khor-Musa a group of five stratified Middle Palaeolithic occupation sites in the Second Cataract of the southern Nile Valley, Egypt. The recovered artifacts include LEVALLOIS FLAKES, DENTICULATES and BURINS, accompanied by well-preserved faunal remains. The term Khormusan was coined by Marks to describe technologically similar extensive Late Middle Palaeolithic sites lying close to the River Nile and contemporary with, or following, the ATERIAN.

Khorramabad a valley in the Luristan section of the Zagros Mountains in western Iran, which contains a series of Middle and Upper Palaeolithic sites, some of which (Kunji, Gar Arjeneh, Yafteh, Ghamari and Pa Sangar) were excavated by Frank Hole and others during the 1960s. The combined results of this work provide a sequence of MOUSTERIAN, Baradostian and ZARZIAN INDUSTRIES that span the Late PLEISTOCENE, a sequence replicating that of SHANIDAR.

Khorsabad a city in Iraq which was a short-lived capital of Assyria. It was one of the first MESOPOTAMIAN sites to be excavated by Emile Botta, beginning in 1843; the excavation was continued by V. Place, and the site was re-examined by G. Loud in the 1920s and 1930s. Khorsabad is the location of Dur-Sharrukin, built over an existing village by the NEO-ASSYRIAN king Sargon II (721–705 BC) as a new capital north of NINEVEH, and used as a fortified place by his successors. The nearly square walls of Sargon's city enclosed roughly 325 ha; the palace complex and arsenal formed separate compounds set in the city walls. The early French work focused on Sargon's palace, and uncovered a fabulous series of wall reliefs and monumental sculpture, much of which w:s lost in the Euphrates while being transported to France.

Khotylevo sites two Palaeolithic localities on the Desna River in Ukraine. At Khotylevo I, Middle Palaeolithic artifacts are buried in ALLUVIUM at the base of the second TERRACE. The molluscan fauna suggests that the alluvium is of last INTERGLACIAL age, although the mammalian remains include reindeer. LEVALLOIS CORES and BIFACES are common among the artifacts. At Khotylevo II (700 m upstream), an Upper Palaeolithic horizon is buried in slope deposits overlying a low bedrock promontory; both the STRATIGRAPHIC CONTEXT and RADIOCARBON dates (23 660 and 24 960 bp) indicate an early LAST GLACIAL MAXIMUM age. The faunal remains are primarily of woolly MAMMOTH. Features include HEARTHS, pits and debris concentrations. The artifacts, which include VENUS FIGURINES, permit assignment to the KOSTENKIWILLENDORF CULTURE or EASTERN GRAVETTIAN. The Khotylevo sites were discovered by Zavernyaev, who conducted excavations at Khotylevo I during 1958–59, and Khotylevo II during 1969–75.

Khryashchi a Palaeolithic locality on the Northern Donets River in the south of European Russia. Artifact assemblages were recovered from ALLUVIUM of the third TERRACE, and from the middle of a series of three buried soils overlying the alluvium. The lower, and possibly the upper, assemblage dates to the late Middle PLEISTOCENE, and represents one of the few firmly dated pre-Late Pleistocene sites on the Russian Plain. (The nearby locality of Mikhajlovskoe, also on the Northern Donets, is another example.) The artifacts comprise archaic FLAKE and CORE tools; no HANDAXES were found. Khryashchi was investigated by Goretskij in 1952, and by Praslov in 1964–66.

Khuan Lukpad the site of a protohistoric industrial and trading settlement near Khlong Thom, Krabi, on the west coast of peninsular Thailand, specializing in the production of glass and stone beads and tin. Imports found at the site (Roman and Indian SEALS, fragments of Middle Eastern glass, and a Chinese mirror and some GLAZED STONEWARES) date to the early–mid 1st millennium AD.

Khufu or **Cheops** an Egyptian king of the 4th DYNASTY, during the OLD KINGDOM, the successor of SNEFRU. Owner of the Great PYRAMID at GIZA, the largest of the ancient Egyptian pyramids, he is otherwise relatively poorly attested in the archaeological record.

Kidder, Alfred Vincent (1885–1963) a pioneering American Southwest archaeologist, perhaps best known for his extensive excavations of the prehistoric PUEBLO at Pecos, close to Santa Fe, New Mexico. Kidder intensively analysed the artifacts, and was able to provide a new framework for Southwest CULTURE HISTORY. Kidder convened the first Pecos Conference in 1927, from which emerged the PECOS CLASSIFICATION. Perhaps less well known are his intensive archaeological surveys and excavations in MAYA archaeology for the Carnegie Institution, and his early use of interdisciplinary techniques.

Kietrz one of the largest URNFIELD cemeteries of the LUSATIAN culture in central Europe, with over 3000 graves, located in Silesia, southwestern Poland. Most of the burials consist of one or more urns filled with cremated bones and placed in pits, but some appear to have had mortuary structures with upright posts erected above them.

Kiev one of the major towns of mediaeval Russia, located on the eastern bank of the Dnepr River in Ukraine. Kiev began in the 10th century AD with the establishment of a fortified town with churches and palaces on a bluff overlooking the river. This town was expanded during the 11th century. Subsequent construction took place both on the bluff and on the riverbanks below. Kiev continued as one of the centres of commerce in mediaeval eastern Europe until it was sacked by the Mongols in the 13th century AD.

Kiik-Koba   a Middle Palaeolithic cave-site in the Crimea, Ukraine. Two occupation levels were identified by the excavator. The age of the occupations is unknown, but the remains of arctic fox and choughs in the upper level indicate cold climatic conditions (early LAST GLACIAL?); GIANT DEER and saiga remains are common. Artifacts from the lower level are crude and battered in appearance, containing few defined tool types. The upper level yielded an assemblage rich in sidescrapers (see SCRAPER) and BIFACIAL FOLIATES. Two burials were also found in the cave, but it is unclear with which level(s) they are associated. One burial contained the remains of a robust adult NEANDERTHAL. The second burial contained the poorly preserved remains of a young child. Kiik-Koba was excavated by Bonch-Osmolovskij in 1924–26.

Kili Gul Mohammad   see QUETTA.

Killke   the ceramic style pertaining to the CUZCO region of Peru, in the LATE INTERMEDIATE PERIOD, the antecedent to INCA style CERAMICS. First identified by John H. Rowe, Killke vessels have globular bodies, a white or buff SLIP, and simple geometric designs painted usually in black, and sometimes in black and red.

kill-site   an archaeological SITE, whose primary function was the killing of single or multiple animals. The site is recognized by its particular location, tool ASSEMBLAGES or TAPHONOMY.

kiln sites   centres in a number of mainland Asian states where GLAZED STONEWARES were manufactured during the early 2nd millennium AD, the best-known wares being produced at Phnom Kulen and Buriram (ANGKOR), Go Sanh (CHAMPA), Kalong and the SUKHOTHAI sites in Thailand, sites in north Vietnam and probably in Burma.

Kilu   a limestone shelter on Buka Island, Northern Solomons, MELANESIA. There are three main phases of occupation, one about 28 000–20 000 bp and a second about 9000–6500 bp; the upper levels of the site contain plain calcareous-tempered pottery dated elsewhere to c.2500 bp. The flaked stone artifacts are primarily undiagnostic SCRAPERS and FLAKES, on some of which plant residues have been identified. Kilu establishes Late PLEISTOCENE occupation of islands off the SAHUL shelf, implying the capacity for regular open-sea voyaging. See also BISMARCK ARCHIPELAGO.

Kilwa   an important trading centre on an island off the coast of Tanzania, with the ruins of many centuries of occupation by Islamic merchants. It was first occupied in the 9th century AD and later became a major mercantile centre on the East African coast, until trade passed into Portuguese hands from the end of the 15th century.

Kimberley point   a PRESSURE-FLAKED BIFACIAL point sometimes with a serrated edge, found mainly in the Kimberley region of Western Australia, but also traded widely in northern and central Australia. Their antiquity is unknown, but point industries in northern Australia generally belong to the AUSTRALIAN SMALL TOOL TRADITION. Kimberley points were still made at European contact and new raw materials such as glass and porcelain were quickly adopted.

Kimhae   a SHELL MIDDEN site of the PROTO-THREE KINGDOMS period on the southern Korean coast in South Kyongsang Province. It is the type-site for Kimhae pottery, a category now hotly contested as to its composition. It traditionally included both earthenware and STONE-

Kimberley point

WARE of the 1st–4th centuries AD, but is now confined by some archaeologists to stoneware alone (compare WAJIL).

kin   a period of time in the CLASSIC MAYA LONG COUNT equalling a single day.

Kinai   a pre-modern district in west central Honshu Island, Japan, consisting of the original 'five home provinces' of Japan: YAMATO, Kawachi, Izumi, Settsu and Yamashiro (see RITSURYO) – now comprising parts of Nara, Osaka and Kyoto Prefectures. The term is widely used in archaeological writings.

Kinki   a modern administrative district in Japan comprising Hyogo, Kyoto, Shuga, Mie, Nara, Osaka and Wayakama Prefectures. It is one of the regional designations often used in archaeological work.

Kintampo   an INDUSTRY associated with the beginning of food production in West Africa, dated to about 3600 BP. Cultural material includes CERAMICS, FLAKED stone tools and a unique scored stone 'cigar', probably used for grinding (see SONGON DAGBE).

Kirillovskaya   an Upper Palaeolithic open-air site in the city of Kiev on the Dnepr River in Ukraine. The remains are buried in slope deposits on the second TERRACE. The site was discovered in 1893 by Khvojko, who conducted the first large-scale excavations (more than 7000 sq m) of an open-air Palaeolithic site here in 1894–1900. Woolly MAMMOTH predominates among the faunal remains, and as many as four MAMMOTH-BONE HOUSES may have been unearthed by Khvojko without being recognized as such. A recently reported AMS RADIO-CARBON date of 19 200 bp supports earlier assignment of the occupation to the late Upper Palaeolithic.

Kisalian   an extraordinarily rich Iron Age complex in southeastern Zaire, which succeeded the KAMILAMBIAN towards the 8th century AD. The Classic Kisalian reached its peak in the 10th century AD, and is associated with graves containing numerous objects in iron, copper and ivory as well as items suggesting contact with the East African coastal trade, and finely made pottery. Kisalian funerary practices indicate the beginning of a hierarchical society in central Africa at the turn of the 1st millennium AD (see SANGA).

Kisapostag   an Early to Middle Bronze Age culture of western Hungary and Slovenia characterized by cemeteries with cremation burials. Although typologically contemporaneous with late ÚNETICE and HATVAN, the use of the cremation burial rite in open cemeteries by the Kisapostag culture in the early 2nd millennium bc foreshadows that of the URNFIELD period several centuries later.

Kisese   a series of sites with impressive rock paintings in the Kondoa region of central Tanzania, including naturalistic animals and ANTHROPOMORPHS. Kisese II has a long sequence of LATER STONE AGE MICROLITHIC stone assemblages dating from 19 000 BP, which overlies a layer characterized by SCRAPERS.

Kish   an important EARLY DYNASTIC city on a former channel of the Euphrates. The site is composed of several separate large mounds that together define an occupation sequence from 'UBAID to mediaeval times. Excavation at Kish occurred as early as the 1850s, but the most informative investigations were those of Ernest Mackay and L. Watelin in the 1920s and early 1930s. Evidence for the earliest occupations is confined to several 'Ubaid sherds; good occupation contexts begin with the JEMDET NASR and run through Early Islamic periods. The most significant contributions of Kish to the archaeology of southern MESOPOTAMIA belong to the Early Dynastic periods at the Ingharra group of mounds. The discoveries here include the 'Y' settlement (Early Dynastic I–II) with its rich burial evidence (including cart burials of the sort also found at UR and SUSA), and the 'A' complex of palace and ZIGGURAT (Early Dynastic IIIa) and cemetery (Early Dynastic IIIb and AKKADIAN); major flood deposits separated the 'Y' and 'A' occupations. The importance of Kish to the 3rd millennium history of southern Mesopotamia is reflected in the textual sources, where it plays a pivotal role in the regional political affairs of competing city-states, and the city may have been the centre of a cultural tradition distinct from that further south in Mesopotamia (see ABU SALABIKH).

Kiskevély   a prehistoric cave-site located near Budapest in north-central Hungary. Artifacts and faunal remains are buried in clay and rubble. The lower cultural layer contains Middle Palaeolithic tools (chiefly sidescrapers – see SCRAPER), apparently dating to the early part of the LAST GLACIAL. GRAVETTIAN (?), Neolithic and younger remains occur in the upper layers.

Kissonerga–Mylouthkia   an early CHALCOLITHIC (mid-4th millennium BC) site in western Cyprus, investigated by Peltenburg in 1976–80, consists of a dense cluster of hollows which contained occupational debris but may not actually have been inhabited.

Kissonerga–Mosphilia   one of the largest Chalcolithic (mid 4th to mid 3rd millennium) settlements on Cyprus, being excavated by Peltenburg. The houses are circular stone structures. Floors and walls were plastered and sometimes painted.

kitchen-garden agriculture   a form of cultivation where garden and tree crops are grown in plots adjacent to dwellings. This form of agriculture is currently an important component of MAYA households' subsistence. Recent work in the Maya area suggests that the clear areas near prehistoric residential mounds, previously identified as plazas, may be kitchen gardens. This idea has implications for understanding the demographics and the agricultural practices of the Maya.

kitchen midden   **1.** *n.* a mound formed by the accumulation of domestic refuse.
2. *adj.* relating to the people who created the MIDDEN. In Scandinavia, particularly Denmark where mounds of shellfish debris (*Kjökkenmöddings*) of up to 2000 cu m have been found, the name 'SHELL MIDDEN' is given to some of the MESOLITHIC groups. See ERTEBØLLE, OBANIAN.

Kition the site of a major Late CYPRIOT settlement in southern Cyprus, which has been excavated by Karageorghis. The site was first occupied in the 13th century BC. The settlers evidently profited from the COPPER trade and built two temples. *Circa* 1200 BC Kition was destroyed, possibly by the SEA PEOPLES. CYCLOPEAN fortifications replaced the earlier MUD-BRICK *enceinte* (enclosure) and the sanctuary was enlarged. The industrial installations constructed alongside the temples suggest that METALLURGY and religion were closely linked. In the 11th century BC, possibly as a result of an earthquake, Kition was abandoned but was re-colonized in the 9th century by the PHOENICIANS, who rebuilt the temples and remained until 312 BC.

kiva a ceremonial chamber, often semi- or completely subterranean and of varying shape, used by contemporary PUEBLO groups of the American Southwest. Prehistoric kivas are thought to have evolved out of earlier PITHOUSE structures.

Kjökkenmöddings see KITCHEN MIDDEN.

Klasies River Mouth a series of caves and overhangs on the Tsitsikama coast of the southern Cape Province of South Africa, which has provided 20 m of clearly stratified deposits forming one of the most complete sequences available for studying the archaeological record and sea-level changes of the Late PLEISTOCENE. Of particular interest are some of the oldest-known remains of anatomically modern HOMO *sapiens*, considered to date to some 100 000 years ago; indications of cannibalism in the Late Pleistocene; and evidence for the systematic exploitation of marine resources such as shellfish by 120 000 years ago. The detailed MIDDLE STONE AGE artifact sequence shows that the HOWIESONS POORT industry is part of the Middle Stone Age rather than transitional between the Middle and LATER STONE AGE as previously thought. The extensive Middle Stone Age sequence is capped by Later Stone Age deposits containing painted stones and burials with numerous shell beads dating to the last 5000 years.

klepsydra 1. a spring located on the slopes of the AKROPOLIS at ATHENS.

2. a water clock. In the law courts at ATHENS one basin containing two *choes* (see CHOUS) would drain into a second basin at a lower level. They would have timed a speech of six minutes.

kleroterion an allotment machine used to decide who would serve on the jury in the lawcourts. Surviving examples, such as the one from the AGORA at ATHENS are made of marble, although it is likely that others were of wood. The front face was divided into several columns, into which a potential juror placed a ticket which would identify him. A bronze tube attached to the side of the machine would allow balls to drop, and depending on their colour, would decide which groups or jurors would be accepted or rejected.

kline a couch used widely in the Greek world. It normally has a head-board, and occasionally a foot-board. The kline was often used to recline on during the SYMPOSIUM. Dining-rooms may be easily recognized on an archaeological site, as the layout of the couches arranged around the walls required that the entrance door to the room had to be offset to one side. See also TRICLINIUM.

knapping the working of stone to produce a tool by applying force to its surface, either by PERCUSSION (direct or indirect) or by pressure. The hard but brittle nature of FLINT and its homogeneous structure made it the preferred knapping material in prehistoric Europe and North Africa. See BULB OF PERCUSSION, HARD HAMMER, SOFT HAMMER, PRESSURE FLAKING, PRIMARY FLAKING, SECONDARY FLAKING, STRIKING PLATFORM.

Kniegrotte   an Upper Palaeolithic cave-site located on the Orla River in eastern Germany. Artifacts and faunal remains (chiefly horse and reindeer) are buried in LOAM and rubble dated by RADIOCARBON to 13 582–10 175 bp. Artifacts include BURINS, borers and a HARPOON; they are assigned to the late MAGDALENIAN.

Knossos   a site on Crete that has been occupied more or less continuously since 6000 BC when the first Neolithic settlers arrived. Neolithic Knossos was discovered by EVANS during his excavation of the MINOAN palace. This was constructed c.1900 BC, destroyed by an earthquake c.1700 BC, and then completely rebuilt. Like MALLIA, PHAISTOS and ZAKRO, Knossos was a multi-storey structure, planned around a central court and designed to serve a range of different functions: political, economic, cultural and religious. As the largest of the Minoan palaces, Knossos is likely to have governed much of Crete. This was certainly the case c.1450–1370 BC when the MYCENAEANS were in control. Even after the final destruction of the palace, Knossos remained prosperous and powerful, emerging as one of the foremost Greek city states on Crete.

Knovíz culture   a Bronze Age URNFIELD regional group of Bohemia and parts of Thuringia and Bavaria between 1400 and 900 bc. A characteristic Knovíz vessel form is the *Etagengefäss*, in which a large bulging vessel has a smaller bottomless pot fused on top of it to form a neck. Essentially similar is the neighbouring MILAVČE group. Knovíz settlements appear to have been small rural farmsteads.

Knowth   a large circular Neolithic burial mound over 60 m in diameter in Co. Meath, Ireland, containing two PASSAGE GRAVES entered from opposite sides of the mound. The passages and chambers are richly decorated with MEGALITHIC ART, as are many of the stones in the kerb which encircles the mound. Around its foot is a series of smaller satellite passage graves. Knowth is one of the three principal elements of the BOYNE VALLEY megalithic cemetery and dates probably from the 4th millennium BC.

Kobystan   a low plateau in Azerbaijan west of Baku and set against the eastern end of the Caucasus mountain range, which is perhaps best known for its corpus of ROCK ART, some of which is Mesolithic and Neolithic in date (the rest being Bronze Age and mediaeval). The earlier series show human and animal figures, often in hunting scenes (drives, bow and arrow). Excavation at rockshelters in the area (e.g. Kjaniza) indicate hunting-gathering communities using a MICROLITHIC (including geometrics) toolkit, who at some point started using pottery without a change in lithic technology or subsistence. The fauna recovered from these sites corresponds well to the animals depicted in the rock art (cattle and onager, with fewer mountain goat and gazelle).

Kodak   a Middle Palaeolithic locality on the lower Dnepr River in Ukraine. A small assemblage of artifacts, including several sidescrapers (see SCRAPER) was recovered from SEDIMENT filling 'an ancient ravine. Among the associated faunal remains are early forms of woolly MAMMOTH and reindeer. Kodak was excavated by Teslya in 1934–35.

Kodiak Tradition a long-lasting tradition (5000 BP to the historic period) that was centred on Kodiak Island and the adjacent mainland of Alaska, and which was characterized by a heavy use of polished slate for artifacts. Subsistence practices concentrated on the hunting of sea-mammals. Towards the end of the period, it was influenced by elements of the THULE culture.

kodja a flaked stone hatchet unique to southwestern Australia, comprising two stones hafted in a ball of resin on the end of a stick. One stone is usually blunt for pounding, while the other is sharpened for chopping. Archaeological examples are known from the last 3000–2000 years.

Koenigswald, Gustav H. Ralph von (1902–82) a Dutch–German palaeoanthropologist, best known for his discoveries of HOMINID remains in Java at NGANDONG in 1933 and SANGIRAN in 1937–9.

Kofun literally 'old mound'; the name of the protohistoric 'Tomb' period in Japan (AD 300–710) featuring YAMATO and RITSURYO state formation and development. Characterized by HAJI ware, SUE ware and MOUNDED TOMBS, the Kofun period is divided into Early (4th century), Middle (5th century) and Late (terminal 5th–7th centuries) phases which are illuminated by the KOJIKI and NIHON SHOKI texts. (See JAPANESE PERIODIZATION.)

Koguryo a protohistoric people of eastern Manchuria related to the PUYO, known from HAN-dynasty texts as horseriders, who became a strong state power in the 4th century AD (see PROTO-THREE KINGDOMS, THREE KINGDOMS). They are famous for their MURAL TOMBS.

Kojiki the earliest surviving chronicle of Japan, compiled in AD 712 under the RITSURYO state. Together with the NIHON SHOKI, it provides protohistoric data for the preceding KOFUN period.

Kökénydomb a Neolithic settlement of Hungary's TISZA culture in which small rectangular houses stood in close parallel rows with narrow alleys between them. Fragments of plaster from the Kökénydomb houses were found; these had been decorated with elaborate incised decoration. Notable CERAMIC artifacts include what have been called 'altars' – enigmatic rectangular or triangular clay pedestals.

Ko Kho Kao a port site on the west coast of peninsular Thailand near TAKUAPA, from which have been recovered fragments of Middle Eastern glass and Chinese GLAZED STONEWARES of the late 8th and 9th centuries AD; it was probably linked by an overland route to the port of LAEM PHO.

Kokkinopilos a group of Palaeolithic open-air sites along the Louros River in northwestern Greece. Artifacts were recovered from the surface and a reddish buried soil thought to date to the early LAST GLACIAL; no faunal remains are reported. The Middle Palaeolithic artifacts include LEVALLOIS CORES, sidescrapers (see SCRAPER) and BIFACIAL FOLIATES. Kokkinopilos was investigated by HIGGS.

Kokorevo a group of six Upper Palaeolithic open-air sites on the Yenisei River in south-central Siberia. At each locality, artifacts and faunal remains are buried in ALLUVIUM of the second TERRACE; among the fauna, reindeer and hare are the most common species. Nine RADIOCARBON estimates from Kokorevo I–IV range between 15 900–12 940 bp. The artifacts include WEDGE-SHAPED MICROCORES, MICROBLADES, sidescrapers (see SCRAPER) and RETOUCHED BLADES. At

Kokorevo I, two bone points with microblades set into their sides were found, one embedded in the shoulder-blade of a steppe bison. Assemblages from Kokorevo I are assigned to the KOKOREVO CULTURE, but those from Kokorevo II and III are assigned to the AFONTOVA CULTURE. The Kokorevo sites were initially excavated by Sosnovskij in 1925–28; later excavations were undertaken by Abramova from 1961–66.

Kokorevo Culture an Upper Palaeolithic culture of south-central Siberia, dating to *c*.20 000–10 000 BP. Diagnostic artifacts include WEDGE-SHAPED MICROCORES, MICROBLADES, RETOUCHED BLADES, side-scrapers and endscrapers (see SCRAPER). The Kokorevo Culture was defined by Abramova in 1979.

Koldewey, Robert (1855–1925) a German architect who established the German participation in the archaeological investigation of MESOPOTAMIA. After working in Anatolia and the eastern Mediterranean, he began excavation in Mesopotamia, where he investigated AL HIBA, Fara, ASSUR and, over an 18-year period, BABYLON. In the latter site, he uncovered the famous ISHTAR Gate, and also the temple of MARDUK, palace of NEBUCHADNEZZAR and other monuments. This work is published in a series of reports that still form the basis for understanding the archaeology of Babylon.

Köln-Lindenthal a site of the LINEAR POTTERY CULTURE near Cologne, in the Rhineland, western Germany, *c*.4300–4100 bc. Excavated by Buttler in 1929–1934, Köln-Lindenthal was one of the earliest attempts to expose a settlement plan. The excavator initially interpreted the large pits as subterranean dwellings and the post structures as granaries. Subsequently, the post structures were identified as LONGHOUSES, with the pits serving as the sources of mud plaster for the house walls. Köln-Lindenthal is unusual among Linear Pottery settlements in that it is encircled by a ditched enclosure in its later phases.

Kolomiishchina one of the best-known village sites of the CUCUTENI-TRIPOLYE culture, in western Ukraine. Kolomiishchina is estimated to cover 27 000 square metres, about half of which has been excavated. The excavator identified the traces of 39 complete or partially preserved structures, from 4 m to over 22 m in length. Most of the buildings were arranged in a circle approximately 100 m in diameter, in the centre of which were two structures. While the presence of ovens suggests that most buildings were houses, others may have been used for storage or as shrines.

Kolomoki a large site in Georgia, USA, covering over 400 000 ha, that comprises numerous BURIAL MOUNDS, as well as a PLATFORM MOUND, and dates to the latter half of the 1st century AD. The size of the complex is indicative of a CHIEFDOM level of social organization, unlike other less socially complex contemporary cultures.

Kolonna a site on the island of Aegina in the Aegean that has been occupied almost continuously since the late 4th millennium. The Bronze Age settlement, which was protected by a series of fortifications, is an extraordinary amalgam of the HELLADIC, CYCLADIC and MINOAN cultural traditions. The site derives its name from the single intact column of the 6th century BC temple of Apollo.

Kommos the site of a MINOAN settlement on the south coast of Crete, excavated by Shaw in 1976–85. It would seem that Kommos served as the harbour town for the palace of PHAISTOS. One monumental structure may have been built so that ships could be kept in dry dock over the winter. In the 10th century BC, after a period of abandonment, a temple was built on the ruins of the Minoan town. This sanctuary remained in use until the Roman period.

Kom Ombo   the site of a TEMPLE in southern UPPER EGYPT constructed by PTOLEMAIC kings and early Roman emperors. The Temple is unusual in having a double axis, a result of its dedication to two principal deities, Haroeris (a form of HORUS) and the crocodile-headed Sobek. To the south of Kom Ombo itself is a substantial tract of agricultural land where, in the 1920s, Vignard excavated a series of upper Palaeolithic sites which produced a series of chronologically overlapping industries now termed the Sebekian, Silsillian and Sebillian (c.15 000 to 9500 BC).

Komornica culture   the name applied to the early Mesolithic assemblages of the area lying between the Oder and Bug drainages in central and northern Poland, roughly contemporaneous with the MAGLEMOSIAN culture in Denmark during the 7th and 8th millennia bc.

Kondoa   see KISESE.

Kongemose   a MESOLITHIC culture of South Scandinavia and Denmark, whose type-site is the lake-settlement of Kongemosen in Zealand. Dating to the late BOREAL and early ATLANTIC (c.5600–5000 bc), the culture lies between the MAGLEMOSIAN and ERTEBØLLE. Known primarily from summer coastal sites devoted to the exploitation of forest species and marine resources, it features large BLADES, axes, bone points and a mainly geometric art.

Königsaue   a Middle Palaeolithic open-air site located northwest of Halle in eastern Germany. Artifacts and faunal remains (e.g. woolly MAMMOTH, reindeer) are buried in a lengthy succession of lake deposits (former Aschersleben Lake); Middle Palaeolithic occupation is dated to the Early GLACIAL. The artifacts include sidescrapers (see SCRAPER) and small HANDAXES.

Kon-Tiki   the replica of a balsa raft of the type observed in the 16th century AD along the coasts of Ecuador and northern Peru, built in 1947 for Thor Heyerdahl. With a crew of five, he sailed the raft from South America to the Tuamotu Archipelago to demonstrate that South American Indians could have reached POLYNESIA. Archaeological evidence, however, suggests that such contact could only have been minor.

Koobi Fora   an area along the northeast shore of Lake Turkana in northern Kenya which has yielded many important early HOMINID fossils and stone artifacts from the period between about 2.5 and 1 million years ago. Of particular interest are the fragmentary remains of more than 150 hominids, including specimens attributed to AUSTRALOPITHECUS *boisei*, possibly *A. africanus*, and HOMO *habilis*. The latter is best known by a relatively large-brained skull numbered 1470, which is dated to about 2 million years ago (see also KARARI, KBS, OLDOWAN).

Koolan 2   a rockshelter in the West Kimberley, Western Australia, with evidence of use of marine resources in the Late PLEISTOCENE and Early HOLOCENE. A minimum age of 27 300 bp makes this the oldest coastal site in Australia. See also MANDU MANDU CREEK, MATENK-UPKUM.

Koonalda Cave   a limestone sinkhole on the Nullarbor Plain, South Australia. Excavations by Alexander Gallus, and later by Richard Wright, showed that the cave was visited between about 24 000 bp and 14 000 bp to mine flint nodules. Finger markings deeper in the cave in complete darkness are presumed to be contemporary with the quarrying. They comprise random meandering lines, together with a few more definite designs such as grids or lattices and concentric circles. Charcoal from the floor dated to about 20 000 bp may be from torches.

Koongine   a limestone cave in southeast South Australia, excavated by David Frankel. Most of the two metres of deposit relates to a 1000–2000 year period of occupation about 9000 bp. The site was only reoccupied within the last 1000 years. The stone assemblage confirms an Early HOLOCENE date for the GAMBIERAN industry. Like other caves in the region, Koongine has finger markings similar to those at KOONALDA CAVE.

Koori or **Koorie**   the name preferred by non-traditional Aboriginal people over much of southeast Australia to refer to themselves. Other names are in use by Aboriginal groups elsewhere.

Korakou   a site in the Corinthia, Greece, which was excavated by BLEGEN in 1915–16 and proved to have been occupied more or less continuously throughout the Bronze Age. It was largely on the basis of the Korakou stratigraphy that WACE and Blegen devised their classification of the HELLADIC pottery sequence. This is also the type-site for the Early Helladic II Korakou culture.

kore   a statue, usually draped, of a female figure. Korai are usually found as dedications in Greek sanctuaries, although some have been found in funerary contexts. An important series have been found in the temple of Hera on Samos as well as on the AKROPOLIS at ATHENS. The clothes of some of the Athenian examples have retained extensive traces of bright colours. Inscriptions show that many of these female statues were set up by men, and thus the choice of sex may be related to the nature of the deity in whose sanctuary the statues were placed. Compare KOUROS.

Korean periodization   the artificial classification of prehistoric and historic eras used by archaeologists and historians for Korea. The major chronological divisions after the Palaeolithic period are: CHULMUN (7000–1000 BC); BRONZE AGE (700 BC–AD 0); IRON AGE (400 BC–AD 300); PROTO-THREE KINGDOMS (AD 0–300); THREE KINGDOMS (300–668); United Silla (668–935); Koryo (935–1392); Yi (1392–1910); Japanese Colonial (1910–45); Modern (1945–present). (See also NEOLITHIC.)

Korman' IV   a Palaeolithic and Mesolithic open-air site on the Dnestr River in western Ukraine. A total of 16 occupation horizons are buried in a thick bed of slope deposits overlying ALLUVIUM on the second TERRACE. The four lowest horizons contain Middle Palaeolithic artifacts, are associated with buried soils, and appear to date to warm intervals preceding and/or following the early cold maximum of the LAST GLACIAL. A sequence of younger horizons, dated by RADIOCARBON estimates and stratigraphic correlation, spans the early and late Upper Palaeolithic (30 000–10 000 bp). Two

Mesolithic horizons are contained in the modern soil. Korman' IV, in conjunction with the MOLODOVA sites, provides a key to the succession of Palaeolithic industries of the Dnestr region. The site was discovered and initially studied by Botez in 1930–31; Chernysh conducted large-scale excavations from 1948–61.

Korolevo a Palaeolithic open-air site located on the Tisza River in the eastern Carpathian basin, Ukraine. Thirteen artifact layers occur in a sequence of LOAMS containing numerous buried soils; stream gravels underlying the loams also contain artifacts. Faunal remains are absent. The lowest two layers are dated by TL and PALAEOMAGNETISM to the late Lower PLEISTOCENE (i.e. › 730 000 BP). Both these and the five overlying layers are assigned to the Lower Palaeolithic, and contain CHOPPING TOOLS, BIFACES, sidescrapers (see SCRAPER) and other tools. Except for the uppermost layer, which is assigned to the Upper Palaeolithic, the remaining layers contain Middle Palaeolithic assemblages (e.g. LEVALLOIS CORES, sidescrapers). Korolevo appears to represent one of the oldest occupations, and provides one of the most important Palaeolithic cultural sequences, in Europe.

Körös an Early Neolithic culture of southern Hungary, part of the complex that includes KARANOVO I, CRIŞ and STARČEVO (sometimes seen in literature as STARČEVO-KÖRÖS). Körös settlements do not form TELLS but rather tend to occur on river levees in this low-lying region. The most common species in Körös faunal assemblages are sheep and goats. The Körös culture is believed to have been the precursor of the LINEAR POTTERY culture that subsequently developed on the Hungarian Plain.

Korpach an Upper Palaeolithic open-air site on the Prut River in Moldova. The lowest occupation level has yielded a RADIOCARBON date of 25 250 bp, and contains an assemblage rich in tool types characteristic of both the Middle and Upper Palaeolithic. The upper levels presumably date to the late Upper Palaeolithic. The site was excavated by Grigor'eva in 1975–76.

Korucu Tepe a small (3 ha) mound on the Altinova plain of eastern Anatolia, in the upper Euphrates drainage, where M. van Loon's work provides a cultural sequence of 140 levels divided into 12 phases that begins with the Early CHALCOLITHIC (around 4500 BC) and runs largely unbroken to the Early Iron Age (to c.800 BC); a mediaeval occupation caps this sequence. The Korucu sequence, a standard for regional comparative chronology, also reflects some of the broader inter-regional patterns of western Asian prehistory, including some connection with the HALAF phenomenon in the early occupations, and a strong connection with the KURA-ARAXES culture during the 3rd millennium. The Late URUK connection found at such nearby sites as ARSLANTEPE is not so apparent at Korucu Tepe; however, the deforestation of the Keban-Altinova region which began at this time may be related to intensified production as a local response to the Late Uruk phenomenon.

Koryo see KOREAN PERIODIZATION.

Kosipe an open site in the NEW GUINEA HIGHLANDS, dating back to c.26 000 bp. The sparse artifacts include WAISTED AXES and TANGED tools.

Kossinna, Gustaf (1858–1931) a professor of German prehistory, beginning in 1902 at the University of Berlin. Kossinna is associated with a nationalistic brand of prehistoric interpretation, which viewed Germany as a centre of numerous prehistoric developments and which took an expansive approach to the distribution of ancestral German peoples. Such views of the central European archaeological record contributed to the ideological base of Nazism during the 1920s and 1930s.

Kostenki–Borshchevo   a group of 25 Upper Palaeolithic open-air sites on the Don River in European Russia. The sites are located on the first and second TERRACES, adjacent to side-valley ravines, on the west bank of the river. The remains are buried in slope deposits containing humic layers and a thin volcanic ASH layer, that permit cross-correlation among many sites. Early Upper Palaeolithic occupations (more than 25 000 bp), associated with remains of horse and other mammals, were found on the second terrace. At five sites, cultural layers underlie the volcanic ash and apparently date to c.36 000–32 000 bp or earlier; these cultural layers contain assemblages assigned to the STRELETS CULTURE and SPITSYN CULTURE. Cultural layers were found in humic horizons above the volcanic ash dating to c.32 000–26 000 bp at eight sites; they contain assemblages of the Strelets Culture and the GORODTSOV CULTURE. Younger cultural layers assigned to late Upper Palaeolithic industries (c.25 000–10 000 bp), and often associated with large quantities of woolly MAMMOTH remains, occur at shallower depths on the second terrace and on the first terrace. Complex feature arrangements, including MAMMOTH-BONE HOUSES, traces of other types of dwelling structures, debris-filled pits, HEARTHS, and debris concentrations, were found at some sites; many items of PORTABLE ART, including IVORY animal and VENUS FIGURINES were also recovered. Excavations were initiated at Kostenki in 1879 by Polyakov; in subsequent years, investigations were undertaken by Spitsyn, EFIMENKO, ROGACHEV, BORISKOWSKIJ, Praslov and others.

Kostenki-Willendorf Culture   an Upper Palaeolithic culture defined on the basis of assemblages from sites distributed across central Europe and the Russian Plain dating to c.30 000–20 000 bp. The assemblages contain BACKED BLADES, SHOULDERED POINTS, and art objects including VENUS FIGURINES. It may be generally equated with the EASTERN GRAVETTIAN INDUSTRY.

Koster   a thick, well-stratified multicomponent site in Illinois, USA. The site was excavated under the direction of Stuart Struever and James Brown in the 1970s and was one of the first major multidisciplinary endeavours of the 'NEW ARCHAEOLOGY'. Twenty-tree cultural horizons, stratigraphically separated over a thickness greater than 10.5 m, range in age from greater than 8700 bp to protohistoric times. The site has served as a benchmark for defining the ARCHAIC period cultural chronology in the American Midwest. Focusing on the interrelationships between people and their changing environment, the site has yielded information on the emergence of sedentism, the rise of broad-based subsistence patterns, and the origins of wild plant cultivation, all during the Archaic period. The site also contributed to the methodology of excavation, including pioneering approaches to deeply buried sites and the application of the flotation technique of recovering fine-grained remains.

Kostienki   see KOSTENKI.

Kostolac   an ENEOLITHIC site in Serbia that has given its name to the

Kostolac group, often considered a late variant of the BADEN culture of the Carpathian Basin.

Kostrzewski, Józef (1885–1969)   a central figure in Polish archaeology during the first half of the 20th century. Kostrzewski founded the department of archaeology at the University of Poznań and was responsible for the excavation of a number of significant sites, including BISKUPIN.

Kosziderpadlás   a settlement of the TUMULUS culture of the Bronze Age about 70 km north of Budapest, Hungary, famous for three large hoards that define the range of bronze artifacts found in similar hoards across central Europe about 1400 BC. Such hoards – with axes and swords decorated in spiral and geometric patterns, spiral bracelets and anklets with rolled ends, and similar elaborate bronze artifacts – mark what is known as the 'Koszider horizon' throughout this region.

Kota Batu   see SANTUBONG.

Kota Cina   see SRIVIJAYA.

Kota Tampan   an open site in peninsular Malaysia, yielding remains of a pebble and FLAKE stone industry, once thought to be very early but now dated to 31 000 BP or later, and classed as Upper Palaeolithic.

Kot Diji   a small, walled site in the upper Sind of Pakistan, excavated in the 1950s by F. Khan, that provides a sequence of Early and Mature HARAPPAN levels. The Early Harappan painted CERAMICS, similar to later products of the AMRI culture, present several decorative motifs later typical of the Mature Harappan, and characteristic Harappan vessel forms also appear; RADIOCARBON dates indicate an early 3rd millennium BC date for these levels at Kot Diji. Following extensive burning, the overlying levels of the site are Mature Harappan in character. The Kot Diji pottery style appears over large areas of the Punjab to the north (e.g. HARAPPA, RAHMAN DERI).

Kotosh   a major ceremonial site in the north-central highlands of Peru, first utilized during the Late PRECERAMIC Period, and whose occupation continued until after the demise of the CHAVIN culture of the EARLY HORIZON. A series of temples was constructed in sequence up a hillside at Kotosh; each temple was filled in and covered over, and the subsequent temple built above it. The lowest temple, the Temple of the Crossed Hands, is the best known. Square in plan, the single doorway is flanked on the interior wall by two small rectangular niches, one on either side. Below each niche, modelled in bas-relief in the mud plaster covering the wall, is a pair of crossed human forearms. One pair is larger than the other, suggesting male–female duality. Around the perimeter of the structure is a low bench, and a fire pit is found in the centre of the floor. This style of religious architecture, and evidence of ritual burning of offerings, is found elsewhere in the northern Peruvian Andes, suggesting the existence of what has been termed by Richard Burger and Lucy Salazar-Burger the *Kotosh Religious Tradition*. This tradition ended with the expansion of the Chavin cult in the Early Horizon. (See HUARICOTO, LA GALGADA.)

kotyle   1. a unit of Greek measure that varied from city to city, ranging from 0.21 to over 0.33 litre.

2. a type of drinking cup with two horizontal handles more usually called a SKYPHOS.

Kou   see SETOUCHI.

Kouklia–Palaepaphos   a site in southern Cyprus that has been the focus of excavations since 1869. There was evidently activity on the site as early as the 3rd millennium BC, but it was in the Late CYPRIOT period that Palaepaphos became a major centre as the rich tombs in the Evreti cemetery testify. *Circa* 1200 BC a magnificent ASHLAR temple was built, presumably in honour of Aphrodite. This was certainly the centre of her apparently licentious cult in the CLASSICAL period. In 498 BC Palaepaphos, then capital of one of the Cypriot kingdoms, was attacked by the PERSIANS whose massive siege ramp was never demolished and has been excavated.

Koumbi Saleh   a site thought to have been the capital of the GHANA empire. Excavations have uncovered a large urban settlement extending over 7 km, with two cemeteries and a mosque. The foundations of the mosque were laid in the 9th century AD, and the site appears to have been abandoned in the 15th century.

kouros (*Gk* 'a youth')   a Greek statue produced in the ARCHAIC PERIOD showing a naked striding figure. The two main uses of such statues were as funerary markers or as dedications in sanctuaries; in both cases related inscriptions seem to indicate that they should be associated with members of the social elites. They are usually larger than lifesize although small examples were made. Their medium is often marble, although there are also bronze and ALABASTER examples. Stone examples could be painted and an example from the AKROPOLIS at ATHENS was given fair hair. The type is thought to have been influenced by Egyptian sculpture. Compare KORE.

Kourounkorokale   a cave close to the Niger River in western Mali, containing a MICROLITHIC and HARPOON industry, with an economy based on fishing, molluscs and hunting. A later phase, featuring microliths, grindstones and decorated pottery, had an economy of hunting and gathering, with little evidence of fishing.

Kow Swamp   a cemetery site in the Murray Valley, Victoria, Australia, dating from 15 000 to 9000 bp and documenting a range of burial practices. The fossil material is robust and archaic-looking, and is crucial to Thorne's hypothesis of a dual origin for the Australian Aboriginal population. Brown has shown that some archaic features in skeletal material from Kow Swamp and COOBOOL CREEK can be accounted for by artificial deformation. The Kow Swamp collection is the largest single Late PLEISTOCENE population in the world. It has now been returned to the local Aboriginal community and reburied.

Kraków–Spadzista   three Upper Palaeolithic sites located on the Rudawa River in Kraków, southern Poland. At Kraków-Spadzista B, EASTERN GRAVETTIAN artifacts (e.g. BACKED BLADES, SHOULDERED POINTS) are buried in LOESS deposits dating to the beginning of the LAST GLACIAL MAXIMUM (23 040–20 600 bp); associated faunal remains are chiefly woolly MAMMOTH, and traces of three MAMMOTH-BONE HOUSES were found. At Kraków-Spadzista A, an AURIGNACIAN assemblage underlies the Eastern Gravettian level.

Kraków–Zwierzyniec   a Palaeolithic open-air site located near the confluence of the Rudawa and Vistula rivers in Kraków, southern Poland. Artifacts and some faunal remains (e.g. woolly MAMMOTH, reindeer) are buried in LOESS and slope deposits. The lower cultural layers contain Middle Palaeolithic assemblages, apparently dating to the Last INTERGLACIAL and subsequent cooler periods. Above a sterile layer, several Upper Palaeolithic assemblages (e.g. endscrapers – see SCRAPER – and BURINS), assigned to the AURIGNACIAN and dating to the INTERSTADIAL preceding the LAST GLACIAL MAXIMUM, were found.

Krapina Cave   a Middle Palaeolithic site located north of Zagreb in Croatia, first excavated by D. Gordajanović-Kramberger in 1899. Artifacts and faunal remains (including red deer, CAVE BEAR and rhinoceros (*Dicerorhinus mercki*)) are buried in deposits of sand and rubble, possibly dating to the Last INTERGLACIAL. The Middle Palaeolithic industry has a predominance of sidescrapers (see SCRAPER). Krapina has yielded over 650 skeletal fragments from dozens of archaic HOMO *sapiens*; once thought to be cut and smashed in a cannibal feast, they are now seen as the traces of a secondary funerary ritual.

Krasnyj Yar   an Upper Palaeolithic open-air site on the Angara River in south-central Siberia. Seven cultural layers are buried in sand and sandy LOAM on the third TERRACE; the age of the occupations is unclear, but they probably date to the LAST GLACIAL MAXIMUM (25 000–14 000 bp). Among the associated faunal remains are reindeer, horse and woolly rhinoceros. The artifact assemblages from the various layers are similar and include WEDGE-SHAPED MICROCORES, MICROBLADES, points and endscrapers (see SCRAPER). Krasnyj Yar was initially investigated by OKLADNIKOV in 1957; subsequent excavations were conducted by Abramova in 1957–59, and Aksenov and Medvedev in 1964–65.

krater   a large Greek vessel made of clay or metal, in which wine and water were mixed.

Kremikovci   an Early Neolithic culture of the Balkans, centred on the highlands of the Bulgarian border in Macedonia. The Kremikovci culture is contemporaneous with, and bears similarities to, the KARANOVO I culture of southern Bulgaria, the STARČEVO culture of Serbia and Bosnia, the KÖRÖS culture of southern Hungary and the CRIŞ culture in Romania. Kremikovci CERAMICS are characterized by white-on-red or black-on-red painted decoration. Kremikovci settlements, such as Vrsnik, Slatina and Kremikovci itself, tend to be low mounds with thick Early Neolithic cultural deposits.

Krems-Hundssteig   an Upper Palaeolithic open-air site located on the Danube in northeastern Austria. Artifacts and faunal remains (e.g. woolly MAMMOTH, woolly rhinoceros) are buried in LOESS deposits. The assemblage, which includes endscrapers (see SCRAPER) and RETOUCHED BLADES and is dated to 35 200 bp, is assigned to the AURIGNACIAN. At the nearby Galgenberg hill, in 1988, a remarkable female figurine of green serpentine was found in an Aurignacian level dated to 31 790 bp.

krepidoma   the base or foundations of a CLASSICAL building, usually stepped.

Krivodol group   an ENEOLITHIC regional group of northwestern Bulgaria broadly correlated with Layer VI at KARANOVO, *c*.3000–2800 bc, and known largely from settlements such as ZAMINETS.

Kroeber, Alfred Louis (1876–1960)   an American anthropologist known primarily for his work in North America, where he supervised NELSON's initial work on California SHELL MOUNDS. He advocated the efficacy of SERIATION, by applying the technique to Zuni POTSHERDS in 1915. Later he conducted fieldwork in Peru, summarized the CERAMICS collected there by UHLE, and used them to develop regional sequences. He excavated in the NASCA region, including the sites of CAHUACHI and ESTAQUERIA. He was also responsible for formally defining the HORIZON style concept.

Kromdraai   a site with fossiliferous PLIO-PLEISTOCENE cave fillings near Krugersdorp in the Transvaal, South Africa, which yielded the first robust AUSTRALOPITHECINE, *Paranthropus robustus*, in 1938 (see STERKFONTEIN, SWARTKRANS).

krotovina   a SOIL feature consisting of an animal burrow filled with soil or SEDIMENT that is usually, but not necessarily, in contrast with the surrounding material into which the burrow was excavated. The filling material is derived from overlying SOIL HORIZONS or sediment STRATA. Different animals produce burrows of different size, shape and orientation; identification of the animals responsible can provide supplementary environmental information based on habitat requirements or restrictions.

Krzemionki   a flint mine in the HOLY CROSS MOUNTAINS of central Poland, in use primarily during the Middle and Late Neolithic by the FUNNEL BEAKER and GLOBULAR AMPHORA cultures. Axes made from the grey and white 'banded' flint from Krzemionki were widely exchanged throughout the Vistula and Oder drainages. At Krzemionki, in a belt 4 km long by about 100 m wide, over 1000 shafts were sunk to depths of between 4 and 15 m. Galleries reaching 30 m in length connected many of the shafts. The Funnel Beaker settlement of CMIELÓW is located 9 km from Krzemionki.

kshemenitsa   a term of Russian derivation used in Eastern Europe to refer to a dense scatter of flint artifacts and DÉBITAGE on a Late Palaeolithic or Mesolithic open site. Within a kshemenitsa, a number of FLAKES can be refitted to CORES, suggesting that these areas were the locations of flint working and related activity.

Kuala Selinsing or **Tanjong Rawa**   a port site in peninsular Malaysia, in use for most of the 1st millennium AD, the finds from which include the remains of a bead industry pottery similar to PONTIAN; and Indian seals and Chinese STONEWARES from surface layers.

Ku Bua   a moderately large (2000 m × 800 m) settlement of the DVARAVATI period near the mouth of the Mae Klong River, south-central Thailand; its roughly rectangular moat possibly dates to the KHMER period of domination, after *c*.AD 1000.

Kudaro   two cave-sites located on the south slope of the Greater Caucasus Mountains (1600 m above sea level) in Georgia. Artifacts and faunal remains are buried in LOAM and rubble. At Kudaro I, the three lowest cultural layers are assigned to the ACHEULIAN, and are associated with the remains of Middle PLEISTOCENE vertebrates (e.g. *Dicerorhinus, Macaca*). The artifacts include BIFACES, CHOPPERS and sidescrapers (see SCRAPER). Small quantities of Middle Palaeolithic artifacts, associated with remains of Late Pleistocene vertebrates including CAVE BEAR and salmon, were found in overlying levels; the tools include points and sidescrapers. The uppermost layers contain late Upper Palaeolithic, Mesolithic and younger remains. Both

Kudaro I and III were discovered and excavated by Lyubin in 1955–87.

kudurru (literally 'boundary') a term applied to a series of stone documents that record land grants or sales during the KASSITE and post-Kassite periods in southern MESOPOTAMIA. These monuments, often placed in temples, are decorated with the symbols of the various gods whose protection guaranteed the land transfers. The term is also applied, anachronistically, to 3rd millennium CUNEIFORM documents in southern Mesopotamia that also deal with land transfers.

Kufr Nigm a site in the eastern Nile DELTA, Egypt, excavated by Zagazig University since 1984. Kufr Nigm contains a cemetery which has yielded material of the ARCHAIC PERIOD, including CERAMIC jars incised with the name of NARMER.

Kuk a site in the Wahgi Valley near Mount Hagen, that has been studied intensively by Jack Golson and documents the development of agricultural systems in the NEW GUINEA HIGHLANDS. The archaeological evidence includes a probable 30 000 year-old hearth, a drain and evidence for clearance at about 9000 bp, a sequence of field systems from about 6000 bp to the present, and evidence of sweet potato cultivation from about 250 years ago. The evidence of water management at 9000 bp has been claimed to represent dryland agriculture and, consequently, an independent centre of plant domestication.

Kukuba a limestone shelter excavated by Ron Vanderwal, and the oldest known site in lowland mainland New Guinea. The lower of the two cultural horizons has a date of c.4000 bp.

Kulichivka an Upper Palaeolithic open-air site on the Ikva River (Styr' tributary) near Kremenets in western Ukraine. Two occupation levels are buried in slope deposits on a bedrock hill overlooking the valley. The lower level is associated with a buried soil and apparently dates to the INTERSTADIAL preceding the LAST GLACIAL MAXIMUM; the artifact assemblage contains tool types characteristic of the Middle and Upper Palaeolithic. The upper level presumably dates to the late Upper Palaeolithic (i.e. 25 000–10 000 bp). Kulichivka was excavated by Savich in 1968–73.

Kůlna Cave a prehistoric cave-site located northeast of Brno in Moravia, Czechoslovakia. Artifacts and faunal remains are buried in deposits of loam and rubble. The lower levels, which are correlated with the Last INTERGLACIAL and Early GLACIAL, contain a Middle Palaeolithic industry with BIFACIAL FOLIATES and DENTICULATES. A younger Middle Palaeolithic industry (e.g. sidescrapers – see SCRAPER – and BIFACES), probably dating to the early LAST GLACIAL, was found in overlying levels. Late Upper Palaeolithic (MAGDALENIAN), Neolithic, Iron Age and later remains occur in the upper layers. Kůlna Cave was excavated by Valoch in 1961–76 and others.

Kulp'o-ri a site in North Hamgyong Province, Korea, attributed to the Middle Palaeolithic based on tool typologies. Rocks for supporting a hut structure 11.5 m × 8 m, excavated in 1964, provided the first evidence of Palaeolithic dwellings in Korea.

Kültepe an important site in Cappadocia near Kayseri in central Anatolia, the best documented of the Old ASSYRIAN KĀRUM, in this case the ancient Kanish. First excavated in the late 19th century, and best known from the work of T. Örgüç begun in 1948, Kültepe consists of a 20 ha mound with an associated settlement outside it; the latter represents the location of the *kārum* and was settled only during the late 3rd and early 2nd millennia BC. Occupation in the mound began in EARLY BRONZE I times and continued (interrupted at several points) to the CLASSICAL period. During the period of the *kārum*, the city was dominated by a fortified palace (covering over 1 ha), and also contained residential structures of varying sizes within a city wall. The lower city, or *kārum*, was a residential and commercial district also enclosed by a wall (defining an area perhaps 3 km in diameter). Divided into five phases (IV–II, Ib, Ia), the period of the Old Assyrian CAPPADOCIAN TRADE corresponds to levels II and Ib (dated to the 19th–18th centuries BC), when Assyrian merchants representing commercial firms in ASSUR resided in the *kārum*, largely adopting the local material culture. The many documents (*c.*15 000) from Kanish provide the richest available picture of a MESOPOTAMIAN trading community. The post-*kārum* levels on the city mound include an early 1st millennium occupation that shows strong material connections both to the 'Syro-Hittite' kingdoms to the southwest (ORTHOSTATS with reliefs) and with the PHRYGIAN kingdom to the west (much 'Phrygian' painted pottery).

Kulupuari   a site on the Kikori River, Gulf Province, Papua New Guinea. Excavations by Jim Rhoads produced the earliest direct evidence for sago palm exploitation and evidence for coastal trading systems preceding the HIRI and MAILU networks, both about 1300 bp.

Kumadzulo   a large Early Iron Age village of the DAMBWA tradition in southern Zambia, occupied between the 5th and 7th centuries AD. It contains remains of remarkably small rectangular pole-and-DAGA structures with large corner posts. Cattle and small stock were herded, while grindstones and iron hoes suggest grain cultivation. Small cross-shaped COPPER INGOTS and a glass fragment attest to trading activity.

Kunda culture   a Mesolithic culture of the BOREAL and ATLANTIC climatic periods of the eastern Baltic littoral, named after the site of Kunda-Lammasmagi on the Gulf of Finland in Estonia. Kunda settlements often contain traces of an elaborate bone and antler INDUSTRY associated with the emphasis on fishing and seal-hunting in the economy. Among terrestrial mammals, elk (*Alces alces*) appears to have been particularly important. The Kunda culture is succeeded by the NARVA culture with the appearance of pottery and the first traces of food production.

Kura-Araxes culture, Eastern Anatolian Bronze Age or **Transcaucasian Early Bronze Age**   a culture complex characterized by a type of black or red highly BURNISHED, handmade pottery that occurs in EARLY BRONZE AGE sites of Transcaucasia (drained by the Kura and Araxes Rivers, hence the designation), eastern Anatolia, and northwestern Iran; closely related pottery also occurs in western Syria (the Red-Black Burnished Ware of 'AMUQ H–I) and northern Palestine (the Khirbet-Kerak ware). Other typical features of the complex are portable hearths and frequently circular houses. In Transcaucasia and adjacent regions, the culture complex exhibits minimal differentiation of settlement sizes and provides little indication of social hierarchy (by grave-goods, architectural variation). At the same time, many settlements are fortified, and intensified agricultural production is evident in field terracing and large water management works. The chronology of the culture complex is still debated, but seems to belong between the later 4th and the later 3rd millennia BC.

kurgan   the Russian term for a burial mound (i.e. a BARROW or a TUMULUS), frequently – but not exclusively – used in connection with ENEOLITHIC and Bronze Age burial practices (see KURGAN CULTURES).

Kurgan cultures   a complex of cultures defined by M. Gimbutas as a key element in a model of cultural development and dispersal in the steppe zone of southern Russia and Ukraine. The Kurgan cultures are distinguished by their use of KURGANS or burial mounds and are differentiated by the subterranean architecture of the burials. The first Kurgan culture is the YAMNAYA, or Pit-Grave, culture, the second the CATACOMB GRAVE culture, and the third the SRUBNAYA, or Timber-Grave, culture. In Gimbutas' model, there were several incursions of the INDO-EUROPEAN–speaking Kurgan cultures into eastern Europe.

Kurru   a site in UPPER NUBIA, the NAPATAN royal cemetery from the late 9th to mid 7th centuries BC. The early TUMULUS tombs, probably the legacy of the KERMA CULTURE, were replaced by steep-sided PYRAMIDS after the conquest of Egypt by the Napatan kings. See also NURI.

Kurtén, Björn (1924–88)   a Finnish palaeontologist who specialized in the study of PLEISTOCENE mammals of the Holarctic, and contributed significantly to knowledge of Pleistocene environments and human palaeoecology.

Kush   an Egyptian term for UPPER NUBIA generally, and for any independent state which established itself in this region during periods of Egyptian weakness (e.g. during the Second INTERMEDIATE PERIOD). See also KERMA, NAPATA.

Kutama   a southern African Late Iron Age tradition which clusters the GUMANYE, Harare, K2, LEOPARD'S KOPJE, MAMBO, MAPUNGUBWE and WOOLANDALE pottery groups, and which is identified with the transition from the Early to the Late Iron Age at the end of the 1st millennium AD.

Kutei   a region of east Borneo which has yielded several 5th century AD SANSKRIT inscriptions of a vaguely Hindu character, but written for local rulers, as well as 9th–10th century statuary related to that of Java.

Kutikina formerly **Fraser Cave**   a limestone cave in southwest TASMANIA, with extraordinarily rich occupation deposits 20 000–15 000 years old sealed beneath a STALAGMITE layer. The excavation of Kutikina in 1981 first established the PLEISTOCENE occupation of southwest Tasmania, now confirmed at numerous other sites. See also NUNAMIRA CAVE, WARGATA MINA.

Kuyavian long barrow   an earthen long BARROW of the FUNNEL BEAKER CULTURE in northern Poland about 3000 BC. Kuyavian barrows are characteristically surrounded by a kerb of large erratic boulders and are sometimes called 'MEGALITHIC', even though they lack true megalithic architecture. In addition, they normally have a very characteristic trapezoidal plan and often occur in groups. Despite their large size, they normally contain single PRIMARY BURIALS, rarely more than two. Key sites are SARNOWO and WIETRZYCHOWICE. They are related to the HUNEBEDS of northern Germany and Holland.

Kwale a site in southeastern Kenya which has given its name to a branch of the Eastern Stream or UREWE tradition of the CHIFUMBAZE Early Iron Age complex. This tradition appeared in southeastern Kenya and northern Tanzania in the 2nd century AD.

kyathos 1. a Greek measure of capacity, six to a KOTYLE. 2. a dipper consisting of a small bowl at the end of a long handle. Silver, bronze and clay examples are known from both the Greek world and ETRURIA.

kylix a Greek stemmed drinking cup usually made of clay or metal.

L

La Adam cave a MESOLITHIC cave-site on the Black Sea coast of Romania. Claims have been made for the presence of early domesticated sheep or goats at La Adam, but the context of these finds is not securely dated and has been called into question.

Laang Spean a prehistoric cave-site in western Cambodia, occupied between *c*.7000 and 500 BC, with evidence of reuse in *c*.AD 900. By *c*.4000 BC the occupants were using a late HOABINHIAN tool-kit and cord-marked and paddle-impressed pottery; succeeding layers contain increasingly elaborate pottery associated with FLAKED stone tools. SUBSISTENCE appears to have been based upon broad-spectrum HUNTING AND GATHERING.

Labastide a MAGDALENIAN decorated cave in the Hautes-Pyrénées, southern France, containing numerous engraved figures on its walls, as well as a huge polychrome horse painting. Rich in HEARTHS and engraved stones, the cave's occupation has been dated to 12 310 bc.

La Brea see RANCHO LA BREA.

La Chapelle-aux-Saints a MOUSTERIAN cave-site in Corrèze, southwestern France, where the burial of an almost complete NEANDERTHAL male adult with severe osteo-arthritis was discovered in 1908 by the abbés Bouyssonie. The bones were studied in detail by Boule in 1911–13, and were for a time regarded as a type-skeleton for Neanderthal man. They are now generally considered to represent an extreme form of Neanderthaler. Middle Palaeolithic stone tools and numerous animal bones were also recovered from the cave.

La Chaussée-Tirancourt a Late Neolithic ALLÉE COUVERTE constructed in *c*.2900 BC in Somme, France, and used for several centuries until infilled and destroyed in *c*.2000 BC. Remains of over 350 individuals were preserved in two separate deposits divided by a chalk fill, 60 in the lower, almost 300 in the upper. The discovery that genetic abnormalities present in the lower layer recurred directly above at the same location in the upper layer suggested that individual families or kin groups each had rights to a different part of the tomb.

Lachish (*Arabic* TELL ed-Duweir) a Palestinian site, chiefly excavated by Starkey from 1932–38. In the CHALCOLITHIC Period natural caves at Lachish were adapted for use as dwellings. During the MIDDLE BRONZE AGE the natural defensive hill was supplemented by a GLACIS. The destruction levels attributed to the Egyptian kings of the early NEW KINGDOM were followed by rebuilding during the LATE BRONZE AGE, including the construction of a major building at the foot of the earlier rampart, termed the 'Fosse Temple'. Lachish seems to have been again destroyed in the 12th century BC and possibly deserted until the 10th century BC when it was occupied by the ISRAELITES. Biblical evidence suggests that Rehoboam constructed the substantial Iron Age fortifications. Lachish was sacked in 701 BC by the ASSYRIANS, an event commemorated in the palace-reliefs from NINEVEH.

Laconian pottery pottery made at SPARTA largely in the 6th century BC. BLACK-FIGURED and BLACK-GLOSSED was produced. Laconian pottery was once thought to have been made in Cyrenaica, Libya, because one well-known cup showed the king of CYRENE, Arkesilas, of c.568–550 BC. The fabric was widely exported and is common in Cyrenaica (see TOCRA), in ETRURIA and in the Greek colonies in Italy.

La Cotte de Saint-Brelade a Palaeolithic cave-site on Jersey, Channel Islands, principally excavated by MCBURNEY in 1961–78, which has produced some ACHEULIAN-style BIFACES, many thousands of MOUSTERIAN artifacts, animal bones including MAMMOTH and rhinoceros concentrations, and 13 teeth attributed to a NEANDERTHALER. Jersey was linked to the continent during periods of low sea level.

lacquer *(East Asia)* the resin of the sumac tree (*Rhus verniciflua*) used as a coating to harden and strengthen cloth, paper, wood, baskets, leather or ceramic objects. Often the lacquer, coloured red or black, is applied directly to the object's surface in many layers; however, objects themselves can be constructed, for example, of layers of cloth or paper each lacquered as they are added to the form. The term 'lacquer ware' in archaeological contexts (see SINAN, TORIHAMA) usually refers to lacquered wooden vessels.

Laem Pho the site of a port on the east coast of peninsular Thailand, near CHAIYA, from which have been recovered fragments of Middle Eastern glass vessels and Chinese GLAZED STONEWARES of the late 8th and 9th centuries AD; it was probably linked by an overland trade route across the peninsula to KO KHO KAO.

Laetoli formerly **Laetolil** a site in northern Tanzania which has yielded fragments of AUSTRALOPITHECINE fossils dating to about 4–3.5 million years ago and attributed to *Australopithecus afarensis* or *A. africanus*. Of particular interest are 3.8 million-year-old footprints of bipedal HOMINIDS preserved in hardened ASH-covered mud.

La Ferrassie a well-stratified rockshelter in Dordogne, France, excavated by PEYRONY and, more recently, by Delporte, which has yielded Middle Palaeolithic material including the burials of two NEANDERTHAL adults and five children and babies; one infant lay beneath a slab with cupmarks on it. The site has given its name to a subdivision of the CHARENTIAN MOUSTERIAN tradition. The Upper Palaeolithic material forms a 10 m stratigraphy including CHÂTELPERRONIAN, AURIGNACIAN and GRAVETTIAN stages, and has proved one of the keys to understanding the Upper Palaeolithic sequence in France. Crude engravings on blocks in the Aurignacian level include animals and possible 'vulvas'.

La Galgada a site in the western slopes of the north highlands of Peru, pertaining to the Late PRECERAMIC and early INITIAL PERIOD. Similar to KOTOSH, the site comprises a series of sequentially built temple structures. Each structure was circular to roughly square with rounded corners, with a bench around the interior perimeter, and a vented fire pit in the centre of the floor. Analysis of the fire pit ash has revealed remains of chili pepper seeds. Each temple structure was filled, sometimes used as a tomb, and covered over prior to the construction of the subsequent temple. In addition to the ceremonial architecture, domestic architecture indicates a resident population numbering in the thousands. The latest ceremonial constructions at the site no longer have a central hearth, and are laid out in a U-shaped configuration. (See HUARICOTO.)

Lagash see AL HIBA.

Lagoa Santa a series of sites in Minas Gerais, Brazil, which display evidence of occupation in the late PLEISTOCENE, with human remains and stone tools found associated with extinct animals such as MASTODON and sloth. The rockshelter of Lapa Vermelha IV, excavated by A. Laming-Emperaire in the 1970s, has a 13 m stratigraphy with occupation back to 15 300 bp, and an industry of QUARTZ FLAKES. The Cerca Grande Complex, of 10 000–8000 bp, features small flakes of rock-crystal, as well as axes, bone PROJECTILE POINTS, and burials, especially in the cemetery of Santana do Riacho with its 50 flexed inhumations. This site also has hundreds of rock paintings, including hunting scenes, from the Planalto Tradition (7000–3000 bp).

La Gorge-Meillet the richest Iron Age chariot burial of the so-called 'Marnian' culture, Marne, France. On the chariot lay the body of a youth equipped with sword, spearheads, bronze helmet, gold bracelet and toilet set of tweezers, ear scoop, and nail cleaner. There were also wheel-made pottery vessels and an ETRUSCAN bronze flagon. Above this principal interment was the body of an older man, possibly a retainer. The burial dates to LA TÈNE Ia, c.475–450 BC.

Lagozza di Besnate a Late Neolithic settlement in Lombardy, Italy, dated to c.3600 BC, consisting of remains of wooden pile dwellings in a PEAT-filled basin. It is the type-site of the Lagozza culture, characterized by finely made black-BURNISHED CARINATED bowls. At ARENE CANDIDE it succeeds the BOCCA QUADRATA (Square Mouth pottery) assemblage. COPPER axes found at Lagozza sites are among the earliest copper objects from northern Italy.

La Graufesenque see SAMIAN WARE.

La Gravette see GRAVETTIAN.

lagynos a type of HELLENISTIC jug produced in various centres in the eastern Mediterranean. It has a low, squat body with a vertical neck with rounded mouth; there is a single strap handle.

Lake Condah a complex of stone structures in southwest Victoria, Australia, studied in detail by the Victoria Archaeological Survey, which includes hut foundations and fish traps. The fish traps exploit small variations in topography to control water flows. The complex postdates the Late PLEISTOCENE volcanic activity in the area which formed the swamps, and analysis of lake levels suggests that the fish-trap system in its present form could not have operated before about 4000 bp. Fish-trap systems are a feature of HOLOCENE southwest Victoria and may have facilitated large ceremonial gatherings See also TOOLONDO.

lake dwelling or **lake village**   a settlement formerly on the edge of a lake, now usually buried by lake-shore sediments or drowned beneath the lake waters. The most famous examples are the pile-dwellings of Switzerland and northern Italy, villages built on wooden stilts to keep them above the damp ground of the lake shore; some may indeed have stood above the lake waters, as ethnographic examples from West Africa illustrate. The Swiss pile-dwellings first came to scholarly notice when lake levels fell in 1853. Other famous lake villages are known in northern Italy (POLADA) and eastern France (CLAIRVAUX-LES-LACS, CHARAVINES), and in southwestern England (GLASTONBURY). See also MONDSEE.

Lake George   a lake in southeast New South Wales, Australia, that has yielded a continuous POLLEN sequence covering the whole of the PLEISTOCENE. An increase in charcoal and expansion of fire-tolerant eucalypts at an inferred date of 120 000 BP has been claimed to indicate the arrival of humans in Australia. This interpretation remains controversial, while the date has been questioned by Wright, who suggests about 60 000 BP as more likely, on the basis of age-depth regression analysis.

Lake Hauroko   the site of a 17th century AD cave burial on an island in this lake on South Island, NEW ZEALAND. The female skeleton was found seated on a bier of sticks and wrapped in a cloak of woven flax with a dogskin collar and feather edging.

Lake Mangakaware   a lakeside PA in the Waikato District, North Island, NEW ZEALAND, with good preservation of artifacts and structural remains. The site covers about 0.2 ha and comprises an artificial mound with a semicircle of houses around an open space (MARAE) and defended by palisades. The site was occupied about AD 1500–1800.

Lake Mungo   see MUNGO.

Lake Ngaroto *pa*   a lakeside fortified settlement in the Waikato District, North Island, NEW ZEALAND, comprising an artificial mound built up as a result of repeated construction of sandy living floors, but with little evidence of substantial structures.

Lake Nitchie   a shaft burial of a large robust male in western New South Wales, Australia, about 6500–7000 bp. The man wore a necklace of pierced teeth from at least 47 Tasmanian devils, an animal now extinct on the Australian mainland.

Lake Sentani   a lake in Irian Jaya, northern New Guinea, where metal objects, including bronze socketed axes and spearheads, were found in a burial mound. The objects are undated, but may relate to the activities of recent Indonesian traders.

lake village   SEE LAKE DWELLING.

Lalibela   an Ethiopian cave with evidence of the Near Eastern domesticates barley, chickpeas and legumes, in association with stone artifacts, pottery and bones tentatively identified as cattle and small stock, dating to the mid 1st millennium BC. This evidence supports the view that agriculture developed at an early date in Ethiopia, but unfortunately does not indicate its exact antiquity.

Lalla   a site in Tunisia with a pre-CAPSIAN BLADELET industry, which differs from and may be earlier than the IBEROMAURUSIAN.

La Madeleine see MAGDALENIAN.

La Marche a Palaeolithic cave-site in the Vienne region of France, only 30 km from ANGLES-SUR-L'ANGLIN, which yielded over 1500 engraved stone slabs, studied primarily by L. PALES. They include figures of humans, carnivores, horses, deer, bison, MAMMOTHS, etc. The site has been dated to 14 280 bp, the early mid-MAGDALENIAN.

Lamb Spring a PALAEOINDIAN site in Colorado, USA, with possible culturally modified camel bones dated to approximately 13 000 BP. Other bones present include MAMMOTH, horse and bison. The site also contains later Palaeoindian components.

La Micoque see MICOQUIAN

lamina a sheet-like unit layer of SEDIMENT defined by STRATIFICATION planes less than 1 cm apart. Horizontal laminae are parallel to bedding planes and CROSS LAMINAE are at an angle to bedding planes. Laminae are a fundamental sedimentary structure used in interpretation of depositional environments of which cultural debris may be a part.

Lancefield Swamp a site in south central Victoria which was the first in Australia where contemporaneity of extinct MEGAFAUNA and artifacts was established. *Macropus titan*, a giant kangaroo, was the dominant species in the bone bed, dated to *c*.26 000 bp. There is no evidence that humans were responsible for the deaths of these animals, though there was some scavenging by *Thylacoleo*, an extinct marsupial carnivore.

landform a configuration of the earth's surface created by a distinct erosional or depositional process or set of processes. Landforms are the principal components that collectively comprise a LANDSCAPE, whether at the scale of mountains and plains, or at the scale of individual valley features. Different landforms have different archaeological implications regarding settlement, resources, and site visibility, preservation and destruction.

landnam a Danish term, meaning literally 'land taking', used to describe episodes of land clearance for cultivation identified in the POLLEN record. The usual *landnam* episode begins with a drop in tree pollen, then a rise in the level of grass and plantain pollen, and then a return of higher levels of tree pollen. The Danish palaeoecologist Iversen argued that such episodes represented the arrival of farmers practising SHIFTING CULTIVATION in which a short period of cultivation was followed by a regeneration of the forest.

landscape the collection of LANDFORMS particular to a region at a particular time. Identifying former landscapes is a key component in understanding archaeological CONTEXT, because it is upon landscapes that human occupation and activities occur.

landscape archaeology see OFFSITE.

langi tombs burial mounds of the Tui Tonga dynasty on Tongatapu, Tonga. The rectangular mounds are faced with slabs of coral limestone. Some contain burial chambers, also built of coral slabs. Most are associated with the ceremonial centre at MU'A on Tongatapu.

Langkasuka an early historic state in the Pattani region of peninsular Thailand, first mentioned in Chinese records of the 6th century AD and still extant early in the 2nd millennium, incorporating YARANG.

Langmannersdorf an Upper Palaeolithic open-air site located in Austria. Three cultural layers are contained in LOESS deposits dating to the LAST GLACIAL MAXIMUM (RADIOCARBON dates of 20 580–20 260 bp). The assemblage includes BURINS and endscrapers (see SCRAPER), and is assigned to the AURIGNACIAN.

L'Anse-Amour a burial site on the coast of southern Labrador, Canada, which contains the remains of an adolescent skeleton, dated to between 7000 and 7500 years ago. The body had been placed face down, with a rock slab on its back. Various grave goods, including a walrus tusk, stone spear points, a bone whistle, an antler HARPOON head, a bone pendant, and OCHRE-covered graphite pieces together with an antler pestle were found with the skeleton. The body had been laid in a deliberately excavated pit, which had then been filled and covered with a mound of stones. The site is one of the earliest of this complexity in the world, and the oldest BURIAL MOUND in North America.

L'Anse aux Meadows a VIKING site in northern Newfoundland, Canada, that was founded at the end of the 10th century AD. The site contains the remains of Scandinavian-style houses and other artifacts of European origin (including an iron smithy). See VINLAND, SKRAELINGS.

Lantian [Lan-t'ien] an Early Palaeolithic site in Shaanxi Province, China, where HOMO *erectus* remains have been found at two localities, Gongwangling and Chenjiawo, dated to *c.*700 000 bp in the Middle PLEISTOCENE. The CORE tools from Lantian have been used to characterize a heavy-tool tradition in Palaeolithic China, in contrast to a FLAKE-tool tradition typified by the ZHOUKOUDIAN finds.

Lanzón see CHAVÍN.

Laoguantai [Lao-kuan-t'ai] see PEILIGANG.

Lapakahi an area on the main island of Hawaii with a settlement pattern typical of dry leeward valleys, with a belt of uncultivable land separating the coastal settlement, established *c.*AD 1300, from the dryland agricultural areas. Compare HALAWA VALLEY, KAWELA, MAKAHA VALLEY.

La Pasiega see EL CASTILLO.

La Pineta see ISERNIA.

Lapita an Oceanic culture complex defined by distinctive dentate-stamped pottery (i.e. stamped with a toothed implement), appearing first in island MELANESIA (ELOUA) *c.*3500 bp and distributed as far east as Fiji and Samoa. Most Lapita sites occur on offshore islands or strandlines and assemblages also include shell artifacts, stone ADZES, and OBSIDIAN from TALASEA and LOU, with material from Lou predominating in later phases. The distinctive pottery style and obsidian suggest long-distance trade. The origins of the complex are controversial. Some researchers propose rapid spread into the Pacific from island southeast Asia, while others see Lapita as an indigenous development in island Melanesia. Lapita is thought to be associated with the spread of AUSTRONESIAN speakers into the Western Pacific and the settlement of POLYNESIA. See also BISMARCK ARCHIPELAGO, NENUMBO, WATOM.

La Quina a Middle and Upper Palaeolithic site complex in the Charente, southwest France, which has given its name to one of the sub-divisions of the CHARENTIAN MOUSTERIAN tradition identified by

BORDES. It was excavated primarily by the Henri–Martins in 1906–36 and 1953–65. Fragments of 27 NEANDERTHALERS were found.

L'Arbreda   see SERIÑA.

La Riera   a well-stratified prehistoric cave-site in Asturias, northern Spain, which has yielded over 55 000 stone artifacts and a large amount of faunal evidence, which indicates intensive red deer and ibex hunting during the Upper Palaeolithic (SOLUTREAN and MAGDALENIAN) phases of occupation. This is followed by an AZILIAN SHELL MIDDEN layer with associated HARPOONS, flint BLADELETS and MICROLITHS, and then clearly distinct ASTURIAN levels with characteristic *conchero* (shell midden) deposits and a tool-kit including QUARTZITE CHOPPERS, picks and sidescrapers (see SCRAPER). The cave was first excavated by the Conde de la Vega del Sella in 1917–18 and has since been investigated by a variety of workers, notably G. Clark and L. Straus in 1976–79. Its occupation began *c*.20 500 and ended *c*.6500 bp.

Larisa or Larissa   a site in Northern Greece where MOUSTERIAN industries have been found. Milojcic defined a FINAL NEOLITHIC Larisa culture characterized by the black polished pottery found at ARAPI, ARGISSA, OTZAKI and SOUFLI, but the belief that this represents a distinct chronological phase would appear to be mistaken. Typical Larisa pottery has in fact been identified in Late Neolithic contexts.

larnax   **1.** a closed box. A gold example was found in the royal tomb at VERGINA. In art, examples are seen being carried by women in scenes which are often linked to the preparation of textiles in the home.
2. a MINOAN-MYCENAEAN clay coffin which usually resembles a rectangular wooden chest. The invariably rather crudely painted decoration on the sides of larnakes sometimes includes religious or funerary scenes.
3. a bath-tub. Such tubs are made of a special fabric which contained straw.

Larnian   a MESOLITHIC INDUSTRY found along the coast of western Scotland and eastern Ireland, named after Lough Larne, and characterized by the presence of SHELL MIDDENS. The early Larnian tool-kits include leaf-shaped points and SCRAPERS; the later Larnian assemblages contain more FLAKES than BLADES and include TRANCHET AXES and very small scrapers made from beach pebbles.

Larsa   the most prominent city in the history of southern MESOPOTAMIA during the early OLD BABYLONIAN period, when it was the political seat of a kingdom that controlled a large part of the region, and contending with the kingdom of ISIN. Archaeological remains of the city form a group of TELLS within an area of about 350 ha, located about 20 km east of WARKA. First explored by Loftus in the mid 19th century, Larsa has been the object of a French investigation, initiated by Parrot in 1933, then again in 1967 and after, which concentrated on the palace of Nur-Adad (1865–1850 BC) and the temple complex known as the E.babbar, dedicated to the god SHAMASH, and used between Old Babylonian and NEO-BABYLONIAN times. The documented settlement history of the site spans the late 3rd millennium (UR III) to mid 1st millennium (Neo-Babylonian) BC.

Lartet, Edouard   (1801–71) a French scholar, known as the founder of the science of Palaeontology, who proposed a classificatory scheme for the Palaeolithic based entirely on recovered animal bones. He worked with CHRISTY excavating many of the well-known rockshelter sites of southern France (AURIGNAC, LE MOUSTIER, LA MADELEINE), and was one of the first to recognize *in situ* MOBILIARY ART.

Lascaux   a MAGDALENIAN cave in the Dordogne, France, discovered by four boys in 1940, which houses the most spectacular collection of Palaeolithic wall-art yet found. Best known for its 600 magnificent paintings of AUROCHS, horses, deer and signs, it also contains almost 1500 engravings dominated by horses. A shaft features a painted scene of a bird-headed man with a wounded bison and a rhinoceros, usually interpreted in shamanistic terms. Stone tools for engraving were found in the cave's engraved zones. Many lamps were recovered, as well as 158 fragments of pigment, and colour-grinding equipment. Scaffolding was used in some galleries to reach the upper walls and ceiling. Much of the cave floor was lost when the site was adapted for tourism, but it was probably never a habitation, being visited briefly for artistic activity or ritual. Charcoal has provided RADIOCARBON dates around 15 000 bc and in the 9th millennium bp. The cave was closed to tourists in 1963 owing to pollution, but a facsimile, Lascaux II, is now open nearby.

Las Chimeneas   see EL CASTILLO.

Las Haldas   a large ceremonial site on the north central coast of Peru, pertaining to the INITIAL PERIOD. The site has a stepped PYRAMID at one end, and a series of smaller mounds and sunken courts extending along a linear axis.

Lasithi   an upland plain on the island of Crete, which has been inhabited since the Neolithic period and which was intensively exploited by the MINOANS.

Las Monedas   see EL CASTILLO.

Last Glacial Maximum or **Late Pleniglacial**   the geological period dating between 25 000–14 000 bp, during which global temperatures achieved the lowest levels of the Upper PLEISTOCENE (127 000–10 000 bp). Massive continental ice sheets developed in the northern hemisphere, and a corresponding fall in sea levels occurred worldwide. Despite harsh climatic conditions, human populations (represented by anatomically modern people and industries of the Upper Palaeolithic) occupied most unglaciated portions of the Old World.

Late Bronze Age   a period in the Levant marked by the increasing incursions of the Egyptian Empire, following the expulsion of the HYKSOS and the bringing of CANAANITE cities under Egyptian control. This period is divided into the phases LBA I (*c.*1550–1400 BC), LBA IIa (*c.*1400–1300 BC), and LBA IIb (*c.*1300–1200 BC).

Late Horizon (AD 1450–1533)   The period in Andean South America during which the INCA Empire expanded to gain political control over the entire Andean region.

Late Intermediate Period (AD 1000–1450)   The period in Andean South America following the collapse of the MIDDLE HORIZON empires, during which distinctive regional cultures emerged on the coast and in the highlands of the central Andes. The best known, and most extensive, was the CHIMÚ culture. The various POLITIES that developed during the Late Intermediate Period were conquered by the INCA Empire. (See also CHANCAY.)

La Tène   a site on the shore of Lake Neuchâtel, Switzerland, with remains of a timber double-bridge spanning a former river bed and a settlement on its southern bank. Abundance of Iron Age metalwork suggests a place where votive offerings were thrown into the water. The material includes over 150 swords, many with decorated scabbards, as well as FIBULAE, spearheads, and other bronze and iron tools and weapons. The site has given its name to the second major division of the European Iron Age (succeeding the HALLSTATT phase) and to the La Tène style of CELTIC art. The La Tène period is customarily subdivided into three parts: La Tène I, *c.*480–220 BC; La Tène II, *c.*220–120 BC; La Tène III, *c.*120– Roman conquest.

Late Period   an era of Egyptian history (*c.*664–332 BC) comprising the 26th to the 30th DYNASTIES, plus the second Persian occupation sometimes called the 31st Dynasty. A period of alternating foreign rule and native kings, ended by the invasion of Alexander the Great.

Late Pleniglacial see LAST GLACIAL MAXIMUM.

lateral-chambered tomb see SEVERN-COTSWOLD.

Later Stone Age   the third and final stage of STONE AGE technology in sub-Saharan Africa, dating from about 30 000 or more years ago until historical times in some areas. In southern Africa, it is particularly associated with the ancestors of the SAN and KHOIKHOIN people known from historical and ethnographic records. Characteristics include abundant evidence for art and personal decoration, burials, and in some, but not all, assemblages, MICROLITHIC stone tools such as BLADELETS, SEGMENTS and small SCRAPERS, which were hafted on handles, and specialized hunting and gathering equipment. Pottery and stone bowls appear at various times and places in the last three millennia, when some Later Stone Age societies also acquired stock and switched to a herding way of life (see KHOIKHOIN).

Before the appearance of stock, all Later Stone Age people were nomadic hunter-gatherers who did not live in settled communities. A great variety of game as well as plant foods, shellfish, fish, birds and insects were consumed. Their societies were probably egalitarian with great emphasis on sharing and reciprocity. The arrival of stock, which involved the maintenance of personal wealth, transformed the social relations of Later Stone Age people (see ALBANY, EARLY LATER STONE AGE, EBURRAN, KHAMI, LOCKSHOEK, MATOPO, NACHIKUFAN, OAKHURST, PASTORAL NEOLITHIC OF EAST AFRICA, PFUPI, POMONGWE, ROBBERG, SAN, SMITHFIELD, WILTON, ZAMBIAN WILTON).

Lathrap, Donald Ward (1927–90)   an American archaeologist specializing in the study of South and Middle America. His most important contribution was the proposal that the lowland Amazon regions were able to support complex societies, in all probability civilizations, long before they arose elsewhere on the continent.

latte   rectangular settings of large stone pillars with hemispherical CAPSTONES which formed the basis of structures. Burials sometimes occur between the uprights. *Latte* appear in the Mariana Islands, Micronesia, about 1000 years ago.

Laugerie Haute   a well-stratified French rockshelter in the Dordogne near LES EYZIES, and excavated by LARTET, PEYRONY, BORDES and others. The site has yielded AURIGNACIAN, GRAVETTIAN, SOLUTREAN and MAGDALENIAN occupation levels, and is one of the type-sites used in the classification of the French Upper Palaeolithic. *Laugerie Basse* is a nearby rockshelter with a wealth of Magdalenian material including many art objects.

laurel-leaf point   a long, thin and elegantly worked leaf-shaped SOLUTREAN FLAKE tool with delicate invasive RETOUCH. The largest laurel leaf found, recovered from Volgu in eastern France, measured approximately 35 cm long but less than 1 cm thick. See also WILLOW-LEAF POINT.

Laurentian   an important late ARCHAIC TRADITION in northern New York and Vermont, and the upper St Lawrence valley (5200–4400 BP). The tradition comprises such PHASES as Vergennes, Brewerton and Vosburg. It is characterized by specific SCRAPERS, slate points or knives, ground stone gouges and stone plummets used as weights for fishing lines.

Laurentide   a continental ice-sheet that originated in northeastern Canada during the WISCONSIN GLACIAL episode, and subsequently spread south and west. The system began to recede about 14 000 BP. The timing of its expansion and retreat, and the dating of its coalescence with Cordilleran glaciers originating in the Rocky Mountains, is crucial to dating the entry of humans into the New World. See ICE-FREE CORRIDOR.

Lauricocha   a region of the highlands of central Peru in which several PRECERAMIC cave-sites have been excavated by Augusto Cardich. The sites represent seasonal hunting camps, and include remains of deer and camelids. In the Lauricocha I period (*c*.8000–6000 bc), PROJECTILE POINTS were triangular in form. In Lauricocha II (*c*.6000–4000 bc), willow-leaf-shaped points were typical. Later occupations have also been identified, extending up to and into the INITIAL PERIOD.

Laurion   the silver mines in Attica, Greece, which were operating from the Bronze Age. Numerous shafts have been sunk exploiting the deep layers of ore. Above ground were extensive processing areas. A washery at Agrileza has recently been excavated by the British School. There were several other mining settlements including Thorikos.

Lausitz Culture   see LUSATIAN.

La Vache   a MAGDALENIAN cave-site in Ariège, French Pyrenees, containing a series of occupation layers and HEARTHS rich in PORTABLE ART. Some of the art objects feature the same pigment-recipes as at nearby NIAUX, and come from layers dating to the 11th millennium bc. The economy was based heavily on ibex and reindeer exploitation.

La Venta   one of the major CEREMONIAL CENTRES of the OLMEC, and one of the largest sites in this region of Mexico. There has been some difficulty in establishing the chronology at La Venta, which RADIOCARBON dates have been unable to resolve. La Venta reached its maximum population and height of power during the Middle FORMATIVE, *c*.850–750 BC. Evidence like the large, parabolically concave mirrors at the site and the appearance of elite residences and public building indicate a shift from the pan-MESOAMERICAN trade network of the Early Formative to increased regionalization, accompanied by social and political evolution. La Venta rose to power after the collapse of SAN LORENZO in *c*.1150 BC, and as the impact of Olmec ritual in the VALLEY OF MEXICO lessened. As with most Olmec sites, the end of the occupation was violent, indicated by the mutilation of the monumental sculpture. Archaeologists suggest La Venta's collapse was caused by the conflict between the apparent CARRYING CAPACITY of the immediate area and the large numbers of workers postulated to construct and maintain the structures at the site.

La Venta is well known for the arrangement of 16 stone figures and six JADEITE axes, in reddish-brown sand under the courtyard floor near the Northeastern Platform. Although this cache is recognized as being placed in a ritual context, its further meaning is unknown. La Venta has four giant Olmec stone heads. The first was discovered by F. Blom and O. LaFarge in 1925. In 1940, STIRLING located three more heads, in a row, at the north end of the site.

Layard, Sir Austen Henry (1817–1894)   a Paris-born British lawyer who, along with Botta, began archaeological excavation in MESOPOTAMIA, each working in competition around Mosul in northern Iraq. Layard became interested in western Asian antiquities while making a trip through Anatolia and Syria. Thinking he had discovered NINEVEH, he began excavation at the NEO-ASSYRIAN city of KALHU in 1845, then in 1849 moved to Nineveh itself. His work unearthed massive palace complexes with associated winged bulls at the gates and extensive archives, then undecipherable, inside. The former now stand in the British Museum. Layard also made soundings at ASSUR, BABYLON and NIPPUR. He produced an extremely popular account of his research, *Nineveh and its Remains*.

layers   see STRATA.

Layzón   see HUACALOMA.

Lazaret   an ACHEULIAN cave-site near Nice, France, excavated by a variety of workers, principally Octobon and de Lumley. Possible evidence has been found for a large hut-like construction, 11 m long, illuminated by two fires, within the cave. The assemblage, dated to RISS III, includes pointed BIFACES and CHOPPERS. Human remains corresponding to two children and one adult have been found. The fauna is dominated by red deer and ibex.

LBK   see LINEAR POTTERY CULTURE.

Lchashen   a Bronze Age site near Lake Sevan in Armenia, where a group of pit graves under stone CAIRNS has yielded traces of 16 wheeled vehicles, 7 wagons and 6 carts, with tripartite disc wheels, and two spoked-wheel chariots. The Lchashen finds have provided some of the most complete evidence of early wheeled vehicles beyond that available from models.

lead-glazed ware   a soft-fired earthenware of HAN-dynasty China with a greenish-grey lead GLAZE, made specifically for funerary deposits. Not only vessels but miniature CERAMIC sculptures of daily scenes and architectural forms occur among this ware. (Compare STONEWARE, CELADON.)

Leakey, Louis Seymour Bazett (1903–72)   a pioneer East African prehistorian especially known for his work at OLDUVAI GORGE in Tanzania. The 1959 discovery of ZINJANTHROPUS at this site by his wife, Mary Leakey, led to intensive early HOMINID research in East Africa.

Leang Burung   **1.** a rockshelter site in southwest Sulawesi, Indonesia, with deposits postdating ULU LEANG (*c*.2000 BC and later); its

assemblage includes late TOALIAN MICROLITHS and Maros points and pottery (see TOALIAN).
2. a rockshelter site in southwest Sulawesi, Indonesia, which has yielded a late PLEISTOCENE (*c.*29 000–17 000 bc) stone industry characterized by unretouched FLAKES, a few similar to the LEVALLOISIAN of Europe. The industry appears in the lowest levels of ULU LEANG, underlying the TOALIAN assemblages.

Lébous a CHALCOLITHIC enclosed settlement in Hérault, France, excavated by J. Arnal, consisting of a dry-stone wall with circular huts or towers attached. Some have interpreted the site as a fortified settlement with towers, others as a livestock enclosure with shepherds' huts. The associated material is of FONTBOUISSE type. A number of similar sites are known, including BOUSSARGUES.

Lefkandi a settlement on the Aegean island of Euboea, which has been the focus for British and Greek excavations since 1965. The Xeropolis headland seems to have been occupied continuously from the later 3rd until the end of the 2nd millennium BC. The earliest level contains the Anatolian-inspired pottery which characterizes the Lefkandi I phase. Late in the MYCENAEAN period the settlement was twice destroyed by fire and then abandoned, presumably in favour of the site associated with the three PROTOGEOMETRIC cemeteries. That at Toumba proved to be centred on an artificial TUMULUS covering a large APSIDAL structure, approximately 45 m long, surrounded by a PERISTYLE of wooden columns. Built *c.*1000 BC, this contained the rich graves of a man and a woman, and may have been a shrine for a hero–cult. Objects from the cemeteries suggest links with the eastern Mediterranean. See also AL MINA.

Łęg Piekarski a richly furnished burial site located in west-central Poland and dated to the 1st or 2nd century AD. Referred to as 'princes' graves', the burials at Łęg Piekarski yielded elaborate silver and bronze vessels and a variety of other high-status items. Burials such as those at Łęg Piekarski and elsewhere in east-central Europe are regarded as evidence for the emergence of local hereditary CHIEF-DOMS at the beginning of the 1st millennium AD.

lehm see LOAM.

Lehringen a Middle Palaeolithic site near Bremen in Lower Saxony, Germany, best known for the discovery of a broken yew wood spear with a sharpened and FIRE-HARDENED tip recovered from between the ribs of a straight-tusked elephant skeleton. The spear was originally 240 cm in length, and has been interpreted as a 'thrusting' spear, as it would probably have been too long to throw accurately.

Leilan, Tell a 90 ha site on the Wadi Jarrah in the Khabur triangle in northwestern Syria. The work of Harvey Weiss in the 1980s identified this city as Shubat Enlil, the capital of SHAMSHI-ADAD I (1813–1781 BC). While a few HALAF sherds appear on the surface of the site and at the base of the stratigraphic sounding, the documented occupation of the site extends from the early 4th to the first half of the 2nd millennium BC, defining a sequence of northern 'UBAID (Leilan VI), URUK-related (Leilan V–IV), NINEVITE 5 (Leilan III), a later 3rd millennium BC occupation (Leilan II), and an early 2nd millennium occupation with Khabur ware (Leilan I). Urbanization of the earlier village began with Leilan III, culminating in Leilan II times in a walled lower town covering some 75 ha, an upper town of 15 ha, and possibly a 10 ha enclosed KĀRUM appended to the lower town wall. The important continuing excavations at Tell Leilan will throw considerable light on the social and political developments in northern Syria during the 3rd and earlier 2nd millennia BC, and especially on the emergence of urban states in the region and on Shamshi-Adad's empire, documents from which have already been recovered at the site.

leilira a large pointed or rectangular BLADE which may be retouched to form a point, or a rectangular SCRAPER-like tool, associated with point industries of the AUSTRALIAN SMALL TOOL TRADITION in northern Australia. They were hafted as spearheads or fighting picks, or as knives.

Leisner, Georg (1870–1957) and **Leisner, Vera** (1885–1972) a husband and wife team of German archaeologists who devoted their lives to the first comprehensive survey and analysis of the MEGALITHIC tombs of Iberia; it was a massive undertaking, the results of which were published in a major series of monographs *Die Megalithgräber der Iberischen Halbinsel* in 1942–65.

leister a two-pronged fork-like spear used in fishing by the present-day ESKIMO. Some Mesolithic and Neolithic barbed bone points were probably used as leister prongs.

lekane an open large basin usually with two horizontal handles. It is often found in Greek domestic contexts and seems to have been an essential household item. It was probably multi-purpose in function, but may have been used for storing liquids.

lekanis a shallow Greek basin normally with two horizontal handles. It is usually fitted with a lid which could be reversed to form a stemmed plate. RED-FIGURED examples are often decorated with scenes of women, and it is possible that the shape was used as a trinket box.

Łęki Małe a complex of TUMULUS burials of the ÚNĚTICE culture in western Poland near Poznań. The central burials in the Łęki Małe tumuli lie in stone cists with wooden ceilings, covered by stone pavements. Grave-goods include bronze axes, daggers, and HALBERDS; gold ornaments; amber ornaments; and pottery vessels. Łęki Małe is comparable with the Únětice burial at LEUBINGEN and the burials of the WESSEX CULTURE.

lekythos a Greek vessel, usually made of clay, which has a narrow neck and was used for perfumed oil.

Lelang [Lo-lang] the name of a HAN-dynasty COMMANDERY founded in 108 BC on the north Korean peninsula near modern P'yongyang. As an outpost in the HEQIN system of controlling border populations, Lelang became a regional trading centre, distributing Han and succeeding Wei court gifts to foreign embassies (e.g. YAYOI, PUJO, YAMATAI) and securing raw materials for central court use. Lelang existed until destroyed by KOGURYO in AD 413 (see CHINESE DYNASTIES, PROTO-THREE KINGDOMS, THREE KINGDOMS). The commandery compound and many of the MOUNDED TOMBS of the Han elite and later Koguryo MURAL TOMBS were excavated by Japanese teams in the 1930s.

Le Lazaret see LAZARET.

Lelesu an undated, less well-known Early Iron Age tradition of the

CHIFUMBAZE complex in central Tanzania.

Le Mas d'Azil a massive river-tunnel and cave-system in Ariège, French Pyrenees, containing occupation deposits from the AURIGNACIAN to the Bronze Age. Its MAGDALENIAN layers are phenomenally rich in cultural material and PORTABLE ART, producing dates in the 12th millennium bc. On the river's left bank, PIETTE first recognized AZILIAN material in 1887 – including perforated barbed points, and the painted pebbles of which this site contained more than all other sites combined – and thus filled the hiatus between the PALAEOLITHIC and NEOLITHIC.

Lemba-Lakkous the site of a CHALCOLITHIC (mid 4th to mid 3rd millennium BC) settlement in western Cyprus, which was excavated by Peltenburg in 1976–83. The houses were circular huts built of stone and PISÉ. The dead were buried INTRAMURALLY in pit graves.

Le Moustier see MOUSTERIAN.

Lengyel culture a broadly distributed culture in eastern Europe, considered to be Late Neolithic in Hungary, Czechoslovakia and Austria, and Early Neolithic in Poland. Named after the type-site of Lengyel in western Hungary, the culture is characterized by a variety of vessel forms including bowls, small AMPHORAE, biconical pots, and pedestalled bowls. The earliest Lengyel pottery (4000–3500 bc) retains many decorative elements that appeared at the end of the LINEAR POTTERY culture, including painted and incrusted designs, but through time decoration virtually disappeared. Late Lengyel (3500–3000 bc) pots have small appliqué bosses. The Lengyel culture saw some of the earliest use of COPPER in temperate Europe. Settlements of the Lengyel culture vary considerably. Many (e.g. POSTOLOPRTY, BRZEŚĆ KUJAWSKI, and OSŁONKI) are characterized by trapezoidal LONGHOUSES, while others are surrounded by defensive works (e.g. HLUBOKE MAŠŮKY, TĚŠETICE-KYJOVICE). Lengyel burials are largely contracted inhumations, either in cemeteries (e.g. JORDANÓW) or in settlements (as at Brześć Kujawski). The Lengyel culture has affinities with the RÖSSEN and TISZA cultures.

Leopard's Kopje a Late Iron Age complex of southwestern Zimbabwe and adjacent areas of the northern Transvaal, South Africa, named after the Leopard's Kopje or Nthabazingwe site in southwestern Zimbabwe. The Leopard's Kopje initial or A phase dates to the 10th and 11th centuries AD. It is represented in the Limpopo Valley by the K2 FACIES and further north in southwestern Zimbabwe by the MAMBO facies. The second or B phase of the Leopard's Kopje tradition continues as the MAPUNGUBWE facies in the Limpopo Valley and the WOOLANDALE facies in southwestern Zimbabwe in the 12th and 13th centuries AD. Societies in this phase are characterized by trade with the East African coast, gold mining and working, the construction of stone walling, class distinction and the development of sacred leadership. These processes led to the ZIMBABWE culture.

Lepcis Magna or **Leptis Magna** a harbour town in the Roman province of Africa, now Libya. The site seems to have been settled by the PHOENICIANS during the 6th century BC. Under the emperor Augustus it seems to have been Romanized and it gained the status of a colony under the emperor Trajan. Excavations have uncovered the FORUM, remodelled under the emperor Septimius Severus, and related administrative buildings. The Hunting Baths are particularly well preserved.

Le Pech de l'Azé   see PECH DE L'AZÉ.

Lepenski Vir   a settlement of complex hunters-fishers, and later farmers, in the Djerdap Gorge of the River Danube in Serbia, excavated by D. Srejović between 1965 and 1971. Eight habitation levels have been divided into three main phases, although the idiosyncratic nature of their contents has led to disagreements over their chronological position. Phases I and II apparently had an economy based on red deer, boar, AUROCHS and fish. The Phase I and II settlement had a total of about 25 trapezoidal structures with wide ends facing the river. Most had a limestone sculpture near the HEARTH with features reminiscent of fish, with bulging eyes and piscine mouths. Fish bones were quite common in the faunal sample from Lepenski Vir. Among terrestrial species, red deer, aurochs and boar comprise most of the sample from Phases I and II. Phase III is an occupation of the STARČEVO culture, with domestic cattle, pigs, sheep and goats. Interpretations of Lepenski Vir vary. Typically, it is seen as a complex foraging adaptation that emerged in the 7th millennium bc. A dissenting point of view places Phases I and II later, in the late 6th/early 5th millennia bc, contemporaneous with early farming communities of the Starčevo culture nearby.

Le Placard   a cave-site in the Charente region of France which has yielded abundant SOLUTREAN and MAGDALENIAN material including 74 well-carved BÂTONS-DE-COMMANDEMENT and numerous decorated and carved objects. Engravings were recently discovered on its walls, and some fallen engraved fragments were stratified between two Upper Solutrean layers. Le Placard was a major industrial and artistic site in both periods.

Lepsius, Karl Richard   (1810–84) a German Egyptologist, chiefly known for the Prussian survey of Egyptian monuments of 1842–45.

Leptis Magna   see LEPCIS MAGNA.

leptolithic, *adj.*   literally 'of small stones', occasionally used to describe INDUSTRIES with many BLADES and blade tools, without any particular dating connotation.

Lerma point   a PROJECTILE POINT type found before 7000 BC in Tamaulipas and Puebla, Mexico, including the site of SANTA ISABEL IZTAPÁN. This laurel leaf-shaped point is similar to those found in the Great Basin in the United States, and is thus suggestive of an adaptation commonly defined as the DESERT TRADITION.

Lerna   a site on the coast of the Argolid, Greece, which was excavated by CASKEY in 1952–58. Lerna was first occupied in the Neolithic period, subsequently abandoned and then reoccupied in Early HELLADIC II. The site was fortified and the House of Tiles was built. This impressive two-storeyed structure, 25 m by 12 m, appears to have served an administrative function and may have been a proto-palace. *Circa* 2200 BC it was, however, burnt down and the radical cultural change which Lerna then experienced suggests that this was an act of violence. Although Lerna never entirely recovered from this setback, archaeologically the Middle Helladic levels have proved extremely informative.

Leroi-Gourhan, André Georges Léandre   (1911–86) a French prehistorian best known for his revolutionary work on PALAEOLITHIC

Lerma point

ART (*Préhistoire de l'Art Occidental*, 1965), seeing it as structured and composed rather than as a random collection of images; and for his excavations at LES FURTINS, ARCY-SUR-CURE and especially PINCEVENT where he pioneered techniques of horizontal excavation, the minute study and moulding of occupation floors, and ethnological reconstruction of prehistoric life.

lesche an enclosed space in the Greek world where people could sit and talk, with perhaps also a dining area. Compare STOA.

Les Combarelles a long narrow cave near LES EYZIES (in Dordogne, France), where hundreds of Palaeolithic engravings were discovered on the walls in 1901. They are dominated by horses, together with bison, bear, reindeer, MAMMOTH and ANTHROPOMORPHS, and are assigned to the mid-MAGDALENIAN (c. 14 000–12 000 BC).

Les Eyzies a village at the centre of the French Dordogne's distribution of Palaeolithic cave and rockshelter sites. The cave of Les Eyzies has yielded MAGDALENIAN and AZILIAN material. See CRO-MAGNON, ABRI PATAUD, LAUGERIE HAUTE, FONT DE GAUME, LES COMBARELLES.

Les Fouaillages a triangular Neolithic CAIRN on Guernsey, Channel Islands, covering a MEGALITHIC CIST towards the narrow end, a closed megalithic cist in the centre, and a PASSAGE GRAVE entered from the middle of the widest end. Pottery of CERNY type was found and RADIOCARBON dates suggested construction in c. 4300 BC. In the 3rd millennium BC the monument was buried beneath a large oval mound.

Les Furtins a MOUSTERIAN cave-site in Saône-et-Loire, eastern France, excavated by LEROI-GOURHAN, where six bear skulls were thought to be deliberately arranged on a limestone slab, and hence evidence of a CAVE BEAR cult. It is now clear that hibernating bears and fallen ceiling fragments produced these finds. Compare DRACHENLOCH.

Lespugue a series of small cave-sites in the Save Gorge, Haute-Garonne, in the French Pyrenees, where R. de Saint-Périer encountered material from the AURIGNACIAN to the MAGDALENIAN. In the Grotte des Rideaux, in 1922, he discovered the famous ivory 'VENUS' of Lespugue. Damaged during extraction, it was found beneath a rock, but seems to have been associated with GRAVETTIAN material.

Les Trois Frères see VOLP CAVES.

Le Tillet a gravel pit at Seine-et-Marne in northern France, with a well-defined LOESS stratigraphy recorded by BORDES, which has yielded a clear sequence of Palaeolithic industries including ACHEULIAN and a MOUSTERIAN assemblage with BOUT COUPÉ-style BIFACES.

Le Tuc d'Audoubert   see VOLP CAVES.

Leubingen   an Early Bronze Age high-status burial of the ÚŇETICE culture located in southeastern Germany. At Leubingen, a timbered mortuary house under a BARROW was erected over the burial of an adult male and an adolescent, probably female. Elaborate grave-goods include not only bronze daggers, chisels, axes and HALBERDS, but also a gold armlet, beads, pins and earrings.

Leukas or **Levkas**   one of the Ionian islands, in Greece, that was the focus of lengthy and detailed investigations by DÖRPFELD, SCHLIEMANN's collaborator, who believed but could never prove that this was the Homeric Ithaca, home of Odysseus. In the Nidhri plain he discovered a richly furnished Early HELLADIC TUMULUS grave cemetery and two Middle Helladic tumuli.

Levallois technique   a prepared-CORE KNAPPING technique which allows the removal of large FLAKES of predetermined size and shape. The top and sides of the core are trimmed to form a *tortoise core*, a STRIKING PLATFORM is prepared, and one or two flakes are struck from the core. The flakes show characteristic preparation scars on the dorsal surface and a faceted striking platform. See DISCOIDAL NUCLEUS TECHNIQUE.

(a)   (b)

Levallois technique Core and flake.

Levantine art   ROCK ART found primarily in ROCKSHELTERS of eastern Spain, comprising small red-painted figures of deer, ibex, humans, etc., including hunting scenes. Traditionally assigned to the MESOLITHIC, it is now thought to date primarily to the Neolithic period.

Levanzo   a small island lying to the west of Sicily, Italy, where GRAZIOSI discovered fine engravings of horses, deer, humans and cattle in the Grotta Genovese, dating to the Upper Palaeolithic (ROMANELLIAN), *c*.10 000 bc.

level   an instrument used in SURVEYING to take vertical measurements for constructing maps and identifying the height of individual artifacts. A level is less sophisticated than a TRANSIT or THEODOLITE, consisting of a focusing or nonfocusing telescope for sightings, some form of level-bubble to level the scope, and a set of cross-hairs. Vertical readings are taken by sighting the level on a graduated stadia rod or levelling staff, to gain a reading of the difference between instrument height and ground surface at base of the rod. Subtracting the stadia rod reading from the height of the level above the ground surface gives the difference in height between ground surface at the instrument station and ground surface at the shot point.

Levkas   see LEUKAS.

Lhokseumawe   a series of marine SHELL MIDDENS on the mid-HOLOCENE coastline of northeast Sumatra, containing HOABINHIAN stone tools, a high proportion of which are SUMATRALITHS.

Liangzhu [Liang-chu]   a site in Jiangsu Province, China, giving its name to one of the Middle and Late Neolithic rice-growing cultures of HEMUDU lineage in the central Yangtze River basin. It is distinguished by JADE artifacts (see ZONG) with intricate incising and relief carvings of the TAOTIE motif. The late Liangzhu culture is contemporaneous with the LONGSHAN cultures of the Late Neolithic further north.

Liaodong [Liao-tung]   the peninsula in Liaoning Province, China, between the BOHAI Bay and the Yellow Sea.

Liaoning see SONGGUK-RI.

libation   a Greek or Roman offering of wine to the gods poured from a PHIALE or PATERA which had been filled from an OINOCHOE.

Libby, Willard Frank   (1908–80) an American chemist who devised and reasoned the fundamentals of the RADIOCARBON DATING method in the early 1950s, for which he won a Nobel prize.

Libyco-Capsian see CAPSIAN.

Li Chi [Li Ch'i]   (1895–1979) a Chinese archaeologist from Hubei Province who took his Ph.D. from Harvard in 1928. Upon returning to China, he conducted the excavations at ANYANG. Moving to Taiwan in 1949, he established the first archaeology department of any Chinese university, at the National Taiwan University in Taipei.

lienzo   a large document similar to a CODEX, made of an animal skin or cloth. The major difference between the two is that a lienzo is either rectangular or irregular, while a codex is a long scroll. In MESOAMERICA the lienzo is frequently, but not always, a map showing elite land holdings. Its name comes from the Spanish for 'linen,' and all surviving specimens are post–conquest.

Lijiacun [Li-chia-t'sun]   see PEILIGANG.

Lima Culture   the culture located on the central coast of Peru during the EARLY INTERMEDIATE PERIOD. A major population centre was the site of CAJAMARQUILLA, and Lima-style CERAMICS show influence from the MOCHE culture of the north coast. Stylistic influences in ceramic design during the MIDDLE HORIZON indicate either conquest by, or interaction with, the HUARI Empire.

Lime Springs   an open site in northeast New South Wales, Australia, with association between artifacts and MEGAFAUNA over a

1.3 metre sequence. DIPROTODON is the most common species, while macropods such as PROTEMNODON also occur. KARTAN material occurs in the upper third of the sequence above a date of 19 300 bp. The site shows evidence of late survival of megafauna in well-watered parts of Australia.

Lindenmeier   a FOLSOM site in northern Colorado, USA. ARCHAIC and Late prehistoric COMPONENTS are also present; the date for the Folsom occupation is approximately 11 000 BP. It was used as a KILL/butchering and camp SITE, and contained a wide variety of artifacts and animal bones. It has been suggested that the site served as a seasonal meeting-place for individual hunting groups or BANDS.

Lindisfarne   an island off the northeast coast of England where St Aidan and other monks from the Scottish island of Iona founded a monastery in AD 634. It became a centre for producing illuminated manuscripts such as the *Lindisfarne Gospel* of c.700, a sumptuous blend of CELTIC and Germanic art. The island was raided by Danes in 793.

Lindner Site, Nauwalabila   **1** a painted sandstone shelter in ARNHEM LAND, northern Australia, with nearly three metres of deposit, going back more than 20 000 years. The lowest levels, older than 18 000 bp, contain artifacts typical of the AUSTRALIAN CORE TOOL AND SCRAPER TRADITION. This is succeeded by an amorphous industry of SCRAPERS and utilized FLAKES. Elements of the AUSTRALIAN SMALL TOOL TRADITION such as points begin to appear from about 6000 bp, but ADZES are only introduced c.3500 bp. The earliest EDGE-GROUND TOOLS date to about 14 000 bp.

Lindow Man   a bog body discovered in 1984 in Cheshire, England, during PEAT cutting. One leg is missing but the rest of the body is relatively well preserved and is that of a young man around 25 years old who had been twice struck violently over the head, garotted, and finally had his throat cut. Like the famous TOLLUND and GRAUBALLE bodies from Denmark, this may have been a ritual sacrifice. RADIO-CARBON dates show that Lindow Man met his untimely end in the 1st or 2nd century AD. Parts of between one and three other bodies have also been found at Lindow.

Linear A   a SYLLABIC script devised by the MINOANS which was in use throughout Crete and on a number of other Aegean islands in Greece in the NEOPALATIAL period (c.1700–1450 BC). The script, which has never been deciphered, was inscribed on clay tablets, evidently administrative documents, on stone vases and bronze DOUBLE AXES.

Linear B   a SYLLABIC script, in use in MINOAN Crete and MYCENAEAN Greece in the period 1450–1200 BC, which Michael VENTRIS deciphered as an early form of Greek. It would appear that the script was devised at KNOSSOS when the Mycenaeans took control and spread to mainland Greece but was effectively restricted to the major palace sites: MYCENAE, PYLOS, THEBES and TIRYNS. Most Linear B inscriptions are on CLAY tablets and document the economic transactions of the palace administration.

Linear Pottery culture or *Linearbandkeramik*   the earliest Neolithic culture of central Europe, distributed broadly from the western Ukraine to eastern France, between c.4500 and 3900 bc. The Linear Pottery culture is frequently called by its German name, *Linearbandkeramik* (LBK), as well as a variety of local names, and

V.G. CHILDE referred to it as 'DANUBIAN I'. The Linear Pottery culture takes its name from the incised lines on its fine pottery, beginning with simple meander and spiral patterns and developing into complex designs, often including punctates (small depressions or pits) and stroked ornamentation. The characteristic vessel form is a 3/4-spherical bowl. The best available evidence indicates that the Linear Pottery culture is derived from the KÖRÖS culture of the northern Balkans. Linear Pottery settlements are concentrated in the LOESS-filled basins of central Europe and are situated primarily on the margins of floodplains. They are characterized by LONGHOUSES with rectangular ground plans, as found at CUIRY-LÈS-CHAUDARDES, KÖLN-LINDENTHAL, BYLANY, and OLSZANICA. The economy of the Linear Pottery culture was based on grain cultivation and on domesticated livestock, primarily cattle.

lingling-o   a type of knobbed earring, made of JADEITE, glass or metal, which is characteristic of SA HUYNH in Vietnam and related sites in the islands (TABON CAVES, KALANAY), and found as a trade item elsewhere in Southeast Asia.

lingling-o

Lipari   an AKROPOLIS site on the island of the same name in the Aeolian group (Italy). Beneath the Castello of Lipari, excavations have revealed a long sequence of occupation stretching back to the Neolithic c.4000 BC. In the Bronze Age, Lipari became an important trading centre, and MYCENAEAN pottery has been found dating to the period 1500–1250 BC. Remains of HELLENISTIC buildings show that the Castello was also important in CLASSICAL times. The volcanic deposits of the island of Lipari were exploited in the Neolithic as an important source of OBSIDIAN used by the farming settlements of southern Italy.

Lisht   the royal NECROPOLIS of Egypt's early 12th DYNASTY that was probably close to the now unknown capital of the time, *Iti-Tawy*. The poorly preserved PYRAMID of King AMENEMHAT I, excavated in 1920, seems to have been the first royal tomb at Lisht. It was followed by the better preserved example of King SENWOSRET I, 2.5 km to the south, which was excavated by Gauthier and Jéquier in 1894 and the Metropolitan Museum of Art in 1908–34. A notable discovery in the MORTUARY TEMPLE of Senwosret's PYRAMID COMPLEX was 10 fine statues of the king, bigger than life-size.

lithics   stone artifacts and TOOLS. Because such MATERIAL CULTURE preserves so well, lithic analysis constitutes an important component of archaeological investigation.

lithofacies   part of a recognized SEDIMENT or rock unit that is differentiated by some aspect of composition or character such as grain size or SEDIMENTARY STRUCTURES. Because characteristics of sedimentary units are closely related to their DEPOSITIONAL ENVIRON-MENT, recognition and description of lithofacies and lithofacies associations is integral to interpretation of depositional environments and the CONTEXT and integrity of related archaeological deposits in those environments.

lithofacies analysis a technique used to identify and interpret DEPOSITIONAL ENVIRONMENTS in which archaeological deposits are found. SEDIMENT bodies are subdivided into constituent LITHOFACIES which are examined in terms of geometry, vertical sequences, and lateral associations. Although arrays and sequences of lithofacies are interpretable in their own right, qualitative or quantitative comparisons are made to lithofacies MODELS, which are generalized summaries of sedimentary characteristics of specific depositional environments, developed from work in modern as well as ancient depositional environments that serve as interpretative guides and predictors.

lithophone a naturally occurring stone, STALACTITE or STALAGMITE which may have been struck by Palaeolithic people to create musical notes.

Little Salt Spring a site in Florida, USA, adjacent to a flooded basin and sinkhole, which is famous for the excellent preservation of prehistoric materials. The earliest components at the site belong to the PALAEOINDIAN period (12 000–8 500 BP) and contain HEARTHS, a well-preserved non-returning oak BOOMERANG, a socketed antler PROJECTILE POINT and the shell of an extinct giant land tortoise with a wooden stake still stuck in it. The succeeding ARCHAIC (6800–5200 BP) comprised an extensive burial, possibly containing up to 1000 individuals. The peat, in which the burials were found, allowed excellent preservation – one skull had the remains of the brain inside. Wooden, bone, shell and stone tools were found, as well as a wealth of PALAEOENVIRONMENTAL data. See REPUBLIC GROVES, WINDOVER.

Little Woodbury an Iron Age farmstead in Wiltshire, England, excavated by Gerhard BERSU in 1938–39, consisting of an oval ditched enclosure within which were found POST-HOLES of one large round house together with a smaller circular structure, four-post granaries and storage pits. It was occupied from the 4th to the 2nd century BC.

Liu Sheng see MANCHENG.

livre de beurre the name of the distinctive BLADE CORES of GRAND PRESSIGNY flint, so called from their yellowish colour and their resemblance in shape to the slabs of butter common in the area in the 19th century.

Ljubljansko Blat a wetland area near Ljublijana in Slovenia, in which a number of Late Neolithic and ENEOLITHIC sites have been found, primarily of the VUCEDOL culture, including traces of COPPER working and casting.

Llano Estacado a large plateau in eastern New Mexico and the Texas Panhandle, USA. During the PALAEOINDIAN period, it was much wetter and more hospitable than it is today, the indigenous fauna including antelope, badger, bison, camel, coyote, fox, horse, jackrabbit, MAMMOTH, muskrat, peccary, prairie dog, raccoon, skunk and wolf. The area contains many Palaeoindian sites, including BLACKWATER DRAW, and has attracted numerous archaeological investigations that have been able to recover detailed information on

0   5   10 cm

livre de beurre

Palaeoindian settlement patterns. Llano Estacado is Spanish for the 'Staked Plain', and the region received its name because early Spanish explorers were forced to stake out their line of march in order to be able to return safely.

Llano Tradition   see CLOVIS.

loam, loehm or **lehm**   a TEXTURE class used in describing SEDIMENT and SOIL consisting of a mixture of SAND, SILT and CLAY that contains 7% to 27% clay, 28% to 50% silt, and less than 52% sand. Other loamy textures exist that have differing percentages of sand, silt and clay constituents. Loams tend to be agriculturally productive soils because of their generally good drainage qualities.

Lobo Tuwa   see SRIVIJAYA.

Lockshoek   a term sometimes used for a 12 000–8000 BP non-MICROLITHIC LATER STONE AGE industry of the OAKHURST complex in the interior of South Africa (replacing the term SMITHFIELD A). It is contemporary with and equivalent to the ALBANY Industry of the southern and eastern Cape Province.

loehm   see LOAM.

loess   an AEOLIAN deposit of massive to horizontally bedded SILT. During GLACIAL times, meltwater streams carried large SEDIMENT loads including large amounts of silt derived from glacial abrasion. These streams were mostly braided with barren expanses of floodplains. Prevailing winds preferentially winnowed silt from exposed flats and fans at the glacial front and redeposited the silt as a blanket deposit in upland areas downwind from the source valleys. It is not uncommon to have beds of SAND interbedded with silt close to source valleys (see COVER SAND). Extensive loess bodies are present in North America, Europe and Asia. Archaeologically, loess is significant for several reasons. Soil EROSION in loess-covered regions during the HOLOCENE has caused substantial redeposition of this silt in colluvial slopes, ALLUVIAL FANS and as valley fill, potentially burying, sometimes deeply, and preserving archaeological sites in these settings. Loess is a deposit rich in nutrients for plants and is excellent for agricultural purposes. The ability of loess deposits to maintain stable vertical walls has been exploited, in China for example, by people who have built dwellings in the thick loess. In central and eastern Europe, loess soil was favoured by the earliest farming communities, especially the LINEAR POTTERY culture in Czechoslovakia, Germany, Poland and the Netherlands, and the CUCUTENI-TRIPOLYE culture in Ukraine.

Lolang   see LELANG.

London (*Lat.* Londinium)   an important port during the early years of the Roman occupation of Britain. Like COLCHESTER it suffered during Boudicca's revolt, but subsequently became the centre of government for the province. The monumental tombstone of the procurator Julius Classicianus who took over in the aftermath of the revolt has been found. Traces of the palace, dating to AD 80–100, have been discovered. Around AD 100 the city received a large BASILICA forming one side of the FORUM. A fort was incorporated into the layout of the city, presumably for the permanent garrison attached to the procurator's staff. A MITHRAEUM has been excavated at Walbrook, which contained various pieces of marble sculpture.

Long Count   a means of counting time devised during the MESOAMERICAN PRECLASSIC period. Using the day (KIN) as the basic unit of measure, the Long Count includes a series of increasingly large units of measure (i.e. UINAL, TUN, KATUN, and BAKTUN), mostly progressing by twenties. The Long Count permits the calculation of days to infinity. The MAYA began their count with the year 3113 BC, with most calculations falling in the 9th, but also the 8th and 10th, baktun.

longhouse   1. (*Neolithic*) an elongated wooden post structure typical of the early Neolithic (*c.*4500–3000 bc) and the later Iron Age (*c.*100 bc–AD 500) of north-central Europe (as well as Late WOODLAND cultures of northeastern North America, particularly the Huron and Iroquois tribes, *c.*AD 1300–1600). The North American longhouses were divided into living quarters for a number of residential groups, while the European structures may have been multi-purpose buildings that served both as dwellings and as stables for livestock.
2. (*Palaeolithic*)   a type of dwelling structure attributed to the Upper Palaeolithic by Soviet archaeologists. The dwelling is reconstructed as an elongated above-ground structure up to 100 m in length, with a central line of interior hearths and, in some cases, an arrangement of debris-filled pits. The walls and roofing are thought to have been supported by wooden poles and large mammal bones. Remains of supposed longhouses were described from KOSTENKI I and IV, and PUSHKARI I during the 1930s; another possible example was reported at AVDEEVO in the 1950s. The interpretation of these features is controversial; they may actually represent several small structures.

***long* kiln [*lung* kiln]**   see JINGDEZHEN.

Longquan [Lung-ch'üan]   see CELADON.

Longshan [Lung-shan]   the collective name of the prominent regional cultures of the Late Neolithic in northern China dating to the 3rd millennium BC. The Longshan period encompasses the trends towards the emergence of civilization (walled sites of HANGTU construction, first metal use, warfare, etc.) and is distinguished by delicate black-polished CERAMICS of complicated shapes. (Compare LIANGZHU, MACHANG, QIJIA.)

Lopburi   a major settlement occupied from the late prehistoric to the historic period, located near the confluence of the Chao Phraya and Pa Sak rivers in central Thailand, adjacent to major COPPER deposits. Lopburi and smaller sites in its catchment region (e.g. BAN THA KAE, NON PA WAI, Lopburi Artillery Centre, HUAI YAI and others) produced copper and bronze during the 2nd and 1st millennia BC, and some sites continued to produce copper and iron into the KHMER period of occupation. Already an important town during the DVARAVATI period, Lopburi became the major centre in central Thailand in the 11th–13th centuries, and it has given its name to the Khmer-influenced art of the region during that period.

Los Millares   a CHALCOLITHIC settlement and cemetery of c.2400 bc in ALMERIA, Spain. The settlement stands on a spur between the River Andarax and a seasonal stream, and is protected by a series of dry-stone walls with circular bastions running across the neck of the promontory. Within the settlement were a series of circular houses, and immediately outside it to the west was a cemetery of some 80 PASSAGE GRAVES. The tombs were of circular 'THOLOS' type with ORTHOSTATIC walls and CORBEL-VAULTED roofs, and were used for communal burial. The rich grave-goods included an IVORY sandal, bone 'idols', COPPER axes and daggers, and pottery decorated with double 'eye' motifs. See SIRET.

lost wax or *cire perdue*   a method of casting awkwardly shaped objects in metal. A wax model of the object is coated in clay and baked, and the melted wax allowed to escape. Liquid metal, poured into the resulting cavity in the mould, assumes the model's shape, and is released when hard by breaking the TERRACOTTA surround – hence each mould can be used only once. First developed in the 4th millennium BC in the Near East, it was used primarily for bronze in the Old World (especially in China), and for gold in South America and MESOAMERICA.

Lothagam   see AUSTRALOPITHECUS.

Lothal   a HARAPPAN town (covering about 7 ha) on an extinct course of the Sabarmati River near the Gulf of Cambay in Gujerat, north-western India, where S.R. Rao's excavations in the 1950s revealed a walled settlement. This contained residential and craft (especially stone beads and COPPER working) areas, a citadel on a platform in the southeast corner of the town, and a large dock along the eastern town wall. Rao has argued from this last feature that Lothal was a Harappan sea port, perhaps engaged in the PERSIAN GULF TRADE (a Dilmun SEAL was a surface find on or near the site), though the 'dock' is more plausibly identified as a water tank. Lothal is also remarkable for the presence of local non-Harappan pottery in Mature Harappan levels, and for the subsequent post-Harappan occupation that shows a strong continuation of the Harappan tradition but with the loss of many salient characteristics (see RANJPUR).

Lough Gur   a series of 16 Neolithic and Early Bronze Age settlement sites on the Knockadoon peninsula on the shores of Lough Gur, Co. Limerick, Ireland. Excavations here have revealed plans of several rectangular Neolithic houses, some associated with BEAKER pottery. More unusual are the enclosures around some of the houses, consisting of a double ring of stones, the revetment or facing of a turf bank which protected the houses against the depredations of livestock. These are dated to *c*.2600 bc. Nearby are a number of MEGA-LITHIC CHAMBERED TOMBS and STONE CIRCLES.

Lou Island   an island in the Manus group, Admiralty Islands, that is an important source of OBSIDIAN in the BISMARCKS and the western Pacific. Lou obsidian first appears at BALOF 2 about 3000 bp and increases in importance over time in LAPITA sites at the expense of TALASEA obsidian. Settlement of the Manus group required an open sea voyage of over 200 km and is currently dated at about 5000 bp. There is a series of short-lived occupation sites and obsidian workshops on Lou, buried by volcanic ASH layers which provide good chronological control. Excavation at the Sasi site, dated to *c*.2100 bp, produced a unique bronze artifact.

loutrophoros   a type of container with an ovoid body, long neck, flaring mouth and two long handles. From the iconography of Athenian RED-FIGURED examples it seems to be linked with women and may have been used for carrying water as part of the marriage ceremony. The shape also appears either in relief or in the round on Attic grave STELAI.

loutrophoros

Lovčičky   a Late Bronze Age settlement in southern Moravia of the URNFIELD period, belonging to the VELATICE group. At Lovčičky, in the centre of an open area surrounded by smaller post houses stood a larger building with the appearance of a 'hall'.

Lower Egypt   the northern part of Egypt, chiefly comprising the Nile DELTA and the area around MEMPHIS. The boundary between Lower and UPPER EGYPT was somewhere between LISHT and MEIDUM on the west bank of the Nile; on the east bank the second NOME of Upper Egypt extended slightly further to the north.

Lower Nubia   that part of the Nile Valley extending southwards from the traditional border of Egypt at ASWAN as far as the Second Cataract of the Nile.

Luangwa   1. a Late Iron Age complex identified with the main pottery style in eastern and most of central and northern Zambia during the 2nd millennium AD. It appeared as a sudden break from the CHIFUMBAZE complex in the 11th century and is considered to have originated in Zaire.

2. EARLIER STONE AGE SANGOAN collections from secondary contexts in river GRAVEL deposits in eastern Zambia, which are characterized by large picks and other CORE tools.

Lubbock   see AVEBURY, LORD.

Lucania   an area of Italy to the south of CAMPANIA adjoining the Tyrrhenian Sea. It contained several Greek colonies including PAESTUM. See also LUCANIAN POTTERY.

Lucanian pottery   a type of RED-FIGURED pottery produced in LUCANIA from the late 5th and through the 4th century BC. One of the initial centres of production was located at METAPONTO, and there are clear links with APULIAN POTTERY. See also SOUTH ITALIAN POTTERY.

'Lucy'   a small 3 million-year-old AUSTRALOPITHECINE, generally attributed to *Australopithecus afarensis*, found at HADAR in Ethiopia in 1975. Forty per cent of the skeleton was recovered, which makes this the most complete specimen of an australopithecine ever found. The name 'Lucy' was inspired by the Beatles' song *Lucy in the sky with diamonds*, which was playing on a tape in the field camp shortly after the remains were found. However, the specimen is not necessarily female.

Luka Vrublevetskaya   an ENEOLITHIC settlement of an early phase of the CUCUTENI-TRIPOLYE culture in Ukraine. Luka Vrublevetskaya provides good evidence for the development of the Cucuteni-Tripolye culture. Eight pit-dwellings were excavated at Luka Vrublevetskaya, contrasting with the PLOSHCHADKI found in later Cucuteni-Tripolye settlements, and one was exceptionally large (43 m long) with 11 hearths arranged down the middle. Numerous female figurines were also found.

Lukenya Hill   a southern-Kenyan boulder-hill containing material from the MIDDLE STONE AGE to the Late IRON AGE. Of particular interest is a long sequence of LATER STONE AGE BACKED MICROLITH INDUSTRIES, which appeared by at least 16 000 BP, and which are associated with a fragmentary human skull described as having features similar to those of modern Negroid people.

lunette   see WILLANDRA LAKES.

Lungshan   see LONGSHAN.

Luni   see APENNINE CULTURE.

lunula   a sheet gold collar of Early Bronze Age date, sometimes with incised geometric decoration similar to that on BELL BEAKERS. Lunulae are of Irish or west British origin but are found also on adjacent parts of the continent. They may have been worn as ritual equipment.

Lupemban   a post-SANGOAN stone industry of parts of central and eastern Africa, dated to 30 000 BP, or considerably earlier, characterized by BIFACIALLY worked CORE tools as well as large side-scrapers (see SCRAPER) and occasional bifacial points (see MWANGANDA).

lur   a Late Bronze Age bronze horn from southern Scandinavia. *Lurer* consist of a long curving tube, cast in sections and expertly fitted together, ending in a circular plate decorated with raised bosses or similar design. Lacking a proper mouthpiece, *lurer* are capable of producing only a limited range of sounds. They are often found in pairs of similar size and tone and were sometimes deposited in bogs as votive offerings.

lunula

Luristan bronzes a heterogeneous group of metalwork styles found in the mountains of west central Iran, spanning the two millennia between about 2600 and 600 BC. Until c.1000 BC this metalwork is essentially indistinguishable from that of other areas of western Asia; after that time (i.e. during the Iron Age) the style becomes more regionally distinctive, especially for weapons and horse equipment. Even in the latter period, however, the Luristan bronzes do not seem to be the products of a single regional or ethnic community. Thus, while denoting the broad region of this metalwork, the term has very little cultural historical meaning.

Lusatian culture or **Lausitz culture** a Late Bronze Age/Early Iron Age (HALLSTATT period) culture of Poland and eastern Germany. The Lusatian culture is known from both URNFIELD cemeteries (e.g. KIETRZ) and settlements. Many larger settlements, such as (BISKUPIN, SENFTENBERG, and SOBIEJUCHY) are fortified. Cattle were the primary Lusatian livestock species, and Ostoja–Zagórski has suggested that the herds were large.

lustral basin a sunken room in MINOAN architecture, entered by a short flight of steps and usually screened off by a parapet. EVANS believed that lustral basins were used for ritual purification but, in certain contexts, they are more plausibly interpreted as bathrooms.

Luxor the modern town which now covers most of what was the ancient city of THEBES (EGYPT)-EAST BANK. In the southern part of the town is the TEMPLE of Luxor, largely constructed under AMENHOTEP III and RAMESSES II, and connected with KARNAK via a processional route.

Lydenburg an Early Iron Age village in the eastern Transvaal, South Africa, occupied between AD 450 and 600, which has given its name to an Early Iron Age group. Of particular interest are a number of unique fired-clay sculpted heads. These are thought to have been used in rituals, such as initiation ceremonies, after which they were deliberately broken and the pieces discarded into deep pits.

lydion a form of pot containing perfumes. The name is derived from Lydia, an area where numerous examples have been found. Many examples were made in western Turkey (see EAST GREEK POTTERY) as well as at ATHENS.

Lyles Hill a Neolithic settlement site, in Antrim, Ireland, type-site together with GRIMSTON in Yorkshire of the Grimston-Lyles Hill pottery style of the British Middle Neolithic (4th millennium BC). The site was enclosed within a continuous bank but no ditch.

Lyngby see BROMMIAN.

M

Maadi an Egyptian PREDYNASTIC site to the south of CAIRO, chiefly excavated by Menghin and Amer in 1930–35. The settlement debris at Maadi is up to 2 m thick and covers an area of approximately 18 ha. The community was probably centrally organized with defined areas for houses and for the large pottery jars and pits which comprised storage areas. The economy of Maadi seems to have relied less on hunting than did MERIMDE. The presence of imports of the GERZEAN of UPPER EGYPT and of EARLY BRONZE AGE Palestine suggests that Maadi may have been an important trading centre. Its period of occupation has been dated to c.3200–3000 BC, immediately preceding the ARCHAIC PERIOD.

Maa-Palaekastro a promontory on the west coast of Cyprus. It is the site of a fortified settlement excavated by Karageorghis in 1979–86, and was first occupied late in the 13th century BC, possibly by the SEA PEOPLES. A fine ASHLAR structure may have been their sanctuary. Early in the 12th century BC this settlement was destroyed by fire, and it would appear that Maa was then taken over for a brief period by MYCENAEAN Greeks who subsequently moved on to KOUKLIA-PALAEPAPHOS.

Maba [Ma-pa] a site in Guangdong Province, China, where transitional fossils between HOMO *erectus* and *H. sapiens sapiens* have been discovered in the Middle Palaeolithic period. (See also JINNIUSHAN.)

Macassans Indonesian traders, mainly from Sulawesi, who visited tropical Australia to collect and process *trepang*, also known as *bêche-de-mer* or *sea cucumber*, an important ingredient in Chinese cooking. The trade seems to have begun about AD 1700 and continued until the end of the 19th century. Archaeological evidence of the trade is common in northern Australia. The Macassan influence on local Aboriginal society can be seen in artifacts, including dug-out canoes and metal tools, art motifs, language and ritual, while Macassan sailing vessels, or *praus*, were depicted in ROCK ART and rock arrangements.

MacEnery   see KENT'S CAVERN.

Machang [Ma-ch'ang]   a Late Neolithic culture in northwestern China of YANGSHAO descent, contemporaneous with the LONGSHAN cultures of the east, dating to 2800–1800 BC.

Machu Picchu   an INCA site northwest of CUZCO, Peru. Situated on a sharp ridge between a large and a small mountain peak, it includes agricultural terraces, habitation structures, religious architecture, and tombs. The site was abruptly abandoned at the time of the Spanish conquest, and the Spanish seem to have shown little interest in it. 'Discovered' by Hiram Bingham in 1911, it has been interpreted as many different things: an Inca fortress, a convent, the lost site of VILCABAMBA, the location of the origin of the Inca dynasty, and ever more fanciful things. John H. Rowe has noted that Spanish documents list a place named 'Picchu' as still belonging to the descendants of the Inca Pachacuti in the 16th century; he argues that the site functioned as a royal estate belonging to Pachacuti.

macrofauna   large animals (compare MICROFAUNA).

macrolith   a large stone tool (compare MICROLITH). See ASTURIAN.

Madai Caves   a series of caves in Sabah, north Borneo, Malaysia, yielding prehistoric remains dating to *c*.9000 BC and later. Agop Atas, the largest, and Agop Sarapad were inhabited from *c*.9000–5000 BC by hunters using pebble and FLAKE tools. After a 4000-year gap, the caves (particularly Agop Atas) were reused between *c*.2000 and 500 BC by people using stone flake tools and pottery similar to that at Leang Tuwo Mane'e in Talaud. The caves were again abandoned, then reused early in the 1st millennium AD.

Mad'arovce   an Early Bronze Age regional culture of the central Danube basin, centred on the Váh drainage in western Slovakia. The Mad'arovce culture emerged towards the end of the neighbouring ÚŇETICE culture and is sometimes considered a late sub-group of Úňetice. As in the case of the OTOMANI culture to the east, Mad'arovce settlements often occur on fortified hilltops, although others occur in lowland valleys.

Maes Howe   the most splendid of the PASSAGE GRAVES in Orkney, Scotland. A long passage with floor, walls and ceiling of massive stone flags leads to a rectangular main chamber with CORBEL-VAULTED roof, the stones of each course sloped to make a smooth-faced vault. Though the top of the vault has been lost, it is estimated that it would originally have been approximately 4.5 m in height. To either side of the main chamber and in the rear wall facing the entrance, small square openings, originally with removable closing blocks, lead to rectangular side chambers. Of the tomb contents nothing now remains, and VIKING RUNIC inscriptions of the 12th century AD within the tomb, which refer to the discovery of a treasure, can probably be discounted. A series of RADIOCARBON dates averaging 2700 BC was obtained from the ditch which surrounds the CAIRN.

Maeva   an impressive complex of 25 MARAE on Huahine, Society Islands, POLYNESIA. Many have now been restored.

Magan   see PERSIAN GULF TRADE.

Magarita   see ITAZUKE.

magatama (*Jap.* 'curved bead')   a JADE or jasper pendant produced in the JOMON, YAYOI and KOFUN periods. During the Kofun period, it attained the status of an imperial emblem, together with the BRONZE MIRROR and sword. Many such curved beads also decorate the gold crowns of SILLA.

Magdalenian   the final West European Upper Palaeolithic INDUSTRY, best known for its art, which seems to have originated in southwest France and spread out to adjacent areas, lasting from *c.*16–10 000 BC. The Magdalenian people hunted primarily deer or ibex, and fished for salmon. Their assemblages include practical but unremarkable stone tools, and well-made bone and antler implements including SPEARTHROWERS, BÂTONS-DE-COMMANDEMENT and barbed HARPOONS. The type-site is the Dordogne rockshelter of *La Madeleine*, France, first excavated by LARTET and CHRISTY, and extremely rich in MOBILIARY ART. See also PALAEOLITHIC ART, PARIETAL ART.

Magdalenska Gora   an Early Iron Age (HALLSTATT period) complex of TUMULI in Slovenia, near STIČNA. Excavated by the Duchess of Mecklenburg in 1905–14, the graves at Magdalenska Gora have yielded a broad range of artifacts from the 7th century BC. Of particular significance are the SITULAE, but also numerous weapons, helmets and body armour. Magdalenska Gora is one of a number of Hallstatt tumuli complexes that include NOVO MESTO in Slovenia and NOVE KOSARISKA in Slovakia.

Maghzalia, Tell   a small ACERAMIC NEOLITHIC site in the Sinjar region of northern Iraq, excavated by N.I. Merpert and R.M. Munchaev as part of their Sinjar project. It provides important evidence for the introduction of sedentary communities and probably farming into the northern MESOPOTAMIAN piedmont. The architecture features rectilinear structures with stone foundations, and contains indirect indications of cultivation as well as more direct evidence of hunting. The lithic industry contains similarities with other aceramic sites in the Zagros (e.g. JARMO) but also with aceramic Neolithic industries of Syro-Palestine.

Maglemosian (from *Danish* 'big bog')   the first MESOLITHIC culture of northern Europe found in Scandinavia, the north Balkans, north Scotland and northern England, and lasting from *c.*8000–5000 BC. The assemblages reflect the exploitation of the POST-GLACIAL forest and riverside environments, with evidence of increased woodworking provided by stone axes and faunal remains indicating the wide variation in diet which included fish and birds. MICROLITHS, picks and bone and antler fishing and hunting tools such as barbed points are characteristic Maglemosian artifacts.

magnetic, *adj.*   **1.** pertaining to magnetism, the ability to be magnetized or affected by a magnet.

2. relating to the earth's magnetic field. See ELECTROMAGNETIC SURVEYING, MAGNETIC SUSCEPTIBILITY, ARCHAEOMAGNETIC DATING, PALAEOMAGNETISM.

magnetic susceptibility   a property of SEDIMENT and SOIL, measured as a ratio of intensity of magnetization of the material to the strength of an applied magnetic field. It is an indication of the concentration of magnetic minerals in the material, such as the magnetite family minerals and haematite. In QUATERNARY LOESS-PALAEOSOL sections, the magnetic susceptibility profile serves as a substitute for climatic data, although the relationship is not fully understood.

Concentrations tend to be greater in palaeosols and less in unaltered loess.

magnetometer   a geophysical instrument that measures the Earth's MAGNETIC field strength, used in ELECTROMAGNETIC SURVEYING to identify changes in the field within SOIL or SEDIMENT that might be caused by subsurface features, HEARTHS or metal objects. The PROTON MAGNETOMETER takes intermittent measurements of absolute field strength. The FLUXGATE, DIFFERENTIAL FLUXGATE and PROTON GRADIO-METERS take continuous measurements of relative vertical change in intensity of field strength.

Magosian   a term formerly widely used in eastern and southern Africa for stone INDUSTRIES containing MICROLITHS and small BLADES as well as MIDDLE STONE AGE artifacts, which were thought to be transitional between the Middle and LATER STONE AGES. The original sample from the Magosi site in Uganda has been shown to be mixed and the term is no longer used.

magoula   see TOUMBA.

Mahaiatea   the largest MARAE ever constructed in Tahiti, Society Islands, POLYNESIA. It was built in AD 1767 by the chieftainess Purea of Papara and described in 1769 by Joseph Banks. Now largely destroyed, it comprised a platform 81 m by 22 m at the base, rising in 11 steps to a height of about 13.5 m. The platform was faced with squared volcanic stone over a basal course of coral blocks, and stood at one end of a walled court 115 m long.

Mahal Teglinos   see GASH.

Mahan   see SAMHAN.

Maiden Castle   an impressive Iron Age HILLFORT in Dorset, England, with several concentric lines of huge chalk ramparts following the contours of the steep-sided hill. Excavations by WHEELER, in 1934–37, showed that beneath the hillfort were traces of a Neolithic CAUSEWAYED CAMP overlain by a later Neolithic long mound over 500 m in length. The first hillfort c.500 BC was a relatively simple affair occupying only the eastern part of the site. The hillfort was considerably extended and strengthened c.250 BC, with highly elaborate entrances at east and west. Traces of round houses and streets have been found in the interior. The fort was besieged and captured by the Romans in AD 43.

Maikop   ENEOLITHIC KURGAN burials in the northern Caucasus Mountains, Russia, dating to the late 3rd millennium BC. Under the main Maikop BARROW was a tripartite mortuary structure. In the central part was the burial of a male, characterized as a 'royal' individual, under a canopy with gold and silver supports. Grave-goods included silver vessels with animal designs (including horses), gold figurines of a lion and two bulls, copper tools, and textiles with elaborate designs. The Maikop burials have given their name to the Maikop culture of the Caucasus, with walled settlements.

Mailu   an island about 15 km off the southeast coast of New Guinea, that was a significant centre in coastal Papuan trading systems. The islanders were middle-men in local and long-distance networks connecting the *kula* and HIRI, manufactured shell valuables and held a monopoly on local pottery manufacture. Archaeological evidence documents some 1500 years of growing regional specialization, culminating in the development of the ethnographic system about 400-500 years ago.

Majninskaya an Upper Palaeolithic open-air site on the Uj River near its confluence with the Yenisei in south-central Siberia. Nine cultural layers are buried in sandy ALLUVIUM of the second TERRACE; they are dated (RADIOCARBON and PALAEOMAGNETISM) to *c*.19 000–9000 bp. Among the associated faunal remains are horse, red deer, AUROCHS and birds. The artifacts include WEDGE-SHAPED MICROCORES, sidescrapers and endscrapers (see SCRAPER), laterally grooved bone points, and a crude ANTHROPOMORPHOUS figurine of fired clay.

Makaha Valley a valley in Oahu, Hawaii, that was first settled *c*.AD 1100. Agricultural terraces, habitation sites and HEIAU have been documented in the course of a detailed archaeological survey. The lower part of the valley was used for dryland cultivation while the much wetter upper valley allowed irrigation of root-crops (*taro*). Compare HALAWA VALLEY, KAWELA, LAPAKAHI.

Makapansgat a fossiliferous cave filling at the Limeworks site near the entrance to the Makapan Valley in the northern Transvaal, South Africa, which has produced important samples of AUSTRALOPITHECUS *africanus* and fossil animal remains (see DART.)

Makarovo a group of four Upper Palaeolithic open-air sites on the Lena River in south-central Siberia. At Makarovo II, two cultural layers are buried in ALLUVIAL deposits of the second TERRACE, and have yielded RADIOCARBON estimates between 11 400–11 950 bp. Both layers contain MICROBLADES and other artifacts typical of the Siberian late Upper Palaeolithic. At Makarovo III, redeposited artifacts are buried in slope sediments on the third terrace along with remains of woolly MAMMOTH, reindeer, and other mammals. The assemblage includes sidescrapers and endscrapers (see SCRAPER) and CHOPPERS, and is thought to date to the early Upper Palaeolithic. At Makarovo IV, weathered artifacts were found in slope deposits on the fourth terrace; they include points, sidescrapers and endscrapers, and are believed to pre-date the LAST GLACIAL MAXIMUM. The first Makarovo site was discovered and investigated by OKLADNIKOV in 1941; much of the subsequent work at these sites was undertaken by Aksenov in 1966–75.

malachite a green COPPER carbonate mineral that is an alteration product of copper ORE deposits. It was used as a source of copper and, when powdered, as a cosmetic.

malacology the study of aquatic and terrestrial molluscs as indicators of past environmental conditions and diet. Certain land snails are good microenvironmental indicators, having very restrictive environmental tolerances for ground cover, vegetation, and moisture regimes. Calcareous SEDIMENT and SOILS in which carbonate mollusc shells are preserved are sampled in a vertical column, the sediment is wet-sieved, and snails are dried, identified and counted. Percentages of species are plotted versus depth, and environmental changes are interpreted from changes in the snail assemblage.

   Edible species of marine and aquatic molluscs give an indication of diet and the subsistence economy. See SHELL MIDDENS.

Malakunanja 2 a sandstone shelter in ARNHEM LAND, northern

Australia, first excavated by Johan Kamminga and re-excavated by Rhys Jones and Mike Smith. The sequence is similar to the LINDNER SITE, NAUWALABILA 1. TL dates from SEDIMENTS associated with the lowest artifacts are claimed to indicate human presence in northern Australia between 50 000 and 60 000 years ago.

Malangangerr a rockshelter in ARNHEM LAND, northern Australia, excavated in 1964–65 by Carmel Schrire. The two-part sequence extends back about 25 000 years. Evidence from 20 000 year-old levels here and at Nawamoyn first established the presence of EDGE-GROUND TOOLS in PLEISTOCENE Australia.

Malaya Sya an Upper Palaeolithic open-air site on the Belyj Iyus River (Chulym tributary) in western Siberia. Artifacts and faunal remains are buried in LOAM and clay deposits on the slope of a side-valley ravine. Among the faunal remains are reindeer, sheep, steppe bison, and woolly MAMMOTH. Three RADIOCARBON estimates, ranging from 34 500–20 370 bp, are reported, and seem generally consistent with the view that the occupation pre-dates the LAST GLACIAL MAXIMUM. The artifacts include large RETOUCHED BLADES and endscrapers (see SCRAPER), and are considered to be representative of the early Upper Palaeolithic, which remains poorly known in Siberia. Malaya Sya was discovered and excavated by Ovodov in 1974.

Mali the West African empire which followed GHANA two centuries later. About AD 1230, a group of Kangaba under their leader Sundiata founded an empire that a century later extended over much of sub-Saharan West Africa under the unifying effect of Islam, until its overthrow by SONGHAY by the end of the 15th century.

Malia or **Mallia** the site of a MINOAN palace, on the island of Crete, constructed c.1900 BC, destroyed by an earthquake c.1700 BC, and then completely rebuilt. The final destruction is dated c.1450 BC. Malia lacks the refinement of the palaces at KNOSSOS and PHAISTOS. More space proportionally is set aside for the storage of agricultural produce, in particular oil and grain. Much of the town around the palace has been uncovered by the French excavators. Of particular interest are two large PROTOPALATIAL complexes, known as the AGORA and Quartier Mu.

Mallowan, Sir Max Edgar Lucien (1904–78) a British archaeologist who worked in the Near East. Beginning as an assistant to C.L. WOOLLEY at UR, Mallowan's career in northern MESOPOTAMIAN archaeology encompassed work at NINEVEH, ARPACHIYAH, CHAGAR BAZAR, Tell BRAK, and Nimrud (KALHU) in the 1930s and 1950s. In addition to field work, he served as director of the British School of Archaeology in Baghdad and also presided over the British Institute of Persian Studies, in both capacities promoting archaeological investigation of western Asia. Mallowan was married to Agatha Christie, who used her excavation experiences as the setting for *Murder in Mesopotamia*.

Mal'ta, an Upper Palaeolithic and Mesolithic open-air site on the Belaya River (Angara tributary) near Irkutsk in south-central Siberia. The Mesolithic layer is buried under the modern soil on the third TERRACE; the more deeply buried Upper Palaeolithic layer overlies a buried soil and is believed to date to the beginning of the LAST GLACIAL MAXIMUM (c.24 000–23 000 bp). Faunal remains associated with the lower layer include reindeer, arctic fox, woolly MAMMOTH and woolly rhinoceros. Excavation uncovered traces of former dwellings, partly constructed with limestone slabs, and a child burial. The artifact assemblage contained prismatic CORES, RETOUCHED BLADES and endscrapers (see SCRAPER). Many ornaments and art objects, including human and animal figurines were found. Mal'ta was excavated by Gerasimov, Sosnovskij and others in 1928–37 and 1956–58.

Malthi a precipitous BRONZE AGE AKROPOLIS in Messenia, Greece, which was excavated by Valmin in 1927–36. Unlike most Middle HELLADIC sites, Malthi was fortified and the houses, although rather ramshackle, appear to have been built to an integrated plan. MYCENAEAN remains are unimpressive except for two THOLOS tombs at the foot of the akropolis.

Maluquer de Motes, Juan (1915–88) a Spanish archaeologist best known for his studies of MEGALITHS in Navarre and his excavations at CORTES DE NAVARRA.

Malwa a plateau in northwestern Madhya Pradesh in western central India, which gives its name to a CHALCOLITHIC culture of the earlier 2nd millennium BC, best known from sites such as NAVDATOLI. The CERAMICS of the culture include a characteristic fine red-slipped ware with elaborate black-painted decoration (Malwa ware), as well as black-painted cream-slipped, black-and-red painted, JORWE and Lustrous Red wares which appear and disappear during the history of the culture. These people were cultivators (wheat, rice, legumes, oil seed plants, fruits) and animal keepers (cattle, sheep, goat, pig) and hunters; while COPPER objects are relatively frequent, lithic (including flint BLADE) industries are strongly represented. Sites with a material culture related to the Malwa culture complex occur well to the south (e.g. NEVASA) and east of the Malwa plateau, marking a wide distribution of the central Indian Chalcolithic.

Malyan, Tal i- an important site, the ancient Anshan, in the Kur River drainage of Fars, southwestern Iran, that represents the upland centre of the succession of POLITIES (ELAM, SUSA) that traditionally warred with southern MESOPOTAMIAN states. The sequence at Malyan spans the later 5th millennium BC to the early 1st millennium AD, with its most important occupation occurring during the Banesh (c.3400–2800 BC) and Kaftari (c.2200–1600 BC) periods. During the Banesh period, the city wall at Malyan enclosed nearly 200 ha, of which 50 ha was filled with architecture; at this time, a strong PROTO-ELAMITE connection is evident. Kaftari-period Malyan occupied some 130 ha, as the centre of a hierarchically integrated settlement system.

Mambo a Late Iron Age phase of the LEOPARD'S KOPJE complex in southern Zimbabwe, dated to the 10th and 11th centuries AD.

mammisi or **birth-house** an independent religious building found associated with the larger cult TEMPLES of the LATE PERIOD/Graeco-Roman Period in Egypt. The mammisi was connected with the mythological birth of the god of the temple concerned, or with giving birth where the deity concerned was female (e.g. the goddess Hathor at DENDERA).

mammoth a genus of elephant (*Mammuthus*) which became adapted to the conditions of the Ice Age in the northern hemisphere. Up to 3.5 m tall with a domed head, sloping back, long shaggy fur and large curving tusks (see IVORY), mammoths were frequently depicted in PALAEOLITHIC ART, and are best known from complete carcasses occasionally unearthed in Siberia and Alaska. Their massive molars comprised a series of vertical, flattened plates which wore to produce a flat but ridged grinding surface. The two main species were the woolly mammoth, *M. primigenius* (northern Eurasia and northern North America), and the Columbian mammoth, *M. columbi* (southern North America). Both subsisted largely on open grassy vegetation, and became extinct between 11 000 and 10 000 BP. See also MAMMOTH-BONE HOUSES.

mammoth-bone house   a type of dwelling structure thought to have been built by the inhabitants of Upper Palaeolithic sites in central and eastern Europe between *c.*25 000 and 12 000 bp. Remains of these structures typically comprise a circular or oval arrangement of woolly MAMMOTH bones and tusks (*c.*4–8 m in diameter), containing a central interior hearth and much occupation debris. The bones and tusks are believed to have provided structural support in regions where wood was scarce. Pits, hearths and debris concentrations are often found immediately adjacent to the bone arrangement (i.e. presumably external to the former structure). One or more mammoth-bone houses have been uncovered at KRAKOW-SPADZISTA in Poland, at DOBRANICHEVKA, MEZHIRICH and KOSTENKI XI in the former Soviet Union, and elsewhere.

Mamutowa   a Palaeolithic cave-site located on the Kluczwoda River north of Kraków in southern Poland. Artifacts and faunal remains (primarily CAVE BEAR) are buried in clay and rubble. Middle Palaeolithic artifacts (e.g. sidescrapers – see SCRAPER) occur in the lowest cultural layers, while overlying levels contain evidence of two early Upper Palaeolithic industries AURIGNACIAN (e.g. split-base bone points) and JERZMANOWICIAN (e.g. LAUREL-LEAF POINTS) probably dating to the INTERSTADIAL preceding the LAST GLACIAL MAXIMUM. The upper layers contain GRAVETTIAN artifacts probably dating to the Last Glacial Maximum. Mamutowa was excavated principally by ZAWISZA in 1873–81 and Kowalski in 1957–74.

Mancheng [Man-ch'eng]   a city in Hebei Province, China, where two Early HAN-dynasty tombs were cut into a rock cliff. They consist of several chambers totalling almost 200 cubic metres of space in which 2800 funeral objects were deposited, including bronze vessels; gold, silver, iron, glass and JADE articles; earthenware; LACQUER ware and silk fabrics. The deceased, identified as Prince Liu Sheng and his wife, wore suits of jade platelets sewn together with gold thread. (Compare SHAFT TOMBS, MOUNDED TOMBS.)

Manching   a very large OPPIDUM of the late Iron Age near Ingolstadt in Bavaria, Germany, dated to the LA TÈNE period of the last few centuries BC. Adjacent to the Danube during this period (although now some distance away from the river), Manching is situated on a low river terrace. A 7 km. MURUS GALLICUS rampart enclosed 380 ha, of which a fraction (about 7 ha) has been excavated. These excavations have yielded thousands of features and hundreds of thousands of artifacts and animal bones. Manching appears to have been a commercial settlement, perhaps a regional market. Skeletal remains with injuries inflicted by metal weapons reflect a violent end to the settlement around 50 BC.

Manchuria   an old name for northeastern (DONGBEI) China, comprising the Sungari and Liao river basins – the latter draining into BOHAI Bay; now parts of Heilongjiang, Jilin and Liaoning Provinces. It derives from the Manchu peoples, speakers of a non-Chinese, ALTAIC language.

Mandu Mandu Creek a rockshelter at Northwest Cape, Western Australia, where the first episode of occupation shows use of marine resources between 25 000 and 19 000 bp. The site was then abandoned, and re-occupied about 2500 bp. See also KOOLAN 2, MATENKUPKUM.

Manetho an Egyptian priest active in the early 3rd century BC. Manetho's history of the kings of ancient Egypt, preserved in the writings of later authors, provides the basis of the relative chronology of Egypt before the invasion of Alexander the Great. See also DYNASTY.

Mangaasi a pottery tradition in Vanuatu, MELANESIA, characterized by incised and applied relief, dating from about 700 BC to about AD 1600. It is quite distinct from LAPITA pottery, but similar wares are found in the northern Solomons and New Caledonia.

mano a one- or two-handed ground stone tool, used with the METATE, to grind vegetable material for food. Manos have a variety of shapes and sizes and have some degree of usefulness in constructing CULTURE HISTORY. This term is most often used in the American Southwest.

manuport any object transported and deposited by humans.

Maori the descendants of POLYNESIANS who settled NEW ZEALAND towards the end of the 1st millennium AD.

Mapungubwe a Late Iron Age site built on and around a hill in the northern Transvaal, South Africa, which has given its name to the southern FACIES of phase B of the LEOPARD'S KOPJE complex. Mapungubwe was occupied between c.AD 1220 and 1270 and is a forerunner of developments at GREAT ZIMBABWE. It seems to have been the capital of a state which controlled trade with the East African coast, and represents a period during which a highly stratified society developed and the wealth and status of ruling chiefs increased greatly.

Maqiao [Ma-ch'iao] see GEOMETRIC POTTERY.

marae an East POLYNESIAN stone temple, very variable in design, but basically a rectangular enclosure with upright stones and a stone platform or AHU. *Marae* are especially characteristic of the later period of eastern Polynesian prehistory AD 1200–1800. In Tonga, Samoa and NEW ZEALAND, the word also refers to an open space within a village. See also HEIAU.

Marajó Island the large island, some 39 000 sq km in extent, at the mouth of the Amazon River, Brazil, extensively investigated by Clifford EVANS and Betty Meggers. Especially at the eastern end of the island are numerous sites comprising artificial mounds, built as platforms upon which villages were located. The largest centre, Os Camutins, includes some 40 mounds. Excavations by Anna C. Roosevelt at the site of Aterro dos Bichos indicate that some 20 large multi-family houses were arranged around an open space and surrounded by a wide earthen wall. The island is characterized by savanna vegetation, not tropical rainforest, and the prehistoric population subsisted on maize, seeds and fish. The site was occupied from

400 BC until about AD 1300.

Marathon   a site in Attica, Greece, that is rich in tombs: an Early HELLADIC CIST GRAVE cemetery, Middle Helladic TUMULI, and a MYCENAEAN THOLOS tomb, in which two horses had been buried as grave offerings. ATHENS' defeat of the Persian army in 490 BC is commemorated by the Soros, the large mound in which the Athenian casualties were buried, and by the tomb of the Plataeans which, if correctly identified, is the communal grave of their Greek allies.

Marca Huamachuco   a large EARLY INTERMEDIATE PERIOD and MIDDLE HORIZON site in the north highlands of Peru, the centre of a major POLITY. During the Middle Horizon the HUARI empire extended its influence into the Huamachuco region, and began construction of the planned centre at Viracochapampa but never completed the site. Huari materials at Marca Huamachuco suggest interaction between the local polity and the empire, but whether or not the polity came under imperial control is unclear.

Mardikh, Tell   see EBLA.

Marduk   a BABYLONIAN god who came to take the place of the SUMERIAN deity ENLIL, now as the ruler of the gods rather than simply their head; this shift in the relationship between the gods reflected the shift towards the greater unencumbered power of MESOPOTAMIAN kingship. Marduk's seat was at BABYLON itself.

Mari   a city of 600 ha, on the middle Euphrates in southeast Syria, that seems to have been founded in the early 3rd millennium and continued to be occupied to the late 1st millennium BC. Within this long settlement history, two periods may be singled out, the third quarter of the 3rd millennium and the early 2nd millennium, when kings of Mari played significant roles in the political affairs of MESOPOTAMIA. André PARROT's work at Mari, begun in the 1930s and continued by a later generation of French archaeologists, has revealed major temple and palace complexes and also major archives belonging to these two periods. The most important of these is the palace of Zimri-Lim (1782–1759 BC), composed of 300 rooms over a 2.5 ha area and containing extremely rich archives informative of many aspects of the early 18th century BC (OLD BABYLONIAN PERIOD) Mesopotamian world; this palace was famous for its size and splendour, and the king of UGARIT expressed a wish to visit it.

Marib   a site on the Wadi Dhana in northern Yemen, southwestern Arabia, associated with the Sabaean kingdom of the SOUTH ARABIAN civilization. Marib is widely known for the dam constructed there across the *wadi*, perhaps first built in the mid 1st millennium BC and used until the mid 1st millennium AD, when its final rupture had regional repercussions. The settlement at Marib forms a 15 ha mound, part of which is still occupied; the famous temple of Haram Bilqis (Awwam) lies on the opposite bank of the wadi. Explored by the Wendell Phillips group in the 1950s, Marib was more recently the object of a German investigation that greatly elucidated the environmental and hydrological aspects of the site.

Mariette, François Auguste Ferdinand   (1821–81)   a French Egyptologist. His main contribution to archaeology, besides an extensive programme of excavation (e.g. SAQQARA), was the founding of the Egyptian Antiquities Service and what was to become the CAIRO Museum.

Marinatos, Spyridon (1901–74)   a Greek archaeologist who, in 1939, first put forward the theory that the end of the MINOAN civilization in the Aegean could have been caused by the volcanic eruption of the island of THERA. His long career in archaeology culminated in the discovery of the buried Bronze Age city at AKROTIRI on Thera.

Maritsa culture   a late Neolithic culture of the eastern Balkans, characterized by the materials from Layer V at KARANOVO, approximately contemporaneous with VINČA C, between c.4000 and 3700 bc. Maritsa pottery reflects the general Balkan trend towards dark pottery, although a special characteristic of it is a tendency for the surface of the vessel to be covered by either incised (narrow) or excised (wide) lines, which are filled with white paint applied after firing.

Mariupol   a Neolithic cemetery of the DNEPR-DONETS culture on the coast of the Sea of Azov in southern Ukraine. The burials at Mariupol were furnished with large numbers of flint tools, pendants and beads made of animal teeth, bone and shells, but no pottery. A number of beads of non-local stone were also found.

Markleeberg   a Lower Palaeolithic open-air site located on the Pleisse River near Leipzig, eastern Germany. Artifacts and faunal remains (e.g. *Mammuthus trogontherii*) are buried in riverine GRAVELS, probably deposited during the late Middle PLEISTOCENE. The artifacts include FLAKES, sidescrapers (see SCRAPER) and occasional HANDAXES.

Marnian   an Iron Age culture of northeastern France characterized by chariot burials, c.475–325 BC. See also ARRAS, LA GORGE-MEILLET, SOMME-BIONNE.

Maroni–Vournes   the site of a major Late CYPRIOT settlement in southern Cyprus, which is being excavated by Cadogan. The site was first occupied c.1600 BC. An impressive ASHLAR structure dates from the 13th century BC.

Maros point   see TOALIAN.

Marquis of Dai [Marquis of Tai]   see MAWANGDUI.

Marseilles (*Gk* Massalia)   a city on the coast of southern France, close to the mouth of the River Rhône, which was traditionally founded in either c.600 or 540 BC. as a colony of Phocaea in western Turkey. An earlier trading settlement may have been located further westwards at SAINT-BLAISE. Excavations have revealed remains of the Roman port, including a well-preserved merchant-ship, and the defences.

Martin's Hundred   the tract of land on the James River close to JAMESTOWN and Williamsburg, Virginia, USA, which was settled by English colonists in AD 1619. The centre of the plantation was Wolstenholme Towne. The settlement was attacked by Indians in 1622, and at least 58 settlers were killed. Excavations have revealed evidence for the massacre, as well as a detailed cross-section of early colonial life in North America. The area was later resettled as Carter's Grove plantation in the 1700s.

Marxist archaeology   the use of principles drawn from Marxist political theory to understand past societies. Social organization and change are explained in terms of conflicts between segments of society, such as those based on class, sex or age. Because of its emphasis on the importance of the economy in determining the particular form of a society, Marxism has proven to be a popular and robust source of archaeological inference, even in non-communist countries. Since Marxist archaeology does not consider other explanations, it is often criticized as being unscientific, especially by PROCESSUAL ARCHAEOLOGISTS, although in fact many of their own assumptions about society are similar to those made by Marxists. Marxist archaeology's EVOLUTIONARY basis has been criticized by POSTPROCESSUAL ARCHAEOLOGY, although the latter remains very sympathetic to the Marxist notion that an understanding of who has power and how that power is exercised is a vital element in explaining social change. See CHILDE.

Masada a Palestinian site, excavated chiefly by YADIN in 1963–65. A fortress-palace complex built by Herod the Great (37–4 BC), Masada was used as a stronghold by the zealots of the Jewish revolt of AD 66–73 and was the scene of their last stand against the Romans, who subsequently garrisoned the fortress.

Mas d'Azil see LE MAS D'AZIL.

Maspero, Gaston Camille Charles (1846–1916) a French Egyptologist, MARIETTE's successor as Director of the Egyptian Antiquities Service.

massebah a standing stone (or group of stones) similar in form to a DOLMEN, but erected in the Levant. It seems to have possessed a cultic purpose (e.g. in CANAANITE contexts as at GEZER and HAZOR) or, when set up by the ISRAELITES, to have commemorated a particular event.

mastaba (*Arabic* 'bench') a superstructure of Egyptian tombs, chiefly of the ARCHAIC PERIOD and OLD KINGDOM, including the royal tombs of the 1st and 2nd DYNASTY. It was a low, rectangular building with a flat roof and vertical or inward-inclined walls, that enclosed the shaft to the subterranean burial chamber. Early MUD-BRICK mastabas were replaced by more elaborate stone structures, often with numerous internal rooms.

mastodon a group of large mammals related to elephants. The most celebrated species, the American mastodon *Mammut americanum*, was utilized by PALAEOINDIANS before becoming extinct about 10 000 BP. Resembling a stocky and slightly elongated elephant, it had a hairy coat and shorter, straighter tusks than its contemporary the MAMMOTH. The word mastodon means 'breast-tooth', and refers to the large hemispherical cusps, about eight in number, that form the crushing surface of each molar. The mastodon subsisted on spruce and pine forests.

mastos a breast-shaped drinking-cup, usually fitted with one horizontal and one vertical handle. BLACK-GLOSSED and figure-decorated Athenian examples have been found.

Maszycka Cave a prehistoric cave-site located on the Prądnik River near Kraków in southern Poland. Artifacts and faunal remains (e.g. woolly MAMMOTH, reindeer) are buried in LOESS deposits. The main cultural layer contains an Upper Palaeolithic assemblage (e.g. RETOUCHED BLADES, endscrapers (see SCRAPER), and bone points) assigned to the MAGDALENIAN and dated by RADIOCARBON to *c.*17 500–16 500 BP. It is associated with human skeletal remains of at least 16 individuals. The uppermost layer contains Neolithic remains.

MAT see MOUSTERIAN OF ACHEULIAN TRADITION.

mataa   a large-stemmed OBSIDIAN FLAKE used hafted as a dagger or spearhead on EASTER ISLAND, and associated with the period of internal conflict of the 18th and 19th centuries AD.

0   3 cm

mataa

Matacapan   a site in the region of the Tuxtla Mountains of the southern Gulf Coast of Mexico, whose sequence begins in the Early PRECLASSIC. The site is best known for its Early CLASSIC settlement, when it was under the influence of TEOTIHUACÁN. Matacapan contains a Teotihuacán *barrio*, or neighbourhood, in the Central Mexican architectural style. Like KAMINALJUYÚ, Matacapan played an important role in Teotihuacán's trade network.

A University of New Mexico-Universidad de Veracrúz archaeological project, begun in the 1980s, has conducted extensive research at the site. This study has incorporated a number of ETHNOARCHAEOLOGICAL projects to address issues of subsistence and ceramic production.

Mataram   the name of the state which dominated central and east Java during the 8th–10th centuries AD. Major sites include the STUPA of BOROBUDUR, the temple complex of DIENG, and numerous CANDI (funerary temples), the most prominent being the PRAMBANAN complex.

Matenbek   a limestone shelter near MATENKUPKUM, in the BISMARCK ARCHIPELAGO, Melanesia, with two episodes of occupation. The earlier occurred about 19 000 bp, while the later began about 8000 bp. The occurrence of *phalanger* (possum) throughout the sequence suggests a PLEISTOCENE human introduction of this species to New Ireland. OBSIDIAN from TALASEA also appears in the basal deposits.

Matenkupkum   a cave in an uplifted coral terrace on New Ireland, BISMARCK ARCHIPELAGO, Melanesia, excavated by Chris Gosden. At *c*.32 000 bp, the site has the earliest evidence for use of marine resources in SAHUL. The stone assemblage comprises mainly UN-RETOUCHED FLAKES from pebbles; OBSIDIAN from TALASEA first appears *c*.12 000 bp. See also KOOLAN 2, MANDU MANDU CREEK.

material culture   the physical remains of humanly made traces of past societies, which constitute the major source of evidence for ARCHAEOLOGY.

mathematics see VIGESIMAL MATHEMATICS.

Matola a coastal SHELL MIDDEN site near Maputo in southern Mozambique, whose pottery is used to define the Matola unit of the first Iron Age farmers in eastern southern Africa. Matola sites date from the 3rd–5th centuries AD and the pottery is similar to KWALE ware from East Africa, which suggests a rapid southwards spread of Iron Age farmers down the East African coast at the beginning of the 1st millennium AD.

Matopo formerly **Southern Rhodesian Wilton** a MICROLITHIC LATER STONE AGE industry from the Matobo Hills in southwestern Zimbabwe, dated to the last 8000 years and also known as the KHAMI Industry.

matrix 1. grains in SEDIMENTS or rocks that collectively are relatively finer than the coarsest material in the sediment or rock. Matrix is the material within which cultural debris, a fossil or any item of note is contained or embedded.
2. the main metal constituent in an alloy.

Matt-painted pottery Middle HELLADIC pottery which has simple decoration in a manganese-based purple-black paint on a pale ground. Although quite common, Matt-painted pottery has a more restricted distribution than MINYAN.

Matupi a cave in northeastern Zaire, with a long sequence of MICROLITHIC LATER STONE AGE collections dating from more than 40 000–3000 BP, representing one of the earliest such occurrences in sub-Saharan Africa. The levels dating to 21 000–12 000 BP contain unusual decorated BORED STONES and drills used in their manufacture.

Mauer jaw or **Heidelberg jaw** a large broken human mandible with small teeth and a receding chin, recovered in 1907 by workmen in a sandpit at Mauer, south Germany, in association with elephant and rhinoceros bones but no artifacts. The jaw has been attributed to an adult male HOMO *erectus* or PRE-NEANDERTHALER, and dated either to the MINDEL GLACIATION, or the GÜNZ–Mindel INTERGLACIAL.

Mauna Kea a basalt ADZE quarry complex on Hawaii, located at an altitude of 3350–3780 m above sea level and extending over about 2000 ha. It comprises a series of extraction areas and workshops with religious shrines and habitation sites. It has been the subject of detailed field research and experimental replication by Patrick McCoy.

Maungaroa Valley a valley on Raratonga, Southern Cook Islands, that like the OPUNOHU VALLEY, has a well-preserved example of POLYNESIAN settlement pattern, and has been surveyed in detail by Peter Bellwood. The MARAE and paved house-platforms were clustered into four settlements, dating between about AD 1600 and 1823.

Maupiti burial ground a site on an islet in the lagoon on Maupiti, Society Islands, POLYNESIA, which yielded 16 flexed and extended burials dating to AD 800–1200. Grave-goods included pearl-shell FISH-HOOKS, ADZES and ornaments of Early Eastern Polynesian type, all paralleled closely at HANE in the Marquesas.

Mauriwi a name attributed in the 19th and early 20th centuries to the earliest inhabitants of NEW ZEALAND, thought to have been conquered by the later MAORI. The 'Mauriwi myth' has now been discredited. They were sometimes confused with the MORIORI of the Chatham Islands.

Mawangdui [Ma-wang-tui] the location near Changsha City,

China, of two Early HAN-dynasty tombs constructed with features of both SHAFT TOMBS and MOUNDED TOMBS. The eastern tomb had a mound 50 m in diameter and 20 m high; underneath was a rectangular shaft with a northern approach ramp leading into the large WOODEN CHAMBER 16 m underground. The last of three nested LACQUER coffins with painted designs contained a female corpse that was so well preserved that an autopsy was carried out on it, resulting in the discovery of tubercular nodules in the left lung. The deceased was identified through inscriptions on the grave-goods as the wife of one of the three generations of men bearing the title of Marquis of Dai. Among the sumptuous grave-goods were three rare musical instruments and an important painting on silk.

Maxton an 11th century AD Early Iron Age site in central Zimbabwe, which has given its name to a late phase of the period. Maxton sites are frequently on hilltops and are associated with stone walling.

Maya one of the high cultures of MESOAMERICA, and one of its major CLASSIC civilizations from about AD 200 to 850. The Maya practised SWIDDEN AGRICULTURE, as well as intensive agriculture, terracing and raised fields, growing maize and other crops, as well as arboriculture, especially of *ramon nuts* (see CHULTUN). Maya culture is well known for its CEREMONIAL CENTRES, STELAE and accomplishments in HIEROGLYPHIC writing (see GLYPH), CALENDRIC SYSTEMS and MATHEMATICS. The term Maya also refers to a culture area, and is typically divided into the lowland and highland Maya. The descendants of the Maya still occupy the region.

POLYCHROME POTTERY is a hallmark of Maya Lowland Classic culture. Maya society supported craftsmen skilled in creating luxury goods as well as monumental buildings. Maya society had an aristocracy, full-time specialists, a government in which religion and ritual played a critical role, and a peasant population to support the elites.

Maya ceremonial centres were associated in some fashion; major centres were linked to minor, as well as to the surrounding rural populations. Probably, major centres were also grouped into larger POLITIES. Kinship played an important role in elite-ranked activities, including political power. The internal organization at different centres implies variable levels of political organization. The ceremonial centres were constructed and supported by the outlying population of farmers. Religion was a central part of Classic Maya culture, but POSTCLASSIC Maya centres appear to have a more secular focus.

Many of the southern Lowland Maya cities collapsed between AD 800 and 850, probably due to a combination of factors including soil depletion through intensive cultivation, and the inadequate management of urban, military and subsistence issues. However, during the period of collapse in the southern Lowlands, centres in the northern Lowlands began to grow (AD 800–1000). The South's decline may have played a role in the North's prosperity, but the subsequent decline of the latter is not yet well understood.

Mayapán a Late POSTCLASSIC MAYA centre in west-central Yucatán, Mexico, with a wall eight kilometres long and up to two metres high encircling the city. Within these walls, in an area of approximately four square kilometres, 3600 mostly residential structures have been mapped. Population estimates range from 6000 to 15 000, but are generally given as 10 000 at its peak. Mayapán is in a relatively infertile part of the Yucatán, and the site was supported through tribute from neighbouring areas. Nobles from these regions were held as hostages at Mayapán to ensure their families and towns would pay the tribute.

Although built over an earlier city, Mayapán held most of northern Yucatán under its control from the time of its founding by the Cocoms lineage (AD 1200 or 1250) until it was sacked c.AD 1400 during a local uprising led by the rival Tutul Xiu family.

Characteristic of Mayapán is the large number of elaborate residences and their close proximity to the main ceremonial structures. The relative lack of religious structures has been explained in terms of the construction of Mayapán at a relatively late date; the prominence of religion in Maya culture had given way to the importance of secular and militaristic issues. The first archaeological investigations at the site were sponsored by the Carnegie Institution of Washington in the 1950s.

Mayor Island   the most important source of OBSIDIAN in NEW ZEALAND in the Bay of Plenty, North Island. Mayor Island obsidian was exchanged throughout New Zealand and may have been the first source to be found and used by the original settlers.

Maysar or **Samad**   a district of the Omani piedmont in southeastern Arabia, where German work focused on excavating an UMM AN-NAR period settlement that contained abundant information on Bronze Age COPPER SMELTING, the chief product for which ancient Magan was known (see PERSIAN GULF TRADE). Other work in the district also provides evidence for Bronze Age agricultural production and burial patterns, as well as Iron Age settlements, fortifications and burials.

McBurney, Charles Brian Montagu   (1914–79) a British prehistorian, best known for his excavations, at the HAUA FTEAH cave in north Africa and at LA COTTE DE ST BRELADE, Jersey.

Meadowcroft Rockshelter   a stratified rockshelter in Pennsylvania, USA, that spans the PALAEOINDIAN, ARCHAIC, Late prehistoric and historic periods, and has revealed a vast array of artifactual, botanical and faunal data. The early dates for the initial occupation of the site have generated much controversy. The lowest level, stratum I, has only charcoal and some RADIOCARBON dates that pre-date 32 000 bp. The overlying level, IIa, which lasts into the Archaic, does contain stone artifacts and radiocarbon dates that might take cultural occupation back to 19 000 bp or earlier. Recent summaries of the available radiocarbon dates by the site's principal excavator, James Adovasio, conservatively place early occupation of the site at c.14 500 BP and possibly as early as c.16 700 BP.

me'ae   ceremonial structures in the southern Marquesas Islands, POLYNESIA. They comprise complex and irregular groups of terraces with platforms (PA'EPA'E) for priests' houses. There are two types: *mortuary me'ae* were built in secluded places and had stone-lined pits for burials; *public me'ae* were associated with TOHUA.

Mechta Afalou   a robust type of modern human associated with the IBEROMAURUSIAN in the Maghreb and contemporaneous BLADELET industries in the Nile Valley. Mechtoid-related forms are restricted to the western and central Sahara during the last 10 000 years.

Mechta-el-Arbi   one of the most important Upper CAPSIAN sites located west of Tebessa in Algeria. It contained the remains of a number of humans of MECHTA AFALOU type.

Medes   an Indo-European speaking people, related to Persians, who moved southward through the Zagros from a still undetermined region (perhaps in Central Asia) during the Iron Age. The Persians eventually settled in Fars in southwestern Iran, while the Medes were present in the region of Hamadan in western Iran by the 9th century BC. The disparate Median groups were unified into a kingdom by Cyaxares in the late 7th century, when an alliance between the Medes, the SCYTHIANS and the newly resurgent BABYLONIAN kingdom attacked and overthrew the NEO-ASSYRIAN empire (between 614 and 612 BC). In the mid 6th century BC, the Persian king CYRUS overran the Medes.

medicine wheel   a type of site located in the northwestern portion of the North American Plains, which comprises stone alignments in the form of radiating spokes, often with central and peripheral CAIRNS. Although their exact purpose is unclear, medicine wheels may have functioned as memorials to important people, played a role in vision quests and other ceremonies, served as boundary or navigation markers, or served as calendars for the observation of the summer solstices and other celestial events. Some medicine wheels may be as old as 5500 BP.

Medinet Habu   part of the site of THEBES (EGYPT)-WEST BANK. The most substantial monument at Medinet Habu is the relatively well-preserved MORTUARY TEMPLE of RAMESSES III, the scenes on whose walls include representations of that king's campaigns against the SEA PEOPLES. Medinet Habu eventually became the most important administrative centre in the Theban area.

megafauna   large-bodied animals like the bison, MAMMOTH, MASTODON and camel, many of which disappeared during the PLEISTOCENE EXTINCTIONS, and which served as major food sources for late Pleistocene hunters.

In *Australia*, there were several species of giant marsupial, among them DIPROTODON, the macropods PROTEMNODON and *Sthenurus*, a flightless bird *Genyornis* and the predator *Thylacoleo*, which became extinct during the Late Pleistocene. The timing of extinctions seems to have varied throughout the continent, with LIME SPRINGS suggesting late survival in better-watered areas, while at Tandou in arid western New South Wales extinctions were complete by 27 000 bp. Any relationship between humans and megafauna has proved difficult to demonstrate, although it is now clear that some species survived well into the period of human occupation of Australia; no KILL SITES are known. See LANCEFIELD.

megalith (*Gk* megas 'large', lithos 'stone')   a large stone. Compare MICROLITH. The term is sometimes used to refer to a MEGALITHIC MONUMENT.

megalithic art   Neolithic engravings found on the megalithic stones of CHAMBERED TOMBS and MENHIRS. The motifs include representational elements such as axes, oxen and human breasts, as well as abstract designs such as spirals, concentric circles, zigzags and triangles. Megalithic art is particularly associated with PASSAGE GRAVES, GAVRINIS in Brittany and KNOWTH and NEWGRANGE in Ireland being among the most notable examples.

MEGALITHIC CULTURE

megalithic culture (*India*)   an Iron Age culture of southern India where the burials present a heterogeneous phenomenon that is nonetheless grouped together under the terms 'megaliths' and 'megalithic culture'. The grave forms include several kinds of urn burials and various forms of CIST, pit and rock-cut graves; stone ALIGNMENTS are also associated with the Iron Age. The disposition of bodies is equally variable: simple inhumation, secondary burial (both single and multiple), and occasionally cremation burial. These variations may correspond to caste differences, as also described in early Tamil writings and found in contemporary practice. Despite their heterogeneous forms, the graves generally contain a BURNISHED black-and-red ware (also found in settlements) and a fairly uniform series of iron tools, weapons, horse equipment and other household equipment. This funerary complex appears to have developed by the beginning of the 1st millennium BC (and perhaps somewhat earlier) and to have endured into the early 1st millennium AD.

megalithic monument   a construction made of large stones. The term is commonly applied to any CHAMBERED TOMB, even if built with small stones. Megalithic monuments are particularly numerous and most thoroughly studied in the Neolithic and Bronze Age of west and northwest *Europe*. See ALIGNMENT, ALLÉE COUVERTE, CROMLECH, DOLMEN, HUNEBED, MENHIR, PASSAGE GRAVE, STONE CIRCLE.

In *West Africa*, on the other hand, the dates of megalithic monuments are uncertain. Upright standing stones have been found in two areas: the largest number are in the Casamance region of eastern Senegal, and consist of circles of laterite blocks, some over 3 m long, used as funerary monuments (see TIEKENE-BOUSSOURA). Megalithic monuments are also found at Tondidiaro in the central delta of the Niger River floodplain in Mali.

In the *Far East*, the term is used in relation to DOLMENS (mostly of the 1st millenium BC) and the later MOUNDED TOMBS.

In *Southeast Asia*, megalithic monuments likewise date to the last millennium BC and later, and include 'menhirs' and 'dolmens' analogous to those of Europe, stone pavements and terraces, large carved stones, stone slab or CIST graves and stone SARCOPHAGI. Apart from the stone burial vats of XIANG KHOUANG in Laos, most large stone remains are found on the Malay peninsula and in the islands, and they appear to be related to burials or ancestor cults. Some (including those of PASEMAH in Sumatra, the BERNAM-SUNGKAI area of the peninsula, and Pasir Angin on Java) date to the last four centuries BC, others (the slab graves of Kidangan, Besuki, Gunung Kidul, and Kuningen on Java) probably date to the 1st millennium AD, and yet others (Tlaga Mukmin and other sites in Sumatra, the Niah pavements, and stones of the peninsula and Sarawak) are more recent still.

In the *Pacific*, megalithic structures are found in parts of POLYNESIA and include ANTHROPOMORPHOUS statues (MOAI) and religious structures (MARAE). See EASTER ISLAND, HA'AMONGA-A-MAUI, PUAMAU VALLEY, TAIPIVAI VALLEY, TAPUTAPUATEA.

Migration theories based on megalithic remains are now discounted in southeast Asia as they are in Europe. It is now accepted that the practice of erecting such monuments arose independently in many different times and places, and for a wide variety of purposes.

megalithic yard   a unit of measurement corresponding to 2.72 feet

(0.829 m) considered by some to underlie the layout of STONE CIRCLES and ALIGNMENTS in Britain and Brittany.

Megaloceros a group of large PLEISTOCENE deer, also known as the 'giant deer'. The best-known species, *M. giganteus*, has been erroneously termed the 'Irish elk'. Although abundant in Ireland, it also occurred widely across Europe and western Asia. Standing up to 1.8 m at the shoulder, the males carried huge palmated antlers spanning up to 3 m. Its remains are occasionally found in Palaeolithic assemblages, and there are rare depictions in CAVE ART (see COUGNAC). It became extinct *c*.10 500 BP.

Megarian bowl a type of handleless Greek drinking-cup made in moulds. The bowls tend to be decorated in relief, for example with scenes of Dionysos or acting, and finished in the BLACK-GLOSSED technique. They were in widespread use in the HELLENISTIC period from the 3rd century BC, and they merge into the red-glossed ARRETINE WARES. The type was first recognized at Megara, although they were produced in other centres such as ATHENS and CORINTH.

megaron a rectangular or APSIDAL-ended structure in Aegean architecture, usually entered through a shallow porch at one end.

Megiddo a Palestinian TELL on a natural hill, the subject of large-scale excavations by Chicago University in 1925–39. First occupied during the late Neolithic, Megiddo was a well-defended town of the EARLY to MIDDLE BRONZE AGE, wealthy even after its capture by TUTHMOSIS III, as shown by the important series of IVORIES recovered from the site. In the Iron Age Megiddo was strongly fortified by ISRAELITES during the early 9th century BC, when a casement wall and gateway, large stables (or storehouses) and an elaborate water-system were constructed.

0 1 2 3 cm

Megiddo Ivory.

Mehrgahr an important site in the Kachi plain of Baluchistan in western Pakistan occupied from some time before 6000 BC until the beginnings of the Mature HARAPPAN in the 3rd millennium BC. The excavations of J-F. Jarrige have revealed ACERAMIC NEOLITHIC occupations in which occur MUD-BRICK domestic architecture and a massive funerary platform. This community cultivated wheats, barley and other plants, some of which were in transitional stages of domestication; the animals initially are mostly wild, but by the end of the aceramic occupation are almost all domesticated sheep, goat and cattle, and seem to have been domesticated locally. The later phases of occupation provide important evidence of social differentiation and craft specialization in this region, contributing to the early 3rd millennium milieu in which the Harappan civilization was formed.

Meidum   the site of the remains of the first true Egyptian PYRAMID, probably started by King Huni of the 3rd DYNASTY, but completed by his successor SNEFRU. Associated with the Pyramid are MASTABAS of the early 4th Dynasty.

Meiendorf   see HAMBURGIAN.

Meir   the site of an important series of rock-cut tombs of the local NOMARCHS of the late OLD-MIDDLE KINGDOM in Egypt. The relief decoration of these tombs was recorded by Blackman in five seasons between the years 1912 and 1950.

Melanesia   the ethnographic and geographical region which comprises New Guinea, the BISMARCK ARCHIPELAGO, the Solomons, Vanuatu, New Caledonia and Fiji. New Guinea was occupied by 40 000 bp, when it was joined to Australia, and the Bismarcks and Solomons (KILU) seem to have been occupied by about 30 000 bp. There may have been an independent development of horticulture in the NEW GUINEA HIGHLANDS in the early HOLOCENE. Settlement of the rest of Melanesia seems to have occurred as part of the expansion of AUSTRONESIAN speakers into the Pacific.

Melka Kontoure   a site near Addis Ababa in Ethiopia particularly noted for its long stone artifact sequence, which dates from more than 1.5 million years ago. It includes OLDOWAN, ACHEULIAN, MIDDLE STONE AGE and MICROLITHIC LATER STONE AGE collections, as well as various HOMINID fragments.

Melkhoutboom   a cave in the eastern Cape Province of South Africa with LATER STONE AGE material spanning the last 15 000 years. Of particular interest is one of the largest and best-studied collections of well preserved plant remains dating to the last 7500 years, which indicates that plant foods formed an important component of the diets of HOLOCENE Later Stone Age people.

Melos   the principal source of the OBSIDIAN in the Cyclades, which was extensively used for chipped stone implements in the prehistoric Aegean. Although obsidian was being acquired from Melos as early as the 10th millennium BC, it would appear that the island was not inhabited on a permanent basis until the 4th millennium. In the Bronze Age the main settlement was at PHYLAKOPI. The CLASSICAL POLIS, devastated by ATHENS in 416 BC, centred on the fortified AKROPOLIS of Ancient Melos.

Meluhha   see PERSIAN GULF TRADE.

Memphis   the capital of Egypt in the ARCHAIC PERIOD and OLD KING-DOM, and thereafter one of the most important cities of the ancient Near East. Very little remains of the city of Memphis, although impressive mortuary/religious structures associated with the capital may be seen on the desert fringe to the west, from ABU ROASH to DAHSHUR, especially at GIZA and SAQQARA.

Menelaion, the   remains that appear to have been the principal MYCENAEAN site in Laconia, Greece. The two mansions, built in the 15th and 14th centuries BC, foreshadow the later palaces in their lay-out. In the 8th century BC the cult of Menelaus and Helen was established, and the remains of their CLASSICAL shrine dominate the site.

menhir (*Old Breton* men 'stone', hir 'long')   a single standing stone. Menhirs are especially characteristic of Britain and Brittany in the Neolithic and Early Bronze Age, though they are also known in more recent periods from other parts of the world, such as Ethiopia and Madagascar.

Menkaure or **Mycerinus** an Egyptian king of the 4th DYNASTY (during the OLD KINGDOM), and owner of the smallest of the three PYRAMIDS of the Old Kingdom at GIZA.

Merimde Beni Salama a site in the western Nile DELTA, Egypt, excavated by Junker in 1928–39. This settlement of small dwellings seems to have been occupied for about 600 years (probably *c.*4900–4300 BC), perhaps with a population as large as 16 000. The Merimde culture largely overlaps with FAIYUM 'A', and with the BADARIAN/AMRATIAN groups of UPPER EGYPT.

Meroe a site in UPPER NUBIA, the capital of a state of the early 3rd century BC to the early 4th century AD, until its conquest by AXUM. *Meroitic* civilization seems to have owed much to the preceding NAPATAN state in its use of ancient Egyptian models for its state architecture, including the royal PYRAMIDS and temples such as that at MUSAWWARAT ES-SUFRA. Meroe has mainly been excavated by GARSTANG in 1910–14, REISNER in 1922–25 and, since 1965, by Shinnie.

Mersin the location of the small but high tell-site of Yümük-Tepe, in coastal Cilicia, south-west Anatolia, that was excavated by J. GARSTANG, who defined 33 major levels. The bulk of this sequence represents Neolithic (levels XXXIII–XXIV) and CHALCOLITHIC (XXII–XII), which bear strong similarities to the 'AMUQ periods A–B and C–F respectively. This sequence contains Halaf ceramics (see HALAF TELL), perhaps locally produced, in levels XIX–XVII, and painted pottery of the 'UBAID style (levels XVI–XV). The architecture of the late Neolithic settlement (level XXIV; the earlier levels presented only traces of walling and floors) comprises large enclosures with many attached silos. During the Chalcolithic, the place was fortified (starting with level XVI), with complexes of rooms set against the walls on either side of a massive gateway. After a long break, occupation at the site resumed with MIDDLE BRONZE AGE to Iron Age settlements (levels XI–III), the last three of which contain ceramic evidence for contacts with the Aegean world (MYCENAEAN to late ARCHAIC Greek pottery). The final two occupations belong to the BYZANTINE and mediaeval periods.

Mesara the largest and most fertile plain on the island of Crete, which has been intensively exploited since the later Neolithic period. The MINOAN palace of PHAISTOS, and Gortyn, the capital of the Roman province of Crete and Cyrenaica, are the two principal archaeological sites.

Mesa Verde a large flat-topped mountain (or *mesa*) in southwestern Colorado, USA, that is the location of some of the most spectacular ANASAZI structures in the American Southwest. Mesa Verde is especially famous for its cliff-dwellings, which are large PUEBLO III multiroomed apartment dwellings built into large rock overhangs on the sides of cliffs. Most famous of these is CLIFF PALACE. The *mesa* was abandoned, along with the rest of the northern Southwest, about AD 1300. The archaeological remains of Mesa Verde were first brought to the attention of European Americans by Richard WETHERILL in 1888.

Mesoamerica a geographical area extending from central Honduras and northwestern Costa Rica north through Mexico to Tamaulipas and Sinaloa. The climate is mainly tropical, but is also dry in some areas; cultivation is primarily SWIDDEN AGRICULTURE, arboriculture, and in some areas by CHINAMPAS. Archaeologists identify a pan-Mesoamerican culture beginning with agricultural village life more than 4000 years ago. This culture became more elaborate through time, up to the beginning of the Christian Era. Culture subareas in Mesoamerica exhibit variations of commonly held traits rather than unique developments. Uto-Aztecan, Mayan, Otomian, Tarascan, Totonacan, Mixtecan, and Zapotecan are the major linguistic and cultural affiliations in Mesoamerica today.

mesocephalic   see CEPHALIC.

Mesolithic   the 'Middle STONE AGE', a period of transition in the early HOLOCENE between the Upper Palaeolithic HUNTER-GATHERER existence of the last GLACIATION and the development of farming and pottery production during the POST-GLACIAL NEOLITHIC. The Mesolithic was a response to changing climatic conditions following the retreat of the glacial ice at $c.8500$ BC. It was of relatively short duration in the Near East, where farming started about 7000 BC; in Britain it lasted until the arrival of Neolithic technology from the Continent during the 4th millennium. Mesolithic tool-kits reflect the need to adapt to the changing environment, and are characterized by the presence of MICROLITHS and stone axes or ADZES used in woodworking.

Mesopotamia (*Gk* '(the land) between the rivers')   the region of western Asia defined by the Euphrates and Tigris rivers together with their tributaries. Although both rivers have their headwaters in the mountain country to the north, these highlands are normally excluded from Mesopotamia proper. The latter is further divided into the northern piedmont and the southern ALLUVIAL zones, the former corresponding roughly to ASSYRIA and the Syrian middle Euphrates, and the latter to the historical designation BABYLONIA or SUMER and AKKAD. These two zones form the central focus of western Asian civilizations from the emergence of complex societies to the collapse of the Mesopotamian tradition at the end of the 1st millennium BC.

metal detector   a GEOPHYSICAL instrument used in ELECTROMAGNETIC SURVEYING to detect metal artifacts hidden by vegetation or shallowly buried in SEDIMENTS or SOIL. Sophisticated metal detectors can be programmed to detect only those artifacts above a certain depth, and to detect only those artifacts of a given alloy.

metallographic examination or **metallographic microscopy**   a method of analysing the manufacturing techniques of metal ARTIFACTS. A cross-sectional slice of a metal artifact is polished, etched to highlight internal structures, and examined under a metallurgical microscope. Reflected light from the microscope enhances uneven surfaces revealing grain size, shape and boundaries, inclusions, fabric, defects and other detail.

metallurgical analysis   the study of metal artifacts and waste products to determine their material source, manufacture techniques and technology, and uses. Analysis may involve METALLOGRAPHIC EXAMINATION and a variety of CHEMICAL ANALYSIS methods.

metallurgy   the art of working metals; it includes various techniques used to improve the practical and aesthetic qualities of metals, including ANNEALING, REPOUSSÉ, soldering, welding and the creation of alloys. See also LOST WAX.

Metaponto (*Lat.* Metapontum)   a Greek colony in southern Italy with HIPPODAMIAN PLANNING. Two temples in the DORIC ORDER may have been dedicated to Hera and Apollo Lycaeus. Recent field-surveys in its hinterland have revealed a pattern of small rural establishments. See LUCANIAN POTTERY.

metate   a flat, ground-stone slab, used as a plate for the grinding of vegetable material, in conjunction with the MANO. Like the mano, they have a variety of shapes and sizes, and have some utility in the construction of CULTURE HISTORY. This term is most often used in the American Southwest. See QUERN.

methodology   the assumptions and theories that determine the methods of archaeological investigation, and the procedures by which archaeological statements are tested.

metope   part of the ENTABLATURE of a building of the DORIC ORDER, placed between TRIGLYPHS. The 7th century BC temple of Apollo at Thermon had clay metopes decorated with mythological scenes and other motifs. However, later temples had metopes which were either plain or sculpted (see PARTHENON).

Metsamor   a site near Yerevan in Armenia at the edge of the Ararat plain, that contains both KURA-ARAXES and LATE BRONZE to Early Iron Age occupations. The latter settlement indicates the existence of pre-URARTIAN states in Transcaucasia. The city covered as much as 100 ha, and contained a fortified citadel and attached 'cultic' area, residential zones, and industrial areas (especially of metallurgical production). Two elite graves discovered within the city suggest burial of retainers with the principal interments (a practice reminiscent of other early states, such as the ROYAL CEMETERY at UR or those of SHANG China): one of the graves contained 50 people, mostly women, in addition to the two central bodies. Moreover, each of these graves contained an inscribed object (in Mesopotamian CUNEIFORM and Egyptian HIEROGLYPHIC), that not only provides chronological evidence (15th–14th centuries BC) but also implies long-distance contacts with the civilizations to the south (reflected also in the several MITANNI SEALS recovered from graves at Artik northwest of Yerevan).

Mezhirich   an Upper Palaeolithic open-air site located at the confluence of the Rosava and Ros' rivers (Dnepr tributary system) in Ukraine. The occupation horizon is buried in slope deposits overlying mixed ALLUVIUM/COLLUVIUM on the second TERRACE; RADIOCARBON dates range between 17 855–12 900 bp. Woolly MAMMOTH predominates among large mammalian remains; small vertebrates, including hare, rodents and birds, are also common. At least four MAMMOTH-BONE HOUSES, with associated pits, HEARTHS and debris concentrations, were uncovered. In addition to the stone artifacts, a large number of non-stone tools, ornaments and art objects were found, including painted mammoth bones. Mezhirich was discovered in 1965, and excavated by Pidoplichko and Shovkoplyas in 1966–74, and by Gladkih and Korniets in 1976–81.

Mezin,   an Upper Palaeolithic open-air site on the Desna River in Ukraine. The occupation horizon is buried in slope deposits overlying bedrock in a side-valley ravine; a recently reported AMS RADIOCARBON date of 15 100 bp supports earlier assignment (on the basis of artifacts and features) to the late Upper Palaeolithic. Woolly MAMMOTH predominates among the fauna, but horse, reindeer, wolf and arctic fox are also common. At least two MAMMOTH-BONE HOUSES, with associated pits, HEARTHS and debris concentrations, were uncovered. In addition to the stone artifacts, a number of non-stone tools, ornaments, art objects, and painted mammoth bones (musical instruments?) were found. Mezin was discovered and initially excavated by VOLKOV in 1908–16; subsequent investigation was conducted by Shovkoplyas in 1954–61 and others.

Miaodigou II [Miao-ti-kou]   a Middle Neolithic culture of China in the YANGSHAO tradition, chronologically falling between Yangshao and LONGSHAN of the central LOESS highlands at *c.*2800 BC. It is known for its painted pottery with spiral designs.

Michelsberg   a Middle Neolithic hilltop enclosure in Baden-Württemberg, Germany, type-site of the Michelsberg culture found in the Rhineland, Belgium and Eastern France in the period 4500–4000 BC. Pottery forms include pointed- and round-based vessels with flaring rim, and flat pottery discs known as *plats à pain* which probably served as lids.

Micoquian   1. (*morphology*) a pointed-*pyriform* (pear-shaped) or *lanceolate* (tapering) BIFACE with a well-made tip.
2. a final ACHEULIAN phase occurring on the Lower-Middle Palaeolithic borderline and contemporary with or just slightly older than the biface MOUSTERIAN. Although originally defined by Hauser in 1916 on the basis of the assemblages from the French site of *La Micoque*, near LES EYZIES, most Micoquian sites are found in Central Europe (e.g. KŮLNA CAVE, KRAKÓW-ZWIERZYNIEC, MUSELIEVO) and some occur in European areas of the former USSR (e.g. KIIK-KOBA, STAROSEL'E).

microblade   a small stone BLADE, typically several centimetres in length, often produced from a conical or WEDGE-SHAPED MICROCORE. Microblades are found in Upper Palaeolithic industries of Eurasia (e.g. EASTERN GRAVETTIAN), but are especially common in the Upper Palaeolithic of Siberia (e.g. DYUKTAI CULTURE). They are also characteristic of Mesolithic and later industries in the circumpolar regions (e.g. ARCTIC SMALL TOOL TRADITION).

microburin tecnhique   a method of producing a MICROLITH by notching and snapping a BLADE. The waste product, which shows characteristic traces of the manufacturing process, is known as a *microburin*.

microfauna   small animals such as rodents or insectivores as compared with macrofauna.

microlith   a small Later Upper Palaeolithic or Mesolithic stone artifact varying in size from approximately 1 cm to 5 cm, and used as the tip of a bone or wooden implement or as an arrow-point. Microliths were either struck as BLADES from very small CORES, or were made from fractured blades using the MICROBURIN TECHNIQUE.

Micronesia   an ethnographic and geographical region comprising the Palau, Marianas, Caroline and Marshall Islands and Kiribati. The archaeology of the region is poorly understood, but Western Micronesia, comprising the Palau and Marianas, was settled within the last 4000 years. The islands of Eastern Micronesia are mainly atolls and were settled more recently. As in POLYNESIA, pottery production ceased in Eastern Micronesia soon after first settlement.

microwear   see USEWEAR ANALYSIS.

midden   a concentration of cultural debris. The term is sometimes used to include the material in which the debris is encapsulated, and modifications of this MATRIX, but can also be used solely for the debris concentration.

Middle Assyrian   a term denoting an important phase of the ASSYRIAN empire. In the LATE BRONZE AGE 'game of nations' expressed in the AMARNA archives, Assyria had long been dominated by the MITANNI state, but in the 14th century BC this relationship was reversed. Starting at the end of the 14th century a series of vigorous Assyrian kings expanded rapidly through northern MESOPOTAMIA and the mountainous region to the north, and briefly occupied BABYLONIA (in 1225, under Tukulia-Ninurta I, 1243–1207 BC). This empire then weakened considerably during a period of dynastic troubles but Tiglath-pileser I (1114–1076 BC) restored Assyrian dominion over largely the same regions (and reached the Mediterranean). As before, questions of succession weakened Assyria, as did severe nomadic disruptions throughout Mesopotamia (see ARAMAEANS, CHALDEANS).

Middle Awash   a river valley in northeastern Ethiopia, which has yielded sites containing a rich HOMINID fossil, archaeological, mammalian and environmental record, dating from the MIOCENE to the HOLOCENE. Of particular interest are the finds of AUSTRALOPITHECINE fossils of the period between about 3.5 and 2.5 million years ago, which are generally attributed to *Australopithecus afarensis* (see HADAR, 'LUCY'), as well as some of the oldest-known stone artifacts in the world. These are of the FLAKED cobble technology of the OLDOWAN Complex and date to between 3 and 2.5 million years ago.

Middle Bronze Age   a period in the Levant associated with the sophisticated urban civilization of the CANAANITES. The period is conventionally divided into two phases, MBA I (*c.*1950–1800 BC) and MBA II (*c.*1800–1550 BC).

Middle Horizon   (AD 600–1000) the period in Andean South America during which the first large-scale imperial expansions took place, politically uniting portions of the central Andean region. In central Peru, the site of HUARI came to control the highlands and possibly the coast. In Bolivia, the site of TIAHUANACO expanded its control over the altiplano, and adjacent regions in Bolivia, extreme southern Peru and northern Chile. These empires pertain to the first half of the Middle Horizon. The second half was a period of political and economic collapse.

Middle Kingdom   a period of Egyptian history comprising the 11th to the 13th DYNASTY (*c.*2023–1633 BC).

Middle Missouri Tradition   see PLAINS VILLAGE INDIAN.

middle-range theory   a set of theories that allow the construction of accurate statements of past behaviour based on the analysis of the contemporary archaeological record. Middle-range theory is considered by some archaeologists to be the essential key to a scientific understanding of the archaeological record. See BRIDGING ARGUMENT, PROCESSUAL ARCHAEOLOGY.

Middle Stone Age   the second stage of STONE AGE technology in sub-Saharan Africa, dating from *c.*150 000 to 30 000 years ago, and roughly equivalent to the Middle Palaeolithic found elsewhere in the Old World. Middle Stone Age assemblages lack HANDAXES and CLEAVERS, and are characterized by FLAKES typically produced by preparing the CORE from which the flake was to be struck. The flakes vary in size and shape, some being triangular and others long, elongated forms termed 'flake-BLADES.' A few were RETOUCHED into DENTICULATES, points and SCRAPERS, or even BIFACIAL points. Some Middle Stone Age assemblages contain tiny blades and BACKED MICROLITHS (see EPI-PIETERSBURG, HOWIESONS POORT). Middle Stone Age assemblages in southern Africa are associated with anatomically modern HOMO *sapiens* (see BORDER CAVE, KLASIES RIVER MOUTH, PIETERSBURG).

Midea see DENDRA.

Midland **1.** a PALAEOINDIAN point type that is essentially an unfluted FOLSOM point.

2. a PALAEOINDIAN COMPLEX found in the North American Plains that is very similar to Folsom, the major difference being in the point type. The two complexes are roughly contemporaneous, although at some sites they are vertically separated, with either being found above the other. The relationship between the two complexes is unclear, some archaeologists seeing the point type simply as a variant of Folsom. The type-site for the complex is the Scharbauer site, near Midland, Texas. The Midland Complex is best represented at the HELL GAP site. The Midland COMPONENT at this site contained possible evidence for structures, indicated by circular patterns of POST-HOLES.

3. From the Scharbauer site was recovered the skeleton (Midland 'Man') of a young woman, one of the earliest acceptable human remains on the North American continent. It dates to over 10 000 BP.

midwestern taxonomic system a hierarchical TAXONOMY devised by William McKern in 1939 and intended to unify archaeological classification in North America. The taxa have no temporal implications. The focus is a complex of TRAITS found in a number of sites. It is the elemental taxon and is implicitly similar to the ethnographic TRIBE. An ASPECT comprises similar foci in a larger region, and a PHASE is defined as a grouping of similar aspects. Other hierarchically larger taxa include the pattern and the base.

Mikhajlovka a stratified ENEOLITHIC settlement in the lower Dnepr valley of Ukraine, which has yielded important data on subsistence, including faunal remains of sheep, goat and cattle, along with horses. Three main settlement horizons occur at Mikhajlovka. The first is an occupation of the CUCUTENI-TRIPOLYE culture, the second an occupation of the SREDNI STOG culture, and the final occupation is of the CATACOMB GRAVE culture.

Mikulčice a focal urban settlement of Greater Moravia, the earliest SLAVIC state-level POLITY in east-central Europe just prior to AD 900. The core of Mikulčice was a stronghold with five APSIDAL churches and a princely residence. Around this fortified area were suburbs with houses and workshops of craftsmen. Greater Moravia fell in AD 907.

Milavče a Middle Bronze Age site in southeastern Bohemia, the type-site of the Milavče group (related to KNOVIZ), which used a TUMULUS burial rite but which shifted from inhumation burial to cremation. Most of the cremations are urnless, but in one richly furnished grave, the ashes were contained in a wheeled bronze cauldron, about 30 cm in diameter.

Miletus   a Greek city at the southern mouth of the Meander valley in Turkey, built on a narrow spit of land. The city was destroyed by the PERSIANS in 494 BC and the new layout reflects HIPPODAMIAN PLANNING. Excavations have revealed administrative buildings (BOULEUTERION, PRYTANEION) as well as the theatre. The harbour mouth was guarded by statues of lions. Its extramural sanctuary was located at DIDYMA. See EAST GREEK POTTERY, FIKELLURA WARE.

millefiori   a type of multi-coloured glass, literally meaning 'a thousand flowers'. The effect is created by fusing together slices from cores of different coloured glass giving a MOSAIC effect.

milpa agriculture   the cultivation of maize fields, often for only a few years, by SWIDDEN AGRICULTURE. *Milpa* is a Spanish corruption of an AZTEC term meaning 'in the fields.'

Mimbres   a regional variant of the MOGOLLON culture, centred in south-central New Mexico, USA. It is most famous for its magnificent CERAMIC tradition, composed of animal and human figures drawn on black-on-white vessels. The rise of Mimbres may have been partly due to the development of a CHACO–Mexican trade, with Mimbres serving as trading middle-men.

Mimi figures   thin, stick-like human figures which are a feature of ARNHEM LAND ROCK ART in northern Australia. They are earlier than X-RAY ART and are disclaimed by contemporary Aboriginal people, who attribute them to *Mimi* spirits.

mina   a unit of Greek weight, the equivalent of the Near Eastern *manah*. It was formed by 100 DRACHMAS, which on the standard at ATHENS weighed 431 g, or on AEGINA 630 g. It has been recognized that items of silver plate could be made to weigh 1 mina: for example, the GOLD-FIGURED PHIALE from DUVANLI.

Mina Perdida   a ceremonial PLATFORM MOUND site located in the Lurín Valley on the central coast of Peru, dating to the early part of the INITIAL PERIOD. Like the contemporaneous HUACA LA FLORIDA, it was probably used for only a few centuries and then abandoned.

Minatogawa   a Late Palaeolithic site in Okinawa Prefecture, Japan, consisting of a limestone fissure in which skeletal remains dating to *c.*16–18 000 bp have been found.

Mindel Glaciation   the second Alpine PLEISTOCENE GLACIAL advance which ended with the onset of the HOLSTEINIAN INTERGLACIAL. See ELSTERIAN.

Ming tombs   the burial sites of the Ming emperors (see CHINESE DYNASTIES) near modern Beijing, one being now open as a site museum. The SPIRIT PATH leading to the tombs includes animal sculptures and bureaucrats in classical pose, nearly double life-size.

Minoan   a term devised by Arthur EVANS for the Bronze Age civilization of Crete – from Minos, legendary ruler of KNOSSOS. On the basis of his excavations, Evans divided the period into three chronological phases, Early (*c.*3000–2000 BC); Middle (*c.*2000–1550 BC); and Late (*c.*1550–1050 BC). He then subdivided these so that each phase has three divisions designated by Roman numerals. The alternative system, proposed by Platon, takes more account of major architectural developments: PREPALATIAL (Early Minoan I–III), PROTOPALATIAL (Middle Minoan I–II), NEOPALATIAL (Middle Minoan III–Late Minoan IIIA1) and POSTPALATIAL (Late Minoan IIIA2–IIIC).

Minshat Abu Omar   a site in the northeastern Nile DELTA, Egypt, which has been investigated by a team from Munich Museum since 1977. Archaeologically, the most important part of this site is the cemetery dating to the PREDYNASTIC/ARCHAIC PERIOD transition, a period which is relatively poorly attested in the Delta. Among the objects found in these graves (which include CERAMIC and stone vessels, slate palettes, jewellery, and COPPER tools) are imports from Palestine and UPPER EGYPT.

Minyan the term which SCHLIEMANN devised for the distinctive Middle HELLADIC pottery which he found during his excavations at ORCHOMENOS, whose legendary ruler was King Minyas. Grey Minyan is particularly common, whereas Yellow Minyan has a more restricted distribution.

Miocene the epoch preceding the PLIOCENE and dating between about 25 and 5 million years ago.

Miriwun a rockshelter on the Ord River, Kimberley, Western Australia, now submerged by Lake Argyle, that was first occupied *c*.18 000 bp. Like many Australian sites, it has strong continuity in economy throughout the sequence, with a wide range of aquatic and terrestrial species represented. Small tools occur in the upper levels from about 3000 bp, while larger notched and DENTICULATED FLAKES and ADZES characterize the lower levels.

Mississippian a series of related COMPLEXES located in the southeastern part of North America (especially along that section of the Mississippi and its tributaries south of St Louis), from approximately AD 800 to the Historic Period. Mississippian influence was also found outside this 'core-area'. The precise nature of the Mississippian is still debated, some archaeologists defining it by the presence of particular types of MOUNDS or pottery of particular styles and/or TEMPER. There is an increased dependence in the Mississippian on the growing of maize, beans and squash, which supplemented hunting-and-gathering, and there is evidence for greater redistribution of resources and centralized political control. See CAHOKIA, SOUTHERN CULT.

Mitanni the most important of the 2nd millennium BC HURRIAN kingdoms with INDO-EUROPEAN elements in elite circles. Mitanni was a player in the game of international power politics in the LATE BRONZE AGE. Of roughly equal status to the HITTITES and Egyptians, Mitanni initially dominated ASSYRIA, and controlled most of northern MESOPOTAMIA and Syria during the 16th and 15th centuries BC. During the 14th century, Assyria rose to prominence, destroying Mitanni in the process.

Mitathal a prehistoric site west of Delhi in Haryana in northern India, excavated by S. Bhan in 1968. It consists of a double mound with two periods of occupation whose CERAMIC and architectural traditions show a continuous development. The earlier period (Mitathal I) contains pottery similar to that belonging to the Early HARAPPAN settlement at KALIBANGAN. In the later period (Mitathal IIA–B), this pottery continues, but with strong Mature Harappan additions, which are also evident in the town layout and other artifacts. These cultural developments indicate that this part of northern India was involved in the milieu from which developed the Harappan civilization, but with a regional flavour.

Mithraeum a Roman temple, often in the form of a BASILICA, to the Persian mystery god Mithras. The cult seems to have been particularly popular with soldiers. An example has been excavated at Walbrook in LONDON.

Mitla   a site in central Oaxaca, Mexico, with CERAMICS dating from MONTE ALBÁN I (900–300 BC), but without structural evidence until Monte Albán III A–V (AD 200–1521). The earlier structures on the site are ZAPOTEC, the later ones are MIXTEC or a Mixtec-Zapotec blend. Some structures were still occupied into the 16th century. Alfonso CASO and Daniel F. Rubín de la Borbolla conducted the first modern excavations in the mid 1930s.

Mixtec   a linguistic and cultural affiliation in the Mexican state of Oaxaca, especially in the Mixteca Alta region in the northwestern part of the state. Linguistic affiliations are today shared by a highly diverse cultural group. The prehistoric Mixtec shared pan-Mesoamerican culture traits with other groups throughout MESOAMERICA.

During the Mesoamerican POSTCLASSIC, the Mixtecs and ZAPOTECS struggled for power in Oaxaca. Early Mixtec dynasties date back to the 7th century AD. The occurrence of Zapotec settlements on top of Mixtec GRAYWARE CERAMICS suggests a certain amount of blending of the two cultures, probably during MONTE ALBÁN V (AD 1250–1521). Mixtec POLYCHROME POTTERY was famous for its LACQUER-like polish and brilliant colours. Mixtec CODICES are among the most important native pictorials produced in Mesoamerica.

Mladeč point   a type of point manufactured from bone, antler or IVORY, with an elongated oval shape. It is found in AURIGNACIAN sites of Central Europe.

Mlu Prei   a cluster of late prehistoric sites in north-central Cambodia, which includes the small sites of O Yak, O Pie Can and O Nari. They were occupied during the transition period from Neolithic (POLISHED STONE ADZES of several types along with a few flaked side-SCRAPERS, and bone PROJECTILE POINTS) to bronze (armlets, axes, axe-chisels, sickles, stone bivalve moulds and clay crucibles, possibly linked technologically to HANG GON in south Vietnam), and then to iron (axes, etc.).

moa   a species of giant flightless birds (order: Dinornithiformes), once common in NEW ZEALAND, which were hunted to extinction by the MAORI between first settlement and the 16th century AD. There were about 13 species in six genera with varying regional distribution. The largest, *Dinornis giganteus* could be up to four metres high, while *Euryapteryx geranoides* was the most commonly hunted. As well as meat, moas provided raw material for bone artifacts and their eggs were used as water containers. At one time, moas were thought to be a key resource and the earliest phase of New Zealand prehistory was defined as the 'moa-hunter period'. It is now clear, however, that moa-hunting was only regionally important, particularly in the South Island.

moai   a colossal stylized stone human figure of a type found on EASTER ISLAND. Most of the 800 to 1000 known were quarried from volcanic TUFF at RANO RARAKU and carved between *c.*AD 600 and 1500. They are up to 10 m high and weigh up to 82 tonnes. Many were transported to the AHU located around the coast, and placed on top, facing inland; some of those on major *ahu* wore a huge cylindrical red stone head-dress from PUNA PAU and had white coral eyes fitted. All the *moai*, probably ancestor figures, were eventually toppled during internal strife.

moated sites   a complex class of protohistoric and early historic sites in Thailand and Cambodia. The best known of these are the settlements encircled by one or more irregular (roughly circular) moats, a large number of which have been found in the Chi-Mun basin of the KHORAT plateau of northeast Thailand. Although many of these sites had late prehistoric phases of occupation, the moats themselves appear to have been added during phases of settlement growth after about AD 300–500, probably acting as source of both dry-season water and edible aquatic flora and fauna. These settlements, many of which were metal- and pottery-producing centres, appear to have dominated surrounding clusters of smaller, unmoated settlements. By AD 600–700 large settlements of the MON states in central Thailand were moated. Rectangular moats and tanks mark some KHMER settlements. The chronology in Cambodia has yet to be established; in Thailand these moats date to the period of Khmer dominance in the 11th–13th centuries AD.

mobiliary art or **chattel art**   a term used to describe portable art, usually carved or engraved stone, bone or antler or small crudely fired clay models, produced during the Upper Palaeolithic. See BÂTON-DE-COMMANDEMENT, VENUS FIGURINE; compare PALAEOLITHIC ART, PARIETAL ART.

Moche/Mochica   the major culture of the north coast of Peru during the EARLY INTERMEDIATE PERIOD. The religious and political focus of the Moche POLITY was centred at the Huaca del Sol and the Huaca de la Luna in the Moche Valley. Moche influence extended as far south as at least the Nepeña Valley, and as far north as Lambayeque, as documented by the distribution of Moche art and architecture. An outgrowth of the earlier GALLINAZO style, Moche CERAMICS were often modelled to depict realistically all manner of animal and plant life, and possibly portraits of Moche rulers. Other vessels were painted in fine-line drawings depicting elaborate themes, such as burials, the presentation of a ritual goblet, and others. Christopher Donnan suggests that most Moche art can be seen to reflect perhaps only 15 or so major themes. The Moche culture has been divided into five phases, the last of which pertains to the MIDDLE HORIZON. In Moche V times, the southern portion of Moche territory was abandoned by the Moche, and they established a new capital in the north, at PAMPA GRANDE. In 1987 the tomb of the so-called Lord of SIPÁN was discovered, in the far northern portion of Moche territory.

Huaca de la Luna is a large artificial platform, 95 by 85 by 20 metres tall, built against the slope of Cerro Blanco, and it probably served a ceremonial function. The Huaca del Sol is a large stepped pyramid (342 × 159 × 40 metres) with a cross-shaped plan, made of some 143 million ADOBE bricks. Makers' marks on the bricks suggest the existence of a labour tax, similar to that of the later INCA empire. Evidence of structures on the summit suggests that the huaca served a political function within the Moche polity. It is perhaps the largest single construction ever built in the prehistoric Andean region.

Mochlos   an island, formerly a peninsula, on the north coast of Crete. An Early MINOAN cemetery of house tombs contained rich offerings, the gold jewellery and stone vases being particularly impressive, and there is also a large Middle-Late MINOAN settlement.

mode   single or multiple ATTRIBUTES whose frequencies change through time and space, and thus are useful in constructing CULTURE HISTORY.

model   a simplified version of reality that allows that reality to be better understood. Models can vary in complexity from a simple distribution map to complex mathematical formulae, and can be both physical representations and purely literary descriptions. Models provide hypotheses that can then be tested with archaeological data.

Modjokerto   see MOJOKERTO.

Moesia   a Roman province of the lower Danube region, extending from Serbia to the mouth of the Danube. In its eastern part, Moesia lay between DACIA to the north and THRACIA to the south. During the 1st century AD, the Romans built a series of defensive walls and forts in southern Romania to guard the Moesia–Dacia frontier. Later, the GETAE came to settle in Moesia.

Mogao [Mo-kao]   see DUNHUANG.

Mogollon   a prehistoric TRADITION in the Mogollon Highlands of eastern Arizona and western New Mexico, USA, which was heavily influenced by both the ANASAZI and the HOHOKAM. As with the Anasazi and Hohokam, the Mogollon tradition is chronologically divided on the basis of architectural and pottery changes. After AD 1000, Mogollon became so heavily influenced by the Anasazi that it is no longer recognizable as an independent tradition and indeed by AD 1450, the term Western Pueblo is often applied to these late manifestations. Maize, bean and squash agriculture was practised, although their reliance on hunting and gathering always remained great, compared to the other two Southwest traditions. The tradition has a number of regional variants: MIMBRES, Pine Lawn, Upper Little Colorado, Forestdale and Point of Pines.

Mohenjo–daro   the best known of the Mature HARAPPAN cities. Mohenjo-daro lies in the Sind region of Pakistan, and was excavated by J. Marshall and E. Mackay in the 1920s and 1930s, with later work conducted by M. WHEELER, G. Dales and, very recently, by Italian, French and German workers. The city covers some 80 ha, divided into a smaller citadel to the east and a larger residential area to the west. The walled citadel, built on a baked-brick platform, contained a number of massive structures (including the Granary, Great Bath, the 'College', among others). The lower settlement was laid out on a regular grid of major and secondary streets, defining residential blocks; most of the individual dwellings in these blocks fall into one of five plans. Numerous craft installations were also present in the lower town, including potting, bead making, shell working, dyeing and metal working. The artifacts recovered in the Marshall/Mackay excavations still provide the basic definition of the Mature Harappan material culture, especially pottery styles, SEALS, weights, bead forms, figurines and metal forms.

'Moi forts' or 'Cham forts'   a series of small circular earthen-walled enclosures located in the foothills along the middle Mekong valley, east-central Cambodia. Although only one site, Mimot, has been excavated, they are classed as late Neolithic, due to the lack of metal and the presence of three types of POLISHED STONE ADZE, with estimated dates c.2500–2000 BC.

Mojokerto or **Modjokerto**   a town near JETIS, Java, which has given its name to the remains of a HOMO *erectus* child (once called *Pithecanthropus robustus, P. modjokertensis,* or *Homo modjokertensis*), dating to *c*.1.5 million years BP or before.

mokkan   literally 'wooden tablets' in Japanese; administrative artifacts known from HAN-dynasty Chinese sites. Their bureaucratic use was adopted by United SILLA in Korea and the RITSURYO state in Japan in the 8th century AD. In Japan, *mokkan* used as tax tallies, work records, task evaluations, etc., have been excavated by the tens of thousands at the HEIJO Palace and other administrative offices around the country; in Korea, many are known from ANAPCHI pond.

Mokram   a group which succeeds the GASH group in eastern Sudan about 3300 BP. There is evidence for a settlement hierarchy and sites contain domestic stock and sorghum.

Molfetta   a Middle Neolithic settlement in the 'Pulo di Molfetta', Puglie, Italy, originally a curious circular cave over 100 m across, but now open to the sky owing to the collapse of the cave roof. On the floor of the former cave are remains of several oval huts with stone footings and WATTLE AND DAUB walls. The pottery consists of red-on-buff painted ware, together with a late variety of IMPRESSED WARE related to the Sicilian STENTINELLO style. A Neolithic cemetery nearby held some 50 crouched burials.

Molino Casarotto   see BOCCA QUADRATA.

Molodova   a group of Palaeolithic and Mesolithic open-air sites on the Dnestr River in western Ukraine. The two most important localities are Molodova I and V, where multiple occupation levels are buried in slope deposits overlying ALLUVIUM on the second TERRACE. At both sites, Middle Palaeolithic artifacts and associated faunal remains (primarily woolly MAMMOTH) are contained in humic LOAMS that appear to represent redeposited buried soils; both sites also yielded evidence for MAMMOTH-BONE HOUSES, which are otherwise unknown from the Middle Palaeolithic. The artifacts include many tools made on BLADES (RETOUCHED blades, points and sidescrapers – see SCRAPER). Most of the Middle Palaeolithic levels apparently date to INTERSTADIALS prior to the beginning of the LAST GLACIAL. Molodova V also contains at least 10 levels that span the full duration of the Upper Palaeolithic; associated faunal remains are chiefly of horse and reindeer. The lower levels (*c*.30 000–25 000 bp) yielded a distinctive early Upper Palaeolithic industry (MOLODOVA CULTURE); the upper levels (*c*.23 000–12 000 bp) contain late Upper Palaeolithic assemblages with large numbers of BURINS. The Molodova sites, in conjunction with KORMAN' IV, provide the most complete and best-dated sequence of Upper Palaeolithic occupation in Ukraine. Molodova I was discovered and first investigated by Botez in 1927–31; subsequent discoveries and excavations at these sites were undertaken by Chernysh in the period 1948–84.

Molodova Culture   an Upper Palaeolithic culture of western Ukraine, represented principally at MOLODOVA V. It spans much of the duration of the Upper Palaeolithic and is divided into phases. The early phase (*c*.30 000–25 000 bp) is characterized by BURINS, large RETOUCHED BLADES, and endscrapers (see SCRAPER). The later phases (*c*.23 000–12 000 bp) have a continuing predominance of burins, along with BACKED BLADES and points. Non-stone tools and art objects are less common than among other Upper Palaeolithic cultures of

Europe.

Moloko   a Late Iron Age complex which appears in the central, southern and western Transvaal of South Africa at *c*.AD 1200–1300. A second phase of the complex starts *c*.AD 1600 with a dramatic increase in the number of stone-built settlements on the grasslands of the southern highveld of South Africa (see SOUTHERN HIGHVELD Types N, V, Z).

Mon   an ethno-linguistic group, related to the KHMER and to various hill groups of mainland Southeast Asia, who formed the earliest states in the lower Irrawaddy valley of Burma, and in the Chao Phraya valley, KHORAT and peninsular regions of Thailand, most dating to the 1st millennium AD (see DVARAVATI).

Mondsee culture   an ENEOLITHIC culture of the Alpine foothills of northeastern Austria, named after a LAKE-DWELLING site on the Mondsee 30 km east of Salzburg. Mondsee CERAMICS are often ornamented with incised geometrical shapes with white incrustation. An important dimension of the Mondsee culture is its involvement with the mining of local Alpine COPPER sources and the manufacture of copper artifacts on a scale larger than hitherto practised.

Mongch'on   an irregularly shaped walled site on the south bank of the Han River in Seoul, Korea. Dating from the late 3rd to late 5th centuries AD, it was probably an important economic and administrative centre of the early PAEKCHE state. Excavated mainly by the Seoul National University Museum from 1985, several pit-houses, storage pits, iron horse-trappings, and bone-plate armour have been recovered from the interior.

Monk's Kop   see MUSENGEZI.

Mont Bégo   a complex of glaciated valleys on the slopes of Mont Bégo, Alpes-Maritimes, France, rich in protohistoric ROCK ART. The principal concentrations are those in the so-called Vallée des Merveilles and at Fontanalba. Representations include stylized figures, abstract shapes and artifacts, including daggers of Early Bronze Age type. Some of the engravings may be still older; but others are as recent as the Middle Ages or later. The 150 000 engravings are scattered over 4000 ha at between 2000 and 2600 m altitude.

Montbolo, Balma de   a small cave in the Pyrénées Orientales, France, excavated by J. Guilaine; halfway up a rock face, very difficult of access, it has Neolithic and CHALCOLITHIC deposits. The Neolithic assemblage is characterized by simple globular vessels with tubular lug-handles and is transitional between Early Neolithic CARDIAL WARE and Middle Neolithic CHASSÉEN. There is a single RADIOCARBON date of 4500 bc for this layer, and others of *c*.2100 bc for a series of Chalcolithic burials.

Monte Albán   a large CEREMONIAL CENTRE located on top of an artificially flattened mountain, 400 m above the city of Oaxaca, Mexico. The CHRONOLOGY developed at this site is the basis for dating all other sites in the state of Oaxaca.

Monte Albán I (900–300 BC), the first period of occupation, already shows a well-developed culture, influenced by the OLMEC ('Olmecoid'), with a knowledge of calendrics, and having the earliest-known form of HIEROGLYPHIC writing. Most of the DANZANTES were carved during this period, as was the inner, or first, building in which they were placed.

During the Monte Albán II, II–III, and IIIA, the site continued to grow, as well as to be influenced by other MESOAMERICAN groups. In Monte Albán IIIB (AD 650–1000) the centre was also influenced by TEOTIHUACÁN. It is this later period that is seen as a 'true ZAPOTEC' period, and also when Monte Albán reached its peak population of 50–60 000 (in the city and surrounding eight square kilometres).

During the subsequent period, Monte Albán IV (AD 1000–1521), the construction of large buildings at Monte Albán ceased, and the emphasis of the region moved to the valley. Monte Albán was essentially abandoned. The MIXTEC entered the area at this time, and throughout this and the overlapping period of Monte Albán V (AD 1300–1521) Monte Albán was used as a cemetery, with earlier Zapotec tombs reused for the Mixtec dead.

Most of our information from the site comes from Alfonso CASO and his collaborators, who spent many years there, beginning in 1931.

Monte Circeo   see GROTTA GUATTARI.

Montelius, Oscar (1843–1921)   a distinguished Swedish prehistorian famous for his TYPOLOGICAL schemes for the European Neolithic and Bronze Age. His detailed subdivision of the Northern Bronze Age (1885) into five successive phases was based on close study of the changing styles of bronze artifacts. He later adapted it to other parts of Europe. Montelius was also a strong adherent of the *ex oriente lux* view, which held that all European culture in later prehistoric times was derived from the ancient civilizations of Egypt and the Near East.

Monteoru culture   a Middle/Late Bronze Age culture of eastern Romania which lasted for much of the 2nd millennium bc. The type-site of Monteoru is a fortified hilltop near Bucharest. In a nearby inhumation cemetery are four large clusters of graves.

Montespan   a Palaeolithic cave-site in Haute-Garonne in the French Pyrenees, where N. Casteret, in 1923, discovered engravings on the walls as well as a series of clay statues and bas-reliefs, most notably a sphinx-like headless bear, over a metre long, made of approximately 700 kg of clay. It seems to guard the cave's low 'sanctuary' where many engravings are found. The site's art is assigned to the middle MAGDALENIAN.

Montet, Pierre (1885–1966)   a French Egyptologist, best known for his work at TANIS and BYBLOS.

Monte Verde   an Early PRECERAMIC (c.13 000 bp) site in southern Chile, one of very few sites that may represent a pre-CLOVIS occupation in the New World. Excavated by Tom Dillehay, the site includes remains of 11 or 12 residential huts, roughly rectangular with shallow clay-lined pits used as braziers, and built of wood frames possibly covered with animal hides. Another structure, whose foundation is compacted sand and gravel, has a wishbone shape and a protruding rectangular platform. Tools were of wood, bone, or stone; stone tools were naturally fractured, or sometimes shaped through PERCUSSION flaking. Some scholars have expressed doubts as to the validity of the early date. Even more hotly disputed is the date of c.33 000 bp from deeper strata, which Dillehay suggests may be associated with human occupation.

Mont Lassois   an Iron Age HILLFORT dominating the upper valley of the River Seine, Côte-d'Or, France, and commanding an easy land route from the Seine to the Rhône-Saône corridor leading to the

Mediterranean. Principal occupation is dated to the second half of the 6th century BC (HALLSTATT D), when Mont Lassois was probably the residence of a powerful CELTIC chieftain. Trade with the Greek colonies of southern France is demonstrated by finds of Massiliote wine AMPHORAE and Attic BLACK FIGURE WARE. Immediately below the hillfort is the rich contemporary burial of VIX.

Moore, Clarence Bloomfield (1852–1936) an American archaeologist, noted for his detailed and intensive investigations of numerous sites in the southeast part of North America. His most famous work was conducted at the MOUNDVILLE and POVERTY POINT sites.

Moose Mountain a MEDICINE WHEEL, located in southern Saskatchewan, Canada. The site comprises a central CAIRN approximately 10 m in diameter, which is surrounded by an ellipse of stones. Radiating from the central cairn are five stone lines, each of which ends in a small stone cairn. A RADIOCARBON date of approximately 2600 BP indicates an initial construction of the site, although a later date of 1700 BP has also been proposed. It has been suggested that the site was aligned with reference to the summer solstice.

Mootwingee a site in western New South Wales, Australia, that is rich in archaeological remains. There are many figurative and nonfigurative engravings on rocky slopes and in shelters, as well as a wide range of stencils of body parts, natural objects and artifacts, including some European items, in shelters. Some of the engravings are of PANARAMITEE type. There are also many surface camp-sites.

moraine a term for a family of depositional LANDFORMS directly resulting from the action of glacier ice. The morphology and origin of the more common moraine types are as follows:

(a) end or terminal moraine – linear ridge transverse to flow of glacial ice, marking maximum extent of ice advance. The ridge forms as the result of a balance between ice advance and ablation of the ice that causes the ice front not to fluctuate for some period of time.

(b) recessional moraine – linear ridge forms due to a pause in the ice front during retreat. End and recessional moraines may form natural dams which support lakes.

(c) ground moraine – plain formed by deposition in the wake of a steadily retreating glacier that may be relatively featureless, have subtle linear rises or minor moraines transverse to glacial flow, or consist of streamlined landforms parallel to ice flow such as flutes or drumlins.

(d) hummocky or·ablation moraine – chaotic low-relief plain resulting from stagnation and downwasting of glacial ice.

(e) lateral moraine – linear ridges along valley walls parallel to ice flow of valley glaciers.

Moraines usually offer different drainage conditions from surrounding terrain so that different vegetational communities might be supported.

Morgan, Lewis Henry (1818–81) one of the founders of American anthropology, whose unilinear scheme of human development – from savagery to barbarism to civilization – greatly influenced future archaeological MODELS of CULTURE HISTORY and the application to the discipline of models drawn from the theory of EVOLUTION.

Moriori   the POLYNESIAN inhabitants of the Chatham Islands, the furthest limit of Polynesian dispersal. Archaeological evidence suggests that the islands were settled from NEW ZEALAND during the Archaic phase, but became isolated after about AD 1400.

Morley, Sylvanus Griswold (1883–1948)   an American archaeologist who studied MAYA civilization. From 1908–14 he recorded Maya GLYPHS. Morley synthesized his own work and that of his peers and, with Sir J.E.S. THOMPSON, proposed an interpretation of Maya civilization that remained accepted and virtually unquestioned for years. This interpretation was based on a study of the large Maya CEREMONIAL CENTRES, proposing that the Classic Maya were not urban dwellers, but farmers who occupied 'vacant centres' only during religious holidays.

In 1915 Morley became a research associate of the Carnegie Institute of Washington. At this time he began surveying the southern Maya lowlands. He also directed the huge Carnegie project at CHICHÉN ITZÁ from 1924–40, and was the first to dredge the Sacred CENOTE there. Morley's contact with modern-day Maya greatly influenced his interpretations of the prehistoric Mayan civilization.

Morse, Edward Sylvester (1838–1925)   an American zoologist credited with the introduction of the modern discipline of archaeology to Japan with his excavation of the OMORI SHELL MIDDEN in 1877 while teaching at Tokyo (Imperial) University.

mortarium   a Roman grinding bowl.

Mortillet, Gabriel de (1821–98)   a French prehistorian who proposed an alternative to LARTET'S classificatory scheme for the Palaeolithic, based on archaeological remains rather than palaeontology. De Mortillet's scheme used type-names such as MOUSTERIAN, AURIGNACIAN and SOLUTREAN which are still used today, but divided the Palaeolithic into time-periods, not CULTURES or TRADITIONS.

Mortlake   see PETERBOROUGH WARE.

mortuary temple   an Egyptian TEMPLE, usually situated close to a royal tomb. The specialized purpose of the mortuary temple was to provide a centre for the performance of rites for the benefit of the dead king. Compare CULT TEMPLE.

mosaic   1. a technique using TESSERAE, especially in the Roman world.
2. a TESSELLATED area often with complex designs and even inscriptions. See also COLOGNE, FISHBOURNE, OSTIA.

Mossbauer spectroscopy   a technique of analysis used to determine the presence and type of IRON-bearing minerals in CERAMICS, and to interpret firing conditions. Iron is one of the few ISOTOPES in which the Mossbauer effect, the recoil-less fluorescence of gamma rays, occurs. Samples are bombarded with gamma rays; the detected amount of absorption by iron nuclei provides information regarding the iron-bearing minerals present.

Motupore   an island in Bootless Bay, near Port Moresby, Papua New Guinea, investigated by Jim Allen. Archaeological material from Motupore, especially the evidence for manufacture of shell valuables and pottery, documents the development of a coastal trading centre, which supplied goods to Papuan Gulf communities between about 500 and 250 years ago. See HIRI.

Motya   a PHOENICIAN harbour town situated on a small offshore island reached from the Sicilian mainland by a causeway. The earliest activity seems to date from the 8th century BC. Extensive excavations by the British and Italians have revealed a *cothon* (artificial dock), the walls, houses, cemeteries and the *tophet* (sanctuary). Although the site is Phoenician, large quantities of Greek pottery, both fine and domestic, have been found. The site provides an important TERMINUS ANTE QUEM of 397 BC, when it was destroyed by the Syracusans and largely abandoned.

Mouillian   see IBEROMAURUSIAN.

mound (*Australia*)   a series of low earth mounds found in southwest and central Victoria, the central Murray, Riverina and Northern Territory of Australia. They are mostly less than 1 m high, being formed primarily through the heaping up of refuse from earth ovens, and were also used as dry camping-places in poorly drained areas. The oldest date from *c.*4000 bp along the Murray River, while they appear in southwest Victoria from *c.*2500 bp.

mounded tombs   a form of elite burial in East Asia constructed with monumental earthen or stone-piled mounds containing various burial facilities such as a WOODEN CHAMBER, clay enclosure, brick or MEGALITHIC stone chamber. Round and square mounds are common; KEYHOLE TOMBS are exclusive to Japan. The tombs and their contents provide the major sources of data for the THREE KINGDOMS period in Korea and the KOFUN period in Japan (see MURYONG, HEAVENLY HORSE TOMB, FUJINOKI, TAKAMATSUZUKA). One of the earliest mounded tombs in China was that of the First Emperor of QIN, and the MING TOMBS are some of the latest. The tombs contain a variety of prestige goods differing in time and space, but including such items as BRONZE MIRRORS, LACQUER vessels, iron swords and armour, funerary pottery (LEAD-GLAZED WARE, SUE ware), gold jewellery, silk, JADES, and horse trappings. HANIWA or a SPIRIT PATH were constructed outside the tombs. (Compare SHAFT TOMBS, MAWANGDUI, MANCHENG.)

Moundville   an important MISSISSIPPIAN site in Alabama, USA, that reached its zenith approximately 300 years before European contact. It comprised about 20 mounds, mostly PLATFORM MOUNDS. Over 3000 burials, of varying social status, have been uncovered at the site, and it is likely that it was part of a CHIEFDOM. Moundville has much evidence for the SOUTHERN CULT, and was first investigated by C.B. MOORE.

Mount Camel   an Archaic midden site covering about 1.5 ha at the north end of the North Island, NEW ZEALAND, and dating to AD 1150–1260. The excavations by Wilfred Shawcross revealed earth-ovens and evidence for a range of activities, including butchering, fish scaling and manufacture of bone and IVORY ornaments.

Mount Cameron West   the most complex art site in TASMANIA, Australia. It features a range of non-figurative engravings on slabs fallen from the cliff. The motifs compare with those of PANARAMITEE ART. However, the space behind the slabs was used as a camp-site in 1350–850 bp, suggesting the engravings are recent.

Mount Carmel   a group of Palaeolithic cave-sites in Israel, excavated primarily by GARROD. The best-known sites are EL WAD, ES SKHUL, TABUN and NAHAL OREN. See also KEBARAN.

Mount Sandel   an Irish Mesolithic site in County Londonderry, which has yielded a series of circular wooden hut-foundations with central hearths, and a distinctive lithic industry including MICROLITHS, TRANCHET AXES and the early appearance of polished stone axes. The site was first excavated by Collins and later by Woodman.

Mount William   a GREENSTONE axe quarry and workshop in central Victoria, Australia, and the centre of an exchange network through most of Victoria and into South Australia and southern New South Wales. First documented in the late 19th century by the anthropologist, A.W. Howitt, it has since been the subject of detailed study by Isabel McBryde.

Mousterian   a term first used for Middle Palaeolithic artifacts recovered from the lower rockshelter at *Le Moustier*, Dordogne, France, excavated by LARTET and CHRISTY. The term was then extended to include assemblages showing a high proportion of FLAKES, RACLOIRS, points, occasional BIFACES and the use of prepared-CORE KNAPPING techniques. The Mousterian has a wide geographical distribution, stretching across Europe and Asia, and from Britain to North Africa. Three major regional variants have been identified, West, East and LEVALLOISO-Mousterian, each with clear sub-groups based mainly on TYPOLOGICAL differences in tool forms. Mousterian occurrences have been dated between the late RISS and the late middle WÜRM (*c.*180 000 to 30 000 BP). They are frequently associated with the occupation of caves or rockshelters and with NEANDERTHAL remains. See also CHARENTIAN.

Mousterian Biface.

Mousterian of Acheulian Tradition (MTA (*French*) or **MAT** (*English*))   the name given by BORDES to one of the MOUSTERIAN variants identified in southwest France on the basis of ARTIFACT TYPOLOGY. The MAT has two recognized sub-types: Type A, with BIFACES, BACKED knives, DENTICULATES and SCRAPERS; developing into Type B, with fewer bifaces and a higher frequency of Upper Palaeolithic tool-types such as BURINS and AWLS.

Movius, Hallam Leonard (1907–87)   an American prehistorian best known for his field work in Northern Ireland and southeast Asia, and for the excavation of the Upper Palaeolithic rockshelter of ABRI PATAUD, France, in 1958–64.

Moxeke   see PAMPA DE LAS LLAMAS.

Mrs Ples   see STERKFONTEIN.

Mšecké Zehrovice   an Iron Age settlement in Bohemia, dated to the LA TÈNE C–D period (c.150–50 BC). Mšecké Zehrovice has been termed an 'industrial village' at which both iron and sapropelite (a type of shale) were worked. Two large contiguous rectangular enclosures, each about 100 m per side, delimited an area which may have had a ritual purpose. The best-known find from Mšecké Zehrovice is the stone bust of a CELT with a curling moustache and wavy hair.

MTA   see MOUSTERIAN OF ACHEULIAN TRADITION.

Mu'a   a ceremonial centre of the ruling dynasties on Tongatapu, Tonga. The ditched and banked earthworks enclose an area of 400 by 500 metres with many house-platforms and LANGI TOMBS. It has never been excavated but, according to tradition, became the residence of the ruling Tui Tonga dynasty about AD 1200, the defences being built about AD 1400.

Muang Fa Daet   a large (approximately 170 ha) late-prehistoric/early-historic settlement in the upper Chi valley, KHORAT, Thailand. It is the largest MOATED SITE in the Khorat, the rectangular outermost of its three concentric moats and the 15 ha reservoir dating to the period of KHMER domination late in the 1st millennium AD. It was a major farming, trading, and BRONZE- and IRON-working site. Material culture of the mid 1st millennium AD resembles that of the state of DVARAVATI, and much of the moated site was sacred Buddhist space.

Muang Sima   a large (over 150 ha) late-prehistoric/early-historic settlement upstream from PHIMAI in the Mun valley, KHORAT, Thailand, occupied by the early 1st millennium AD. By the 7th and 8th centuries AD, the twice-enlarged MOATED SITE appears to have been the centre of a small INDIANIZED state called, according to the inscription from the site, Šrî Canâśa. Buddhist remains of the period are similar to those of DVARAVATI.

Muara Jambi   see SRIVIJAYA.

mud-brick   a brick dried in the sun, used for construction in dry climates. See also ADOBE, SEBBAKH.

Mud Glyph Cave   a site located in Tennessee, USA, that comprises a series of almost inaccessible 'galleries' containing a rich collection of prehistoric art, constructed from incisions cut into the natural mud of the cave walls. Designs are mostly ANTHRO-POMORPHOUS, but ZOOMORPHS as well as abstract designs identical to ones on contemporary artifacts (including the SOUTHERN CULT) are also present. The cave was used from AD 420–1750, with heaviest use between the 12th and 16th centuries. See MISSISSIPPIAN, WOODLAND.

Muge   the location of Mesolithic *concheiros* (SHELLMOUNDS) near the mouth of the Tagus, Portugal, excavated in the 1880s and 1950s. Their dates lie between 7350 and 5150 bp, the ATLANTIC period, and they contain a MICROLITHIC industry together with QUARTZITE pebbles and grindstones, as well as bone points and axes of red deer antler like those of Lyngby (see BROMMIAN). The 3 *concheiros* of Muge yielded over 230 burials, the most important European Mesolithic funerary assemblage.

Mulloy, William Thomas (1917–78)   an American archaeologist who developed the cultural chronology of the northwest Plains, USA, especially at Pictograph Cave, Montana. He is best known for his important work on EASTER ISLAND from 1955 onwards, especially the excavation and restoration of ORONGO and several AHU with their MOAI.

Mumba-Höhle   an impressive rockshelter near Lake Eyasi in northern Tanzania, first dug by Margit Kohl-Larsen in 1938, and one of a very few excavated deeply stratified sites in East Africa. Its 9 m deposit spans much of the last 125 000 years and contains material from the MIDDLE STONE AGE to the IRON AGE.

mummification   the artificial treatment of a cadaver, with the aim of preserving a life-like appearance, a body that has been treated in this way being popularly known as a *mummy*. The earliest attempts at mummification by the Egyptians were during the OLD KINGDOM, but only in the NEW KINGDOM were techniques developed (major removal of internal organs, effective use of desiccating agents, subcutaneous padding) which made mummification possible on a reasonably large scale. Not only people but also sacred animals and birds were treated in this way. All stages of the procedure were accompanied by elaborate rituals.

It is thought that the practice was inspired by the natural desiccation of bodies in the desert sand, and the term is often extended to bodies preserved accidentally in this way in other parts of the world, such as Peru.

Mummy Cave   a deeply stratified site in the mountains of western Wyoming, USA, with 38 distinct levels, the earliest dating to before 7300 BC, and the latest dating to the 16th century AD.

Mumun   literally 'no decoration' in Korean; the tradition of 'plain pottery' of the Korean peninsula, succeeding CHULMUN pottery in c.1500 BC and lasting to AD 300 in the PROTO-THREE KINGDOMS period. It was the dominant pottery type from the Bronze Age through the Proto-Three Kingdoms period. Mumun-pottery sites without bronze fit unconformably between the Chulmun and Bronze Age (e.g. HUNAM-RI). (See KOREAN PERIODIZATION.)

Mundigak   a prehistoric site northwest of Kandahar in the upper Helmand drainage in southern Afghanistan, where the excavations of J-M. Casal in the 1950s provided an important cultural sequence (Mundigak I–VII). The first five of these periods form a succession of occupations from the 5th to the early 2nd millennium BC. By the Mundigak IV period (later 3rd millennium), the settlement had grown from a village to a town covering some 7 ha and containing a large colonnaded 'palace' building and other monumental structures within a walled citadel. At the same time (especially in Mundigak III–IV), the pottery and various small finds indicate increasing interaction with surrounding regions, including Turkmenistan (GEOKSJUR, NAMAZGA III), Baluchistan and the Early HARAPPAN Indus region. The later two periods (Mundigak VI–VII) belong to the Iron Age.

Mungo   a now dry lake with an associated LUNETTE in the WILLANDRA LAKES, western New South Wales, Australia. In 1969, the remains of a cremated human female (Mungo 1) dated to c.26 000 bp were found, the oldest evidence of cremation in the world. The remains of a man were later found (Mungo 3), this time an extended inhumation covered with red OCHRE and dated to c.30 000 bp. There are also many occupation sites, including artifact scatters, HEARTHS and freshwater SHELL MIDDENS. TL dating places the hearths between 31 400 and 36 400 years ago.

Munsell colour chart   a widely used colour identification system with a standardized method of description and notation of colours of SEDIMENT, SOIL, CHERT, pottery and rock. The method facilitates communication of colours to those familiar with them but unable to see samples firsthand. It consists of an atlas of charts of colour chips that are numerically graduated scales with visual increments of hue, value and chroma. Components of value and chroma correspond to the perceptual attributes of lightness and saturation, respectively. *Hue* refers to the range of perceptions from red to blue, and back to red. *Value* refers to the degree of darkness or lightness of the colour. *Chroma* refers to brightness of the colour, or to the degree to which a colour differs from a grey of the same lightness.

Münsingen-Rain   an Iron Age cemetery near Bern, Switzerland, of 170 flat graves dating from Early LA TÈNE to the beginning of Middle La Tène *c.*200 BC. Grave-goods include swords, spears, FIBULAE and in one instance a necklace of amber beads. Careful analysis of the grave-goods has allowed the individual burials to be placed in chronological order by SERIATION.

Munyama   a Ugandan cave on Buvuma Island in Lake Victoria with an early BACKED MICROLITH INDUSTRY dating to *c.*15 000 BP.

mural tombs   MOUNDED TOMBS of East Asia with painted FRESCOES on the walls of the interior stone chamber; particularly associated with KOGURYO but also occurring in China and Japan (see TAKAMATSUZUKA). Koguryo murals can be divided into genre paintings, portraits and directional deities of the Chinese tradition.

Mureybet   an important late-EPIPALAEOLITHIC (NATUFIAN) and ACERAMIC NEOLITHIC (to PPNB) settlement on the middle Euphrates excavated by Maurits van Loon and Jacques Cauvin. It is a key site for understanding the emergence of food production in north Syria. The architectural sequence shows the transition from circular to rectilinear structures during the PPNA, during which time the community was heavily involved in morphologically wild cereals (especially einkorn) which were probably being cultivated. Together with ABU HUREYRA, Mureybet provides a detailed picture of the origins of food production and village life on the middle Euphrates, between 8500 and 6800 BC.

Murray Black Collection   a large collection of skeletal material collected between 1937 and 1950 by George Murray Black in the central Murray Valley, Australia. None of the material was properly excavated and thus lacked contextual data, though most was mid to late HOLOCENE in date. It included the COOBOOL CREEK material. The collection has now been returned to Aboriginal communities in the Murray Valley for reburial.

murus gallicus   a term used by Julius Caesar in his account of the Gallic Wars to describe the defences of the CELTIC OPPIDUM of Avaricum (Bourges). This was a timber-laced rampart, with heavy beams in the front face tied to similar beams in the rear face by cross-members and held in place by iron nails. The spaces between the beams were filled by regular courses of stone walling. Evidence of *murus gallicus* defences has been found at a number of late-Celtic oppida.

Muryong   an early 6th century AD king of PAEKCHE whose MOUNDED TOMB is near Kongju City, Korea. Chinese-style bricks bearing moulded decoration were used to construct the chamber, whose contents were intact upon excavation in 1971. They included a bronze chopstick and spoon set, precious toiletry goods, small glass sculptures, and an inscribed plaque identifying the deceased.

Musang Cave   a cave in northern Luzon, north Philippines; its early phase is represented by a FLAKE industry dated c.12 000 to 9000 bc; following a gap there is a Neolithic assemblage dated to c.3500 BC or later, with links to DIMOLIT and Arku Cave, and possible Taiwanese Neolithic connections.

Musawwarat es–Sufra   a MEROITIC site in UPPER NUBIA, excavated by Hintze in 1960–70. A colonnaded temple is the central building in a complex of monumental stone buildings, which also include large enclosures identified as elephant pens.

Muselievo   a Palaeolithic open-air site on the Osm River near its confluence with the Danube in Bulgaria. The main cultural layer is buried in rubbly LOESS overlying a limestone promontory. The artifacts, which appear to have been partly redeposited, include BIFACIAL FOLIATES and sidescrapers (see SCRAPER); this layer may date to the early cold maximum of the LAST GLACIAL.

Musengezi   a 13th century AD Late Iron Age group of the LUANGWA Tradition, best known from burial caves in northern Zimbabwe. The site of Monk's Kop yielded about 70 skeletons buried sitting upright and wrapped in bark cloth and palm fibre matting, surrounded by pottery.

Mushroom Rock   a painted sandstone shelter near Laura, southeast Cape York, Australia, with four metres of deposit. The site was first occupied in the Late PLEISTOCENE. The sequence falls into the two phases common in Australia, with the earlier AUSTRALIAN CORE TOOL AND SCRAPER TRADITION giving way to the AUSTRALIAN SMALL TOOL TRADITION. OCHRE was found throughout the deposits.

mutisalah   a kind of small opaque reddish–glass bead found frequently in metal age (late 1st millennium BC) sites in maritime Southeast Asia, and most probably manufactured in south India.

mutule   a projecting flat slab found under the CORNICE in CLASSICAL buildings of the DORIC ORDER.

Mwanganda   an undated elephant butchery site in northern Malawi, comprising the bones of a single elephant together with numerous SCRAPERS and a few CORE axes attributed to the LUPEMBAN industry. It is of interest because it apparently preserves a discrete episode of activity.

Mwulu's   a cave near Pietersburg in the northern Transvaal, South Africa, which provided the type sample for the MIDDLE STONE AGE PIETERSBURG industry. This is succeeded by deposits containing the MIDDLE STONE AGE BAMBATA-like Mwulu Industry.

Mycenae   the site, in the Argolid, Greece, of the first major MYCENAEAN excavations, initiated by SCHLIEMANN in 1876. He was followed by TSOUNTAS, WACE, MYLONAS and TAYLOUR. Mycenae appears to have been a relatively insignificant Middle HELLADIC site, but it rose to prominence at the end of the period when the two SHAFT GRAVE CIRCLES were built for the members of a royal family which must have controlled much of the northeastern Peloponnese. Subsequently the elite were buried in the nine THOLOS tombs which include the magnificent Treasury of Atreus. The citadel of Mycenae was first fortified in the 14th century BC, and the defences were strengthened in the 13th century when the Lion Gate was constructed. On the summit of the AKROPOLIS stood the palace of the ruler. Late in the 13th century Mycenae was devastated, possibly by an earthquake, and suffered a further destruction in the 12th century. Mycenae never recovered and emerges from the Dark Ages as a minor Argive town.

Mycenaean, *adj.* relating to the civilization of late Bronze Age Greece. The SHAFT GRAVE CIRCLES at MYCENAE constitute one of the earliest manifestations of the Mycenaean civilization, which originated in the Peloponnese in the 16th century BC and spread to central Greece and subsequently across the southern Aegean. In the 14th and 13th centuries palaces were built at Mycenae, PYLOS, THEBES and TIRYNS. Their role as administrative and economic centres is evident from the LINEAR B documents written by the palace scribes. A spate of destructions *c.*1200 BC apparently led to the decline and eventually the collapse of the civilization.

Mycerinus see MENKAURE.

Mylonas, George (1898–1988) a Greek archaeologist who excavated at Ayios Kosmas, ELEUSIS, MYCENAE and OLYNTHUS. He was Secretary-General of the Archaeological Society of Athens in 1979–88.

Myrina a city on the west coast of Turkey, where excavations in the cemeteries during the 19th century revealed hundreds of TERRACOTTA figurines, mainly HELLENISTIC in date.

Myrtos a site on the southern coast of Crete. An Early MINOAN settlement, occupied *c.*2600–2200 BC, was excavated on the hill of Fournou Korifi by Warren, and at Pyrgos Cadogan has uncovered a NEOPALATIAL country house, built *c.*1550 BC and destroyed by fire *c.*1450 BC.

Myrtou-Pigadhes the site of a Late CYPRIOT settlement and sanctuary in northern Cyprus, excavated by du Plat Taylor in 1949–51. The sanctuary, which was built *c.*1400 BC and remained in use until *c.*1175 BC, contained a magnificent ASHLAR altar crowned by HORNS OF CONSECRATION.

N

Nabatake see ITAZUKE.

Nabta Playa a low-lying 100 sq km basin in the eastern Sahara of southern Egypt. A site dated to 8100 bp has yielded unparalled assemblages of wild plant foods, as well as CERAMICS and domestic cattle. Caprids were present by 6700 bp. A large aggregation site dated to 7000–6000 BP, used in the rainy season, may have associated MEGALITHS.

Nachikufan Zambian LATER STONE AGE MICROLITHIC industries named after Nachikufu Cave in northern Zambia. These industries were originally regarded as a single local tradition, the 'Nachikufan

Industrial Complex', which was divided into several phases, but its continuity is no longer upheld. The 'Nachikufan I' is now regarded as a more widespread industry dating to between c.20 000 and 12 000 BP, characterized by very small pointed BACKED BLADELETS and various SCRAPERS, as well as relatively early examples of BORED STONES (see MATUPI). Later phases of the Nachikufan are more restricted geographically.

naga long walled avenues divided by crosswalls into separate rectangular enclosures, found only in the central part of Viti Levu, Fiji. Similar structures, but without crosswalls, occur on Vanua Levu. They were associated with male initiation ceremonies.

Nagada see NAQADA.

Nagyrév the initial culture in the tripartite sequence of the Hungarian Early Bronze Age defined by Moszolics on the basis of the stratigraphy at TÓSZEG, where the Nagyrév culture precedes the HATVAN and FÜZESABONY. In its earlier stages, Nagyrév shows connections with the VUČEDOL group (c.2000 BC), while later it reflects contemporaneity with ÚŇETICE (c.1800 BC). Nagyrév vessels are characterized by extremely high constricted necks.

Nahal Mishmar a Palestinian site discovered in 1960; it consists of a cave containing a cache of 630 CHALCOLITHIC COPPER objects of the GHASSULIAN culture, with incised and solid decorative elements, including 240 mace-heads, 80 'sceptres' and 10 crowns.

Nahal Oren a site on the western slope of MOUNT CARMEL, Israel, excavated by Stekelis in 1941 and 1954–60, and by Noy and HIGGS in 1969–71. The stratified deposits revealed occupation from KEBARAN to early ACERAMIC NEOLITHIC (PPNA) times. The PPNA settlement consisted of many circular stone structures set along the *wadi* terraces, and contained a rich material culture of chipped stone, ground stone tools, bone tools, stone vessels and some art objects. The NATUFIAN settlement also contained circular stone structures, and an important group of 36 burials. The Kebaran levels (16 300–13 850 BC) are less well known.

Nahua a group of tribes in Central Mexico, originally from the north, the last and best-known of which were the AZTECS.

Nahuatl a Uto-Aztecan language. Groups speaking Nahuatl migrated into MESOAMERICA from its northern frontier, GRAN CHICHIMEC. The name Nahuatl is commonly used for the language of the AZTECS.

naiskos a small Greek temple or shrine.

Naj Tunich a cave in southeast Guatemala where 8th century AD MAYA cave art was discovered in 1980. It comprises almost 100 paintings and a few PETROGLYPHS, mostly HIEROGLYPHIC texts and human figures. Many of the major paintings were vandalized in 1989.

Nakamine a Palaeolithic site in Miyagi Prefecture, Japan, which has yielded stone tools sandwiched between layers dated to 150 000 and 300 000 bp. These argue for Early Palaeolithic occupation of the Japanese islands.

Nakbe a MAYA urban centre in northern Guatemala, 13 km from EL MIRADOR to which it was joined by a causeway. The site, whose name means 'by the road' in Yucatec Maya, was seen from the air in 1930, but first visited in 1962 by Ian Graham. It comprises two main clusters of platforms and mounds, including a PYRAMID 50 m high. Occupied between c.3000 and 1000 BP, Nakbe was a major centre only in the middle PRECLASSIC (*c*.3000–2300 BP) when maize and squash were already being grown here. It may have been eclipsed by the rise of El Mirador, and was abandoned for a millennium until reoccupied in the late CLASSIC by small communities.

Nakhon Pathom a very large (3700 × 2000 m) protohistoric and early historic settlement in the lower Chao Phraya valley, central Thailand, which is thought to have been the capital of the state of DVARAVATI for a time. The first three phases of the Phra Pathom CHEDI may date to this period and earlier. The rectangular moat may have been added during the period of KHMER power, after *c*.AD 1000.

Nakhon Si Thammarat a city on the east coast of peninsular Thailand. The pre-modern phases of its occupation are represented by three sites: Muang Nakhon Si Thammarat, of the 15th–18th centuries AD; Muang Phra Wieng, a moated settlement and Buddhist centre, probably the capital of TAMBRALINGA; and the *c*.8th–15th century site Ban Tha Rua, apparently the port associated with the capital.

Namazga-depe a site in Turkmenia on the north slope of the Kopet Dagh, where excavations of B.A. Kuftin and I.N. Khlopin in the 1950s to 1970s produced the standard chronological framework for the CHALCOLITHIC and BRONZE AGE of western Central Asia. This sequence contains six phases, numbered Namazga I (earliest) to VI (latest), which spans the ENEOLITHIC (i.e. Chalcolithic; NMZ I–III, *c*.4800–3000 BC) and Bronze Age (NMZ IV–VI, *c*.3000–1500 BC); the sequence thus covers the time from the ANAU IA Neolithic culture to the beginning of the Iron Age (Yaz I, see YAZ-DEPE). The site of Namazga-depe itself grew from the size of a small town (about 15 ha) in its early occupation to that of a small city (about 50 ha) during the Namazga IV–V times (most of the 3rd millennium), before collapsing in its final 'tower' phase (about 2 ha) in the late 3rd/early 2nd millennium BC.

NAN languages see PAPUAN LANGUAGES.

Nan Madol a town and ceremonial centre on Ponape in the Caroline Islands, MICRONESIA. Built in a tidal lagoon, it covers about 70 ha and comprises 92 artificial rectilinear platforms built of coral rubble with basalt facings, surrounded by channels. The complex is protected by two breakwaters. It is divided into two sections: the southern part was mainly for houses of the nobility and public and ceremonial activities; while the northern part was for priests' houses, and includes the chiefly burial enclosure of Nan Douwas. The complex was never finished and is assumed to have been built within the last few centuries at a time when the CHIEFDOMS of Ponape were unified under a single dynasty.

Nanna the SUMERIAN god, equivalent to the AKKADIAN god Sin, who was the oldest son of ENLIL, and was connected to the moon and to fertility; his principal city was UR.

naos 1. a shrine, usually monolithic, within which the image of an Egyptian deity was housed. The largest naoi are those where a TEMPLE's main cult-statue was kept, in the sanctuary.
2. a Greek temple which may be placed within a TEMENOS. See, for example, PARTHENON.

Napata a district in UPPER NUBIA, including the sites of KURRU, GEBEL BARKAL, NURI and Sanam. Napata was the seat of a kingdom (called KUSH by the Egyptians) to which it gives its name, which flourished between the late 9th and early 3rd centuries BC.

Naqada   a site in UPPER EGYPT, where PETRIE and Quibell's 1894 excavations produced the first substantial evidence of the Neolithic in Egypt and provided the basic framework for the PREDYNASTIC sequence of Upper Egypt. See AMRATIAN and GERZEAN.

Nara   see JAPANESE PERIODIZATION, HEIJO.

Naram-sin   the grandson of SARGON and the last great ruler of the AKKADIAN empire, who, conventionally in 2254–2218 BC, managed to sustain his grandfather's conquests, putting down a series of rebellions, and campaigned against foreign enemies in Syria and to the east. The Akkadian empire began to fall apart under the rule of his son Sharkalishari. Even so, Naram-sin became identified with this collapse in CUNEIFORM literature: in the poem 'Curse of Akkad', Naram-sin takes the part of the unjust king whose impious acts invite divine retaliation in the form of invasion and disaster. Just as Sargon provided the positive paradigm of kingship, so Naram-sin supplied the counter-example.

Narmer   an Egyptian king, ruling in UPPER EGYPT in the late PRE-DYNASTIC Period, and possibly to be equated with the legendary King Menes who united Egypt at the beginning of the ARCHAIC PERIOD. Narmer is best known from the 'Main Deposit' of ritual objects at HIERAKONPOLIS.

Narosura   an important southern Kenyan PASTORAL NEOLITHIC site covering at least 8000 sq m, dating to between the 9th and 5th centuries BC. The stone industry is characterized by OBSIDIAN geometric BACKED MICROLITHS and BURINS, as well as ground stone axes and stone bowls. The abundant pottery, decorated with incisions and comb-stamping, is frequently BURNISHED and is known as *Narosura Ware*. Most of the animal bones represent domestic stock, but there is no evidence for cultivated crops.

Narva culture   a Neolithic culture of the eastern Baltic littoral, in the 4th and 3rd millennia BC, occurring in Lithuania, Latvia, Estonia and portions of Poland and Belarus. At two key sites, Osa and Narva-town, Narva assemblages overlay those of the Mesolithic KUNDA culture. Many artifact categories show continuity from Kunda to Narva, with the addition of pottery in the form of pointed-base pots with straight or S-profiles and oval bowls. Other important sites include SARNATE in Latvia and Sventoji in Lithuania.

Nasca or **Nazca**   the major culture of the south coast of Peru during the EARLY INTERMEDIATE PERIOD. An outgrowth of the earlier PARACAS culture, Nasca CERAMICS are painted in up to 16 colours, depicting plants, animals, humans, supernatural creatures and elaborate geometric designs. Stylistically the ceramics have been divided into nine phases, the first of which is an extension of terminal Paracas culture. During phases 2–4 (c. AD 200–500), which can be termed Early Nasca times, ceramics were depicted with fairly realistic designs. CAHUACHI served as the central ceremonial focus of the culture, and construction of the site continued through this period. There is little evidence of complex political organization at this time, and people lived in small villages adjacent to arable land. The dead were buried in large cemeteries, most of them located near Cahuachi.

In Nasca phase 5, a transitional phase, new elements were added to ceramic designs, which became increasingly abstract. New constructions at Cahuachi ceased, and a system of horizontal wells, PUQUIOS, may have been established. New settlements were established in previously unoccupied portions of the valleys. In phases 6 and 7 (c.ad 550–700), Late Nasca times, ceramic designs became extremely abstract and complex, and warriors were depicted with increasing frequency. Most small villages were abandoned, and population aggregated into large settlements, some of them in defendable locations. The dead continued to be buried in cemeteries near Cahuachi, suggesting that the site continued to serve as a ceremonial centre, but no new constructions were made there. Nasca phases 8 and 9 may pertain to the MIDDLE HORIZON when the region came under the influence of the HUARI empire.

Nasca lines or **geoglyphs**   straight lines, geometric shapes and representational designs found on the desert plain in the NASCA region of the south coast of Peru. The lines were created by clearing the surface of the ground of small red-brown stones, and exposing the lighter-coloured soil beneath. Many of the straight lines radiate outward from points located at small hills or the end of low ridges, suggesting a largely ceremonial function. Various living forms are depicted as well, including birds, whales, a monkey, a spider, an ANTHROPOMORPHOUS owl and others. The figures are mostly concentrated along one edge of the plain, and some are stylistically similar to designs painted on Early Nasca CERAMICS.

The straight lines have a much wider distribution, and seem to date not only to the EARLY INTERMEDIATE PERIOD, but to later periods as well. The lines were reported by the Peruvian archaeologist, Toribio Mejía Xesspe, and then by the American, Paul Kosok. Kosok introduced one of his students, a German mathematician named Maria Reiche, to the region in the late 1940s; she has since devoted her life to the study of the lines. She believes that the figures represent constellations, and that many straight lines have astronomical significance. Other researchers have suggested that the lines were ceremonial pathways, and may have pointed toward sacred places, especially mountains. See CEQUE.

Nasera   an impressive boulder-hill in northern Tanzania, originally excavated in 1932 by L.S.B. LEAKEY, who called it Apis Rock. It contains a 9 m deep deposit of MIDDLE and LATER STONE AGE remains.

Native Americans   the past and contemporary aboriginal inhabitants of North America. It is used to differentiate these peoples from North Americans of European or other descent.

Natufian   the terminal EPIPALAEOLITHIC culture complex of the Levant, dated to c.12 500–10 000 BP, and named after the site of Wadi en-Natuf in Palestine. Natufian assemblages contain geometric MICROLITHS, bone artifacts such as points, spearheads and fish-hooks, and tools such as flint sickle-blades, pestles and mortars that indicate the harvesting of cereals. As yet there is no clear evidence of the deliberate sowing of crops, and faunal remains suggest that the Natufian people were primarily settled or semi-settled hunters with relatively elaborate burial rituals. A number of large settlements contain substantial permanent architecture, food storage facilities, a large amount of fixed and portable grain-pounding and -grinding equipment, and cemeteries that indicate differential wealth and status within communities. Initially confined to a central Levantine core area,

Natufian groups later appear in the middle Euphrates Valley, southern Jordan and the Negev. They were the first settled occupants of JERICHO. See also EYNAN, MOUNT CARMEL.

natural levee   a depositional LANDFORM consisting of low linear ridges adjacent to and paralleling either side of ALLUVIAL channels. Natural levees form as channels overflow their banks; flow velocity and depth of flood waters decrease immediately outside channel boundaries, depositing the coarser material of the suspended load adjacent to the channel. Repeated overbank flooding leads to levee growth. Natural levees in alluvial valleys are slightly better-drained landscape positions than other FLOODPLAIN landforms, and archaeological material is often on and buried within them, reflecting their utilization.

Naucratis   a Greek trading settlement in the Nile Delta, Egypt, excavated by PETRIE and others. The finds are dominated by Greek fine pottery. Many of the SHERDS are inscribed with the names of Greek deities and they seem to have been dedicated in the sanctuaries. The earliest pottery from the site is Transitional CORINTHIAN POTTERY which is traditionally dated to c.630–620 BC.

Navan   an Iron Age enclosure and royal residence in Co. Armagh, Ireland. Earliest remains are of a round house with associated stockade occupied from 700–100 BC; the skull of a Barbary ape from North Africa indicates the special nature of this first Navan settlement. In c.100 BC the site was transformed by the construction of a massive circular timber building 43 m across standing within a great circular banked and ditched enclosure. The timber building was later burned down and covered by a monumental CAIRN. Iron Age Navan is identified with the historical Emhain Macha, royal seat of the Ulaid, the pre-Christian kings of Ulster.

Navdatoli   an important site on the Narmada River in western Madhya Pradesh in western central India. Sankalia's investigation of Navdatoli together with Maheshwar on the opposite bank of the river provides evidence of Lower and Middle Palaeolithic, Chalcolithic, Iron Age and mediaeval occupations. The Chalcolithic occupation, dated to the 2nd millennium BC, presents four phases distinguished by changes in the pottery: a painted black-and-red ware and a black-painted cream slipped ware occur in the first phase, while JORWE ware appears in the third and fourth phases; the painted MALWA ware occurs throughout this sequence. In all these levels the architecture consists of rectilinear or circular huts of bamboo and daub. The Chalcolithic levels present important information on subsistence in this part of India during the 2nd millennium BC (a focus on wheats and a wide variety of legumes, with addition of rice in the second phase). After a flood deposit, this occupation is followed by several periods belonging to the late 1st millennium BC and early 1st millennium AD, during which architecture shifts from single room dwellings in smaller settlements to monumental architecture and towns, correlated with the CERAMIC sequence NORTHERN BLACK POLISHED to RED POLISHED wares.

naveta (*Lat.* 'little boat')   a stone-built CHAMBERED TOMB shaped like an upturned boat with rounded prow and squared stern. *Navetas* are found on the Balearic Islands and date from the later Bronze Age (c.1500–800 BC). See also ELS TUDONS.

Naville, Henri Edouard (1844–1926) a Swiss Egyptologist who excavated at ABYDOS, DEIR EL-BAHRI, and in the DELTA (e.g. BUBASTIS).

Nazca see NASCA.

Nderit ware formerly **Gumban A** one of several distinct pottery wares associated with PASTORAL NEOLITHIC sites in Kenya and northern Tanzania, but not well defined chronologically or spatially. It is characterized by wedge-shaped impressions over large areas of the pot's surface, and often has deep scoring inside the pot.

Ndondondwane an important mid 8th century AD Early Iron Age village in the Thukela River Valley of central Natal, South Africa. Of particular interest are the remains of structures interpreted as stockades, nearly 2000 fragments of waste from the manufacture of IVORY bangles, and pieces of large CERAMIC sculpture. These include large eyes, horns and crocodile-like jaws on a scale larger than the LYDENBURG heads. Also of interest is the earliest date for domestic chicken in southern Africa.

Neanderthal(ers) see HOMO.

Nea Nikomedeia or **Nea Nikomidhia** a site in Macedonia that was excavated by Rodden in 1961–64 and proved to be one of the earliest Neolithic sites in Greece, occupied in the Early Neolithic period only. A large structure in the centre of the mound contained a number of female figurines and is thought to have served a ritual purpose.

nearest-neighbour analysis a method of determining the extent to which two-dimensionally located points are randomly distributed. The technique has been especially useful to archaeologists studying the distribution of sites over the landscape and their relationship to each other.

Nebuchadnezzar II (604–562 BC) the great royal figure of the NEO-BABYLONIAN empire, well known from the Biblical accounts of his activities in Judea and Samaria. At the beginning of his rule, Babylonia controlled much of MESOPOTAMIA proper, but was under pressure from a resurgent Egypt and its allies in Palestine. Nebuchadnezzar defeated the Egyptians and, famously, conquered the petty states of the Levant, including JERUSALEM, many of whose inhabitants were deported to BABYLON. Most of the monumental buildings at Babylon are his work. The Neo-Babylonian empire did not long survive his death. After three short reigns, Nabonidus (555–539 BC) occupied the throne; this king is notorious for his 10-year withdrawal from Babylon to the city of TAYMA in northwestern Arabia, possibly because of a quarrel with the entrenched power of the MARDUK priesthood at Babylon. His neglect of affairs of state made CYRUS's conquest of Babylonia both easier and welcomed by the populace.

Necker Island a small barren island off the Hawaiian chain; despite being uninhabited at European contact, it is rich in remains of houses, cultivation terraces, and 33 HEIAU of an unusual and standardized form. It is not known whether these result from occasional visits from the main Hawaiian islands or a resident population.

necropolis a cemetery, literally 'a city of the dead'.

Nefertiti an Egyptian queen, the chief wife of AKHENATEN. Nefertiti seems to have played a more prominent role in public life than was usual among consorts of Egyptian kings, and is identified by some scholars with the monarch named Smenkhare who briefly succeeded Akhenaten.

Nelson, Nels (1875–1964)   an American archaeologist who worked in both California and the American Southwest. He is famous for his substantial contribution to the archaeological interpretation of stratigraphy in his work in the Galisteo Basin of New Mexico, especially at the site of San Cristobal Pueblo. He was influenced in this by his earlier excavations of California SHELL MOUNDS, under the direction of Alfred KROEBER and Max UHLE, as well as by innovations in the excavation of various European Palaeolithic sites.

Nelson Bay   a coastal cave, containing a 6 m deep deposit, on the Robberg Peninsula in the southern Cape Province, South Africa. A sterile deposit separates basal MIDDLE STONE AGE material from the upper layers which contain successive LATER STONE AGE industries. The faunal remains document habitat changes caused by sea-level rise and vegetation changes at the end of the PLEISTOCENE.

Nemi   the site of a grove of Diana in the Alban Hills just outside ROME. In 1929 remains of two ships were found in the lake, perhaps those used by the emperor Caligula. These were subsequently destroyed during fighting in the Second World War.

Nenana Complex   a prehistoric CULTURE or COMPLEX in south-central Alaska dating to *c*.12 000–10 500 bp, characterized by small BIFACIAL PROJECTILE POINTS (including CHINDADN POINTS) and a lack of MICROBLADE technology. It represents the earliest firmly dated set of archaeological remains in Alaska. The complex was defined by Powers and Hoffecker in 1989.

Nene Valley ware   a type of Roman pottery, formerly known as Castor ware, produced near Peterborough in England from the 2nd to the 4th centuries AD. The different shapes, which include tumblers, were decorated with a dark SLIP and had added decoration in white; some show elaborate hunting scenes.

Nenumbo   a LAPITA site dating to *c*.1100 BC in the Main Reef Islands, Santa Cruz group. Excavations by Roger Green allowed identification of different activity areas. Faunal remains include pig, chicken, fish, dugong and sea turtle. Artifacts include shell ornaments and OBSIDIAN from TALASEA. The Lapita pottery shows a particularly wide range of motifs.

Neo–Assyrian   the famous political period of the Assyrian empire in the Iron Age. It was basically an extension of the MIDDLE ASSYRIAN patterns of empire building. After the troubles that produced the collapse of the earlier Assyrian empires, the next expansionary episode belonged to the 9th century BC, identified with AŠŠURNAṢIRPAL II (883–859 BC) and his immediate successors. This empire was not long lived, as the question of succession to the throne again weakened the Assyrian expansionary impulse. The intervening period of military mediocrity lasted until the reign of TIGLATH-PILESER III (744–727 BC) who began the creation of the famous Assyrian empire that is reflected in the Old Testament, and among whose rulers are the well-known Sargon (721–705 BC), Sennacherib (704–681 BC), Esarhaddon (680–669 BC) and Assurbanipal (668–627 BC). The Assyrian empire, which at its largest extent stretched from ELAM to Egypt, was destroyed by an alliance of BABYLONIANS and MEDES in 612 BC.

Neo-Babylonian period a long period of political weakness, social disruption (see ARAMAEANS, CHALDEANS), economic decline through the first part of the 1st millennium BC culminating in the absorption of BABYLONIA into the NEO-ASSYRIAN empire (by 688 BC). After several unsuccessful attempts, a rebellion in the 620s managed to evict the Assyrians, and Nabopolassar (625–605 BC) took the throne of Babylonia. In alliance with the MEDES, Nabopolassar managed to destroy the Assyrian state (between 616 and 612 BC), and the Babylonians occupied much of northern MESOPOTAMIA and Syria. This empire was consolidated by NEBUCHADNEZZAR II but lasted only until 539 BC, when the Persian CYRUS invaded and occupied Babylon.

Neolithic a term introduced by Sir John LUBBOCK in 1865 to describe the period of antiquity in which people began to use ground stone tools, cultivate plants, and keep domestic livestock (in contrast to the PALAEOLITHIC), yet still used stone instead of metals for tools. In a number of parts of the world, such as western Europe, the appearance of pottery was also added as a hallmark of the Neolithic. The dating of the Neolithic is quite variable, begining in the Near East in the 8th millennium bc and lasting into the 2nd millennium bc in the more northerly parts of Europe. Over the last century, the term has become progressively more equivocal. For instance, in the Near East, the first food production occurs before pottery (see PRE-POTTERY NEOLITHIC); in Japan, pottery appears among foraging populations without food production (see FUKUI, KAMIKUROIWA). COPPER METALLURGY appears at the end of the Neolithic, leading some to designate this transition to the BRONZE AGE as the ENEOLITHIC. In the minds of most Old World archaeologists, the term retains a certain basic utility as a convention of scholarly communication, which serves to differentiate a society with evidence of food production from those without it on one hand and from those with bronze metallurgy on the other.

In *East Asia* the Chinese Neolithic (6000–2000 BC) includes all social development from the beginning of agricultural society to social stratification; the late Neolithic is often referred to as the LONGSHAN period. It is succeeded directly by the SHANG period of state formation, known also as the early Chinese Bronze Age. In Japan and Korea, the POSTGLACIAL ceramic HUNTER-GATHERERS (JOMON, CHULMUN) are also termed Neolithic for their possible horticultural activities, though cultivation of domesticates occurs later. See CHINESE DYNASTIES, KOREAN PERIODIZATION, JAPANESE PERIODIZATION.

Neolithic Revolution see BROAD SPECTRUM.

Neopalatial the period of the New or Second palaces, in the chronological system for MINOAN Crete devised by Platon: Middle Minoan III–Late Minoan IIIA1 (*c*.1700–1375 BC) in the traditional chronology.

nephrite iron calcium magnesium silicate of the amphibole mineral group that occurs in low-grade metamorphic rocks and is widely distributed. Nephrite is the more common of the two varieties of JADE; the other variety is the tougher, more compact, JADEITE. Nephrite ranges from white to dark green but can be blue and black, and was used for jewellery and ornamental carvings. See also GREENSTONE.

network analysis the study of interconnected SITES or points. Analysis is aimed at understanding the reasons for the particular configurations of the network, whether they be economic, social or geographical.

neutron activation analysis   a physical technique of CHEMICAL ANALYSIS used to determine the composition of a wide range of materials found in archaeological contexts. A specimen is bombarded with neutrons which interact with nuclei in the sample to form radioactive ISOTOPES that emit gamma rays as they decay. The energy spectrum of the emitted rays is detected with a counter, and constituent elements and concentrations are identified by the characteristic energy spectrum of emitted rays and its intensity.

Nevali Çori   a prehistoric site near Samsat on the Euphrates River in southwestern Turkey. The recent work of H. Hauptmann has revealed an ACERAMIC NEOLITHIC settlement that contains significant new information on cultic activities of the PPNB complex. The excavations reveal a series of buildings with stone foundations, one of which differs from the others in architectural detail and accoutrements. Here the floor is paved with stone slabs and in the middle of one room is an upright stone STELA. Broken stelae occur elsewhere in the site, one of which (incorporated into the wall of a structure) bears a human face in high relief. Later occupation at the site includes HALAF–period circular dwellings, and EARLY BRONZE I walling and pits with which are associated COPPER slags and crucibles.

Nevasa   a locality in the headwaters of the Godavari River, on the northern Deccan plateau of Maharastra in western central India, which presents a rich prehistory studied by M.D. Deshpande and H.D. Sankalia. Palaeolithic materials occur within the river SEDIMENTS, and Sankalia has proposed the name 'Nevasan' to refer to the Middle Palaeolithic industry of central India. The next reported occupation is identified by JORWE ware, and belongs to the regional CHALCOLITHIC of the later 2nd millennium BC; the Jorwe pottery at Nevasa displays some idiosyncratic characteristics. The levels of this culture contain remains of houses constructed with wooden posts and plastered floors. Double urn burials (mostly of children) occur under floors; beads strung on a thread of silk and cotton were in one of these burials. Following the Jorwe period settlement is one belonging to the late 1st millennium, where in multiroomed structures occur black-and-red wares, 'Russett coated painted' ware, other wares of the late Iron Age in southern India and some SHERDS of NORTHERN BLACK POLISHED WARE. The next phase represents a basic continuation of the latter, but now with an introduction of RED POLISHED WARE and of AMPHORAE, ROULETTED WARE and other products of the Mediterranean world, indicative of a connection with Rome by the maritime trade early in the 1st millennium AD (hence the designation 'Indo-Roman' for this period).

new archaeology   a development in the 1960s aimed at making archaeology more scientific, now more often referred to as PROCESSUAL ARCHAEOLOGY. It proposed that archaeology should openly state its assumptions and use specific scientific procedures derived from POSITIVISM. Some New Archaeologists believed that laws of human behaviour were obtainable by using the correct METHODOLOGIES. Key elements in new archaeology were cultural EVOLUTION and GENERAL SYSTEMS THEORY. See DEDUCTION, DEDUCTIVE-NOMOLOGICAL, HYPOTHETICO-DEDUCTIVE REASONING, INDUC-

TION.

New Forest ware a type of Roman pottery produced in the New Forest area of southern England especially in the 3rd and 4th centuries AD. Various shapes were produced including cups, flagons and MORTARIA. The plain surface is decorated with added white decoration. The fabric has a limited distribution, with most of the fine-wares travelling no further than 80 km from the kilns.

Newgrange the most famous of the Irish PASSAGE GRAVES, part of the BOYNE VALLEY cemetery, Co. Meath. The large kidney-shaped mound, dated to *c*.3100 BC, is over 100 m in diameter and 13 m high. A kerb of large stones carved with wavy lines, lozenges, triangles and similar motifs encloses the base of the mound. MEGA-LITHIC ART is also represented on several of the ORTHOSTATS of the passage and chamber. The chamber itself is of cruciform plan and is roofed by a tall CORBELLED VAULT. Above the outer entrance to the passage is the roof box, a small opening designed to allow sunlight to shine along the passage and into the chamber for 17 minutes at sunrise on 21 December, the winter solstice. The current appearance of the Newgrange mound, with a near-vertical façade of white QUARTZ blocks above the kerb, is a result of a contentious modern reconstruction.

New Guinea Highlands an area between 1300 and 2300 m above sea level which was unknown until the 1930s. The population comprises MELANESIAN speakers of PAPUAN LANGUAGES and is characterized by small-scale acephalous political organization, although it has some of the most intensive agricultural systems and highest population densities in the Pacific. The prehistory of the Highlands goes back at least 26 000 years (see KOSIPE) and a long sequence of development of agricultural systems has been documented in areas like the Wahgi Valley (see KUK) dating back at least 6000 years.

New Kingdom a period of Egyptian history comprising the 18th to the 20th DYNASTY (*c*.1550–1070), an era of imperial expansion and subsequent decline.

New Zealand the southernmost and only temperate land mass settled by POLYNESIANS, except for the Chatham Islands. New Zealand was first settled about 1000 years ago and involved the adaptation of tropical agriculture to temperate conditions in the North Island. Subsistence in the cooler South Island was primarily based on hunting and gathering. The sequence has commonly been divided into two phases: an earlier Archaic phase, associated with MOA-hunting and Early Eastern Polynesian artifact assemblage and a later Classic MAORI phase with elaborate wood carving, fortified settlements (PA) and a society resembling that described by COOK and others at European contact.

Nezwiska a site of the LINEAR POTTERY CULTURE in Ukraine, on the eastern fringe of Linear Pottery distribution. Settlement remains included a large surface structure 12 by 7 m with several HEARTHS. Although it is elongated, the structure at Nezwiska is different in its construction and proportions from the large timber LONGHOUSES that characterize Linear Pottery settlements in central Europe.

Ngamuriak a Neolithic open-air site in southwest Kenya where extensive excavations revealed stone tools and pottery of the

ELMENTEITAN tradition, dating to c.2000 BP. The animal bones and teeth belong almost exclusively to domestic cattle and sheep/goats. The former represent the earliest evidence for *humped* cattle in eastern Africa. Features at the site include part of a hut floor and accumulations of animal dung. OBSIDIAN used in tool manufacture was obtained from the Rift Valley, more than 100 km away.

Ngandong   a site in the SOLO River valley in east Java which has yielded remains of PLEISTOCENE fauna (later than TRINIL) and advanced HOMO *erectus* (SOLO MAN) of c.100 000 years ago, with which a stone industry of choppers and RETOUCHED FLAKES has been traditionally associated (see CHOPPER/CHOPPING TOOLS), but these may have been washed down from higher TERRACES. See von KOENIGSWALD.

Ngaro   see NDERIT.

Ngilipitji   a QUARTZITE quarry in eastern ARNHEM LAND, whose products, including LEILIRA BLADES, were key items in traditional exchange in northern Australia. Techniques of quarrying and point manufacture have recently been studied with the traditional owners.

Niah Cave   the West Mouth site at Niah in Sarawak, north Borneo, that is one of the major prehistoric deposits of island Southeast Asia containing human remains, the best known of which is the 'deep skull', a HOMO *sapiens* skull recovered from a depth associated with RADIOCARBON dates of c.38 000 bc. which would make it amongst the earliest in the region. However, excavation of the site was not carried out by archaeological strata, and the carbon and the skull were recovered from different parts of the cave, making it more likely that the skull represents a much later inhumation cut into earlier levels. Other deposits include a series of flexed, seated and fragmentary burials more securely dated to 12 000–1500 bc; extended burials in wooden coffins or mats of the last two millennia BC; and jar burials and cremations ranging in date from c.?1500 BC to after AD 1000. Distinctive pottery appears by c.2500 BC along with Neolithic POLISHED STONE ADZES, and metal appears by the 1st millennium AD.

Niaux   a huge cave in Ariège, in the French Pyrenees, where Palaeolithic drawings were discovered on the walls in 1906. Prehistoric visitors had explored all 2 km of galleries, and left some footprints. No trace of occupation has been found. The 'Salon Noir' houses six panels of black animal figures (bison, horse, ibex, deer) of different sizes. Figures are sparser elsewhere, but include some engravings in the clay floor. Recent analysis has shown that some black figures were first sketched in charcoal, and six different pigment 'recipes' have been detected. Dates for the same recipes at nearby LA VACHE assign much of Niaux's art to the late MAGDALENIAN of the 11th millennium bc and this is confirmed by a RADIOCARBON date of 10 940 bc from charcoal in a Salon Noir bison figure.

Nichoria or **Nikhoria**   the site of a MYCENAEAN settlement in Messenia, Greece, excavated in 1969–73. A substantial 15th century BC structure, rebuilt in the 14th century, may be an early palace, and there were at least two THOLOS tombs.

niello   powdered sulphides of COPPER and silver, heated to produce a bluish-black plastic substance which was used to decorate metalwork, in particular the inlaid daggers from the SHAFT GRAVE circles excavated at MYCENAE.

Nietoperzowa Cave or **Jerzmanowice**   a prehistoric cave-site located on the Bêdkówka River, northwest of Kraków in southern Poland. Artifacts and faunal remains (primarily CAVE BEAR) are buried in LOAM and rubble deposits. The lower cultural layers contain Middle Palaeolithic assemblages (e.g. sidescrapers – see SCRAPER – and BIFACES) dated by stratigraphic correlation to the end of the Middle PLEISTOCENE, Last INTERGLACIAL, and Early GLACIAL. Above a sterile layer lie several early Upper Palaeolithic layers containing LAUREL-LEAF POINTS which are assigned to the JERZMANOWICIAN industry; the lowest of these layers yielded a RADIOCARBON date of 38 500 bp. Neolithic and later remains occur in the uppermost layer. Nietoperzowa was excavated by Roemer in 1878–79, Chmielewski in 1956–63 and others.

Nihewan [Ni-ho-wan]   a basin and stratigraphic formation in Hebei Province, China. The SANDS and CLAYS of the Nihewan Formation were originally dated to between 3 and 1.52 million years ago; now they are thought to be 1 million years old, but they still include some of north China's earliest Palaeolithic tools (QUARTZITE CHOPPERS and FLAKES). The mammalian fauna of the Nihewan Formation belongs to the Lower PLEISTOCENE and is characterized by an early form of horse.

Nihon Shoki or ***Nihongi***   the second-earliest surviving chronicle of Japan, compiled in the 8th century AD as part of the RITSURYO state's effort at legitimizing the ruling dynasty. These political documents include imperial genealogies, legendary events and reign chronicles; their use in archaeology provides data for the protohistoric KOFUN period. (See also KOJIKI.)

Nikhoria   see NICHORIA.

Nîmes (*Lat.* Nemausus)   a colony founded by the emperor Augustus in France. Extant remains include the mid 1st century AD AMPHITHEATRE designed by Titus Crisius Reburrus. It could hold some 21 000 people. The *Maison Carrée* is a temple dating from the 1st century BC. Water brought by AQUEDUCT to the town (see PONT DU GARD) was redistributed from the *castellum*.

Nimrud   see KALHU.

Nineveh   a walled city covering some 750 ha at the time of the NEO-ASSYRIAN empire, that has provided its steady stream of excavators (beginning with Emile Botta in 1842) with a wealth of Neo-Assyrian art, architecture and texts, including the famous winged bulls that grace the British Museum and the library of Assurbanipal. The city walls incorporate two mounds, Kuyunjik (the citadel) and Nebi Yunus (the arsenal), which correspond to the separate citadel and arsenal compounds that were standard in Neo-Assyrian cities. Most attention has been paid to the Kuyunjik mound, beginning with H. LAYARD's and H. Rassam's work on the palaces of Sennacherib (704–681 BC) and Assurbanipal (668–627 BC). The Kuyunjik mound was also the setting of M. MALLOWAN's deep sounding at the ISHTAR temple. This work established a long sequence whose earliest levels begin with a HASSUNA occupation (Nineveh 1). The regional implications of the Nineveh sequence have been overtaken by later work, though the term k'NINEVITE 5' is still current in the archaeological literature. Mallowan's deep sounding also recovered one of the most famous pieces of later 3rd millennium art work, the life-size bronze head of an AKKADIAN king, often identified as SARGON

NINEVITE 5

(the founder of the Akkadian empire at the end of the 24th century BC).

Ninevite 5 1. a style of painted pottery and the accompanying incised and excised decorated wares; the term is derived from Max MALLOWAN's deep sounding at NINEVEH.
2. an archaeological period or horizon in northern MESOPOTAMIA. Recent work (at Telul Thelathat, LEILAN, Tell Mohammad 'Arab) has firmly dated this pottery to c.2900–2500 BC, and has defined stylistic changes within the period, notably the chronological priority of the painted over the incised wares.

Ninstints the finest *in situ* example of North American Northwest Coast architecture and monumental art. This large multilineage village site is located on Anthony Island, off the coast of British Columbia, Canada, and comprises standing superstructures of buildings, living floors, roof beams and 21 standing mortuary poles, some of which date to the early 1800s. The earliest occupation of the site is dated to approximately AD 360, and the village was abandoned in 1888. The village was occupied by the prehistoric and historic Haida.

Nintoku the 17th emperor of Japan, as given in the traditional list for the 5th century AD and the name of the KEYHOLE-shaped MOUNDED TOMB, the largest in Japan measuring over 485 m long, specified as his mausoleum in Osaka Prefecture.

Nippur a city of southern MESOPOTAMIA, one of the great cultural centres of the Mesopotamian world, that has been the object of successive American excavations, beginning with those of John Peters in 1889 and continuing to McGuire Gibson's work today. The city, covering some 75 ha, was first occupied by late 'UBAID times, and continued to be inhabited into the 1st millennium AD. Nippur was a religious and scribal centre, though was never a political capital; in SUMERIAN myth, Nippur was the city of the god ENLIL and the meeting place of the divine assembly. The archaeological investigations of the city have provided an extremely detailed sequence of pottery that covers most of the pre-Islamic periods of southern Iraq, much of which comes from a deep sounding in the INANNA temple precinct. Excavations at the site have also produced a wealth of CUNEIFORM archives (particularly cultic texts of various periods and economic texts of the KASSITE and ACHAEMENID periods). And in addition to the religious architecture of EARLY DYNASTIC and UR III dates (e.g. the Inanna precinct, the Enlil ZIGGURAT), the Nippur excavations have recently exposed OLD BABYLONIAN residential architecture, the social and economic history of which can be interpreted with the aid of contemporary documents.

Nishiyagi a site in Hyogo Prefecture, Japan, where a 5 cm × 27 cm wooden board dating to the Palaeolithic period has been excavated. Preserved by waterlogging and bearing whittling scars, it is dated to 50 000–70 000 bp, adding to the debate as to whether there was an Early Palaeolithic in Japan. (See HOSHINO.)

Nissan Island a MELANESIAN island, halfway between the BISMARCK ARCHIPELAGO and the Solomons, where recent work at several sites has identified a sequence of LAPITA stratified above earlier material. The pre-Lapita deposits date back to c.5000 bp and are ACERAMIC NEOLITHIC; they do, however, contain TALASEA OBSIDIAN, indicating long-distance sea voyaging in the pre-Lapita period.

Nitovikla   the site of a fortress in eastern Cyprus, which was excavated by Sjöqvist in 1929. The fortress was built in the Middle CYPRIOT period, presumably to defend the Karpass peninsula against sea raids from Anatolia and Syria; it was destroyed, and then rebuilt in Late Cypriot I.

Nitra   a large cemetery of the LINEAR POTTERY culture in southern Slovakia which has provided a considerable amount of data on mortality, age and sex ratios, and differential burial treatment during the Early Neolithic. Seventy-five percent of the male burials, particularly those of older individuals, had grave-goods, including SPONDYLUS shell ornaments and SHOE-LAST axes.

Nitriansky Hrádok   a fortified site of the BOLERÁZ culture at the transition from the ENEOLITHIC to the Early Bronze Age in Slovakia in the late 3rd/early 2nd millennium BC. The fortifications at Nitriansky Hrádok are characterized by a double ditch and timber-framed rampart, with elaborate 'inturned' gateway construction. Numerous artifacts include antler cheekpieces for horse-bits.

nitrogen dating   a RELATIVE DATING technique applied to bone. In the burial environment, bone collagen decomposes releasing nitrogen, a major component, at a fairly uniform slow rate. The relative ages of bones in similar burial environments can be compared by examining the remaining nitrogen content, assuming bones initially have similar amounts of collagen. Nitrogen concentrations are determined by CHEMICAL ANALYSIS.

Niuheliang   see HONGSHAN.

Njoro River Cave   one of the earliest sites of the ELMENTEITAN industry of the PASTORAL NEOLITHIC in Kenya, dated to about the 12th century BC. It functioned as a cemetery for cremated burials, each of which was accompanied by a stone bowl, pestle and mortar. An elaborately decorated wooden vessel, thought to be associated with milking, and a gourd were also recovered.

Nkope   an Early Iron Age site in southern Malawi which has given its name to a branch of the Eastern Stream of UREWE Tradition of the CHIFUMBAZE Complex of the early 1st millennium AD. It is thought that a migration from the Nkope area resulted in the appearance of the GOKOMERE Complex in Zimbabwe around AD 500.

Nkudzi   a Late Iron Age cemetery on the southwestern shore of Lake Malawi, dating to the late 18th–early 19th centuries AD. Abundant grave-goods attest to a period of trade with the East African coast, as well as slave raiding.

Noailles burin   an Upper Palaeolithic FLAKE tool RETOUCHED to give several chisel-like edges. Named after the cave of Noailles in Corrèze, France, it characterizes a FACIES of the Upper PERIGORDIAN (the 'Noaillian') dating to c.27 000 bp. See BURIN.

nodule   a rounded to irregular relatively hard mass of mineral matter formed in a SOIL that exhibits massive internal structure formed by the localized deposition of minerals from solution. Nodules that formed under differing environmental conditions may differ mineralogically, isotopically and radiometrically. These characteristics may aid PALAEOENVIRONMENTAL reconstruction and age determination of the conditions under which they formed. Compare CONCRETION.

Nok   a valley in central Nigeria which has given its name to an Early Iron Age culture characterized by distinctive broken TERRACOTTA human and animal figures, which are interpreted as altar figures associated with an agricultural fertility cult. Nok settlement sites at TARUGA and Samun Dukiya date to between the 5th and 3rd centuries BC.

nomarch the chief official of an Egyptian NOME. The power of a nomarch, usually most pronounced during an INTERMEDIATE PERIOD, may be seen in the often lavish tombs they built for themselves (e.g. BENI HASSAN, EL-BERSHEH).

Nombe a rockshelter in the NEW GUINEA HIGHLANDS with evidence of occupation going back 25 000 years. Extinct species, including THYLACINE and PROTEMNODON, occur in the PLEISTOCENE levels with WAISTED AXES.

nome an administrative district of ancient Egypt. By the Graeco-Roman period, whose temples are the major source of surviving lists of nomes, there were 22 in UPPER EGYPT and 20 in LOWER EGYPT.

nomothetic, *adj.* pertaining to general laws and principles of human behaviour. It is the opposite of IDIOGRAPHIC.

Non Chai a large (approximately 38.5 ha) late-prehistoric settlement in the upper Chi valley, KHORAT, Thailand, apparently settled *c*.600 500 BC. Iron appears in basal layers. Peak economic activity occurred between *c*.200 and 100 BC, at which time local pottery was traded to the Songkhram basin sites about 100 km to the north. The site was abandoned by about AD 300. The early date of abandonment may explain the lack of moats (see MOATED SITES).

Non Dua a late-prehistoric moated settlement (see MOATED SITES) in southern KHORAT, Thailand, occupied from *c*.600 500 BC to *c*.AD 800. The local economy included rock-salt extraction and trade.

Non Nok Tha the most extensively excavated prehistoric settlement in the KHORAT region of Thailand, occupied from *c*.3000–500 400 BC, and then abandoned for a number of centuries before being reoccupied late in the 1st millennium AD. The prehistoric occupation spans the transition from Neolithic to bronze-working on the site. Unlike the nearby sites of BAN CHIANG and BAN NADI, it appears to have been abandoned before iron was in general use.

Non Pa Wai one of a cluster of prehistoric COPPER-extracting and SMELTING sites in the Khao Wong Prachan valley, near LOPBURI in the hills dividing the KHORAT plateau from the Chao Phraya valley in Thailand. Finds at this site and those of *Non Ma Kla* and *Nil Kam Haeng* include thousands of crucibles, tuyères, ore fragments, cup moulds for casting INGOTS and clay bivalve moulds for casting such items as axe-, spear- and arrow-heads, and bracelets. Estimated dates are *c*.1500–250 BC.

non-site archaeology see OFF-SITE ARCHAEOLOGY.

Noricum an Iron Age POLITY (sometimes referred to as a 'kingdom') in the eastern Alps, with its seat at Magdalensberg in Austria. Noricum flourished during the last centuries BC and was linked to the Italian peninsula by close trading connections. Mining and iron working were significant economic activities. Around 15 BC, Noricum was absorbed by the Roman Empire.

normative, *adj.* relating to a view of CULTURE, whereby an individual society has a uniform and standard way of doing things, so that these social norms are represented by particular homogeneous patterns in the archaeological record.

Norşuntepe   a 10 ha prehistoric site in the Keban plain on the upper Euphrates River in eastern Anatolia, where H. Hauptmann's excavations have revealed a sequence of occupation from CHALCOLITHIC to Iron Age times. The earliest levels show connections with the HALAF and 'UBAID horizons, but are not well known. During the occupation contemporary with the Late URUK period, architecture becomes more elaborate and contains a probable COPPER foundry. Copper workshops continue to be present in the subsequent EARLY BRONZE levels, whose CERAMICS reveal connections both to the south (pottery comparable to 'AMUQ G materials) and to the northeast (KURA-ARAXES culture). At the end of the Early Bronze period, the multiple-building architecture is replaced by a single large complex, perhaps a rural manor house. The later occupations are less substantial. The evidence for copper production at Norşuntepe during the late 4th millennium BC has added significance when combined with similar evidence at the nearby site of Tepecik, where the Late Uruk phenomenon is more strongly represented. In both cases, the copper production was based on the important Ergani copper sources, and was arguably stimulated by demand in southern MESOPOTAMIA.

Northern Archaic Tradition   a cultural tradition of the North American arctic and subarctic dating to *c.*6000–4000 bp. The most characteristic artifact type is the SIDE-NOTCHED POINT, although assemblages also contain oval BIFACES, endscrapers (see SCRAPER) and notched pebbles (net-sinkers?); MICROBLADES have been recovered from some sites, but may represent mixture of materials from other traditions. The Northern Archaic Tradition is widely thought to reflect a population intrusion from more southerly latitudes; it was defined in 1968 by Anderson.

Northern black polished ware   a very fine grey ware with a lustrous black surface (actually ranging from silvery-white to brown) produced by coating the surface with an alkali flux and firing in a reducing atmosphere. This ware was made from 500 BC (or slightly earlier) until the 1st century BC, and had a distribution from the lower Ganges in the east into the Punjab in the west. NBPW characterizes the urban kingdoms of early historical India, the social setting of the Buddha.

Northern zone   the steppe region south of the Gobi desert along the northern edge of agricultural China, comprising Inner Mongolia, the ORDOS and southern DONGBEI regions. Within this zone developed several local BRONZE AGE cultures with nomadic connections in the 1st millennium BC.

Norton   a series of Arctic Alaska cultures, essentially coastal in orientation, dating from approximately 1000 BC–AD 1000 that contain the first evidence for the use of CERAMICS in the region. The CHORIS CULTURE, which is the earliest manifestation of the tradition, is characterized by pottery that is Asiatic in origin, is fibre-tempered and has linear-stamp decorations. The IPIUTAK CULTURE, dated to the end of the tradition, lacks 'classic' Norton forms, such as pottery.

Nové Košariská   an Early Iron Age complex of TUMULI near Bratislava in Slovakia, dated to the HALLSTATT C and D periods. Of the seven tumuli at Nové Košariská, five have been excavated to reveal elaborate central timber-lined chambers with cremation burials in many different vessels (between 20 and 80 in each tumulus), but relatively few bronze weapons or luxury items.

Nové Mesto an Upper Palaeolithic open-air site located on the Váh River in western Slovakia (Czechoslovakia). Artifacts were found at many levels in a deep succession of LOESS and slope deposits. The lowest buried soil, correlated with the final warm phase of the Middle PLEISTOCENE, yielded isolated FLAKES. Middle Palaeolithic artifacts (e.g. sidescrapers – see SCRAPER) were recovered above the Last INTERGLACIAL soil, while an overlying soil (corresponding to the Early GLACIAL?) yielded a LAUREL-LEAF POINT (SZELETIAN?). The uppermost buried soil contains artifacts assigned to the EASTERN GRAVETTIAN.

Novgorod an early urban centre in northwestern Russia 160 km south of St Petersburg. Founded in the 9th century AD, Novgorod came to control a vast territory in the 14th and 15th centuries, extending to the Arctic Ocean and beyond the Ural Mountains. Excavations at Novgorod have revealed evidence of extensive craft production and involvement of the city's merchants in a vast trading network. Among the most interesting finds from Novgorod are over 700 letters written on birch-bark between the 11th and 15th centuries. Extensive waterlogged deposits account for the good preservation.

Novo Mesto an Early Iron Age settlement and complex of TUMULI in Slovenia, dated to the HALLSTATT D period.in the 5th century BC. A stone wall enclosed a 2.5 ha settlement centre. Nearby, 10 large tumuli, averaging 30 m in diameter, have been excavated. The number of inhumation burials in each ranges from 20 to 35. Finds include bronze SITULAE, breastplates, and helmets, as well as ornaments of Baltic amber.

Novye Ruseshty or **Novi Ruseşti** a multiperiod Neolithic and EN-EOLITHIC site in Moldova. The first occupation at Novye Ruseshty was of the LINEAR POTTERY culture, while later layers belong to the CUCUTENI-TRIPOLYE culture. Nearby was the location of the KARBUNA hoard, and a number of COPPER objects have been found in Cucuteni-Tripolye contexts at Novye Ruseshty itself.

Noyen-sur-Seine a Middle Neolithic enclosure consisting of a system of palisades cutting across a meander of the River Seine, Seine-et-Marne, France. In a later phase the enclosure was replaced by an interrupted ditch enclosure, smaller in area and cutting across the first. Within the enclosures domestic debris indicates a settlement-site including hearths, storage pits, pottery and stylized female TERRACOTTA figurines. To the east of the enclosure in PEAT deposits of an old arm of the Seine, Mesolithic organic remains have been found (c.7000–5000 BC), in particular a dugout canoe and basketry fish-traps.

Ntereso an open site in northern Ghana with evidence of an as yet undated early occupation with MICROLITHIC tools, bone HARPOONS, small axes and pottery.

Nthabazingwe see LEOPARD'S KOPJE.

Nubia that part of the Nile Valley stretching from ASWAN in Egypt as far south as the Khartoum district in the Sudan, and conventionally divided into UPPER and LOWER NUBIA. See also A-GROUP, C-GROUP.

Nubian Rescue Campaign an international effort, coordinated by

UNESCO between 1960 and 1980, to limit the loss of archaeological data as a result of the building of the ASWAN High Dam and the subsequent flooding of much of LOWER NUBIA by the newly created Lake Nasser. The campaign had two main objectives: the survey and excavation of as many as possible of the archaeological sites which would be destroyed by Lake Nasser; and the dismantling and re-erection of the most important TEMPLES in the affected area (e.g. ABU SIMBEL, PHILAE, KALABSHA).

nucleus   see CORE.

Nunamira Cave formerly **Bluff Cave**   one of several recently excavated limestone caves in southwest TASMANIA, Australia, which have particularly rich PLEISTOCENE occupation deposits. The site was first occupied *c*.30 500 bp and abandoned about 12 000 years ago. See also KUTIKINA, WARGATA MINA.

nuraghe (*pl.* **nuraghi**)   a circular stone defensive tower with CORBEL-VAULTED internal chambers dating from the Middle and Late Bronze Ages on Sardinia (*c*.1500–800 BC). Some, such as BARUMINI, were strengthened by the addition of substantial outer fortifications with further stone towers in the 1st millennium BC. The later part of the Nuraghic period is noted also for its bronze figurines and votive models.

Nuri   a site in UPPER NUBIA, the successor to KURRU as the main royal PYRAMID cemetery of the NAPATAN kings during the mid 7th to early 3rd centuries BC.

Nus–i Jan   one of the few excavated plausibly MEDIAN sites. It lies in the Malayer valley of Luristan in western Iran. D. Stronach's work revealed a small fortified settlement of the late 8th century BC that contained a columned hall, a fort and several shrines; one of the latter is identified as a fire-temple that was intentionally filled with shale when the place was abandoned. This architectural reminder of Median cultic practices may not be directly associated with Zoroastrianism, but surely belongs to the general cultural background of this important religious system. A later PARTHIAN settlement also exists on the site.

Nuzi   the small (4 ha) site of Yorgan Tepe near Kirkuk in north-eastern Iraq where the excavations by Edward Chiera and others in the 1920s and 1930s recovered evidence for occupation from 'UBAID to Sassanian times. Many of the earlier levels of the site are poorly understood, and Nuzi takes its importance from a collection of Old AKKADIAN texts (when the place was named Ga.sur) of the 23rd century BC and from the wide exposure of mid 2nd millennium occupation associated with the kingdom of Arrapkha and with the MITANNI. The abundant texts recovered from the latter occupation provide the richest available documentation of the Mitanni empire, and for the sociopolitical character of 2nd-millennium petty kingdoms in northeastern Iraq. Nuzi also gives its name to a style of painted pottery strongly associated with Mitanni domains but widely distributed in mid 2nd millennium western Asian sites.

nymphaion   an elaborately decorated semicircular monumental CLASSICAL fountain-house, often with niches filled with sculpture. The name is derived from Caves of the Nymphs.

O

Oakhurst   a cave in the southern Cape Province of South Africa containing over 3 m of LATER STONE AGE material. The basal layers dating to *c*.12 000–8000 BP preserve material ascribed to the ALBANY or Oakhurst industry (formerly SMITHFIELD A). Some researchers include this industry together with the LOCKSHOEK and POMONGWE industries in an Oakhurst Complex. This is characterized by quadrilateral FLAKES larger than those in preceding or succeeding assemblages. MICROLITHS are very rare and there are few formally patterned artifacts other than SCRAPERS more than 20 mm long, although there are numerous bone tools at some sites.

oasis   a fertile patch in a desert. The five major oases of the western desert of Egypt (Siwa, Bahariya, Farafra, Dakhla and Kharga) were considered as peripheral border regions by the ancient Egyptians. Kharga Oasis has produced industries of the Lower and Middle Palaeolithic discovered by Gardner and CATON-THOMPSON in 1930–33. Apart from the settlements of the OLD KINGDOM and First INTERMEDIATE PERIOD in Dakhla Oasis, the oases do not seem to have been substantially occupied in the historic period until the 1st millennium BC.

Oaxaca   see VALLEY OF OAXACA.

Obanian, *adj.*   denoting a group of KITCHEN MIDDEN settlements found along the western Scottish coast and dating to the Late Mesolithic, between *c*.3065 and 3900 bc. The sites have yielded rather poor stone implements but well preserved bone and antler artifacts designed to exploit the coastal environment, including HARPOON heads and finger-shaped objects identified as 'limpet scoops'.

obelisk   an ancient Egyptian monolithic monument, consisting of a tall, thin, square shaft tapering to a pyramidal peak. Obelisks were usually cut from a hard stone, particularly granite from ASWAN, and were typically erected in pairs before the PYLON of a TEMPLE. The sides of an obelisk were inscribed with columns of HIEROGLYPHIC text referring, in a self-laudatory manner, to the king who caused it to be erected. This form of monument was used from the OLD KINGDOM onwards, but the largest surviving examples (up to 30 m in height and 450 tons in weight) were products of the NEW KINGDOM.

Oblazowa   an Upper Palaeolithic cave-site located along the Bialka River in southern Poland. Artifacts and faunal remains (e.g. reindeer, arctic fox) are buried in cave deposits, apparently dating to the beginning of the LAST GLACIAL MAXIMUM. The artifacts include an endscraper (see SCRAPER), BLADES and a polished fragment of a woolly MAMMOTH tusk that represents a BOOMERANG.

obol   a small unit of Greek COINAGE, derived from the word for a spit. Six obols were the equivalent of one DRACHMA, literally a handful. Iron spits, probably an early form of currency, have been excavated in the sanctuary of Artemis Orthia at SPARTA. At ATHENS the silver obol weighed *c.*0.72 g, and on AEGINA it weighed 1.05 g. Multiples of the obol could be issued such as the *triobol* (3) and the *tetrobol* (4).

Obora   see KAMEGAOKA.

Obre   a complex of Neolithic settlements on the Bosna River near Sarajevo in Bosnia. The settled area at Obre I covered an area of about 1.5 ha, with rectangular houses similar to those at KARANOVO I and ANZA arranged in rows. Obre II was occupied somewhat later, by the BUTMIR culture, related to VINČA. Situated halfway between the Adriatic coast and the inland Morava corridor, Obre has yielded pottery from both areas, which has been interpreted as reflecting possible TRANSHUMANT pastoralism.

obsidian   a naturally occurring volcanic glass, easily chipped to form extremely sharp (though brittle) edges; this makes it a desirable raw material for tools. In western Asia, important obsidian sources occur in central and eastern Anatolia, the neighbouring Transcaucasus, and southwest Arabia. Chemical characterization studies of these flows and of obsidian artifacts from ancient sites (through TRACE ELEMENT ANALYSIS) have pinpointed sources and documented traffic in obsidian through western Asia, both within regions nearer to the sources and in those much further away; as in the Aegean (see MELOS) this traffic seems to begin with the Neolithic. Obsidian was also an important trade item in MESOAMERICA, and many of the basic tools of prehistoric households there were made of this material. See also OBSIDIAN HYDRATION DATING.

Obsidian was an important resource in the Pacific and was widely exchanged. The most important sources are in MELANESIA where TALASEA obsidian was exploited as far back as 19 000 bp at MATENBEK, with obsidian from LOU coming into use in the Late HOLOCENE. There are also many sources in NEW ZEALAND, the most important being MAYOR ISLAND, and obsidian was widely used from first settlement. It was also important on EASTER ISLAND (see MATAA).

obsidian hydration dating   a chemical dating method used to date OBSIDIAN ARTIFACTS. It is based on the diffusion of atmospheric and SOIL water into fresh surfaces of obsidian, beginning immediately after they are exposed. A distinct hydration rind grows inward and it thickens with time. The rate of thickening, or hydration rate, is also a function of temperature and to a lesser degree chemical composition of the obsidian. This rate can be CALIBRATED for a region and composition, by CROSS-DATING and FISSION TRACK DATING methods. In regions where hydration rates have been determined, ages in excess of 100 000 years have been calculated.

Oc Eo   the most famous protohistoric site in Southeast Asia, located in the Mekong delta, south Vietnam, and once connected with the state of FUNAN. The urban enclosure comprises five rectangular ramparts and four moats, covering 450 ha, and bisected by a canal linked to other sites and waterways giving access to the sea. Structural remains and finds at this early port site date mainly to the 1st millennium AD, the heaviest use of the site being between the 2nd and 7th centuries. Imports include Chinese bronzes, Indian beads, SEALS and other jewellery, Roman medallions of the 2nd century AD, and jewellery from the Mediterranean. Local manufactures include glass and stone beads, and jewellery of tin, bronze and gold. The canals linked the town to docks at Ta Kev, and to inland sites like Angkor Borei and Da Noi.

ochre soft varieties of the iron oxide minerals haematite, limonite and goethite, widespread weathering materials of iron-bearing minerals, used as a pigment for painting and pottery SLIPS, personal decoration, and on skeletons. Red ochre is haematite, whereas limonite and goethite produce brown, yellow and black colours.

Ochre Coloured Pottery a distinctive CERAMIC of post–HARAPPAN northern India. OCP is a poorly fired ware to which a red wash or SLIP has been applied. The ware belongs to a family of Late Harappan ceramics (e.g. Late Siswal, Bara, Cemetery H) which are poorly systematized or understood, and OCP tends to be an elastic term. Generally speaking, these Late Harappan ceramics belong to the 2nd millennium BC. They may be grouped with similar pottery as a style derived from the Harappan tradition, and are broadly dated to most of the 2nd millennium BC.

Ocsöd-Kovashalom a Late Neolithic site of the TISZA culture, located on the Körös River in eastern Hungary. Neolithic finds and settlement features are spread over an area of 21 ha, concentrated on three small elevations. These settlement nuclei yielded traces of a number of small rectangular post structures that had undergone several episodes of rebuilding over the occupation span of the settlement. Associated with these were a number of household features, including ovens, storage pits, rubbish pits, and burials.

oculus (*Lat.* 'eye') the central opening at the top of a dome, such as that in the Pantheon at ROME.

odeum or **odeon** a Roman covered concert hall usually with tiered seating. A good example is that of Agrippa in the AGORA at ATHENS.

Odmut a cave-site in the Montenegran alps, on the Piva River, Montenegro. The lower layers at Odmut resulted from a long Mesolithic occupation (8100–6650 bc). Sixty-five per cent of the Mesolithic faunal sample consisted of ibex, 25% of red deer, and the remainder of roe deer, pig and bear. Fish bones and antler HARPOONS were also found. Later layers contained an Early Neolithic IMPRESSED WARE occupation, above which were Late Neolithic, ENEOLITHIC and Early Bronze Age deposits.

Oelknitz an Upper Palaeolithic open-air site located on the Saale River in eastern Germany. Artifacts and faunal remains (e.g. horse, reindeer) are buried in deposits dated by RADIOCARBON to 12 542–11 750 bp. Among the tools are BACKED BLADES, endscrapers (see SCRAPER), BURINS and bone points; art objects include stylized VENUS FIGURINES. The assemblage, which is assigned to the MAGDALENIAN, is considered typical of this region ('Oelknitz Group').

Offa's Dyke a linear earthwork of ANGLO-SAXON England, *c.*192 km in length, and built by King Offa of Mercia in the late 8th century AD as a frontier between his kingdom and that of Powys. This large earthen bank and quarry ditch lies close to the modern border of England and Wales.

off-site archaeology, **non-site archaeology** or **landscape archaeology** an approach, especially in archaeological survey, where the unit of analysis is the ARTIFACT rather than the SITE. Off-site archaeology recognizes that many of the material consequences of human behaviour are ephemeral and will not conform to standard definitions of sites, and documents the distribution of humanly-modified materials across the landscape.

ogam or **ogham** a CELTIC script of northwest Europe comprising about 20 letters represented by tally marks on either side of or crossing a horizontal baseline. Of uncertain origin, it is thought to have been created in the 2nd or 3rd century AD. Most inscriptions are found in Ireland and Wales (in ancestral Gaelic), but the script is also found in Scotland by the 8th century (in an unknown tongue). Claims have been made for ogam inscriptions in many parts of the New World, especially North America, but most scholars treat these with extreme scepticism.

Ohaba-Ponor a Palaeolithic cave-site located on a tributary of the Mureş River in the southern Carpathian Mountains of western Romania. Artifacts and faunal remains are buried in deposits of LOESS and clay; among the faunal remains are woolly MAMMOTH and reindeer. Most of the cultural layers contain assemblages dominated by sidescrapers (see SCRAPER) and points, and are assigned to the Middle Palaeolithic. The uppermost layer apparently contains a small Upper Palaeolithic assemblage. Ohaba-Ponor was excavated by Nicolăescu-Plopşor in 1954–55 and others.

Ohalo II see KEBARAN.

oinochoe a Greek jug made from precious metal, bronze or clay. It seems to have been used for pouring wine at the SYMPOSIUM and it is often shown in conjunction with a PHIALE during the pouring of LIBATIONS at an altar. See CHOUS.

Ojin the 16th emperor of Japan as given in the traditional list for the 5th century AD, and the name of a KEYHOLE-shaped MOUNDED TOMB, 415 m long, specified as his mausoleum in Osaka Prefecture.

Okhotsk a deep-sea fishing culture of Northeast Asia, between the 8th–14th centuries AD, on coastal areas of northeast Hokkaido, Japan, and southern Kurile and Sakhalin Islands. (Compare SATSUMON.)

Okladnikov, Aleksei Pavlovich (1908–84) a Soviet archaeologist and specialist in Siberian and Central Asian prehistory. Okladnikov discovered and excavated the NEANDERTHAL burial at the site of TESHIK TASH in Uzbekistan, and investigated many important Siberian Palaeolithic sites, including UST'-KAN CAVE, ULALINKA, MAKAROVO, KRASNYJ YAR, BURET' and others.

Old Babylonian period a chronological designation, roughly dated between 2000 and 1600 BC, for a time of competing kingdoms in southern MESOPOTAMIA which were eventually conquered by HAMMURABI of BABYLON. During the first half of the period, the political landscape of southern Mesopotamia was composed of many kingdoms, many of them ruled by AMORITE dynasties; ISIN and LARSA were two of the more important of these kingdoms, and these two cities supply the term 'Isin-Larsa period' in referring to the first quarter of the 2nd millennium BC. The second half of the Old Babylonian period contained the large kingdom that Hammurabi created, his successors gradually lost, and Murshili I the HITTITE king destroyed in his raid on Babylon (in 1595 BC according to the conventional chronology). Archaeological work on Old Babylonian settlements is well represented throughout southern Mesopotamia.

Oldbury a rockshelter located in Kent, in one of the few areas of Britain with caves suitable for occupation during the Palaeolithic period. The site, which has yielded many typologically Middle Palaeolithic artifacts including BIFACES and well-made FLAKE tools, was excavated by HARRISON in 1890.

Old Copper Culture   a related series of late ARCHAIC complexes in the upper Great Lakes area of Canada and the United States that shared the use of beaten native COPPER. The metal was shaped into a wide variety of utilitarian tools. The copper tools may have also carried some degree of social prestige.

Old Cordilleran   a tradition, recognized most easily by a distinctive leaf-shaped, bi-pointed lanceolate point (Cascade type), that is found throughout Pacific North America. The tradition is best recognized at the FIVE MILE RAPIDS SITE in levels dated to about 9800 BP, with earlier dates possible. The tradition has a terminal date of about 7000 BP. The Old Cordilleran Tradition may have cultural ties to such southerly located complexes as SAN DIEGUITO.

Old Crow   a series of locales along the Old Crow River in the Yukon, Canada, that were once thought to contain the earliest indisputable artifact in the New World, a piece of caribou leg-bone that had been worked into a tool used to de-flesh animal hides. A RADIOCARBON date obtained from the tool in the 1960s was approximately 27 000 bp, although the tool was very similar to ones made by recent DENE peoples. In 1986, a new and more accurate technique of radiocarbon dating was applied to the bone, and this gave a date of only 1350 bp, thus destroying claims to the tool's antiquity.

Oldishi   a Kenyan PASTORAL NEOLITHIC pottery tradition, which is divided into southern, eastern and northern FACIES. NAROSURA Ware is a phase of the southern facies.

Old Kingdom   a period of Egyptian history comprising the 3rd to the 8th DYNASTIES (*c.*2700–2160 BC), sometimes referred to as the 'PYRAMID Age' from the monumental tombs of its more powerful kings.

Oldowan   an EARLIER STONE AGE INDUSTRY and COMPLEX represented at OLDUVAI GORGE and other African sites, dating from before 2 million to about 1.6 million years ago and later, and presumed to have been made by HOMO *habilis*. It is characterized by the production of small FLAKES removed from alternate faces along the edge of a cobble. Many Oldowan flaked cobbles or 'CHOPPERS' show signs of use and were probably opportunistic tools, but the purpose of the flaking seems to have been the production of small sharp flakes which could be used as cutting or scraping tools. The utility of such flakes for cutting has been confirmed by experiments.

Olduvai Gorge   an important locality in northern Tanzania containing a series of sites in sediments in an ancient lake basin, from which the longest cultural sequence in the world has been recorded. Research by Louis and Mary LEAKEY, and other workers, has uncovered numerous HOMINID remains and large collections of animal bones as well as stone artifacts dating from *c.*1.9 million years to less than 10 000 years ago. Of particular interest are the finds of ZINJANTHROPUS in 1959, and the first fossils to be named HOMO *habilis* in the early 1960s. These finds sparked intensive studies of early humans at sites throughout East Africa, on which most current knowledge of early humans is based (see DEVELOPED OLDOWAN, OLDOWAN).

Oleneostrovski Mogilnik a large MESOLITHIC cemetery located on Lake Onega in northern Russia. One hundred and seventy burials (out of an estimated 400) have been excavated, yielding more than 7000 artifacts. Variation in grave-goods has indicated the existence of differential access to wealth and of inherited status positions.

Ollantaytambo an INCA site in the Urubamba Valley, near CUZCO, Peru. The site comprises a planned town, trapezoidal in outline, and a ridge-top 'fortress' that includes both domestic and ceremonial architecture. Originally a royal estate belonging to the Inca Pachacuti, it was used as a fortress by Incas rebelling against the Spanish.

Olmalenge a Kenyan PASTORAL NEOLITHIC pottery TRADITION, which is divided into a northern FACIES in the Turkana region and a southern facies in the Nakuru Basin.

Olmec the first complex civilization to emerge in MESOAMERICA, and a distinctive art style. The Olmec civilization began during the Mesoamerican Early PRECLASSIC (at least 1200 BC) and ended *c.*400 BC. This culture was marked by CEREMONIAL CENTRES, beautiful art work in JADEITE and shell, sculpture, and the first HIEROGLYPHIC writing system (see GLYPH). The Olmec culture represents a shift to a village-and-centre, rather than a village, social order. The earliest of the ceremonial centres is SAN LORENZO located near the Gulf of Mexico coast.

The Olmec also produced an art style expressed primarily through sculpture, and realistic in its rendition of natural and supernatural forms. The WERE-JAGUAR is a central theme of this style. Elements of Olmec style and iconography are found throughout Mesoamerica during the Middle Preclassic period. Sculptures range from small jadeite figures to huge stone heads standing almost 2 m tall.

Olorgesailie an informative EARLIER STONE AGE ACHEULIAN locality in southern Kenya with remarkable accumulations of thousands of HANDAXES, CLEAVERS and other stone artifacts, now dated to between 900 000 and 700 000 years ago. Most of the assemblages have probably experienced some post-depositional sorting or movement from water action. This probably also played a role in the accumulation of the remains of many extinct giant gelada baboons found at one site, which some archaeologists interpret as the result of HOMINID hunting (see ISAAC).

Olsen–Chubbuck a KILL-SITE in Colorado, USA, in which at least 200 bison were driven into an *arroyo* (a deep, dry stream cutting). The site is approximately 8500 years old and dates to the Firstview COMPLEX of the PLANO tradition. Its analysis was one of the first aimed at providing information on the specific strategies of PALAEOINDIAN hunting and butchering techniques.

Olszanica a settlement of the LINEAR POTTERY culture in southern Poland near Kraków, located on a LOESS-covered plateau. Excavations revealed 13 LONGHOUSES of varying dimensions. House 6, measuring 41.5 m long, has been interpreted as the dwelling of a high-STATUS individual, while in a smaller house imported OBSIDIAN and SHERDS of BÜKK pottery from Hungary were found. RADIOCARBON dates point to the late 5th millennium bc.

Oltome a Kenyan PASTORAL NEOLITHIC pottery TRADITION, within which KANSYORE Ware probably represents a FACIES.

Olympia a major PANHELLENIC sanctuary in the western

Peloponnese of Greece. Athletic events were part of the festival associated with the TEMENOS of Zeus. German excavations have uncovered remains of the temple of Zeus, in which was placed the CHRYSELEPHANTINE statue of the god, one of the SEVEN WONDERS; the workshop of Pheidias in which it was created has also been found. The temple was decorated with architectural sculpture. Inside the *temenos* was a temple of Hera and other buildings including THESAUROI. There were also numerous private dedications; only the bases for the now lost bronze statues remain. Traces of the STADIUM have been uncovered.

Olynthus a city in northern Greece destroyed in 348 BC. It provides a TERMINUS ANTE QUEM for the development of BLACK-GLOSSED pottery. Excavations have revealed houses fitting into HIPPODAMIAN PLANNING.

Omari a cluster of settlements/cemeteries to the south of CAIRO, Egypt, excavated by Debono in 1943–52. Omari seems to represent a community of a transitional phase between the two major PREDYNASTIC sites of LOWER EGYPT, MERIMDE and MAADI.

Omo a river in southern Ethiopia which has exposed a complex series of riverine and lake shore deposits laid down at intervals during the last four million years. Of particular interest is the 1 km thick Shungura Formation dating between 3 and 1 million years ago, which contains a rich fossil vertebrate sequence, including gracile and robust AUSTRALOPITHECINES, HOMO *habilis* and *H. erectus*. Layer F of this formation, dating to between 2.4 and 2 million years ago, contains concentrations of FLAKED and battered QUARTZ pebbles, which differ from OLDOWAN collections of this period. Detailed dating with POTASSIUM-ARGON, PALAEOMAGNETISM and faunal comparisons makes Omo a valuable reference sequence for comparisons with other sites of this age in East Africa.

Omori a Late to Final JOMON SHELL MIDDEN site near Tokyo, Japan, where the first formal archaeological excavation in the Western sense was carried out in 1877 by Edward S. MORSE.

Ondratice a group of Middle Palaeolithic open-air localities situated northeast of Brno in Moravia (Czechoslovakia). Artifacts are buried in the modern soil (formed on LOESS); no faunal remains are preserved. The cultural layer contains a mixture of Middle and Upper Palaeolithic tool types (e.g. endscrapers and sidescrapers – see SCRAPER – and RETOUCHED BLADES); its age is unknown. Ondratice was investigated by ABSOLON in 1928, Valoch in 1965 and others.

Ongbah Cave a badly disturbed site in west-central Thailand near the Three Pagodas Pass, close to a major trade route to Burma, and a source of lead. While there appears to have been HOABINHIAN period occupation (*c.*9000 BC), the best-known remains from the cave come from later (3rd–2nd century BC) burials: iron implements, bronze bangles similar to those from BAN DON TA PHET, stone beads and fragments of at least five DONG-SON cast-bronze drums.

Onion Portage a deeply stratified coastal site in northwest Alaska. The site has evidence for occupation from at least 8500 BP and possibly earlier, and contains COMPLEXES belonging to the AMERICAN PALAEOARCTIC, NORTHERN ARCHAIC, ARCTIC SMALL TOOL TRADITIONS, as well as later prehistoric INUIT cultures.

opisthodomos a shallow room which served as an entrance for the

ADYTON of a CLASSICAL temple. It is found at the rear of a temple, and is often entered through two columns placed between two stub walls (see ANTA). Compare PRONAOS.

Oplontis or **Torre Annunziata**   an extensive seaside VILLA destroyed during the eruption of Vesuvius in AD 79 (see also HERCULANEUM, POMPEII) and excavated from the 1960s. The building seems to have been undergoing reconstruction at the time of the destruction, with some of the walls stripped for redecoration. However, the remaining wall paintings were in good condition and show architectural settings including columns in the CORINTHIAN ORDER.

Opunohu Valley   the site of a detailed survey by Roger Green on Moorea, Society Islands, POLYNESIA. About 500 structures were recorded, including terraces, houses, MARAE and shrines, most dating to the 18th century AD. The analysis successfully related settlement organization to ethnographically recorded social structure.

oppidum   a term used by Caesar to denote the fortified native towns he encountered in his campaigns in Gaul in 58–51 BC, now by extension used for all fortified CELTIC towns; they are distinguished from HILLFORTS by their combination of residential, industrial, market and administrative functions. See ENSÉRUNE, ALÉSIA, BIBRACTE, ENTREMONT, GERGOVIA.

optical emission spectrometry   a physical technique used to identify trace elements in stone and metal artifacts and CERAMICS that may aid in identifying the material source. A sample is bombarded with a laser beam or other energy source, exciting the atoms; as the atoms relax they emit light of a wavelength characteristic of the constituent atoms. The wavelength spectrum and intensity are analysed for the type and concentrations of constituent elements present.

opus caementicium   Roman concrete work.

opus incertum   a Roman construction technique by which irregular blocks of stone were attached to a concrete core.

opus quadratum   a Roman construction technique consisting of squared blocks. It is the equivalent of ASHLAR masonry.

opus reticulatum   a Roman construction technique where blocks are laid on a concrete core so that the edges are placed on a diagonal, thus forming a criss-cross pattern.

opus sectile   a Roman construction technique using marble of different colours laid in a geometric or other ornamental pattern, as part of the decoration for floors or walls.

opus signinum   a Roman construction technique for flooring, consisting of crushed brick set in mortar.

oracle bones   divination bones – usually shoulder blades (*scapulae*) or tortoise under-shells (*plastrons*) – of the SHANG culture region of northern China. Used in scapulomancy to divine messages from the ancestors, they are inscribed variously with the charge, answer, and name of the diviner. They have been discovered at the ZHOU site of QISHAN and the Shang site of ANYANG, dating to the late 2nd millennium BC. The inscriptions are the earliest examples of coherent Chinese script (compare WUCHENG), and those deciphered from Anyang allow reconstruction of the Shang kinship system and some aspects of the economic and political systems. Oracle bones are preceded in the Chinese Neolithic period by uninscribed divination bones, and the pottery marks on YANGSHAO, LONGSHAN and some other CERAMICS have been interpreted as incipient writing systems.

Orangia   a MIDDLE STONE AGE open site in the southern Orange Free
State, South Africa, now inundated by a dam, which has given its
name to an early Middle Stone Age PIETERSBURG–like FLAKE-BLADE industry, the Orangian.

Oranian   see IBEROMAURUSIAN.

orchestra   an area which served as the dancing-floor for Greek
religious events. With the construction of permanent theatres, the
orchestra became the area at the foot of the tiers of seats in the
semicircular auditorium where acting took place. Actors gained access
to the orchestra by means of a PARADOS. With the advent of the
SKENE, the function and size of the orchestra diminished.

orchestra Plan of a theatre.

Orchestra Shell Cave   a cave near Perth, Western Australia, with
occupation deposits dating back at least 6500 years. Finger markings
resemble those from KOONALDA CAVE and from a number of sites
such as KOONGINE CAVE in the Mount Gambier district of South
Australia.

Orchomenos   the home of the legendary King Minyas in Boeotia,
Greece, after whom SCHLIEMANN named the distinctive Middle
HELLADIC MINYAN pottery which he found during his excavations. A
large FRESCOED Late Helladic structure is tentatively identified as a
palace and the magnificent THOLOS tomb, known as the Treasury of
Minyas, is proof that Orchomenos was a major MYCENAEAN centre.
Later remains include the impressive fortifications of the CLASSICAL
city and a fine 4th century BC theatre.

Ordos   the desert region in the 'hook' of the Yellow River in northern China, location of a Palaeolithic 'Ordos culture' (see SHUIDONGGOU). Small bronze animal sculptures produced in this region during the 1st millennium BC have been referred to as 'Ordos bronzes' (compare SHANG, ZHOU). Both these terms have fallen out of use; the area is now referred to as the NORTHERN ZONE.

ore   a mineral, or mineral aggregate, from which a prized constituent, usually a metal, can be profitably exploited.

orientalizing   **1.** a decorative scheme found especially on Greek pottery. Motifs and images, such as sphinxes, lions, PALMETTES, and lotus plants from the countries bordering the eastern Mediterranean, appear from the late 8th century BC. The style is probably the result of renewed contact with Syria, PHOENICIA and Egypt. See AL MINA.
2. a chronological period in Greece forming the link between the Early Iron Age and the ARCHAIC. It spans the late 8th century BC and continues through the 7th; it saw the rise of narrative in Greek art.

Orongo   a ceremonial village of about 50 stone houses with CORBELLED roofs standing 300 m above the ocean at the edge of the Rano Kau volcanic crater on EASTER ISLAND. Some houses contain PICTOGRAPHS, while one enclosed a richly carved MOAI. Rich in PETROGLYPHS of vulvas and of birdmen holding eggs, Orongo was the site of the annual birdman ritual, which involved obtaining the first sooty-tern egg from a nearby islet, and which persisted until *c.*AD 1878. Probably built in the 16th century AD, it was excavated and restored by MULLOY and others.

Oronsay   a small island in the Inner Hebrides, Scotland, best known for a series of at least six coastal Late Mesolithic SHELL MIDDEN sites dated to *c.*3700–3200 bc which have provided abundant well preserved faunal remains, including large numbers of coalfish bones. Excavations by Mellars in 1970–79 revealed that small groups of people moved seasonally from site to site.

orthostat   a large upright stone supporting the capstone or roof of a chamber or passage in a MEGALITHIC tomb.

Osan-ri [Osanni]   an early Neolithic site in Kangwondo Province, Korea. It has produced the earliest RADIOCARBON dates yet for CHULMUN pottery, in the 7th millennium BC.

oscillum   an ornament, normally made of marble, suspended from the ARCHITRAVE of a PERISTYLE in a Roman house. Some are circular with reliefs cut on both faces, whereas others may be in the form of theatrical masks.

Oseberg   see CLINKER-BUILT.

Oshara   see PICOSA.

Osiris   an Egyptian deity, depicted as an anthropoid figure with MUMMIFIED body, plumed crown and the crook and flail emblems of kingship. He was primarily the god who ruled the Underworld after his murder by his brother SETH. Osiris was the brother and husband of ISIS and the father of HORUS. He was especially revered at ABYDOS, where his tomb was thought to be situated.

OSL   see THERMOLUMINESCENCE.

Osłonki   a settlement of the LENGYEL culture (*c.*3500–3300 bc) in north–central Poland, 8 km west of BRZEŚĆ KUJAWSKI. Like Brześć Kujawski, Osłonki is characterized by trapezoidal LONGHOUSES and numerous burials scattered among them. The burials are striking for the number of copper artifacts they contain. In one, the skull of a woman was decorated with a 'diadem' in which copper strips had been wrapped around a belt of perishable material, presumably leather or cloth.

ossuary or **osteotheke**   a charnel house used for multiple, typically SECONDARY, INHUMATIONS.

osteoarchaeology   a branch of archaeology that deals with human anatomy, especially bony structure or organization, in the context of archaeological deposits.

osteodontokeratic   see DART.

osteotheke   see OSSUARY.

Ostia   a major port at the mouth of the Tiber serving ROME. It seems to have been established in the 4th century BC. In AD 42 its facilities were increased by the construction of breakwaters under the emperor Claudius at a site slightly removed from the actual mouth of the Tiber. The emperor Trajan constructed a hexagonal inner harbour in which over 100 ships were able to moor. This was surrounded by warehouses, and was connected to the river by a canal. Its international relations are underlined by the Square of the Corporations, where merchants from various parts of the Mediterranean had offices; their origins, such as SABRATHA in Tripolitania or Narbonne in Gaul (France), were stated by inscriptions set in MOSAICS. Substantial remains include tenement houses, baths and a synagogue.

ostrakon   a POTSHERD. At ATHENS, names could be incised on the ostraka, and these pieces could be cast to expel a citizen from the city for a period of 10 years (hence 'ostracize'). One well contained 190 ostraka inscribed with the name of Themistokles, and it is possible that they were prepared before the vote for the illiterate. Ostraka could also be used for making lists or even practising the alphabet.

In Egypt, ostraka (potsherds or a flake of stone, typically limestone) were used as a cheap and readily available vehicle for short texts, usually in HIERATIC or DEMOTIC, of a semi-permanent nature such as letters. Ostraka were also used for artists' sketches and preliminary drawings. Ostraka from the NEW KINGDOM are especially numerous, the site most associated with them as a source of evidence for the life of a community being the workmen's village of DEIR EL-MEDINA.

Otakanini   a PA of ring-ditch type on an island in Kaipara Harbour, North Island, NEW ZEALAND, excavated by Peter Bellwood. Like KAURI POINT, the site shows a sequence of fortifications beginning about AD 1500.

Otomani   an Early Bronze Age culture of eastern Slovakia and Transylvanian Hungary and Romania, essentially the equivalent of the FÜZESABONY culture in the central Hungarian sequence. Otomani CERAMICS feature large, pointed bosses, and bronze artifacts, especially weapons, are also elaborately ornamented. A number of Otomani settlements are known, particularly fortified ones at BARCA and SPIŠŠKY STVRTOK, which also provide evidence for social differentiation.

Otzaki   the site of an ACERAMIC NEOLITHIC–Early Bronze Age settlement mound in Thessaly, Greece, excavated by Milojcic in 1953–55. Otzaki has been a key site in reconstructing the Thessalian cultural sequence, but the stratigraphy is not as clear as Milojcic believed. In particular it would appear that the supposedly FINAL NEOLITHIC LARISA phase is in fact Late Neolithic.

'Oueli   a small mound near LARSA, excavated by the French group working at the latter site, that provides a deep sequence of 'UBAID culture deposits, the base of which is earlier than the 'Ubaid 1 (ERIDU) period. The excavators have proposed the label 'Ubaid 0 for these earliest levels, and have provisionally assigned a dating of c.5800–5500 BC to them. Although some surface pottery collections had previously been tentatively identified as pre-'Ubaid 1, 'Oueli provides the first stratigraphic confirmation of such an early settlement on the southern MESOPOTAMIAN ALLUVIUM. The decorated CERAMICS show similarities with SAMARRAN pottery.

Ounan Point   a pointed BLADELET with basal stem, found in North African Late PLEISTOCENE and HOLOCENE industries, such as the Ounanian and Early Neolithic of the Eastern Sahara.

ovate   a refined ACHEULIAN BIFACE with an oval or elliptical outline and a flat or deliberately twisted profile. Many ovates have a TRANCHET finish.

Owo   the most easterly Yoruba kingdom in Nigeria, where an excavation at Igbo Laja revealed a concentration of TERRACOTTA sculptures dated to the early 15th century AD. Many of the terracottas of human heads have a striking resemblance to those from IFE, while others are stylistically similar to those from BENIN.

oxygen isotope analysis   isotopic analysis that examines the $^{18}O/^{16}O$ ratio of materials; changes in ratio are often interpreted as having palaeoclimatic significance, particularly in the analysis of DEEP SEA CORES. Such cores preferably sample ocean bottom SEDIMENT rich in carbonate skeletons of *Foraminifera*, small benthic and planktonic marine organisms. The isotopic ratio in the marine fossils is the same as that of the water in which they lived. *Foraminifera* sampled from cores have revealed cyclic fluctuations in the $^{18}O/^{16}O$ ratio, which are interpreted as evidence primarily for continental ice volume change in response to GLACIAL–INTERGLACIAL cycles. The isotopic fluctuations arise as isotopically lighter ^{16}O is preferentially evaporated from oceans. During glacial episodes the ^{16}O is preferentially stored in glacial ice, and oceanic $^{18}O/^{16}O$ ratios are relatively low in response to the addition of the isotopically lighter enriched water that was stored in glaciers. At least 11 cycles have been recognized, and formed the basis for re-evaluating the classical model of four glacial episodes.

Because temperature variations are correlated with changes in atmospheric $^{18}O/^{16}O$ ratios, oxygen isotopic analysis has also been used to identify seasonal changes in ice cores, interpret temperature variations during SPELEOTHEM precipitation, and examine isotopic variations in tree ring climatic relationships.

Oxyrhynchus (*Arabic* Bahnasa)   a site in Middle Egypt. The activities of SEBBAKH-diggers and the excavations of Grenfell and Hunt in 1897 and 1903–07 produced many thousands of fragments of literary and nonliterary PAPYRI from the rubbish-dumps of the Graeco-Roman town.

Oyu   a town in Akita Prefecture, Japan, where two Late JOMON-period STONE CIRCLE sites are located. Both have two nested circles, the outer 135–150 m across and the inner 35–47 m across, and associated 'sundial' arrangements of a standing stone and surrounding pavement to the northwest. Such stone circles have been found to contain burials in shallow pits under the alignments.

Ozette   a village site located in Washington State, USA, which was occupied from about the 15th century AD to the Historic Period, and consists of a row of longhouses and individual dwellings. Excellent preservation at the site allowed recovery of houses as well as wooden boxes, baskets and various artifacts, some of which were beautifully carved and decorated with shells and teeth.

Ozieri   a Late Neolithic culture of Sardinia, named after the cave-site of San Michele near Ozieri. Ozieri material is known from caves, village settlements and rock-cut tombs. It is characterized by the high-quality pottery, with a polished or BURNISHED surface incised with flamboyant designs including zigzags, hatched triangles, arcs, festoons and stars. The CARINATED shapes recall CHASSÉEN and LAGOZZA pottery, but the decoration is unique. Classic Ozieri decorated ware has been dated to c.4100–3500 BC at the Grotta di Filiestru (Bonu Ighinu).

P

pa   a MAORI term meaning fortified place. The best-known *pa* are ditched and banked enclosures of various types, but some were built in swamps and defended by palisades. Relatively few have been excavated, but most are Classic Maori in date. There is often evidence of occupation before defences were constructed. See KAURI POINT, LAKE MANGAKAWARE, LAKE NGAROTO, OTAKANINI, TE AWANGA.

Pacariqtambo   a region to the south of CUZCO, Peru, the place of origin of the INCA royal DYNASTY according to oral tradition. The original Inca ancestors, the four brothers Ayar and their four sister-wives, were said to have emerged from a cave with three windows on the mountain called Tambotoco. They organized the people into 10 groups, and thence migrated north. The last remaining brother, Manco Capac, founded Cuzco.

Pacatnamú   a large MIDDLE HORIZON and LATE INTERMEDIATE PERIOD site in the Jequetepeque Valley on the north coast of Peru, excavated by Christopher Donnan. The site is located on a promontory, bounded by the ocean on one side and steep cliffs on another. Large defensive walls impede access along the remaining side. Within the walled portion of the site are more than fifty truncated pyramid complexes – mounds, courtyards and enclosures. The site was occupied first in the Middle Horizon, and it may represent the south-ernmost extent of the MOCHE V POLITY. The site was abandoned near the end of the Middle Horizon, and reoccupied later in the Late Intermediate Period; it was abandoned again at about the time that the CHIMU polity expanded into the region.

Pachacamac   a large ceremonial site on the central coast of Peru, first established during the MIDDLE HORIZON, when it may have been under the control of the HUARI empire, or it may have been an independent POLITY. The site, excavated by UHLE, was a major pilgrimage centre, and still functioned as such at the time of the Spanish conquest. People from throughout the Andean region came to consult the oracle at Pachacamac. Branch oracles were established in other regions as well, these being considered 'wives' of Pachacamac. When the INCA conquered the region they allowed the centre to continue to function, and added their own Temple of the Sun to the site, along with other constructions.

Pachamachay a PRECERAMIC cave-site at 4300 metres altitude, in the central highlands of Peru. Excavated by John Rick, the site was a base-camp located in the high PUNA zone, occupied year round by a small group who made infrequent trips out to other resource zones, and who subsisted almost entirely on meat. The site has a very early date of 11 800 bp, but most of the occupation seems to date to between 9000 and 2000 bp.

Pacheco a MIDDLE HORIZON site in the Nasca Valley on the south coast of Peru at which a major HUARI offering-deposit was found. The deposit, excavated by Julio C. TELLO, comprised hundreds of intentionally smashed polychrome vessels, buried in a large unstructured pit. There were remains of other structures as well, but details are unknown; the site was destroyed in the early 1950s.

Pacitan or **Patjitan** a region of south-central Java where, along the Baksoko River, stone tools were found which MOVIUS classified as CHOPPER/CHOPPING-TOOLS of assumed middle and late PLEISTOCENE date. Recent work indicates that these large tools formed only part of a pebble and FLAKE INDUSTRY (with possible HOABINHIAN affinities) of the late Pleistocene and early HOLOCENE.

Padah Lin cave-sites in the mountains of east Burma, not far to the west of SPIRIT CAVE, with early hunter-gatherer remains dating to *c.*11 000 BC, amongst the earliest-known HOABINHIAN ASSEMBLAGES.

Padang Lawas see SRIVIJAYA.

Padina a multi-period site in Serbia, located on the River Danube several kilometres upstream from LEPENSKI VIR. The two major occupations of the site are a 'pre-Neolithic' level contemporaneous with Lepenski Vir I and II, and a Neolithic layer with STARČEVO pottery. Burials occur in both phases, among the houses.

Padre Island the site, off the coast of Texas, of the remains of three Spanish treasure ships (out of a fleet of four) that were wrecked in AD 1554. The site is especially important because it contains some of the few such treasure ships that have been scientifically excavated, documented and published.

Paekche an early historic state succeeding Mahan (see SAMHAN) on the Korean peninsula (*c.*AD 300–662) that was in competition with KOGURYO and SILLA and had diplomatic and military relations with YAMATO in Japan. Its first capital was in or near MONGCH'ON Fortress near modern Seoul, thence removed to Ungjin (modern Kongju) and Sabi (modern PUYO), both in South Ch'ungch'ong Province. Its remains mainly consist of stone-stepped or earthen MOUNDED TOMBS in these areas (see MURYONG), although excavations and survey in modern Puyo have determined the positioning of the gridded-city constructed in the 7th century on the Tang model (see CHINESE DYNASTIES), including the locations of several Buddhist temples. (Compare CHANG'AN, HEIJO, ANAPCHI.)

pa'epa'e elaborate, well built, rectangular house-platforms in the Marquesas Islands, POLYNESIA.

Paestan pottery a type of SOUTH ITALIAN POTTERY produced at PAESTUM perhaps under the influence of SICILIAN POTTERY (see also CAMPANIAN POTTERY). It is unlike the other types of South Italian pottery in that some of the craftsmen signed their work; at the moment Asteas and Python are known. Production seems to have started near the middle of the 4th century BC.

Paestum (*Gk* Poseidonia) a coastal Greek colony in LUCANIA, Italy, founded *c*.600 BC. It is notable for a major series of temples in the DORIC ORDER which were rediscovered in the 18th century. They were dedicated to Argive Hera (the 'Basilica'), Poseidon and Athena ('Ceres'), and range in date from the mid 6th century to the mid 5th century BC. A Roman FORUM was inserted over some of the sanctuary areas in the 3rd century BC; buildings include a shrine to the emperor and a temple of Peace. There are also traces of an AMPHITHEATRE within the walled city. Some of the local tombs were decorated with murals, one of the more famous being the 5th century BC 'Tomb of the Divers'. See PAESTAN POTTERY.

Pagan an urban and Buddhist religious centre in upper Burma, capital of the Burman state formed in the mid 9th century AD and conquered by Mongol armies late in the 13th century, famous for the *c*.5000 large and small temples and STUPAS built there over the centuries, the best known of which are the Kyanzittha, Ananda, Shwezigon and Nanpaya of the 11th century, the Sapada, Thatbinnyu and Shwegugyi of the 12th, and the Mahabodhi, Kondawgyi, Mingalazedi and Tilominlo of the 13th.

Paglicci an Italian prehistoric cave-site on the Adriatic coast with a detailed stratigraphy, best known for its GRAVETTIAN material dating from *c*.24 700–20 000 bp, including two burials covered in OCHRE, and its CAVE ART.

Paiján a PRECERAMIC tradition found in the north and central coast and highlands of Peru. Characteristic points are triangular, with a long narrow stem; they are never FLUTED. The Paiján tradition probably post-dates the PALAEOINDIAN FISHTAIL POINT tradition, and may have developed out of the EL INGA complex. The Paiján tradition may represent the first adaptation to the exploitation of maritime resources on the coast of Peru.

Painted Grey ware a pottery type characteristic of Iron Age sites in northern India, from the eastern Punjab and northern Rajastan to the central Ganges. Of a fine, thin and well fired grey fabric, its decoration is black- or red-painted geometric designs. The ware, dated roughly 900–500 BC, is commonly associated with Indo–Aryan movements into northern India, though this is far from proven.

Palaeoasiatic a postulated early 'race' of HOMO *sapiens sapiens* of northeastern Asia, including the POSTGLACIAL CHULMUN and JOMON inhabitants of the Korean peninsula and Japanese islands, and the modern AINU. It is thought to have been replaced in the former area by TUNGUS-speaking migrants.

palaeoeconomy a school of archaeological thought headed by E.S. HIGGS concerned with the long-term determinants of human behaviour, specifically those concerned with the relationship between humans and their environments. Palaeoeconomy was strongly in-

Painted Grey ware

fluenced by concepts drawn from animal ETHOLOGY.

palaeoenvironment   the ancient environment. Palaeoenvironments can be reconstructed using a variety of techniques, such as ARCHAEOZOOLOGY and PALYNOLOGY. This kind of information is invaluable to an archaeologist, since it is assumed that the environment plays a fundamental role in determining many aspects of behaviour.

Palaeoindian   of late PLEISTOCENE and early HOLOCENE cultures of North America, with a terminal date of approximately 7000 BP, depending on the precise area. Palaeoindian groups were mobile HUNTERS AND GATHERERS, often of now-extinct MEGAFAUNA, and probably used a spear technology, although use of the ATLATL is not impossible.

Palaeolithic   literally the 'Old STONE AGE', the technological division of PREHISTORY covering the period from the first appearance of tool-using humans to the retreat of the GLACIAL ice in the northern hemisphere at *c*.8500 BC and the emergence of the MESOLITHIC. Palaeolithic people lived as HUNTER-GATHERERS without agriculture and without formal pottery production. The Palaeolithic has traditionally been subdivided into three successive phases based mainly on ARTIFACT TYPOLOGY, although there is a growing awareness that such a classificatory approach may not be entirely valid, considering the vast time span and the varying climatic and geographical conditions involved. The Lower Palaeolithic is the period of early HOMINID PEBBLE TOOL and CORE TOOL manufacture. More technologically advanced tools appear in the Middle Palaeolithic, with a developing aesthetic and religious awareness and the appearance of NEANDERTHALERS. The Upper Palaeolithic is the period of fully modern humans, HOMO *sapiens sapiens*, a period of delicate stone and bone tool manufacture and the development of PALAEOLITHIC ART.

These terms have been used throughout the Old World, though primarily within Eurasia. The New World equivalent is PALAEOINDIAN.

In *East Asia*, the subdivisions are somewhat different from those farther west. The Palaeolithic period in China divides into Early (1 000 000–73 000 BC), Middle (*c*.73 000–40 000 BC), and Late (40 000–10 000 BC), typified by the remains at ZHOUKOUDIAN Loc. 1 and Upper Cave. Some dates by PALAEOMAGNETISM suggest a 1.7 million-year bp start to the Chinese Palaeolithic (see YUANMOU), but these are under review. In Korea and Japan, sites have been attributed up to 400 000 bp, but few of the datings before 50 000 bp are generally accepted

PALAEOLITHIC ART

(see SOZUDAI, SOKCHANG-RI, BABADAN A, ZAZARAGI, KULP'O-RI, HOSHINO, NISHIYAGI, NAKAMINE). The majority of sites in these countries thus belong to the Late Palaeolithic. The dual tool traditions of China (see LANTIAN) are joined by BLADE technologies c.30 000 bp, with small blades appearing at 28 000 bp. Heavy FLAKES (see SETOUCHI) and blades in Late Palaeolithic Japan are replaced by MICROBLADES (see YUBETSU) at 14 000 bp, and overall BIFACIAL flaking at 12 000 bp. CERAMICS appear in the terminal Palaeolithic record of Japan (see FUKUI). (See also AKASHI, ARAYA, DINGCUN, IWAJUKU, JINNIUSHAN, KEHE, MABA, MINATOGAWA, NIHEWAN, SHIYU, SHUIDONGGOU.)

Palaeolithic art   The art of the last Ice Age that is usually divided into three groups: (a) portable or MOBILIARY ART, comprising a wide variety of forms, from engraved stones to carvings in antler or ivory. Thousands of such pieces are known from Spain to Siberia; (b) deep engravings or bas-reliefs on large blocks of stone, known from southwest France; (c) cave-art or PARIETAL ART, known primarily in Spain, France and Italy. It includes a range of techniques from finger-markings and engravings to bas-relief sculpture, and painting. It comprises animal figures (mostly adults drawn in profile, and dominated by horse and bison), much rarer ANTHROPOMORPHS, and abundant non-figurative motifs and 'SIGNS'. Some is on open view, but much is hidden or inaccessible. Some engravings of the period have recently been found on rocks in the open air. Art in Europe appears early in the Upper Palaeolithic (see VOGELHERD, HOHLENSTEIN-STADEL, GEISSENKLÖSTERLE), and becomes abundant in the SOLUTREAN and especially MAGDALENIAN periods. Art of similar antiquity is also known on other continents (see PEDRA FURADA, APOLLO 11, KOONALDA, EARLY MAN, KAMIKUROIWA, etc.). Much of the European art appears linked to a complex mythology and incorporates a distinct set of rules: early interpretations such as 'art for art's sake' or hunting magic are now recognized as far too simplistic.

palaeomagnetism   the magnetic polarization of magnetic particles in rocks and SEDIMENT in alignment with the Earth's MAGNETIC field at the time of rock formation and sediment deposition. Palaeomagnetism can be used in STRATIGRAPHY for correlation. Past reversals in the earth's magnetic field are recorded in susceptible deposits and independently dated by other methods; the youngest reversal dates to about 700 000 bp. With time, the magnetic poles also wander on a smaller scale which causes regional variations in declination (angle between magnetic and true north) and inclination (angle of vertical inclination from a horizontal plane). Measurement of these parameters on materials of different ages can be used to build regional chronologies that can be independently dated. See ARCHAEOMAGNETISM.

palaeontology   the study of the remains, origin and evolution of life forms through time. Fossils may provide PALAEOENVIRONMENTAL information based on habitat restrictions. The unique sequencing and non-repeating nature of evolution provides a biostratigraphic tool for RELATIVE DATING and CORRELATION. See STRATIGRAPHY.

palaeopathology   a branch of pathology that deals with anatomical and physiological abnormalities in humans in ancient contexts. Sometimes used in determining the cause of death in individuals, palaeopathology is also useful in studies of nutrition, exercise and disease in ancient populations.

palaeopedology   the study of the genesis, character, STRATIGRAPHY and geomorphic, temporal and PALAEOENVIRONMENTAL significance of buried fossil soils (PALAEOSOLS) formed on LANDSCAPES of the past, all of which affect the interpretation of any associated archaeological record. Palaeopedology can help identify FEATURES, characteristics and processes that resulted from, or were influenced by, people and their manipulation and exploitation of landsystems.

palaeoserology   a branch of serology that deals with serums and their reactions and properties, primarily in humans, in ancient contexts. Such studies generally require the preservation of body tissue, which is rare except in the case of some mortuary practices or in unusual MATRICES.

palaeosol   BURIED SOIL formed on a LANDSCAPE of the past or under different extrinsic and intrinsic factors, processes and conditions than the present day, which has temporal significance and is a source of PALAEOENVIRONMENTAL information. Palaeosols are preserved in a variety of DEPOSITIONAL ENVIRONMENTS including PLEISTOCENE LOESS sequences, where they aid in interpretation of GLACIAL – INTERGLACIAL sequences, and alluvial river valleys, colluvial HILLSLOPE and ALLUVIAL FAN environments, where sedimentation also tends to be episodic. See PALAEOPEDOLOGY.

Palaepaphos   see KOUKLIA-PALAEPAPHOS.

palaestra   an open exercise area often surrounded by PORTICOS. In the Greek world it might form part of a GYMNASIUM complex which would include a STADIUM. Alternatively it might be connected to THERMAE.

Palaikastro   the site of a MINOAN settlement on the island of Crete. The NEOPALATIAL town is particularly impressive, the blocks of houses laid out on either side of paved streets, but despite the fact that Palaikastro was a populous and evidently prosperous settlement, no palace has as yet been discovered. On Petsophas, above Palaikastro, a PEAK SANCTUARY has been excavated.

Palenque   a MAYA centre on the western frontier of the Maya Lowlands in the state of Chiapas, Mexico. It reached its height during the Late CLASSIC, coming to power as TEOTIHUACÁN was in its decline. Palenque collapsed between AD 810 and 830.

In 1952 the archaeologist Alberto Ruz discovered the burial chamber of Pacal, the greatest ruler of Palenque who died in AD 683 at the age of 80. The spectacular burial was beneath the floor in the Temple of Inscriptions.

Palermo Stone   a diorite STELA, one fragment of which is now in Palermo, with others in London and Cairo. The complete monument was a year-by-year record of the reigns of the kings of Egypt from the 1st to the 5th DYNASTY, and is a major source of information regarding the chronology of the OLD KINGDOM.

Pales, Léon   (1905–88) a French prehistorian best known for his pioneering work on PALAEOPATHOLOGY, his studies of footprints in caves, and especially for his 25-year decipherment of the hundreds of engraved slabs from LA MARCHE.

Palliser Bay   an area at the south end of the North Island of NEW ZEALAND which has been the subject of a detailed regional study by archaeologists from the University of Otago. The sites include settlements, burials and fields for sweet potato cultivation, but no storage pits. The area is today at the limit of sweet potato cultivation, but was first occupied as early as AD 1100. It was abandoned about AD 1400 as a result of environmental degradation and climatic change.

Palmela   a cemetery of four CHALCOLITHIC rock-cut tombs near the Tagus estuary in Setubal, Portugal. The tombs have a passage leading to a 'man-hole' entrance, originally closed by a fitted door slab, beyond which is a kidney-shaped chamber, originally used for collective inhumation. The tombs were rich in BEAKER material, including over 50 Beakers along with copper knives and fragments of gold foil. Also present was the distinctive leaf-shaped copper blade known as the Palmela point, which is found in Beaker assemblages throughout Iberia and along the Mediterranean and Atlantic coasts of France.

palmette   a stylized palm-frond often used as a decorative motif in Greek and Roman art. They were used in a variety of ways and in different media which included architecture (see ANTEFIX) and pottery (see BLACK-GLOSSED).

Palmyra   a city dependent on trade between Syria and the east. Under the emperor Septimius Severus it gained the status of a Roman colony. Remains of the city include colonnaded streets and the temple of Bel. Communal tombs in towers were marked by plaques in high relief showing the deceased.

palstave   a bronze axe type in which the blade is divided from the heel by a ridge, with shallow grooves on either side of the heel to facilitate hafting. In Europe, the palstave was a MIDDLE BRONZE AGE development from the flat and flanged axes of the EARLY BRONZE AGE, the new design being intended to improve the efficiency of hafting, but ultimately giving way to the still more efficient socketed axe of the LATE BRONZE AGE.

palynology or **pollen analysis**   the study of fossil and living pollen and spores including their production, dispersal and applications. Palynology, developed by Swedish botanist Lennart von Post, is utilized in PALAEOENVIRONMENTAL reconstruction, identifying natural and human-induced vegetation changes, and developing relative CHRONOLOGIES. The resilient *exine* (outer coating) of the pollen and spores of plants, mosses and ferns is preserved in ANAEROBIC environments, such as lakes and BOGS, and some acidic and dry soils, such as in caves.

Samples are preferably collected in a CORE, and the pollen is concentrated by chemical treatments and fine mesh wet SIEVING, then stained, mounted on slides, examined and counted under a microscope. Identification is aided by unique combinations of morphological features on the exine. A pollen diagram is constructed that consists of the pollen count data, expressed as percentages for each taxon and plotted versus depth, which represents relative time. An absolute pollen diagram illustrates the numbers of pollen grains of a given taxon deposited on a unit area per unit measure of time, and requires numerous RADIOCARBON ages. Diagrams are zoned, based on changes in pollen assemblages or influx rates. Inferences about past environments and environmental change are made from sequential changes in zone composition and are based primarily on studies of modern pollen production, dispersal, SEDIMENTATION, reworking, preservation and relationships to modern environments.

Pollen zonation can be used as a RELATIVE DATING tool. Pollen

0   5 cm

palstave

zones may be recognized and correlated regionally, although they may well be DIACHRONIC. In some circumstances, pollen zones may be related to archaeological deposits, thus providing some indication of age. See ABSOLUTE POLLEN COUNTING.

Pampa de las Llamas or **Moxeke**   a major INITIAL PERIOD ceremonial centre in the Casma Valley of the north-central coast of Peru. The site follows a linear axis, with the large mound of Moxeke near one end, and Huaca A at the other. Parallel to the central axis are rows of small, contiguous U-shaped structures. Huaca A, excavated by Thomas and Shelia Pozorski, is built according to a rigid, bilaterally symmetrical plan, and may have served as a storage facility.

Pampa Grande   a MIDDLE HORIZON, MOCHE V site in the Lambayeque region on the far north coast of Peru. After the abandonment of the Huacas del Sol and Luna, and the southern portion of Moche territory, a new capital was established at Pampa Grande. The site covers over four square kilometres, and includes truncated pyramids, residential architecture and storage facilities.

Pampa Ingenio   SEE NASCA LINES.

Panaramitee art   an art-style, widely distributed in Australia, but best known from the arid centre, which is characterized by pecked engravings depicting a limited range of motifs, dominated by bird and animal tracks, and circles. Crescents, dots, spirals, lines and mazes also occur. Panaramitee art has long been thought to be ancient. Engravings were excavated at INGALADDI in the lower levels dating to 5000 to 7000 bp and the lowest deposits at EARLY MAN SHELTER, c.13 000 bp, covered Panaramitee-style engravings. Recent CATION RATIO dating at KAROLTA has suggested that Panaramitee-style engravings may have been executed over c.30 000 years. See also MOOTWINGEE, STURTS MEADOWS.

pan-grave culture   a semi-nomadic cattle-herding people of the Eastern Desert of Egypt who flourished during the Second INTER-MEDIATE PERIOD (c.1633–1550 BC) and were so called because of their distinctive round or oval shallow graves which have been found throughout UPPER EGYPT and LOWER NUBIA. Their material culture has much in common with the C-GROUP. The pan-grave people served as mercenaries during this turbulent period of Egyptian history and con-tinued in a similar role as the police force of NEW KINGDOM Egypt, when they were called the Medjay.

Panhellenic, *adj.*   literally 'all Greek'. It is applied to regional, rather than local, sanctuaries which attracted dedications from across the Greek world. See DELPHI, OLYMPIA.

Panlongcheng [Pan-lung-ch'eng]   an early SHANG-period site in Hubei Province, China, thought to be the southernmost outpost of the Shang political system in the 15th–13th centuries BC. A walled town of 7.5 ha was accompanied on the outside by numerous elite burials containing ERLIGANG-style bronzes (see ZHENGZHOU), poor burials, pottery and stone tools and bronze manufacturing.

Pannonia   an area of modern-day Hungary west and south of the River Danube incorporated into the Roman Empire as a province in AD 10. Pannonia became one of the more prosperous Roman frontier provinces in central Europe and was the location of numerous VILLAS. Its principal town was Aquincum, on the site of the Buda section of modern Budapest.

Papuan languages   a group of over 700 languages spoken mainly in New Guinea, but also elsewhere in MELANESIA and the islands of eastern Indonesia. They are widely believed to be descended from the languages of the first people to migrate into Melanesia. They are also referred to as Non-Austronesian (NAN) languages.

papyrus   the flexible writing material produced from the marsh plant *Cyperus papyrus*. The pithy stem of the papyrus plant was cut into thin slivers and laid out in two overlying rows running vertically and horizontally, which were then pounded, forming a homogeneous whole as the starch present in the released sap dried. Papyrus was produced on a relatively large scale in Egypt, from at least as early as the 1st DYNASTY until the extinction of the plant in Egypt during the Middle Ages, and was used for a wide range of documents from letters and administrative records to religious texts.

Paquimé   see CASAS GRANDES.

Paracas   the major EARLY HORIZON culture on the south coast of Peru, showing direct influence from the religious centre at CHAVÍN. The Paracas culture is known primarily from tombs and associated funerary artifacts. The type-site, the Paracas NECROPOLIS, was dis-covered by KROEBER and excavated by TELLO. Paracas textiles are some of the finest prehistoric textiles known anywhere in the world. Tapestries were woven and embroidered with elaborate depictions of mythical creatures, and then used as mummy wrappings (see MUMMIFICATION). Painted cotton textiles with pure Chavín designs have also been found. Paracas CERAMICS were typically incised with geometric or representational designs, especially felines, and painted after firing with resin-based paints. The Paracas style is the direct antecedent of the NASCA tradition.

paradigm   a set of assumptions, objectives and METHODOLOGIES that determine the specific procedures of scientific investigation. Examples of paradigms in archaeology include BEHAVIOURAL ARCHAEOLOGY, CULTURE HISTORY, PROCESSUAL (NEW) AND POSTPROCESSUAL ARCHAE-OLOGY.

parados   an entrance or exit used by actors entering an ORCHESTRA (see figure) of a theatre. It lies between the seats and the SKENE.

Paranthropus   see AUSTRALOPITHECUS.

Parhae   see BOHAI.

parietal art   literally 'art on walls'; the term is extended to cover prehistoric works of art on any non-movable surface, including blocks, ceilings and floors. See LEVANTINE ART, PALAEOLITHIC ART. Compare MOBILIARY ART.

Parmana   a region of the Middle Orinoco drainage, Venezuela. Research by Anna C. Roosevelt has documented a shift in subsistence from root crops, especially manioc, to the cultivation of seed crops, particularly maize, roughly 800–400 bc. Maize cultivation in turn led to a sharp increase in population density, and provided the basis for the later emergence of CHIEFDOM-level societies.

Paroong Cave   one of several limestone caves in the Mount Gambier district, South Australia, with deeply incised, pounded or abraded motifs, especially circles. The style has recently been termed the Karake style by Robert Bednarik, who has suggested it is PLEISTOCENE in age.

Parpalló Cave   a well stratified prehistoric cave situated near Gandia, on the Valencia coast, Spain, and excavated by PERICOT in 1929–31. The site has a characteristic GRAVETTIAN layer including BACKED BLADES, BURINS and endscrapers (see SCRAPER), followed by a sequence of SOLUTREAN levels featuring barbed and TANGED points, and then four MAGDALENIAN levels with typical stone, bone and antler artifacts including MICROLITHS, needles and HARPOONS. Over 5000 small stone plaques, engraved and painted with animal motifs, and scores of decorated bones were found in the Palaeolithic levels of the cave. The Mesolithic occupation phase includes typical MICROBURINS, and is followed by Neolithic and later-period material.

Parrot, André   (1901–80) a French theologian, one of the great for-mative generation of MESOPOTAMIAN archaeologists. Parrot's major contribution to the field was his long-term project at MARI. In the 1920s he worked at several sites (including BAALBEK and BYBLOS) in the French protectorates in the Levant. In the early 1930s he shifted to Mesopotamia, where he ended the French work at TELLO and began exploration at LARSA; in 1933 Parrot began his excavation at Mari, which continued under his direction for the next 40 years. Also involved in the government museum service (eventually becoming director of the Louvre), Parrot produced a history of Mesopotamian archaeology, one of the best ever written.

Parthenon   a highly decorated temple on the AKROPOLIS at ATHENS dedicated to Athena. The building in the DORIC ORDER was started in 447 BC as part of a programme of construction by the statesman Perikles, although it overlies an earlier temple which was either destroyed by the Persians in 480 BC or started by the general Kimon in the 460s and later abandoned. The Parthenon contained an elaborate CHRYSELEPHANTINE statue of the goddess. The PEDIMENTS were filled with scenes of the conflict between the deities Athena and Poseidon over Attica, and the Birth of Athena. The METOPES show battles between Lapiths and Centaurs, the gods and the giants, Greeks fighting Amazons, as well as events at TROY. Although the temple was of the Doric Order, a continuous frieze was placed along the upper walls of the CELLA (a feature of the IONIC ORDER), and was thus partially obscured by the outer colonnade. It showed a procession of horsemen, chariots, sacrificial animals and officials which moved along both sides of the Cella to meet at the east end with the gods seated on Olympus and the folding of the dress for the goddess. Many of the sculptures were removed by ELGIN and are now in the British Museum.

Parthians the inhabitants of Khorasan in northeastern Iran, who removed themselves from BACTRIAN Greek domination in the mid 3rd century BC, and then during the 2nd century BC formed an empire that incorporated Iran and most of MESOPOTAMIA. The Parthians are perhaps best known historically for their intermittent wars with the Romans, including the defeat of Crassus at Carrhae in 53 BC and the temporary loss of Mesopotamia to TRAJAN (in AD 115–117). The Parthian empire was overthrown early in the 3rd century AD by the SASSANIANS in southern Iran. The English phrase 'Parthian shot' derives from the typical Parthian military tactics of mounted bowmen, who could fire at the enemy while retreating.

particle size analysis or **grain size analysis** the analysis of the grain size distributions used to characterize and describe archaeological SEDIMENTS or SOILS, identify subtle depositional trends, and address specific research questions. Particle size distributions are not diagnostic of a particular depositional agent, process or environment, but may aid in characterization and interpretation of these parameters. For determining SAND, SILT and CLAY percentages, various SEDIMENTATION methods are utilized that are based on laws of settling velocity of particles. Microscopy methods are also available. For determining size distribution of fine GRAVEL and sand, SIEVING is performed. Particles greater than PEBBLE size are measured directly.

Pasemah a plateau in southwest Sumatra famous for its 'MEGALITHIC' remains, including stone slab graves and large sculpted boulders bearing figures of animals and warriors wearing metal armour, swords and beads similar to those found in Iron Age burials of the last centuries BC, and carrying DONG SON bronze drums. Sites include Tegurwangi, Tanjungara, Pagaralam, Gunungmegang, Pematang and Batugajah.

Paso a lakeshore SHELL MIDDEN in north Sulawesi, Indonesia, containing OBSIDIAN FLAKE tools and bone points pre-dating the TOALIAN (c.6500 BC); similar forms appear in basal ULU LEANG and Agop Sarapad (MADAI CAVES).

passage grave a type of CHAMBERED TOMB in which the chamber is reached from the edge of the covering mound via a long passage.

Passo di Corvo a Middle Neolithic enclosure in Puglie, Italy, surrounded by concentric ditches. Within the ditches are traces of approximately 100 circular hut compounds. These contained rectangular houses on low stone footings associated with red painted pottery. There is a single RADIOCARBON date of c.5200 BC. Several hundred enclosures of this type are known on the Tavoliere plain.

Passy-sur-Yonne a cemetery in Yonne, France, of Middle Neolithic long mounds, up to 300 m in length, represented today only by their surrounding ditches. From a broad east end, interrupted by a central 'entrance' gap, the monuments tail away to a narrow western extremity. Individual burial in a deep pit near the east end of the structure is the general rule. Associated pottery includes early Middle Neolithic CERNY and indicates a date of c.3800 BC. Similar cemeteries are now also known from the Caen area of Normandy.

Pastoral Neolithic of East Africa a general term for pre-Iron Age food-producing societies in East Africa. Although the term refers only to pastoralism, it is in fact uncertain whether or not crops were cultivated as well. The route by which food production reached East Africa may have been from Ethiopia or the Sudan. The earliest Pastoral Neolithic sites are on the plains of northern Kenya and date to the middle 3rd millennium BC. Southern Kenyan Pastoral Neolithic sites date from the end of the 2nd millennium BC and the tradition continues until the appearance of iron working in the last few centuries BC and first centuries AD. The Pastoral Neolithic is not found south of northern Tanzania. Several Pastoral Neolithic traditions have been recognized, but are generally not well defined chronologically (see ELMENTEITAN, KANSYORE, NAROSURA, NDERIT, NJORO RIVER CAVE, OLDISHI, OLMALENGE, OLTOME).

patera a rounded bowl, often bronze, of the Roman period usually attached to a long handle. Its shape probably made it suitable for the pouring of LIBATIONS.

patina 1. the outermost surface of an ARTIFACT that differs in colour, texture, lustre or composition from the remainder of the artifact, resulting from chemical, physical or biological alteration in response to surrounding soil environmental conditions. Numerous processes may obscure or destroy surface detail including corrosion, dissolution, precipitation, abrasion and replacement.
2. a porous bluish or white weathering, caused by alkaline conditions which slowly affect the surface of flint when exposed to the atmosphere or to rainwater. A green patina caused by corrosion can affect bronze objects.

Patjitan see PACITAN.

patu a short MAORI fighting club made of wood, bone or stone. Finds of whalebone and wooden clubs comparable to Maori *patu* at VAITO'OTIA, Society Islands, suggests they may have been part of the Early Eastern POLYNESIAN assemblage introduced to NEW ZEALAND by the first settlers.

Paviland Cave the Goat's Hole Cavern at Paviland, Gower Peninsula, in Wales, that has yielded early Upper Palaeolithic material of c.38 000 to 10 000 years ago. (AURIGNACIAN and CRESWELLIAN), including the earliest-known British ceremonial burial, identified by Buckland in 1823 as the 'Red Lady of Paviland' but which was actually an OCHRE-covered male burial; dating to 26 350 bp, it was accompanied by IVORY objects.

Pavlov an Upper Palaeolithic open-air site located near the Dyje River in southern Moravia in Czechoslovakia. The cultural layer is contained in LOESS deposits, and yielded RADIOCARBON dates of 26 730–26 000 bp; among the faunal remains are woolly MAMMOTH, horse and reindeer. Traces of over a dozen former structures with central hearths were encountered. The artifacts include small RETOUCHED BLADES, Gravette points and animal figurines of fired loess, and are assigned to the EASTERN GRAVETTIAN.

Payne, Humfry (1902–36) the director of the British School at Athens from 1929 to his death. While Assistant Keeper in the Coin Room at the Ashmolean Museum in Oxford he prepared what is considered to be a definitive study of ARCHAIC Corinthian art, *Necrocorinthia* (1931). See CORINTHIAN POTTERY. It was this interest which led him to conduct work in the Archaic sanctuary at PERACHORA. After some further fieldwork on Crete at KNOSSOS he turned to preparing an illustrated catalogue of the Archaic sculpture from the Athenian AKROPOLIS (SEE KOUROS, KORE).

Pazyryk a complex of BARROWS in the ALTAI Mountains of Central Asia, dating to the 5th to 3rd centuries BC. The Pazyryk tombs are characterized by exceptional preservation of their contents. Timber burial chambers were covered by stone CAIRNS, under which the ground was permanently frozen to a depth of seven metres. Not only did artifacts of wood, leather, skin and wool survive, but also the mummified bodies of the occupants of several tombs. The Pazyryk burials are believed to be high-status individuals of nomadic peoples related to the SCYTHIANS.

peak sanctuary a MINOAN cult place in the mountains of Crete. The sacred status of peak sanctuaries was indicated by deposits of votive offerings rather than by monumental architecture.

peat a sedimentary body of dark brown or black, partially decomposed organic matter preserved under ANAEROBIC conditions in an environment containing excessive moisture. Peats are important sources of PALAEOENVIRONMENTAL information; macrobotanical remains, pollen, beetle parts, gastropods and even human remains are usually well preserved and can be RADIOCARBON dated. Peat could also have been used as a fuel source when dried. (See LINDOW, TOLLUND, GRAUBALLE.)

pebble a size subdivision of GRAVEL CLASTS that ranges between 4 and 64 mm in diameter, according to the Wentworth-Udden classification system. Crude, early tools were often made from pebble-size clasts and are referred to as *pebble tools*.

Pécel a Late ENEOLITHIC regional variant of the BADEN culture in southwestern Hungary, known primarily from cemeteries.

Pech de l'Azé a well-stratified Palaeolithic tunnel-cave in the Dordogne, France, with six distinct ACHEULIAN levels dating to the RISS GLACIATION, followed by six MOUSTERIAN levels dated to the WÜRM glaciation. Excavated principally by BORDES, it contains numerous HEARTHS of various kinds. ESR dating of animal teeth shows occupation between 232 000 and 53 000 years ago.

Pech Merle a major cave in the Quercy region, France, where Palaeolithic paintings and engravings were first discovered in 1922. About 60 animal figures (dominated by MAMMOTH) are known, together with numerous dots and signs. The most famous figures are a frieze of black drawings, and the 'spotted horse' panel. The art has been assigned to three phases, from 20 000 to 10 000 BC, and a RADIOCARBON date of 18 400 bp has been obtained from a butchered reindeer bone left in front of the horse panel. The cave was never inhabited by Palaeolithic people, and their scant traces (including footprints) suggest a series of brief visits.

Pecos Classification a culture stage sequence devised by the first Pecos Conference of 1927 to organize prehistoric material from the American Southwest. It was later restricted to the ANASAZI tradition of the northern part of the region. Architecture and CERAMICS are the primary elements defining the stages. The individual stages are Basketmaker I–III and PUEBLO I–V, and show increasing social, architectural, subsistence and technological complexity.

pediment a triangular recess usually found at both ends of CLASSICAL temples and treasuries, often filled with sculpture. It is located above the ENTABLATURE. See TYMPANON.

pedogenesis the total interaction of physical, chemical and biological factors, processes and conditions that cause a SOIL to evolve, as expressed by SOIL HORIZONS. Through pedogenesis, archaeological deposits can be displaced, mixed, sorted or buried. Pedogenic processes continuously interact with depositional and erosional processes that result in the SOIL PROFILE. If SEDIMENTATION processes overwhelm pedogenesis, the former land surface soil is buried and becomes a PALAEOSOL.

pedology the study of the genesis, characteristics, distributions and uses of SOILS. Proper interpretation of the CONTEXT and integrity of archaeological deposits associated with soils requires identification and understanding of the soils, or the pedology. See also PALAEOPEDOLOGY, PALAEOSOL.

pedoturbation a general term applied to the set of processes by which SOILS are disrupted, mixed, sorted or materially cycled to different degrees of homogenization by a variety of physical, chemical and biological agents. Both the land surface and layers within the soil, and any associated cultural debris, may potentially be affected, including total or partial destruction of feature boundaries and interiors.

Pedra Furada or **Toca do Boqueirão do Sítio da Pedra Furada** a huge painted sandstone rockshelter in the Piauí region of eastern Brazil, excavated by Niède Guidon in the 1970s and 1980s, at which a long sequence of possible HEARTHS have yielded RADIOCARBON dates back to c.47 500 bp. Fallen painted wall-fragments have been found STRATIFIED in layers dating to 12 000 and possibly 17 000 bp, indicating the presence of ROCK ART by that period. While the upper layers of the site represent an undisputed post-PALAEOINDIAN occupation, some researchers have questioned the identification of crude QUARTZITE PEBBLE and FLAKE tools and hearths in lower levels.

Pefkakia the site of a Late Neolithic–Bronze Age settlement mound in Thessaly, Greece, excavated by Theocharis in 1957 and by Milojcic in 1967–72. Pefkakia has been a key site in reconstructing the Thessalian cultural sequence, and the presence of CYCLADIC, MINOAN and Trojan imports has made it possible to link this securely into the Aegean chronological framework.

Pei Wenzhong [Pei, Wen-chung] (1904–82) a Chinese Palaeolithic archaeologist who graduated from the Geology Department of Beijing University and joined the ZHOUKOUDIAN excavations in 1928. From 1935 to 1941 he studied in France, returning with a Ph.D. from the University of Paris to become the Director of the Cenozoic Laboratory of the Geological Survey of China. In the postwar period, he was a Research Fellow of the Laboratory of Vertebrate Paleontology of the Chinese Academy of Sciences. Pei was a pioneer of TAPHONOMIC studies of bone breakage.

Peiligang [P'ei-li-kang] a cluster of Neolithic sites in Henan Province, China, and namesake of the earliest millet-based culture of northern China which includes or is parallel to CISHAN, Laoguantai and Lijiacun.

Pejeng the findspot in Bali of a large bronze drum dating to the early 1st millennium AD, a locally made variant of the DONG SON drum tradition, ancestral to the recent *moko* drums of eastern Indonesia. Decorative styles relate Pejeng drums to ceremonial bronzes in the east, including elaborate axes from Roti and Savu, and a flask from Sulawesi.

Pekárna a prehistoric cave-site located east of Brno in Moravia, Czechoslovakia. Artifacts and faunal remains (e.g. reindeer, arctic fox) are buried in rubble and LOAM. The lower cultural layers contain assemblages assigned to the EASTERN GRAVETTIAN, with some associated Middle Palaeolithic artifacts. Above these lie two MAGDALENIAN cultural layers containing endscrapers (see SCRAPER), borers, bone/antler points, and a HARPOON; art objects include bones engraved with depictions of animals. Neolithic and later remains occur in the upper layers. Pekárna was excavated by ABSOLON and others.

Peking Man see ZHOUKOUDIAN.

pelike a large container with two vertical handles probably used for water or wine at a Greek SYMPOSIUM. The term is of modern, not ancient, usage and refers to a type of AMPHORA where the greatest diameter is below the mid-point.

Pella see BERENICE.

Pelos-Lakkoudes see GROTTA-PELOS.

Pengelly, William (1812–94) one of the first British archaeologists to demonstrate the true antiquity of British PALAEOLITHIC ARTIFACTS by showing that stone tools clearly made by humans were contemporary with the remains of extinct animals. This contradicted the then widely accepted chronology of Archbishop Ussher (1581–1656) which dated the Creation to 4004 BC. Pengelly excavated in Devon at KENT'S CAVERN and WINDMILL CAVE, BRIXHAM.

Pengkalan Bujang see SRIVIJAYA.

Pentelic marble a white marble quarried from mount Pentelikon in Attica, Greece. It was widely used for public buildings, such as the PARTHENON.

Perachora a Greek sanctuary located on a promontory jutting into the Bay of CORINTH and excavated by PAYNE. In the Early Iron Age a sanctuary of Hera was established which attracted a wide range of offerings including IVORIES. Round the harbour were found traces of a STOA and a temple of Hera Akraia.

percussion technique the group of methods used to strike a FLAKE from a CORE. *Direct* percussion means simply hitting a core with a hammer, either HARD or SOFT. *Indirect* percussion involves the use of a punch placed between the core and the hammer to direct the force of the blow precisely to the STRIKING PLATFORM, a method probably used to produce BLADES. *Anvil* percussion, or 'block on block' percussion, is the striking of a core against a fixed hardstone anvil; while the *bipolar* technique involves resting the core on a stationary anvil and striking it with a hammer, producing a flake with a BULB OF PERCUSSION at each end.

Pergamon the capital of a HELLENISTIC kingdom in Turkey dating to 283–133 BC. The steep-sided AKROPOLIS was decorated with a range of elaborate buildings. The focus is the theatre which lay above a long terrace, itself dominated by a temple of Dionysos. Remains of the library, once containing some 200 000 volumes (many written on parchment), have been found. One of the most spectacular monuments is the Altar of Zeus which was decorated with a continuous sculpted relief showing a *Gigantomachy* (battle between gods and giants); parts are now in Berlin. In the Roman period a temple of Trajan was constructed. In the lower city a sanctuary of Asklepios was reached by a ceremonial way.

Pericot García, Luis (1899–1978) a Spanish archaeologist, best known for his meticulous excavation over three seasons in 1929–31 and subsequent publication of the PARPALLÓ cave, as well as his work on northeast Spanish MEGALITHS.

periglacial environment an environment characterized by severe frost action in non-GLACIAL conditions and dominated by processes and features influenced by cold climates, including ground ice, mass movements, production of relatively large amounts of weathered debris, often strong wind activity at times, resulting in substantial AEOLIAN deposits of SILT and SAND, and valleys with bedload-dominated streams. It is often associated with the area fringing modern and PLEISTOCENE glaciers and areas of PERMAFROST, but conditions vary widely with altitude, latitude and climatic parameters.

Perigordian a classificatory division of the French Upper Palaeolithic proposed by PEYRONY and named after the French Périgord region. It viewed the CHÂTELPERRONIAN as the 'Lower Perigordian' developing into the GRAVETTIAN or 'Upper Perigordian'. This scheme is not now widely accepted, as it is based on ARTIFACT TYPOLOGY rather than STRATIGRAPHIC evidence, and it assumes the contemporary parallel development of the Perigordian and AURIGNACIAN cultures.

Peristeria one of the most prosperous and powerful Early MYCENAEAN (*c.*1550–1400 BC) settlements in Messenia, Greece. The four THOLOS tombs, although disturbed, contained splendid offerings and the East House may have been a palatial residence.

peristyle a colonnade which is found (a) on the exterior of buildings such as temples, and (b) within the courtyard of a HELLENISTIC or Roman house.

Perjamos or **Periam** a TELL site near Arad in western Romania, the type-site of the Early–Middle Bronze Age Periam culture, largely contemporaneous with the OTOMANI or FÜZESABONY culture to the north and northeast. Stratified sites like Periam and Pecica, as was the case at TÓSZEG, provide a detailed chronological sequence for the first half of the Bronze Age in this part of the Carpathian Basin.

permafrost continuous or discontinuous perennially frozen ground, overlain by the active layer, a surface zone up to about 3 m thick that undergoes seasonal freezing and thawing, formed under cold climatic conditions. During QUATERNARY GLACIAL episodes, permafrost extended to lower latitudes in North America, Europe and Asia. Amelioration of climatic conditions left relict LANDFORMS, such as PINGO scars, ICE WEDGE casts and patterned ground, as indicators of former permafrost in these areas.

Persepolis the ACHAEMENID ceremonial centre, situated on a wide plain within the Zagros Mountains of Fars in southwestern Iran, one of the great architectural treasures of world history. Darius I (521–486 BC) moved the Achaemenid seat from Pasargadae (where stands the tomb of CYRUS the Great (559–530 BC)) to Persepolis. Here he and the kings that followed built, on a large terrace, a series of columned buildings (the Persian *apadana* refers to a columned hall) that are today identified as palaces, treasury, harem, and Apadana proper. Perhaps the most famous of the Persepolis monuments is the terrace staircase, on the stone walls of which are depicted the bearers of tribute from all the parts of the Achaemenid empire. While the tombs of several later kings are at Persepolis itself, the nearby cliff face at Naqsh-i Rustam contains the rock-cut burial chambers of Darius I and his three successors; Naqsh-i Rustam also presents some Middle ELAMITE (late 2nd millennium BC) and SASSANIAN (earlier 1st millennium AD) inscriptions. Alexander the Great, following his victory over the last Achaemenid king, burnt Persepolis in 330 BC.

Persian Gulf trade the active maritime trading of the 3rd and early 2nd millennia BC between MESOPOTAMIA – especially Lagash (TELLO) and UR – and three places whose names appear at various times in the CUNEIFORM texts of southern Mesopotamia: Dilmun, Magan and Meluhha. The combination of textual evidence and archaeological analysis indicates that Dilmun corresponds to the BARBAR culture area in the Persian Gulf, and that Magan probably relates to the UMM AN-NAR and related cultures in southwestern Arabia (possibly extending to the southern coast of Iran); less certainly, Meluhha is usually identified in the HARAPPAN culture area. To southern Mesopotamia, the Persian Gulf trade was a principal source of copper produced in Magan (see MAYSAR), as well as a variety of semi-precious stones and other goods shipped from the Iranian plateau and elsewhere; the chief products exported from Mesopotamia were textiles and grain. Owing to the commercial wealth generated by this trade, and to the abundant artesian water of the place, Dilmun also held an important place in SUMERIAN mythology, as a sort of Eden.

Persians see ACHAEMENIDS, MEDES.

Peschiera a Bronze Age LAKE DWELLING at the foot of Lakeand Garda in Veneto, Italy. Dredging operations in the 19th century recovered a mass of Late Bronze Age metalwork (c.1250–1100 BC) along with pottery and other artifacts, and the remains of the timber piles which supported the houses. Among the bronzes are FIBULAE of violin-bow form, the world's oldest safety-pins.

Petén a part of the MAYA Lowlands, MESOAMERICA. The Petén is a geographical and cultural area including the southern two-thirds of the Yucatán; it is also a modern department of Guatemala. The environment is that of a lowland rain forest. TIKAL and UAXACTÚN in the northeastern Petén, and ALTAR DE SACRIFICIOS in the southwestern part of the region, have materials dating from the PRECLASSIC to the Late CLASSIC.

Peterborough Ware a Neolithic pottery tradition of southern Britain comprising successive *Ebbsfleet*, *Mortlake* and FENGATE styles. Poorly made and crudely decorated, the vessels were principally intended for everyday domestic use.

Peterborough Ware (a) Fengate style (b) Ebbsfleet style.

Petersfels a southern German cave-site lying to the northwest of Lake Constance, near Baden, excavated most recently by G. Albrecht (1974–79). It shows evidence of MAGDALENIAN occupation during a cold period including some jet artifacts which may represent figurines, HARPOON-heads, BURINS, AWLS, BACKED BLADELETS and decorated BÂTONS-DE-COMMANDEMENT. The remains of at least 1200 reindeer dominate the fauna, exploited primarily in the autumn.

Petit-Chasseur, Sion a Late Neolithic and CHALCOLITHIC burial complex in the Valais, Switzerland, consisting of one large MEGALITHIC chamber (M VI) and several smaller tombs. The large chamber stands within a triangular stone pavement, with large engraved ANTHROPOMORPHOUS stone STELAE in front. Despite much later disturbance, M VI can be dated to the Late Neolithic period. Twenty-six of its stelae have been found re-used in smaller tombs of slightly later date containing BEAKER material, and it is clear that the original megalith M VI was also emptied of its primary contents and re-used at that period. The figures on the stelae are equipped with triangular daggers of a form paralleled in 3rd millennium BC contexts in northern Italy, and thus testify to transalpine contacts at this early period.

Petra a city in modern Jordan which rose to importance during the HELLENISTIC period. It is best known for its temples and tombs cut in the rock faces.

Petralona a Middle Palaeolithic cave-site located near Thessalonika in eastern Greece. A series of occupation levels are contained in clay, LOAM and rubble deposits. Among the faunal remains are giant deer (see MEGALOCEROS), red deer and CAVE BEAR. The dating is problematic; estimates range from the early LAST GLACIAL to the early Middle PLEISTOCENE. Artifacts include SCRAPERS, CHOPPING TOOLS and spheres, and have been characterized as 'early MOUSTERIAN'. They are associated with a human skull that is widely assigned to a very archaic form of HOMO *sapiens*.

Petreşti culture   an ENEOLITHIC culture of Transylvania in northwestern Romania, contemporaneous with the early stages of the CUCUTENI-TRIPOLYE culture to the east and the GUMELNIŢA culture to the southeast. Petreşti pottery is decorated with brown parallel lines in elaborate patterns prior to firing.

Petrie, Sir William Matthew Flinders (1853–1942)   an English Egyptologist, a major figure in the development of the science of archaeology. His insistence on the importance of all material recovered from a site was in marked contrast to the excavation techniques of most of his predecessors and contemporaries, as was his use of these data (e.g. SEQUENCE-DATING). An energetic excavator of Egyptian sites (e.g. KAHUN, NAQADA, ABYDOS, MEMPHIS) he concentrated his activities after 1926 on Palestine, where he carried out pioneering work (e.g. at Tell EL-AJJUL).

petroform   a line of rocks or boulders placed on the ground in the shape of an animal, mythological figure or other shape.

petroglyph   see ROCK ART.

petrological analysis or **petrological microscopy**   a technique utilizing a petrological microscope for identifying mineral constituents of ARTIFACTS based on the optical behaviour of polarized light as it passes through a THIN SECTION. Minerals refract the light in different diagnostic ways because of differences among crystal lattice characteristics that allow their identification.

Peu–Richard   a Late Neolithic enclosure in Charente, France, with concentric rock-cut ditches and out-turned entrances, type-site of the Peu-Richardien culture of western France, which is characterized by pottery with flamboyant incised or channelled decoration including so-called *oculi* or double-eye motifs, *c*.3500–2800 BC.

Peyrony, Denis (1869–1954)   a French schoolteacher who became the foremost prehistorian in the Dordogne region. He discovered the CAVE ART at FONT DE GAUME, Bernifal and Teyjat, and carried out pioneering excavations at major sites such as LA FERRASSIE and LAUGERIE HAUTE. He proposed the two-stage PERIGORDIAN system, and created the prehistory museum of LES EYZIES.

Pfupi   a term previously used for LATER STONE AGE material from southwestern Zimbabwe, now generally replaced with KHAMI or MATOPO.

Pfyn   a Middle Neolithic culture of northeastern Switzerland related to the MICHELSBERG culture of the Rhineland. Typical pottery includes round and flat-based vessels, and simple copper objects and crucibles are occasionally found. The Pfyn culture is represented at a number of Neolithic LAKE-DWELLINGS, including the well preserved village of Thayngen-Weier.

Phaistos   the site of a MINOAN palace on the island of Crete, constructed *c*.1900 BC, destroyed by an earthquake *c*.1700 BC, and then rebuilt. The final destruction is dated *c*.1450 BC. Although not as large a palace as KNOSSOS, Phaistos shares the same basic layout and is in some respects superior architecturally, the residential block being particularly impressive. It must be assumed that Phaistos controlled the fertile MESARA plain.

Phalaborwa a copper and iron ore mining town in the eastern Transvaal, South Africa, where a long Iron Age sequence dating back to the 8th century AD has been investigated. There are hundreds of sites where the ore was SMELTED to extract copper and iron, which were then worked into a variety of tools and ornaments.

pH analysis a technique for measuring the hydrogen ion concentration, the pH, of a SOIL or SEDIMENT that is an indication of acidity or alkalinity. The pH in part governs, but is also influenced by, what chemical processes occur, and gives an indication of the likelihood of preservation of some types of cultural remains. Bone, shell and carbonate lithic debris may dissolve where pH is acidic, whereas preservation is likely in calcareous material where pH values are relatively high.

Pharaoh a title used today as a synonym for the king of ancient Egypt, derived from the Egyptian term 'Great House', which originally referred to the palace but came to be applied to the royal personage during the NEW KINGDOM.

phase a term, whose specific definition varies depending on who is using it and where it is being used, but which generally refers to an archaeological unit defined by specific ARTIFACTS and other cultural TRAITS that make the unit distinguishable from other similarly defined units. The phase is fairly restricted in time and space. It is similar in conception to the FOCUS (with the addition of a temporal dimension) of the MIDWESTERN TAXONOMIC SYSTEM and the Old World CULTURE, and is often implicitly used to represent a distinct prehistoric people.

phiale a shallow Greek dish which could be used either as a drinking vessel or for pouring LIBATIONS (see OINOCHOE). The name frequently appears in temple inventory lists of plate, and, since extant examples in silver seem to have been made to a round number of units, they were probably a convenient way to stack and count bullion.

Philae an island in the Nile near ASWAN, on the southern border of LOWER EGYPT. The most important of the complex of TEMPLES built on Philae is that of the goddess ISIS, to whom the island was considered sacred; the nearby island of Biga was the preserve of her mythological husband OSIRIS. The earliest standing monument from Philae dates from the reign of Nectanebo I (380–362 BC) but most of the building on the site was initiated by the PTOLEMAIC Kings and early Roman Emperors (e.g. the Kiosk of Trajan). The temples of Philae were dismantled and re-erected on the nearby island of Agilkia during the NUBIAN RESCUE CAMPAIGN.

Philia the type-site for the CHALCOLITHIC III (mid 3rd millennium BC) Philia culture in northern Cyprus, which is characterized by red polished pottery. The Philia culture may have been introduced by settlers from Cilicia.

Philistines one of the SEA PEOPLES whose occupation of southern Palestine marks the beginning of the Iron Age in that region. The five chief cities of the Philistines (the 'Pentapolis') were ASHKELON, ASHDOD, GAZA, Gath and Ekron. See fig. overleaf.

Phimai a large late-prehistoric/early historic moated settlement in the middle Mun valley, KHORAT, Thailand, occupied before 600 BC. Between c.200 BC and AD 300 it was a major regional iron-working and trading centre. Phimai Black Pottery of this period is found

Philistines A Philistine coffin.

throughout the upper Mun basin, in large quantities within a radius of 50 km, and in smaller quantities further afield. Although perhaps overshadowed by MUANG SIMA in the mid 1st millennium AD, it became a major regional commercial, administrative and sacred centre under KHMER rule in the 11th to 13th centuries (see ANGKOR).

Phocaean ware   a type of Roman red-glossed pottery produced especially from the 4th to the 7th centuries AD. It was made on the west coast of Turkey and its products have a wide distribution, especially in the eastern Mediterranean.

Phoenicians   a Semitic people, the cultural heirs of the CANAANITES, who flourished as traders from their ports of BYBLOS, SIDON and TYRE during the 1st millennium BC. They are credited with the founding of CARTHAGE and the invention of the alphabet.

phosphorus survey or **phosphate analysis**   a technique used to identify, through the analysis of SOIL phosphorus concentrations by various methods, human settlements and activity and burial areas within sites. Excrement and bone are relatively high in phosphorus content, so that human activity and remains tend to produce comparatively large concentrations of phosphates. Identification of such areas implies a need to understand the distribution and range of naturally occurring phosphorus because variations may occur with vegetational abundance and type, and with SOIL HORIZON.

photogrammetry   a technique of constructing maps, making scale drawings of sites and structures, or determining measurements, over a range of scales, from photographs, aerial or otherwise. Maps are made, usually from AERIAL PHOTOGRAPHS, from multiple projections with distortion of the photographs taken into account.

photomicrograph   a photograph of anything that can be viewed in magnification through a microscope taken for permanent documentation and to facilitate communication. It is taken by a camera built in or mounted on any type of microscope, including a SCANNING ELECTRON MICROSCOPE, PETROLOGICAL MICROSCOPE, optical microscope, or binocular microscope. Items of archaeological interest might include palaeobotanical remains, THIN SECTIONS, USE-WEAR on ARTIFACTS, and structures of metals.

Phrygians a people who, at the collapse of the HITTITE empire and the attendant movements of peoples, moved into central Anatolia, probably from a region east of the Black Sea, by the middle of the 12th century BC. Here they founded a kingdom that encompassed most of Anatolia, bordering URARTU and ASSYRIAN client states to the east. They are best remembered, via Greek literature, for two kings whose names have become clichés, Midas and Gordias. The Phrygian kingdom was destroyed by the CIMMERIAN invasion at the end of the 8th century BC, though Phrygian traditions continued into CLASSICAL times in Anatolia.

Phu Lon a copper-mining and ore-processing site near the Mekong River on the northern fringes of KHORAT, Thailand. It is one of a number of metal-extracting and working sites in the hills ringing the plateau, and was apparently in use between c.1750–1425 and 300–275 BC.

Phung Nguyen a site in north Vietnam which has given its name to the late Neolithic–early Bronze transition period in the region, tentatively dated to c.2300–1500 BC (somewhat later than General Period A of KHORAT), and preceding DONG DAU, characterized by POLISHED STONE ADZES and traces of bronze.

Phu Wiang a small plateau south of NON NOK THA in the upper Chi basin, KHORAT, Thailand, on which are located a group of prehistoric sites (Don Sawan, Don Wat Kao, Don Kok) inhabited between c.3000 and 2500 BC. The term is used to describe the group, and the transitional Neolithic–Early Bronze phase they characterize in the region.

Phylakopi the site of a Bronze Age settlement on the Aegean island of MELOS, excavated by British archaeologists in 1896–99, 1911 and 1974–77. The remains of three successive 'cities', respectively Early (= Phylakopi I), Middle, and Late CYCLADIC, were discovered. The third city had close cultural ties, initially with MINOAN Crete and subsequently with MYCENAEAN Greece. The administrative centre appears to have been the MEGARON. The Mycenaean cult centre has also been identified.

phytoliths microscopic biogenic opal silica bodies secreted by or deposited in plants, that are incorporated into the SOIL upon decay of plants and often preserved. Different plants produce phytoliths with different characteristic shapes and sizes, although not all morphologies are unique to individual species; identification of phytoliths collected from stratified sections may indicate the character of past vegetation.

Picosa culture a late ARCHAIC CULTURE, often called the elemental Southwestern culture, that emerged about 3000 BC in the American Southwest. Its name comes from an amalgamation of the previously defined Pinto Basin culture of southern California, southern Nevada and western Arizona, the Cochise culture of southeastern Arizona and southwestern New Mexico and the Oshara tradition of the Four Corners region. It is considered by some archaeologists to be ancestral to the later ANASAZI, HOHOKAM and MOGOLLON traditions.

pictograph see ROCK ART.

Piedmont Tradition a late ARCHAIC TRADITION in northeastern North America that is characterized by particular stemmed PROJECTILE

POINTS and lithic assemblages.

Pietersburg   a term sometimes applied to South African early MID-DLE STONE AGE artifact assemblages dating to the late Middle PLEISTOCENE or early Late Pleistocene, and characterized by numerous long parallel-sided FLAKE-BLADES, many of which have minimal RETOUCH or utilization damage on the sides (see MWULU'S, ORANGIA).

Piette, Edouard (1827–1906)   a pioneering French prehistorian who excavated some major sites in southwest France (see LE MAS D'AZIL, BRASSEMPOUY). The first person to bridge the gap between the Palaeolithic and the Mesolithic through his discovery of the AZILIAN, he was also extremely open-minded, being one of the very few scholars to accept ALTAMIRA's authenticity from the start, and a staunch believer in animal control before the Neolithic period. He amassed the greatest collection of Palaeolithic PORTABLE ART, and gave it to the nation. He also introduced H. BREUIL to prehistory.

Pikillacta   a MIDDLE HORIZON site near CUZCO, Peru, that served as a HUARI administrative centre. The site measures over 800 metres square, and comprises planned architecture of Huari style. Portions of the site were never completed, but excavations by Gordon McEwan demonstrate an extensive Huari occupation, and MIDDEN area. A sector of the site comprises small, ovoid, contiguous structures thought by some to be storehouses, although McEwan argues that they were habitation structures.

Pikimachay   a large PRECERAMIC cave-site in Ayacucho, central highland Peru. Its excavator, Richard S. MacNeish, argued that he had identified very early, pre-CLOVIS phases dating to between 20 000 and 11 000 bc, associated with the bones of extinct sloth. However, these phases have been largely discounted as representing human occupation. Other levels in the cave demonstrated a long preceramic occupation, beginning about 9000 bc.

Piklihal   a prehistoric locality in eastern Karnata in southwestern India, where F. Allchin's work defined a series of Neolithic and MEGA-LITHIC GRAVE period occupations. The Neolithic settlements, beginning around 2100 BC and continuing through much of the 2nd millennium, contain a series of circular beaten-earth floors ringed with stone (presumably to support a perishable superstructure). The earliest of these settlements, which may be associated with the Deccan ASH MOUNDS, has a fauna of cattle, sheep and goat; creation of small farm plots by terracing on hillsides also belongs to this early Neolithic phase. The late Neolithic occupations (later 2nd and early 1st millennia BC) continue along much the same lines, and are similar to other sites in the southern Deccan such as HALLUR and TEKKALAKOTA. The pottery, which in the early Neolithic was hand-made, is now made on a slow wheel, and some of it bears a resemblance to late JORWE pottery to the north. The subsequent 'Megalithic' to early historic occupations present a sequence of pottery that covers most of the 1st millennium BC and continues into the early 1st millennium AD; this sequence contains various BLACK-AND-RED WARES, white-painted black-and-red wares, 'Russet-coated' ware, Indian imitation ROULETTED WARE, and RED POLISHED ware. Iron appears throughout this latter sequence.

pile dwellings   see LAKE DWELLINGS.

pillar crypt   a basement room in MINOAN architecture which contains one or two pillars. Their primary function was clearly structural but the fact that some were incised with sacred symbols, such as the DOUBLE AXE, led EVANS to speculate that they were also the focus for cult activities.

Piltdown Man   skeletal remains recovered from Piltdown, Sussex, England, by Dawson in 1912–15, which were believed to represent the 'missing evolutionary link' between ancient and modern humans. In 1953 the bones underwent a stringent examination which revealed them to be a deliberate forgery, consisting of fragments of a modern human skull and a female orang-utan mandible. The identity of the perpetrator(s) of the hoax is still uncertain.

Pincevent   an extensive Late MAGDALENIAN open-air site in Seine-et-Marne, northern France, which was discovered during commercial sand quarrying in 1964, and excavated by LEROI-GOURHAN until 1985. The project pioneered large-scale horizontal excavation in the west European Palaeolithic and new techniques such as latex moulds of living-floors, and was a training school for generations of archaeologists. Around 9–10 000 BC there were at least 15 occupations here, interspersed with the Seine's flood LOAMS. Over 100 habitation structures (tents) and 20 large HEARTHS have been found. The fauna, almost entirely reindeer, points to occupation from early summer to early winter. The site has provided many examples of CONJOINED FLINTS.

pingo   a LANDFORM that consists of a conical mound formed by a buried body of ground ice up to 40 m high and 600 m wide. Open-system pingos form under discontinuous PERMAFROST in lowland areas underlain by permeable GRAVEL and SAND. Closed-system pingos form under continuous permafrost when shallow lakes freeze under certain conditions. Relict pingos, identified by a circular ridge with a central basin, often filled with PEAT, are used as indicators of the extent of permafrost and the PERIGLACIAL environment.

Pinto Basin   see PICOSA CULTURE.

Piraeus   the main port of ATHENS, to which it was linked by the construction of the 5th century BC Long Walls which ran for more than 6 km. The city itself was laid out in HIPPODAMIAN PLANNING. Traces of *trireme* (warship) sheds have been found. Extant remains include a small HELLENISTIC theatre.

Pirak   a 9 ha prehistoric site on the Kachi plain of Baluchistan in western Pakistan, where J-M. Casal's excavations revealed a post-HARAPPAN cultural sequence of seven phases (Pirak IA–B, II, IIIA–C) that covers most of the 2nd millennium and the early 1st millennium BC; although Mature Harappan pottery occurs on the surface of the site, none exists in stratigraphic context. In addition to a succession of MUD-BRICK architecture (which includes a large platform in the first period, and large rooms with niches in the later periods), the Pirak sequence is characterized by a painted pottery of a dense geometric style seemingly derived from the earlier painted pottery of the QUETTA tradition, without a hint of Harappan survivals. In the earlier phases, the painted decoration is monochrome, but becomes bichrome (black and red on buff) in later phases. The Pirak sequence revealed several regionally important 'events'. Beginning with the lowest levels (perhaps 1800 BC), rice, sorghum and millet occur among the cultigens at the site, marking their early appearance in the

Indus region, and indicative of intensified agricultural production. At the same time, both horse and camel bones appear among the fauna, as do figurines of these two animals. And beginning in Pirak II (in the third quarter of the 2nd millennium BC), and becoming more common in later levels, iron appears.

pirri graver   a recently defined Australian tool type, with a moderate to pronounced underside curvature, extensive flaking on the opposite face, and a RETOUCHED cutting edge on the narrow end of the tool. Pirri gravers are up to 80 mm long, 40 mm wide and 25 mm high. Ethnographic examples were hafted for use as engraving tools for making grooves on wooden artifacts. Their distribution is not well known, but seems to correspond broadly to that of the TULA.

0   2 cm

pirri graver

pirri point   a symmetrical leaf-shaped or triangular point up to 60 mm long, unifacially worked, with invasive flaking, sometimes by pressure, on the dorsal surface. The STRIKING PLATFORM may be removed by trimming the butt. Pirri points belong to the AUSTRALIAN SMALL TOOL TRADITION and are widely distributed in arid Australia, mainly in South Australia and the Northern Territory. The Aboriginal term *pirri* refers to wood-engraving tools. It has been mistakenly applied to unifacial points which were sometimes re-used for engraving. See PIRRI GRAVER.

pisé, *adj.*   (of walls) formed from mud or clay. Compare MUD-BRICK and WATTLE AND DAUB.

Pitcairn Island   one of a number of isolated islands in the Pacific which had prehistoric occupants at some time but were uninhabited at European contact. Evidence of occupation from Pitcairn and neighbouring islands goes back to *c*.AD 1100 and includes stone platforms with ANTHROPOMORPHOUS statues, PETROGLYPHS, stone FISHHOOKS and ADZES, and domestic pig remains. The material resembles NEW ZEALAND Archaic assemblages. See also NECKER ISLAND.

Pit-Comb ware a complex of incipient agricultural groups of the forest zone around the southern Baltic and glacial outwash of central and eastern Poland, named for their pottery which is characterized by comb-stroked decoration and pronounced pits. Related groups are the PITTED WARE CULTURE of central Sweden and Finland, and the NARVA culture of Estonia. The makers of Pit-Comb Ware are poorly known, largely from surface finds and a few sites. Few data are available on subsistence, and some have referred to Pit-Comb Ware as a 'ceramic Mesolithic' or 'paraneolithic' culture.

Pit-Grave culture see YAMNAYA CULTURE.

Pithecanthropus see JAVA MAN, MOJOKERTO.

Pithekoussai see ISCHIA.

pithos a large Greek storage jar, used for items such as olive oil, wine and grain. In the Aegean the dead were sometimes buried in pithoi.

pithouse a subterranean or semi-subterranean chamber used by prehistoric inhabitants of the American Southwest as their primary habitation structure. The pithouse was most popular in the period AD 200–900, and is thought to have been used primarily by individual families. It evolved into the KIVA.

Pitted-Ware culture foraging groups in Sweden and Finland of the 3rd to 1st millennia BC, part of a larger circumpolar complex of later HOLOCENE foragers. Pitted-Ware communities of the northern Baltic region relied to a large degree on seal hunting and pig raising. In addition, ornaments of amber were manufactured extensively.

Pitt-Rivers, General Augustus Lane-Fox (1827–1900) a pioneer of scientific excavation and recording. After a military career he inherited the Rivers estates in southwest England in 1880, and over the following 25 years excavated a series of prehistoric and Romano-British sites on his estates, including Wor Barrow, South Lodge and Bokerly Dyke, which he published in the four-volume report *Excavations in Cranborne Chase* (1887–98). In these works he stressed the importance of STRATIGRAPHY and the precise recording of the location of all finds. Pitt-Rivers was also the first Inspector of Ancient Monuments in England and Wales.

Pizarro, Francisco (1475–1541) a Spanish adventurer who, impressed by the gold of Peru in the 1520s, returned there in 1532 with 180 men and destroyed the empire of the INCAS, who thought the Spaniards were gods returning as prophesied in legends. The founder of modern Lima, he was assassinated in 1541.

Plain of Jars see XIANG KHOUANG.

Plain Pottery see MUMUN.

Plains Village Indian a collection of archaeological cultures found on the Central and Eastern plains of North America in the period AD 900–1850. Despite regional variation, Plains Village Indians were characterized by large habitation structures in permanent or semi-permanent settlements that were often fortified; pottery; and some degree of reliance on corn horticulture. Along the Missouri River in present-day North and South Dakota, there developed the

Middle Missouri Tradition. In the 1400s, drought forced an abandonment of the Central Plains, and its former occupants moved into the Middle Missouri area to form the Coalescent Tradition.

Plainview 1. a PLANO PROJECTILE POINT, distinguished by parallel sides and a concave base, although much internal variety exists. A variant named Firstview was identified at the OLSEN-CHUBBUCK site.
2. a site in Texas that is the type-site for the COMPLEX.
3. a Plano complex associated with the Plainview point and characterized by non-diagnostic stone and bone tools.

plane table a drawing board that is mounted on a tripod used in conjunction with an ALIDADE. Drafting paper is attached to the table, which is then levelled with an alidade. A map is constructed directly on the drafting paper by sighting through the alidade the point to be mapped, while aligning the alidade straight edge so that it intersects the point on the map representing the mapping station, drawing a line along the straight edge, and scaling the calculated distance along the line to the measured point. The technique is somewhat dated, being replaced by PHOTOGRAMMETRY and other methods.

Plano a PALAEOINDIAN TRADITION in North America, characterized, in the west, by the hunting of bison and the development of diverse PROJECTILE POINT styles and complexes, such as AGATE BASIN and HELL GAP, Cody and Frederick. The Plano Tradition dates from approximately 10 000–7000 BP.

plano-convex brick a characteristic brick-form of the EARLY DYNASTIC (and especially of the E.D. II–III) period in southern MESOPOTAMIA, this term refers to bricks that are flat on one face and domed on the other, often with thumb-impressed holes on the latter surface. These bricks were used, with a great deal of mud mortar, in vertical courses inclined in alternating directions to create a 'herring-bone' pattern.

plastered skulls a series of prehistoric skulls that are among the most famous discoveries at JERICHO, Israel. They had been covered in plaster and then painted to render the visage of the dead individual, usually with cowry shells set in the orbits. Such skulls occur in PPNB contexts at several sites in Syro-Palestine (e.g. Ramad, Beisamun). This practice seems to be an elaboration of the common practice of separating head from body of the dead for separate burial, a custom already present in PPNA times, when groups of skulls were buried together.

platform mounds earthen flat-topped mounds that were surmounted by buildings, which served as habitation and/or ceremonial structures. See CAHOKIA, MISSISSIPPIAN.

playa a low-relief dry lake basin in arid or semi-arid regions where runoff collects, forming a temporary lake that eventually evaporates. When dry, the playa is subjected to AEOLIAN erosional and depositional processes. FOSSIL BEACH ridges around playa lakes sometimes have associated archaeological deposits that may become either deflated lags, or buried as the result of aeolian activity.

Pleistocene Epoch a geochronological division of geological time, following the PLIOCENE. The Lower Pleistocene begins c.1.8 million years ago; the Middle c.730 000 years ago; and the Upper c.127 000 years ago. It ends c.10 000 bp. See PLEISTOCENE SERIES.

Pleistocene extinctions the mass extinction of fauna both large (including the MAMMOTH and the horse) and small, in North America and elsewhere at the end of the PLEISTOCENE. Explanations for the extinctions range from massive environmental change or human over-hunting to a combination of both.

Pleistocene Series   the chronostratigraphic division (see STRATIGRAPHY) of the QUATERNARY SYSTEM defined by deposits, overlying PLIOCENE deposits, containing evidence of humans and their development and resulting from alternating GLACIAL and INTERGLACIAL processes and conditions in response to multiple major environmental changes. In some classification systems, the Pleistocene Series is equivalent to the Quaternary system, being its only series. In other classification systems, the Quaternary system is divided into the Pleistocene Series and HOLOCENE Series, the rank accorded the Holocene Series varying regionally. In this case the division is usually taken to be 10 000 bp.

Pleniglacial   see LAST GLACIAL MAXIMUM.

Pliocene   the epoch dating between *c*.5 million years ago and the beginning of the PLEISTOCENE.

Plio–Pleistocene   the latter part of the PLIOCENE and the early part of the PLEISTOCENE, i.e. the period between about 5 and 1 million years ago.

Pločnik   a stratified flat settlement in southern Serbia, whose name is often used in connection with the late phase of the VINČA culture, 3950–3300 bc. At the three-metre deposits at Pločnik, three occupation layers were distinguished. The bottom two are late Vinča, while the uppermost is of the BUBANJ-HUM group. In the Bubanj-Hum levels, four hoards of copper tools include cast shaft-hole axes.

ploshchadki   a Russian term for house floors consisting of a clay layer covering a base of horizontal logs, usually hardened by fire. Such house remains are characteristic of the CUCUTENI-TRIPOLYE culture, but also occur in the GUMELNIŢA, PETREŞTI and VINČA cultures, reflecting a widespread construction practice in southeastern Europe during the Late Neolithic.

ploughmarks or **plough scars**   scars, identified by sharp physical discontinuities in SOIL colour or TEXTURE in upper SOIL HORIZONS, seen in excavation profiles or plan view, that mark the location, depth and type of previous agricultural practices. Ploughmarks associated with the modern soil indicate cultivation and possible displacement of associated archaeological deposits.

Plussulien   a Neolithic quarry in Côtes-du-Nord, France, used for approximately 2000 years (4000–2000 BC) for the production of polished stone axes of 'type A' dolerite. The site consists of outcrops of dolerite, remains of HEARTHS used in fire-setting, and massive accumulations of debris. Among this were found many HAMMERSTONES and grinders for crushing the blocks of dolerite and shaping the axes. Polished stone axes of Plussulien dolerite are found as far away as the Alps, the Pyrenees and southern Britian.

pluvial   1. *n.* a wet climatic episode, marked by high lake levels as indicated by various lines of evidence, including FOSSIL BEACHES. These moist episodes apparently were not SYNCHRONOUS world-wide but rather varied somewhat in age with latitude. High lake levels and other favourable ecological changes accompanying these periods of increased precipitation led to increased human occupation and activity in areas that otherwise were of limited attraction.

2. *adj.*   pertaining to or due to rain.

pochteca   a class of long-distance merchants in AZTEC society. These traders travelled to foreign lands, and often acted as spies during their expeditions.

Pod Hradem   an Upper Palaeolithic cave-site located northeast of Brno in Moravia, Czechoslovakia. Artifacts and faunal remains are buried in rubble and 'cave earth' deposits. The lower layers contain some artifacts, including a LAUREL-LEAF POINT, assigned to the SZELETIAN, and a younger early Upper Palaeolithic industry (e.g. RETOUCHED BLADES) was found in overlying layers; both industries are associated primarily with CAVE BEAR remains and dated to the middle of the LAST GLACIAL. Late Upper Palaeolithic artifacts, associated with reindeer remains, occur in the upper layers.

point   a broad category of stone artifacts, including a variety of pointed tools flaked on one or both sides. See also SIDE-NOTCHED, SHOULDERED, LAUREL-LEAF, WILLOW-LEAF, and SWIDERIAN POINTS.

point bar   a depositional alluvial LANDFORM located on and just behind the convex bank of meandering streams that is a series of accretionary ridges and swales, formed and modified as the stream floods and the meander bend migrates. The slightly better drained ridges were often loci of human activities related to exploitation of aquatic and wetland resources.

Polada   an Early Bronze Age LAKE DWELLING in Lombardy, Italy, type-site of the Polada culture (*c.*2200–1600 BC). This includes cultural features directly derived from BEAKER ASSEMBLAGES, such as WRISTGUARDS and v-perforated buttons, alongside features of indigenous origin. Many Polada sites are waterlogged and have revealed a wide range of organic remains, including long bows, crook ARDS, dug-out canoes and spoked wheels.

Polesini   an Upper Palaeolithic site near Rome, Italy, excavated by Radmilli in 1952–56 which yielded thousands of stone tools and faunal remains dominated by red deer, primarily exploited in winter. The site is best known for its engraved MOBILIARY ART, dating to the 11th millennium bp.

Poliochni   the site of a prehistoric settlement on the Aegean island of Lemnos, which was excavated by della Seta in 1931–36 and by Bernabo Brea in 1951–56. Poliochni was first occupied in the FINAL NEOLITHIC period. The Early Bronze Age settlement, one of the largest in the Aegean, had fine houses, wide streets and massive stone fortifications, but eventually suffered a catastrophic destruction. After a period of abandonment Poliochni was reoccupied, but the Middle and Late Bronze Age levels have largely been eroded.

polis   a Greek state incorporating a city, smaller towns and villages, and its territory.

polished stone adze   a CHOPPING/cutting tool, bevelled on one side, characteristic of the Neolithic of much of Southeast Asia. It seems to have developed from earlier EDGE-GRINDING techniques, in some places appearing as early as 6000 BC and continuing in use in metal-poor regions into the 1st millennium AD. The adzes were generally flaked to shape from a large CORE, then ground and polished over most or all surfaces. Many were traded as roughed-out forms ('blanks') to be polished by the recipient. The basic adze form, common to most areas and phases, is the simple quadrangular shape (rectangular or trapezoidal), probably ancestral to other forms. It appears early in Thailand (SPIRIT CAVE) and Taiwan. Differences between rectangular and oval/lenticular cross-sections appear to relate to the hardness of stone used rather than, as once believed, to different cultures. Three major groupings have been suggested: one in southern China, characterized by Duff's type 2A, stepped 1A and slightly shouldered 1B which are associated with southern LUNG-SHANOID and other contemporary cultures, and which seem to connect with forms in Taiwan, the Philippines and Polynesia; the northern Indochinese focus is characterized by simple types which frequently have oval or lenticular cross-sections (see SAI YOK, BAN KAO); the third focus encompasses the Malay peninsula and much of western Indonesia. The development sequence and migration model proposed by Heine Geldern on the basis of adze types are no longer accepted.

polished stone adze Shouldered adze type 1B.

polity a term used by Renfrew to describe small-scale but politically autonomous early states found, for instance, in MYCENAEAN Greece and ETRUSCAN Italy.

Polivanov Yar a Neolithic settlement of the CUCUTENI-TRIPOLYE culture in Ukraine, located on a high promontory across which a ditch and bank were constructed to complete the defences. INGOTS of SMELTED COPPER at Polivanov Yar point to trade contacts with the Carpathian-Balkan region to the west.

pollen analysis see PALYNOLOGY.

Polyanitsa a TELL site of the ENEOLITHIC GUMELNIŢA culture in northeastern Bulgaria. Excavation of eight habitation levels has revealed densely packed rectangular houses, many with party walls or separated by narrow alleys, set within a rectangular palisade. The living quarters appear to have been relatively uniform in size, consisting of a basic module of a large room with a HEARTH. Interior posts supported a roof.

polychrome pottery *sensu stricto*, pottery that is decorated with more than two colours, but very often applied to any pottery that has more than one colour in its decoration.

Polynesia a region of widely scattered islands in the central Pacific, distributed roughly in a triangle with the Hawaiian Islands, EASTER ISLAND, and NEW ZEALAND at its corners. It is fairly homogeneous in terms of ethnicity, language and social organization. It is divided into two regions, with some differences in material culture and religion:

POLYNESIAN OUTLIERS

Western Polynesia includes Tonga, Samoa and Tuvalu; while Eastern Polynesia includes the Society, Cook, Austral, Marquesas, Tuamotu and Hawaiian Islands, as well as Easter Island and New Zealand. Pottery production seems to have ceased in Western Polynesia about AD 300, and the only pottery found in Eastern Polynesia seems to have been imported from the west.

Polynesian outliers nineteen small islands with Polynesian-speaking populations in MELANESIA, to the east of the Solomons, New Hebrides and New Caledonia, and on the southern fringes of MICRONESIA.

Pomongwe 1. a LATER STONE AGE industry of southwestern Zimbabwe, dated between 10 800 and 9400 bp, and characterized by SCRAPERS and virtually no other patterned stone artifacts. Some researchers view it as a regional industry within the OAKHURST Complex.
2. a cave with many fine rock paintings, especially of giraffe, in the Matobo Hills of southwestern Zimbabwe, which has a long sequence of stone industries and faunal remains.

Pompeii a town in CAMPANIA, Italy, buried under ASH after the eruption of Vesuvius in AD 79. The site was rediscovered in the mid 18th century and a large part of its *c.*65 ha have been excavated. The oldest part of the city lay in the FORUM area, and the street layout has a different orientation to the rest of the city. Extensive remains include houses, workshops, an AMPHITHEATRE, a PALAESTRA and various civic buildings. Many of the private houses had decorated wall plaster which has been categorized into four styles. Outside the gates were cemeteries, and beyond them large residential establishments such as the VILLA of the Mysteries. See also FIORELLI.

Pong Tuk on the Mae Klong River in west-central Thailand, the find-place of a late-Roman bronze lamp (*c.*5th–6th century AD) similar in form to CERAMIC lamps found at other sites in the vicinity: U THONG, KU BUA, and NAKHON PATHOM.

Pont du Gard part of the 40 km long AQUEDUCT taking water to NÎMES. Where the line crossed the River Gard a three-stage aqueduct was constructed, taking the water some 49 m above the river. The present length of the upper storey is 275 m.

Pontian a site in peninsular Malaysia of a boat burial of the early centuries AD associated with pottery similar to that from KUALA SELINSING, with decorative motifs also noticed at OC ÈO. The boat is of Southeast Asian type (see SHIPWRECKS).

Pontic ware a type of BLACK-FIGURED pottery produced in ETRURIA in the ARCHAIC period. The style seems to have been influenced by techniques used in Attica, CORINTH and Ionia.

Pontnewydd Cave a cave-site in north Wales which has yielded Middle PLEISTOCENE HOMINID remains representing at least three individuals, an important series of dates (170–230 000 BP) and an industry once believed to be atypical MOUSTERIAN, but now accepted as Upper ACHEULIAN with the use of prepared-CORE flaking techniques. The lithic artifacts are made from local hard stones which are difficult to KNAP, and which give all the tools a rather primitive appearance. The cave has been investigated since the end of the 19th century, most recently by H.S. Green.

porphyry a type of stone quarried in the eastern Egyptian desert.

There are three main types: red (*rosso antico*), green and black. Many sculptures in this medium seem to be linked to the Roman imperial family; therefore it is thought that the quarries were under direct control of the emperor.

portal dolmens or **portal tombs**   MEGALITHIC tombs with above-ground chambers consisting of a heavy capstone, supported on three or more uprights in such a way that the capstone slopes markedly downwards from front to back. Whether these distinctive monuments were originally hidden within a covering mound is unclear. Portal dolmens are found in Wales and Cornwall, but are most common in western Ireland, especially in the Burren area (e.g. Poulnabrone, Co. Clare).

Port Arthur   a penal settlement on the Tasman Peninsula, south of Hobart, TASMANIA, Australia. The complex was begun in AD 1830 and finally closed in 1877 after a brutal history. A range of structures survives at Port Arthur itself, while other buildings associated with the penal colony occur elsewhere on the peninsula. From 1979 to 1986, Port Arthur was the subject of an intensive archaeological programme associated with the management of the site, and therefore occupies a key place in the development of historical archaeology in Australia.

Port aux Choix   the site of an ARCHAIC cemetery of over 100 burials located in northwestern Newfoundland, Canada, that is dated between the late 3rd and late 2nd millennia BC. The burials were accompanied by grave-goods, which included OCHRE, polished slate artifacts, barbed bone points, toggled bone HARPOON heads, shell beads and combs, needles, knives and SCRAPERS made variously from bone, IVORY and antler.

Port Essington   a site on the Cobourg Peninsula, northeast of Darwin in Australia's Northern Territory, which was excavated by Jim Allen in 1966 and is a pioneering example of historical archaeology in Australia. The Victoria military settlement lasted from AD 1838 to 1849 and was the third unsuccessful attempt by the British to settle tropical Australia. The surviving structures include Cornish round chimneys, while artifacts of bottle-glass are evidence of Aboriginal presence at the site.

portable art   see MOBILIARY ART, PALAEOLITHIC ART.

Porticello   a shipwreck site in the Straits of Messina between Italy and Sicily. Although the site had been looted, the cargo is known to have consisted of lifesize bronze statuary, AMPHORAE, INGOTS, ink-pots and fine pottery. It dates to *c*.440–430 BC.

portico   a colonnade, usually forming part of a building such as PALAESTRAE. Porticos often bordered gardens in Roman houses.

Portland Vase   see CAMEO GLASS.

positivism   a school of philosophy initially associated with Auguste Comte in the 18th century. There is an emphasis on the 'testability' of statements and the separation of data from the theories that explain them, especially as propounded in a variant of positivism termed *Logical Positivism*. Positivism has become somewhat *passé* in contemporary philosophical theory, but it became, and remains, the primary theoretical basis of NEW ARCHAEOLOGY.

Postclassic period   (AD 750/900–1250)   the period following the collapse of CLASSIC PERIOD civilizations in MESOAMERICA. This collapse did not occur simultaneously throughout Mesoamerica, hence the variable beginning date for the period. Mesoamerican cultures during the Postclassic tended to be more secular than those of the Classic period.

postglacial, *adj.* referring to or happening during the period of time following a GLACIAL episode. See INTERGLACIAL.

posthole a hole dug into the ground and into which the base of an upright post is placed. Even after the post itself has rotted away, the posthole remains archaeologically recognizable, because the SEDIMENT with which it is filled is often of a different TEXTURE or colour from the surrounding SOIL. The pattern of postholes in a site can provide invaluable evidence on the size and shape of houses and other structures. The American term for posthole is *postmold*.

Postoloprty a Neolithic site of the LENGYEL culture in Bohemia, in which a 33 m-long trapezoidal LONGHOUSE with bedding trenches (similar to those at BRZEŚĆ KUJAWSKI and OSŁONKI) had four features interpreted as hearths spaced down its centre. B. Soudský argued that these represented the habitation areas of four separate families, by analogy with LONGHOUSE divisions among the Iroquois of North America.

Postpalatial the period after the destruction of the palaces, in the chronological system for MINOAN Crete devised by Platon, Late Minoan IIIA2–IIIC (*c.*1375–1100 BC) in the traditional chronology.

postprocessual archaeology a school of archaeological thought that rejects most of the tenets of the NEW or PROCESSUAL archaeology. It is based on the notions that culture must be understood as sets of symbols that evoke meanings, and that these meanings vary depending on the particular contexts of use and the specific histories of both ARTIFACTS and the people who use them. MATERIAL CULTURE is also vital to the control and exercise of social power over individuals. Explanation of human behaviour cannot be reduced to ecological factors, but rather must be sought within the cultures themselves, as specific, often idiosyncratic, responses to particular conditions.

potassium–argon dating an isotopic dating method based on the radioactive decay of ^{40}K to the stable ISOTOPE ^{40}Ar. The method is used primarily to date lava flows and TUFFS, both of which could be in STRATIGRAPHIC sequences with archaeological deposits, and the PALAEOMAGNETIC reversal timescale by dating ocean floor basalts. When originally formed, these deposits have no ^{40}Ar because the heat at time of emplacement has driven it away. The age is based on the known HALF-LIFE of ^{40}K, the constant proportion of ^{39}K and ^{40}K in rocks, and the $^{40}K/^{40}Ar$ ratio with both isotopes being measured in the sample. The method is routinely applied from about 100 000 to 30 million years, the theoretical upper limit is several orders of magnitude greater.

Potočka Cave an Upper Palaeolithic site located in the mountains of Slovenia (*c.*2000 m alt). Artifacts and faunal remains (chiefly CAVE BEAR) are buried in cave deposits dating to the LAST GLACIAL. The small Upper Paleolithic assemblage includes sidescrapers (rare) and endscrapers (see SCRAPER), and RETOUCHED BLADES, and is assigned to the AURIGNACIAN. Potočka Cave was excavated by Brodar.

potsherd a fragment of a pot. See also OSTRAKON.

Poverty Point a site in Northern Louisiana, USA, which belongs to the WOODLAND STAGE. The site comprises a huge octagonal earthwork, approximately 1.8 km in diameter. The earthwork itself is composed of six individual ridges that surround a central plaza. There is no evidence of agriculture at the site. Poverty Point objects are small irregularly shaped baked clay pieces, the precise function of which is unknown. They may have been used as an equivalent of boiling stones to facilitate the heating of water. The associated Poverty Point COMPLEX dates from 1300 BC to at least 400 BC.

pozzolana   a volcanic dust found in central Italy, especially at Pozzuoli (*Lat.* Puteoli). It was used to strengthen Roman concrete, as well as for lining water channels.

PPNA, PPNB, PPNC   see PRE-POTTERY NEOLITHIC.

Praia das Maças   a pair of Chalolithic CHAMBERED TOMBS near Lisbon, Portugal, the first rock-cut, the second with dry-stone super-structure roofed by a CORBELLED VAULT. The rock-cut tomb contained decorated slate plaques, an alabaster comb, and other material of Late Neolithic or earliest Chalcolithic type, with a RADIOCARBON date of 2300 bc. The later tomb, blocking the entrance to the earlier monument, was over twice as large and contained *c.*150 burials, with BEAKER pottery, PALMELA points and a TANGED dagger. It has a radio-carbon date of 1690 bc.

Prambanan   a complex of Hindu and Buddhist temples, many of them CANDI, near Yogyakarta in central Java, built by the rulers of MATARAM in the late 8th and 9th centuries AD. Best-known temples include Loro Jonggrang, Candi Sewu and Plaosan. Kalasan and Ratu Baka are nearby.

Preceramic   see PRE-POTTERY NEOLITHIC, ACERAMIC NEOLITHIC.

Preceramic Period   (*c.*9000(?) to 1800 bc) the period in Andean South America beginning with the first human occupation of the region and ending with the introduction of CERAMIC ARTIFACTS; the Preceramic is sometimes divided into six phases on the coast of Peru. The general date at which human occupation first took place is a matter of dispute, with some researchers claiming to have found evidence for late PLEISTOCENE occupations, prior to 9000 bc. (See MONTE VERDE, PEDRA FURADA.) Very few such sites stand up to close scrutiny. But there is little dispute that in the Early Preceramic a PALAEOINDIAN tradition spread through South America, evidenced by lithic complexes including FLUTED stemmed 'FISHTAIL' POINTS at such sites as EL INGA and FELL'S CAVE. This is followed by a long period, termed by some the ARCHAIC PERIOD, during which foraging popula-tions occupied much of the continent. Both domestic architecture and ceremonial architecture emerged at this time. (See ASANA.) The Late Preceramic (sometimes called the Cotton Preceramic, or Preceramic VI in coastal Peru) was a period in which sedentary villages began to appear with some regularity on the coast, and agriculture began to supply an increasing portion of the diet. Monumental ceremonial architecture, and widespread religious traditions also occured in the Late Preceramic (See KOTOSH, EL PARAISO). The period ends with the introduction of pottery and the start of the INITIAL PERIOD. In other parts of South America, pottery was adopted much earlier: in Amazonia *c.*7600 bp (see TAPERINHA), and in northwest Colombia *c.*5200 bp. See FORMATIVE.

Preclassic period   (2000 BC to AD 250)   the period in which most traits of MESOAMERICAN culture appear that distinguish it from South

American and North American cultures. The OLMEC is the first of the Mesoamerican cultures to appear in the Preclassic, early in the period. In the MAYA area, the later portion of the Preclassic is often referred to as the PROTOCLASSIC PERIOD. The earliest writing (GLYPHS) in Mesoamerica occurs in this period.

Předmostí   a Palaeolithic open-air site on the Bečva River in north-eastern Moravia, Czechoslovakia. Artifacts and faunal remains are buried in LOESS and slope deposits; many details are obscured by missing data. Middle Palaeolithic artifacts, probably dating to the Early GLACIAL, are associated with a buried soil in the lower part of the sequence. Upper Palaeolithic cultural layers (AURIGNACIAN and EASTERN GRAVETTIAN) were found in the upper levels, associated with numerous woolly MAMMOTH bones (about 1000 individuals) and dated by RADIOCARBON to 26 870 bp. A mass grave containing the remains of 20 individuals, apparently associated with the main Eastern Gravettian layer, was discovered in 1894. The site is rich in bone and IVORY tools, pendants, and PORTABLE ART including female figurines, a mammoth carving, and a remarkable stylized female figure engraved on a tusk.

Pre–Dorset   a series of early Arctic CULTURES and COMPLEXES characterized by MICROBLADES, knives, SCRAPERS and BURINS. The Pre-Dorset economy was based on the hunting of seal and walrus, and also of land animals in some areas. It originated in the western part of the continent in the 5th millennium BP and spread east to northern Greenland. It is part of the ARCTIC SMALL-TOOL TRADITION and, as its name implies, is the basis of the later DORSET CULTURE which emerged about 3000 BP.

Predynastic, *adj.*   relating to Egypt before it became a unified state in *c.*3000 BC. See BADARIAN, AMRATIAN, GERZEAN, MERIMDE BENI SALAMA, OMARI and MAADI.

prehistoric period or **prehistory**   any period for which there is no contemporary documentary evidence. It constitutes the major segment of the human past, and is the major object of study in ARCHAEOLOGY. See HISTORIC PERIOD, PROTOHISTORIC PERIOD.

pre–Neanderthal   a name given to the makers of the ACHEULIAN INDUSTRY, believed by some to develop into classic NEANDERTHALERS.

Prepalatial   the period before the construction of the palaces, in the chronological system for MINOAN Crete devised by Platon: Early Minoan I–III (*c.*3000–2000 BC) in the traditional chronology.

Pre-pottery Neolithic   an early phase of the Neolithic of the Near East, during which agriculture was practised (presumably as a consequence of the intensive use of wild cereals by the preceding NATUFIAN communities) but pottery, the other major innovation of the period, was not yet produced. Domesticated animals also appear in the later phases of this period. The term was coined by KENYON. Its two subdivisions, based on the excavations at JERICHO, are Pre-pottery Neolithic A (PPNA, *c.*8500–7600 BC) and Pre-pottery Neolithic B (PPNB, *c.*7600–6000 BC). Recent work at 'AIN GHAZAL suggests the existence of a third terminal phase, the PPNC dated to 6200–5900 BC. See also ACERAMIC NEOLITHIC.

pre-projectile point complex   a COMPLEX proposed by Alex Krieger that encompasses the earliest archaeological evidence for humans on the North American continent. Its most important characteristic is that it lacks time-diagnostic stone PROJECTILE POINTS.

pressure flaking   a SECONDARY RETOUCH technique involving the use of a compressor of antler, bone, hard wood or stone to apply direct pressure to the edge of a PRIMARY FLAKE. Fine flat flakes may be detached with great precision by this method, which is particularly associated with some tools in the later SOLUTREAN of France, as well as with some New World points. Heating flint can be helpful to the technique.

Přezletice   a Lower Palaeolithic open-air site located near Prague in Czechoslovakia. Artifacts are buried in lake deposits that apparently pre-date the Middle PLEISTOCENE (> 730 000 BP) on the basis of PALAEOMAGNETISM and associated fauna, especially MAMMOTH; the ASSEMBLAGE includes CHOPPING TOOLS, crude BIFACES and FLAKES.

Priene   a Greek city located on the north side of the Meander valley in Turkey. Its original site is unknown but in the 4th century BC it was refounded on a rocky spur of Mount Mykale opposite MILETUS. The lower city was laid out in a grid pattern (see HIPPODAMIAN PLANNING). The AGORA and surrounding public buildings (e.g. BOULEUTERION, PRYTANEION), the STADIUM, the theatre, the temple of Athena and some houses have been excavated. The AKROPOLIS is situated on top of a sheer cliff above the lower city.

primary cremation   the cremating of a deceased individual on a pyre in the grave. Compare SECONDARY CREMATION.

primary flake   a mechanically struck unretouched stone FLAKE produced during KNAPPING. Compare RETOUCH.

primary inhumation   the initial burial of a deceased individual. Compare SECONDARY INHUMATION.

probe or **soil probe**   a tool used for exploring subsurface STRATIGRAPHY or the presence of archaeological debris that is similar to a CORE but less expensive and incapable of penetrating more than several metres. A probe may consist of a short hollow tube, or a rod of spring steel with a ball-bearing welded to the tip and a handle on the opposite end, both of which are pushed by hand into the ground.

processual archaeology   see NEW ARCHAEOLOGY.

profile 1.   *n.* a vertical section that exposes lateral relationships and vertical STRATIGRAPHY of SEDIMENTS, SOILS and rocks, soil horizonation, and if present, archaeological FEATURES, structures and relationships.

2. *n.* the graphic representation of a profile.

3. *vb* to draw a profile.

proglacial, *adj.*   of or pertaining to LANDFORMS, deposits, processes and environments beyond the margin of GLACIAL ice, such as lakes, streams, LOESS, and PERIGLACIAL features.

projectile point   a generic term for the tip of a projectile. It can be made of bone, stone, metal or any other suitable material. See ATLATL, BOW-AND-ARROW and SPEARPOINT. The TOOL changed in shape through time and so is invaluable in the reconstruction of CULTURE HISTORY.

Prolom II   a Middle Palaeolithic cave-site in the Crimea, Ukraine, containing four occupation levels. The age of the occupations is unclear, but the remains of reindeer and arctic fox indicate cold climatic conditions (early LAST GLACIAL?); saiga is the most common species. The artifact assemblages are primarily composed of sidescrapers (see SCRAPER), but include some BIFACIAL FOLIATES and worked bone; they are assigned to the AK-KAYA CULTURE. Prolom II was discovered in 1973 by Kolosov, who conducted excavations during 1981–82.

pronaos a shallow porch through which the CELLA of a Greek temple was entered and the cult-statue approached. Compare OPISTHODOMOS.

prondnik a type of stone artifact representing an asymmetrical scraping tool flaked on both sides. Prondniks are found in some late Middle Palaeolithic sites of Central Europe (MICOQUIAN).

prondnik

propylon the entrance gate to a CLASSICAL TEMENOS. On the AKROPOLIS at ATHENS a simple gate was replaced in 437 BC by the monumental Propylaia built on the same orientation as the PARTHENON. It included a *pinakotheke* (picture gallery) which also served as a dining-room (see SYMPOSIUM).

Prošek, František (1922-58) a Czech archaeologist and Palaeolithic specialist who was instrumental in establishing the stratigraphic position and significance of the SZELETIAN in the Palaeolithic of Central Europe.

proskenion or **proscenium** a single-storeyed structure placed in front of the SKENE and protruding into the ORCHESTRA (where see figure) of a CLASSICAL theatre. It was often faced with half-columns. It was probably used as a raised stage.

Proskouriakoff, Tatiana (1909–85) a Siberian-born MESOAMERICAN archaeologist, epigrapher and artist. Proskouriakoff focused on deciphering the historic content of MAYA GLYPHS. Before her work, the emphasis on understanding Maya glyphs was limited to more esoteric (e.g. astronomy and religious) matters. With that of Heinrich Berlin, Proskouriakoff's research established the use of STELAE to document dynastic sequences. She also deciphered glyphs relating to conflict. These two types of glyphs added substantial depth to the understanding of Maya civilization.

Prosymna see ARGOS.

Protemnodon an extinct species of giant kangaroo, found at several sites in Australia and New Guinea including LANCEFIELD and NOMBE. See also MEGAFAUNA.

prothesis the lying-in-state of a corpse in the Greek world. The scenes on pottery are usually located in the home, and the deceased is normally shown surrounded by mourners. The scenes are particularly common on the ceramic monumental funerary markers at ATHENS in the 8th century BC. See also EKPHORA.

Protoclassic period (*c.*50 BC–AD 250) that period at the end of the PRECLASSIC PERIOD, and immediately preceding the CLASSIC PERIOD, in MESOAMERICAN culture. Cultures of this period have transitional styles between the Preclassic and Classic cultures, occurring contemporaneously with other Preclassic cultures and earlier than Classic period cultures. The term is generally limited to the MAYA area.

Protocorinthian see CORINTHIAN POTTERY.

Proto–Elamite, *adj.* denoting the earliest texts written in a language that can be identified as ELAMITE during the 3rd millennium BC. These texts are of two distinct kinds, separated in time. The earlier is analogous to the URUK IVa texts from the EANNA SOUNDING at WARKA, but using a very different sign list; these date to the very late 4th/early 3rd millennia BC. The later texts are composed in the so-called 'linear script', which dates to the late 3rd millennium BC. The first kind of texts appear at SUSA in the ACROPOLE 1 level 16, and also in a number of sites on the Iranian plateau (SIALK, Tepe MALYAN, Tepe YAHYA, SHAHR-I SOKHTA), usually associated with a distinctive CERAMIC assemblage and style of SEAL. This constellation of material traits, and especially the writing system, is called Proto-Elamite in the archaeological literature. The distribution of these materials seems to reveal a concern for control over critical routes of communication and access to traded exotic materials, and the Proto–Elamite phenomenon is often seen as analogous to the slightly earlier Late Uruk expansion.

Protogeometric the pottery made in Greece *c.*1050–900 BC, and by extension, the period as a whole.

protohistoric period or **protohistory** **1.** the period following PREHISTORY and preceding the appearance of written records in the HISTORIC PERIOD. In parts of Europe, the term denotes the period between the Bronze Age and the Roman conquest when writing was already in use in other areas of the world.
2. a period when non–literate aboriginal peoples had access to European goods, but had not yet entered into actual face-to-face contact with them.
3. period(s) during which some historical documentation is available but fragmentary, or not directly from the society under examination. In East Asia, the ORACLE BONES and bronze inscriptions respectively make the SHANG and ZHOU periods protohistoric. The Late Bronze Age (for East Asia) and PROTO-THREE KINGDOMS and THREE KINGDOMS periods of the Korean peninsula and the YAYOI and KOFUN periods of the Japanese islands, are variously illuminated from Chinese sources (see HOUHANSHU, WEIZHI) and later local historic records (see KOJIKI, NIHON SHOKI, SAMGUK SAGI) of those societies. (See CHINESE DYNASTIES, KOREAN PERIODIZATION, JAPANESE PERIODIZATION.)
4. the period AD 1250–1519 following the POSTCLASSIC in MESOAMERICA, in which the reorganization of that period becomes solidified. Historical and native documents and eyewitness accounts exist for this period, which ends immediately before the Spanish conquest of 1521.

protome the forepart or upper part of a figure. The term is often applied to griffins mounted on the rim of bronze cauldrons as well as to TERRACOTTA figurines.

proton gradiometer see MAGNETOMETER.

proton magnetometer   see MAGNETOMETER.

Protopalatial   the period of the Old or First palaces, in the chronological system for MINOAN Crete devised by Platon, Middle Minoan I–II (c.2000–1700 BC) in the traditional chronology.

Protosesklo   a term sometimes used for the Greek Early Neolithic period, or an Early Neolithic phase, in Thessaly. See also SESKLO.

Proto-Three Kingdoms   the PROTOHISTORIC period of the Korean peninsula (c.AD 0–300), also known as the Late Iron Age or LELANG period, which led into the THREE KINGDOMS period of KOGURYO, SILLA and PAEKCHE state formation. The archaeology of the Proto-Three Kingdoms period is mainly that of LELANG and KOGURYO in the north and the SAMHAN in the south, the latter consisting of MUMUN, WAJIL and KIMHAE pottery finds, stone CIST and jar burials, and a few settlement sites – mainly SHELL MIDDENS and (ditched) villages on hilltops. Both bronze and iron were in use, with iron being produced at many shell midden sites along the southern Korean coast. (See also KOREAN PERIODIZATION.)

provenance or **provenience**   the source, place of origin, or location of something. Debris collected in site survey or excavation, sites, and raw material sources are usually assigned a provenance within a three-dimensional reference system. The horizontal reference system is usually some form of GRID tied to a reference DATUM. The vertical dimension is usually referenced to a vertical datum.

proximal, *adj.*   close to the centre or to the point of origin or attachment. For example, proximal ALLUVIAL FAN is the apex area of the fan just beyond a valley mouth, and adjacent to a mountain front, valley wall or ESCARPMENT; the proximal end of a long bone is the end at which it is attached to the body. Compare DISTAL.

prytaneion   a building in which the *prytaneis*, effectively an inner executive council of a Greek city, could meet. Compare BOULEUTERION.

Przeworsk culture   a Late Iron Age culture over much of the Vistula and Bug drainages, named after a site in southeastern Poland and dated to the LA TÈNE period. The Przeworsk group is known primarily from graves, which have yielded a number of characteristic FIBULAE and other metal artifact types.

psephoperibombetrios   a type of Greek drinking cup with a hollow rim into which pellets were inserted. When shaken, a rattling sound was given, either to attract attention for more wine or perhaps to accompany music during the SYMPOSIUM. Many of the examples are 4th century BC KANTHAROI.

pseudo-isodomic, *adj.*   denoting a Greek masonry style, with squared blocks placed in alternating wide and narrow layers. See ASHLAR.

Ptolemy   a name borne by all the kings who ruled Egypt between 304 and 30 BC. The founder of the DYNASTY, Ptolemy Lagus, was a general of Alexander the Great who established himself in Egypt on the fragmentation of the Macedonian Empire following Alexander's death. Although, in many ways, Egypt functioned as a HELLENISTIC state during the Ptolemaic Period, the traditional forms of art and architecture were continued, especially in the building of TEMPLES to Egyptian gods which were inscribed with HIEROGLYPHIC texts.

Puamau Valley   the site on Hiva Oa, Marquesas, POLYNESIA, of a group of large stone ANTHROPOMORPHOUS statues up to 2.5 m high. These are the largest such statues in Polynesia outside EASTER ISLAND. See TAIPIVAI VALLEY.

public archaeology   a generic term for that branch of ARCHAEO-LOGY that deals with the impact of contemporary construction and other developments on archaeological SITES, and the various laws enacted to mitigate the threat. It has spawned an industry aimed at preserving archaeological sites, which is known in Great Britain as Rescue Archaeology, and in the United States as Salvage Archaeology or CULTURAL RESOURCE MANAGEMENT. In some countries, such as the United States, the protection of antiquities is extended to shipwrecks in both fresh and salt water.

Pucara   an EARLY INTERMEDIATE PERIOD culture of the Peruvian altiplano. The site of Pucara includes a monumental sunken court surrounded by structures, and walls made of dressed stone slabs. Pucara CERAMICS are elaborate, including painted and incised designs, and may be related to ceramics of the late PARACAS culture. The iconography of Pucara ceramics anticipates that of the MIDDLE HORIZON styles of TIAHUANACO and HUARI.

Pueblito   see TAIRONA.

pueblo   1. a Spanish term for village applied to the historic and contemporary town sites of American Southwest Pueblo Indians. The pueblos are 'apartment-like' complexes of small interconnected rooms, up to four storeys high, made of WATTLE AND DAUB. See ADOBE.
2. (**Pueblo**) a culturally homogeneous, linguistically diverse group of NATIVE AMERICANS who inhabit the American Southwest. They are believed to be the successors of prehistoric ANASAZI, HOHOKAM and MOGOLLON groups. See KIVA, PITHOUSE.
3. specific stages in the Anasazi cultural tradition.

Pueblo Bonito   a major site in CHACO CANYON, New Mexico, USA, comprising a large PREHISTORIC PUEBLO, constructed by the ANASAZI in two main building periods: 1) the early part of the 10th century AD; 2) the latter half of the 11th century. The site was first excavated by George Pepper and Richard WETHERILL of the Hyde Expedition in 1897–99, and later between 1921–27 by Neil Judd and the National Geographic Society. The site comprises over 300 ground-floor rooms (with an estimated 650 in total), and at least 32 KIVAS (including 2 great kivas).

Pujo   an early historical place-name occuring on silver SEALS excavated from tombs near the HAN–dynasty LELANG COMMANDERY on the Korean peninsula. The seal inscriptions *Pujo Yegun* and *Pujo Chang* are interpreted as titles given to men of Pujo (eastern Korea?) prior to and just after the establishment of Lelang, indicating the cooperation of peninsular natives in territorial acquisition and administration by the Han.

pulsed induction meter   a GEOPHYSICAL instrument used in ELECTROMAGNETIC SURVEYING to detect primary metals and, under favourable conditions, other shallow or shallowly buried FEATURES. A magnetic field is generated and induced as pulses to the ground which produces eddy currents in metal objects and responsive soils. The currents are detected by a receiver.

Pulumelei   a site on Savai'i, Samoa, which is one of the most spectacular monuments in the Pacific. It is a flat-topped stone mound, 12 m high and 60 m by 50 m at the base. A sunken ramp at either end leads to the top, where there are remains of structures. It is undated, but surrounded by other structures, and may have been the focus of ceremonial activity.

puna   the highest Andean ecozone, devoted to herding of camelids and hunting of wild camelids and other game. Because of the danger of frost, agriculture is rarely practised, and few permanent settlements are found on the puna. Remains of PRECERAMIC hunter-gatherer cultures have been found widely here. Work by John Rick suggests that groups in central Peru lived in sedentary settlements, subsisting on a diet of mostly meat. Other researchers suggest that such groups practised TRANSHUMANCE, and occupied puna sites on a scheduled, seasonal basis.

Puna Pau   a quarry on EASTER ISLAND, source of a soft red *scoria* (volcanic rock) used to make the huge cylindrical head-dresses (*pukao*) placed as late embellishments on some major MOAI. How this was achieved is still uncertain.

Punt   an area on the coast of eastern Africa, possibly close to the Sudan/Eritrea border, to which the ancient Egyptians sent naval trading expeditions for exotic products. The best-known expedition to Punt is that depicted in the reliefs at DEIR EL-BAHRI.

puquio   one of a series of semi-subterranean AQUEDUCTS found in the NASCA region, Peru. Each puquio functions as a horizontal well, tapping groundwater and directing it through a subterranean tunnel and/or an open trench to a small reservoir. While some believe the puquios to have been built by the Spanish during the Colonial period, archaeological evidence indicates construction *circa* the 6th century AD, by the NASCA culture. Thirty-five puquios remain in use at present; their original number may have been 40.

Purépecha see TARASCANS.

Puritjarra   a sandstone shelter in the CLELAND HILLS, central Australia. The first substantial use of the site occurred 22 000–18 000 bp, though it was sporadically used earlier. There were other episodes of intensive occupation at *c.*15 000 and 12–13 000 bp. The stone assemblage includes small elongated FLAKES and large flakes. Puritjarra clearly demonstrates occupation of the Australian arid zone prior to the LAST GLACIAL MAXIMUM.

Purron phase   a phase (2300–1500 BC) during the period of food collecting and incipient plant cultivation in the TEHUACÁN VALLEY, Mexico. During this phase there is a substantial increase in the amount of agricultural products in the diet, and a concomitant decrease in reliance on meat. Dates for this phase are difficult to establish, and derive more from knowing the end of the ABEJAS and start of the AJALPAN phases than from firm dates associated with Purron phase materials.

Pushkari I   an Upper Palaeolithic open-air site located on a bedrock promontory above the Desna River in Ukraine. The occupation HORIZON is buried in LOESS, and yielded a RADIOCARBON date of 16 775 bp. Woolly MAMMOTH predominates among the fauna. According to BORISKOWSKIJ, a small LONGHOUSE is represented by a linear arrangement of three HEARTHS and associated small pits and debris. Pushkari I was excavated by Rudinskij in 1932–33 and by Borsikowskij in 1937–39.

Puskaporos a prehistoric rockshelter located along the Szinva River in the Bükk Mountains of northeastern Hungary. Artifacts and some faunal remains (including CAVE BEAR and woolly rhinoceros) are buried in clay and rubble deposits. The lower cultural layer contains a Middle Palaeolithic assemblage (age unknown) with LAUREL-LEAF POINTS and sidescrapers (see SCRAPER). Late Upper Palaeolithic, Neolithic and younger remains occur in the upper layers.

Putnam, Frederic Ward (1839–1915) an important figure in the development of professional archaeology in North America. He made major contributions to the study of the MOUNDS of Midwestern North America and of the antiquity of humans on the continent (which he believed to pre-date the end of the last GLACIATION.)

Putun see CHICHÉN ITZÁ, COZUMEL.

Puuc a region in the north-central part of the MAYA area of Mexico, with a distinctive architectural style. Puuc architecture is characterized by MOSAIC façades carved in stone: usually the decorations are rain-god masks and earth-god façades. Typically, the mosaics are contrasted with areas of minimal or no decoration. UXMAL is one of the best-known Puuc centres. The Puuc architectural style spread beyond the Puuc region itself, throughout the northern plains of the Yucatán. See also RIO BEC-CHENES and GREATER PETEN.

The Puuc region was slow in reaching CLASSIC Maya status. It was the last variant of Classic Maya culture. The Classic Maya collapse was delayed in the Puuc region for about 100 years. During this time, Puuc cities probably took advantage of the instability of the cities in the southern lowlands. The Puuc collapse was probably caused by a combination of factors, including those that brought down the rest of the Maya centres.

Pu'uhonua or 'city of refuge' the best-preserved example of such a refuge, now reconstructed, at Honaunau on the west coast of Hawaii. It comprises an enclosure built by walling off a peninsula, with three HEIAU. By tradition, the complex was first built in AD 1450 and was still in use in the early 19th century.

Puyo 1. the Korean pronunciation of Chinese 'Fuyu', an ethnic group in the northern Manchurian basin known to the HAN Chinese, with whom the political elite of both PAEKCHE and KOGURYO states claimed ancestral affiliations.

2. the name of a modern city in South Korea, known earlier as Sabi and serving as the last Paekche capital, re-modelled on CHANG'AN.

Pyla-Kokkinokremos the site of a Late CYPRIOT settlement in southern Cyprus, excavated by Dikaios in 1952 and by Karageorghis in 1981–82. The site was occupied in the late 13th century BC, possibly by the SEA PEOPLES who built massive fortifications but then abandoned Pyla for KITION.

pylon a monumental gateway, the usual entrance to an Egyptian TEMPLE from the MIDDLE KINGDOM onwards. The pylon consisted of two wide, massive towers flanking a comparatively small gateway into the temple. Large grooves down the front of each tower would be used for insetting tall wooden flagpoles, while pairs of colossal statues and OBELISKS were often erected in front of the pylon.

Pylos the best-preserved of the MYCENAEAN palaces, located on the hill of Epano Englianos in Messenia, Greece, and revealed by BLEGEN's excavations between 1939 and 1952–66. The 'Palace of Nestor'

415

was built in the 14th century BC and destroyed by fire late in the 13th century. The large archive of LINEAR B tablets recovered from the palace indicates that the ruler of Pylos exercised political and economic control over much of Messenia.

P'yonhan   see SAMHAN.

pyramid   **1.** (*Egypt*) a structure of stone or brick with a square base and four straight sides converging to a point at the apex, having evolved from the STEP PYRAMID. It is the central monument of a PYRAMID COMPLEX. The pyramid was the preferred form of tomb for the kings of the OLD and MIDDLE KINGDOM, the royal burial being in a chamber within or below the pyramid itself. The largest Egyptian pyramid is that of KHUFU at GIZA, its base being 230 m long and with an original height of 146 m. The use of the pyramid as a royal tomb was revived by the kings of NAPATA and MEROE. Compare ZIGGURAT.
2. (*New World*) one of a wide range of religious or funerary mounds throughout the Americas. At first they were merely constructed of earth or rubble; later examples were given facings of MUD-BRICK or stone. In most cases they were truncated pyramids, with religious structures placed on a flat platform at the top (hence TEMPLE MOUND, PLATFORM MOUND). See TEOTIHUACÁN, CAHOKIA, CHICHÉN ITZÁ, etc.

pyramid complex   the structures associated with royal PYRAMIDS of the OLD KINGDOM and MIDDLE KINGDOM in Egypt. The major elements were:

(1)   the Valley Temple, often with a quay on the River Nile, and probably used for ceremonies connected with the MUMMIFICATION of the king.

(2)   the Causeway, an enclosed passageway from the Valley Temple to the Mortuary Temple, used as the approach to the tomb during the royal funeral, and probably the slipway for transporting blocks used in the construction of the pyramid.

(3)   the MORTUARY TEMPLE.

(4)   the royal pyramid itself.

(5)   a subsidiary pyramid, of uncertain function. Satellite pyramids, for the burials of important female members of the immediate royal household, were often located close to or within the royal pyramid complex.

(6)   subsidiary burials of members of the extended royal family and officials of the king, often in regular rows of MASTABA tombs.

(7)   pits containing full-sized boats (e.g. like those associated with the Pyramid of KHUFU).

Pyu   an ethno-linguistic group once dominant in central Burma, whose language was probably related to Burmese.

pyxis   a lidded box in Greek archaeology.

(1)

(2)

pyramid complex

(3)

(5)

(4)

carp's tongue sword

Q

Qafzeh   an Israeli prehistoric cave-site excavated by Neuville in 1933–36 and by Vandermeersch in 1965–79, best known for the remains of seven adults and ten children recovered from the MOUSTERIAN occupation levels. Dated to *c*.95 000 BP by TL on flint tools, and to 100 000 BP by ESR on animal teeth, they are thought to be archaic or proto–CRO-MAGNONS rather than NEANDERTHALERS.

Qala'at al Bahrain   a low TELL, covering about 18 ha on the north coast of Bahrain, which provides the key archaeological sequence for the central portion of the Persian Gulf, spanning the mid 3rd millennium BC to mediaeval periods. The lowest levels (I–II) belong to the BARBAR culture, and represent one of its best-known settlements. The town was walled and its gate contained a concentration of SEALS, sealings, Indus weights, occasional CUNEIFORM texts and exotic raw materials, all reflective of the PERSIAN GULF TRADE. Later occupations include a KASSITE period settlement (period III) and several towns of the 1st millennium BC; a SASSANIAN to Islamic fortress lies on the northern edge of the site.

Qasr es-Sagha   an Egyptian site in the northern FAIYUM, with an unusually undecorated TEMPLE, probably of the MIDDLE KINGDOM.

Qasr Ibrim   a site in LOWER NUBIA, now partially submerged by Lake Nasser. Archaeological evidence indicates an almost continual, and chiefly military, occupation of this fortified cliff from at least as early as the NEW KINGDOM to its abandonment in AD 1812. Qasr Ibrim has been the focus of a major series of excavations by the Egypt Exploration Society since 1963.

Qermez Dere   a late EPIPALAEOLITHIC to early ACERAMIC NEOLITHIC site just southeast of Jebel Sinjar in northern Iraq, where T. Watkins' recent excavations have defined seven phases of occupation. Structures are evident only in the later phases, with a succession of semi-rectangular pit dwellings with plastered walls and floors, each of which contains a plastered STELA in its centre; the last house, deliberately destroyed and filled, also had six human skulls placed within it. The lithic industry bears strong resemblances to that found further west on the Euphrates River, especially in the earliest phases of MUREYBET; this westward connection had already been noticed at later sites such as Tell MAGHZALIA. The community's subsistence was focused on cereals, legumes and nuts, and on cattle, equids, gazelle, sheep/goat, and many small animals and birds; these all seem to be wild. Qermez Dere stands at the beginning of documented habitation on the northern MESOPOTAMIAN plain.

Qijia [Ch'i-chia]   a protohistoric culture of northwestern China contemporaneous with the LONGSHAN and early SHANG cultures at *c*.2000 BC. It is distinguished by Neolithic traditions of painted pottery, animal husbandry (sheep?), and use of copper artifacts.

Qilakitsoq   a site on the west coast of Greenland where the mummified remains (see MUMMIFICATION) of eight humans were found, dating to between AD 1425 and 1525. The bodies, buried in two adjacent graves, ranged in age from a six month old baby to three females of about 50. All the bodies were the remains of children or women. Not only was their clothing still preserved, but the last meal could be identified in the stomach of one mummy, and facial tattoos on five of the adults were visible. The bodies belonged to members of the archaeologically defined THULE culture. See SKRAELING.

Qin [Ch'in]   one of the ZHOU states in protohistoric China, whose last ruler unified all Zhou states in 221 BC and became the first emperor (*Qin Shihuangdi*) of a united China (see CHINESE DYNASTIES). He was buried in a large MOUNDED TOMB near Xian City, *c.*400 m square, which allegedly contains a scale-version of the palace, rivers of mercury, and cocked crossbows to deter plunderers. A TERRACOTTA army of over 7000 lifesize soldiers, discovered in 1974, was made at his instigation and buried in three long pits near his tomb for eternal protection. Though the Qin Dynasty was short-lived, the standardization of weights and measures, coinage and the development of a state infrastructure by Qin Shihuangdi laid the basis for a stable, centralized state in the HAN Dynasty.

Qingliangang [Ch'ing-lien-kang]   a Neolithic culture of the 5th millennium BC on the eastern seaboard of China, succeeding HEMUDU and merging with DAWENKOU. It is distinguished by its unpainted, openwork pedestalled CERAMICS (compare YANGSHAO pottery). A major site is Songze.

Qishan [Ch'i-shan]   a site in Shaanxi Province, China, identified with the capital of the pre-dynastic ZHOU peoples prior to their take-over of the SHANG in 1027 BC (see CHINESE DYNASTIES). Excavations in 1979 revealed inscribed ORACLE BONES and HANGTU foundation platforms for palace buildings.

Quanterness   a PASSAGE GRAVE in Orkney, Scotland, of MAES HOWE or Quanterness/Quoyness type, dated to *c.*3000 BC. A long, low passage leads to the principal chamber, which is of rectangular plan with a tall CORBEL-VAULTED roof. Six smaller side chambers, also corbel-vaulted, are arranged around the main chamber. Exacavations by C. Renfrew in the main chamber and one of the side chambers yielded remains of 157 individuals, giving an estimated total for the whole tomb of 394 individuals. Construction is dry-stone throughout, and the tomb is covered by a large circular CAIRN.

Quanzhou [Ch'üan-chou]   a late-13th century AD Song (see CHINESE DYNASTIES) shipwreck at Houzhu, Fujian Province, China. The ship, 24 m long, was keeled, with 13 internal compartments, constructed shell first. (Compare SINAN.) See also SHIPWRECKS.

quartz   a hard silicon dioxide mineral that is an important constituent in most igneous, metamorphic and sedimentary rocks. Quartz is typically colourless to white, but with traces of other oxide impurities it takes on nearly a full spectrum of colours. Quartz SAND is sometimes used as TEMPER in pottery.

quartzite   a metamorphic rock consisting mostly of QUARTZ. Most quartzites are altered quartz sandstones. It is a dense, hard rock that is able to fracture concoidally; flaked tools were made from quartzite, when available, in the absence of CHERT or FLINT. Quartzite was also used as a heavy monumental building stone. Small rounded quartzite

COBBLES made ideal HAMMERSTONES and HANDAXES.

Quaternary Period   a major GEOCHRONOLOGICAL subdivision (see STRATIGRAPHY) of geological time. See QUATERNARY SYSTEM.

Quaternary System   a major chronostratigraphic subdivision (see STRATIGRAPHY) of GEOLOGY, characterized by deposits resulting from alternating GLACIAL and INTERGLACIAL processes and conditions in response to multiple major environmental changes. The base of the Quaternary System is defined by basal deposits that overlie PLIOCENE deposits. Much of the evidence for the history of humans is preserved in deposits of the Quaternary System. The base is recognized as time-transgressive but is variably taken to be about 1.8 to 2.45 million years.

Quechua   1. the language of the INCA empire, called *Runa Simi* by them. Several dialects of the language are still widely spoken in the Andean region, especially in Peru and Bolivia.
2. the Andean ecozone in which grains, especially maize, are grown in hillside plots. The quechua zone is typically extensively terraced.

quern   a large grindstone (see also METATE). The most common forms are: the *saddle-quern*, where material was ground on an immobile concave stone; and the *rotary quern*, where one stone is rotated by another by hand, animal, water or wind power.

Quéroy   a cave-site in Charente, France, with stratified deposits from the beginning of the Middle Neolithic to the LA TÈNE Iron Age. The Late Bronze Age levels (*c*.800 BC) yielded several SHERDS bearing incised symbols, some representational (ZOOMORPHIC or ANTHROPOMORPHOUS) others abstract (geometric). Similar signs have been found on potsherds in other parts of central and southern France and constitute a form of proto-writing, probably for religious use. Beneath the occupation deposits are remains of TUNDRA species which accidentally fell into the cave towards the end of the last Ice Age, including horse, reindeer and saiga antelope.

Quetta   a valley of Baluchistan in western Pakistan where the survey and excavations by W. Fairservis produced a standard chronological sequence for the region. The sounding at Kili Gul Mohammad indicated four periods (KGM I–IV) and that at Damb Sada'at three (DS I–III), which dovetail (KGM IV just prior to DS I); the combined results provide a cultural sequence that begins around 5000 BC and continues to the later 3rd millennium BC. A number of distinctive pottery styles appear in this sequence, which thus provides a valuable framework for relative chronology.

Quetzalcóatl   a principal deity in Late POSTCLASSIC central Mexico. The word means 'Precious Feather Serpent' in NAHUATL. The deity took a number of forms, including the wind god (*Éhecatl*) and the morning star (*Tlahuizcalpantecuhtli*). Many circular buildings in MESOAMERICA are associated with Quetzalcóatl in his various forms: the centre of his cult in the Late Postclassic was CHOLULA. The Yucatec Maya term for Feathered Serpent is *Kukulkán*. Depictions of feathered serpents on temple columns in the Yucatán have been used to suggest central Mexican influence among the MAYA.

Quetzalcóatl played a significant role in the Spanish conquest. CORTÉS arrived in the BASIN OF MEXICO during a period in which diviners predicted the return of Quetzalcóatl. This prophecy greatly influenced the way in which Moctezuma II initially received and treated Cortés.

Quimbaya   a late-prehistoric culture (AD 300–1600) in western Colombia, South America, known especially for its goldwork, representing some of the most advanced METALLURGICAL techniques in the prehistoric New World. Quimbaya CERAMICS were sometimes modelled, and decorated with negative painting and incision.

quipu   a mnemonic device used by the INCA, made of a thick cord from which descended a series of strings, sometimes of different colours. Knots were placed in the string, their size and position denoting numerical value. A special class of bureaucrats, called *quipu-camayoq*, were charged with keeping the imperial records, and 'reading' the quipu.

Quiriguá   a small MAYA centre in the southern Lowlands of Guatemala, one of the first Maya sites to be studied thoroughly, having been discovered shortly before it was visited in 1840 by Frederick CATHERWOOD. Some of the first excavations at the site were by Alfred P. Maudslay in 1881, and by Edgar Lee Hewitt in 1910. Evidence of conflict between COPÁN and Quiriguá strengthened arguments of warfare and capture as important aspects of CLASSIC Maya art and culture. The largest STELA ever erected by the Maya, Stela E, almost 11 m tall, was found here.

Qujialing [Ch'ü–chia–ling]   see HEMUDU.

Qumran   the site close to the Dead Sea, Israel, of a community of the Essenes, a Jewish sect who lived there from *c.* the 1st century BC to the 1st century AD. Their religious writings seem to have been hidden in nearby caves during the period when the Romans put down the Jewish Revolt, events which probably led to the end of the community. These documents, known as the Dead Sea Scrolls, were discovered in 1947, and were recently dated by AMS/RADIOCARBON to the last two centuries BC and the 1st century AD.

Qurum or **Ras al Hamra**   the area in which the long-term Italian project on the coast near Muscat in Oman in southeastern Arabia revealed evidence for mid-HOLOCENE hunting/gathering maritime adaptations on the Indian Ocean. Several of these sites also contain extensive cemeteries, which provide important documentation of the pathologies and gene pools of these populations.

Qustul   see BALLANA.

R

Ra   see RE.

Rachmani or **Rakhmani**   the site of a Neolithic–Bronze Age settlement mound in Thessaly, Greece, excavated by WACE and Thompson in 1910. The FINAL NEOLITHIC Rachmani culture is characterized by crusted red, pink and white pottery.

racloir   see SCRAPER.

Radial-Decorated Pottery Culture   see BADEN CULTURE.

radiate   a coin on which the Roman emperor wears a pointed solar crown, particularly from the 3rd century AD. Although once thought to be the equivalent of two DENARII, the coin's weight in silver suggests an equation of 1.5 denarii.

radiocarbon an unstable, or radioactive, ISOTOPE of carbon with atomic mass 14 that is produced in the atmosphere and assimilated into living plants and animals in equilibrium with the atmospheric ^{14}C content. Radiocarbon is the basis for RADIOCARBON DATING, the method most frequently used by archaeologists. ^{14}C has a HALF-LIFE of 5730 years; it was originally calculated by Willard F. LIBBY, to be 5568 years and this value is utilized in calculating radiocarbon ages.

radiocarbon dating a RADIOMETRIC DATING technique for determining the age of late QUATERNARY carbon-bearing materials, including wood and plant remains, bone, PEAT and calcium carbonate shell. The method is based on the radioactive decay of the ^{14}C ISOTOPE in the sample to nitrogen, with the release of β particles that is initiated when an organism dies and ceases to exchange ^{14}C with the atmosphere. After death the ^{14}C content is a function of time and is determined by counting β particles with either a proportional gas counter or a liquid scintillation counter for a period of time. The method yields reliable ages back to about 50 000 bp and under extreme conditions to about 75 000 bp. See RADIOCARBON, LIBBY, ACCELERATOR MASS SPECTROMETRY, ISOTOPIC REPLACEMENT, HARD WATER EFFECT, CALIBRATION.

radiography or **x-radiography** a physical technique of analysis in which a sample is bombarded by small wavelength, high-energy electromagnetic radiation, usually x-rays, to study its composition and structure. The specimen is placed on a radiosensitive surface, usually photographic film, and is irradiated by x-rays. The structure and composition of the sample affects the passage of x-rays by differential absorption. An image is recorded on the film consisting of darker and lighter tones reflecting the intensity of x-rays that passed through the sample, and therefore the structure. Radiography is particularly applicable to metals such as iron that are subject to corrosion; the weathering products and uncorroded material absorb the x-rays differentially, as do some decorative materials that may have been added to the metal object. Radiography has also been applied successfully to the examination of SEDIMENTARY STRUCTURES in slab samples of fine-grained SEDIMENT, rocks and ceramic sections, as well as to mummies and other biological remains. Microradiographic techniques have been developed to examine the atomic structure of crystalline substances (see X-RAY MICROSCOPY).

radiometric dating or **radiometric assay** dating using a method based on the decay of radioactive ISOTOPES and yielding absolute age estimations, usually reported with a standard error. These methods include RADIOCARBON DATING, URANIUM SERIES DATING and POTASSIUM–ARGON DATING.

Radomyshl' an Upper Palaeolithic open-air site located in the upper reaches of a side-valley ravine that empties into the Teterev River (a tributary of the Dnepr) in European Russia. The occupation horizon is buried in LOAM near the ground surface (recently eroded by local deforestation). The faunal remains are almost exclusively of woolly MAMMOTH, and are mostly grouped into concentrations; a pit and several hearths were also uncovered. It has been suggested that the site is of early Upper Palaeolithic age, because the artifacts include tool types characteristic of the Middle and Upper Palaeolithic; however, an ACCELERATOR MASS SPECTROMETRY RADIOCARBON date of 19 000 bp has recently been reported. Radomyshl' was excavated by Shovkoplyas between 1957 and 1963.

Rahman Dehrl a 22 ha site in the western Punjab (the Derat Jat region of Pakistan) at which F.A. Durrani's investigations greatly illuminate the millennium (roughly 3400–2500 BC) leading up to the Mature HARAPPAN civilization. Here the early levels contain a regional style of painted pottery, while the ceramic assemblages of subsequent phases are increasingly dominated by the KOT DIJI style. Throughout this pottery sequence occur a large number of GRAFFITI on SHERDS, which, it has been suggested, may be an antecedent to the Harappan script. By its later phases, the settlement is walled and divided into two sections by a major thoroughfare, with a clear orthogonal street plan that may also be a precursor to Mature Harappan urbanism.

Raimondi stela see CHAVÍN.

raised beach see FOSSIL BEACH.

Rajghat the site of Old Banaras on the River Ganges in eastern Uttar Pradesh, India, where A.K. Narain's excavations provided an eight-phase periodization (Rajghat IA–VI), representing the time between *c*.800 BC and the mid 2nd millennium AD. Rajghat IA contains a variety of pottery characteristic of this formative period in the middle Ganges: black-and-red and black slipped wares, both sometimes white painted, as well as red wares. NORTHERN BLACK POLISHED WARE appears in Rajghat IB (beginning around 500 BC), a time when a number of embankments were constructed against flood waters and a major channel dug between the Barna and Ganges rivers. NBPW continues in Rajghat IC (though in a coarse version) and a grey ware appears, as do cast coins. The first baked-brick architecture and large multi-room buildings appear in Rajghat II, perhaps 200 BC, and red wares begin to replace the earlier pottery; these characteristics are further emphasized in later periods belonging to the 1st millennium AD (Rajghat III–IV). The Rajghat sequence presents a separate cultural milieu for the emergence of urban life in the middle Ganges basin from that found further west in the Ganges-Yamuna doab (alluvial plain) represented by HASTINAPURA; this regional cultural distinction endured until the NBPW horizon spanned the Gangetic drainage (by about 500 BP).

Rakhmani see RACHMANI.

Ramesses a name borne by 11 Egyptian kings of the NEW KINGDOM. The most renowned was Ramesses II, who reigned between *c*.1279 and 1213 bc and was probably the most active builder of new monuments, and usurper of existing ones, of all the monarchs of Ancient Egypt. The major political event of the reign of Ramesses II was the much-commemorated, though probably indecisive, battle with the HITTITES at KADESH.

Rancho La Brea a late QUATERNARY faunal locality and prehistoric site located near Los Angeles, California, USA. Large numbers of vertebrate remains dating between *c*.40 000 and 11 000 BP are buried in asphalt deposits representing ancient tar seeps. Younger deposits contain a human skull dated to *c*.9000 BP and some artifacts (including MANOS and wooden spear points).

Ranis Cave or **Ilsenhöhle** a prehistoric and historic site located near the River Saale in eastern Germany. Artifacts and faunal remains (of e.g. woolly MAMMOTH, reindeer) are buried in clay, silt, sand and rubble. The lowest layer contains a small assemblage assigned to the Middle Palaeolithic. Overlying layers contain assemblages with both Middle and Upper Palaeolithic elements (e.g. endscrapers – see SCRAPER – and BIFACIAL FOLIATES) dating to the middle of the LAST GLACIAL MAXIMUM. Late Upper Palaeolithic (GRAVETTIAN, MAGDALENIAN), Bronze Age and historic remains occur in the upper layers. Ranis Cave was excavated by von Breitenbuch in 1926–32 and by Hulle in 1932–39.

Ranjpur a prehistoric site just south of LOTHAL in coastal Gujerat in northwestern India, that provides clear evidence for the Mature and Late HARAPPAN succession in this part of the Harappan world. S.R. Rao's excavations in the 1950s defined five periods (Ranjpur I, IIA–C, III). Ranjpur I is an occupation containing a MICROLITHIC industry (perhaps dated to 3000 BC), and separated from later levels by a silt deposit. The Mature Harappan settlement of Ranjpur IIA includes many of the typical artifacts of this civilization (e.g. baked bricks and drains, GRAFFITI on pottery, stone weights, triangular TERRACOTTA cakes, beads); the pottery is also Harappan but does show some regional variation. Ranjpur IIA provides evidence for rice cultivation in the Mature Harappan; Lothal provides similar evidence, and this may represent an economic variation of Mature Harappan civilization. Harappan characteristics diminish in Ranjpur IIB–C: some disappear entirely (e.g. some typical pottery forms, stone weights, terracotta cakes); others are modified, in that the technological qualities of the pottery deviate from the Mature Harappan standards, and construction becomes less substantial. At the same time, new elements appear in the material culture (e.g. new animal motifs on painted pottery, the class of red BURNISHED pottery named 'Lustrous Red Ware'). In Ranjpur III the Lustrous Red ware becomes common, and a black-and-red ware (often decorated with white paint) also appears. This sequence of Late Harappan materials is repeated in other sites of the region (e.g. Lothal, Rodji).

Rano Raraku a volcanic crater on EASTER ISLAND where most of the MOAI were quarried in the soft TUFF. One of the world's most remarkable sights, it is filled with almost 400 unfinished statues in all stages of completion, in its inner and outer wall, with many finished moai erected either facing the crater-lake or outside on the plain. Thousands of flaked basalt hand-held picks lie discarded at the site. Most quarrying occurred between c.AD 1000 and 1500.

Rapa Nui see EASTER ISLAND.

Ras al Mawra see QURUM.

Ras Shamra see UGARIT.

rath a type of ring fort found in Ireland and southwest Wales; in Wales dated to the late Iron Age/Roman period (1st century BC–4th century AD); in Ireland mainly to the early Christian period, c.5th–10th centuries AD.

Rawlinson, Sir Henry Creswicke (1810–95) a British army officer and diplomat, whose work on the trilingual inscription at BISITUN in western Iran was instrumental in the decipherment of the CUNEIFORM languages of western Asia. Beginning in the 1830s, he produced a translation of the Persian text by 1851, and that of the

BABYLONIAN by 1857. Although Rawlinson did produce several academic publications on his work in the mid 19th century, he subsequently returned to politics and diplomacy, and among other things sat in Parliament and was minister to the Iranian court.

Raymonden   see CHANCELADE.

Re or **Ra**   an Egyptian deity chiefly associated with the sun, and usually depicted as a hawk-headed man with a sun-disc on his head. Re's chief cult centre was the city of HELIOPOLIS and he was especially important during the OLD KINGDOM, being closely associated with the Kings of the 4th and 5th DYNASTIES. In the NEW KINGDOM Re is most importantly attested in the composite deity AMEN-Re, state god of the Egyptian Empire.

Real Alto   a site of the VALDIVIA culture located near the coast of Ecuador, at which the emergence of early complex social organization has been documented. In its earliest occupation (Valdivia I–II, roughly 3500–3200 bc), the site comprised a small village laid out in a U-shaped configuration. Later, the site included public architecture, and evidence of social inequality (Valdivia III, 3200–3000 bc).

Reclau Viver   see SERIÑA.

Redcliff   a complex series of fossiliferous cave fillings at a limestone quarry in central Zimbabwe, containing MIDDLE and LATER STONE AGE assemblages, Iron Age GOKOMERE pottery, and carnivore accumulations.

red-figured, *adj.*   denoting a technique used to decorate pottery. During the decoration of the pot, the area of the figure is left empty ('reserved') and the detail is painted in (contrast BLACK-FIGURED). The red of the clay, which was sometimes heightened by a wash, would contrast with the black gloss. The technique appeared at ATHENS in the late 6th century BC (see ATHENIAN POTTERY) and it remained popular down to the 4th century BC. It was produced in smaller quantities at CORINTH, although in Italy there were several centres from the late 5th century (see SOUTH ITALIAN POTTERY).

Red Lady of Paviland   see PAVILAND.

Red polished ware   a pottery type produced in south Asia during the first three centuries AD. It is a fine red ware with red or orange SLIP that is highly BURNISHED. This pottery is most commonly found near the coast of northwestern India (in and around Gujerat), but is also found in the Gangetic plain and in the interior further south. Because the ware is comparable in many respects (but very different in vessel forms) to Roman products, it is often thought to represent an imitation of Mediterranean pottery and specifically of ARRETINE, examples of which occur in Indian sites (e.g. ARIKAMEDU).

refitting   see CONJOINING.

Reinecke, Paul (1872–1958)   a German archaeologist in Munich who defined the basic periodization of the Bronze and Iron Ages in central Europe between 1902 and 1911. Largely on the basis of TYPOLOGY in hoard finds from southern Germany, Reinecke divided the Early and Middle Bronze Age into four periods, A to D. He also recognized the continuity of the Iron Age from the Late Bronze Age, particularly on the basis of burial finds, and applied the term HALLSTATT to this whole period. His scheme is still used in modified form.

Reisner, George Andrew (1867–1942)   an American Egyptologist. A prolific excavator, his best-known sites are GIZA (including the PYRAMID of MENKAURE and the tomb of HETEPHERES), Naga ed-Der,

SAMARIA and in NUBIA (especially KERMA and NAPATA).

rejoining   see CONJOINING.

relative dating   dating methods that measure differences in age utilizing an ordinal scale. For example, relative dating methods would include sequencing of events or materials relative to another but without linkage to ages in years before present (bp) or calendar years. Principal relative dating techniques include STRATIGRAPHY and stratigraphic CORRELATION. Compare ABSOLUTE DATING.

relict soil   SOIL which formed on a pre-existing LANDSCAPE or under extrinsic and intrinsic factors, processes and conditions different from today, but which was not buried, so that it has been subjected to later PEDOGENESIS, possibly under different conditions from those under which it acquired its original properties and characteristics. Because relict soils may represent a relatively large amount of time, archaeological debris of widely different periods may be superimposed, with little if any STRATIGRAPHIC separation, and a greater chance of mixing of components.

Remedello Sotto   a cemetery in Lombardy, Italy, of 117 flat graves holding individual inhumations, type-site of the CHALCOLITHIC Remedello culture of the Po valley and Veneto in the 3rd millennium BC. Typical grave-goods include fine bifacially flaked daggers of flint (possibly imitating metal types), as well as triangular COPPER daggers, copper axes and awls. See also RINALDONE.

Repolust Cave   a Palaeolithic cave-site located on the Mur River in southeastern Austria. Artifacts and faunal remains (e.g. CAVE BEAR (predominant), woolly MAMMOTH) are buried in cave deposits, apparently dating to a warm interval (Last INTERGLACIAL?). The lowest two layers contain an undated assemblage of Lower or Middle Palaeolithic character (e.g. sidescrapers – see SCRAPER – and DENTICULATES).

repoussé, *adj.*   denoting a technique used in the manufacture of jewellery whereby a design is embossed on the back of a sheet of metal with a hammer and punches. The term is also used of decoration worked on the front, although this technique is more correctly called *chasing*.

Republic Groves   an ARCHAIC cemetery in Florida, USA, which produced remarkably well preserved human and animal bone, stone artifacts, wooden stakes and other burial goods. Human nerve tissue was recovered from some of the skulls. See LITTLE SALT SPRING, WINDOVER.

rescue archaeology   see PUBLIC ARCHAEOLOGY.

resistivity meter   a GEOPHYSICAL instrument used in RESISTIVITY SURVEYING to identify buried FEATURES and structures based on differences in resistance in the SOIL. The instrument detects resistance offered by the soil as an electric current is passed through it. Anomalous readings may indicate the presence of archaeological disturbances.

resistivity surveying   a reasonably inexpensive GEOPHYSICAL SURVEY method used to locate buried FEATURES and structures with a RESISTIVITY METER. An electrical current is passed through the SOIL between electrodes, and the resistance is recorded. Differences in registered ground resistance are in response to the differing conducting capabilities of the soil and features. A decrease in resistance is facilitated by an increase in soil moisture. Limitations arise in distinguishing natural from cultural features if the GEOLOGY or soils of an area are highly variable. Also, the survey should be conducted under as uniform conditions as possible: any changes in soil moisture content, for example over the course of a day, or from rainfall, will affect the results. Compare ELECTROMAGNETIC SURVEYING.

retouch or **secondary flaking**   the working of a PRIMARY FLAKE, usually by the removal of small fragments of stone, to form a tool.

Rhodesian Man   see BROKEN HILL.

rhythmite   a SEDIMENTARY STRUCTURE consisting of rhythmically bedded couplets of LAMINAE or BEDS that have no temporal implications or connotation. If it can be demonstrated that couplets were deposited annually, they are referred to as VARVES.

rhyton   a Greek vessel, made of metal, clay or stone, sometimes in the form of an animal head, which was used to pour LIBATIONS.

Riace   a coastal resort in southern Italy where two lifesize bronze statues of naked warriors were found. A date in the 5th century BC seems likely. No traces of a shipwreck have been found and it is possible that they were jettisoned when their ship ran into trouble. They may have formed part of a cargo of booty looted from Greece.

Richey–Roberts Clovis Cache   a CLOVIS site, located in Washington State, USA, comprising 30 artifacts and bone and antler fragments. Of special interest is the recovery of 14 Clovis points, some of which are 23 cm long, all recovered from a two square metre excavation unit. The points showed wear patterns and signs of use-breakage, which counters arguments that because of their length they may have been purely ceremonial. Hypotheses for the site's function include a tool cache, a flint-knapper's hut, a hunting shrine, a shaman's hut, or even the burial of a high-status individual.

Richmond, Sir Ian Archibald (1902–65)   director of the British School at Rome. He later excavated Roman sites in Britain, which led to the publication of *Roman Britain* (1948).

Riemchen   a German term referring to a brick form typical of the Late URUK period in MESOPOTAMIA. The brick is long and thin with a roughly square cross-section, and was used both to construct bonded walls and to produce patterns on the façades of public buildings of the time. The term gives its name to one of the buildings in the Eanna precinct at WARKA, the *Riemchengebäude*.

Rikhta   a Middle Palaeolithic open-air site on the Rikhta River in central Ukraine. Artifacts were recovered from shallow depths in sand overlying redeposited TILL; no faunal remains were found. The age of the artifacts, which may include material from different time periods, is unknown. Numerous BIFACIAL FOLIATES are present among the tools. Rikhta was excavated by Smirnov during 1974.

Rillaton cup   a gold cup found in a WESSEX CULTURE grave in Cornwall, England, in 1837. The burial consisted of a stone cist beneath a burial mound, and along with the cup there was a bronze dagger and pottery. The cup is of BEAKER shape but dates several centuries later to the late Wessex culture *c.*1650–1400 BC. The cup was given to King William IV after its discovery, and for many years was used by King George IV to hold his collar studs, but was eventually given to the British Museum in 1936.

Rim   an open site in northern Burkino Faso, Africa, from which a sequence of three archaeological phases dating between 12 000 and 1000 years ago has been recognized. Although no organic remains were found, it is believed that a date of 3600 bp for the start of the second phase is associated with a food-producing society (see KINTAMPO).

Rinaldone a cemetery in Lazio, Italy, consisting of eight flat graves with individual inhumations, type-site of the CHALCOLITHIC Rinaldone culture of Tuscany and Lazio, related to the north Italian REMEDELLO culture. Burials include both single graves in flat grave cemeteries and collective inhumations in rock-cut tombs. Richest in metal of all the Italian Chalcolithic groups, Rinaldone graves contain COPPER flat axes, daggers and HALBERDS, as well as flaked flint daggers. Rinaldone material is also found at the village site of Luni sul Mignone. It dates from *c*.3000–2200 BC.

Ringkloster a Danish Late Mesolithic (ERTEBØLLE) site which is unusual in being situated over 10 km inland. However, the recovery of a piece of whalebone in the upper layers of the site indicates contact with the coast.

Rinyo-Clacton see GROOVED WARE.

Rio Bec-Chenes a regional architectural style during the lowland MAYA CLASSIC PERIOD. The style included MOSAIC façades rather than the modelled STUCCO of the GREATER PETEN group. See also PUUC.

Riparo de Romito, Papasidero an Italian cave-site, near Cosenze, Calabria, discovered in 1961 and excavated by GRAZIOSI in 1963–68. Its 8 m stratigraphy contained GRAVETTIAN, EPIGRAVETTIAN (18 700 bp) and ROMANELLIAN (10 960 bp) material; the Romanellian level yielded three graves, each containing a male and female. One male was a 17 year-old dwarf, the earliest known in the world (11 150 bp). A large block beside the graves bore engravings of bulls.

Riparo Tagliente a rockshelter in the Verona region of Italy, whose 3 m stratigraphy contains material from the MOUSTERIAN, early AURIGNACIAN, and final EPIGRAVETTIAN (13 330–12 000 bp). The latter period yielded a number of animal and abstract engravings on stones.

Ripiceni-Izvor a prehistoric open-air site on the Prut River in eastern Romania, located 200 m north of STANCA RIPICENI CAVE. Cultural levels are contained in LOESS and ALLUVIAL GRAVEL overlying a bedrock TERRACE; associated faunal remains include woolly MAMMOTH and wild ass. The lowest level is buried in the gravel and comprises FLAKES assigned to the Lower Palaeolithic. The six overlying levels are assigned to the Middle Palaeolithic and contain sidescrapers (see SCRAPER) and BIFACIAL FOLIATES; RADIOCARBON dates of 46 400–40 200 bp should be treated as minimum estimates. The upper levels contain AURIGNACIAN (?), GRAVETTIAN, and post-Palaeolithic assemblages. Ripiceni-Izvor was excavated by Moroşan in 1929–30 and Nicolăescu-Plopşor in 1961–64.

Ripoli a Neolithic ditched settlement in Abruzzi, Italy, which has given its name to the Ripoli Trichrome Painted Ware of the central Italian Middle Neolithic (*c*.4500–3500 BC). Typical decoration is a band of triangles in dark brown and red paint on a buff background. Ripoli pottery is one of a series of Italian trichrome painted wares, which includes the Capri style of SW Italy and Sicily and the Scaloria style of APULIA.

Riss Glaciation the penultimate Alpine GLACIAL advance which started *c*.250 000 years ago and lasted over 100 000 years. See also SAALIAN.

Ritsuryo   a Japanese term referring to the code of laws adopted in AD 702, thus marking the shift from YAMATO to Ritsuryo state administration. The Ritsuryo state of the Nara period utilized the Tang-dynasty model of capital city (see CHINESE DYNASTIES, JAPANESE PERIODIZATION, CHANG'AN, FUJIWARA, HEIJO) from which emanated several trunk routes (-do), e.g. the Hokkai-do, HOKURIKU-do, TOKAI-do, SAN'IN-do, SAN'YO-do, Saikai-do. These formed the foci of regional administrative districts, known by the route names, which were further divided into provinces containing a provincial capital with attached Buddhist monastery and nunnery, and county seats; many of these early historic administrative sites including DAZAIFU have been excavated throughout Japan, some yielding MOKKAN. The names of some of the road-districts are still used in the archaeological literature for discussing regional cultural development.

river terrace   see TERRACE.

Rivnač culture   an ENEOLITHIC culture of Bohemia, known primarily from a number of small ditched and palisaded sites such as HOMOLKA in the late 3rd millennium bc. The Rivnač culture is related to the BADEN culture slightly to the southeast.

Roaix   a rock-cut tomb or HYPOGEUM in Vaucluse, France, containing remains of several hundred individuals in two distinct layers. The burials in the lower layer of c.2150 bc were accompanied by daggers and arrowheads of flint, simple round-based pots and almost 2500 beads of shell, greenstone, turquoise, copper and glass paste. The upper layer of c.2090 bc was more poorly furnished, and from the position of the skeletons, and the presence of flint arrowheads embedded in them, has been interpreted as a war grave.

Robberg   a LATER STONE AGE MICROLITHIC industry of the southern and eastern Cape Province, South Africa, dated to between c.18 000 and 12 000 BP, and characterized by BLADELET CORES yielding numerous bladelets less than 25 mm long. The few formally patterned artifacts include various SCRAPERS and some BACKED BLADE-LETS, as well as worked bone and ostrich eggshell beads.

Robinson, George Augustus (1788–1866)   a London-born Hobart bricklayer who was employed in Australia by Lieut.-Governor Arthur between 1829 and 1834, to undertake a series of expeditions to establish friendly relations with the Tasmanian Aborigines and later to induce them to settle at WYBALENNA on Flinders Island in Bass Strait. From 1835 to 1839 he presided over the Wybalenna settlement. In 1839, he became Chief Protector of Aboriginals in Victoria, a post he held until 1849. The daily journals Robinson kept during his travels in TASMANIA and Victoria provide valuable information about Aboriginal culture shortly after the European invasion.

rock art   prehistoric or historic graphic markings on suitable cliff, cave or rock surfaces, made for a variety of purposes such as religious rites, the depiction of historical or mythological narratives, as territorial markers, or simply as decoration. The term encompasses *petroglyphs*, which are carvings made into the rock face, *engravings* (incisions), or *pictographs*, which are made of pigments derived from a variety of mineral or organic substances.

rocker jaw   a distinctive anatomical feature of POLYNESIAN populations, where the lower edge of the mandible is convex and thus does not sit firmly on a flat surface.

rockshelter or **abri**   a natural concavity or hollow in a rock wall, usually along a valley, large enough for occupation or activities and providing its occupants with some shelter from the elements. The hollows can form in a variety of ways depending upon the type of rock; these include rock fall, spalling, grain by grain attrition, solution, river valley flooding and scour, or a combination of these.

rock-temple   an Egyptian TEMPLE cut into a solid outcrop of rock, rather than built as a free-standing masonry structure, particularly in the sandstone cliffs of NUBIA. See ABU SIMBEL.

Rocky Cape   a site in northern TASMANIA which provides the longest continuous sequence from a coastal MIDDEN anywhere in Australia. The main chamber of the South Cave has 3.5 m of occupation deposit and was used 8000–3800 bp. The deposits seal an inner chamber, also with occupation, the surface of which is an intact living floor dating to 6800 bp. The North Cave was used from 5500 bp. The sequence documents, from about 3500 bp, the loss of bone tools and fish remains, and increasing replacement of local raw materials with exotic fine-grained CHERTS.

Rogachev, Aleksandr Nikolaevich (1912–84)   a Soviet archaeologist and Palaeolithic specialist who excavated at AVDEEVO, but devoted most of his attention to the study of the stratigraphy and remains (including former structures) at the KOSTENKI-BORSHCHEVO sites on the Don River.

Romanelli   a coastal cave-site near Lecce, Italy, with a sparse lower industry which has been classified as either MOUSTERIAN or Upper Palaeolithic, followed by an Upper Palaeolithic '*Romanellian*-type' industry which is dated to *c.*12 000 BP and includes geometric MICROLITHS and artwork, including *c.*200 plaquettes with engravings of animals and geometric motifs. There are meanders and abstract designs engraved on the walls.

Rome   a major urban settlement in Italy beside the River Tiber. Early traces of settlement, dating back to the 9th century BC, have been found on the hills. These include traces of huts, some of which have recently been excavated on the Palatine. Down to the 6th century Rome was under the influence of the Etruscans (see ETRURIA), but afterwards became an important centre in its own right. Historical events led to its expansion and its conquests were reflected in the richness of the architecture.

The focus for the city was the FORUM, which was surrounded by political (see COMITIUM, CURIA) and religious buildings. The emperor Augustus played a major part in beautifying the city with structures such as the ARA PACIS, his family mausoleum and the forum Augustum. Later emperors also added to the city with further markets and civic amenities (see TRAJAN'S COLUMN). The large population was catered for by gladiatorial events and chariot-racing which required specialized structures (see CIRCUS, COLOSSEUM). Further recreational facilities were provided by THERMAE which required substantial quantities of water (see AQUEDUCT). Burials were outside the city (see CATACOMB, COLUMBARIUM). Extensive warehousing facilities were required to feed the population; food was brought up-river from OSTIA.

Rongorongo   an abbreviated term for the enigmatic 'script' from EASTER ISLAND, surviving on 29 pieces of wood, and comprising parallel lines of engraved characters, each alternate line being upside down. Possibly a post-European contact phenomenon, the characters seem to be symbols or 'cue-cards' expressing ideas, rather than a true phonetic writing system.

roomblock a single or double row of rooms, in sites of the American Southwest, made either from WATTLE AND DAUB or masonry slabs. The roomblock partially surrounded either a PITHOUSE or KIVA. Individual rooms were used as living quarters, storage areas, or for specialized activities like corn grinding.

Roonka a complex of open sites on the Lower Murray River, South Australia, some of which date back to 18 000 bp. The area seems to have been exclusively a cemetery 7000–4000 bp. From about 4000 bp the area was more intensively used both for habitation and for burials. The Roonka burials show a wide diversity of mortuary practices and many individuals were buried with grave-goods.

Rop a central Nigerian rockshelter with two horizons of MICRO-LITHIC stone artifacts, the upper of which dates to about 2000 BP and is associated with CERAMICS.

Roquepertuse a late Iron Age sanctuary in Bouches-du-Rhône, France, perched on a small rocky outcrop, the site of a skull or severed-head cult. Three stone pillars supported a lintel carved with a frieze of horses' heads in low relief. Niches in the pillars held human skulls, all male and under 40 years old. Other sculpture included a fine double-head and figures squatting cross-legged. The sanctuary is probably of late 3rd or 2nd century BC date, and was destroyed by the Romans during their conquest of Provence in 123 BC.

Rosetta Stone a basalt STELA discovered in 1799 at Rosetta, a town in the extreme northwest of the Nile DELTA, during the Napoleonic occupation of Egypt. The trilingual inscription on the stone, a decree issued in 196 BC by King PTOLEMY V, is written in Egyptian HIEROGLYPHIC, DEMOTIC and Greek script, and was instrumental in the important early work on the decipherment of hieroglyphs by CHAMPOLLION. The Rosetta Stone is now in the British Museum.

Rössen culture a Neolithic culture of central and southern Germany and the Rhineland which developed from the LINEAR POTTERY culture. Named after a cemetery near Halle with 70 burials, the Rössen culture is characterized by pottery with complex incised geometrical motifs, particularly 'hanging chevrons', zigzags and diamonds. A number of Rössen settlements are characterized by trapezoidal LONGHOUSES, some of which are extremely long (e.g. 50 m at Deiringsen-Ruploh, 60 m at Bochum-Hiltrop).

Rouffignac a huge cave-site in the Dordogne, France, with important Mesolithic (SAUVETERRIAN) occupation layers at the entrance, dating from 9150 to 8370 bp. MAGDALENIAN engravings were first discovered inside by speleologists in 1947. The further discovery of hundreds of painted and engraved figures in 1956, heavily dominated by over 100 MAMMOTHS, caused a major controversy which remains unsettled. Very few specialists outside France accept that *all* of the cave's figures are authentic; a few are almost certainly modern.

rouletting a technique used to decorate pottery.
(a) on Greek pottery it appears in the early 4th century BC. It seems to have been applied by a strip of metal as the pot was turned on the wheel, leaving a band of even decoration normally on

the inside. A more accurate term would be *chattering*.

(b) on Roman pottery the decoration was applied by a wheel. It is often found on the exterior of vessels, especially on the rim.

(c) on pottery from peninsular India, that was made of a coarser fabric than the Mediterranean product. It is found also on forms derived from the NORTHERN BLACK POLISHED wares of northern India. This rouletted ware is usually considered an imitation of Roman imports, but at ARIKAMEDU it first appears before the Roman imports there, and the Indian product may begin in the very late 1st millennium BC.

Routsi the site of a MYCENAEAN THOLOS tomb in Messenia, Greece, which was excavated by MARINATOS in 1956–57. The lavish grave-offerings included bronze weapons, gold, amber and glass jewellery, and fine pottery.

Royal cemetery the most famous discovery of WOOLLEY's excavation at UR in southern MESOPOTAMIA. It consists of a group of some 1500 tombs ranging from the later EARLY DYNASTIC to the UR III PERIOD, mostly belonging to the Early Dynastic III (*c*.2600–2300 BC). The size, structure, and wealth of these graves varies tremendously. The richest, belonging to the king Meskalamdug and his immediate successors (roughly 2500 BC), are multiple vaulted chambers with access by ramps; these burials contained an immense amount of precious materials (gold, silver, lapis lazuli, exotic shell, ETCHED CARNELIAN BEADS) and provide many of the famous artifacts of the SUMERIAN civilization (the 'royal standard of Ur', inlaid stringed instruments, the electrum helmet of Meskalamdug, the female attendant's headdress, the gold figure of a ram caught in a thicket, etc.). Other prominent features of the royal burials were the accompanying soldiers and servants (up to 74 individuals, often women), and the presence of carts drawn by equids, a feature matched in roughly contemporary burials at KISH, SUSA and other places.

Roy Mata a chief of Efate Island, New Hebrides, South Pacific, who was buried in *c*.AD 1265 on Retoka Island together with about 35 other individuals, 22 of whom were male–female pairs. The collective burial was excavated in 1967 and suggested that, when buried, the males had been alive but unconscious, while the females had been conscious. Rich ornaments accompanied many of the burials.

Rozhok I a Middle Palaeolithic open-air site on the coast of the Sea of Azov in European Russia. Six cultural levels are buried in slope deposits representing an ancient ravine fill. The occupations appear to date to the earlier part of the LAST GLACIAL. Steppe bison predominates among the faunal remains. The artifacts include sidescrapers (see SCRAPER) and many typical Upper Palaeolithic forms (e.g. endscrapers). Rozhok I was discovered and excavated by Praslov during 1961–62.

Rudna Glava the site of prehistoric COPPER mining in eastern Serbia. The shafts at Rudna Glava, sometimes 20 m or more in depth, following veins of malachite, contained pottery of the VINČA culture. The extent of the shafts at Rudna Glava indicates that early COPPER METALLURGY in southeastern Europe required significant investment in the extraction of raw material.

Ruins Tradition see GREAT ZIMBABWE.

runes a script created in North Germany or Scandinavia around the

4th century AD, comprising 24 characters. The runic script, based on Latin, was developed in the ANGLO-SAXON and VIKING kingdoms, and is found primarily on memorial stones, as well as on artifacts. See MAES HOWE.

Runnymede a settlement site on the banks of the River Thames in Surrey, England, with occupation levels of the Middle Neolithic (c.3700–3300 BC) and Late Bronze Age (c.900–700 BC), well preserved beneath riverine ALLUVIUM. The Neolithic deposits are notable for their high density of material including intact HEARTHS. Remains of the Late Bronze Age settlement include a large round-house and parts of two sub-rectangular buildings.

Rzuczewo a settlement site on the Bay of Gdańsk in northern Poland, which gives its name to a sub-group of the broader CORDED WARE/SINGLE GRAVE complex of the Late Neolithic. Settlements of the Rzuczewo culture (known in German as the *Haffkustenkultur*) have post dwellings erected on terraces along the shoreline. The Rzuczewo culture had a maritime economy, relying to a large degree on fishing and sealing, as well as on the use of domesticated livestock.

S

Saalian cold stage the penultimate cold stage in North Europe, spanning c.200 000 to 125 000 BP, following the HOLSTEINIAN and preceding the EEMIAN. Its Alpine equivalent is the RISS, in North America the Illinoian, and in Britain the Wolstonian, named after the type-site of Wolston in Warwickshire.

Sab Champa a late prehistoric and early historic moated settlement in the Pa Sak valley, central Thailand, adjacent to copper deposits, and the site of a bronze-working industry.

Sabratha a coastal city in the Roman province of Africa, now Libya. It seems to have been settled by the PHOENICIANS by the mid 5th century BC. Excavations by KENYON revealed substantial remains of the Roman civic and religious buildings.

Saccopastore a Palaeolithic site in a quarry near Rome, Italy, which has yielded two small NEANDERTHALOID skulls, associated with a few MOUSTERIAN tools and dated to the Last INTERGLACIAL.

sacral horns see HORNS OF CONSECRATION.

Sacsayhuaman the INCA 'fortress' located on a hilltop adjacent to CUZCO in Peru. The site constituted the head of a puma, the planned shape of the site of Cuzco. One side of the hilltop is flanked by three parallel zigzag walls made of huge blocks of cut and fitted stone. On the summit are the remains of various structures, including the foundations of a round tower that was dismantled by the Spanish. Probably originally planned as a Temple of the Sun, the site was used as a fortress by the Incas during the siege of Cuzco, when they tried to defeat the Spanish invaders.

Sagvar an Upper Palaeolithic open-air site in Hungary. Artifacts and faunal remains (e.g. reindeer) are buried in LOESS deposits. The two cultural layers yielded RADIOCARBON dates of 18 900–17 760 bp. The artifacts (e.g. endscrapers, see SCRAPER) are assigned to the GRAVETTIAN.

Sagvardzhile   an Upper Palaeolithic and Neolithic cave-site on the Shavitskhali-Dzevrula River in western Georgia. Artifacts and faunal remains are buried in rubble, clay and loam layers that overlie ALLUVIUM. The lowest cultural layer (V) contains redeposited artifacts and remains of red deer, bison and horse. The assemblage includes many typical Middle Palaeolithic tools (e.g. points and SCRAPERS) and is thought to date to the early Upper Palaeolithic (30 000–25 000 bp?). Four *in situ* cultural layers overlie level V; little information is available on their contents. Above these layers lie more redeposited Palaeolithic remains, some of which are mixed with Neolithic material. Sagvardzhile was excavated by Kiladze in 1951–52.

Sahel   an Arabic word meaning 'shore' and used to refer to the grassland zone on the southern fringes of the Sahara Desert, occupied by pastoral people.

Sahul shelf   the continental shelf which comprises Australia, including TASMANIA, and New Guinea. At times of low sea level, the Sahul shelf has been exposed as dry land, Australia and New Guinea forming a single land mass with a common prehistory. By extension, the term 'Sahul' is often used for this land mass.

Sa Huynh   a site on the central coast of Vietnam which has given its name to a culture thought to be proto-CHAM, active *c.*600 BC–AD 100?, with widespread sea trading links (see KALANAY). Most assemblages known are from jar burials, which are closely paralleled by those in the Philippines, north Borneo and Sulawesi. Characteristic artifacts associated with this iron-using culture are the LINGLING-O earrings and double-headed animal pendants of JADEITE found at a number of sites in Vietnam, Palawan (in the Philippines), Sarawak and Thailand (BAN DON TA PHET). Major sites include HANG GON urnfield, Phu Hoa, Tam My; Long Thanh and Binh Chau represent formative phases.

Sai   an island in UPPER NUBIA, containing an important cemetery of the KERMA CULTURE.

Saint Acheul   see ACHEULIAN.

Saint-Blaise   a settlement close to the mouth of the Rhône in France. Greek pottery from as early as the 7th century BC has been found, as well as quantities of Etruscan BUCCHERO. It may have been the site of an early trading post taking advantage of the route up into central France, and was later replaced by the colony at Massalia (see MARSEILLES). Extant remains of the HELLENISTIC town include substantial stretches of wall.

Saint-Césaire   a prehistoric rockshelter in the Charente-Maritime, France, which was excavated by F. Lévêque in 1976–87 and yielded AURIGNACIAN, CHÂTELPERRONIAN and MOUSTERIAN layers. A NEANDERTHAL skeleton found in the Châtelperronian and dated to *c.*36 300 BP (by TL on burnt flints) may represent one of the latest dated Neanderthalers.

Saint-Michel-du-Touch   a Neolithic enclosure consisting of a series of successive palisades and interrupted ditches across a promontory between the rivers Garonne and Touch, Haute-Garonne, France. Within were large rectangular pits, possibly for ritual use, and over 300 smaller rectangular and circular structures, originally interpreted as hut bases but now thought to be cooking hearths. There was also a large rectangular pit containing two richly furnished burials. The material associated with all these structures was of CHASSÉEN type, and a sequence of RADIOCARBON dates indicates occupation c.4500–3400 BC.

Sais (*Arabic:* Sa el-Hagar) a site in the Western Nile DELTA, capital of Egypt during the 26th DYNASTY (in the LATE PERIOD). The attempts of the Saite kings to re-create Egypt's magnificent past must have made Sais an impressive city, but little now remains of this much-denuded site. The numerous sculptural masterpieces to have come from Sais are largely the product of the digging for SEBBAKH, which caused the destruction of the TELL.

Sai Yok a cave-site in west-central Thailand on the upper Khwae Noi River, utilized during three broad periods: a pre-ceramic phase with PEBBLE TOOLS of a broadly HOABINHIAN type (c.?10 000–8000 BC); a Neolithic phase with parallels at BAN KAO; and an historic-period phase. The term is occasionally attached to the pebble tools of the region.

Sakazhia a Palaeolithic cave-site on the Tskhaltsitela River in western Georgia. Middle Palaeolithic artifacts were found in a sequence of LOAM and rubble layers in one portion of the cave; faunal remains are predominantly of CAVE BEAR. The assemblages (generally small) contain many points, SCRAPERS and DENTICULATES. One of the lower levels of the sequence produced some human skeletal fragments that are classified as NEANDERTHAL. An Upper Palaeolithic assemblage was excavated from another portion of the cave. Associated faunal remains are primarily of steppe bison; the artifacts include BACKED BLADES and points. The age of the occupations is unknown. Sakazhia was discovered and excavated by Shmidt and Kozlowskij in 1914; subsequent investigations were conducted by Nioradze in 1934–37 and 1974–80.

Sakkara see SAQQARA.

Salamis a coastal city in eastern Cyprus occupied from the Bronze Age. CHAMBER TOMBS of the Early Iron Age contained the cremated remains of members of the social élites which evoked the heroic burials recorded by Homer.

Salcuţa a stratified site in southwestern Romania, important for its ENEOLITHIC levels which have made it the type-site for the Salcuţa culture, c.3500 bc, in layers II and III. Salcuţa pottery is characterized by dark BURNISHED ware similar to that of contemporaneous Balkan cultures such as GUMELNIŢA. Layer IV at Salcuţa contained unpainted pottery with affinities to COŢOFENI and BADEN.

Saldanha Man see ELANDSFONTEIN.

Saliagos an islet off Antiparos in the Aegean, the site of a Late Neolithic settlement which was excavated by Evans and Renfrew in 1964–65. The quantity of fish bones recovered suggests an economy based, at least to some extent, on maritime resources.

Salvage archaeology see PUBLIC ARCHAEOLOGY.

Salzgitter-Lebenstedt a northwest German open-air MOUSTERIAN hunting site near Hanover dated to c.50 000 BP, which has yielded an eastern Mousterian assemblage with some typical western Mousterian artifact-forms.

Salzofen Cave   a prehistoric cave-site located in the mountains (2000 m alt.) of southeastern Austria. Artifacts and faunal remains (chiefly CAVE BEAR) are buried in LOESS and rubble deposits. The lower cultural layer contains several artifacts (SCRAPER, FLAKES) assigned to the Middle Palaeolithic. Neolithic remains occur in the uppermost levels.

Samad   see MAYSAR.

Samaria   a Palestinian site, excavated by Harvard University in 1908–10 and Crowfoot in 1931–35, best known as the capital of the northern Kingdom of Israel. Samaria was founded by King Omri (c.882–871 BC), who built the 'upper city' consisting of a palace defended by walls of ASHLAR masonry. Samaria was captured by the ASSYRIANS in 721 BC, but was later an important HELLENISTIC city. Objects of the ISRAELITE Period found at Samaria include OSTRAKA and IVORY plaques similar to those from NIMRUD.

Samarra   an Islamic city of the Abbasid dynasty (mid 8th to mid 10th century AD, a golden age of Islamic civilization), founded as the new capital in AD 836 on the River Tigris, north of Baghdad in central Iraq. The continuing explorations of the city are a rich source of information on early Islamic architecture, public monuments and town planning. E. Herzfeld's work early this century revealed a prehistoric cemetery with inhumations containing a distinctive type of painted pottery, subsequently named *Samarran ware*.

Samarran culture complex   an archaeological culture of east-central Iraq (along the middle Tigris River) dating to the second half of the 6th (and early 5th) millennium BC. It is best known from the sites of Tell es SAWWAN and CHOGA MAMI. These two sites provide the stratigraphic and stylistic basis for distinguishing three phases of the culture, of which the Early contains a coarse ware decorated only by incision, the Middle a painted style that incorporates dynamic naturalistic scenes as well as dense geometric designs, and the Last more open geometric painted design and an absence of naturalistic motifs. Middle Samarran painted pottery appears as imports on many sites belonging to the Standard HASSUNA and Middle HALAF cultural periods. The subsistence economy of Samarran communities involved irrigation agriculture, a significant step towards the formation of MESOPOTAMIAN civilizations, and also herding of sheep, goat and cattle.

Sambor Prei Kuk   an early historic urban centre to the southeast of ANGKOR in Cambodia, apparently the capital of the pre-Angkor KHMER state of Iśanapura of the 7th–8th century AD, probably referred to by the Chinese as ZHENLA.

Samguk Sagi   *Records of the* THREE KINGDOMS, the earliest surviving history for Korea, compiled by Kim Pu-sik in AD 1185.

Samhan   literally 'three HAN' in Korean, the collective name of the Mahan, P'yonhan and Chinhan groups of protohistoric peoples in the southern half of the Korean peninsula during the PROTO-THREE KINGDOMS period, as known from the Chinese dynastic histories (see WEIZHI, HOUHANSHU). Small POLITIES among the Samhan are thought to have given rise to the protohistoric states of PAEKCHE, KAYA and SILLA.

Samian ware   a type of Roman red-glossed pottery mistakenly thought to have been produced on Samos. Numerous production centres have been identified. The earliest were in southern Gaul

(France) at sites such as La Graufesenque, but the production spread northwards into central and eastern Gaul as well as to Britain (see COLCHESTER) The forms, type of decoration and stamps have allowed a detailed chronology to be established and the ware is thus important when found in a stratified context. See TERRA SIGILLATA.

Sampung   a village in east-central Java which has given its name to a mid-HOLOCENE INDUSTRY characterized by bone tools and stone points similar to the Maros points of the TOALIAN of Sulawesi. Sites include Gua Lawa, Gunung Cantalan, Petpuruh, Sodong, Marjan.

Samrong Sen   a late prehistoric (c.1000 BC) settlement and burial site in central Cambodia, the finds of which indicate occupation during the transition from the use of POLISHED STONE ADZES to bronze (stone bivalve moulds for sickles, axes, arrowheads, fish hooks, bells). Similar moulds have been found at a series of small sites near the Laotian border in the vicinity of MLU PREI and at Long Prao in the south. Links have been suggested with GO MUN bronzes in north Vietnam.

Samuilitsa II   a Middle Palaeolithic cave-site located on the Iskr River in central Bulgaria. Ten cultural layers are contained in a succession of clay, sand and rubble, which apparently dates to the earlier LAST GLACIAL; the uppermost levels yielded a RADIOCARBON estimate of 42 780 bp. The artifact assemblages are relatively homogeneous, and include SCRAPERS and BIFACIAL FOLIATES.

Samun Dukiya   see NOK.

San or **Bushmen**   indigenous hunter-gatherer people of southern Africa who formerly lived throughout the region and spoke a variety of languages. Many became absorbed into agricultural societies since the arrival of KHOIKHOIN herders and Iron Age BANTU-speaking peoples during the last two millennia. Their territories were further diminished by the arrival of European colonists, and after about AD 1850 many were exterminated by settlers in the interior of South Africa. Traditionally, they lived a nomadic hunting and gathering existence in an egalitarian society comprising small bands of about 20 people which amalgamated at certain times of the year. Men hunted game with bows and arrows, while women gathered their staple diet of plant foods. Although the small groups of San still living in the Kalahari no longer live a traditional way of life, sensitive use of their historical and ethnographic record can provide valuable insights into the interpretation of LATER STONE AGE archaeological remains and ROCK ART from southern Africa (see KHOISAN).

San Agustín   a region of highland Colombia, South America, in which are found numerous large (about 30 metres in diameter) artificial mounds, containing stone-lined chambers that probably served as tombs or shrines. The region is best known for the stone sculptures, sometimes found inside the chambers. A common depiction is a human form with feline features; other animals and birds are also depicted. The dating of the sculptures is debated, with estimates all falling in the period between 500 BC and AD 1500.

sanctuary   see TEMENOS.

sand   1. a size term for SEDIMENT or SOIL particles, from 0.05 to 2 mm in diameter. As a particle size term, the definition of sand-size particles is independent of mineral composition or other properties other than size. See also CLAY, SILT.

2. a TEXTURE term used in describing sediment and soils, defined, depending on the classification system used, as containing a certain percentage of sand-size particles relative to silt- and clay-size particle content. Sand is sometimes used as TEMPER in pottery manufacture.
3. a descriptive term for a sediment body (deposit) composed primarily of sand-size particles.

Sandai (*Chinese* 'three periods') the XIA, SHANG and ZHOU of PROTOHISTORIC China (see CHINESE DYNASTIES).

Šandalja I a Lower Palaeolithic site located on the Istrian Peninsula in Croatia. Artifacts and faunal remains (e.g. macaque) are contained in a BRECCIA filling an ancient KARST cavity that probably dates to the Lower PLEISTOCENE. The artifacts include CHOPPING TOOLS.

San Dieguito complex a late PALAEOINDIAN complex, located in California, southwest Nevada and western Arizona, USA, that comprises leaf-shaped BIFACES (either points or knives), CHOPPERS, SCRAPERS and HAMMERSTONES. It post-dates CLOVIS in local sequences. See OLD CORDILLERAN, VENTANA CAVE.

Sanga an important Iron Age cemetery in southeastern Zaire, dating from the end of the 1st millennium AD to the last two centuries. Considerable wealth in the form of KISALIAN iron and copper objects and pottery is associated with the main period of usage dating to the 11th and 12th centuries AD.

Sangamonian Age a major North American geochronological subdivision (see STRATIGRAPHY) of the PLEISTOCENE EPOCH ranging from about 125 000 to 75 000 bp. See SANGAMONIAN STAGE.

Sangamonian Stage a major chronostratigraphic subdivision (see STRATIGRAPHY) of the PLEISTOCENE SERIES encompassing deposits of the last INTERGLACIAL episode defined, in the upper American Midwest, as those occurring above TILLS of the preceding GLACIAL episode (Illinoian Age) and buried by LOESSES of WISCONSINAN AGE. The stage is based on a well-expressed warm climate PALAEOSOL, the Sangamon Geosol. Although the boundaries are recognized to be time-transgressive, they are placed at about 125 000 and 75 000 bp. See EEMIAN.

Sangiran the key site in the SOLO River valley of Java for the study of faunal and human evolution in the region, which has also given its name to a stone small-FLAKE industry identified by Von KOENIGSWALD as Middle PLEISTOCENE. More recently it has been suggested that many of the 'flakes' are natural, and that those which are human-made are from the High Terrace Gravels, and are thus of late Pleistocene or HOLOCENE date.

Sangoan a stone INDUSTRY or complex named after Sango Bay on Lake Victoria in Uganda. The name is applied to SOME EARLIER STONE AGE assemblages from forested areas of equatorial and southeastern Africa. Most Sangoan samples are selected or collected from secondary contexts and they may have been produced over a long period in the Middle PLEISTOCENE. HANDAXES and CLEAVERS are relatively rare in the Sangoan, which is characterized by light duty tools as well as crude pick-like tools called *core axes*. A suggestion that the Sangoan represents an adaptation to wooded areas has not been supported by recent evidence.

San'in a pre-modern district (see RITSURYO) along the western north coast of Honshu Island, Japan, widely used in archaeological writings.

It comprises portions of modern Kyoto and Hyogo Prefectures, and Tottori and Shimane Prefectures.

San José Mogote an important FORMATIVE, or PRECLASSIC, site in the VALLEY OF OAXACA, Mexico. The large nucleated village was involved in the manufacture and trade of shell ornaments and magnetite mirrors. Kent Flannery's research at San José Mogote was most important for the systematic investigation of MESOAMERICAN culture at the household and community level.

San Lorenzo a major OLMEC centre in the Gulf Coast Lowlands of Veracruz, Mexico; it was a large nucleated village with a population estimated at 1000. The centre flourished during the Early FORMATIVE. The collapse of San Lorenzo *c.*1150 BC was abrupt and violent: monuments and sculptures, including Olmec heads, were defaced and architecture dismantled. LA VENTA came to power after San Lorenzo collapsed.

The labour requirements to build and maintain the centre necessitated a large population, but at the same time this population was forced to maintain agricultural fields farther away from the site. The collapse of San Lorenzo is thought to have resulted from these conflicting pressures.

Sanskrit a language in the Indo-Aryan branch of INDO-EUROPEAN, and the literary language of Hindu religious texts. The oldest of these texts, the *vedas* and including the *Rigveda*, were written down by the mid 1st millennium BC, following an oral tradition that originated perhaps during the mid 2nd millennium BC in northwestern India. Standardized by grammatical treatises of the 5th century BC, classical Sanskrit was used in Brahminical writings up to around AD 1000, and a form of Sanskrit continues in use as a vehicle for learned writings. The oral tradition behind Vedic Sanskrit provides the basis for arguments about the migration of Indo-Aryan speakers into the subcontinent, and specifically about possible archaeological reflections of this migration (e.g. the GANDHARA GRAVE CULTURE COMPLEX, PAINTED GREY WARE, COPPER HOARD).

Santa Isabel Iztapán a MAMMOTH KILL-SITE in southeast Chiapas, Mexico, dating to 9250 years ago. Straight-based and slightly stemmed, lanceolate, and leaf points were found in association with the two imperial mammoths (*Mammuthus imperator*). Other tools at the site include an OBSIDIAN BLADE, side SCRAPERS, and a semilunar knife. Based on these tools, a combination of hunting techniques (lance-ambushing and dart-stalking) are inferred.

Santorini see THERA.

Santubong a complex of sites on the coast of Sarawak, north Borneo, the remains of a major port of the 10th–13th centuries AD, probably connected with the state the Chinese called Po-ni. Local industries included iron, processed from the iron-rich slag-like lateritic clays of the area; and exports, like those of the contemporary ports of KOTA CINA and LOBO TUWA on Sumatra, included gold and forest products. Local pottery is similar to that of the Malacca Straits, and it seems likely that the inhabitants of coastal sites were Malay-speaking. Port sites of the Sarawak and Brunei coast connected or overlapping in date with Santubong include Gedong, Ensika, Kupang, Tanjong Kubor, Sungei Lumut and Kota Batu, the last probably replacing Santubong as the major port by the 15th century.

These sites must have formed a port hierarchy similar to that of ŚRIVIJAYA.

sanukite   a type of andesite produced in the Inland Sea region of Japan by now-extinct Miocene volcanoes; it is named after the old province of Sanuki. It was used extensively in this region during the Palaeolithic and POSTGLACIAL periods (JOMON, YAYOI) for stone tools (see SETOUCHI).

San'yo   a pre-modern district bordering the Inland Sea on western Honshu Island, Japan (see RITSURYO) widely used in archaeological writings. It comprises modern Yamaguchi, Hiroshima and Okayama Prefectures and a portion of Hyogo Prefecture.

Sao   an INDUSTRY from the Chari Basin in Chad, Africa, associated with sites on mounds above flood-waters of the river. It is poorly documented, but is probably contemporary with DAIMA and is thought to date to the late 2nd millennium BC.

Saoura   a basin in the northwestern Sahara with a long sequence, including OLDOWAN, ACHEULIAN and ATERIAN remains. Good PALYNOLOGICAL and GEOMORPHOLOGICAL data have provided useful information on past environments.

Sapalli-depe   a 4 ha site in southern Uzbekistan, excavated by A. Askarov, containing three periods of Middle to Late Bronze Age occupation, the lower two of which define the Sapalli phase in the regional chronology (at some time in the mid to later 3rd millennium BC). The site contained a central square fortification (82 m to a side) with internal blocks of rooms. Askarov recovered a large number of INTRAMURAL burials which have excellent preservation of organic materials; at least four of the graves contained silk textiles, indicating contacts to the east with China.

Saqqara or **Sakkara**   a site in LOWER EGYPT, the largest of the cemetery-sites associated with MEMPHIS. Saqqara contains a vast array of monuments including royal MASTABA tombs of the ARCHAIC PERIOD; 15 royal PYRAMIDS, chiefly of the OLD KINGDOM, the first and most important being that of DJOSER; the SERAPEUM and other animal galleries; and large numbers of important private tombs from the Archaic Period to the Graeco-Roman Period, but especially of the Old Kingdom associated with the royal pyramids of that date.

sarcophagus (*Gk* 'flesh-swallowing')   a kind of stone that was reputed among the Greeks to consume the flesh of dead bodies, and hence was used for coffins. The term is now applied in archaeology to any stone chest used to contain a corpse. In Egypt, the sarcophagus held the MUMMY. Large rectangular sarcophagi often contained at least one wooden coffin. Most sarcophagi of the LATE PERIOD are notable for their anthropoid shape, their outer form being modelled with the contours of the human body and features of the face/head.

In the CLASSICAL world, the term denotes a container of clay or marble that held a corpse. In the Greek cities of western Turkey, such as CLAZOMENAE, in the ARCHAIC and Classical periods, they could be decorated in a technique closely related to pottery painting. In the Roman period elaborately carved sarcophagi were produced in several centres and exported over long distances.

Sardis   a city on the Gediz Cay plain, some 90 km inland from Izmir in western Anatolia, associated with Croesus and the Lydians.

Although earliest evidence for settlement in the region belongs to the EARLY BRONZE AGE, the first documented occupation of the city occurred in LATE BRONZE AGE times (the evidence of the stratigraphic sounding in the 'House of the Bronzes'); later occupation extends through the 1st millennium BC up to late CLASSICAL times. The Lydian city, of the 7th and 6th centuries BC, contained an AKROPOLIS and walled lower settlement covering perhaps as much as 250 ha. Other salient aspects of the city are gold works (at 'Pactolus North', where areas of furnaces and cupellation are documented) and the grave mounds of the 'royal cemetery' (at Bin Tepe). After the conquest by CYRUS the ACHAEMENID (in the early 540s BC), the city became a *satrapal* (provincial) capital.

Sargon　(*c*.2330–2280 BC) the founder of the AKKADIAN empire in the late 24th century BC, who was the first successful empire builder of MESOPOTAMIA. Originally associated with KISH, Sargon founded a new capital at AGADE.

Sarka style　a late variant of LINEAR POTTERY that occurs in western Bohemia, *c*.3900 bc, parallel to the development of the ZELIEZOVCE style in Slovakia and southern Poland. Sarka vessels are painted in black spirals on buff fabric before firing.

Sarmizegethusa　a Late Iron Age town in eastern Romania, seat of the DACIAN state founded by Burebistas in the 1st century BC, also known by its modern name of Gradistea Muncelului. Sarmizegethusa was composed of several separate precincts over an area 3 km long. Next to a hilltop citadel is a sanctuary area with several shrines or temples. At the foot of this hill is an industrial area where bronze and iron products and pottery were manufactured.

Sarnate　a site of the NARVA culture on the coast of Latvia, on the edge of a swampy lagoon. Large lenses of shells of the water chestnut *Trapa natans* have been found at Sarnate, some covering several square metres up to 40 cm thick, around hearths within houses. Some preserved wooden mallets still had fragments of water chestnut shells embedded in their faces. A variety of other wooden artifacts have also been found at this waterlogged site. A similar site is that of Sventoji on the coast of Lithuania.

Sarnowo　the site of KUYAVIAN long BARROWS in north-central Poland, *c*.3100–2900 bc. The nine trapezoidal-plan barrows at Sarnowo are oriented with the narrow ends facing northwest. Under one of the barrows traces of ARD–marks have been preserved. Both the barrows and the ard-marks belong to the FUNNEL BEAKER CULTURE.

sarsen　a type of sandstone from the Marlborough Downs of northern Wiltshire, England. Sarsen was used in several Neolithic monuments of the region, including the AVEBURY STONE CIRCLE and the WEST KENNET long BARROW, and at STONEHENGE where the principal circle and its lintels, the five great TRILITHONS and the Heel Stone are of this material.

Sarup　two overlapping Neolithic enclosures in Funen, Denmark, with interrupted ditches. The earlier and larger enclosure, Sarup I, belongs to the FUCHSBERG phase at the transition from the Danish Early to Middle Neolithic, *c*.3400 BC. A substantial palisade with only a single main entrance stood behind two parallel lines of interrupted ditches. This was followed *c*.120 years later by Sarup II, a smaller enclosure of similar but slighter construction. Some 12 Neolithic enclosures of this type are now known from southern Scandinavia, other examples being TOFTUM and Büdelsdorf.

Sassanian a Persian empire established in AD 224 after a revolt against PARTHIAN rule. The Sassanians controlled much of western Asia until the Arab Islamic invasion in AD 651. At its largest, the empire extended from Transcaucasia and western Central Asia in the north to the Indus and southern Arabia in the east and south, and to the frontier with the Romans and BYZANTINES in the west. This large region was controlled by a relatively centralized political and military apparatus, and the Sassanian intensification of economic production induced considerable settlement growth in regions such as southern MESOPOTAMIA.

Satingpra a region on the east coast of peninsular Thailand, with sites, including Kok Moh, which span the later 1st and early 2nd millennia AD, possibly associated with LANGKASUKA.

Satruper Moor a wetland region in Schleswig-Holstein in northern Germany, containing a complex of sites representing the transition from foraging to sedentism in northern Europe c.3500–3000 bc. A number of sites can be attributed to the ERTEBØLLE/ELLERBEK culture, with pointed-base pots. From these sites there have been claims for bones of domestic animals and cereal pollen which have not been substantiated.

Satsumon a type of incised-motif pottery related to HAJI ware on early historic Hokkaido, Japan. The Satsumon culture existed between the 4th–14th centuries AD. (Compare OKHOTSK.)

sauceboat a vessel, usually made of clay but occasionally of metal, which is extremely common in mainland Greece and in the Cyclades in mid–late 3rd millennium BC contexts. It seems likely that sauceboats were used for drinking rather than pouring, but their precise function is unclear.

Sautuola, Marcelino Sanz de (1831–88) a Spanish landowner who excavated in ALTAMIRA and, with his daughter, discovered the Palaeolithic paintings there. Unable to persuade the scholarly establishment of their authenticity, he died a broken and bitter man, his honour and honesty still in question. He was not vindicated until 1902.

Sauveterrian a Mesolithic culture which follows the AZILIAN in France in c.9000 bp, and whose influence spread into Britain where it is contemporary with the Later MAGLEMOSIAN. The assemblages contain many geometric MICROLITHS but axes are rare. The culture is named after rockshelters in Sauveterre-la-Lémance, Lot-et-Garonne, France.

Sawwan, Tell es a prehistoric site, 2–3 ha in size, on the Tigris River near Samarra, which is the best-known SAMARRAN period site. B. Abu al-Soof's work there established this class of painted pottery as more than a luxury ware and provided a developmental sequence for it. Excavations during the 1960s revealed the greater part of the village, divided into five architectural levels. From its beginning the community was enclosed by a ditch, and later by a ditch and wall. The later phases of occupation are famous for their 'T'-shaped buildings, a floor plan that also occurs, in modified form, in 'UBAID sites further south (see KHEIT QASIM). A large group of burials occur under the floor of a building in the initial settlement. The crops include (in addition to emmer and einkorn) six-rowed barley, bread wheat and flax, all correlated with early irrigation; domesticated sheep and goat appear, while the other fauna (including cattle) is morphologically wild. The RADIOCARBON dates (uncalibrated) span the second half of the 6th millennium bc.

Sayil a Lowland MAYA site located in the PUUC region in Yucatán, Mexico, which reached its peak during the Late CLASSIC period. Recent work by an American archaeological team in 1983–88, under the co-direction of Jeremy Sabloff and Gair Tourtellot, has involved both extensive and intensive survey, as well as excavation, at Sayil and the surrounding area. The resulting data are often quite different from those traditionally gained from excavations. At the site, CHULTUNS under residences and palaces were used as reservoirs. PHOSPHATE tests of the soils in the 'plazas' associated with raised residential platforms suggest that these areas were KITCHEN GARDENS instead. The findings of the Sayil Project challenge some of the traditional interpretations of Maya culture.

scanning electron microscopy a technique used to examine the microscopic and submicroscopic structure, relief and morphology from about 20× to 50 000× and greater magnification, as well as to determine the chemical identity, of nearly any material for which a sample can be prepared. A scanning electron microscope (SEM) forms an image of a sample as it is scanned at an adjustable angle by a high-energy electron beam. Backscattered and secondary electrons and x-rays emitted from the sample have differing wavelengths that vary with surface topography and elements present. The signal from these emissions is processed and an image of the object is displayed on a television-like screen. Emitted x-rays are characteristic of the elements present. They can be analysed for chemical composition and spatial distribution under the coverage of the electron beam (see BETA-RAY BACKSCATTERING). In addition to the great advantage of magnifying power, the SEM is capable of a great depth of field, which makes it more useful than a light microscope in many cases.

scapulomancy see ORACLE BONES.

scarab an Egyptian STAMP SEAL, in use from the MIDDLE KINGDOM, whose oval base carried an incised design or the name and titles of the owner. The back of the seal was in the form of the dung beetle *Scarabaeus sacer*.

scarab

scarp see ESCARPMENT.

scarred tree a eucalypt from which a slab of bark has been removed to make a container, shield or canoe, or which has toe-holds cut into it for climbing. Scarred trees are common in south-eastern Australia.

Scharbauer see MIDLAND.

Schela Cladovei a Late Mesolithic/Neolithic site in western Romania, along the River Danube about 40 km downstream from LEPENSKI VIR. Twenty Mesolithic burials of adults and children at Schela Cladovei were arranged with their feet towards a hearth. Two of the burials contained red OCHRE. A later layer contained materials of the Neolithic CRIŞ culture.

Schliemann, Heinrich (1822–90) a German businessman who was convinced that the cities described by Homer had once existed. His excavations at TROY in 1874–90, MYCENAE in 1874–78 and TIRYNS in 1884–85 proved that he was essentially correct, but his desire to fit the finds to his theories, and his sometimes unscientific approach have led modern archaeologists to criticize him. There is no doubt, however, that Schliemann pioneered the study of the MYCENAEAN civilization.

Schönfeld group a Late Neolithic group of southeastern Germany whose origin has been a matter of debate. Some have seen it as a regional group of CORDED WARE, while another point of view links it to the TIEF-STICHKERAMIK of the late FUNNEL BEAKER culture. The Schönfeld CERAMICS are distinctive in that the shallow, parabolic bowl is the dominant vessel form, often with patterns of incised zigzag lines.

Schroda a 9th century AD capital and religious centre of some importance in the northeastern Transvaal, South Africa, attributed to the ZHIZO phase of the Early IRON AGE. It documents the initiation of trade between the southern African interior and the East African coast, which later led to the rise of MAPUNGUBWE and GREAT ZIMBABWE.

Scoglio del Tonno a headland projecting into Taranto harbour, Puglie, Italy, site of Middle and Late Bronze Age settlement with sherds of Late HELLADIC III pottery, indicating contact with MYCENAEAN traders from the Aegean *c.*1300 BC.

scraper a prehistoric RETOUCHED FLAKE tool with a thick working edge, probably used to scrape skins or for woodworking. *Sidescrapers*, or *racloirs*, have the retouched working edge along the long edge of the flake; an *endscraper*, or *grattoir*, has a rounded retouched end and is often made on a BLADE.

Scythians the inhabitants of the steppes of southern Russia and Kazakhstan in the mid 1st millennium BC, known from archaeological finds and the writings of CLASSICAL authors like Herodotus. They appear to have had a horse-riding aristocracy that ruled a settled agricultural population. Various precursors of the Scythians have been identified, including the SRUBNAYA (Timber-Grave) culture of southern Russia. Scythian burials, known from sites such as the mounds at PAZYRYK, are particularly elaborate, and many artifacts are decorated with fantastic animal motifs.

While the related CIMMERIANS were harassing Anatolia, Scythian groups moved south through the Caucasus, and occupied URARTU territory in northwest Iran by the early 7th century; these people and related groups are often cited in connection with the LURISTAN

scraper (a) Endscrapers (b) sidescraper.

BRONZES. The Scythians were defeated by Cyaraxes the MEDE later in the same century. A second major episode involved Scythians from Central Asia who, under pressure from other nomadic groups from Chinese Turkistan (chiefly the Yueh-chi), moved west across Iran and south into the Indus region in the late 2nd century BC. These movements, which destroyed the Greek kingdoms of Bactria and north India, brought the Saka of the ACHAEMENID and Indian texts to places like TAXILA. The Saka were soon followed by the Yueh-chi, who gave rise to the Kushana kingdom of the early 1st millennium AD in north India and Afghanistan.

Seacow Valley or **Zeekoei Valley** a river valley in the northeastern Cape Province of South Africa, which has been the subject of intensive archaeological survey by C. Garth Sampson, resulting in the identification of over 14 000 STONE AGE sites. Of particular interest are detailed studies of the CERAMIC sequence dating to the millennium prior to the arrival of European settlers in the 1760s. This has provided unique information on the spatial and territorial organization of Stone Age SMITHFIELD hunter-gatherers, as well as on hunter-gatherer/herder interactions.

seal a device of stone, bone, IVORY or wood with an INTAGLIO design, that was impressed upon nodules of wet clay in order to identify, secure or authenticate the object to which the clay had been attached. In this respect the role of seals in the development of writing systems was clearly fundamental. Because of their use by those in authority, seals were a powerful status symbol and were sometimes accorded talismanic properties. See also CYLINDER SEAL, STAMP SEAL.

sealing see BULLA.

Sea Peoples a collective term for various population groups in the eastern Mediterranean, at least some of whom seem to have been of Aegean origin, who migrated into the Levant in c.1200 BC. They seem to have been responsible for the destruction of cities such as UGARIT and ALALAKH, but were repulsed from Egypt by Kings Merenptah and RAMESSES III, a victory illustrated on the walls of MEDINET HABU. See PHILISTINES.

sebbakh (*Arabic*) a term used to refer to the degraded MUD-BRICK of ancient buildings, utilized as a cheap source of fertilizer by arab peasants. The practice of digging for sebbakh in the last century, and the early years of this, produced many of the objects now in museums and private collections, albeit with little record of their archaeological provenance.

Sebekian see KOM OMBO.

Sebillian see KOM OMBO.

Sechín Alto a large INITIAL PERIOD ceremonial site in the Casma Valley of the north-central coast of Peru, perhaps the largest site occupied at that time. The site comprises a series of PLATFORM MOUNDS and plazas, arranged along a linear axis. The largest pyramid measures 40 m in height. (See also PAMPA DE LAS LLAMAS.)

secondary cremation the practice of removing the remains of the deceased individual from the pyre to the grave. Compare PRIMARY CREMATION.

secondary flaking see RETOUCH.

secondary inhumation the practice of removing the remains of the deceased individual, initially buried or exposed elsewhere, to the grave or OSSUARY. Compare PRIMARY INHUMATION.

Secondary Products Revolution a series of changes in Late Neolithic material culture and subsistence data, interpreted by Andrew Sherratt and others as indicating a shift from floodplain horticulture to a greater reliance on domestic livestock, particularly for their 'secondary products': traction power for wheeled vehicles and the plough; wool; and milk.

sediment individual grains or aggregate grains of mineral and organic material, that have been or are in the process of being eroded and transported from site of origin, and deposited by water, wind, ice or people. Sediment provides part of the physical CONTEXT of archaeological deposits. As soon as material is culturally deposited, archaeological artifacts are fundamentally sediment grains subjected to the same surface or near-surface physical, chemical and biological processes as surrounding natural grains. In an archaeological site, sediment may be created and deposited directly by people, re-deposited by people, or derived from the decay of humanly made structures. Material moved, modified or otherwise related to human activity in the past is sometimes referred to as 'archaeological sedi-ment'. Sediment characteristics and layering (see STRATIGRAPHY) are studied both on and off archaeological sites to reconstruct palaeoenvironments and to identify physical context.

When affected by soil-forming processes, or PEDOGENESIS, sediment is altered and may take on SOIL properties such as SOIL HORIZONS.

sedimentary structure fundamental observable properties of SEDI-MENTS, defined by composition, size, shape, orientation and grain packing, generated by physical, biological, chemical and diagenetic processes. Many sedimentary structures are generated by the move-ment and SEDIMENTATION of particles in a fluid medium at or near the interface of that medium with a substrate, such as a river bed. In these cases, the type and scale of sedimentary structure are a function of the conditions of flow, fluid properties and sediment properties. As such, sedimentary structures are sources of process and environmental information. When examined with reference to a vertical series of sediments or deposits over an area, the succession of sedimentary structures provides information about past depositional environments and environmental change, both of which can have an impact on the integrity and interpretation of archaeological deposits (see LITHOFACIES ANALYSIS.)

sedimentation a process whereby transported SEDIMENT is deposited by agents such as water, wind or ice. Depending on the conditions of sedimentation, pre-existing surface archaeological deposits may be buried intact, or with considerable redistribution of material.

segment or **crescent** a small stone tool made on a BLADE or BLADE-LET, shaped like a portion of a circle, with BACKING along a curved arc opposite a straight unretouched edge (see RETOUCH), which was hafted, possibly as a projectile tip or as part of a cutting implement. They occur typically in some sub-Saharan African HOWIESONS POORT and LATER STONE AGE assemblages (see WILTON), and are widespread in North Africa, especially in Sudanese Neolithic sites. The term *crescent* is now outdated.

segment Examples.

Sehonghong a large rockshelter in eastern Lesotho, with a sequence of periodic STONE AGE occupation dating from about 70 000 BP MIDDLE STONE AGE HOWIESONS POORT-like material to LATER STONE AGE hunter-gatherer remains as late as AD 1872. Of particular interest is a late date of about 20 000 BP for final Middle Stone Age material.

Seibal a MAYA Lowland centre in south-central Petén, Guatemala, which peaked from AD 770–900 while other cities in the Southern Lowlands were declining. Archaeologists suggest the influx at the site of non-CLASSIC Maya (Putun) from the Gulf Coast prompted its development at this time.

Seine-Oise-Marne (SOM) culture a Late Neolithic culture of the Paris basin area of northeastern France (3400–2800 BC). The culture is known best from collective burials in rock-cut *hypogées*, semi-subterranean funerary houses, and ALLÉES COUVERTES such as LA CHAUSSÉE-TIRANCOURT. The typical SOM pottery type is the coarse-ware flat-based flower pot. There are few associated settlement sites.

Selevac a Late Neolithic site of the VINČA culture (B–C phases) located in the Morava valley of Serbia. Selevac is a large settlement, with archaeological material covering an area of 53 ha. Within the three metres of archaeological deposits, the lower levels indicate the vertical replacement of structures, while the later levels show horizontal displacement. The houses were constructed of timber posts, with WATTLE AND DAUB walls. The faunal assemblage indicates that wild animals were more common in the lower levels, scarcer in the upper ones.

Selinunte (*Gk* Selinous, *Lat.* Selinus) a Greek colony in southwestern Sicily traditionally founded by the Sicilian city of Megara Hyblaea in 651 or 628 BC. A series of temples of the DORIC ORDER have been found; Temple E had relief METOPES on mythological themes. A complex series of fortifications have been found on the AKROPOLIS. Some of the earliest material from the site has been found in the TEMENOS of *Malophoros* ('apple-carrier') to the west of the city. The foundation of the colony provided a fixed point for the dating of Early CORINTHIAN POTTERY on the scheme devised by PAYNE. Recent excavations have now revealed earlier pottery.

SEM see SCANNING ELECTRON MICROSCOPE.

Sembiran an extensive port site in north Bali, Indonesia, with remains ranging from the 1st to the 12th centuries AD. Early remains include Indo-Roman ROULETTED WARE (see ARIKAMEDU), a sherd bearing an early Indian script, imported glass beads and fragments of a mould for casting a bronze drum of the PEJENG variety. It was a major Indonesian port on the spice trade route. See BUNI.

Semenov, Sergei Aristarkhovich (1898–1978) a Soviet archaeologist who first developed the technique of microscopic analysis of wear patterns on artifacts in order to determine their function(s). Although Semenov devoted particular attention to the analysis of wear on Palaeolithic stone and bone tools, he also studied artifacts from later time periods.

Semibratny the Seven Brothers' TUMULI in the Kuban, Georgia. These rich SCYTHIAN burials, mostly of the 5th century BC, were accompanied by numerous horses. Although containing fine examples of Scythian craftmanship, the burials included important examples of Greek GOLD-FIGURED silver plate.

Senftenberg a Late Bronze Age fortified site of the LUSATIAN culture in eastern Germany. Surrounded by a bank-and-ditch enclosure, the interior of Senftenberg is occupied by rectangular-plan post structures in irregular rows, although not as densely packed as at the roughly contemporaneous site of BISKUPIN.

Senwosret or **Sesostris** the name of four of the monarchs of Egypt's MIDDLE KINGDOM who, with the four kings named Amenemhat, constitute the majority of the 12th DYNASTY, a period of Egyptian strength from *c*.1963–1786 BC.

septal slab an upright stone slab across the floor of a MEGALITHIC CHAMBERED TOMB, dividing it into separate segments.

Sepulcros de Fosa cemeteries of individual crouched inhumations in simple pits or stone cists, found in the Catalonia region of northeast Spain in the Middle Neolithic period (5th–4th millennia BC).

sequence dating a method developed by PETRIE to date AMRATIAN and GERZEAN graves at the Egyptian site at Hu (Diospolis Parva). The system employed was a SERIATION based on the overlapping lifespans of artifact types to produce a relative chronology of the graves by their contents.

Serabit el-Khadim the chief ancient Egyptian site in an area of the southwestern Sinai exploited for its deposits of turquoise and copper ore. The major monument at Serabit el-Khadim is the TEMPLE of the goddess Hathor, 'Mistress of Turquoise', which was active from the 12th until the 20th DYNASTY, and which contains STELAE erected both by kings and by the officials connected with the mining expeditions which worked in the area.

Serapeum   a funerary complex at SAQQARA in Egypt where the APIS bulls were interred after MUMMIFICATION. Before the reign of RAMESSES II the bulls were buried in individual tombs, surmounted by small chapels; subsequently a series of underground galleries was constructed with side chambers for the great stone SARCOPHAGUS of each bull. The Serapeum, discovered by MARIETTE, was a place of pilgrimage, and the votive STELAE left by worshippers (c.1200 of which have been recovered, from the NEW KINGDOM to the PTOLEMAIC period) are an important source of information.

serdab (*Arabic* 'cellar')   a chamber found within some Egyptian MASTABAS of the OLD KINGDOM, appearing during the reign of DJOSER and relatively widespread in the cemeteries at GIZA and SAQQARA after the reign of MENKAURE. The serdab contained a statue of the tomb-owner which magically benefited from the produce brought to the adjoining offering-room, through an eye-level slot in the dividing wall. The use of the serdab declined with a change in mortuary practices towards the end of the Old Kingdom.

Sered'-Mačanské vršky   a Mesolithic dune site in the Váh valley near Nitra in Slovakia, the type-site of the Sered' group, the name given to the Mesolithic assemblages of western Slovakia. The Sered' group is distinguished by the extremely small size of its geometrical MICROLITHIC tools. Unusually for dune sites, there is good preservation of bone at Sered', and a faunal assemblage of red deer, roe deer, wild pig, bison and hare is reported, as well as fish bones.

seriation   a RELATIVE DATING technique, in which artifacts are temporally organized, according to their relative popularity. *Evolutionary seriation* is based on changes that represent essentially technological improvements. An example of this is the THREE AGE SYSTEM. *Similiary* or *stylistic seriation* is based on gradual changes in the frequencies of stylistic ATTRIBUTES, so that the greater the similarity in style, the closer in age artifacts are to each other.

Seriña or **Serinya**   a series of cave-sites in Girona, northeast Spain, comprising occupation in the MOUSTERIAN and the Upper Palaeolithic. The MAGDALENIAN is best represented at Bora Gran d'En Carreras, and the SOLUTREAN at Reclau Viver. Excavations by N. Soler at *L'Arbreda* since 1972 have uncovered a detailed sequence at the transition from Middle to Upper Palaeolithic, with RADIOCARBON (AMS) dates of 40 400 bp for the Upper Mousterian and c.38 500 bp for the start of the AURIGNACIAN.

serpentine   a group of relatively common water-bearing magnesium silicate minerals that principally occur in altered ultrabasic rocks rich in olivine and pyroxenes. Serpentine-rich rocks are referred to as *serpentinites*. The most common are green and greenish-blue. Serpentine minerals were used in the manufacture of fine stone tools, vessels, jewellery and architectural decorations.

Serpent Mound   see GREAT SERPENT MOUND.

Serra d'Alto   a Neolithic village in Basilicata, Italy, defended by three concentric ditches, which has given its name to the Serra d'Alto pottery style (*c*.4500–3500 BC). This attractive pottery has decoration of rectangular meanders in black or dark purple paint on a buff surface, and though commonest in APULIA was traded widely, reaching even Lake Garda in the north and Malta in the south.

Sesklo a site in Thessaly, Greece, that was first occupied late in the 7th millennium BC, in the ACERAMIC NEOLITHIC period. By the Middle Neolithic, the period of the Sesklo culture characterized by elegant red-on-cream decorated pottery, the site had grown to a considerable size and the large MEGARON complex on the AKROPOLIS suggests a central authority. Subsequently destroyed by fire, Sesklo was reoccupied in the Late Neolithic period and remained a substantial settlement throughout the Bronze Age.

Sesostris see SENWOSRET.

sestertius a Roman bronze coin, four of which made a DENARIUS.

Seth an Egyptian god, the mythological brother and murderer of OSIRIS, and contender with HORUS for the vacant kingship. Generally regarded as a deity with negative connotations he was, however, occasionally revered; for example, in the Eastern DELTA during the HYKSOS period, because of Seth's identification with the god BAAL. Seth was represented as an anthropoid deity with the head of an unidentified mammal.

Setouchi 1. the Japanese name for the Inland Sea region of western Japan.
2. a Late Palaeolithic stone-working technology for producing side-blow FLAKES using local SANUKITE. Such flakes were used for fashioning Kou knives among others, a tool type named after the Kou site in Osaka Prefecture, other types of knives being produced on classic BLADES.

settlement pattern study a type of archaeological study to record all human-made features of the landscape, relating them to their natural topographic setting and locating them in time. The importance of these studies is the broad regional perspective of cultures and how they change through time, incorporating population estimates, and the distribution of population centres across time and space. In MESOAMERICA, settlement pattern studies enable the archaeologist not only to link regional centres together, but to observe the distribution of archaeological materials from non-elite contexts.

Seven Brothers' Tumuli see SEMIBRATNY.

Seven Wonders a HELLENISTIC list, probably drawn up in the 2nd century BC, of monuments considered the most outstanding ever created. The compilation, which reflected the Greeks' confidence about comprehending the world and the works of humankind following the campaigns of Alexander the Great, comprised: the Egyptian PYRAMIDS, the Hanging Gardens of BABYLON, the Mausoleum of HALICARNASSUS, the Artemision of EPHESUS, the CHRYSELEPHANTINE statue of Zeus at OLYMPIA, the Pharos at ALEXANDRIA, and the Colossus of Rhodes.

Severn-Cotswold a group of Neolithic burial monuments in southwestern Britain consisting of a long mound, tapering towards one end, with one or more PASSAGE GRAVES. The two principal varieties are: the *axial-chambered tombs* such as WEST KENNET, where the passage entrance opens from the centre of the broader end of the mound; and the *lateral-chambered tombs* such as HAZLETON, where two MEGALITHIC chambers are entered from opposite sides of the mound midway along its length.

Sevso treasure   a hoard of Roman silver treasure, which appeared on the art market with rumoured find-spots in both Yugoslavia and the Lebanon. The name is taken from the owner's inscription on one of the dishes.

Shaar ha-Golan   a Palestinian site excavated by Stekelis from 1943 to 1952. It is the type-site of a Neolithic culture of the Jordan Valley termed the Yarmukian, the most distinctive artifact of which is a schematic pebble or clay figurine.

shabti or **ushabti**   a figurine found in Egyptian tombs of the MIDDLE KINGDOM onwards, often in large numbers, and usually in the FORM of a mummy bearing agricultural implements. The shabti was intended to serve as a magical replacement should the deceased be called upon to perform tasks of manual labour in the netherworld.

Shaft Grave Circles A and B   sites at MYCENAE that were excavated by SCHLIEMANN in 1876 and by Papadhimitriou *et al* in 1952–54. The circles were enclosed by a low stone parapet and contained approximately 30 graves altogether, most of which were shaft graves. The spectacular offerings suggest that the rulers of Mycenae must have been buried in the grave circles, which were in use in the later 17th and 16th centuries BC.

shaft grave

shaft tombs   a type of monumental burial structure used by the SHANG elite of northern China (see XIBEIGANG), consisting of a deep central shaft at the bottom of which was constructed a WOODEN CHAMBER for holding a wooden coffin and grave-goods. One to four sloping ramps led into the chamber, producing in the last instance a cruciform tomb plan. (Compare MAWANGDUI, MANCHENG, MOUNDED TOMBS.)

Shahdad   a complex of settlements in the Kirman province of Iran, dated from the late 4th millennium BC to Islamic times, which is important for its three excavated cemeteries. These latter, not yet adequately published, document the emergence of stratified societies during the 3rd millennium of southern Iran, whose elites amassed material wealth in styles that reflect wide-ranging contacts with surrounding civilizations. Surface survey on the settlement itself reveals areas of semi-precious stone workshops and of a major copper-smelting industry; some excavation of the latter area has taken place, revealing complexes of furnaces and workshops dated to the second half of the 3rd millennium BC.

Shahr-i Sokhta   a site located in the Seistan district of Iran, and excavated by M. Tosi during the 1960s and 1970s, containing a sequence spanning the late 4th to early 2nd millennium BC. Beginning with a size of under 20 ha, the settlement grew to cover nearly 100 ha by the late 3rd millennium, before collapsing to under 10 ha in the early 2nd millennium BC. The site is a fundamental reference for understanding urbanization and complex societies in the Bronze Age of eastern Iran and Afghanistan, and provides a wide range of evidence for subsistence and craft production, social stratification, interregional exchange and other relations, and other social questions.

Shamarkian   a MICROLITHIC stone industry found in 8000–6000 year-old sites in the Sudanese Nile Valley.

Shamash   see UTU.

Shamshi–Adad I (c.1813–1781 BC)   the first of the great rulers of ASSYRIA, who originated in a tribal group located near MARI on the River Euphrates. By undetermined means, he created an empire in northern MESOPOTAMIA that stretched from the middle Euphrates in the west to the mountains in the east; although he did not directly control northern BABYLONIA, some of the kingdoms there (including that of HAMMURABI of Babylon) were his clients. With his capitals at ASSUR and Shubat-Enlil (Tell LEILAN), Shamshi-Adad placed as governors his elder son at Ekallatum (in the north of Assyria) and his younger son at Mari, the source of most of the textual evidence about this ruler. On his death, the brothers could not control their inheritance, and the empire collapsed.

Shang   the second of the CHINESE DYNASTIES in the PROTOHISTORIC SANDAI period, 16th–11th centuries BC. Shang originated as the name of a Bronze Age people, who are now said to have ruled the Shang state – known by a characteristic set of bronze weapons (e.g. GE), ritual vessels (e.g. JUE, DING) of the Erligang and Anyang styles and ORACLE BONE inscriptions. The major Shang sites are ZHENGZHOU, PANLONGCHENG and ANYANG. (Compare WUCHENG, XIAJIADIAN.)

Shanidar   a cave in the Zagros foothills near Erbil in northeastern Iraq, where excavations by Ralph Solecki in 1950–60 revealed a Palaeolithic sequence including MOUSTERIAN, Baradostian (the Upper Palaeolithic BLADE INDUSTRY of the Zagros region) and Mesolithic levels. The site provides the type assemblage for the Baradostian industry (33 000–27 000 BP), but is best known for the burials of NEANDERTHALS recovered from the Mousterian levels dating to 60 000–44 000 BP. One may have had flowers placed in the grave.

Shaqadud   a Sudanese site covering some two hectares with three metres of deposit containing early KHARTOUM NEOLITHIC material dated to c.5500 bp separated from a late Neolithic occupation dated to between 4200 and 3600 bp by a break.

shard   see POTSHERD.

Shechem   a Palestinian site excavated by Sellin in 1913–34 and WRIGHT in 1956–64. Building works of the MIDDLE BRONZE AGE resulted in a massively fortified site, including a GLACIS of the HYKSOS Period, at which time Shechem seems to have controlled the territory from MEGIDDO to GEZER. The subsequent destruction level has been attributed to the campaigns of AHMOSE. The rebuilding of Shechem in the LATE BRONZE AGE included fortifications and a temple containing a MASSEBAH, while ISRAELITE Shechem was, before the founding of SAMARIA, the short-lived capital of the Kingdom of Israel.

shell midden or **shell mound**   an archaeological deposit consisting primarily of mollusc shells resulting from food procurement activities. Shell middens are important sources of information on diet, subsistence economy, aquatic harvesting patterns and techniques, and seasonality. See also KITCHEN MIDDEN.

shengwen [sheng-wen] (*Chinese* 'cord motif')   coarse pottery with textured surface decoration in early POSTGLACIAL Chinese sites, pre-dating the Neolithic wares of CISHAN and HEMUDU. It is comparable though not similar to JOMON pottery in Japan, CHULMUN pottery in Korea, and corded-ware in the DAPENGENG culture of Taiwan.

sherd   see POTSHERD.

shifting cultivation   a method of cultivation, very common in tropical forests where soils are thin, in which a field site, or swidden (see SWIDDEN AGRICULTURE) is cleared and then used for a very short period of time until its fertility is depleted, whereupon the cultivation site is relocated to fresh soil. Shifting cultivation is often associated with slash-and-burn, a method of land clearance in which standing vegetation is cut, allowed to dry, and then burned prior to the planting of crops. Evidence for land clearance from LANDNAM episodes in pollen diagrams from temperate Europe led to the hypothesis that shifting cultivation was practised there during the NEOLITHIC, but evidence of long-term settlement and thick fertile soils contradicts such a model.

Shilla   see SILLA.

shipwrecks   the remains of sunken ships; those in Southeast Asian waters, dating to the 1st and early 2nd millennia AD, indicate that most shipping in the region was carried in locally built sewn-plank and lashed-lug vessels built with layered hulls and incorporating no iron. Small sea-going vessels had double outriggers, but the larger ones, despite the illustrations on BOROBUDUR, probably did not. Those in the Gulf of Siam and off Vietnam, dating to the 13th–15th century AD (Koh Khram, Phu Quoc, etc.) have established the contemporaneity of some Thai and Vietnamese CERAMICS. Two wrecks, one in QUANZHOU (Ch'uan chou) Bay and one off the Paracel Islands, indicate that by the 13th–15th century Chinese vessels were also carrying cargoes to and from Southeast Asia. No Indian vessels have yet been found in Southeast Asian waters.

Shirataki   see YUBETSU.

Shiyu [Shih-yu]   a Late Palaeolithic site in Shanxi Province, China, yielding a fossil human occipital bone and 14 animal species, primarily horse and donkey, giving a RADIOCARBON date of *c*.28 000 bp. The lithics include small scrapers and points, and MICROLITHIC CORES and BLADES.

Shizhaishan [Shih–chai–shan]   a cemetery site in Yunnan Province, China, where the distinctive regional DIAN bronze culture was documented in 1956. Contemporaneous with the HAN Dynasty, the grave-goods consisted primarily of bronze and iron weapons and tools, with unique representational motifs of animals and ethnic peoples of the region. Bronze cowrie containers and drums, the latter related to those of DONG SON, are the characteristic types of Dian.

shoe–last adze or **celt**   a long, thin chisel-shaped ground–stone tool characteristic of the LINEAR POTTERY culture. The function of the shoe-last adzes is the subject of some discussion. While the majority of scholars believe them to have been woodworking tools, some have argued that the shoe-last adzes served as ARD-shares or hoes for cultivation.

shoe-last adze

Short Count   a 52-year cycle in the MAYA system, based on a sequence of 13 KATUNS. See also CALENDAR ROUND.

Shortugai   a prehistoric settlement on the Amu Darya (Oxus River) in northeast Afghanistan discovered in the 1970s by H. Francfort in an extension of the French work at the Graeco-Bactrian town of Ai Khanum. In its lower two levels it contained a Mature HARAPPAN settlement. Located 600 km from the northern edge of the Indus ALLUVIUM, it contains a typically Harappan material culture (dated to the second half of the 3rd millennium BC) and has an associated irrigation system. The Badakshan source of lapis lazuli is accessible from the site, and a considerable amount of lapis occurs in the site; for these reasons, Shortugai is often identified as a Mature Harappan trading colony. The subsequent two periods of occupation belong to the 'Beshkent' culture, a probably semi-nomadic culture of southern Tadjikistan/eastern Bactria, best known from cemeteries and dated to the first half of the 2nd millennium.

Shoshong   see TOUTSWE.

shouldered point   a category of stone point manufactured on a BLADE, exhibiting a notch on one side of the base, and sometimes flaked partially or wholly on both sides. Shouldered points are especially characteristic of some Upper Palaeolithic industries of Europe (SOLUTREAN and EASTERN GRAVETTIAN).

shouldered point

Showlow   a prehistoric PUEBLO ruin in Arizona, USA, which provided timbers enabling the modern DENDROCHRONOLOGY sequence to be tied to the prehistoric sequence for the first time.

Shriver   a site in Missouri, USA, containing a WOODLAND occupation, what appears to be a FOLSOM occupation and, underlying that, an assemblage of CHERT FLAKE tools. Neither of the levels can be reliably dated, except by THERMOLUMINESCENCE of the chert itself, which gave dates of approximately 10 700 BP and 13 000 BP. The 'pre-Folsom' materials are similar to other hypothetically contemporary assemblages.

Shu   see ZHOU, DIAN.

Shubat Enlil   see LEILAN.

Shuidonggou [Shui-tung-kou]   a Late Palaeolithic site in Ningxia Hui Autonomous Region, China, yielding bison remains, numerous ostrich eggshell fragments, and classic BLADE artifacts. Originally assigned to the 'ORDOS culture,' the assemblage is characterized by prepared-platform NUCLEI highly varied in shape, marginally RETOUCHED FLAKES and pebble tools.

Shulaveri–Shomu culture   a culture, named after two Neolithic sites on the Kura River in eastern Georgia and western Azerbaijan (Transcaucasia), that represents a local Neolithic to early CHALCOLITHIC phenomenon, characterized by small sites (never more than 5 ha) containing usually small round domestic structures, and by a hand-made coarse pottery decorated only by incision or applied knobs and other elements; at the bottom of some sites (e.g. Shulaveri) pottery is uncommon, perhaps implying a recent adoption of this technology. Subsistence focused on cultivation of a variety of cereals (wheats, barleys, millet), as well as legumes and grapes; irrigation seems to have been practised from the earliest phases of the culture. The fauna concentrates on domesticated cattle and sheep/goat, while hunting is minimally represented. The Shulaveri-Shomu culture seems to date (on the basis of a few CALIBRATED RADIOCARBON determinations) to the mid 6th to early 5th millennia BC.

Shul'gantash Cave   see KAPOVAYA CAVE.

Shulgi   (2094–2047 BC) the successor to Ur-Nammu, the founder of the UR III dynasty. Shulgi created the Ur III empire. Quiescent until halfway through his reign, he undertook a bureaucratic reform that greatly centralized state control over economic life, and at the same time undertook a series of campaigns that brought into his administrative control a large area extending up the Tigris River and through the adjacent sections of the Zagros Mountains down to SUSA. This small empire endured only half a century, collapsing in the reign of Shulgi's third successor Ibbi-sin (2028–2004 BC).

Sialk, Tepe an important prehistoric site near Kashan on the Iranian plateau that provides an interrupted cultural sequence that spans from the Neolithic to the Iron Age. R. GHIRSHMAN's excavations in the 1930s defined six major phases, the last two represented chiefly by Cemeteries A and B of Iron Age date. The earlier four phases (Sialk I–IV, each divided into two or more subphases) form an unbroken succession from the early 6th to the early 3rd millennium BC, the various subphases of which all exhibit external connections. Most of these connections are to other upland sites of Iran, and provide a stratigraphic anchor for regional chronologies. In Sialk IV, on the other hand, the two subphases indicated involvement in the Late URUK and PROTO-ELAMITE phenomena. Since Sialk lies on the Great Khorasan Road (connecting MESOPOTAMIA with Central Asia and ultimately with East Asia), these connections with the Mesopotamian world are often understood as reflecting trading ventures.

Siassi Islands islands in the Vitiaz Strait between New Guinea and New Britain, that were occupied by traders with exclusive control over exchange westward of pottery and eastward of OBSIDIAN and sago. As in south coastal Papua, the ethnographically documented system appears within the last few hundred years, but ancestral versions date back 1500–2000 years. See also HIRI, MAILU.

Sibri a small settlement near MEHRGAHR in the Kachi plain of eastern Baluchistan in Pakistan, investigated as part of J-F. Jarrige's Mehrgahr project, which contains many artifacts with very strong similarities to Central Asian cultures to the north. This connection is reinforced by the South Cemetery at Mehrgahr, where much of the material culture is virtually identical with Central Asian forms. A recently discovered burial near QUETTA repeats this pattern, while earlier discoveries in Baluchistan and parts of the Sind had hinted at this northern connection. Considerable controversy exists over the precise dating of these materials, and how they should be interpreted in the prehistory of the northern subcontinent.

Sicilian pottery a type of SOUTH ITALIAN POTTERY decorated in the RED-FIGURED technique which seems to have been produced from the late 5th century BC. There appear to have been several production centres including SYRACUSE, Himera and possibly Centuripe. The style seems to have had an impact on PAESTAN and CAMPANIAN POTTERY.

sickle sheen a silica deposit or polishing that may occur along the working edge of flint tools during the harvesting of many plant types, and particularly of the Gramineae. The resulting 'sickle sheen' is often used to infer subsistence patterns, namely the consumption of wild or cultivated cereals. The inference is a weak one, however, since these plants may be put to other uses.

side-notched point a type of stone point, chipped on both faces and exhibiting notches on both sides near the base; in some cases, the notches are shallow and wide, forming a stemmed base. Side-notched points are diagnostic of the NORTHERN ARCHAIC TRADITION in North America

side-notched point

Sidescraper   see SCRAPER.

Sidi Abderrahmane   a series of beach and cave deposits in a quarry near Casablanca in Morocco, which have yielded a sequence of abundant ACHEULIAN stone artifact collections linked to sea-level changes, as well as a mandible fragment attributed to HOMO *erectus*.

Sidon   a city situated on the Mediterranean coast of Lebanon, that was a major centre of the PHOENICIANS. Little archaeological work has been undertaken on the ancient city, which lies beneath the modern town.

sieving   a technique of PARTICLE SIZE ANALYSIS used to determine the size grades of PEBBLE GRAVEL, SAND and coarse SILT in SEDIMENT, SOILS and archaeological deposits. A weighed sample is placed on the top sieve of a series of nested sieves, stacked with progressively smaller mesh size towards the bottom. Sieve mesh sizes are standardized so that the sized sample fractions are amenable to statistical analysis. The stack is mechanically agitated, and the material retained in each sieve, representing a size fraction, is weighed and its percentage of the total calculated. Wet sieving, sometimes as part of a flotation technique, is performed to recover small cultural remains from sites.

Sigatoka   a stratified DUNE site on Viti Levu, Fiji, which has produced a discontinuous pottery sequence. The lowest levels, *c.*500 BC, contain LAPITA material, with some unusual forms. Above this, paddle-impressed pottery dated to *c.*AD 200 occurs.

Signal Butte   a stratified site located in western Nebraska, USA, which has a discontinuous occupation sequence stretching from approximately 4500 BP to the Historic Period. It provided an invaluable initial CULTURE HISTORY for the Great Plains of North America.

signs   apparently non-figurative representations found either engraved or painted in PALAEOLITHIC PARIETAL ART, including certain often-repeated forms such as *tectiforms* ('hut shapes') or *claviforms* ('club-shapes') which are regionally restricted and may be 'ethnic markers'.

Silbury Hill   a huge conical chalk mound, 40 m high and 160 m in diameter, surrounded by a broad, deep quarry ditch. Located in Wiltshire, England, it is part of the AVEBURY complex of Neolithic monuments. Excavations, most recently by R. Atkinson, have failed to reveal any trace of a burial within or beneath the mound, and its purpose and significance are unclear, though the effort required to build it *c*.2600 BC would have surpassed even that for the great Avebury HENGE.

Silk route   the collective name for several overland and ocean routes of trade between China and the western Mediterranean between the 1st and 8th centuries AD. From CHANG'AN, capital of China's HAN Dynasty, the primary route led west through the Gansu corridor into the Tarim basin at DUNHUANG. Separate routes ran around the northern and southern edges of the Takla Mahan desert, meeting in the west at Kashgar to continue into Turkmenia in Central Asia.

Silla   a PROTOHISTORIC state on the Korean peninsula (*c*.AD 300–935) that was in competition with KOGURYO and PAEKCHE until 668 and had diplomatic and military relations with YAMATO in Japan. In 668 it unified the peninsula under the rule of United Silla. The capital remained in Kyongju, where large MOUNDED TOMBS of the 5th and 6th centuries have produced much fine gold work (see HEAVENLY HORSE TOMB). In the 7th century the capital was redesigned on the Chinese gridded-city plan (see CHANG'AN, compare HEIJO), and the ANAPCHI pond was constructed.

Silsillian   see KOM OMBO.

silt   **1**. a size term for SEDIMENT or SOIL particles, from 0.002 to 0.05 or 0.06 mm in diameter. As a particle size term, the definition of silt-size particles is independent of mineral composition or other properties apart from size. See also SAND, CLAY.
2. a TEXTURE term used in describing sediments and soils, defined, depending on the classification system used, as containing a certain percentage of silt-size particles relative to sand- and clay-size particle content.
3. a descriptive term for a sediment body (deposit) composed primarily of silt-size particles that is typically soft and plastic when moist. LOESS deposits consist primarily of silt-size particles, and would be described as silt.

silver-figured, *adj.*   denoting a technique used to decorate Greek and Etruscan bronze and gold. Either silver figures were attached to the other metal, or silver foil was placed over relief decoration.

Silver Leaves   one of the earliest-known Iron Age sites south of the Zambezi River, located in the eastern Transvaal, South Africa, and dated to the 3rd–4th centuries AD. Of particular interest are seed impressions of cultivated bulrush millet, *Pennisetum americanum*, representing the earliest evidence for crop cultivation in the region.

sima   a row of vertical tiles placed at the edge of a CLASSICAL roof above the CORNICE, forming a gutter. It was normally made of clay which could be painted. Water was thrown clear of the building by the use of elaborate spouts often in the form of lions' heads. See also ANTEFIX.

Similaun Man   a CHALCOLITHIC man, aged about 20, whose body was found in the Similaun Pass in the Tirolean Alps, Italy, in 1991. The corpse, which seems to have become air-dried at high altitude before being enveloped by a glacier *c*.5000–5500 years ago, was clothed in a skin tunic and leggings stuffed with straw for insulation. His leather boots were filled with straw and birch wood chippings. He had a stone necklace, a wooden-framed backpack, a copper-tipped axe, a bow with a quiver of 14 arrows, and a leather pouch containing flints and tinder. Scars on his torso, back and inner knees may be tattoos or tribal markings.

Sin   see NANNA.

Sinan   the site of an early 14th century AD Yuan ship (see CHINESE DYNASTIES) wrecked off the southwestern Korean coast at Mokpo, South Cholla Province, and discovered in 1976. It has seven compartments, constructed shell first, with a V-shaped cross-section. Its cargo was enormous, including nearly 17 000 CERAMICS, half of them CELADON; 18.5 tons of coins; and many metal, stone, wooden and LACQUER objects.

Sinanthropus   see ZHOUKOUDIAN.

Sinda   the site of a Late CYPRIOT settlement in eastern Cyprus, excavated by Furumark in 1947–48. The site, which was first occupied in the 13th century BC, was massively fortified but nevertheless experienced two major destructions, possibly inflicted by the SEA PEOPLES, and was eventually abandoned early in the 12th century BC.

Single Grave culture   a Danish Neolithic culture dated *c.*2800–2400 BC, part of the North European CORDED WARE complex. The Single Grave culture is characterized by single inhumations (predominantly male) under round BARROWS, accompanied by stone battle axes and Corded Ware BEAKERS. The burial mounds are sometimes multi-phase, with a primary mound at the base covered over by later heightenings, each with a central burial. This gives rise to the typical three-phase Single Grave sequence of *under-grave, bottom-grave* and *over-grave.* Few settlement sites are known.

Sion   see PETIT-CHASSEUR.

Sipán   a complex of tombs in the Lambayeque region of the far north coast of Peru, pertaining to the MOCHE culture of the EARLY INTERMEDIATE PERIOD. Discovered by looters in 1987, the site contains an unknown number of intact royal, or at least incredibly lavish, tombs. Excavations are being carried out by Peruvian archaeologist Walter Alva. The tomb of the Lord of Sipán, the excavation of which has been completed, included a central personage buried in a wooden box, filled with a spectacular variety of artifacts, including a necklace of large gold beads in the form of peanuts. He was surrounded by four other individuals and a dog, and numerous CERAMIC vessels. Another human, presumably meant to guard the tomb, was buried above the main chamber with his feet cut off. These tombs are perhaps the first intact, elaborate Moche burials excavated by professional archaeologists.

sipapu   a small hole in the floor of some KIVAS that gives access to the lower world in PUEBLO mythology. Sipapus have been identified, by HOMOLOGY, in some prehistoric kivas.

Sipontian   see COPPA NEVIGATA.

Siret, Henri (1857–1933) and **Siret, Louis** (1860–1934)   Belgian engineers working in the ALMERIA region of Spain from 1880; keen amateur archaeologists, the Siret brothers were the first to reveal the amazing richness of the CHALCOLITHIC and BRONZE AGE of southeast Spain, with their excavations at many key sites including LOS MILLARES, EL ARGAR and Tabernas.

Sirikwa Holes   circular depressions, 5–10 m in diameter, sometimes with stone walling around the circumference, which functioned as cattle byres in Iron Age sites of the Western Highlands of Kenya, during the first half of the 2nd millennium AD.

Si Satchanalai   the main industrial centre of the state of SUKHOTHAI in north-central Thailand. Over 600 kilns have been located in the vicinity of the old town, which produced pottery and STONEWARE over a period of several hundred years. The best known of the wares (the brown-GLAZED Chalieng wares, under-glaze black on cream Sukhothai wares and the green-glazed CELADONS), collectively called 'Sawankhalok' after the present name of the district, date to the 14th–16th centuries AD but earlier phases of production at the Ban Ko Noi site may date to the period of MON domination before the mid 13th century.

Sitagroi   a prehistoric settlement mound in Greek Macedonia invest-igated by Gimbutas and Renfrew in 1968–69. The excavations at Sita-groi made it possible to correlate the Neolithic and Early Bronze Age sequences of the Balkans and the Aegean, and proved that COPPER METALLURGY was an independent development in the Balkans.

site   any place where there is evidence for past human behaviour. A site can be as small as an isolated find, which is either a single ARTIFACT or a small number of artifacts from which few inferences can be drawn, or as large as an ancient city. Sites are classified according to their function, although different regions of the world tend to have different terms for specific types of site. Major types in-clude a domestic/habitation site (the primary residential locus); a KILL-SITE; and a processing/butchering site (where animal carcasses were stripped of their meat and other useful resources). There are, however, many other types.

site catchment analysis   the definition of the site catchment, the total area from which the contents of a SITE have been derived, and an assessment of the catchment's economic potential, according to the principles of PALAEOECONOMY. See SITE EXPLOITATION TERRITORY.

site exploitation territory   the territory surrounding a site that is habitually exploited by the site's inhabitants. It is a central concept in PALAEOECONOMY, which proposed a MODEL for site exploitation territories of a one-hour walking distance for farmers, and a two-hour walking distance for HUNTER-GATHERERS.

site formation processes   see FORMATION PROCESSES.

site structure   the arrangement of the various components at a place, including the distribution of ARTIFACTS, FEATURES, facilities and activities. The concept of site structure applies to both behavioural and archaeological contexts. Often done in the context of ETHNOARCHAEOLOGICAL studies, site structural analysis identifies how the organization and use of space relate to other aspects of the cultural system.

The space required for most activities depends on the physical con-straints of the human body. Because the proportions of the human body have remained relatively constant through time, we can develop an understanding of the constant relationship between activity types and the space needed to perform those activities. This knowledge can then be taken to the archaeological record. Additional ethnoarchaeological studies of site structure identify other factors in-fluencing the organization and use of space. These factors include length of occupation, number of people at the site, types of facilities necessary for a given activity, and the nature of the materials resulting from the activity. Site structural analyses from contemporary or ethnographic contexts are then used to make WARRANTING ARGUMENTS in the context of the archaeological record.

Sittard a LINEAR POTTERY settlement in Limburg, the Netherlands, excavated by P.J.R. Modderman. Over 30 houses, many of them LONGHOUSES, were excavated, and it is estimated that between three and six were occupied at any one time, somewhat fewer than at the contemporaneous site of ELSLOO nearby.

situla a CLASSICAL bucket-shaped container, with a single swinging handle across the rim. Silver and bronze examples are often found in burials in Macedonia and Thrace.

Six's technique a technique used to decorate 6th century BC ATHENIAN POTTERY, and first discussed by Jan Six in 1888. The black surface of the pot was overpainted in red or white, and the detail was cut through, showing the black surface of the pot (contrast BLACK-FIGURED).

Skara Brae a Neolithic village of stone-built houses preserved beneath a later sand dune on Orkney, Scotland. The houses are of sub-rectangular internal plan and are linked together by covered passageways. Built-in furnishings of stone included dressers, beds, wall cupboards and limpet tanks. The villagers kept cattle and sheep, but cereal farming and fishing with limpet bait were also important. Two phases of occupation have been identified spanning six centuries *c.*3100–2500 BC.

Skateholm a group of southern Swedish Mesolithic fishing sites on the coast of Scania which used to be on small islands in a lagoon. They were discovered and excavated by Lars Larsson in 1980–84, and include domestic areas and over 80 graves of men, women and juveniles. The site of Skateholm 4 is dated to 6000–5500 BP.

skene 1. a Greek temporary shop or building.
2. a permanent stage-building, of several storeys, for a theatre placed behind the ORCHESTRA (where see figure). It could be used as a backdrop for a play, as well as for storing equipment. In the Roman period the skene could be decorated with statues. See PROSKENION.

Skhul see ES-SKHUL.

Skorba a Maltese temple complex with earlier deposits beneath. A four-apse temple with a central apse of the TARXIEN phase (*c.*3000–2600 BC) has been added to a three-apse temple of the preceding *Ggantija* phase (*c.*3600–3000 BC). Excavations beneath the temples revealed an oval hut of the *Ghar Dalam* (IMPRESSED WARE) phase (*c.*5000 BC), and nearby was an oval-roomed building of the *Red Skorba* phase (*c.*4300–4000 BC), thought from the presence of figurines to be a shrine, precursor of the later temples.

Skraeling a term applied to the aboriginal inhabitants of Greenland by Norsemen who settled the island in the late 10th century AD. The Skraelings are probably represented archaeologically by the THULE culture. See QILAKITSOQ.

skyphos a type of Greek drinking vessel, normally a deep cup with two horizontal handles mounted near the rim. See KOTYLE.

slash-and-burn see SHIFTING CULTIVATION, SWIDDEN AGRICULTURE.

Slavs a complex of ethnic groups speaking related languages that emerged during the second half of the 1st millennium AD in eastern

Europe, although some have traced their roots to antecedents like the VENEDIANS. The emergence of state-level POLITIES in the lands of the Slavs began with Greater Moravia, centred on MIKULCIČICE, in the 9th century AD and in west-central and southern Poland in the 10th century. Further east, nodes of trade and commerce emerged at localities like NOVGOROD and KIEV. The basic unit of all these communities was the stronghold – the GRÓD or *hrad*.

slip   a mixture of clay and water that is applied to the surface of a pot before firing to improve the pot's smoothness and decrease its porosity. See CERAMICS.

slopewash   a general term for COLLUVIUM consisting of a typically, but not necessarily, poorly sorted deposit located on and at the base of HILLSLOPES. Slopewash is the result of soil EROSION upslope, downhill SEDIMENT transport and final SEDIMENTATION. Soil erosion may result from a number of processes, some human-induced. Erosion and transport may result in the incorporation and displacement of archaeological deposits. Deposition at the base of the slope may include cultural debris redeposited from upslope locations, and it may result in the burial of intact and previously redeposited artifacts.

Słupia Stara   an Iron Age metallurgical site of the VENEDIAN people in the HOLY CROSS MOUNTAINS of central Poland, dated to the 1st and 2nd centuries AD. At Słupia Stara, the neighbouring site of *Słupia Nowa*, and several other sites in the vicinity, clusters of several hundred iron SMELTING furnaces about a metre in diameter are found in parallel rows.

smelt, *vb*   to separate metal from ORE, usually by heating in a HEARTH or furnace.

Smenkhare   see NEFERTITI.

Smith, Sir Grafton Elliot   (1871–1937) an Australian-born anatomist who, along with his student and later colleague W.J. Perry, unswervingly advocated a hyper-diffusionist view that all civilizations, if not all cultures, including those in the New World, originated as a result of influences from Ancient Egypt.

Smith, Worthington George   (1835–1917) a British amateur archaeologist who pioneered the scientific excavation and detailed recording of Palaeolithic sites and exposed sections. He is best known for his illustrations of flint artifacts and his CONJOINING of flint FLAKES.

Smithfield   a LATER STONE AGE INDUSTRY of the South African interior, originally thought to be contemporaneous with the WILTON. The designation is now applied to a complex post-dating the Wilton in the South African interior between AD 1300 and 1700. See SEACOW VALLEY.

Smyrna   see IZMIR.

Snaketown   a large site in Arizona, USA, excavations of which provided much basic information for the formulation of the HOHOKAM sequence. The site covers over 1 sq km and has 60 refuse mounds. At its peak of use, the site contained a BALL COURT, a large habitation area comprising PITHOUSES built around a central plaza, and extensive irrigation ditches. Craft specialization was also apparent, not only in pottery but also in shell. Such items as copper bells and distinctive pottery figurines are highly suggestive of contact with MESOAMERICAN cultures.

Snefru   an Egyptian king, founder of the 4th DYNASTY. Building works which should probably be ascribed to him are the two PYRAMIDS at DAHSHUR and at least the completion of that at MEIDUM.

Snettisham   a location in Norfolk, England, where a single field has yielded nine hoards of Iron Age treasure comprising almost 200 gold, silver and bronze TORCS or neck-rings, as well as bracelets and coins, dating to *c.*70 BC. The most spectacular object is one massive torc of gold-rich electrum.

Soan   the name given to a Lower Palaeolithic industry of the Punjab (Pakistan and Northwest India) which was encountered in a group of sites by de Terra and Patterson during their geological and archaeological explorations of the region in the 1930s. The term encompassed both HANDAXES and CHOPPER/CHOPPING TOOLS. Much of this material, together with the GEOMORPHOLOGICAL units from which it was gathered, has been redated to Middle Palaeolithic times, and the Soan seems to have no archaeological validity.

soapstone   see STEATITE.

Sobiejuchy   a lakeside settlement of the Late Bronze Age/Early Iron Age (HALLSTATT period, LUSATIAN culture), in north-central Poland, 12 km north of BISKUPIN. Sobiejuchy was surrounded by a double palisade filled with stones and earth, and was occupied for about 75 years. The settlement of Sobiejuchy was destroyed by fire, as was the case at Biskupin, and skeletons were found in the settlement debris with arrowheads embedded in the bones.

soft hammer, bar hammer or **cylinder hammer technique**   the use of a hammer made of bone, antler, wood or some other relatively soft material, to remove flat FLAKES during flint KNAPPING. Flakes struck with a soft hammer have a characteristic appearance, being relatively long and thin with a diffuse BULB OF PERCUSSION. Compare HARD HAMMER TECHNIQUE.

soil   1. unconsolidated mineral or organic matter at and near the land surface that is the product of and influenced by PEDOGENESIS: the interacting pedogenic, depositional and erosional processes and factors along with environmental factors that have through time physically, chemically, biologically and morphologically altered pre-existing material from its original conditions. The alterations form differentiated layers (see SOIL HORIZON) with respect to the land surface that comprise a soil.

Archaeological deposits are often associated with soils because for a soil to form, some type of dynamic balance of the land surface is implied since it takes time for pedogenic processes to be expressed; the longer a favourable 'stable' surface on which a soil is forming is exposed, the greater the likelihood of occupation and discard of debris. Archaeological deposits associated with soils are subject to the same environmental conditions, processes and factors as the soil.

Soils also have temporal significance because it takes time for pedogenic alterations to occur. Although not all soils may be ISOCHRONOUS across a landscape, they are often a useful means of CORRELATION. See also PALAEOSOL.

2. (*engineering*) all unlithified material whether it has been altered or not. Often any available engineering drilling records are consulted for subsurface information about an archaeological site or area prior to archaeological investigations, making the distinction between this and

the foregoing definition important.

soil conductivity meter a GEOPHYSICAL instrument used in ELECTROMAGNETIC SURVEYING to identify metal objects and shallow pit features with different conductivity from the surrounding SOIL.

soil geomorphology the study of the interaction of PEDOGENIC and GEOMORPHIC processes as applied to interpretation of old and new LANDSCAPES. By definition, archaeological debris was deposited on former landscapes. After deposition, it was then subject to alteration by both pedogenic and geomorphic processes, potentially resulting in burial, mixing, redistribution or removal. The physical CONTEXT of archaeological material is best determined and evaluated by an integrated SOIL geomorphic approach. See GEOMORPHOLOGY, PEDOGENESIS.

soil horizon a layer in a SOIL or soil material, developed through PEDOGENESIS, that differs from overlying or underlying genetically related layers in chemical, physical or biological properties and characteristics. Sequences of genetically related soil horizons make up the SOIL PROFILE which reflects the environmental conditions under which it formed.

soil probe see PROBE.

soil profile 1. a vertical sequence of SOIL HORIZONS expressed as a result of PEDOGENESIS acting over time. Different soil profiles with different soil horizons evolve under different extrinsic and intrinsic factors, processes and conditions. The soil profile therefore provides environmental or, in the case of PALAEOSOLS, palaeoenvironmental information, such as clues to vegetation type and prevailing climate.
2. a vertical section, exposed either in excavation or naturally, that reveals soil horizons. Ideally, the excavation should be deep enough to expose the entire succession of soil horizons. See PROFILE.

soil stratigraphy a specialized branch of STRATIGRAPHY concerned with identification of SOILS as stratigraphic units (pedostratigraphic units) and their chronological ordering. A pedostratigraphic unit is a formally defined three-dimensional, laterally traceable, buried SEDIMENT or rock body, consisting of one or more SOIL HORIZONS (e.g. PALAEOSOLS), and is not to be confused with the sequencing of soil horizons within a SOIL PROFILE. In stratigraphic sequences where multiple palaeosols occur, soil stratigraphic study provides information for palaeoenvironmental reconstruction, monitoring environmental change, and dating pedological and depositional episodes.

soil structure the physical arrangement of SEDIMENT into secondary aggregations referred to as *peds* as the result of PEDOGENESIS. SOIL structure is defined by the size and shape of peds, and the degree to which cohesive forces bind sediment particles within and between peds. Soil structure is a principal soil property noted in describing and interpreting soils.

Sokchang-ri [Sokchangni] a Palaeolithic site in South Ch'ungch'ong Province, Korea, with 12 cultural layers, dug by Sohn Pow-key (Son Bo-gi) from 1962. Layer 1 yielded OBSIDIAN SCRAPERS, rhyolite BURINS, prismatic CORES and an occupational floor dated to *c.*20 000 bp. Layer 6 gave a RADIOCARBON date on charcoal to *c.*30 000 bp, and heavy QUARTZITE tools in the lower layers are dated to the Middle PLEISTOCENE by comparison with ZHOUKOUDIAN artifacts.

Soleb a site in UPPER NUBIA, capital of KUSH under TUTANKHAMEN. It is notable for the TEMPLE of AMENHOTEP III (*c.*1391–1353 BC) and a cemetery of the NEW KINGDOM. The site was extensively examined by Pisa University from 1957–77.

solifluction the process of mass movement of water-laden SOIL and SEDIMENT material as the result of the thawing of frozen ground. Solifluction can cause disruption or displacement of archaeological deposits, as well as result in burial in downslope landscape positions. COLLUVIUM deposited as the result of solifluction can be found as HILLSLOPE veneers, colluvial wedges and fans at the base of HILLSLOPES, and as valley fill.

Solo a river in central and east Java, the terraces of which have yielded remains of early humans, PLIOCENE, PLEISTOCENE and early modern fauna, and stone tools of uncertain association. The geological beds of archaeological interest, clearly exposed at SANGIRAN, are: *Pucangan* (lower-middle Pleistocene, *c.*3–2 million years BP at base, containing pre-modern JETIS fauna with which the earliest HOMINID remains, the MOJOKERTO child, are linked); *Kabuh* (middle Pleistocene, *c.*1.4–0.7 million years BP at base, containing pre-modern TRINIL fauna and JAVA MAN HOMO *erectus* remains); *Notopuro* (volcanic soil formation marking the transition to upper Pleistocene); and *High Solo Gravels* or *High Terrace* (upper Pleistocene, *c.?*0.5 million years BP at base, containing modern NGANDONG fauna associated with SOLO MAN and *H. sapiens*, and stone tools distinctly different from the ACHEULIAN).

Solo Man (HOMO *erectus soloensis*) an advanced HOMINID, somewhat more archaic than European NEANDERTHALS, found at NGANDONG and Sambungmacan in the Solo valley of Java; it may possibly be later than PEKING MAN but is at a similar evolutionary level. See DUBOIS.

Solomon king of the united kingdom of Israel and Judah. His reign (*c.*965–928 BC) saw a good deal of building activity at many sites including JERUSALEM.

Solutrean or **Solutrian** a western European Upper Palaeolithic INDUSTRY which appears to have developed in the Rhône valley area of France, following AURIGNACIAN influence at about 19 000 BC, and which lasted approximately 3000 years. The type-fossils are the LAUREL-LEAF POINT (Earlier Solutrean) and the SHOULDERED POINT (Later Solutrean). Solutrean flint artifacts represent some of the best examples of Palaeolithic KNAPPING technology, and the assemblages also contain some fine bone work. Many decorated caves in France can be assigned to this period. The name is derived from the French open-air site of *Solutré*, Saône-et-Loire, excavated most recently by J. Combier; it has material from the MOUSTERIAN to the late MAGDALENIAN, and specialized in the exploitation of horse herds, rounded up against the foot of a craggy hill.

SOM see SEINE-OISE-MARNE.

Somerset Levels a wetland region of southwestern Britain, famous for its preserved prehistoric organic remains. These include the Neolithic SWEET TRACK and the Iron Age villages of GLASTONBURY and Meare.

Somme-Bionne a Marnian chariot burial in Marne, France, equipped with ETRUSCAN bronze beaked flagon and Attic RED-FIGURE KYLIX, dating to LA TÈNE Ia, *c.*450–420 BC.

Somme-Tourbe see LA GORGE-MEILLET.

Sondershausen   a cemetery of the LINEAR POTTERY culture in eastern Germany. Twenty-eight inhumation burials were found at Sondershausen, with the skeletons in a contracted position lying on their sides. Ornaments of SPONDYLUS shell occurred in both male and female burials.

Songguk-ri [Songgungni]   a Bronze Age site in South Ch'ungch'ong Province, Korea, where a stone CIST burial yielded in 1974 the first Liaoning-type dagger found on the peninsula. Excavation of the associated village site in 1985 revealed two pit-houses dated to the 5th century BC.

Songguk-ri Liaoning-type dagger.

Songhay   a 15th–16th century AD West African empire, which controlled virtually the entire great bend of the River Niger by means of wealth based on Saharan trade.

Songon Dagbe   one of more than 100 large SHELL MOUNDS at the Ebrie Lagoon in the Ivory Coast dating to c.2400 bp. Contact with areas further north is suggested by the presence of several KINTAMPO 'cigars'.

Songze [Sung-tse]   see QINGLIANGANG.

Son Vi   type-site of a pre-HOABINHIAN stone tool industry located at cave-sites around the Red River valley in northern Vietnam, dating to c.18 000–9000 BC, and characterized by unifacially flaked pebbles, rare bifacially worked pebbles, CHOPPERS, side-SCRAPERS and 'round-edged' pebbles. The industry precedes Hoabinhian phases at Con Moong and Hang Pong 1, the transition occurring c.10 000–9000 BC.

Sopot Lengyel   an ENEOLITHIC culture of the northwestern Balkans, viewed as a regional variant either of the LENGYEL or of the VINČA cultures in the late 4th millennium bc.

Sopron   an Early Iron Age cemetery (HALLSTATT C period) located in western Hungary 60 km southeast of Vienna. In the cremation burials found under BARROWS at Sopron were a number of unusual urns with incised human figures which depict people spinning, weaving on an upright loom, playing the lyre, dancing, and riding on horseback. Other individuals lead horse-drawn wagons, herd animals and hunt. Male figures are depicted wearing trousers, the earliest-known representation of this garment in temperate Europe.

Soroki   a complex of sites in the middle Dniester valley of Moldova which have provided most of the data on the late Mesolithic/early Neolithic BUG-DNIESTER culture. Located on a low terrace, the earliest occupations at Soroki (c.5600 bc) are ACERAMIC and have an exclusively hunting and fishing economy. Later levels (c.4800 bc) have much the same sort of economy, but include pointed-base vessels unlike those of the CRIŞ culture nearby. Claims have been made for evidence of local domestication, particularly of pigs, at Soroki, although the data are equivocal.

soros a Greek burial mound. One of the best known contained the Athenian dead from the battle of MARATHON in 490 BC. See also MAGOULA, TOUMBA.

Sotira-Teppes a site in southern Cyprus that was excavated by Dikaios in 1947–54 and is the type-site for the Neolithic II (later 5th millennium BC) Sotira culture which is characterized by combed ware. The settlement, which was surrounded by an enclosure wall, consists of circular and oval stone and MUD-BRICK houses. The dead were buried in a simple pit-grave cemetery at the foot of the hill. In 1981–83 Swiny excavated a CHALCOLITHIC PHILIA culture (mid 3rd millennium BC) settlement and cemetery at *Sotira-Kaminoudhia*.

Soufli the site in Thessaly, Greece, of an ACERAMIC Neolithic–Bronze Age settlement mound and a LARISA phase cremation cemetery excavated by Theocharis and Biesantz in 1958.

Sounion the promontory in Attica, Greece, on which was constructed the temple of Poseidon. This dated to the mid 5th century BC.

souterrain a long stone-built chamber sunk into the ground and roofed with stone slabs, usually beneath a house or settlement and intended for cold storage. Souterrains are found in Scotland, Ireland, Cornwall (where they are known as *fogous* and date to the 2nd and 1st centuries BC) and Brittany, where the earliest belong to the mid 1st millennium BC.

South Arabian civilization a group of kingdoms that developed during the 1st millennium BC and lasted until the mid 1st millennium AD, in the region of southwestern Arabia roughly corresponding to modern Yemen. The most famous of these kingdoms include the Minaeans, Qatabanians, Sabaeans and Himyar. Sharing a system of writing and further united, by many common cultural attitudes and materials, these states were based both on exploiting the agricultural potential of this mountainous area and, more famously, on producing and exporting incense (frankincense and myrrh). The attention paid to these groups by Greek and Roman writers as well as in several Biblical episodes (especially the 'queen of Sheba') is due almost entirely to the commercial aspect of the South Arabian states, which were proverbially wealthy.

Southeastern Ceremonial Complex see SOUTHERN CULT.

Southern Cult a COMPLEX of motifs and objects, also known as the Southeastern Ceremonial Complex, found throughout the southeastern part of North America during the MISSISSIPPIAN, that appears to be almost a true HORIZON in the 13th century AD. The 'cult' was probably not a religious cult in the modern sense of the word, and was probably tied into widespread exchange networks. Distinctive motifs include the cross, 'sun circle', swastika and an eye-and-hand motif.

Southern Highveld Settlements Iron Age farms of the early 2nd millennium AD, located on the extensive grasslands of the southern highveld area of the Orange Free State and Transvaal, South Africa. The farmers built numerous stone walls to enclose cattle byres and courtyards around houses. Many of these structures still stand today and have been classified as Types N, V and Z settlements, which are associated with the MOLOKO Complex and the dispersal of the ancestors of the modern Sotho-Tswana people.

Southern Rhodesian Wilton   see KHAMI, MATOPO.

South Italian pottery   a type of pottery that was produced in the Greek colonies in southern Italy and Sicily, particularly from the late 5th century BC. There were various centres of production: see APULIAN, CAMPANIAN, GNATHIAN, LUCANIAN, PAESTAN and SICILIAN POTTERY.

Sozudai   a controversial Palaeolithic site in Oita Prefecture, Japan, excavated by C. Serizawa, who claims a date of 400 000 bp on geological grounds and tool comparisons with ZHOUKOUDIAN. Many archaeologists do not accept that the tools are of human manufacture; some accept a date of only 70 000 bp.

spacer-plate   a flat rectangular or sub-rectangular plaque of amber or jet, with a complex arrangement of through-borings to serve as a separator for the strings of a multi-strand necklace. Amber spacer plates are found as components of necklaces of amber beads in graves of the Early Bronze Age WESSEX CULTURE, and contemporary examples of jet are known from burials in east Yorkshire, England.

spacer plate Necklace with spacer plates; detail of spacer plate.

spall   see BURIN.

Sparta   the main urban centre of Laconia on the banks of the river Eurotas in Greece. An important sanctuary, dating from the Early Iron Age, was that of Artemis Orthia where numerous ivory, bone, lead and ceramic offerings have been found. In the Roman period the sanctuary was remodelled by the construction of a theatre. Another sanctuary was that of Athena Chalkioikos, a structure decorated with bronze plates. See LACONIAN POTTERY.

Spaulding, Albert Clinton   (1914–90) an American archaeologist who contributed much to the development of modern archaeological theory, especially PROCESSUAL ARCHAEOLOGY. He engaged in a famous series of debates with James FORD on the nature of the archaeological TYPE, and also advocated the adoption of explicitly scientific and quantitative methods by the discipline.

Spear Hill   a complex of 28 sites in the Pilbara region of Western Australia with a wide range of PETROGLYPHS similar to those of GALLERY HILL.

spearpoint   the tip of a projectile used for throwing or stabbing. See PALAEOINDIAN, PROJECTILE POINT.

spearthrower   a long stick with a hooked end designed to hold a spear. The implement is used to extend the reach of the arm, producing a stronger and longer throw. In Europe antler spearthrowers, often beautifully carved, developed during the MAGDALENIAN phase. See ATLATL.

specific gravity   a physical property of all solids and liquids defined by the ratio of the mass of a body to the mass of an equal volume of distilled water at prescribed temperature conditions. Knowing the specific gravity of the pure metals can help in calculating by means of a simple non-destructive analysis the composition of a metal ARTIFACT if it is a two-component alloy, and preferably if one of the alloy components is known. The property is also utilized in preparations for HEAVY MINERAL ANALYSIS.

speleothem   a secondary mineral deposit, usually carbonate, precipitated in air-filled caves from seeping waters enriched in carbonate. Geographically widespread periods of speleothem growth (as *stalagmites* and *stalactites*) and ISOTOPIC composition of speleothems may provide palaeoclimatic information. They can be dated by the URANIUM SERIES dating method. Periods of speleothem growth near coastal or river valley areas of carbonate rock can provide information on past sea-level or river-level fluctuations. Speleothem deposition can potentially bury earlier archaeological deposits.

sphinx   a mythological beast usually with a lion's body and a man's head or face. As a motif in Egyptian art the sphinx was used as a depiction of royal power, and therefore only the king was shown in this form. The largest representation of an Egyptian sphinx is also one of the earliest, the Great Sphinx at GIZA, associated with the PYRAMID COMPLEX of King KHAFRE. Representations of ram-headed lions termed *crio-sphinxes*, and associated with the god AMEN, are found from the NEW KINGDOM, most notably as statues flanking the roads between the TEMPLE of LUXOR and the complex at KARNAK.

sphyrelaton   a bronze statue made by the technique of hammering bronze plates over a core. The plates were secured by nails. The technique is a precursor to the LOST WAX technique, and three statues dating to the 8th century BC have been found in the temple of Apollo at Dreros on Crete. The technique was also used to produce colossal statues, some of which survived into the Roman period.

Spiennes   Neolithic flint mines in Belgium covering an area of 60 ha. The earliest are opencast pits, but deep shafts with underground galleries later became necessary as the more accessible deposits were exhausted. A second less-extensive flint mine series at Petit-Spiennes *c.*1 km to the west became the site of a double-ditched enclosure in the MICHELSBERG period, running across the shafts and dumps of the earlier mining complex.

Spina   a harbour town located at the mouth of the River Po in Italy. It seems to have been occupied by the Etruscans and was probably founded in the early years of the 5th century BC. Its extensive cemeteries (Valle Trebba and Valle Pega) have yielded large quantities of imported ATHENIAN POTTERY. The site may have served as an outlet for agricultural produce from the Po Valley and slaves from Central Europe which could be shipped down the Adriatic to the urban centres of the Greek world. Its rise in fortune contrasts with the decline of Massalia (see MARSEILLES), perhaps seeing a new emphasis on the Alpine Passes rather than on the Rhône Valley.

Spirit Cave   one of numerous limestone rockshelters in the KARST uplands of north Thailand, occupied intermittently from before 9000 BC until c.5500 BC. Stone implements of the lower layers fall within the range associated with the HOABINHIAN. After c.6000 BC these are mixed with cord-marked and BURNISHED pottery and with flaked and EDGE-GROUND or POLISHED STONE ADZES and small slate knives similar to those later used to harvest rice in the region. The presence of these knives suggests that a transition occurred at this time from broad-spectrum hunting and gathering and incipient horticulture to greater dependence upon rice as a staple. While no rice remains were found at the site, rice husks were recovered at the site of *Banyan Valley Cave*, 30 km to the east, along with small slate knives. This site was occupied by c.3500 BC and continued in use into the 1st millennium AD. A third rockshelter in the region, *Steep Cliff Cave*, utilized between c.5500–3500 BC, appears to have been used as a seasonal hunting campsite.

spirit path   the rows of stone sculptures arranged facing the path up to Chinese MOUNDED TOMBS from the HAN Dynasty onwards. Their function was to guard or honour the deceased. The sculptures often include people and animals, of three-quarters to double life-size. Decadent examples are seen at the MING TOMBS outside Beijing.

Spiro   a site, located in eastern Oklahoma, USA, which comprises eight mounds of varying size, one of which had served as both a TEMPLE MOUND and BURIAL MOUND. The largest of these, the Craig mound, was 11 m in height. Much of the site has been destroyed by pot-hunting. It contained a rich assemblage of artifacts associated with the SOUTHERN CULT. See ETOWAH, MISSISSIPPIAN, MOUNDVILLE.

Spišsky Stvrtok   a Bronze Age fortified site of the OTOMANI culture in eastern Slovakia. The hill top settlement of Spišsky Stvrtok is surrounded by a stone and earth rampart 170 m in circumference, plus an outer stone wall. One part of the site is termed the 'acropolis', in which the houses had stone foundations and in one of which was a hoard of gold and bronze artifacts. The houses outside the 'acropolis' were of simpler construction. This distinction has been interpreted as indicating social differentiation, with the members of the elite living in the 'acropolis.'

Spitsyn Culture   an early Upper Palaeolithic culture defined chiefly on the basis of the lowest level of KOSTENKI XVII on the Don River in European Russia, dating to c.40 000–30 000 bp. It is characterized by BURINS, RETOUCHED BLADES and SCRAPERS; some bone tools and ornaments (e.g. perforated fox teeth) are also present. The Spitsyn assemblages represent a very early but fully developed Upper Palaeolithic industry that contrasts sharply with the contemporaneous STRELETS CULTURE.

Spondylus gaederopus   a species of marine shell found in the eastern Mediterranean, widely used in Neolithic Europe for ornaments, including bracelets, discs and beads. These ornaments are found in many sites from southeastern to northwestern Europe, including those of the LINEAR POTTERY culture in Czechoslovakia, Germany and the Netherlands.

Spring and Autumn period see ZHOU.

Spy a prehistoric cave-site near Liège, Belgium, best known for the late 19th century discovery of three damaged NEANDERTHAL skeletons, the first ever found associated with MOUSTERIAN artifacts. The upper layers of the cave yielded Upper Palaeolithic material.

square-mouth see BOCCA QUADRATA.

Squier, Ephraim George (1821–88) an American antiquary who, with Edwin H. DAVIS, described and analysed hundreds of mounds and enclosures in the Ohio and the Mississippi Valley. Their resulting book *Ancient Monuments of the Mississippi Valley* was a remarkable volume for its time, and still stands as a pioneering work in American archaeology, even though they concluded that the mounds were too sophisticated to have been constructed by the ancestors of contemporary Indians. As part of his research on Mound Builder origins, Squier also conducted archaeological work in central America, Peru and Bolivia. See ATWATER, HAVEN, THOMAS.

Sredni Stog culture an Early ENEOLITHIC culture of the Dnepr basin of Ukraine, of the late 4th/early 3rd millennia bc. It is seen as the precursor of the YAMNAYA culture of the Late Eneolithic and is known from a number of settlements and cemeteries including DEREIVKA. The Sredni Stog culture is particularly important for its role in the domestication of the horse.

Śri Kṣetra an early name for the town of Prome in lower Burma, capital and Buddhist religious centre of the state of the same name in the early–mid 1st millennium AD, later absorbed by PAGAN.

Śrivijaya a major early trading state in the Malacca Straits in Southeast Asia, probably structured like the later Malacca Sultanate, controlling ports of Sumatra and peninsular Malaysia during the 7th–8th centuries AD and again in the 10th–13th centuries, periods of booming trade in Asian waters. The capital has traditionally been placed at Palembang, but most early remains apart from inscriptions of the 7th century have been found elsewhere. The largest port by the 12th century was Muara Jambi (near Jambi) which has a number of temple remains, large quantities of Chinese CERAMICS and coins. Other large sites possibly connected with the later phase of Śrivijaya include such ports as Kota Cina (northeast Sumatra, 11th–14th century), Lobo Tuwa (northwest Sumatra, 11th–12th century), Kampong Sungei Mas (Kedah, Malaysia, 10th–11th century) and Pengkalan Bujang (Kedah, Malaysia, 11th–14th century), all of which have yielded large quantities of Chinese STONEWARE and Middle Eastern glass; Kota Cina and Pengkalan Bujang also share types of local pottery. The 12th–14th century complex of Buddhist temples of Padang Lawas, northeast Sumatra, may also be connected, along with smaller religious sites of the interior of Sumatra, such as Muara Takus.

Srubnaya culture or **Timber Grave culture** a Bronze Age culture of the steppes of the Volga and Don basins in southern Russia, succeeding the YAMNAYA culture. Srubnaya burials contain remains of horse trappings, and settlements have significant percentages of horse bones in their faunal samples, leading to the belief that mounted pastoralism was the dominant form of subsistence and settlement.

stadial a climatically cold episode of relatively short duration represented by deposits and processes characteristic of GLACIAL conditions. Compare INTERSTADIAL. See also STRATIGRAPHY.

stadium a long narrow running track, often surrounded on three sides by banks, sometimes tiered with seating. The name is derived from the term for the measurement of 600 (ancient) feet (178 m). An elaborate starting-gate has been excavated at Isthmia near CORINTH. Stadia were normally attached to major sanctuaries where athletic games took place (see DELPHI, OLYMPIA), but they were also among the public buildings of a Greek city.

stage a general level of cultural development, which can be regional, continental or even global in distribution. *Sensu stricto*, the concept has no temporal implications, but in practice it is often used as an integral part of the CHRONOLOGICAL sequencing of CULTURE HISTORY. Examples are the ARCHAIC, WOODLAND AND FORMATIVE.

stalactite/stalagmite see SPELEOTHEM, TRAVERTINE.

St Albans (*Lat.* Verulamium) a Roman town (*municipium*) in England built on the site of an earlier Iron Age capital. The early town was laid out in a grid pattern and traces of timber-framed shops have been found lining Watling Street. The town was destroyed by Boudicca (see COLCHESTER), but was rebuilt with a monumental FORUM which was opened in AD 79 by the governor Agricola. In addition to temples linked to strictly Roman cults, buildings apparently dedicated to native deities have been found. In the 2nd century a theatre was constructed. See also WHEELER.

stamnos a round-mouthed jar, with two horizontal handles mounted on the upper part of the body. It is a shape often decorated in the RED-FIGURED technique at ATHENS.

stamped decoration a technique normally used to decorate plain wares (see BLACK-GLOSSED). It first appears on ATHENIAN POTTERY in the middle of the 5th century BC, and frequently consists of patterns of PALMETTES. From the 4th century it was used in conjunction with ROULETTING. Figured stamps were also occasionally used. The stamp was cut onto the end of a rounded stick and applied by a circular motion.

stamp seal a SEAL that is pressed into the sealed material, rather than rolled as is a CYLINDER SEAL. In Bronze Age western Asia, the form as well as iconography of stamp seals tends to be correlated with culture areas; thus it is square in the Indus, round in the Persian Gulf (BARBAR), and COMPARTMENTED in Central Asia (BACTRIAN BRONZE AGE)

Stanca Ripiceni Cave an Upper Palaeolithic site on the Prut River in eastern Romania, located 200 m south of RIPICENI-IZVOR. Four cultural layers occur in the succession of cave deposits; among the associated faunal remains are horse, reindeer and steppe bison. The lowest assemblage includes BIFACES, SCRAPERS and BURINS, and probably dates to the earlier Upper Palaeolithic (i.e. › 25 000 bp). The three overlying levels apparently date to the late Upper Palaeolithic; the uppermost assemblage includes geometric MICROLITHS.

Stanwick an extensive late Iron Age enclosure in Yorkshire,

England, consisting of ditches and banks defining an area of some 300 ha around a small central nucleus. Originally interpreted as an encampment built by the CELTIC Brigantes in the 1st century AD in their resistance to the Romans, and the largest 'HILLFORT' in Britain, it is now thought to be no more than an enclosed private estate or demesne containing a number of residential compounds.

Star Carr   a waterlogged Earlier MAGLEMOSIAN lakeside settlement in Yorkshire, England, excavated by J.G.D. Clark in 1949–51 and dated to the 8th millennium bc. The damp conditions have led to the preservation of wooden tools and a large number of bone and antler ARTIFACTS, including 187 barbed points, 'mattock heads' of elk antler, and a group of perforated red deer frontlets which may have been worn as ceremonial or hunting masks. The faunal remains indicate summer occupation, probably by people based on the coast.

Starčevo culture   the earliest Neolithic culture of the western Balkans, named after a settlement site north of the Danube near Belgrade in Serbia, part of a broadly distributed complex of cultures that includes KARANOVO I, KREMIKOVCI, KÖRÖS and CRIŞ, *c*.5500–5000 bc. Starčevo settlements in the southern Balkans are generally TELLS, but further north in Serbia they are usually flat sites, reflecting an adaptation to the temperate continental environment. In the more northerly Starčevo sites, cattle bones exceed those of caprines in quantity, suggesting a shift from the pattern seen in the earliest Neolithic sites in the Near East, Greece and the southeastern Balkans. At LEPENSKI VIR, a Starčevo occupation lies over the settlement of complex foragers.

Staré Hradisko   a Late Iron Age OPPIDUM in Moravia, first occupied in the mid 2nd century BC and abandoned about a century later. Staré Hradisko has provided important information on manufacturing, including pottery-production using kilns. The interior of Staré Hradisko is subdivided by palisades into smaller units, possibly separate farmsteads.

star mound   a stone or earth structure in Samoa, about 2 m high and 10–15 m in diameter, with several projecting arms. Their function is unknown, but was probably religious. They are apparently recent in date.

Starosel'e   a Middle Palaeolithic cave-site in the Crimea. Artifacts and faunal remains were found throughout a thick deposit of LOAM and rubble; the presence of arctic fox and reindeer indicates cold climatic conditions (early or middle LAST GLACIAL?). The tools are primarily SCRAPERS and BIFACIAL FOLIATES. A mass of wild ass remains (at least 287 individuals), appears to be associated with the occupation, and has been interpreted as evidence that entire herds were driven over cliffs near the site. The skeleton of a child and isolated bones of an adult, both assigned to anatomically modern humans, were also found in the cave, but their relationship to the occupation is considered problematic. Starosel'e was excavated by Formozov during 1952–56.

state   a type of society, characterized by a strong, centralized government, socio-economic class divisions and a market economy. Populations are normally very large, and have cities and monumental architecture. It represents the most complex form of social organization.

stater   the Greek electrum and silver coin equivalent to the Near Eastern *shekel*. It was also the same as a *didrachm* (see DRACHMA).

statue–menhir   a standing stone with carving of schematic human figures, some in relief, others simply engraved lines. Found in southern France, northern and eastern Italy, and on Corsica and Sardinia, they include female figures with breasts and necklaces, and heavily armed male warriors. Most statue-menhirs are of Late Neolithic to Early Bronze Age date, but Iron Age examples are also known, e.g. in northern Corsica.

status   an individual position or rank in society, and the responsibilities and privileges that go with it. Status can be either *achieved*, whereby an individual works to gain a particular status in the course of his/her lifetime, or *ascribed*, in which status is gained by being born into a particular class or family.

steatite or **soapstone**   a soft, white to green massive rock consisting mostly of the CLAY mineral *talc*, a magnesium silicate that forms by hydrothermal alteration of ultrabasic rocks or by low-grade metamorphism of siliceous dolomites. The softness of steatite lends itself to carving and it was used to produce figurines and other carvings, jewelery, vessels, seals and decorative stone works. Steatite is fire resistant and was used to make moulds for metal casting.

Steep Cliff Cave   see SPIRIT CAVE.

Stein, Sir Mark Aurel (1862–1943)   an archaeologist, Hungarian by birth and British by choice, who was perhaps the greatest archaeological explorer of central and western Asia. His early training in SANSKRIT took him to India, where he developed an interest in antiquities to the north. Beginning in 1892 and continuing until 1930, Stein made four trips through western China and Khotan, where he documented a great many mediaeval monuments and caravan routes. Stein was made Superintendent of the Indian Archaeological Survey in 1910, a post he held until 1929, and he made a number of exploratory archaeological tours through Baluchistan and many parts of Iran, in which he located many important sites and made soundings in a number of them.

Steinheim   a German site near Stuttgart where a female HOMINID skull with prominent brow-ridges and certain similarities to the SWANSCOMBE skull was recovered in 1933 from GRAVELS dated to the HOLSTEINIAN interglacial. The skull belongs to an early form of HOMO *sapiens* with specific NEANDERTHAL characteristics.

stela or **stele**   an upright stone slab, often inscribed or carved in relief, and sometimes painted. In Egypt, the term denotes an upright slab (of stone or other durable material), usually with a rounded or flat top, upon which texts and illustrations intended to be of a permanent nature were inscribed. Funerary stelae were located in the publicly accessible superstructures of tombs; their subject matter related to the wellbeing of the deceased. Commemorative stelae were, typically, erected in TEMPLES as a record of a particular event, such as an endowment made to the temple by the king. Votive stelae recorded an individual's veneration of a particular deity or deities.

In MESOAMERICA, carved stone shafts are usually found with temples. Work by PROSKOURIAKOFF and others in deciphering them has demonstrated that they are historical monuments recording the exploits and genealogy of rulers (see e.g. QUIRIGUÁ).

Stellmoor see AHRENSBURGIAN, HAMBURGIAN.

Stentinello a Neolithic village site near Syracuse in Sicily, Italy, enclosed by rock-cut ditches, type-site of the Sicilian Stentinello culture (*c*.5600–4400 BC). The characteristic pottery is a development of CARDIAL or IMPRESSED WARE, with exuberant decoration covering the whole surface of the pot, sometimes with white chalky incrustation.

Stephens, John Lloyd (1852–1905) an early explorer of the MAYA Lowlands. A New York lawyer, Stephens travelled with the Englishman Frederick CATHERWOOD, in 1841 and 1843, and documented a number of little-known or unknown Maya sites. The accounts of these explorations, along with Catherwood's extraordinary drawings, provided an introduction to the ancient Maya lowlands civilization.

step pyramid a transitional form of Egyptian royal tomb, between the MASTABA of the early ARCHAIC PERIOD and the true PYRAMID of the OLD KINGDOM. The only known completed step pyramid is that of DJOSER.

Sterkfontein a series of fossiliferous cave fillings dating from perhaps 2.5 million years ago, near Krugersdorp in the Transvaal, South Africa. Since 1936, the site has produced the largest collection of AUSTRALOPITHECINE fossils in southern Africa. These are of the gracile species *Australopithecus africanus*, and include a complete adult skull described by Robert Broom as *Plesianthropus transvaalensis* and nicknamed 'Mrs Ples'. A remarkably complete cranium found in 1976 is attributed to HOMO *habilis*, thought to have been the manufacturer of EARLIER STONE AGE artifacts, variously described as DEVELOPED OLD-OWAN B or early ACHEULIAN (see KROMDRAAI, SWARTKRANS).

Steward, Julian Haynes (1902–72) an American archaeologist and ethnographer who worked on South American and Great Basin cultures, and was a major proponent of the re-emergence of evolutionary and ecological thought in American anthropology and archaeology. He argued that culture was heavily influenced by the specific local environment, and that regularities could thus be sought to explain cultural change.

Stichbandkeramik see STROKE-ORNAMENTED POTTERY CULTURE.

Stična an Early Iron Age fortified settlement with an associated group of BURIAL MOUNDS near Ljubljana in Slovenia, dated to the later part of the HALLSTATT period. The hill-top settlement at Stična was fortified by earth and stone walls which enclosed an area of about 32 ha. Over 6000 graves are known from the cemeteries, found primarily in about 140 burial mounds. Stična is located amidst iron deposits and a number of iron-SMELTING sites, which resulted in the development of this locality as a commercial centre.

Stirling, Matthew Williams (1896–1975) an American archaeologist, best known for his extensive work on the OLMEC, including the sites of LA VENTA, SAN LORENZO, TRES ZAPOTES and Cerro de las Mesas.

stirrup jar or **false-necked amphora** a CERAMIC container used to transport oil or perfume. First found in MINOAN Crete but more typical of MYCENAEAN Greece, they were widely exported.

stoa a Greek multi-purpose colonnaded building, single- or double-storeyed. Stoas could serve as a seat for magistrates, as house shops and as dining-rooms. They are often found lining the edge of an AGORA or a TEMENOS, where they would have provided shade from

stirrup jar

the sun or protection from the rain. The stoa adjoining the agora at ATHENS was decorated with painted plaques showing scenes from the battle of MARATHON (see SOROS).

Stone Age   1. the oldest and longest division of the traditional 'THREE AGE SYSTEM' devised by THOMSEN to classify the PREHISTORIC Period on the basis of technology. The Stone Age covers the period from the first production of stone artifacts to the first use of metals, and is of varying length in different areas of the world. It may be further subdivided into the Palaeolithic (Old), Mesolithic (Middle) and Neolithic (New) Stone Age.
2. (*sub-Saharan Africa*) the first and longest stage of human technology, beginning some 2.5 million years ago, and continuing in some areas until the 19th century AD, characterized by the production of tools made from stone as well as from other materials such as bone and wood. It is equivalent to the term Palaeolithic used in Europe and elsewhere (see ACHEULIAN, GOODWIN, EARLIER, MIDDLE and LATER STONE AGES, MIDDLE AWASH, OLDOWAN).

stone circle   a ring of standing stones, sometimes surrounded by a ditch. In the British Isles, almost 1000 stone circles are known dating from the Neolithic and Early Bronze Age, famous examples being those of CALLANISH, AVEBURY and STONEHENGE.

Stonehenge   a major Neolithic and Early Bronze Age ritual monument in Wiltshire, England. In its form (phase I *c.*3200 BC) Stonehenge was a typical HENGE monument surrounded by a bank with internal ditch *c.*100 m diameter, and a ring of 56 AUBREY holes (later used for cremation burials) immediately inside the ditch. In phase II, *c.*2200, some 80 BLUESTONES were brought to the site from the Preseli Hills of southwest Wales and set up in a double horseshoe arrangement. At the same time, the first section of the Avenue was built, flanked by banks and ditches and running over 500 m·downhill from the entrance to the monument. About 100 years later (phase IIIa), these bluestones were removed and the present SARSEN circle with lintels enclosing a horseshoe arrangement of five massive sarsen TRILITHONS was put in place. Several centuries later (phase IIIc), the bluestones were re-erected in a circle and horseshoe shadowing the sarsens. The final stage (phase IV) came in the Middle or Late Bronze

Age when the Avenue was extended some 2000 m to the east. Well known for its summer solstice orientation, Stonehenge has been interpreted as the temple of a sun or sky cult. Its social importance is reflected in the high density of Early Bronze Age burial mounds of the WESSEX CULTURE in the vicinity, including the Winterbourne Stoke and Normanton Down cemeteries, the latter including the famous BUSH BARROW.

stone line a descriptive term for a subsurface sheet of stones one layer thick within a SOIL which, when cut in vertical profile, appears as a line. Stone lines may consist wholly or in part of archaeological debris. Stone lines have various origins, including buried residual lag deposits on EROSION surfaces, stony STRATA inherited from stratified material, and PEDOTURBATION with selective size-sorting. The contextual interpretation of any archaeological debris in stone lines depends upon proper interpretation of stone line genesis. See also STONE ZONE.

stoneware a CERAMIC fired above 1000 °C and distinguished from earthenware by the formation of the mineral *mullite* in the ceramic body during firing. It is usually grey in colour, owing to firing in a reducing atmosphere in a kiln. In East Asia, stoneware was sporadically produced from the SHANG Dynasty onward, but mass production did not begin until the 3rd century AD, when the technique was transferred to the Korean peninsula and then to Japan from KAYA. See SUE.

stone zone a descriptive term for a subsurface BED of stones or stony material within a SOIL that is greater than one layer of stones thick. Stone zones may consist wholly or in part of archaeological debris. As with STONE LINES, stone zones have multiple origins, the correct assessment of which is necessary for the interpretation of any archaeological debris contained within the zone.

Stradonice a large Iron Age OPPIDUM in Bohemia, settled in the 2nd century BC during the LA TÈNE period. Stradonice was a production centre, particularly of fine painted CERAMICS. In addition, it contained a mint for coins, which are found within a 30 km radius.

Strandloper 1. 'beachcomber'. The innumerable SHELL MIDDENS along the southern African coast are popularly attributed to Strandlopers, who were incorrectly thought to have subsisted exclusively on a marine diet.
2. a South African coastal LATER STONE AGE industry of the last 2000 years, characterized by pottery, large FLAKES, flaked cobbles and rare RETOUCHED stone artifacts.

Stránská Skála a Lower Palaeolithic former cave-site located near Brno in Moravia, Czechoslovakia. Artifacts are buried in cave, slope and LOESS deposits that apparently antedate the Middle PLEISTOCENE (> 730 000 BP) on the basis of PALAEOMAGNETISM and associated fauna (e.g. sabre-tooth cat). The artifacts include CHOPPING TOOLS and FLAKES.

Strashnaya Cave a Middle Palaeolithic site in the Altai region of Siberia. Redeposited artifacts and faunal remains are buried in a deep sequence of LOAM and rubble. Among the faunal remains are woolly MAMMOTH, steppe bison, red deer, horse and many others; the absence of arctic species indicates occupation during a mild climatic interval (prior to the LAST GLACIAL?). The artifacts include LEVALLOIS CORES, SCRAPERS and some DENTICULATES. Strashnaya was excavated

STRATA

in 1969 and 1970 by OKLADNIKOV and Ovodov.

strata (*Sing.* **stratum**) or **layers**   informal SEDIMENTATION units greater than one centimetre thick, usually incorporated in BEDS.

stratification   a structure in sedimentary rocks or SEDIMENT produced by deposition of more or less tabular units such as BEDS, STRATA and LAMINAE. Changes in depositional conditions and sediment supply cause changes in sediment composition, TEXTURE and internal sedimentary structures, resulting in deposition of a unit contrasting with the immediately underlying unit, and thereby giving rise to stratification. Stratification is the basis for STRATIGRAPHY, which has archaeological implications regarding environmental interpretation, sequencing of events and construction of CHRONOLOGIES.

stratigraphy   the study of the formation, composition, sequence and CORRELATION of STRATIFIED SEDIMENT, SOILS and rocks. Stratigraphy is the principal means by which the CONTEXT of archaeological deposits is evaluated, chronologies are constructed and events are sequenced. It is governed by a number of stratigraphic principals developed to help order materials and events in time and space. Among the underlying principals are:

(a) law of superposition – older BEDS or STRATA are overlain and buried by progressively younger beds or strata.

(b) law of cross-cutting relationships – a feature that cuts across or into a bed or stratum must be younger than that bed or stratum.

(c) included fragments – fragments, material or debris from an older bed may be incorporated in a younger bed, but not *vice versa*.

(d) correlation by fossil inclusions – strata may be correlated based on the sequence and uniqueness of their floral and faunal content.

These principals carry no implications for absolute age or age differences, although CHRONOMETRIC DATING techniques may aid in establishing temporal relationships.

Stratigraphy applied to archaeological concerns has variously been called 'archaeostratigraphy' or 'archaeological stratigraphy'. The stratigraphy of an archaeological site is invaluable for interpreting the sequence of deposition of the site, and thereby the relative ages of artifacts, features and other phenomena in the site.

Straubing group   an Early Bronze Age regional group of Lower Bavaria, Germany, during the early 2nd millennium bc, sometimes classified as a regional variant of the ÚŇETICE culture.

Strelets culture   an early Upper Palaeolithic culture defined on the basis of several assemblages from the Oka-Don Lowland of the European Russia dating to *c.*40 000–25 000 bp; it exhibits some geographic and temporal variation. The earliest Strelets assemblages (e.g. lowest level of KOSTENKI I) reflect heavy emphasis on Middle Palaeolithic tools and techniques of production; the former include SCRAPERS, POINTS and BIFACES. Later assemblages (e.g. SUNGIR') contain a higher percentage of typical Upper Palaeolithic forms such as scrapers and BURINS, as well as some non-stone tools and art objects. The most diagnostic tool type throughout the sequence is a small triangular bifacial point with a concave base.

strigil   a rounded bronze or silver scraper used in the Greek and Roman worlds to remove olive oil which was applied after bathing or taking exercise in the GYMNASIUM. On ATHENIAN POTTERY strigils are shown in the hands of athletes, often in conjunction with an ARYBALLOS.

striking platform   the part of a CORE which is struck to produce a FLAKE (where see figure), and which becomes partially detached from the core with the flake. The striking platform may be plain, or it may be prepared or flattened by removing small facets to produce a longer and thinner flake.

Stroke-Ornamented Pottery culture   an Early/Middle Neolithic culture of west-central Europe (Bohemia, southwestern Poland, eastern and southern Germany) which follows the LINEAR POTTERY culture in this area between c.4000 and 3800 bc. On Stroke-Ornamented Pottery, the continuous incised lines that characterize Linear Pottery disappear and are replaced by lines of small stroke-like jabs or depressions. LONGHOUSES of the Stroke-Ornamented Pottery culture (often called by its German name, *Stichbandkeramik*) are often slightly trapezoidal in plan.

Strong, William Duncan (1899–1962)   an American who was a pioneer in Plains archaeology. He helped develop the Direct Historical Approach of working back through archaeological sequences from the known historical past, and made significant contributions to the development of a distinct archaeological theory in the years between the two world wars.

structural archaeology   a branch of archaeology, closely linked to POSTPROCESSUAL ARCHAEOLOGY, that studies CULTURE as a set of symbols and codes that determine how individuals act in a society. Culture must be viewed as more than just an adaptation to the environment. These structural codes connote particular meanings to members of society, meanings that can change depending on their particular context. Thus, a safety pin used in association with a baby has one set of meanings, but connotes an entirely different meaning if used as decoration by a punk rocker. Structural archaeology is concerned with how individuals manipulate the meaning of MATERIAL CULTURE, as embedded in structural codes, in order to make new statements and to create new meanings. Because of its concern with the meanings evoked by the symbolic nature of material culture, structural archaeology is virtually synonymous with what is often called *symbolic* or *cognitive* archaeology.

stucco   a lime plaster, especially that used for creating interior architectural elements such as masks or for providing a surface for walls.

stupa   a Buddhist monument, usually built to contain relics associated with the Buddha or other holy people or sacred texts; miniature stupas might also be built as votive offerings, and Hindus of the Jainist sect built stupas in commemoration of saints. They occur throughout the Buddhist world, and tend to be constructed in places sacred to Buddhism, but the architectural form varies in different regions (domed in northern India, multi-stage pagodas in China, Japan and Korea, terraced temples in Java). One of the best-known Indian stupas is the 2nd century BC complex at Sanchi (in Madhya Pradesh), which comprises domed stupas on circular bases, enclosed by stone railings ornamented with carved reliefs showing events in Buddha's life and mythological figures.

Sturts Meadows a PANARAMITEE site in western New South Wales, Australia, about 40 km from MOOTWINGEE. The engravings occur on a series of mudstone outcrops extending for over a kilometre. RADIO-CARBON dating of carbonate DESERT VARNISH on the engravings has yielded a minimum age of 10 000 bp.

Subalyuk a Middle Palaeolithic cave-site located in the Bükk Mountains of northeastern Hungary. Artifacts and faunal remains are buried in clay and rubble deposits; ibex predominates in the lower levels, but CAVE BEAR predominates in the upper. Middle Palaeolithic tools (chiefly SCRAPERS) occur in both lower and upper levels, and appear to pre-date the LAST GLACIAL. Human skeletal remains, exhibiting classic NEANDERTHAL characteristics, were found in the upper levels.

Sub–Atlantic climatic period the last of five POSTGLACIAL climatic periods of northern Europe defined on the basis of POLLEN ANALYSIS by Blytt and Sernander, beginning *c.*1500 bc. The Sub-Atlantic period is characterized by a continuation of the trends towards dampness and coolness that began during the preceding SUB-BOREAL period.

Sub–Boreal climatic period one of five POST-GLACIAL climatic and vegetational periods defined by Blytt and Sernander on the basis of POLLEN ANALYSIS, dated between *c.*3000 and 1500 bc. In northern Europe, the Sub-Boreal has been thought of as a cooler and drier period, especially in contrast to the preceding warmer and more humid ATLANTIC period, but it now appears that in central and.southern Europe the climate became moister because of the southward displacement of the polar air masses and the resultant climatic perturbation.

Suberde a small ACERAMIC NEOLITHIC settlement near Lake Sugla in southern Turkey, excavated by Jacques Bordaz in the 1960s and 70s. It presents a later 7th millennium BC example of a relatively permanent community that seems to have relied heavily on hunting (sheep, goat, cattle, pig) and some harvesting of possibly wild cereals (an inference based on SICKLE SHEEN and grinding equipment). The case of a possibly specialized hunter's village in a landscape of farming communities is also presented at MUREYBET and UMM DABAGHIYAH.

Submycenaean the transitional phase which bridges the Late HELLADIC and PROTOGEOMETRIC periods in Mainland Greece. Although characterized on the basis of the pottery from cemeteries in Attica, Submycenaean is also attested stratigraphically on sites in Central Greece and the Peloponnese. It would appear to have been a relatively short phase and is currently dated *c.*1050–1020 BC.

subsistence that part of the overall economy of a society concerned with the acquisition, production and distribution of food resources.

Sue a Japanese grey, unglazed STONEWARE of the late 5th–14th centuries AD, derived from the KAYA stoneware traditions on the Korean peninsula. Originally imported and then centrally produced in Japan for funerary use, it was deposited in MOUNDED TOMBS of the KOFUN period for containing food offerings. Within the RITSURYO state, it became a standardized court service ware, and production sites were decentralized to the provinces to supply additional regional administrative headquarters. Compare HAJI.

Sukhaya Mechetka or **Volgograd** a Middle Palaeolithic open-air site on the Volga River at Volgograd in European Russia. The occupation horizon rests on the surface of a buried soil thought to be of Last INTERGLACIAL age, underlying a thick bed of slope deposits. Among the heavily weathered faunal remains, steppe bison is the most common species. The artifacts include both SCRAPERS and BIFACIAL FOLIATES. Along with KHOTYLEVO I, Sukhaya Mechetka represents one of the few Last Interglacial sites on the Russian Plain. The site was discovered by Grishchenko in 1951, and excavated by Zamyatnin from 1952–54.

Sukhothai   an early Thai state in north-central Thailand, founded in the mid 13th century AD, expanding outwards from its core towns of Sukhothai and SI SATCHANALAI late in the century, then coming under the influence of the state of Ayuthya in the 15th century. Its best-known remains include the Ram Khamhaeng inscription of AD 1292 (the first known record written in Thai language), a collection of Buddha images of a distinctive style (to which the state has given its name), and a range of GLAZED STONEWARE vessels (characterized by under-glaze decoration in black/brown on a cream SLIP) produced by kilns in the town during the 14th–15th centuries, and forming part of the repertoire of the much larger industry at Si Satchanalai.

sumatralith   a unifacially flaked discoid stone tool, often formed on a thin slice of the CORTEX of a large pebble, characteristic of some HOABINHIAN assemblages in Southeast Asia, particularly in coastal SHELL MIDDENS in north Sumatra. See fig. on p.214.

Sumerian king lists   a group of CUNEIFORM documents assembled in the early 2nd millennium BC in southern MESOPOTAMIA, that offer a partly mythical and partly historical summary of ruling dynasties. Beginning with the lowering of kingship from the heavens, the list begins with a series of kings, first at ERIDU and then at other cities, who ruled for tens of thousands of years; this series ends with the FLOOD. Afterwards, kingship was once again lowered, first at KISH and then at other cities; the earlier of these kings reigned hundreds of years but regnal spans soon became biologically plausible and some of these rulers (especially at Kish) are known from contemporary EARLY DYNASTIC documents (see GILGAMESH). The list continues to the early 2nd millennium. In addition to its mythical aspects, the king list is not an attempt at history, as it presents contemporary rulers as sequential in time, and does not include many important dynasties (e.g. that of Lagash; see TELLO). Rather, the variations of list have a political purpose, namely to validate contemporary royal authority by lineally tracing kings at the time of their composition to the beginnings of kingship in southern Mesopotamia.

Sumerian question   the traditional academic question of Sumerian origins, in both a cultural and, especially, a linguistic sense. The Sumerian language has no known relatives, and is poorly understood, making impossible the kinds of comparative analyses found in INDO-EUROPEAN studies. To the extent that the archaic CUNEIFORM texts of southern MESOPOTAMIA (i.e. those of the Late URUK and JEMDET NASR periods, in the later 4th millennium BC) are comprehended, the language is already Sumerian. Some elementary Sumerian vocabulary (some place names, terms in basic economic activities) is often argued to be adopted from some pre-Sumerian population, implying a movement of Sumerian speakers into a southern Mesopotamia that was already occupied by settled agriculturalists. However, this linguistic argument is contested, and the archaeological record reveals no perceptible break in a continuous cultural development. In short, the Sumerian question is a problem not at present open to solution.

Sumerians   people speaking and writing Sumerian who are the earliest documented inhabitants of southern MESOPOTAMIA. Sumerian is unrelated to any other known language, and considerable controversy surrounds the question of Sumerian origins (see SUMERIAN QUESTION). The Sumerians, along with AKKADIAN-speaking elements in southern Mesopotamia, created in the late 4th and 3rd millennia BC a tradition of social and political organization, art, literature and religious observation that greatly influenced neighbouring cultures and provided many of the central features that defined the Mesopotamian world until the end of its existence.

sun-dagger   see FAJADA BUTTE.

Sundaland   the enlarged Southeast Asian continental region created by the drop in sea levels during periods of GLACIATION, which connected much of western Indonesia to the mainland.

Sungir'   an Upper Palaeolithic open-air site on the Klyaz'ma River (Oka tributary) near Vladimir in European Russia. After the Pechora Basin sites (e.g. BYZOVAYA), it is the northernmost Palaeolithic site in Europe. The occupation horizon is associated with a buried soil in slope deposits overlying a bedrock promontory, and appears to date to *c*.25 000 bp, although RADIOCARBON estimates range between 25 500 and 14 600 bp. Reindeer is the most common species among the fauna. The site is best known for its spectacular burials, which contain three complete skeletons and numerous associated ornaments and art objects, including ivory spears, bracelets, brooches, ivory beads (*c*.10 000) and over 200 perforated fox teeth. The artifacts, which include small triangular bifacial points and many typical Middle Palaeolithic forms, have been compared to the STRELETS CULTURE assemblages from KOSTENKI. Sungir' was discovered in 1955, and excavated by BADER during 1956–70.

sun temple   a religious structure built by kings of the 5th DYNASTY of Egypt for the worship of the sun-god RE. Architecturally the sun temple resembles the PYRAMID COMPLEXES of the same period, with valley temple and causeway leading to the Upper Temple. The main elements of the Upper Temple were a large open court, containing an altar, which stood before a monumental, squat, masonry-built OBELISK. Of the six sun temples known to have been built, only those at ABUSIR and ABU GHURAB have so far been located.

survey or **surveying**   1. the examination of the surface of the earth for archaeological SITES, and their recording and preliminary analysis. Because of constraints of time and money, many surveys are sample surveys, in which only a portion of the total area under consideration is actually examined. Samples can be drawn either intuitively, in which the archaeologists only look at those areas in which they feel sites will be found; or they can be statistically generated using a variety of techniques. The latter type of sample is more representative of the total area, and thus more accurate.
2. the three-dimensional plotting of a site, its FEATURES and ARTIFACTS, using a variety of techniques borrowed mostly from civil engineering. Techniques can range in sophistication from a hand-held

compass and hand-drawn map, to computer- and satellite-assisted location systems. See EXCAVATION, TRANSIT, THEODOLITE, PLANE TABLE, ALIDADE.

Susa   one of the great sites of western Asia, lying in the Khuzistan lowlands in southwestern Iran, at the southeastern edge of the MESOPOTAMIAN alluvial plain. Systematic excavation here began in the 1880s, and has been continued over the past century by a succession of French teams. These efforts reveal an unbroken succession of occupation from around 4000 BC to early mediaeval times. The archaeology of Susa does not present a single encompassing cultural sequence, but rather a series of sequences from separate excavation areas loosely tied together by CERAMIC parallels and periods in the city's history (see ACROPOLE OF SUSA). The cultural and political history of Susa traces multiple cycles of looking towards the civilizations of southern Mesopotamia to the west and of integrating with peoples in the mountains to the east; in the latter connection, Susa was traditionally associated with Anshan (Tepe MALYAN) in Fars. Susa was frequently controlled or deeply influenced by a succession of Mesopotamian neighbours, but just as frequently was the centre of autonomous ELAMITE states, and often invaded BABYLONIA. Susa's success in the latter regard is reflected in the numerous pieces of famous Mesopotamian art that have been recovered there (including the Victory STELA of NARAM-SIN, HAMMURABI's law code, and many KASSITE KUDURRU).

Susquehanna Tradition   a late ARCHAIC TRADITION in northeast North America that is characterized by particular stemmed points and knives. Some of the earliest point styles may have evolved from earlier PIEDMONT TRADITION forms.

Sutton Hoo   a group of 6th and 7th century AD burial mounds in Suffolk, England, marking the royal cemetery of the Wuffingas, early ANGLO-SAXON kings of East Anglia. The fame of the site rests on the discovery in 1939 of a richly furnished ship-burial beneath mound 1, with sword, shield and decorated helmet of Swedish style, large gold belt buckle with intricate animal interlace, and purse and cloak clasps with designs in multi-coloured glass. There were also Merovingian gold coins from France and silver vessels from BYZANTIUM, providing further testimony of the importance of the deceased, who may have been the powerful East Anglian ruler Raedwald (d. 625). The site has been excavated by C.W. Phillips and, more recently, by M. Carver.

Swanscombe, Barnfield Pit   a well stratified British Lower Palaeolithic site by the River Thames which has yielded a fragmented skull belonging to an early form of HOMO *sapiens* with strong NEANDERTHAL characteristics. Typical CLACTONIAN artifacts have been recovered from the Lower Gravel, an ACHEULIAN pointed BIFACE assemblage has come from the Middle Gravel, and the Upper Loam has produced a refined OVATE Acheulian assemblage.

Swarling   see AYLESFORD.

Swartkrans   a cave with a series of fossiliferous deposits, thought to date between 1.8 and 1 million years ago, close to STERKFONTEIN and KROMDRAAI in the Transvaal, South Africa. The site has produced a large sample of robust AUSTRALOPITHECINE remains since 1948. Stone artifacts attributed to the DEVELOPED OLDOWAN are present, while polished and scratched pieces of bone are thought to have been used to dig up edible bulbs. Fire-blackened bones dating to between 1.5 and 1 million years ago may be the oldest known direct evidence for the use of fire in the archaeological record.

Sweet Track   a Neolithic timber trackway preserved in the water-logged PEAT deposits of the SOMERSET LEVELS, England, and excavated by J. and B. Coles. The track was an ingenious raised plank walkway running for 1800 m across wet reed swamp from the southern end of the Levels to Westhay island. DENDROCHRONOLOGY has dated the construction precisely to the winter of 3807/3806 BC, making it Europe's oldest road.

swidden agriculture   a system of farming in which fields are prepared by cutting down the natural vegetation, letting it dry and burning it off. This technique serves to clear the field and enrich the soil with nutrients from the ash. Swidden fields are generally productive for no more than a few years, after which the farmer moves to a new area and repeats the process. Swidden agriculture is common throughout much of MESOAMERICA. See also SHIFTING CULTIVATION.

Swiderian   a late Upper Palaeolithic industry of Poland characterized by BURINS, SCRAPERS and SWIDERIAN POINTS. Swiderian sites are associated with DUNE deposits dating to the end of the PLEISTOCENE (*c.* 11 000–9000 BP). See also BROMMIAN.

Swiderian point   a type of stone point manufactured on a BLADE, with a stemmed base flaked on both sides. It is found in sites of the SWIDERIAN industry in Poland.

Swiderian point

Swidry   a group of Upper Palaeolithic open-air sites located along the Vistula River in Poland. Concentrations of artifacts (including SCRAPERS, BURINS and SWIDERIAN POINTS) are deposited on sand DUNES thought to date to the end of the PLEISTOCENE (*c.* 11 000 BP). These sites are assigned to the SWIDERIAN CULTURE.

Swieciechów flint   a variety of flint from the HOLY CROSS MOUNTAINS of central Poland (compare CHOCOLATE FLINT, CMIELÓW). It is dark grey to black in colour with flecks of white or light grey. It was exploited primarily by communities of the FUNNEL BEAKER culture and was distributed over a broad area in the Bug, Vistula and Oder drainages. Swieciechów flint is commonly found in the form of very large BLADES up to 30 cm long, and axes.

Sydney Cove   a well preserved wreck found in 1977 on Preservation Island in the Furneaux Group, Bass Strait, Australia, and the subject of detailed archaeological research since then. Wrecked in

1797, she was the first merchant ship to founder in Australian waters after the settlement of New South Wales; her cargo of spirits attests to the importance of the rum trade in the colony. Expeditions mounted after the wreck established the existence of Bass Strait.

syllabic, *adj.* denoting scripts such as LINEAR A and B in which each of the signs represents a syllable.

symbolic archaeology see STRUCTURAL ARCHAEOLOGY.

Symbolkeramik CHALCOLITHIC pottery of ALMERIA found at LOS MILLARES and similar sites, decorated with incised *oculi* or 'rayed sun' motifs, sometimes in pairs.

symposium a male drinking-session held at the end of a Greek meal. Scenes of the symposium frequently appear as the decoration on Greek pottery. These show the wide range of activities which took place in addition to drinking, such as music, singing, games and sexual intercourse. Many of the vessel forms for Greek pottery are connected to the symposium either as cups or for containing or mixing the wine and water. See AMPHORA, KRATER, PELIKE, KLINE.

synchronic or **synchronous,** *adj.* occurring simultaneously or at the same time. The term is often used in CORRELATION of events or bounding surfaces of STRATIGRAPHIC units, or to characterize the equivalency of age across a widespread bounding surface. Compare DIACHRONIC. See also ISOCHRONOUS.

Syracuse a Corinthian colony in southeastern Sicily, traditionally founded *c.*734 BC. The city took advantage of the fine natural harbour. The earliest settlement was on the island of Ortygia, whereas later settlement was on the mainland in the area known as Achradina. A series of temples were constructed in the 6th century BC in both the DORIC and IONIC ORDERS. The temple of Athena was later incorporated into the cathedral. On the mainland are remains of the theatre, as well as the quarry which also served as a prison in the late 5th century BC. The city was defended by the Euryalus fort. In 21 BC the city became a Roman colony. Roman remains include a substantial AMPHITHEATRE constructed in the 3rd century AD.

Syuren' I an Upper Palaeolithic cave-site in the Crimea, Ukraine. Three occupation horizons are buried in a thick bed of sand and rubble. The most common species among the faunal remains are saiga and arctic fox, the latter indicating cold climatic conditions. The age of the occupations is unclear; they are thought to date to the earlier Upper Palaeolithic on typological grounds. Many elements typical of the Middle Palaeolithic (e.g. points) and AURIGNACIAN industry (e.g. keeled endscrapers, see SCRAPER) are present. Along with ADZHI-KOBA, Syuren' I represents one of the rare Upper Palaeolithic sites of the Crimea. The site was investigated by Merezhkovskij in 1879–80, and by Bonch-Osmolovskij in 1926–29.

Szakalhát-Lebo group a Middle Neolithic culture of the Tisza River valley in eastern Hungary, succeeding the Alföld variant of the LINEAR POTTERY CULTURE south of the Körös River, and preceding the TISZA culture between *c.*4100 and 3800 bc. Settlements of this group such as Csóka have small rectangular single-room structures. The figurines resemble those of the early phases of the VINČA culture immediately to the south, but the pottery is decorated in patterns associated with the Alföld Linear Pottery variant.

Szeleta Cave a prehistoric cave-site located on the Szinva River in the Bükk Mountains of northeastern Hungary. Artifacts and faunal remains (CAVE BEAR (predominant), reindeer and woolly MAMMOTH) are buried in rubble and 'cave earth' deposits. The lowest cultural layer comprises a small quantity of Middle Palaeolithic (?) artifacts. The overlying layer contains an assemblage (including LAUREL-LEAF POINTS and SCRAPERS) assigned to the early Upper Palaeolithic SZELETIAN industry; it yielded a RADIOCARBON date of › 41 700 bp. Szeletian assemblages also occur in the upper layers, the youngest of which yielded a date of 32 620 bp, and Neolithic remains were found near the surface. Szeleta Cave was excavated by Hillebrand in 1906–13 and VÉRTES in 1966.

Szeletian   an early Upper Palaeolithic industry of Central Europe characterized by BIFACIAL FOLIATES and sidescrapers (see SCRAPER); later assemblages contain more endscrapers and RETOUCHED BLADES. The industry dates to the middle of the LAST GLACIAL, and appears to develop from the local Middle Palaeolithic (MICOQUIAN). The Szeletian was defined by PROŠEK in 1953.

Szelim   a prehistoric cave-site located near the River Danube in north-central Hungary. Artifacts and faunal remains (including CAVE BEAR (predominant), reindeer, and woolly MAMMOTH) are buried in LOESS and clay. The lower cultural layer contains a Middle Palaeolithic assemblage (e.g. sidescrapers – see SCRAPER) that probably dates to the beginning of the LAST GLACIAL. Late Upper Palaeolithic, Neolithic and younger remains occur in the upper layers.

T

taap knife   a saw-knife, known only from the southwest of Western Australia, comprising small stone chips mounted in a row on a wooden handle. In ethnographic specimens, the chips are unretouched and irregular in shape, but BACKED MICROLITHS may have been used in the past.

Tabon Caves   a series of caves on Palawan in the Philippines which have produced remains ranging in date from *c*.22 000 bc to the late metal age. The skeletal material of Tabon Cave (*c*.22 000–20 000 bc) is younger than dates at NIAH, but perhaps more securely dated, and it falls within the same date range as LEANG BURUNG 2 in Sulawesi. Later remains at the caves include jar burials of the 1st millennium BC and later, related both in form and in contents (LINGLING-O, double-headed animal pendant) to SA HUYNH on the Vietnamese coast and KALANAY in the islands.

Tabun   a prehistoric cave-site in the MOUNT CARMEL complex, Israel, excavated by GARROD from 1929–34, which has yielded NEANDERTHAL-like human remains. The archaeological levels have been classed as successively TAYACIAN, Final ACHEULIAN, JABRUDIAN, AMUDIAN and LEVALLOISO-MOUSTERIAN. RADIOCARBON dates range from 51 000 to 38 800 BP; ESR dates from *c*.200 000 to 90 000 BP.

Taforalt   a large Moroccan cave, excavated by J. Roche, with a long sequence from MOUSTERIAN, through ATERIAN to an IBEROMAURUSIAN SHELL MIDDEN on top. A large Iberomaurusian cemetery of 185 people, including 100 children, of MECHTA-AFALOU type, is dated to 11 900 bp. The site's lowest Iberomaurusian layers have been dated to *c*.22 000 bp.

Tagalagal a Neolithic site at a boulder-hill in northeastern Niger, dating to *c*.9300 bp, which has provided some of the oldest dates for CERAMICS in the Sahara. Stone tools include BURIN-like FLAKES and delicate arrowheads, as well as much grinding equipment.

taiga see BOREAL FOREST

Taima–Taima a site in Venezuela at which were found MASTODON bones and a small quantity of stone tools. It has been suggested by R. Gruhns and A.L. Bryan that the site represents a pre-CLOVIS occupation, between 12 000 and 15 000 years ago. Other scholars question whether the tools were truly associated with the bones.

Taipivai Valley a site on Nuku Hiva in the Marquesas Islands in Polynesia, with many stone structures. These include VAHANGEKU'A, and ANTHROPOMORPHOUS stone statues of a type also known from the PUAMAU VALLEY.

Tairona a late prehistoric culture in northeastern Colombia, organized at the level of a CHIEFDOM. One of the larger sites is Pueblito, which includes as many as 3000 houses, as well as public architecture. Most sites are villages, with a central PLATFORM MOUND.

Tajín see EL TAJÍN.

Takamatsuzuka a MOUNDED TOMB of KOFUN-period dating to the late 7th century AD. Located in Nara Prefecture, Japan, the small round mound, 18 m in diameter and 5 m high, contains a stone chamber with plastered walls bearing painted murals of the Chinese directional symbols (see MURAL TOMBS). These were first assigned to KOGURYO influence, but recent opinion favours a Tang attribution (see CHINESE DYNASTIES). The tomb belonged to an aristocrat of the YAMATO state with continental connections.

Takuapa an early historic settlement and religious centre in peninsular Thailand, connected to the port at KO KHO KAO, with remains indicating contact with South India in the early 2nd millennium AD.

Talasea an OBSIDIAN source on the north coast of New Britain, BISMARCK ARCHIPELAGO. Talasea obsidian first occurs in Late PLEISTOCENE contexts at MATENKUPKUM and MATENBEK, and is widely distributed in early LAPITA sites throughout MELANESIA; in later Lapita sites, it tends to decline in importance relative to LOU obsidian.

talatat stone blocks of relatively small size (the Arabic term refers to three hand-breadths) used in Egypt for the rapid construction of TEMPLES of the AMARNA PERIOD.

talayot a massive Bronze Age dry-stone tower, usually with central chamber, found on the Balearic Islands. Roughly equivalent to the Sardinian NURAGHE, talayots display a broader range of forms with circular, square and stepped examples. Many later became the centre of a small village of dry-stone houses.

talc see STEATITE.

talent a unit of Greek and Near Eastern weight. It was the equivalent of 60 MINAS; at ATHENS it would have weighed 25.86 kg, and on AEGINA 37.80 kg.

Talgai   the site in southern Queensland of the first human fossil skull found in Australia, in 1886. The cranium is robust and archaic-looking, resembling the KOW SWAMP material. It has not been firmly dated, but the deposits in which it was found have a minimum age of 14 000 to 16 000 bp.

Tamar Hat   a small, but very rich Algerian cave, probably a camp for hunting Barbary sheep, with 3 m of IBEROMAURUSIAN remains. These show only gradual change through time, indicating re-use of the site by people and their descendants for nearly 5000 years. This is the only Iberomaurusian sequence excavated to bedrock, where it is dated at *c*.20 600 bp. (See ARAMBOURG.)

Tamaya Mellet   one of several sites in the Tamesna of Niger in Africa, containing bone HARPOONS associated with lacustrine fauna at *c*.9400 bp (see 'AQUALITHIC').

tambo or **tampu**   a waystation along the INCA road system. Tambos were located a day's travel apart, and equipped with storehouses and rest houses. More elaborate tambos were established every four or five days' travel apart. Stationed at each tambo were runners, *chaski*, who carried messages in relay fashion throughout the empire.

Tambo Colorado   an INCA administrative centre located in the Andean foothills in the Pisco Valley of south coastal Peru. The site is well preserved, including red-painted walls which give the site its name. It lies along an important Inca road connecting the coast with VILCAS GUAMAN.

Tambo Viejo   a large site in the Acarí valley of the south coast of Peru. It was occupied during early NASCA phases of the EARLY INTER-MEDIATE PERIOD, and represents an extension of Nasca culture to the south. A part of the site was reoccupied during INCA times, when it served as a TAMBO along the royal highway of the Inca.

Tambralinga   an early historic state located in peninsular Thailand in the later 1st and early 2nd millennium AD, centred probably on NAKHON SI THAMMARAT, and possibly encompassing CHAIYA.

Tampanian   the stone tool INDUSTRY of KOTA TAMPAN.

tampu   see TAMBO.

Tanagra   a town in Boeotia, Greece, best known for the discovery in the late 19th century of numerous TERRACOTTA figurines in its cemeteries. Many date from the HELLENISTIC period. More recently MYCENAEAN CHAMBER TOMBS have been excavated in the area.

Tang   see CHINESE DYNASTIES.

tang   a projection at the base of a tool or weapon which could be attached to a handle or shaft.

Tanis   probably the most important archaeological site in the Nile DELTA of Egypt, the chief excavations being carried out by PETRIE in 1883–86 and by MONTET in 1929–51. It is best known for the rich, and largely intact, royal tombs of the 21st and 22nd DYNASTIES (*c*.1070–715 BC) which were constructed within the precincts of the great TEMPLE of the god AMEN. It seems likely that much, if not all, of the large quantity of comparatively early material excavated at Tanis (e.g. of the OLD KINGDOM, MIDDLE KINGDOM, RAMESSES II) was transported there by kings of the 21st and 22nd Dynasties to adorn their building works at the site.

Tanjong Rawa   see KUALA SELINSING.

Tanum   a major concentration of Scandinavian prehistoric ROCK ART in Bohuslän, Sweden. The designs are pecked on glacially smoothed rock surfaces and depict ships, ploughing scenes, warriors armed with spears and battle axes, carts, and possible sun discs. The many-oared ships, sometimes with fighting warriors, are particularly characteristic. Dating is difficult but the Tanum art is attributed mainly to the later Bronze Age.

taotie [t'ao-t'ie]   a Chinese Neolithic design motif first occurring on JADE objects of the LIANGZHU culture, then adapted to bronze in the SHANG period. In its earlier form it is thought to represent a person wearing a cap of rank; later, it evolved to form a mythic animal figure with claws, horns, etc. See ANYANG.

taotie

Taperinha   a prehistoric riverine SHELL MIDDEN of several hectares near Santarem, northern Brazil, where investigations by Anna Roosevelt have proved that this part of the lower Amazon has the oldest pottery in the New World, dated by AMS and TL to the 8th millennium BP (see also PRECERAMIC, FORMATIVE).

taphonomy   the study of the transformation of materials into the archaeological record. Originally the term was limited to the examination of these processes for living organisms (i.e. processes affecting the composition and completeness of a skeleton after the animal's death). Unlike ETHNOARCHAEOLOGY, the focus of taphonomic studies is the understanding of the processes resulting in the archaeological record *per se*. See also ACTUALISTIC STUDY.

Taputapuatea   a MARAE on Raiatea, Society Islands (Polynesia), which was a centre for the worship of the god Oro. The surviving platform (AHU) is 40 m by 7 m and faced with coral slabs up to 4 m high. Shell from the platform fill is dated to the 17th century AD.

Tara   the Hill of Tara, Co. Meath, seat of the pre-Christian and early Christian High Kings of Ireland. It is encircled by the RATH na Riogh, the 'Fort of the Kings', a large enclosure like that at NAVAN with ditch inside bank and therefore non-defensive in nature. At the centre of the enclosure are two conjoined raths or ringforts probably of early Christian date, with a third rath just outside the enclosure. The earliest monument on the Hill, within the Rath na Riogh, is the Mound of the Hostages, a small Neolithic PASSAGE GRAVE dated *c.*2800 BC.

Tarascans or **Purépecha** a people of Central Mexico, contemporaries of the AZTECS but not under their subjugation. Their original capital was *Tzinzunzan*; later it was *Pátzcuaro*.

Tardenoisian   the final MESOLITHIC culture identified in southwest France following the SAUVETERRIAN and characterized by the presence of geometric MICROLITHS but few woodworking tools. The Tardenoisian is found in Iberia and central Europe but did not spread to Britain, possibly because of the newly formed English Channel. The Tardenoisian shows definite Neolithic influences. It is named after the French site of Fère-en-Tardenois, Aisne.

Tarentum (*Gk* Taras)   a colony of SPARTA in southeastern Italy founded in the late 8th century BC. It takes advantage of a fine natural harbour. There is also some MYCENAEAN pottery. The earliest city was located on the peninsula now occupied by the Citta Vecchia. Tombs of the ARCHAIC PERIOD have yielded large numbers of imported Greek pots. In the CLASSICAL period Tarentum may have been a production centre for some APULIAN POTTERY as well as TERRACOTTA figurines.

Tarquinia   the greatest of the ETRUSCAN cities, in Tuscany, Italy, with remains of a powerful wall and the base of the great central temple, the Ara della Regina which had TERRACOTTA winged horses in its PEDIMENT; both were built in the 4th/3rd century BC. To the east the important VILLANOVAN cemetery of Selciatello (10th to 7th century BC) relates to the earliest period of the city's development; the principal Etruscan cemetery, with burial mounds covering FRESCOED rock-cut tombs, is at Monterozzi to the south. Tarquinia was absorbed into the Roman confederacy in 353 BC and enjoyed several more centuries of prosperity before post-Roman decline and destruction by Arab raiders in the Early Middle Ages. The city was served by the port of GRAVISCA.

Tarsus   a prehistoric site in coastal Cilicia, southwestern Anatolia, where H. Goldman's excavations in the 1930s and 1950s at a location called Gözlü Kale produced a sequence that complements that of MERSIN; together they provide the basic framework for the region. Although the Tarsus excavation reached late Neolithic and CHALCOLITHIC levels, these are contained in a very small exposure and are more fully known at Mersin. The subsequent levels, opened over larger areas, contained a series of Early Bronze Age occupations not evident at Mersin. During this time the settlement changed character several times, with the first fortification appearing in EBA II level; the pottery and small finds, which previously had correlated with the 'AMUQ sequence (up through 'Amuq F), now find more similarity with Anatolian forms to the northwest (as far away as TROY II–IV). The Middle Bronze Age levels contain a painted pottery similar to that at Tell ATCHANA (XVI–VIII), followed by Late Bronze Age occupations that include a walled HITTITE temple compound and a large Hittite administrative building. The site also contains an important series of Iron Age deposits, as well as later (to the early mediaeval period) occupation.

Tărtăria   a Late Neolithic site in west-central Romania where in a VINČA pit were found three unbaked clay tablets with incised signs, which some have claimed bear a resemblance to signs from JEMDET-NASR and URUK in MESOPOTAMIA. There is about a 1000-year discrepancy between the Tărtăria tablets and the later Mesopotamian symbols, suggesting that the resemblance is coincidental. Since then, similar tablets have been found in a slightly later context at GRADESNITSA in Bulgaria.

Tartessos   an early trading state at the mouth of the River Guadalquivir in southern Spain, referred to by East Mediterranean writers of the 8th century BC as a source of gold, silver, tin and lead.

Taruga   a central Nigerian Iron Age site where TERRACOTTA figures of the NOK culture were found in association with large quantities of domestic pottery and iron SMELTING debris and furnaces. These are dated between the 5th and 3rd centuries BC and are among the oldest so far discovered in West Africa.

Tarxien a Late Neolithic temple complex in Malta, comprising remains of four temples. The first, of which little survives, was built in the Ggantija phase c.3300 BC. Two further temples of four-apse type (the South and East Temples) were built at the beginning of the following Tarxien phase c.3000–2500 BC. The South Temple is particularly fine, with carved running spirals and the lower part of a large standing statue originally c.2.75 m tall. A door in the right-hand rear apse leads into the Central Temple, of six apses with central niche, the fourth and last in the sequence. The temples were abandoned c.2500 BC and the area became a cem. ery of inurned cremation burials in the so-called Tarxien Cemetery phase c.2500–1500 BC.

Tasian an early phase of the BADARIAN. The term was coined by Brunton, from the site of Deir Tasa, but it is not now generally regarded as a valid description of a distinct cultural group.

Tasmania an island that, during the PLEISTOCENE, was part of SAHUL but was cut off from mainland Australia by rising sea levels about 8000 bp. Occupation of southwest Tasmania by 30 000 bp is now well established (see NUNAMIRA CAVE) and numerous other extraordinarily rich sites in the area document the adaptation of the southernmost humans during the Pleistocene (see KUTIKINA, WARGATA MINA). Tasmania did not share in the developments associated with the AUSTRALIAN SMALL TOOL TRADITION on the mainland, and EDGE-GROUND TOOLS, MICROLITHS and the DINGO are all absent. The simplicity of the Tasmanian material culture at European contact has long been fascinating to anthropologists and archaeologists. Changes did, however, occur in HOLOCENE Tasmania and are well documented by the ROCKY CAPE sequence. The arrival of Europeans was disastrous for the Tasmanians, who were almost exterminated during the 19th century (see ROBINSON, WYBALENNA).

Tasmanian tiger see THYLACINE.

Tassili n'Ajjer a rugged massif in southeastern Algeria, famous for its ROCK ART, which covers most of the Saharan sequence and includes wild animals, human figures, domesticated cattle and chariots.

Tata a Middle Palaeolithic open-air site located near the River Danube in north-central Hungary. Artifacts and faunal remains (e.g. woolly MAMMOTH (predominant), extinct horse, and wild ass) are buried in LOESS deposited between layers of spring SEDIMENT; the cultural layer apparently dates to the early LAST GLACIAL. The tools include sidescrapers (see SCRAPER), BIFACES and some Upper Palaeolithic types. Tata was excavated by VÉRTES in 1958–59 and others, and yielded a carved and polished segment of mammoth molar, and a fossil with an engraved line on it, both dating to c.100 000 bp.

taula a Bronze Age ritual monument found on the Balearic Islands, consisting of two carefully cut stone slabs balanced one on top of the other, sometimes with mortise-and-tenon joint, to form a 'T'. The largest taula, at Trepuco, is 4 m high.

Taung a 2 million year-old fossiliferous deposit at a quarry in Bophuthatswana, South Africa, which produced the first AUSTRALOPITHECINE fossil in 1924. This so-called 'Taung baby' consisted of the face and *endocranial* (brain) cast of a young child, named *Australopithecus africanus* by DART in 1925.

Tautavel or **Caune de l'Arago** a cave-site in the Pyrénées-Orientales, in southern France. Excavations by H. de Lumley since 1964 have revealed a 10 m stratigraphy containing Middle PLEISTOCENE/Lower Palaeolithic material. Associated with an archaic TAYACIAN industry on QUARTZ were a number of human remains, notably the front part of a skull. Opinions are divided about classing these as HOMO *erectus* or as archaic NEANDERTHALERS; dating is also complex, but it is thought they lie between 320 000 and 200 000 BP.

Tawantinsuyu the name given by the INCA to their empire. It means 'the four inextricably linked quarters.'

Taxila a great city in northwestern Pakistan, explored by J. Marshall and later by others, that contains three major settlements, Bhir, Sirkap and Sirsuleh. Bhir is an unplanned walled town whose earliest levels date to around 500 BC and which continued in use up to the founding of Sirkap. Sirkap is a planned settlement founded in the 2nd or 1st century BC and lasting into the 2nd century AD; here blocks of buildings are laid out on a regular grid of streets, and an interior wall divides the place into upper and lower cities. Sirsuleh was an early Kushan foundation (perhaps 1st or 2nd century AD), and continued this succession of cities. At Sirkap, the upper city contains the Hathial mound group where recent excavation has revealed earlier settlements. Hathial A contains at least two phases of occupations, the earlier with CERAMIC parallels to the KOT DIJI tradition (dated perhaps 2000 BC) and the later a settlement belonging to the middle phase of the GANDHARA GRAVE culture (dated around 1000 BC). Hathial B (the 'citadel' of Sirkap), on the other hand, contains a sequence that spans the range 700 BC to AD 100.

taxonomy a system of classifying ARTIFACTS or other cultural material into discrete units or *taxa,* based on their similarities to each other. Taxonomy is the basis of the organization of archaeologically recovered MATERIAL CULTURE.

Taya, Tell a site in the northwestern Sinjar area of northeastern Iraq containing extensive stone architecture that is largely visible on the surface. Julian Reade's programme in the late 1960s to early 1980s of excavation and extensive mapping indicates that the site was occupied from very late EARLY DYNASTIC times into the early 2nd millennium BC (Khabur ware), with later NEO-ASSYRIAN, PARTHIAN and Islamic settlement also present. Most of the visible architecture belongs at the beginning of this sequence, and formed a walled inner area of dense architecture covering 65 ha and an outer zone of more scattered buildings over another 90 ha. The mapping project presents one of the clearest pictures of town layout yet available for a large settlement in 3rd millennium MESOPOTAMIA.

Tayacian a rather nebulous term which has been used to describe probably unconnected Lower and Middle Palaeolithic industries which have no BIFACES and no well-made FLAKE tools. The name was derived from material at LA MICOQUE in LES EYZIES-de-Tayac. See FONTÉCHEVADE.

Taylour, Lord William (1904–89) a British archaeologist whose principal excavations were at MYCENAE, where he uncovered the cult centre, and at Ayios Stefanos in Laconia.

Tayma   an Iron Age city in the Hejaz region of northwestern Arabia, best known as the place where Nabonidus (555–539 BC), the last king of the NEO-BABYLONIAN empire, resided for ten years. Its archaeology is poorly known. A contiguous series of large walled compounds, one of them enclosing a small mound, form the centre of the town, with large walls extending from these to enclose nine square kilometres. Set in one of the latter walls is an excavated cultic area, formed as a linear series of rooms set on a natural rock outcrop; one of these rooms contains a stone block, on two sides of which are carved cultic scenes with an iconography derived from the MESOPOTAMIAN world (probably ACHAEMENID). A number of STELAE with Aramaic inscriptions also belong to this part of the 1st millennium BC.

Te Awanga   a fortified ridge PA, at Tiromoana, Hawkes Bay, NEW ZEALAND. Excavations by Aileen Fox revealed remains of palisades, a large rectangular house and distinctive raised-rim sweet potato storage-pits. Unusually early dates from storage pits suggest that these features may date back to the earliest settlement, although old timber may have been used. See also KAURI POINT, OTAKANINI.

Tegdaoust   see AWDAGHAST.

Tehuacán Valley   a semi-arid highland valley in Puebla, Mexico. The valley, about 1800 m above sea level, has one of the longest continuous archaeological sequences in MESOAMERICA (7000 BC–AD 1520). Research in the valley was conducted primarily by Richard MacNeish in the 1960s. His work, primarily in cave and rockshelter sites, documented changes in subsistence from a period of hunting and gathering and incipient agriculture (AJUEREADO and EL RIEGO PHASES) to a major reliance on domesticated foods (ABEJAS and PURRON PHASES). Archaeological materials from the earlier phases are considered part of the DESERT TRADITION. The Tehuacán Valley research represents significant findings in the origins of agriculture, and the shift to dependence on agriculture, in Mesoamerica.

Tekkalakota   a prehistoric site of the southern Deccan in Karnataka, southwestern India. Nagaraja Rao's excavations here in the 1960s revealed two successive occupations (Tekkalakota I–II) dated to the 2nd millennium BC. Both occupations contain the mud or stone floors of circular (sometimes rectilinear) huts in which were various pieces of household equipment; these dwellings are scattered on a hill slope. Around and in the settlement are burials, which in Tekkalakota I are secondary and in Tekkalakota II are usually extended or in urns. Metal objects, though rare, occur in both periods; mostly copper tools, although gold is also present in the earlier period. The fauna emphasizes domesticated cattle, while finger millet and *horse gram* (a legume) exist in Tekkalakota I. This cultural configuration, found also in other sites of the region (e.g. Bramagiri, HALLUR, PIKLIHAL) represents a food-producing adaptation to the hill country of southern India.

Telanthropus   a genus previously used for early HOMO fossils from SWARTKRANS.

Telarmachay   a PRECERAMIC (9000–2000 bp) rockshelter located on the PUNA of central Peru, at an altitude of 4420 metres. Excavations by Danièle Lavallée indicate that the site was seasonally occupied, and that *in situ* camelid domestication took place there. She argues that structured mobility was a more likely subsistence adaptation than the sedentary occupation suggested by Rick in the case of PACHAMACHAY.

Teleilat Ghassul   the Palestinian type-site of the GHASSULIAN, chiefly excavated by Mallon and Koppel in 1929–38 and by the British School of Archaeology in 1967–78. Tuleilat Ghassul is particularly known for its polychrome geometric and figurative mural paintings on the walls of the rectangular MUD-BRICK houses, which were often lime-plastered.

Tell   for sites beginning 'Tell', see under other element of name.

tell (*Arabic* 'mound' or 'hill')   a major archaeological feature of settlement sites in the Near East. A *tell* is an artificial mound created by the accumulation over centuries of stratified layers of disintegrated MUD-BRICK walls and cultural debris, brought about by new phases of occupation being built upon the ruins of their predecessors on the same site. The terms *tal, tepe, depe* and *hüyük* refer to the same phenomenon in areas adjacent to MESOPOTAMIA. As a site type, *tells* are variable in size, comprising the extremely low mounds of villages as well as those of major cities, and may refer to a single mound or a series of connected mounds. In many places in western Asia ancient *tells* are still being occupied, that at Erbil in northern Iraq being a famous example.

Tellem   a pre-Dogon society with large NECROPOLISES in the Bandiagara escarpment of Mali, Africa, dated between the 11th and 16th centuries AD.

Tello, Julio Cesar (1880–1947)   a Peruvian archaeologist of mostly native ancestry, educated in science and medicine in Peru, and in anthropology at Harvard. He excavated at many of the major sites in Peru, including CHAVÍN, PARACAS, HUARI, PACHECO and PACHACAMAC. He argued that Chavín was the first major civilization in the Andes, a view that has only recently fallen from favour. Tello founded what is today called the National Museum of Anthropology and Archaeology in Lima; he is buried in a courtyard on the museum grounds.

Tello   a site identified as Girsu, the capital of the Lagash city-state in early southern MESOPOTAMIA; the French work at Tello, begun by Ernst de Sarzec in 1887 and continued by various others until 1933, revealed for the first time the character of SUMERIAN civilization. Although poorly executed by modern standards of stratigraphic control, de Sarzec's work recovered many important pieces of Sumerian art (e.g. the 'STELA of the Vultures', the silver vase of Entemena, the statues of GUDEA) and also a significant corpus of EARLY DYNASTIC III and UR III CUNEIFORM texts. The latter represent the richest available body of written evidence for the social, political and economic affairs of the Early Dynastic III Mesopotamian city-states, and also provide valuable evidence for the GUTIAN 'dark age' and Ur III administrative practices. The rulers of Lagash include the line of Enannatum, which fought a protracted border war with Umma, the later Uruinimgina (Urukagina) who is known for his administrative and religious reforms, and the post-AKKADIAN Gudea famous for his statues and building programmes. Girsu was occupied from late 'UBAID to OLD BABYLONIAN times, and also has a late 1st millennium BC palace.

Tembeling   a river valley of the interior of peninsular Malaysia with sites yielding Neolithic and metal age remains. The former include the curved stone 'Tembeling knife' from such sites as Nyong, and the latter include iron tools (see TULANG MAWAS) and a DONG SON bronze drum from Batu Pasir Garam.

temenos   a Greek sanctuary or sacred precinct at a cult centre (see AKROPOLIS, DELPHI, OLYMPIA). It could contain numerous buildings such as the NAOS, housing the main cult, and a series of THESAUROI, STOAS, as well as dedications from worshippers.

Temet   a Neolithic site in northeastern Niger, Africa, dated to about 9500 BP, and covered by more than 6 m of DIATOMITE deposits. The stone industry contains BLADES, BLADELETS and MICROLITHS, indicating the association of these types.

Temnata Cave   a Palaeolithic site located in central Bulgaria. Artifacts and faunal remains (e.g. woolly MAMMOTH, bear) are buried in deposits of clay and rubble. The lowest cultural layer contains a Middle Palaeolithic assemblage (sidescrapers – see SCRAPER – predominate among tools), which may date to the early cold maximum of the LAST GLACIAL. A younger Middle Palaeolithic assemblage with BIFACIAL FOLIATES was found outside the cave. The upper levels in the cave contain AURIGNACIAN and GRAVETTIAN assemblages. Temnata Cave was investigated by Kozłowski and others.

temper   crushed material added to a clay to improve its firing qualities. Temper may be stone, various organic materials or broken pottery. See CERAMICS.

temple   a building with a religious function. The structure of the many imposing temples of the CLASSICAL world has been studied in particular detail (see ADYTON, ANTA, CELLA, OPISTHODOMOS, PRONAOS).

In *Egypt*, archaeological evidence, especially the well-preserved examples of the Graeco-Roman Period (e.g. EDFU), indicates that from at least as early as the NEW KINGDOM the basic layout of an Egyptian temple was composed of a number of well-defined elements:

(1) the PYLON;

(2) an open *courtyard,* with colonnades on at least the lateral sides and often also at the front and rear;

(3) the HYPOSTYLE HALL;

(4) the *sanctuary,* which was the central element of a CULT TEMPLE, containing the image of the deity, usually housed within a NAOS.

The number of these elements within any individual temple, especially pylons, courtyards and hypostyle halls, was largely the result of additions and alterations by successive kings. The sacred precinct of a town, including the temple and its associated buildings, was surrounded by a massive MUD-BRICK enclosure wall. See fig. overleaf.

temple mound   an artificial hill constructed of earth and stone on which stands a temple or some other ceremonial building. In MESOAMERICA, these structures are terraced, or stepped. In some cases, as in the Temple of Inscriptions at PALENQUE, temple-mounds served as tombs.

Temple Mound Period   the period following the BURIAL MOUND period, when many cultures in eastern North America built large PLATFORM MOUNDS. It begins approximately AD 800 and continued to the time of European contact. It is often used synonymously with the MISSISSIPPIAN.

temple An Egyptian temple.

Temple of the Crossed Hands   see KOTOSH.

Templo Mayor   see TENOCHTITLÁN.

Tenerian   a Neolithic industry of the Tenere Desert and surrounding areas of Niger, Africa, dating to between 6500 and 4500 BP, and associated with a pastoral economy that was possible in the climatic conditions that prevailed in the Sahara at the time.

Tenochtitlán   the great AZTEC capital, located where Mexico City now stands. The city was founded in AD 1325 on an island in Lake Texcoco. The Aztecs reclaimed the swampland in this part of the lake, building artificial islands on which houses and other structures were placed, and constructing CHINAMPAS and other agricultural plots. It was linked to the mainland by three causeways.

Tenochtitlán was an excellent example of planned urban growth. Through the city ran six major north-south, and two major east-west canals, with smaller canals feeding into them. Houses along streets and canals were on stone-faced platforms. The city had between 60 and 70 wards, corresponding to kinship units. Each ward had communally constructed public buildings. The wards were divided between four principal districts. The district of Tlatelolco held a large market.

At the centre of Tenochtitlán was the major ceremonial precinct. Palaces, temples, BALL COURTS and other public buildings were arranged around plazas. The *Templo Mayor* (Great Temple) dominated the precinct. It comprised a truncated pyramid, on which were two temples, one dedicated to the Aztec patron god, Huitzilopochtli, and the other to the rain god, TLALOC.

Tenochtitlán fell to CORTÉS in 1519, while under the rule of Moctezuma II, and later of Cuauhtémoc. By 1522, the city had virtually disappeared. The ruins of residences filled the canals, and the Spaniards disassembled buildings and used the stone in the construction of their own city.

Teotihuacán ('place of the gods' in NAHUATL)   a major site in the northeastern part of the BASIN OF MEXICO, in the Teotihuacán Valley. Outstripping CUICUILCO, located at the southern end of the Basin, in power, size and population, by AD 100 Teotihuacán had about 40 000 inhabitants. At its peak, between AD 450–650, Teotihuacán was the largest city in the preindustrial world, with a population of at least 200 000. It was a planned urban centre from its inception.

Teotihuacán's rise to power is attributed to its advantageous position on a trade route, its monopoly over an important OBSIDIAN source, the favourable conditions for intensive agricultural production in the Basin, and the religious significance of the site. Teotihuacán controlled much of the obsidian manufacture and trade throughout MESOAMERICA, and its position on a natural trade route to both the south and east allowed it to control the trade of other goods also. Both KAMINALJUYÚ and MATACAPAN, as well as other centres, were under the domination of Teotihuacán. Evidence for this influence is seen in the predominance of Teotihuacán art and architectural styles. Other sites (e.g. TIKAL, MONTE ALBÁN and CHOLULA) also show evidence of interaction with Teotihuacán. At some times, military strength was involved in Teotihuacán's occupation of these centres; but at others, it appeared limited to commercial or religious influence.

At the heart of the city's 20 sq km is a complex of major structures, including the huge PYRAMIDS of the Sun and Moon (that of the Sun is 210 m square at the base, and 64 m high), distributed along a central road called 'The Street of the Dead'.

In 1971 a ceremonial cave was discovered under the Pyramid of the Sun. It has been suggested that the location of the temple, as well as the city as a whole, may be related to the cave. Teotihuacán was probably an important religious site, to which many made pilgrimages. This aspect of the city probably also increased its influence throughout much of Mesoamerica.

After AD 650, the population of Teotihuacán began to decline. By 750, the city had been destroyed. Currently, there are no satisfactory explanations for the demise of Teotihuacán. Climatic deterioration and invasion by semi-nomadic groups are the two commonly given reasons for its fall. The archaeologist George Cowgill has also suggested that the inefficiencies of the bureaucratic system played a role in its end.

Leopoldo Batres carried out the first major excavations at Teotihuacán in 1905. More recently, Ignacio BERNAL undertook excavations at the site, René Millon conducted a detailed mapping project of the city, and William T. Sanders carried out a settlement pattern survey of the Basin of Mexico.

Tepe   for sites beginning 'Tepe', see under other element of name.

tephra   a general term for all air-borne volcanic ejecta emanating from a volcanic vent during eruption. Tephra includes volcanic dust, ASH, cinders, lapilli, scoria, pumice, bombs and blocks, any of which can cause rapid burial of cultural debris. Tephra beds cover a broad area and are deposited essentially instantaneously, making them ideal STRATIGRAPHIC markers. Furthermore, most tephra can be dated by POTASSIUM-ARGON DATING and FISSION TRACK DATING methods. See TEPHROCHRONOLOGY.

tephrochronology   a dating method utilizing ages, widespread distribution, and CORRELATION of TEPHRA layers and the application of the results. Ages can be determined radiometrically by POTASSIUM-ARGON DATING and RADIOCARBON DATING, and radiogenically by FISSION TRACK DATING. Because tephra BEDS are essentially ISOCHRONOUS they provide throughout their extent limiting ages on overlying and underlying material, including archaeological deposits. Identification of multiple tephra beds may provide bracketing ages for intervening STRATA. Tephrochronology has also been used to date and correlate glacial advances, sea level changes, and ALLUVIAL FANS.

tepidarium   a warm room in a Roman bath-house. Attached to it was a plunge-bath which would have made the atmosphere of the room humid. See THERMAE.

terminus ante quem (*Lat*. 'the end before which')   a term used to provide fixed points in the STRATIGRAPHY of a site or in the relative dating of ARTIFACTS, *before* which something occurred. For example, the presence of Early Ripe CORINTHIAN POTTERY at SELINUNTE, thought to have been founded in 629/8 BC, provides a *terminus ante quem* for the production of that style of pottery. The presence of datable material such as pottery or coins above a destruction layer would provide a *terminus ante quem*. Compare TERMINUS POST QUEM.

terminus post quem (*Lat*. 'the end after which')   a term used to provide fixed points in the STRATIGRAPHY of a site or in the relative dating of ARTIFACTS, *after* which something occurred. For example, the lack of pottery decorated with ROULETTING at MOTYA, a site destroyed in 397 BC, is thought to be a *terminus post quem* for the introduction of the technique. The presence of datable material such as pottery or coins STRATIFIED under a destruction layer would likewise provide a *terminus post quem*. Compare TERMINUS ANTE QUEM.

Ternifine　an ACHEULIAN site in Algeria from which three well-preserved human mandibles and a skull fragment attributed to HOMO *erectus* were recovered.

Terra Amata　a French Lower Palaeolithic site located in Nice and excavated by de Lumley in 1966 who dates it to the MINDEL GLACIATION (*c.*380 000 BP). It has been claimed that the site may have been used annually for 15 successive years by ACHEULIAN hunter-gatherers who built fires and erected tent-like constructions during the late spring or early summer.

terra sigillata　a type of Roman pottery, normally red-glossed, to which were applied stamps often bearing the name of the potter. It was produced in several centres, especially in the western Mediterranean: see ARRETINE WARE, SAMIAN WARE.

terrace　**1.** a LANDFORM consisting of a level to gently sloping former alluvial surface, restricted to a valley, elevated above the active FLOODPLAIN, and bordered on one side by a valley wall or SCARP ascending to a higher terrace, and on the other side by a scarp descending to a lower terrace or the modern valley floor. Terraces form as the result of changes in stream regimen, caused by numerous factors, and can be either erosional or depositional in origin. Terraces may exhibit relict floodplain landforms, providing the basis for interpreting former valley conditions, processes and environments. Terraces are often favoured loci for human activity because of their intermediate position between upland and bottomland resources, and their relatively well-drained LANDSCAPE situation. Archaeological deposits associated with terraces are equal in age or younger than the terrace. Older archaeological deposits may be buried in alluvial fill beneath the terrace. Where multiple terraces exist in a valley, successively lower terrace levels are progressively younger, a fact that can be used to advantage in archaeological SURVEYING, tempered by the possibility that younger terrace veneer deposits may be present and obscure the archaeological record. See BENCH.

2. a landform consisting of a level to gently sloping former platform elevated above current sea level, lake levels or dry lake beds. This type of terrace can have associated beach ridge (see FOSSIL BEACH) landforms and wave-cut platforms (see BENCH). Marine terraces form as a result of oscillations of sea level, common during the QUATERNARY, caused by the interaction of vertical changes in sea and land levels. Archaeological material associated with this type of terrace are no older than the activity that created the terrace. Marine terraces, and associated archaeological deposits, may be submerged as the result of later, higher sea level stands.

terracotta　'baked earth', or fired clay, which is still quite porous; artifacts are mostly in the form of figurines, simple vessels, tablets or loom weights. See CERAMICS.

terracotta army　see QIN.

terramara (*pl.* **terremare**)   the name given to Middle Bronze Age settlements in the Emilia region of northern Italy, on account of their rich black organic occupation deposits, used as fertilizer by local farmers.

Těšetice-Kyjovice   a site of the LENGYEL culture in southern Moravia, which includes a circular enclosure with a ditch about 60 m in diameter with four entrances oriented approximately to the cardinal points of the compass. Within the enclosure were two concentric palisades, with gates at the points where entrances break the ditch. Traces of settlement occur outside the enclosure, the function of which is uncertain.

Teshik Tash   a Middle Palaeolithic cave-site with five levels of a MOUSTERIAN industry, located at 1800 m altitude in Tadjikistan in Central Asia, and excavated by A.P. OKLADNIKOV in 1938–39. Teshik Tash, dated to *c.*44 000 BP, is best known for its NEANDERTHAL child burial. Subsequent work in the region has revealed a large number of Mousterian sites whose industries have been divided into several distinct FACIES.

tessellated, *adj.*   (of Roman MOSAIC floors) formed by TESSERAE.

tessera   a small cube of stone, glass or tile set in concrete and used to form part of a Roman MOSAIC.

tetrastyle   **1.** four columns forming the façade of a CLASSICAL building such as a NAISKOS.
2. four columns placed in a square pattern, such as at the four corners of an IMPLUVIUM within the ATRIUM of a Roman house.

Teufelsbrücke   an Upper Palaeolithic site located on the Saale River in eastern Germany. Five cultural layers, apparently dating to the end of the PLEISTOCENE, are buried in sediments at the entrance of a nearly collapsed rockshelter. Faunal remains include horse, reindeer and arctic fox. The assemblages contain bone points and HARPOONS, and are assigned to the late MAGDALENIAN. A RADIOCARBON date of 13 025 bp has been obtained.

Téviec   a small island off the coast of Brittany, France, containing a SHELL MIDDEN excavated by the Péquarts in 1928–34. It has a MESOLITHIC cemetery of 10 graves which have yielded 23 burials, some accompanied by stag antlers, shell jewellery and red OCHRE, and associated with 'ritual' HEARTHS. The site has been dated to 6575 bp.

texture   **1.** a property of SEDIMENT and SOILS defined by the relative proportions of GRAVEL, SAND, SILT and CLAY size particles that is in part a function of DEPOSITIONAL ENVIRONMENT. Soil texture class names are assigned to soil or sediment with specific ranges of percentages of sand, silt and clay. Boundary percentages and class names vary according to which of the several recognized texture classification systems is used.
2. the size, shape and arrangement of constituent grains in igneous, metamorphic and sedimentary rocks. Rock texture is an important criterion in various rock classification schemes. The texture of ARTIFACTS is one property that in combination with others may help to identify material source. CERAMICS can be described by texture defined by the geometrical aspects of its constituents, which may provide clues as to the origin and manufacturing techniques and technology.

Thames pick   a term occasionally used for a large and crudely made MESOLITHIC TRANCHET axe.

Thapsos a Middle Bronze Age cemetery of *c*.400 rock-cut tombs in Sicily, Italy, mostly reached by a vertical shaft and used for collective inhumations. Type-site of the Thapsos culture of eastern Sicily, it is characterized by decorated pottery, bronze swords and daggers, and MYCENAEAN imports including pottery and FAIENCE beads.

Thebes the site of a MYCENAEAN palace in Boeotia, Greece, identified on the basis of the FRESCOES, jewellery and in particular the LINEAR B tablets which have been discovered in excavations under the modern town. The layout of the palace remains uncertain, and investigation of CLASSICAL and Mediaeval Thebes, the most powerful city in Boeotia, is equally problematic.

Thebes (Egypt)–East Bank the city of Waset in UPPER EGYPT, called Thebes by the Greeks, was one of the most important cities of ancient Egypt. On the east bank of the Nile was the main part of the city itself; it is now mostly overbuilt by the modern town of Luxor, apart from the TEMPLE largely constructed by AMENHOTEP III and RAMESSES II, while a short distance to the north was the temple of KARNAK.

Thebes (Egypt)–West Bank the NECROPOLIS of the ancient city of Waset, and the largest concentration of standing monuments in Egypt. These fall into two major categories: MORTUARY TEMPLES and royal/private tombs, the latter being dug chiefly into the cliffs and valleys of the Theban mountain, while the former are mostly sited on the narrow desert plain between the mountain and the cultivated land close to the Nile. Both types of monument are best represented by examples of the NEW KINGDOM. The most important Mortuary Temples are those of Nebhepetre Montuhotep and HATCHEPSUT (both at DEIR EL-BAHRI), RAMESSES III (at MEDINET HABU), Ramesses II ('the Ramesseum'), Seti I, and the COLOSSI OF MEMNON. The largest concentrations of royal tombs are at el-Tarif (11th DYNASTY), Dra Abu el-Naga (17th Dynasty) and the VALLEY OF THE KINGS, while the burials of several members of the royal families of the 19th–20th Dynasties are to be found in the Valley of the Queens.

theodolite a SURVEYING instrument consisting of a focusing telescope that is able to pivot on both horizontal and vertical planes; scales for measuring vertical and horizontal angles; and some type of levelling device. It is used to survey and map sites and surrounding environments, to plot excavation units and debris, and for topographic mapping. See TRANSIT.

Thera or **Santorini** the volcanic island in the Cyclades which erupted cataclysmically *c*.1500 BC, burying the prehistoric settlement at AKROTIRI under a thick layer of TEPHRA. MARINATOS suggested that it was this eruption which caused the collapse of the MINOAN civilization, but the destruction of sites on Crete appears to have occurred at least a generation later.

Thericleian ware a form of decoration described in literary sources and essentially belonging to the late 5th, 4th and 3rd centuries BC. Silver, *terebinth* wood (from pistachio trees) and clay seem to be the three main media used. Various characteristics are noted which include ribbing and a black colour (see PSEPHOPERIBOMBETRIOS). Extant candidates seem to be the BLACK-GLOSSED pottery. The name is derived from the name of Therikles, a Corinthian potter, who is said to have developed the technique.

thermae a bath-complex in the Roman world which contained not only rooms of different temperatures (see FRIGIDARIUM, CALDARIUM, TEPIDARIUM) but also exercise areas (see PALAESTRA). See also APODYTERIUM.

Thermi   the site of a Bronze Age settlement on the Aegean island of Lesbos, excavated by Lamb in 1929–33. Thermi was colonized early in the 3rd millennium BC by settlers who had close links with sites in northwestern Anatolia and who also traded with the Cyclades. The settlement grew to a considerable size and was eventually fortified before being abandoned. After several centuries Thermi was resettled and was finally destroyed by fire, apparently in the 13th century BC.

thermoluminescence (TL)   a radiogenic dating technique developed for dating fired archaeological material; suitable for dating QUATERNARY SEDIMENTS deposited in a range of depositional environments, particularly LOESS, other AEOLIAN deposits, and COLLUVIUM; and still undergoing refinement. Sediments and materials buried in them are exposed to radiation from decay of radioactive ISOTOPES which causes energy in the form of displaced electrons to be stored in electron traps within mineral crystal lattices. When heated or exposed to light, trapped electrons in the crystal lattice are freed, releasing energy in the form of light referred to as thermoluminescence. The signal is a measure of the accumulated radiation exposure, or equivalent dose: the longer the exposure or the stronger the radiation level, or dose rate, the greater the emitted thermoluminescence of a sample. When archaeological material such as pottery is fired, any stored energy in mineral grain inclusions is released and the thermoluminescent clock is reset. Upon burial, the mineral inclusions begin to store energy anew.

A new technique, *optically stimulated luminescence* (OSL), measures the luminescence emitted by a mineral when exposed to visible light, for example green laser. TL and OSL can be used on the same minerals, such as quartz, and produce dates back to about 300 000 years.

thesauros   a treasury resembling a NAISKOS located in a TEMENOS as a store for the valuables of distant states. An elaborate series of thesauroi have been excavated leading up the sacred way at DELPHI. Many were highly decorated with sculpture, and thus served to make a statement about the importance of the city which had dedicated them. For example, the so-called Siphnian treasury had CARYATIDS on the porch, and a continuous sculpted frieze.

Thiessen polygons   polygons constructed around SITES (or features) on the landscape in such a way that the area enclosed by each polygon is nearer to the site used to define the polygon than it is to any other site. The resulting pattern serves as a MODEL for understanding, amongst other things, the exploitation territories of individual settlements. The areas so defined can be tested against archaeological data for their closeness of fit.

thin section   a sample chip that has been ground down to a paper-thin (0.03 mm thick) sheet and mounted on a glass slide beneath a cover slip. It is used in PETROLOGICAL ANALYSIS of the mineralogical composition of CERAMICS, stone ARTIFACTS and SOILS.

tholos   a round chamber with attached rectilinear entrance passage in Greek architecture, in particular the CORBEL-VAULTED MYCENAEAN tombs, also known as *beehive* tombs, exemplified by the Treasury of Atreus at MYCENAE.

tholos A beehive tomb.

Thomas, Cyrus (1825–1910)   an American scholar famous for his pioneering studies of the mounds of the American Midwest. After careful and detailed analysis, Thomas was able to demonstrate that these mounds had been built by the ancestors of contemporary NATIVE AMERICANS. See ATWATER, DAVIS, HAVEN, SQUIER, POWELL.

Thompson, Sir John Eric Sidney (1898–1975)   an English ethnographer and archaeologist who worked in the MAYA area. In 1926, Thompson joined the Carnegie Institution excavations in the Yucatán. He was a pioneer in the study of Maya HIEROGLYPHIC writing. Thompson also studied the contemporary Maya, suggesting that aspects of Precolumbian culture had persisted to modern times. Thompson was the first New World archaeologist to be knighted.

Thomsen, Christian Jurgensen (1788–1865) a   Danish antiquary and curator of the National Danish Museum of Antiquities, most famous for devising the THREE AGE SYSTEM. The first *ethnoarchaeologist* (using modern people's stone tools to explain the uses of PREHISTORIC ARTIFACTS), he also called for osteological studies, chemical analysis of pot-residues, and study of the mutual relationships of artifacts in graves.

Thorikos   an area in Attica, Greece, that lies just north of the Laurion hills and is a rich source of metallic ores from which COPPER, silver and lead were being extracted as early as the 3rd millennium BC. In the MYCENAEAN period, Thorikos evidently prospered since two THOLOS tombs were constructed on the AKROPOLIS. In the 5th and 4th centuries BC, ATHENS exploited the Laurion mines intensively and a number of ore refineries were built, but the most impressive CLASSICAL structure is an unusual elliptical theatre. See LAURION.

Thoth   an Egyptian deity, usually depicted as an ibis-headed man, although the baboon was also an animal sacred to this god. Thoth was particularly associated with the activities of scribes and was later identified with the Greek god Hermes. His main cult-centres were at HERMOPOLIS MAGNA, and Hermopolis Parva in the DELTA.

Thracia or **Thrace**   the eastern part of the Balkan peninsula north of the area of Greek settlement, extending to the shores of the Black Sea. In the 5th century BC Thracia encompassed the territory of modern Bulgaria and Romania. In the 4th century, its leader Seuthes established a state-level POLITY on Greek and Macedonian models, with a capital at Seuthopolis, but this state was short-lived. By the 2nd century AD, Thracia had become a province of the Roman Empire, territorially equivalent to the southern part of modern Bulgaria.

Three Age System   a MODEL devised by Christian THOMSEN for organizing the ARTIFACTS on display at the National Museum in Copenhagen. The system was first publicized with the opening of the museum in 1819, and was later expanded in a formal guidebook written by Thomsen in 1836 (the first English translation appeared in 1848). The system has become the primary organizational framework for the whole of European PREHISTORY. The model proposes that European prehistory can be broken into three successive stages, each one marked by changes in the dominant technology: STONE AGE; BRONZE AGE; IRON AGE.

Three Kingdoms   1. in China, the Wei (AD 220–265), Shu Han (AD 221–263) and Wu (AD 222–280) Kingdoms of the Three Kingdoms/ Six Dynasties period, which succeeded the HAN Dynasty (see CHINESE DYNASTIES) 2. on the Korean peninsula, the PROTOHISTORIC kingdoms of KOGURYO, PAEKCHE and SILLA, existing independently from *c.*AD 300 until 668, when the peninsula was unified under Silla (see also KAYA, KOREAN PERIODIZATION).

Thule   a prehistoric ESKIMO culture that originated in Alaska about AD 900, and spread eastward as far as Greenland about AD 1000 as a result of climatic improvement, although it retreated westward again after AD 1300. The culture was dependent on the hunting of sea-mammals, although caribou and other land animals were also taken. Western Thule used a coarse pottery which was later replaced by soapstone vessels. Stone was not commonly used for artifacts, the preferred media being bone, IVORY and antler. The Thule were the SKRAELINGS encountered by the VIKINGS in the 10th century AD. See QILAKITSOQ.

Thunderbird site   a PALAEOINDIAN and ARCHAIC campsite in Virginia, USA, which is part of a series of sites known as Flint Run. The Thunderbird site includes both processing and hunting sites. POSTHOLES may be the remains of the oldest structures in North America (approximately 11 000 BP), although their association with the CLOVIS level is not certain, and they may date to the succeeding Archaic.

thylacine or **Tasmanian tiger**   a flesh-eating marsupial predator which became extinct on the Australian mainland about 3000 bp, possibly as a result of competition with the DINGO, but which survived in TASMANIA until the 20th century.

Tiahuanaco or **Tiwanaku**   a major MIDDLE HORIZON site located on the altiplano of the central Andes in Bolivia, probably the capital of an empire. The central core of the site comprises a ceremonial district, 500 × 1000 metres in extent. This includes a large sunken rectangular plaza, the Kalasasaya, as well as the Akapana, a large U-shaped mound surrounding a spring. Near the Kalasasaya is the monumental Gate of the Sun. Originally a single slab of andesite (it is presently broken into two pieces), it was cut to form a large doorway, with niches on either side. Above the doorway is an elaborate bas-relief frieze depicting a central deity, the Staff Deity, a human standing on a low stepped platform, wearing an elaborate headdress with appendages ending in the heads of animals, and holding a staff in each hand. He is flanked by rows of ANTHROPOMORPHOUS birds.

Along the bottom of the panel are a series of anthromorphous faces, much like the face of the Staff Deity.

The site had a substantial population numbering probably in the tens of thousands. Investigations by Alan Kolata indicate that Tiahuanaco reorganized agriculture in the altiplano, building systems of raised fields to bring marshy land under cultivation and to increase production of potatoes. The distribution of Tiahuanaco artifacts and architecture suggests that it was the capital of a major empire that extended into southernmost Peru, northern Chile, most of Bolivia, and adjacent Argentina. Although Tiahuanaco shares some aspects of its iconography with HUARI, especially the Staff Deity and associated figures, the two cultures are separated by a sharply defined boundary. Only one Huari site, Cerro Baul, is found in Tiahuanaco territory, in extreme southern Peru; its defensive location suggests that relations between the two POLITIES was not entirely amicable.

Tianko Panjang a cave-site in the interior of central Sumatra, yielding an OBSIDIAN MICROLITH industry characterized by unRETOUCHED FLAKES and chips of c.9000 bc and later; upper levels contain pottery.

Tiaret a region of Algeria where many CAPSIAN sites are found.

Tiefstichkeramik a style of pottery decoration that characterizes the FUNNEL BEAKER culture of the North European Plain in Germany and Holland between c.3000 and 2700 bc. 'Tiefstich' decoration consists of short, deeply incised strokes in bands and zigzag patterns. It is closely associated with the HUNEBED tombs of the North European Plain.

Tiekene-Boussoura a funerary MEGALITHIC site in eastern Senegal, dating to the 6th–8th centuries AD. Thirty monuments with nine circles of upright stones enclosing multiple burials with pottery were found, suggesting a highly stratified society contemporaneous with GHANA.

Tiemassas a Senegalese site with an undated MICROLITHIC INDUSTRY containing geometric microliths as well as leaf-shaped and hollow-based PROJECTILE POINTS.

Tievebulliagh a Neolithic axe factory in Co. Antrim, Ireland, source of many of the Group IX porcellanite axes; a second source is the small offshore island on Rathlin some 24 km to the north. Group IX axes are widespread in Ireland and are also found in mainland Britain.

Tiglathpileser III a king of ASSYRIA, founder of the later Assyrian empire. After the 9th century NEO-ASSYRIAN empire collapsed (following the reign of Shalmaneser III; see AŠŠURNAṢIRPAL II), the next great king was Tiglathpileser III (744–727 BC), who restored and extended the empire, and reorganized provincial administration. During his reign, BABYLONIA was effectively brought within the empire as a client state. Sargon II (721–705 BC) further enlarged the empire, campaigning extensively in Syro-Palestine and in URARTU and other mountainous regions around Assyria, and engaged in a protracted war with the CHALDEAN king Merodach–baladan in southern Babylonia. These two kings established the 'classic' Assyrian empire that provided later western Asian empires with the model of imperial rule.

Tikal one of the largest of the Southern Lowland MAYA centres, located in Guatemala. The earliest buildings at the site date to 800 BC, from which time construction continued for over 1000 years. At its height, it covered 120 square kilometres. Evidence of influence from

TEOTIHUACÁN is thought to have come from the ruler Curl Nose, and later his son, Stormy Sky. Curl Nose who may have been from KAMINALJUYÚ, married into the ruling dynasty at Tikal.

The site is most significant for the results of an extensive mapping project carried out by the University Museum of the University of Pennsylvania, from 1956–70, under the direction first of Edwin Shook and then of William R. Coe. During the course of the project, the substantial number of domestic structures mapped made Maya archaeologists re-evaluate the notion that Maya ceremonial centres were non-urban, occupied only during certain events. The residences identified implied a substantial population for the centre, estimated at between 45–75 000. To accommodate such a population, archaeologists had to reconsider their assumptions about the agricultural system of the Precolumbian Maya. Work by Dennis Puleston suggests that the very nutritious *ramon nut* was an important food source, in addition to corn, beans and squash. Puleston found an association between the distribution of housemounds, ramon trees and CHULTUNS. Chultuns provide an effective place to store the ramon nuts.

tiki   see HEI TIKI.

Tilemsi   a north/south-oriented valley that ends at the River Niger at Gao in Mali, Africa. It was probably one of the main routes followed by pastoralists who moved southwards after the desiccation of the Sahara after about 4 500 BP (see KARKARICHINKAT).

Tilkitepe   a prehistoric site to the southeast of Lake Van in eastern Anatolia, which represents the northernmost well-documented representation of the HALAF culture (Halaf sherds do occur into Transcaucasia). Excavated principally in the 1930s by E. Reilly and K. Lake, the stratigraphic and contextual control of the Halaf material is poor, and allows a basically typological approach to the recovered materials. Later occupations also occur, represented by later CHALCOLITHIC and some EARLY BRONZE AGE (KURA-ARAXES culture) pottery. Tilkitepe lies near some of the OBSIDIAN sources by Lake Van, and many commentaries on the Halaf phenomenon invoke this proximity as an example of controlled access to this widely traded material.

till   an aggregate of material, consisting typically but not necessarily of massive, unsorted or poorly sorted DIAMICTON, deposited directly by GLACIAL ice, and not significantly resedimented after original deposition. Till is direct evidence of GLACIATION, and is often associated with MORAINE LANDFORMS. Much of the material in the environment directly in front of a glacier is descriptively diamicton, but not all diamicton is till, and much of it may be series of debris and SEDIMENT flow deposits, caused by the reworking of till in this water-rich environment. Several types of till are recognized, deposited in the supraglacial or subglacial environment, based on associated sediment types, landforms and STRATIGRAPHIC sequence.

Tillya-Depe   a small (1 ha) site in southern Bactria in northwestern Afghanistan, excavated by V.I. Sarianidi in the 1970s. It consists of a series of Iron Age (Yaz complex) levels (see YAZ-DEPE) dated to the first half of the 1st millennium BC, the early levels containing a central fortified architectural platform. The site is perhaps most famous for the group of 'royal tombs' dug into its surface after abandonment; these had extremely rich contents, including many gold vessels and jewellery, and are dated to the late 1st millennium BC (perhaps Kushan).

Timber Grave Culture see SRUBNAYA CULTURE.

Timna a series of COPPER-SMELTING sites in southern Israel, exploited from the CHALCOLITHIC to the Roman Period and excavated by Rothenberg in 1964–77. The most remarkable structure located at Timna is a small temple of the goddess Hathor, showing Egyptian interest in the area during the NEW KINGDOM.

Timonovka two Upper Palaeolithic open-air sites on the Desna River near Bryansk in European Russia. The occupation horizons at each locality are buried in LOESS and slope deposits overlying a bedrock promontory. Collectively, the sites have yielded RADIOCARBON dates of 15 110–12 200 bp. The heavily weathered faunal remains are predominantly woolly MAMMOTH. Timonovka I was originally reported to contain evidence of large semi-subterranean dwellings, but these features have been revealed as ICE-WEDGE CASTS; however, the remains of at least two MAMMOTH-BONE HOUSES may be represented. Timonovka I was discovered and initially excavated by Voevodskij in 1927; subsequent excavations were conducted by GORODTSOV in 1928–33 and ROGACHEV in 1955. Timonovka II was discovered and excavated by Grekhova during 1965–67.

tin a malleable metallic element typically added to other metallic elements to form alloys, most notably bronze, for the manufacture of artifacts. Most tin is extracted from the tin oxide mineral *cassiterite*.

Tinkayu a series of sites in Sabah, north Borneo, near the edge of an ancient lake, yielding a sophisticated PEBBLE and FLAKE INDUSTRY based on local CHERT, characterized by bifacially flaked lanceolate knives and large tabular BIFACES, dating *c.*28 000–17 000 BP, preceding the industry of the BATURONG CAVES.

Tintan a HOLOCENE site in northern Mauretania, Africa, which yielded 50 individuals highly reminiscent of the MECHTA-AFALOU type.

Ti-n-Torha two rockshelters in the ACACUS of southwestern Libya. Ti-n-Torha East is dated to between 9350 and 7730 bp and contains evidence for fishing, fowling and hunting, especially of Barbary sheep. Ti-n-Torha North dates to between 7440 and 5260 bp and was occupied by pastoralists with small stock and cattle.

tipi ring a circle of stones found in the Northern Plains of North America, thought to be the remains of weights used to keep in place the wall of a skin lodge or *tipi*. There are probably millions of these sites in the Northern Plains.

Tîrpeşti a stratified site of the CUCUTENI-TRIPOLYE culture in northeastern Romania. Surrounded by a ditch, it is relatively small, but shares many characteristics with the larger Cucuteni-Tripolye sites in terms of location, organization, and presence of figurines.

Tiryns a site in the Argolid, Greece, that was once coastal but has since been stranded some distance from the sea. The German excavations, initiated by SCHLIEMANN in 1884, have revealed a large, circular, Early HELLADIC structure which may have served as a communal granary and suggests a relatively sophisticated economic system. The massive CYCLOPEAN fortifications and the MYCENAEAN palace, built in the 14th–13th centuries BC, indicate that Tiryns remained a major centre but must surely have been dominated by MYCENAE politically.

TISZA CULTURE

Tisza culture a Late Neolithic culture of eastern Hungary, centred on the Tisza River, contemporaneous with the LENGYEL culture of east-central Europe and sharing many of its characteristics, between *c.*4000 and 3600 bc. Both TELL and horizontal settlements are known. Tisza CERAMICS are characterized by a wide variety of forms, including footed and pedestalled bowls. They are frequently decorated with incised lines in complicated geometrical patterns that cover their entire surface. Red, yellow and white paint is applied after firing.

Tiszapolgár culture an ENEOLITHIC culture of eastern Hungary, successor to the TISZA culture between 3500 and 3000 bc, named after the large cemetery site at *Tiszapolgár-Basatanya*. The pottery continues the Tisza tradition of pedastalled bowls and other similar forms, but is characterized by an almost total lack of decoration save for small lugs and bosses, a phenomenon similar to the late phase of the LENGYEL culture to the northeast. At Tiszapolgár-Basatanya, 156 contracted inhumations occurred in individual pits with a vessel and often a copper shaft-hole hammer-axe or other tool.

Tito Bustillo a cave-site in Asturias, northern Spain, named after one of its discoverers in 1966 and containing a wealth of PORTABLE and PARIETAL ART of the Upper MAGDALENIAN. It is especially notable for a polychrome panel of horses and deer, for the westernmost depictions and bones of reindeer, and for a number of engraved stones dating to the Upper Magdalenian (14 250 bp). The cave was blocked immediately after this period.

Tiwanaku see TIAHUANACO.

TL see THERMOLUMINESCENCE.

Tlaloc the rain and fertility god of Late POSTCLASSIC AZTEC central Mexico. Depictions of Tlaloc at sites outside the region, including the centres of KAMINALJUYÚ and COPÁN, are used as further evidence of TEOTIHUACÁN'S influence at these places. The earliest depictions of such a goggle-eyed being occur in the late PRECLASSIC at CUICUILCO.

Tlapacoya and Tlatilco see BASIN OF MEXICO.

tlatoque the ruler of a city-state in the BASIN OF MEXICO during AZTEC rule. These petty kings were supported by produce cultivated on communal land and by tribute in labour and service. The tlatoque generally claimed descent from QUETZALCÓATL through the 'TOLTECS', thus strengthening his right to rule through his divine lineage.

To'aga a deeply stratified coastal site on Ofu Island, Samoa, with evidence of occupation spanning the entire Samoan sequence, and unusual preservation of shell and bone. The oldest deposits date to 3700–3300 BP and may be LAPITA. The succeeding assemblage dates to 2500–1900 BP and is characterized by plain CERAMICS, and shell FISH-HOOKS and ornaments, some of which are comparable to Early Eastern POLYNESIAN material from the Marquesas and Society Islands.

Toalian a mid-HOLOCENE (6000 BC and later) stone FLAKE and BLADE INDUSTRY of Sulawesi, Indonesia, characterized by backed flakes and MICROLITHS, including Maros POINTS.

Toca de Esperança a PRECERAMIC site in eastern Brazil, whose earliest level yielded a date of 295 000 bp. The bones of extinct PLEISTOCENE fauna were associated in this level with what have been claimed to be very crude chipped stone tools. Most scholars are very sceptical of the early date; if accurate, the site would represent a HOMO *erectus* occupation in the New World, which is regarded as

0   3 cm

Toalian Maros points.

extremely unlikely.

Toca do Boqueirão   see PEDRA FURADA.

Tocra (*Gk* Taucheira)   a Greek city in Cyrenaica, Libya, probably founded in the late 7th century BC. Imported ARCHAIC Greek pottery was found in votive deposits in the sanctuary of Demeter and Kore.

Toftum   a Neolithic enclosure in Jutland, Denmark, consisting of a causewayed ditch, double on the west side. Material recovered was of the transitional Early/Middle Neolithic FUCHSBERG phase, *c*.3400 BC. See also SARUP.

Togolok   **1.** a group of Late Bronze Age sites in the Murghab delta in southeastern Turkmenia. Togolok sites are generally smaller than those of the GONUR phase, though Togolok 1 is perhaps 15 ha, and some others are equally large. As with the Gonur phase, many aspects of the material culture are similar to the BACTRIAN Late Bronze Age.
2. a chronological phase (dated perhaps to the second quarter of the 2nd millennium BC) that shows considerable continuity with the preceding Gonur phase.

Togueres   habitation areas above the flood plain of the interior delta of the Niger River in Mali, Africa, which have yielded rich archaeological material of agricultural fishing people. Excavated sites include *Toguere Dowpil,* occupied between 1000 and 500 BP, and *Toguere Galia,* with dates between 1000 and 800 BP.

Tohoku   a modern district of northern Honshu Island, Japan, often used in archaeological writings. It comprises Aomori, Iwate, Akita, Yamagata, Miyagi and Fukushima Prefectures. (See EMISHI, JOMON, KAMEGAOKA.)

tohua   ceremonial dancing grounds unique to the Marquesas Islands, Polynesia, comprising rectangular flat earthen areas, surrounded by raised platforms used either for temples or as seating for spectators. One of the largest *tohua* is VAHANGEKU'A in the TAIPIVAI VALLEY.

Tokai   a pre-modern district of Japan (see RITSURYO) bordering the Pacific seaboard, often used in archaeological writings. It comprises modern Tokyo Metropolitan District and Chiba, Ibaragi, Saitama, Kanagawa, Shizuoka, Aichi and Mie Prefectures. (See TORO.)

tokens   small clay geometric objects (spheres, discs, cones, ovoids, cylinders and so forth) found in many early Neolithic sites of western Asia (Levant, the Taurus and Zagros Mountains and their piedmont zones). The work of D. Schmandt-Besserat suggests that these clay geometrics give rise ultimately to writing. Similarly shaped clay 'counters' occur within hollow clay BULLAE (envelopes) that are sealed by a CYLINDER SEAL impression, a characteristic of Late URUK southern MESOPOTAMIA. These same bullae might also bear impressions of the tokens themselves, representing the content of the bulla. From this form of accountancy to writing numbers on a tablet (i.e. the flattened bulla) is a short step; soon thereafter, words were added to the numbers to clarify the accountancy. This progression is observed at the ACROPOLE of SUSA and (with some stratigraphic circularity) at WARKA (EANNA SOUNDING).

tokens

Tolbaga an Upper Palaeolithic open-air site on the Khilok River near Lake Baikal in south-central Siberia. The main cultural layer is buried in slope deposits on a TERRACE of medium elevation. Associated faunal remains include woolly rhinoceros, steppe bison and reindeer; two of the bones yielded dates of 34 860 and 27 210 bp. Among the artifacts are RETOUCHED BLADES, sidescrapers and end-scrapers (see SCRAPER), points, BURINS and a piece of carved bone representing the head of a bear. Redeposited artifacts and faunal remains were found in overlying sandy LOAM layers. Tolbaga is an important Siberian early Upper Palaeolithic locality; it was discovered and excavated in the 1970s by OKLADNIKOV and others.

Tollund Man an Iron Age bog body discovered in the Tollund Fen, central Jutland, Denmark, in 1950. Naked except for a pointed leather cap, he lay in the bog on his right side with a noose around his neck. Stomach contents showed that his last meal had been a gruel containing barley, linseed, knotweed, dock and camomile but no meat. Possibly a ritual sacrifice or an executed criminal, Tollund Man is thought to have met his end in the 3rd century BC.

'Toltec' one of the important cultures of MESOAMERICA, whose in-fluence lasted from AD 900 to 1100. The AZTECS claimed to be descended from the 'Toltecs;' and, to date, much of our understand-ing of the 'Toltecs' comes from ethnohistoric sources. These sources contain legend and myth, as well as fact. Archaeologists are currently reassessing their understanding of the 'Toltecs,' and are using the archaeological record to supplement other sources. The 'Toltecs' have been depicted as spreading their influence throughout Mesoamerica through military conquest and coercion, but the archaeological evidence for this is not clear. At TULA, the 'Toltec' capital, symbols of militarism, death and blood are prevalent.

Tomba di Giganti see GIANT'S GRAVE.

Tomskaya an Upper Palaeolithic open-air site on the Tom' River (Ob' tributary) in Tomsk, western Siberia. A small assemblage of artifacts was found in association with the disarticulated skeleton of a woolly MAMMOTH, buried in LOESS-like LOAM overlying ALLUVIUM of the third TERRACE. The remains have yielded a date of 18 300 bp. The artifacts include BURINS and RETOUCHED BLADES. Tomskaya apparently represents a KILL-SITE, which is rare among Palaeolithic sites in Russia. It was excavated by the zoologist Kashchenko in 1886.

Tondidiaro   see MEGALITHIC MONUMENT.

Tongsamdong   a Neolithic SHELL MIDDEN site in South Kyongsang Province, Korea, dating to c.4500–1500 BC. JOMON pottery and OBSIDIAN from Kyushu among the CHULMUN remains document oversea interaction with Japanese island inhabitants.

tool   an ARTIFACT used for a specific task.

Toolondo   the remains of a fish-trap system, in southwest Victoria, Australia, comprising earth-cut channels. Excavations by Harry Lourandos established that the system fell out of use about 200 years ago. As in the case of LAKE CONDAH, the antiquity of the system remains unknown.

topography   the physical configuration of the LANDSCAPE, usually expressed with particular reference to relief and contour. A detailing of site topography is fundamental in archaeological site description. Often this includes construction of a topographic map, where three-dimensional relief is expressed in two dimensions by the use of contour lines, representing intersections of a set of imaginary equally spaced horizontal planes at prescribed ALTITUDES with the land surface. Contour lines are identified by altitude, preferably relative to a formally recognized sea level, but sometimes to a relative local DATUM. Several SURVEYING instruments can be used to construct local topographic maps, including the TRANSIT, THEODOLITE and LEVEL.

Toprakkale   **1.** a site on the eastern shore of Lake Van in eastern Anatolia, which, together with the related monuments around the lake, represents the centre of the URARTIAN state (roughly 850–600 BC). Toprakkale itself contains a large temple complex and associated storerooms and residential area that were subject to 'excavation' in the 19th century, yielding a great many bronzes, carved IVORY, and possibly silk. Elsewhere in the Van area are a series of fortified sites with the typically Urartian extensive storerooms; temples at various places, including that at Adilcevas which retains some of its wall paintings; the rock-cut tomb of Argishti I (786–764) at Tushpa; and monumental inscriptions in various localities. Urartian texts also refer to a large number of irrigation works in the Van area. Recent Turkish work at Van has focused on the citadel and palace of Argisti I; excavation in the mound of Van Kalesi has exposed Urartian levels overlying a sequence that begins in the EARLY BRONZE AGE.
2. a class of BURNISHED fine red ware characteristic of the Urartian period.

torc or **torque**   a neckring, usually of gold, worn by CELTIC warriors and sometimes found in Late Iron Age hoards or graves. One of the finest examples is the SNETTISHAM torc.

Tordos   see TURDAŞ.

Torihama   an Initial-Early JOMON site in Fukui Prefecture, Japan, where waterlogging has preserved evidence of horticultural practices, as well as many bone and wood artifacts such as a dugout canoe, paddles, hunting bows, tool hafts, wooden bowls and a LACQUER comb. Remains of gourds and beans at 5000–3500 BC suggest mid-HOLOCENE extension of control over garden crops in western Japan well before the adoption of rice agriculture (see ITAZUKE).

Toro   a Late YAYOI site in Shizuoka Prefecture, Japan, known for its unbounded village plan and wet-preserved wooden tools and architectural remains. Excavated in 1948 as the first inter-disciplinary project of the Japanese Archaeologists' Association, it has long served as the type-site for the rice-growing Yayoi period despite being in the marginal TOKAI region (compare ITAZUKE). Several pit-houses and raised granaries have been reconstructed as a historical park; excavated paddy-field systems adjoin the village, but the cemetery has not been recovered. (Compare YOSHINOGARI.)

Torralba and Ambrona   two large Lower Palaeolithic Spanish lakeside sites, 2 km apart, 150 km northeast of Madrid, which have been excavated by numerous workers, most recently Howell, Aguirre, Butzer and Freeman. The sites have yielded ACHEULIAN tools and the remains of many partially dismembered animals, particularly straight-tusked elephants and horses. Many of the bones are water-transported, but it is possible that some artifacts were used to kill or at least butcher some of the animals. The sites belong to the Middle PLEISTOCENE, somewhere between 300 000 and 700 000 BP.

torre   a circular dry-stone tower of Bronze Age date (2nd millennium BC) found in southern Corsica. Though in some ways equivalent to the Sardinian NURAGHE, the Corsican torre was capped by a CORBELLED VAULT covering the principal chamber, and was not topped by a fighting platform. A torre is the central feature of the FILITOSA promontory fort.

Torre Annunziata   see OPLONTIS.

Torre in Pietra   a Palaeolithic site *c.*25 km to the south of Rome, Italy, which has yielded an ACHEULIAN industry of probable RISSIAN age with associated faunal remains, and an early dating MOUSTERIAN assemblage.

tortoise core   see LEVALLOIS TECHNIQUE.

Torwa   see KHAMI.

Tószeg   a TELL site in eastern Hungary near Szolnok on the Tisza River, where a stratigraphy several metres in depth has defined the chronological sequence of the Early Bronze Age in this region. A variety of periodizations have been proposed during the mid 20th century by CHILDE, Tompa and Moszolics. Moszolics' chronology from the early 1950s is generally still used, with the settlement layers at Tószeg providing the NAGYRÉV-HATVAN-FÜZESABONY sequence between 1800 and 1300 bc.

toumba or **magoula**   in Greek archaeology an artificial mound or TELL.

Toutswe   an Iron Age phase or group in eastern Botswana, Africa, named after the large settlement of *Toutswemogala,* which achieved prominence at the same time as K2 and MAPUNGUBWE. Massive vitrified deposits at sites such as Toutswemogala, Bosutswe and Shoshong are accumulations of animal dung which caught fire in the past and which testify to herding on a substantial scale.

trace elements   elements that occur naturally in minor amounts in minerals in SOILS and SEDIMENT. Trace element suites can be identified by various analyses and may serve as 'fingerprints' for some ARTIFACT raw material sources. Source identification can lead to further interpretations of trade and economic systems.

trademarks   see GRAFFITI.

tradition   1. long-term continuity in either individual technologies or ATTRIBUTES.

2. a temporally ordered series of archaeological PHASES or CULTURES that show cultural similarities to each other.

trait   an element of an archaeological CULTURE or technology.

Trajan's column   a column at ROME, some 38 m high, decorated with a continuous spiral relief frieze, surmounted by a statue of the emperor, celebrating the DACIAN wars in the Balkans conducted by the emperor Trajan (AD 98–117). It formed part of the FORUM of Trajan, and the ashes of the emperor and his wife Plotina were placed in its base. The frieze provides a narrative of the campaigns and is an invaluable source of information on Roman and Dacian armour, weapons and other military matters.

tranchet axe   a large MESOLITHIC axe with a cutting-edge formed by the intersection of two FLAKE scars removed by the TRANCHET TECHNIQUE.

tranchet technique   1. the precise removal of a large flat FLAKE from the tip of a BIFACE, so that the edge of the tranchet flake scar forms a straight cutting-edge.

2. a northern and northwestern MESOLITHIC technique used to create or resharpen the cutting-edge of an axe or ADZE, by striking a thick flake from the tip. The resultant tranchet flakes have a highly distinctive appearance.

Transcaucasian Early Bronze Age   see KURA-ARAXES CULTURE.

transhumance   a subsistence strategy, in which human groups copy the seasonal or periodic movement, between fundamentally different environmental zones, of the animals on which they rely for food. This movement is often altitudinal and is determined by seasonally changing climate and resource availability. In Europe and the Old World, the term is usually restricted to pastoralist farmers and their livestock, whereas in the New World the term is often used more generally for any well-defined animal/human migration. The identification of prehistoric transhumance patterns was one of the principal aims of many studies of PALAEOECONOMY.

transit   a SURVEYING instrument capable of measuring horizontal and vertical angles and horizontal distances. Similar to a LEVEL, ALIDADE and THEODOLITE, it consists of a focusing telescope for long sightings. Unlike the level and alidade, however, the telescope is mounted on a graduated base used to measure horizontal angles. It also has a striding level to level the scope, either a bulls-eye level or two bubble levels perpendicular to one another to level the instrument on the tripod on which it rests, a vernier scale for measuring vertical angles, stadia and cross hairs for determining distances with measurements taken from a stadia rod, and a compass for determining magnetic north and taking compass bearings. The telescope can also pivot on a horizontal transverse axis to reverse its line of sight. The transit is used for the same purposes as a theodolite. It cannot, however, be used to construct a map in the field simultaneously, as can be done with a plane table and alidade.

transmission electron microscopy   a technique used to examine the internal and surface structure and morphology of a wide range of materials. An extremely thin sample is prepared either by grinding it to a fine powder which is mounted on a carbon film, or by reproducing the surface of the sample in one of several ways. A high energy electron beam is focused so that it passes through the sample. An image of the sample is enhanced by magnification and projected so that it can be photographed if desired. Unlike in SCANNING ELECTRON MICROSCOPY, the sample must be extremely thin for the beam to penetrate it and reveal internal structures. Otherwise, many of the same tasks can be performed with both instruments.

travertine or **tufa**   a light-coloured, compact calcite deposited from solution in ground and surface waters at springs, seeps and in caves. Porous varieties may be referred to as calcareous tufa, calcareous sinter or spring deposits. Banded varieties are often referred to as *onyx* or onyx marble, although onyx is actually a CHALCEDONY. Cave *stalactites* and *stalagmites* are formed of travertine. Travertine deposits are potential sources of palaeoenvironmental information, as fossils and organic remains may be incorporated and preserved. Dense travertine with little or no detrital contamination is a candidate for URANIUM SERIES DATING and ISOTOPIC analysis.

TRB culture   an Early and Middle Neolithic culture of northern Europe characterized by the use of a Funnel-Necked BEAKER (*Trichterrandbecher*) with globular body and out-turned rim. Five regional groups can be distinguished, with largely separate development: the west group in the Netherlands, sometimes associated with HUNEBEDDEN; the southern group in Germany with Baalberge and Salzmünde variants; the southeastern group in Czechoslovakia; the eastern group in Poland; and the northern group in Denmark and Sweden, sometimes found in MEGALITHIC tombs and at enclosures such as SARUP and TOFTUM. Copper was worked in the southeastern group, and products distributed among the eastern and southern groups, reaching even the northern group as shown by the BYGHOLM hoard.

Trebenište   an Iron Age burial site of the HALLSTATT D period (*c*.600 BC) in Macedonia, where a large KRATER of Greek origin, resembling the one from VIX, was found. Trebenište represents the most northerly penetration of Greek goods into lands adjacent to Greece during this period (although in western Europe there is ample evidence of trade with Greece at this time).

tree-ring dating   see DENDROCHRONOLOGY.

Trelleborg   a VIKING fortress in Zealand, Denmark, of *c*.AD 1000, comprising a central circular fortification, 13.6 m in diameter, with four gates. These serve two main streets dividing the interior into four quadrants, each containing four barrack buildings arranged in a square. Each building was boat-shaped, 30 m long and 8 m wide.

trephination or **trepanation**   a surgical technique whereby small sections of cranial bones were removed. The cuts were made by scraping or sawing, or, less commonly, by drilling a series of adjacent round holes. After removal of the bone piece, the head was wrapped, and in many cases the patient survived the operation and the bone grew back. Trephination is found especially in the south coast PARACAS culture of Peru, dating to the EARLY HORIZON, but the practice was also used elsewhere in the world and in other periods.

Tressé a Late Neolithic ALLÉE COUVERTE in Ille-et-Vilaine, France, with a paved chamber over 10 m long roofed by seven capstones. ORTHOSTATS of the terminal chamber were carved with four pairs of small breasts. Material recovered included Late Neolithic coarse ware pottery and BLADES of GRAND PRESSIGNY FLINT.

Tres Zapotes an OLMEC CEREMONIAL CENTRE in southern Veracruz, Mexico. The site is poorly known except for its sculptures, including Olmec heads. Occupied from 1000–600 BC, Tres Zapotes became the most important centre after LA VENTA was destroyed. Matthew STIRLING excavated here, beginning in 1938.

Trialeti a high plateau region south of Tbilisi in southern Georgia (Transcaucasia), where B.A. Kuftin's exploration of KURGANS during the 1930s produced one of Georgia's most widely known archaeological cultures. Of variable size and internal structure, the Trialeti Bronze Age kurgans contain single burials, often accompanied by a four-wheeled cart. The grave-goods include a range of painted wares and an extremely rich inventory of metal objects (cups, buckets, weapons, jewellery in gold, silver, tin, bronze, copper), sometimes with an extremely rich iconography. Kurgans in other parts of central Transcaucasia have since been found with a comparable cultural inventory; however, the corresponding settlements are very rarely reported. The date of the Trialeti, conventionally 'Middle Bronze Age', is debated and may be pushed back into later Early Bronze times, but certainly begins by around 2000 BC and lasts to the mid 2nd millennium BC.

Trianda the site of a MINOAN colony, on the Aegean island of Rhodes, founded in the 16th century BC, presumably to facilitate trade between Crete and Cyprus. After the destruction of the Minoan palaces in the 15th century, MYCENAEANS may have settled at Trianda but the site was abandoned in the 14th century.

triangulation a SURVEYING technique in which a network of triangles is laid out, and an unknown point is located by measuring the angles and distances formed by the lines of sight between the point in question and two known points of a triangle. A base line of known length is established between two control points that serves as one side of one of the triangles. Calculation of distances to other points is then a matter of trigonometric calculations using angles shot with a TRANSIT or other surveying instrument.

tribe a form of social organization that comprises a centrally organized collection of bands. See BAND, CHIEFDOM, STATE.

Trichterrandbecher see TRB CULTURE.

triclinium the dining-room of a Roman house. The name is derived from the three couches (see KLINE) placed around the walls of a square room. Tables with food would be placed in front of the couches. Some large houses might have several triclinia.

triglyph part of the ENTABLATURE of a Greek building of the DORIC ORDER, alternating with a METOPE. The triglyph had three elements separated by two vertical grooves.

trilithon two upright stones supporting a third to form a kind of arch or doorway. A horseshoe arrangement of five huge SARSEN trilithons is the central feature of STONEHENGE. The island of Tonga has a massive coral trilithon, *c*.5 m high, of AD 1200 (see HA'AMONGA).

Trinil a site in the SOLO River valley of Java. It has given its name to the PLEISTOCENE fauna of *c*.1.3 million to 500 000 BP, which succeeds that of JETIS, apparently adapted also to an open forest environment. HOMO *erectus* (JAVA MAN) remains are less robust than those of Jetis. See DUBOIS.

Triple Alliance an alliance formed in AD 1428, when the Aztec-Mexica of TENOCHTITLÁN joined with the Texcoco and the state of Tacuba to overthrow the city-state of Azcapotzalco. Eventually, the AZTECS came to dominate the alliance. The rise of the Triple Alliance ended the competition between city-states in the BASIN OF MEXICO that had begun with the fall of TEOTIHUACÁN.

Tripolye see CUCUTENI-TRIPOLYE.

Troy see HISARLIK.

Trundholm a bronze wheeled model of a horse pulling a disc, covered with gold leaf probably to represent the sun. The model dated to *c*.1650 BC was found in 1902 in the Trundholm bog, Zealand, Denmark, where it may have been deposited as a ritual offering.

Truso an early mediaeval Baltic trading port described by the ANGLO-SAXON traveller Wulfstan in the 9th century AD. Although the location of Truso has not yet been established through archaeological research, it is believed to have been located at the eastern edge of the delta of the Vistula River. According to Wulfstan's account, he arrived at Truso after a seven-day voyage from HAITHABU.

Trzciniec culture an Early Bronze Age/Middle Bronze Age culture of the Vistula and Bug drainages in eastern Poland. It continues many cultural traits that emerged at the end of the Neolithic in the CORDED WARE culture, including both the CERAMIC forms and flint industry. At the same time, there appear a small number of bronze artifacts. primarily imports from areas to the west and south. Trzciniec graves are primarily under TUMULI, although cremations are also known. Dating is somewhat uncertain, but generally thought to be between 1600 and 1300 bc.

Tsangli the site of a Neolithic–Bronze Age settlement mound in Thessaly, Greece, excavated by TSOUNTAS in 1905 and by WACE and Thompson in 1910. The Late Neolithic Tsangli culture is characterized by grey-on-grey and matt-painted pottery.

Tshangula a cave in the Matobo Hills of southwestern Zimbabwe, containing a sequence of MIDDLE STONE AGE and LATER STONE AGE assemblages, which has given its name to a late Middle Stone Age industry postdating 30 000 BP, also known as the Umguzan. It contains BACKED MICROLITHS and ostrich eggshell beads as well as Middle Stone Age artifacts, but is not well documented.

Tshitolian a LATER STONE AGE INDUSTRY named after the Tshitolo Plateau in southern Zaire, dating from *c*.14 000 to 5000 BP and distributed in Angola, Zaire, Gabon and Cameroon in equatorial Africa. It is characterized by BACKED MICROLITHS, small CORE axes, picks and foliate points.

Tsodilo Hills an important ROCK ART region with many painted LATER STONE AGE rockshelters as well as Iron Age sites near the Okavango Swamp in northwestern Botswana. The rock art includes red paintings of a variety of animals, including scenes with domestic animals, grids, spoked circles and handprints, as well as cupmarks.

Tsountas, Christos (1857–1934) a Greek archaeologist who excavated at MYCENAE from 1877 to 1902. He investigated a number of settlement sites in Thessaly, in particular DIIMINI and SESKLO, and he also excavated extensively in the Cyclades.

tufa see TRAVERTINE.

Tufariello see APENNINE CULTURE.

tuff a clastic sedimentary rock consisting of compacted volcanic ASH. Tuff may bury and preserve archaeological deposits, and can usually be dated by the POTASSIUM–ARGON DATING method.

Tula a modern town in the state of Hidalgo, Mexico, that has been identified with Tollán, the legendary capital of the 'TOLTECS', by Wigberto Jimenez Moreno and Jorge Acosta in the 1940s. The site began gaining importance in AD 800, after TEOTIHUACÁN fell. Tula reached its greatest extent between AD 900–1100. Military symbols are a major theme at the site. It is famous for the Atlantean statues, standing nearly 5 m tall, that supported the roof of PYRAMID B. Tula was destroyed in AD 1156. After its decline, Central Mexico had no central power until the appearance of the AZTECS.

tula or **tula adze** a hafted chisel used in arid central Australia for working hardwoods. It is made on a thick FLAKE with a prominent BULB and a convex bulbar surface. Repeated resharpening of the semicircular working edge opposite the obtuse-angled STRIKING PLATFORM results in a distinctive 'slug'. See also ADZE.

tula Adze flakes.

tulang mawas ('monkey bone') a long-shafted, socketed iron axe unique to the Iron Age (*c.*300 BC) of peninsular Malaysia, normally found in hoards and perhaps used as units of value rather than as tools. Other socketed tools of the industry are distantly related to those from BAN DON TA PHET.

Tule Springs a site near Las Vegas, Nevada, USA, which was originally considered to have evidence for human occupation, in the form of HEARTHS and ARTIFACTS, which pre-dated 28 000 BC. More recent work at the site has suggested that the earliest date for human use of the site is no greater than 11 000 BP.

Tulúm a POSTCLASSIC MAYA site on the east coast of Yucatán, Mexico. It is a fortified site, facing the sea and surrounded on three sides by a wall 6 m thick and between 3 m and 5 m high. The city, an important trading centre, has a planned design in a concentrated pattern with residences around the CEREMONIAL CENTRE. The buildings at Tulúm are architecturally inferior to those of the CLASSIC Maya.

tumulus   a mound of earth or stones, usually covering a burial or burials. The TUMULUS CULTURE is a Middle Bronze Age culture of southern Germany known mainly from inhumations beneath round barrows; it is not to be confused with the Armorican Tumulus Culture of Brittany, represented at KERNONEN, with close parallels to the WESSEX CULTURE of southern Britain. See also TOUMBA, SOROS, BURIAL MOUNDS.

Tumulus Culture   a Middle Bronze Age culture of the central Danube region in Czechoslovakia, Austria and Bavaria, following the ÚŇETICE culture, c.1500–1200 bc. Named after the prevalent burial rite under round mounds of earth and stone (a practice obviously not limited to this period), the Tumulus Culture reflects the continuation of a number of earlier trends in CERAMICS and metalwork, with greater elaboration of forms and decorative techniques. The Tumulus burial rite was followed by the URNFIELD burial pattern.

tun   the basic unit in the CLASSIC MAYA LONG COUNT equalling 360 days.

Tuna el-Gebel   the site of a major cemetery in Middle Egypt, the NECROPOLIS of the site of HERMOPOLIS MAGNA. Foremost among the mortuary monuments are the LATE PERIOD/Graeco-Roman tombs, especially that of the High Priest of THOTH, Petosiris, and the underground galleries containing the burials of sacred ibises and baboons. Nearby is a rock-cut STELA marking the boundary of the city of Akhetaten (see EL-AMARNA).

tundra   the region between ice caps and tree line of lower arctic latitudes, characterized by treeless vegetation consisting of mosses, lichens, sedges, grasses and stunted shrubs growing on PERMAFROST. During the QUATERNARY, tundra and tundra-like conditions were translated southward during GLACIAL episodes as continental ice sheets expanded.

Tungus   an ethno-linguistic group of eastern Eurasia, especially in the Siberian region. Speakers of Tungusic languages, belonging to the ALTAIC language family, are thought to have infiltrated the Korean peninsula in the Bronze Age (1st millennium BC), resulting in a replacement of the PALAEOASIATIC population of the earlier CHULMUN Neolithic period. This migrational hypothesis has yet to be confirmed.

Turdaş or **Tordos**   a site in Transylvania, northwestern Romania, which has given its name to a variant of the VINČA culture, roughly equivalent to Vinča A/B, sometimes differentiated as the 'Turdaş culture'.

Turville-Petre, Francis Adrian Joseph (1901–42)   an English archaeologist, whose brief career was confined to Palestine under the British Mandate. In 1925 he discovered the 'Galilee Skull' in Zuttiyeh Cave, still the earliest HOMINID skull (at least 150 000 BP by RADIOMETRIC dating) from the Levant. In 1931 he directed the first detailed investigation of Kebara Cave, MOUNT CARMEL, which identified the late Palaeolithic (20 000–12 500 BP) culture known as KEBARAN.

Tustrup   a Neolithic mortuary house of c.2900 BC at the centre of a cemetery of MEGALITHIC tombs in Jutland, Denmark. The sub-rectangular structure, open on one side, was of dry-stone construction but boarded internally with a combination of split oak trunks and megalithic ORTHOSTATS. On the floor were 28 highly decorated pottery vessels and beneath one of the walls was a sand-filled pit which may have held a burial.

Tutankhamen a comparatively minor Egyptian king of uncertain parentage of the 18th DYNASTY, ruling *c.*1336–1327 BC, and whose reign saw the end of the AMARNA PERIOD. Tutankhamen is best known for the discovery of his virtually undisturbed burial in the VALLEY OF THE KINGS by CARTER in 1922. The splendid contents of this remarkable tomb are now housed in the CAIRO Museum.

Tuthmosis the name of four of the monarchs of Egypt's 18th DYNASTY (early NEW KINGDOM). Tuthmosis I and III were both active military campaigners who extended the Egyptian Empire in Palestine and NUBIA.

Twickenham Road see KAPWIRIMBWE.

Tylissos the site of a MINOAN settlement on the island of Crete. The impressive NEOPALATIAL houses excavated by Hazzidakis in 1909–13 suggest that Tylissos must have been a local administrative centre.

tympanon or **tympanum** a vertical face which forms the rear of a PEDIMENT. The 7th century BC temple of Artemis on Corfu has the tympanon carved in high relief.

type a specific ARTIFACT, which serves to represent the *taxon* of which it is a member. Types are very often 'idealized' versions, from which actual specimens deviate to a lesser or greater extent. See also INDEX FOSSIL.

typology the classification of a contemporary series of ARTIFACTS by dividing them into TYPES and sub-types based upon a consideration of qualitative, quantitative, morphological, technological and functional ATTRIBUTES. Typologies are often constructed to help in the formation of chronologies and CULTURE HISTORY.

Tyre a site on the coast of Lebanon, a little-excavated city of the PHOENICIANS. See also SIDON and BYBLOS.

tzolkin the sacred almanac, having 260 days, that was part of the CALENDAR ROUND used in MESOAMERICA. It consists of 20 named days combined with 13 numbers. The almanac is referred to as the tzolkin by MAYA scholars, although this may not have been the name used by the Maya themselves. NAHUATL speakers call the almanac the *Tonalpohualli*.

U

Uan Muhuggiag a cave in the ACACUS Mountains of Libya, well-known for its rock paintings. Excavations revealed two occupations by pastoral people: the first about 7500 bp and the second, which included pottery, about 4800 bp.

Uaxactún a MAYA centre of moderate size in the southern Maya Lowlands, about 40 km north of TIKAL. It was one of the most extensively studied Maya sites in the first half of this century. Much of the work at the site was done for the Carnegie Institute of Washington by Oliver Ricketson in 1926–30 and by A. Ledyard Smith in

1931–37. This research focused on an increased understanding of elite Maya culture. The CERAMIC sequence at Uaxactún provides the basis for the whole of Lowland Maya chronology.

'Ubaid culture complex   a set of items of material culture associated with the 'Ubaid culture. The initial settlement of southern MESOPOTAMIA by food-producing communities is identified archaeologically by this culture. Although still not fully understood, the date of the 'Ubaid seems to cover the second half of the 6th and most of the 5th millennia BC. The culture is characterized by a style of painted pottery that changes through time, giving rise to a four-part division, 'Ubaid 1–4 (the first two of these are also called ERIDU and HAJJI MOHAMMAD respectively); the recent excavations at 'OUELI contain a long pre-'Ubaid 1 sequence that is tentatively being named 'Ubaid 0. Other materials characteristic of the 'Ubaid are baked clay sickles and other equipment and flaked chert hoes. During the 'Ubaid period, towns coalesced within clusters of villages along river and irrigation channels, and contained massive architecture, usually identified as temples (see ERIDU). While the earlier phases of the 'Ubaid are restricted to the southern Mesopotamian ALLUVIUM, the later phases appear through a large region of western Asia, from the Persian Gulf in the south to coastal Syria in the northwest. North and west of southern Mesopotamia, the cultural horizon is often called the Northern 'Ubaid; several sites (e.g. Tell AQAB, Tepe GAWRA) indicate a gradual rather than abrupt transition to 'Ubaid pottery styles from HALAF antecedents, while the CHOGA MAMI Transitional pottery represents a geographical or chronological transition between SAMARRAN and 'Ubaid styles. See AL 'UBAID.

Ubeidiyeh   an early ACHEULIAN site lying near Lake Kinnerath in the Jordan Valley, Israel, best known for its PEBBLE TOOL and FLAKE INDUSTRY, which is somewhat similar to that recovered from OLDUVAI GORGE (Bed II) and which represents one of the earliest sites in this region. The assemblage has been classified into three phases: Phase I includes CHOPPERS and CHOPPING TOOLS; Phase II has polyhedrons and picks; and Phase III is similar to Phase II but of a later date. Phase III is followed by an occupation level which contains similar artifacts but with the addition of primitive BIFACES. Some fragments of HOMO *erectus* have been found, and the whole site is dated to *c*.1 million BP.

Ugarit (*mod.* **Ras Shamra**)   an important Bronze Age city of coastal Syria. Excavations at Ugarit by C. Schaeffer and his successors, begun in the 1920s, provide the most detailed picture of petty kingdoms of Syro-Palestine during the LATE BRONZE AGE, in this instance a client state of the HITTITE empire. This picture is based both on archaeological remains (architecture, art work and small finds) and on texts, the latter revealing social, political, economic and cultic affairs. Excavation at Ras Shamra also gives important information on earlier periods. The place was first settled by an ACERAMIC NEOLITHIC community in the late 7th millennium BC, and deep soundings have traced a largely unbroken cultural sequence (with strong parallels to the 'AMUQ sequence) through the MIDDLE BRONZE AGE (earlier 2nd millennium BC), when Ugarit was a small kingdom involved in the interregional politics of the time (see MARI, OLD BABYLONIAN PERIOD).

Uhle, Max (1856–1944)   a Peruvian archaeologist, one of the first to use artifact style and stratigraphic associations to establish a chronological sequence. He undertook excavations in the major coastal valleys of Peru, and his collections were taken to the Lowie Museum at Berkeley, California. He is perhaps best known for his excavations at PACHACAMAC, and for his synthesis of the first broad regional chronology for the central Andean region.

uinal a period of time in the CLASSIC MAYA LONG COUNT equalling 20 days.

Ulalinka a Paleolithic open-air site on the Ulalinka River in the Altai region of Siberia. Upper Palaeolithic artifacts are buried in LOESS-like LOAM overlying clay and coarse gravel deposits. The gravels yielded an assemblage of fractured rocks that are purportedly artifacts; both the status of the artifacts and the dating of the gravels are problematic. Some researchers believe that the assemblage represents a CHOPPING TOOL industry of early PLEISTOCENE age. The site was discovered by OKLADNIKOV in 1961.

Ullastret an early Iron Age town in Girona, northwest Spain, consisting of a triangular hilltop enclosure protected by a stone wall with circular towers. Within the defences were rectangular stone-built houses, cisterns, paved streets and a market place. Abundant finds of Greek pottery and coins testify to close contacts with Greek colonies nearby on the Mediterranean coast. The town was founded in the 6th century BC and destroyed by fire shortly after 200 BC.

Uluburun see KAŜ.

Ulu Leang a rockshelter site in southwest Sulawesi, Indonesia, the basal layers of which date to the early HOLOCENE (*c*.8000–6000 bc) and contain FLAKE tools similar to those of LEANG BURUNG 2, with additional types of stone and bone tool which were further elaborated in the TOALIAN assemblages of succeeding layers of the site and at LEANG BURUNG 1. Upper layers have yielded metal-age jar burials (late BC–early AD) and rice by *c*.AD 500.

Uluzzian a lithic industry recognized in 1963, and found in a score of Paleolithic caves and open-air sites in Italy. Comprising abundant SCRAPERS, DENTICULATES, small curved backed points and characteristic crescents, it occurs after the final MOUSTERIAN and ends as a contemporary of the early AURIGNACIAN. The oldest RADIOCARBON dates for the industry exceed 33 000 bp.

Umguzan see TSHANGULA.

Umm an-nar a small coastal island in Abu Dhabi in the Persian Gulf on which is a Bronze Age settlement together with a series of contemporary tombs. Excavated by a Danish group in the 1950s and 1960s, the settlement and more particularly the tombs established the archaeological character of the Bronze Age in southeastern Arabia. While the settlement remains largely unreported, the burials – the funerary architecture, pottery and small finds – defined an archaeological culture, dated roughly 2500 to 2000 BC, that is distributed through much of southeastern Arabia, and which may be identified with the ancient CUNEIFORM place-name Magan (see PERSIAN GULF TRADE).

Umm Dabaghiyah a small prehistoric site in the Jezirah in northern Iraq that provided one of the first indications of a pre-HASSUNA occupation of MESOPOTAMIA. Diana Kirkbride's excavations revealed an architectural sequence composed of small rooms in long blocks arranged around a central space. This community kept some domesticated animals, but relied heavily on hunting (especially onager); some domesticated cereals are present, but these are often argued to have been imported (perhaps in exchange for animal skins) and not locally cultivated, since the region of the site is not suited to dry farming. The material culture of Umm Dabaghiyah includes a range of painted, incised, BURNISHED and plain wares, some of which bear resemblances to 'archaic' Hassuna materials. The same material culture occurs at Tell Sotto and at Telul Thalathat.

umu ti   large earth-ovens, common in Canterbury and Otago, South Island, NEW ZEALAND, used for cooking the roots of the cabbage tree *Cordyline australis*.

unconformity   a surface of non-deposition that appears as a break between two rock or SEDIMENT units in a sequence. Unconformities arise from changes in depositional conditions to conditions of EROSION or non-deposition. Recognition of unconformities on and off archaeological sites is significant because they may represent substantial periods of time for which a depositional record is lacking.

underwater archaeology   the SURVEY, EXCAVATION and analysis of submarine archaeological remains, most often the remains of sunken ships. Underwater archaeology was pioneered in the Mediterranean, but is now used in many other places where such techniques are suitable.

Úñetice or Aunjetitz   an Early Bronze Age culture of Bohemia and adjacent areas of Bavaria, southeastern Germany and southwestern Poland, whose name is taken from a cemetery north of Prague. Its origin is uncertain, although the NAGYRÉV culture and BELL BEAKER culture are often mentioned as playing a role. Úñetice burials, particularly the rich inhumations at LEUBINGEN and ŁĘKI MAŁE, have been compared with those of the contemporaneous WESSEX CULTURE in their opulence and indications of social differentiation. Úñetice is generally dated between 1800 and 1500 bc.

unguentarium   a container for perfumed oil. In the HELLENISTIC period the name is usually applied to a small ceramic container, often found in tombs. In the Roman period the name is applied to glass containers of a variety of shapes.

Upper Egypt   a geographical term for that part of the Nile Valley stretching to the south of LOWER EGYPT as far as ASWAN.

Upper Nubia   a geographical term for that part of the Sudanese Nile Valley from the 2nd Cataract as far south as Khartoum.

Upper Republican   an ASPECT located in the central Plains of North America, which dates to AD 1000–1450, and is characterized by cord-roughened pottery, semi-subterranean earth lodges, and an equal dependence on the growing of corn, beans and squash, and on hunting and gathering. Abandonment of western Upper Republican sites may have been caused by a widespread drought.

Upper Swan   an open site on an ALLUVIAL TERRACE of the Swan River, Western Australia. Dated to 38 000 bp, it is one of the oldest firmly dated sites in Australia. The assemblage of QUARTZ and QUARTZITE FLAKES and flake tools is not typical of the AUSTRALIAN CORE TOOL AND SCRAPER TRADITION.

Ur   a site in southern MESOPOTAMIA, already popularly known by its identification with Abraham and the CHALDEANS, which was established by the excavations of Leonard WOOLLEY and others during the 1920s and 30s as one of the most important in the region. Occupation at Ur began during 'UBAID times, in the 6th–5th millennia BC, when the town covered up to 10 ha; it grew in size and importance during the 3rd millennium, reaching 50 ha by the late EARLY DYNASTIC period when the city was an important factor in regional affairs. In the last century of the 3rd millennium BC, the city was the ceremonial centre of the UR III empire which briefly controlled much of Mesopotamia and the adjacent zones of the Zagros. The city lost its political importance in the following centuries, though it remained an important trading centre of the PERSIAN GULF TRADE and grew slightly in size (to 60 ha). The place continued to be inhabited until the late 1st millennium, but at reduced scale and prosperity. Notable features include: the evidence for early settlement in southern Mesopotamia; the extreme wealth of royal and other elite burials, as well as the differences in wealth seen in other graves in the ROYAL CEMETERY; the 3rd millennium religious architecture, principally the ZIGGURAT of NANNA/Sin the moon god; the layout of early Mesopotamian cities and the residential architecture and street plans; and a rich body of texts that range from the early 3rd millennium to the late 1st millennium BC.

Ur III period a period named after the third dynasty of UR according to the SUMERIAN KING LISTS. Ur III denotes the last century of the 3rd millennium during which Ur managed to control much of MESOPOTAMIA and the adjacent Zagros highlands. The dynasty was initiated by Ur-nammu (2112–2095 BC), who extended his power over most of southern Mesopotamia; the empire was largely a creation of his successor SHULGI. The period is marked by close bureaucratic control over many aspects of economic life, reflected in the enormous numbers of economic texts from administrative centres such as Drehem (a small site near NIPPUR). The Ur III state collapsed under ELAMITE and AMORITE military pressure, perhaps exacerbated by economic over-intensification and administrative rigidity.

uraeus the coiled serpent shown on the forehead in depictions of Egyptian kings as a symbol of royalty.

uranium series dating a group of ISOTOPIC dating methods based on the decay series of the radioactive uranium isotopes ^{238}U and the far less abundant ^{235}U to the stable isotope of lead. In most cases they are based on measurements of the activity of one of the uranium isotopes and a relatively short-lived daughter isotope expressed as isotopic ratios. When precipitated as a trace constituent in surface minerals, the uranium begins producing daughter isotopes. Ideally, samples are chosen that chemically have behaved as closed systems, and for which the ratio used to calculate sample age was initially zero.

Dating methods, and respective age ranges, include measurement of $^{230}Th/^{234}U$ (1–350 ka); $^{231}Pa/^{235}U$ (1–300 ka); $^{234}U/^{238}U$ (100–1000 ka); U-trend (10–1000[?]); ^{226}Ra (0.5–10 ka); $^{230}Th/^{232}Th$ (5–300 ka); $^{231}Pa/^{230}Th$ (5–300 ka); and, $^{4}He/U$ (20–400[?] ka).

Material datable by uranium series methods includes, in order of reliability, aragonitic coral, SPELEOTHEM, TRAVERTINE, mollusc shells, marl, bone and teeth, caliche and calcretes, organic matter including PEAT and wood, and detrital sediment. Much of this material has either direct archaeological application, or indirect application through CHRONOMETRIC DATING of archaeological or palaeoenvironmental contexts.

Urartu   a kingdom of the 1st millennium BC in the mountains north of ASSYRIA (encompassing northwest Iran, northeast Anatolia and Armenia) that represents the last of the important HURRIAN-speaking states of western Asia. Coming into existence probably during the 11th century BC, the Urartu state was a perennial obstacle to Assyrian empire building, especially between 900 and 600 BC; at the same time, Urartian art, and especially iconographic expressions of power, reveals a heavy debt to Assyrian culture. Although the most important centres of the kingdom were around Lake Van (see TOPRAKKALE), other major centres existed elsewhere (especially on the Ararat plain, see KARMIR BLUR). Indeed, the Urartian state seems to have been comparatively decentralized, this being perhaps an adaptation to the nature of its mountainous setting.

Urewe   an Early Iron Age pottery style from southwestern Kenya, northwestern Tanzania, Rwanda, eastern Zaire and southern Uganda, in Africa, associated with the first iron-making communities in the region. It dates from the last few centuries BC to the first few centuries AD (see KATURUKA), and gives its name to one of the traditions of the CHIFUMBAZE Complex.

Urfirnis   the GLAZE-like paint used on Greek pottery of the Middle Neolithic and Early HELLADIC periods. The name comes from the German for primitive glaze.

Urnfield complex   a term used to refer to the period between c.1200 and 800 BC in central Europe, spanning the Late Bronze Age and Early Iron Age, in which the burial rite consisted of cremation burials in urns in large open cemeteries, as at KIETRZ in Poland. The Urnfield complex is generally equated with the HALLSTATT sequence defined by REINECKE, although the pattern of burial spread beyond the core Hallstatt region. Within the Urnfield complex are entities such as the LUSATIAN culture, known also from settlements like BISKUPIN and SENFTENBERG.

Uruk period   a period named after the site of WARKA (Uruk), that marks the crystallization of the MESOPOTAMIAN tradition and the emergence of the Mesopotamian state societies. Conventionally dated between roughly 3800 and 3100 BC, CALIBRATED RADIOCARBON dates suggest that the Uruk period begins in the late 5th millennium BC and ends around 3400 or 3300 BC. The period is marked by urban development, elaborate religious centres within cities, the development of a writing system and of CYLINDER SEALS and their application to administrative procedures, mass production of pottery and other goods, and sophisticated art. The Late Uruk period is further marked by the appearance of this material culture outside southern Mesopotamia, notably at SUSA, GODIN TEPE and elsewhere to the east and HABUBA KABIRA to the northwest (the 'Uruk expansion'). Occurring prior to the advent of the more literary uses of writing, social and political interpretations of the Uruk period rest largely on archaeological evidence and some backward extrapolation from EARLY DYNASTIC patterns.

Usatovo culture   a late regional variant of the ENEOLITHIC CUCUTENI-TRIPOLYE culture, named after the site of Usatovo, Ukraine, on the northwestern coast of the Black Sea, where there are a settlement, two barrow (or KURGAN) cemeteries, and two flat-grave cemeteries. Numerous artifacts point to connections with cultures to the southwest and west, including central Europe and the Aegean. Usatovo is believed to represent a distinctive local development of social differentiation and long-distance exchange in the period between 2600 and 2100 bc.

usewear analysis or **microwear analysis**   the examination of the surface and working edge of an ARTIFACT for signs of use, either damage or residue, often by means of a high-powered microscope. The technique is principally used in the study of stone tools, which suffer diagnostic damage or polishing when used to cut, saw or pierce other materials.

ushabti   SEE SHABTI.

Ushki   a group of five prehistoric open-air sites in central Kamchatka in Siberia. Cultural layers are buried in sandy LOAMS along the shore of Big Ushki Lake. At Ushki I, four Neolithic levels overlie three levels assigned to the Upper Paleolithic. The uppermost (5) contains WEDGE-SHAPED CORES and sidescrapers (see SCRAPER), and has been dated to the early HOLOCENE (8790 bp). Layer 6 has been dated to 10 760–10 360 bp, and contains a DYUKTAI CULTURE assemblage associated with traces of former dwellings with tunnel entrances. The lowest layer (7) has yielded dates of 14 300–13 600 bp and further evidence of former dwellings; artifacts include stemmed BIFACIAL POINTS and perforated stone ornaments, but MICROBLADE technology is lacking. The Ushki sites were discovered and excavated by Dikov in 1961–76.

usnu   a platform or small mound found in important INCA sites, on which stood the Inca emperor when holding court. Often the usnu is associated with water channels, and liquid offerings were made there. Astronomical observations may have been made from the usnu in CUZCO.

Ust'-Kan Cave   a Middle Paleolithic site in the Altai region of Siberia. Artifacts and faunal remains are buried in layers of LOAM and rubble. The most common animals are mountain sheep and hare; the absence of arctic species indicates that the remains date to a relatively mild climatic interval (probably prior to the LAST GLACIAL). The artifacts include LEVALLOIS CORES, sidescrapers (see SCRAPER) and points. Ust'-Kan was discovered and investigated by OKLADNIKOV in 1954.

Ust'-Kova   a prehistoric open-air site on the Angara River in central Siberia. Several cultural layers are contained in deposits of sand and clay on the second TERRACE. Artifacts of the Iron Age and Bronze Age are buried in the modern soil; beneath the latter lies a sand containing Mesolithic and Neolithic remains. Three Upper Palaeolithic horizons were tentatively identified in the underlying clay. All of the horizons are associated with faunal remains of woolly MAMMOTH, reindeer and other mammals. Artifacts from the lowermost horizon, which yielded RADIOCARBON dates of 32 865–28 050 bp, include large BLADES and points. The middle level, dated to 23 920 bp, contains various tool forms, including sidescrapers and end-scrapers (see SCRAPER) and BIFACES. The upper horizon, dated to 14 220 bp, produced bifaces, BURINS and other tool types, but not the

MICROBLADE technology that is so characteristic of the later Upper Palaeolithic in Siberia. Ust'-Kova was discovered in 1937 by OKLADNIKOV, and excavated by Drozdov in 1969–81.

U Thong a large (1690 m × 840 m) late prehistoric/early historic moated settlement in central Thailand located near trade routes to the west. Finds at sites in the old city (Tha Muang) and vicinity include Indian beads similar to those at BAN DON TA PHET (*c*.300? BC), a Roman coin of Victorinus (3rd century AD), and coins once thought to be from FUNAN, but now dated to the 7th–8th century AD and linked to the MON state of DVARAVATI and contemporaries. The site, which has Buddhist and Hindu remains, and evidence of a bead-producing industry, may have been a palace centre at one time; it was annexed by the state of KAMBUJA early in the 2nd millennium. The name is attached to a style of Buddhist art dating to the 12th–15th centuries.

Utqiagvik an INUIT site, located in Barrow, Alaska, comprising 60 historic and prehistoric house remains. The most significant find at the site was that of the remains of five bodies, trapped in their house by a winter coastal ice-surge. Three of them, belonging to two young girls and an adolescent male, were skeletons only. The other two, however, were the frozen remains of a woman in her 20s and one in her 40s. Autopsies revealed that the individuals had been well-nourished, although subject to occasional periods of food short-age. They had suffered from excessive consumption of meat and fat and from inhalation of smoke. A RADIOCARBON date of 440 bp (the same period as the QILAKITSOQ find) was taken from a vertebra of the older woman. Clothing and hunting tools were also well preserved. See THULE, SKRAELING.

Utu a SUMERIAN god, equivalent to the AKKADIAN god Shamash, an offspring of ENLIL and connected to the sun; the symbol of light, both literally and metaphorically, he was the god of justice, before whom legal contracts had to be sworn and whose name was invoked in the various MESOPOTAMIAN law codes. His symbol, the winged sun disc, became a standard representation of royalty.

Uvarov, Count Aleksei Sergeevich (1828–84) a major figure in the early development of archaeology in prerevolutionary Russia. Uvarov organized the Imperial Russian Archaeological Society in 1864 and the first archaeological congress in 1869. He also conducted excavations at Chersonese in the 1850s, the Merian graves, and the Upper Paleolithic site of Karacharovo on the Oka River in 1877.

Uxmal the largest and best known of the PUUC MAYA sites, occupied during the Late CLASSIC. Uxmal enjoyed its heyday in the period AD 800–1000. The site is extremely well planned and an excellent example of the Puuc style of architecture. This style includes large masonry buildings with a veneer of well-cut stone and decoration on the upper portions of the structures. Uxmal is connected by a paved causeway (*sacbe*) to a second Puuc site, KABÁH. Various aspects of Puuc sites suggest that the 'Classic Maya' did not collapse, but rather shifted from south to north during the POST-CLASSIC (or 'Decadent') period.

V

Vădastra culture   a Middle/Late Neolithic culture of southwestern Romania in the late 5th millennium bc, occurring to the north of the VESELINOVO culture of Bulgaria. It was contemporaneous with the early stages (A/B) of the VINČA culture of the western Balkans in its earlier stages, and later part of a complex of Late Neolithic groups that include the MARITSA and BOIAN cultures. Cattle phalanges from two Vădastra sites had osteological characteristics that suggested the use of the animals for traction.

Vahangeku'a   one of the largest TOHUA in the TAIPIVAI VALLEY, Nuku Hiva, Marquesas, Polynesia. It comprises an artificial terrace, 170 m by 25 m, faced by a 3 m wall of basalt blocks. The open area is surrounded by massive PA'EPA'E. Excavations by Robert Suggs in 1957 showed that it was built over several centuries and reached its final form close to European contact.

Vailele   a series of large earthen mounds built as house platforms on the island of Upolu, Samoa, which date to the most recent aceramic period of Samoan prehistory. Two excavated mounds sealed occupation deposits containing ADZES and plain pottery dating to 300 BC–AD 200.

Vaillant, George Clapp (1901–45)   an American archaeologist who worked in the MAYA Lowlands and the BASIN OF MEXICO, and established some of the basic chronologies used in these areas.

vaisselle blanche   pseudo-ceramics produced during the ACERAMIC NEOLITHIC (PPNB) of Syria, Lebanon, and the east bank of the River Jordan (e.g. the sites of ABU HUREYRA, Buqras, Ramad, Labweh, AIN GHAZAL). This white ware was made from lime mixed with ashes and built into large vessels in coils; its surface was smoothed, and it was then left to dry rock-hard. These vessels are occasionally decorated with painted bands.

Vaito'otia   an Early Eastern POLYNESIAN site of c.AD 800, on Huahine, Society Islands, with good preservation of organic materials in waterlogged deposits. Structures include wooden storehouses on piles and an enigmatic basalt upright on a coral base. Plant remains found include kava, gourd, coconut and pandanus. Besides FISH-HOOKS and shell artifacts, wood and whalebone hand–clubs similar to MAORI PATU were found.

Val Camonica   a glaciated valley in the Alpine foothills of Lombardy, Italy, with a rich collection of prehistoric ROCK ART, conventionally divided into four chronological phases (NEOLITHIC, CHALCOLITHIC, BRONZE AGE and IRON AGE) with subdivisions. Motifs are pecked in the glacially smoothed rock surfaces, and include daggers, chariots, warriors and warfare, sun motifs, ploughing scenes, men and animals, and geometric designs. Some of the daggers resemble those of the Chalcolithic REMEDELLO culture of the Po plain.

Valders Advance   the last major GLACIAL advance of the

527

PLEISTOCENE in North America, which lasted until approximately 10 000 BP.

Valdivia   an early FORMATIVE period site (*c*.3200 bc) on the coast of Ecuador, which gives its name to Formative period culture in Ecuador. Early CERAMICS located at the site by Betty Meggers, Clifford EVANS and Emilio Estrada were, at the time (1960s), the earliest known in the New World (but see PRECERAMIC). Having no known antecedents for this fairly well-made pottery, decorated with a variety of plastic techniques, they suggested that Valdivia ceramics were directly related to the JOMON ceramics of Japan. This idea was never widely accepted, and antecedents to Valdivia ceramics were eventually found.

Vallée des Merveilles   see MONT BÉGO.

Valley of Mexico   see BASIN OF MEXICO.

Valley of Oaxaca   a large plateau lying in the southern part of the Sierra Madres in the state of Oaxaca, Mexico. The valley is a highland area, elevation 1550 m above sea level.

The valley has a long sequence of occupation, beginning about 5500 BC. Some of the first cities in Mexico emerged in the Valley of Oaxaca. The work of Kent Flannery, especially at SAN JOSÉ MOGOTE and other FORMATIVE sites, has greatly increased our understanding of urban development in MESOAMERICA. The largest centre in the valley was MONTE ALBÁN. The valley was subsequently occupied by the MIXTECS and the ZAPOTECS.

Valley of the Kings   part of THEBES (EGYPT)–WEST BANK. With the adjacent West Valley, the Valley of the Kings contained tombs prepared for almost all the known kings of the NEW KINGDOM from TUTHMOSIS I to RAMESSES XI, plus some members of the immediate royal family and high court officials. The best known of the tombs in the Valley of the Kings is that of TUTANKHAMEN.

Vallonnet   a southeastern French Lower Paleolithic cave-site, discovered in 1958 at Roquebrune-Cap-Martin, Alpes-Maritimes, and excavated by Barral in 1959 and by de Lumley in 1962, which has yielded nine pieces of an unrefined PEBBLE and FLAKE INDUSTRY and a fauna datable to *c*.900 000 BP.

vallum   1. a Roman defensive rampart.
2. the flat-bottomed ditch with two parallel banks which ran to the south of HADRIAN'S WALL, in northern Britain. It is thought to have marked the southern boundary of the frontier zone.

Van Heekeren, H. Robert (1902–74)   a Dutch archaeologist best known for his work in Indonesia, especially his excavations on Java and Sulawesi, and for his important books *The Stone Age of Indonesia* (1957/1972) and *The Bronze-Iron Age of Indonesia* (1958).

Van Riet Lowe, Clarens 'Peter' (1894–1956)   a South African civil engineer and public relations man for archaeology, who discovered many archaeological sites in the course of his work and, with GOODWIN, wrote the 1929 classic *The Stone Age cultures of South Africa*.

Vapheio   the site of a 15th century BC MYCENAEAN THOLOS tomb in Laconia, Greece, which was excavated by TSOUNTAS. Although plundered, the tomb contained an intact grave-pit in which a rich and no doubt powerful individual had been buried with bronze weapons, fine jewellery and two superb decorated gold cups.

Varna   a Late ENEOLITHIC cemetery site of the GUMELNIŢA culture (KARANOVO VI) located in eastern Bulgaria, containing some of the richest burials known from the 4th millennium bc. Some 200 graves have been excavated at Varna, a number of which are *cenotaphs* (a mortuary monument to an individual whose remains lie elsewhere). An extraordinary number of gold artifacts were found in the Varna graves, including diadems and earrings, while copper artifacts, pottery, and flint tools are common. The differentiation in the richness of grave-goods has led to the interpretation that the Varna cemetery indicates nascent social ranking in southeastern Europe.

varves   a SEDIMENTARY structure consisting of rhythmically bedded couplets of LAMINAE or BEDS that demonstrably were deposited in the course of a year. Annually laminated sediments are deposited in freshwater lakes and lakes influenced by proximity to glaciers, and occur as different types, depending on lake chemistry, physical processes and sediment input over the course of the seasons of a year. Varved lake sequences are usually an excellent source of palaeoenvironmental information that can be applied to the interpretation of nearby archaeological sites. In addition to detailed information on seasonal and environmental change, varves provide information on rates of change in vegetation history, the role of fire in forests under natural and management conditions, and the effects of people on erosion and other drainage-basin processes.

Varves can be used in geochronological studies and as a CHRONOMETRIC DATING method because varve couplets are deposited annually. However, unless tied to modern SEDIMENTATION or a known benchmark, varved sequences may be only FLOATING CHRONOLOGIES. RADIOCARBON DATING of organic constituents can provide a general age estimate for varved sequences. On the other hand, varve sequences can be used to CALIBRATE other dating techniques. The method was developed in 1878 by Baron Gerard de Geer, a Swedish geologist.

vase-support   a pottery vessel consisting of a hollow cylindrical (or more rarely cuboid) base supporting a dished upper surface. The outer faces and broad flat rim are often richly decorated with incised triangle, chevron and chequer-board designs. The earlier theory, reflected in the name, that they may have been stands for round-based pots has been superseded by their identification as incense-burners. They are a characteristic feature of the Middle Neolithic CHASSÉEN culture.

Vasić, Miloje (1869–1956)   a Serbian archaeologist who began the systematic excavation of the TELL site at VINČA in 1908. Vasić recognized the importance of the Vinča site for the establishment of the Neolithic chronology of the western Balkans, but linked it closely with developments in the Aegean area, a theme taken up in the English-language literature by V.G. CHILDE.

Vasiliki   the site of a MINOAN settlement on the island of Crete, excavated by Seager early this century and more recently by Zois, who has demonstrated that the Early Minoan II (*c*.2600–2200 BC) 'House on the Hill', a multi-storey structure regarded by some as a prototype Minoan palace, is in fact two large houses. The mottled black, red and brown pottery known as Vasiliki ware was abundant in these Early Minoan II levels.

Vatcha   a LAPITA site on Ile des Pins, New Caledonia, Melanesia.

There are two episodes of occupation, the younger of which has a date of 2855 bp.

Vedbaek Bøgebakken   a Danish Mesolithic cemetery on Zealand which, although there had been at least three previous excavations at Bøgebakken, was discovered only during construction work in 1975 and subsequently excavated by Brinch Petersen. The site, which is dated to *c*.4800 BC, has yielded 17 graves with the remains of 22 individuals, some accompanied by grave-goods and apparently covered in red OCHRE. The burials included two young mothers buried with their new-born infants and what appears to be a family group of a father, mother and one-year-old child. The site has been dated to the early ERTEBØLLE phase.

vegetational climax   a model which attempts to explain vegetational succession as a series of phases culminating in a terminal phase which exists in a state of dynamic equilibrium with the prevailing environmental conditions. The model has been discounted as an explanation for vegetational community evolution, because it has been demonstrated that they are not predictable systems.

Veii   a city in south ETRURIA situated 18 km to the north of ROME. It seems to have been settled in the VILLANOVAN PERIOD and was destroyed by Rome in 396 BC. The site occupies a large plateau, some 195 ha, which in the 5th century BC was enclosed by a wall. A sanctuary has been excavated at Portonaccio. The ridge of the temple carried large TERRACOTTA statues of deities.

Velatice group   a regional Late Bronze Age group of the URNFIELD burial tradition in Moravia, dated to the 12th century bc (HALLSTATT A). In addition to burial finds, settlements of the Velatice group are also known, the most important being LOVČIČKY.

Vénat   a Late Bronze Age metal hoard (*c*.700 BC) from Charente, France found buried in a large pottery vessel in 1893. The hoard contained 2720 bronzes including 133 swords, 126 spearheads, 125 socketed axes and 440 bracelets, some with geometric decoration. Among the swords were several of CARP'S TONGUE type, but the hoard as a whole was a mixture of Atlantic and continental bronze-working traditions.

Venedians   a Late Iron Age people of the lower Vistula basin in Poland, from the 1st century BC (late LA TÈNE) to the 6th century AD. Venedian settlements and burials have yielded a rich array of iron and bronze ARTIFACTS, and iron working was particularly important at sites in the HOLY CROSS MOUNTAINS such as SŁUPIA STARA.

Ventana Cave   a stratified site in southwestern Arizona, USA, with occupation levels over 11 000 years old. The lowest level contains stone tools, as well as the bones from numerous extinct PLEISTOCENE animals. The generalized hunting and gathering pattern suggests similarities with the roughly contemporary SAN DIEGUITO COMPLEX of California.

Ventris, Michael (1922–56)   a British scholar and architect who, in 1952, deciphered the LINEAR B script as an early form of Greek. This discovery revolutionized our knowledge of the MYCENAEAN civilization.

'Venus' figurines   the popular but erroneous name for the small female statuettes of the Upper Paleolithic. They are found from southwest France to European Russia, and also in Siberia. Those of western Europe (see BRASSEMPOUY, LESPUGUE, GRIMALDI) are of IVORY or stone;

very few have any stratigraphic context, but all have been subjectively assigned to the GRAVETTIAN period. In central Europe (see WILLENDORF, DOLNÍ VĚSTONICE) they are of stone, baked LOESS or ivory, while those of the east (see AVDEEVO, GAGARINO, KHOTYLEVO, KOSTENKI, MAL'TA) are of ivory and span a period from 25 000 to 12 000 BP. Not a homogeneous set of objects, they depict females of a wide variety of ages and physical types. The few with enormous breasts and buttocks are usually seen as emphasizing fertility, but they are not representative of the genre.

Vergina the royal capital of Macedonia in northern Greece. An extensive TUMULUS cemetery of the Early Iron Age has been explored as well as part of the HELLENISTIC palace. Excavations by Manolis Andronikos at the so-called Royal Tomb discovered an extremely rich burial which included quantities of IVORY and silver items. Inside a gold LARNAX were found the cremated remains of a male. Reconstructions of the skull, and comparisons with royal portraiture, have raised the possibility that this was the burial of Philip II, the father of Alexander the Great.

Vértes, Laszlo (1914–68) a Hungarian archaeologist and Palaeolithic specialist who excavated many of the most important Palaeolithic sites in Hungary, including VÉRTESSZÖLLÖS, ISTÁLLÓSKÖ, SZELETA CAVE, TATA and JANKOVICH.

Vértesszöllös a Lower Paleolithic open-air site on the Átalér River, near its confluence with the Danube, in north-central Hungary. Artifacts and faunal remains are buried in LOESS and spring deposits on the fourth TERRACE. The fauna (e.g. *Dicerorhinus etruscus*) indicates a Middle PLEISTOCENE age, and the spring deposits yielded URANIUM SERIES dates of 350 000–175 000 bp. The artifact assemblages contain PEBBLE CHOPPING TOOLS and unspecialized FLAKE tools, and are included in the BUDA industry. They are associated with human skeletal remains considered intermediate between HOMO *erectus* and *H. sapiens*. Vértesszöllös was investigated by VÉRTES in 1963–65.

Verulamium see ST ALBANS.

Veselé an Early Bronze Age fortified site of the MAD'AROVCE culture in southwestern Slovakia, *c.*1800–1700 bc. In the interior of the fortified area were numerous storage pits and houses with beaten earth floors, hearths, and burnt wall daub.

Veselinovo culture a Middle/Late Neolithic culture of southern Bulgaria in the late 5th millennium bc, material of which is found in Layer III at KARANOVO, which is contemporaneous with the early stages (A/B) of the VINČA culture. Veselinovo vessel forms include pear-shaped and cylindrical beakers with flat bases or cylindrical legs, often with a characteristic curving handle with an upper knob.

Věteřov culture an Early Bronze Age culture of Moravia, contemporaneous with the MAD'AROVCE culture of western Slovakia (the two are often considered together). Their material culture contained a mixture of elements from the Hungarian Early Bronze Age and the ÚNĚTICE culture of Bohemia.

Victoria West a LEVALLOIS-like technique for preparing CORES for the removal of a single FLAKE, associated with EARLIER STONE AGE assemblages from the interior of South Africa.

Vicús a late EARLY HORIZON culture of Piura, on the far north coast of Peru. The modelled and painted CERAMICS exhibit stylistic similarity to early MOCHE ceramics.

vigesimal mathematics   a base-20 place-notation system employed in MESOAMERICAN writing systems, primarily that of the MAYA, for counting periods of time. More accurately, it is a *modified* vigesimal system because the 20 × 20 position was calculated as 20 × 18 (known by the Maya as the TUN). Its best-known application was the LONG COUNT of the Maya calendar: the units were KIN (1 day), UINAL (20 days), tun (360 days), KATUN (7200 days) and BAKTUN (144 000 days).

Vikings   Scandinavians of *c*.AD 700 to 1100 who were great boat-builders (see CLINKER-BUILT) and navigators. They reached the Mediterranean and the Black Sea, and BYZANTIUM, and also raided the rivers and coasts of western Europe, including LINDISFARNE, the Isle of Man and the Irish coast. In 865 their raids on England led to their conquest of most of the eastern part of the country, with their capital at YORK (JORVIK). In the 10th century they briefly colonized Greenland and portions of the North American coast, but had abandoned these settlements by the mid 15th century because of worldwide climatic deterioration. See L'ANSE AUX MEADOWS, SKRAELINGS, THULE, VINLAND.

Vikletice   a cemetery of the CORDED WARE culture in Bohemia with 164 graves, 138 of which contained grave-goods. It is difficult to reconcile the existence of such a cemetery with the model of Corded Ware nomadic pastoralism that has often been proposed.

Vila Nova de São Pedro   a CHALCOLITHIC fortress at Santarém, Portugal, consisting of a massive dry-stone rampart with semicircular bastions, on a massive rammed-earth platform surrounded by a rock-cut ditch and traces of concentric outer defensive circuits. Three phases of occupation have been recognized, the first pre-dating the construction of the fortifications. Excavations in the interior have recovered copper axes, chisels and daggers, together with evidence of metalworking. Pottery included BEAKER material and local wares, dating to the 3rd millennium BC.

Vilcabamba   an INCA site established after the Spanish conquest in the eastern Andes north of CUZCO, Peru. After attempting to defeat the Spanish by means of a siege of Cuzco, the Inca rebels fled north, stopping at various locations, and finally settling at Vilcabamba. Although Hiram Bingham argued that MACHU PICCHU was the location of Vilcabamba, the American explorer Gene Savoy located the actual site in 1964, at a place called Espíritu Pampa.

Vilcas Guamán   a large INCA administrative centre near Ayacucho, located along the royal Inca highway north of CUZCO, Peru. It was the symbolic centre of the Inca universe. A large four-stepped USNU of dressed stone was erected at this site.

villa   a Roman residence, including palace complexes such as Hadrian's Villa at Tivoli outside Rome, luxurious private dwellings (see OPLONTIS), urban dwellings (see HERCULANEUM, POMPEII), and more humble rural dwellings.

Villanovan period   the Early Iron Age phase of the Po Valley, ETRURIA and parts of CAMPANIA in Italy, defined by artifacts from the type-site of Villanova near Bologna (*c*.900–700 BC). Cremation was often practised and the ashes could be buried in hut-shaped urns (see IMPASTO). Their metalwork, in gold and bronze, often shows affinities with Central Europe as well as with other parts of Italy. The Villanovan culture provided the foundations for the emergence of the Etruscan city-states in the 8th century BC.

Villeneuve-Tolosane a Middle Neolithic village covering *c*.30 ha on a Garonne river terrace in Haute-Garonne, France. Excavations have revealed enclosure ditches, storage pits, a length of palisade trench and over 700 shallow circular and rectangular pits containing cobbles, which probably served as communal hearths. Associated material was of CHASSÉEN type, and RADIOCARBON dates suggested occupation from *c*.4250–3600 BC. Thousands of cereal grains were recovered, and one pit contained over 50 000 snailshells.

Vinapu a site with important AHU on EASTER ISLAND. Vinapu II, dating to *c*.ad 857, has a typically POLYNESIAN facing of rough, vertical slabs, while Vinapu I, of *c*.ad 1516, has a famous façade of beautifully fitted blocks, often erroneously compared with the CYCLOPEAN blocks of the INCAS at CUZCO. Both ahu carried a series of MOAI.

Vinča a TELL site on the River Danube near Belgrade, in Serbia, initially excavated by VASIČ between 1908 and 1912. The deep (9 m) stratigraphy of the Vinča tell provides a sequence that spans the period between *c*.5000 and 3500 bc. The lowest levels at Vinča contain STARČEVO material, while the upper levels have yielded habitation levels from all phases of the Vinča culture. V.G. CHILDE attempted to tie the Vinča sequence to the sequence from Troy (HISARLIK) in the Aegean, but the advent of RADIOCARBON DATING showed this correlation to be spurious.

Vinča culture a Late Neolithic culture of the western Balkans, centred on the Danube and Morava valleys in Serbia, between *c*.4500 and 3500 bc. The Vinča culture succeeds the STARČEVO culture in this region and is divided into four phases (A–D). Vinča fine pottery is black or dark grey and is decorated by channelling and BURNISHING. Both extensive open settlements, such as SELEVAC, and compact TELL settlements, such as Vinča itself, are known. Numerous ANTHROPOMORPHOUS figurines are found on Vinča sites, suggesting ritual activity. COPPER artifacts and evidence for copper mining at sites like RUDNA GLAVA represent some of the earliest METALLURGY in prehistoric Europe.

Vindija Cave a Paleolithic site located near Zagreb in northwestern Croatia. Artifacts and faunal remains are buried in clay, sand and rubble deposits. The lower cultural layers contain tools (predominantly sidescrapers – see SCRAPER) assigned to the Middle Palaeolithic. The basal layer, which contains remains of *Dicerorhinus mercki*, is dated to the Last INTERGLACIAL; younger Middle Palaeolithic layers appear to span the early PLENIGLACIAL (*c*.115 000–60 000 bp). Overlying layers are dated to the middle and late Pleniglacial, yielding assemblages assigned to the AURIGNACIAN (lower) and GRAVETTIAN (upper). Numerous human skeletal fragments were recovered from Vindija, including NEANDERTHAL remains from an upper Middle Palaeolithic level, and anatomically modern remains from the Gravettian level.

Vindolanda a Roman fort and civilian settlement of the late 1st/early 2nd century AD at Chesterholm, northern England, lying just south of HADRIAN'S WALL on the earlier frontier of Stanegate. Excavated by Robin Birley in 1969–89, its main structures include a military bath-house, an inn, houses and mausolea. A wide range of leather and wooden remains have survived. Among the most important finds are over 1000 fragments of letters and documents written in ink on thin slivers of wood, which are providing an unparalleled insight into life in a frontier province of the Roman Empire.

Vinland the VIKING name for the portion of North America visited by Leif Erikson in the 10th century AD, probably in the vicinity of L'ANSE AUX MEADOWS, although some historians have proposed the coast of Maine as its correct location. See SKRAELINGS.

Viracochapampa see MARCA HUAMACHUCO.

vitrified fort a type of Iron Age HILLFORT with dry-stone timber-laced rampart, found in Scotland, in which the timber-lacing has been fired, probably by accident or hostile action, causing the stone core of the rampart to fuse.

Vix an Iron Age burial mound, 42 m across and 6 m high, at the foot of MONT LASSOIS, Côte-d'Or, France. A sub-rectangular wooden chamber beneath the mound held a rich burial of HALLSTATT D date (late 6th century BC). The body of a woman wearing a solid gold TORC or diadem lay on a dismantled wooden cart. The torc was one of several outstanding imports from the CLASSICAL world, including also ETRUSCAN bronze vessels and an Attic BLACK FIGURE cup. The most notable import, however, was a huge bronze KRATER 1.64 m high, decorated around the neck with an embossed frieze of foot soldiers and chariots. The krater, for mixing wine, is of Greek manufacture and is thought to have been made either at SPARTA or at the Greek colony of TARENTUM in southern Italy.

Vladimirovka one of the largest sites of the CUCUTENI-TRIPOLYE culture in Ukraine, with over 200 huts of the PLOSHCHADKI type arranged in five concentric circles.

Vlasac a transitional Mesolithic–Neolithic site located in the gorges of the River Danube known as the Iron Gates in Serbia. The settlement at Vlasac is similar to the one at LEPENSKI VIR, although smaller in size. The large number of human skeletons from the Vlasac cemetery has provided one of the best samples of palaeoanthropological data for this period.

Vogelherd a Paleolithic cave in Württemberg, southwest Germany, excavated by G. Riek in 1931, which has yielded MOUSTERIAN layers followed by two important AURIGNACIAN occupation levels: the lower assemblage includes refined RETOUCHED BLADES, BURINS, endscrapers (see SCRAPER) and many bone points with split bases; the upper assemblage includes a similar stone tool-kit but a different style of bone point with a rounded section. Carved IVORY animal figurines, including MAMMOTH, horse and bison, were recovered from both Aurignacian levels. There is MAGDALENIAN occupation above.

Volga–Oka culture a complex of transitional Mesolithic–Neolithic groups of the forest zone of the Central Russian Plain north and east of Moscow. The Volga-Oka culture is related to the 'Forest Neolithic' groups of the Baltic zones, such as the PIT-COMB POTTERY culture and the NARVA culture, and represents a similar adoption of pottery by local hunter-gatherer populations, but with little evidence of food production. Rather, hunting and fishing appear to have been the central economic activities.

Volgograd see SUKHAYA MECHETKA.

Volgu see LAUREL-LEAF POINT.

Volkov, Fyodor Kondrat'evich (1847–1918) a Ukrainian archaeologist influential in the development of Palaeolithic studies in Russia. A former student of de MORTILLET, Volkov conducted the first excavations at the Upper Palaeolithic site of MEZIN, and trained the noted Russian Palaeolithic archaeologist EFIMENKO.

Volos the site in Thessaly of ancient Iolkos, in Greek legend the home of Jason, which appears to have been occupied more or less continuously from the Early Bronze Age until the HELLENISTIC period. A large structure, built in the 14th century BC and reconstructed in the 13th century BC, might be a MYCENAEAN palace. An intact THOLOS tomb was discovered at Kapakli, just north of Volos.

Volp Caves a cave system around the Volp River in Ariège (French Pyrenees), comprising three sites. *Enlène*, a MAGDALENIAN occupation site containing numerous HEARTHS, has an area of paving and a wealth of PORTABLE ART including over 1100 engraved stones. It has produced dates between *c.*12 000 and 11 000 bc. In *Le Tuc d'Audoubert* in 1912 the three Bégouën brothers discovered animal engravings on the walls and, in a chamber at the end of the cave, two clay bison in haut-relief. The Tuc's sparse occupation material has been dated to 12 400 bc; in 1914 the brothers discovered the cave of *Les Trois Frères*, a largely uninhabited extension of Enlène containing hundreds of parietal engravings and some paintings, especially in the profusely engraved 'sanctuary' dominated by a 'sorcerer' figure. Links of style and pigment with Enlène's portable art assign most of the wall art to the 12th millennium bc.

volute a spiral scroll found on CAPITALS of the IONIC ORDER.

vomitorium the access way to the CAVEA of a Roman theatre or AMPHITHEATRE.

Vounous the site of a large Early CYPRIOT (late 3rd millennium BC) cemetery in northern Cyprus. The tombs consisted of a roughly oval rock-cut chamber entered through a short DROMOS. The grave-offerings include TERRACOTTA models which depict cult scenes.

Vrysi see AYIOS EPIKTITOS-VRYSI.

Vučedol group a Late Neolithic group of the central Balkans, named after the site of Vučedol on the Drava River in northern Croatia and Slovenia. The Vučedol group (or phase) succeeds the BADEN culture and the KOSTOLAC group. Other sites of the Vučedol group are found at LJUBLJANSKO BLAT.

Vulci a city in ETRURIA. Excavations have revealed traces of an Etruscan temple and Roman houses. The exploration of the cemeteries during the 19th century yielded significant quantities of Greek pottery, which were dispersed throughout European collections. It also seems to have been a production centre for bronzes.

W

Wa   the early historic Chinese name for some inhabitants of the Japanese islands in the YAYOI period.

Wace, Alan (1879–1957)   a British scholar and archaeologist who was Director of the British School at Athens from 1914–23. He undertook excavations in Laconia and in Thessaly and, most extensively, at MYCENAE.

Wadi Kubbaniya   an extensive series of Egyptian Late Palaeolithic sites on the west bank of the River Nile south of ASWAN, investigated by F. Wendorf and others since 1978. The sites have yielded rich evidence for early plant domestication, with grinding stones, mortars and pestles and well-preserved carbonized plant remains including wheat and barley, dated by RADIOCARBON to between 18 250 and 16 960 bp.

Wadi Shatt er-Rigal   a dried watercourse in UPPER EGYPT whose valley walls bear over 800 PREDYNASTIC rock engravings and later GRAFFITI, the most important of the latter being of the MIDDLE KINGDOM.

Wairau Bar   an Archaic burial ground and MIDDEN site at the mouth of the Wairau River, South Island, NEW ZEALAND. Investigations at this site in the 1940s allowed Roger DUFF to define the so-called 'MOA-hunter period'. Dated to AD 1100–1350, the burials have unusually rich grave-goods. The artifacts from Wairau Bar are paralleled in early sites in the Marquesas and Society Islands.

waisted axe   a large stone tool with a flaked cutting edge and a flaked notch on either margin, giving a waist for hafting. Waisted axes have been found in PLEISTOCENE contexts: in New Guinea at KOSIPE, NOMBE and Yuku; on the HUON PENINSULA; and in Australia, on KANGAROO ISLAND.

Wajak   a now-destroyed site in east-central Java, at which two fossilized HOMO *sapiens* crania were found; associations and dates are lacking, but it is thought that Wajak Man is younger than SOLO MAN, being late PLEISTOCENE or early HOLOCENE.

Wajil   a hard-fired, reduced, unglazed earthenware of the Korean PROTO-THREE KINGDOMS period. (Compare MUMUN, KIMHAE.)

Wakankar, Vishnu Sridhar (1919–88)   an Indian archaeologist and ROCK-ART specialist, best known for his studies and excavations at BHIMBETKA.

Walker Road   an early prehistoric open-air site on the Nenana River in south-central Alaska, USA. The cultural layer is buried in LOESS and wind-blown sand deposits overlying an ancient TERRACE; it has yielded four RADIOCARBON dates between 11 820–11 010 bp. There is evidence of a former dwelling structure with central HEARTH. The assemblage contains CHINDADN POINTS and endscrapers (see SCRAPER), and has been assigned to the NENANA COMPLEX. Walker was discovered and initially investigated by Hoffecker in 1980–84; excavations were conducted by Powers in 1985–88.

Wallacea   a zone of islands between the Southeast Asian Sunda shelf and the SAHUL SHELF. There has never been a complete land bridge between the islands, and the resulting water crossings formed a barrier to the spread of animals and humans into Australia and New Guinea.

Wandjina figures   an Aboriginal term in the Kimberley region of Western Australia for ancestral spirits, depicted in large ANTHROPO-MORPHIC bichrome or polychrome paintings. The figures have prominent eyes and the head is surrounded by a 'halo', often with radiating lines. Wandjina figures are the most recent art in the area, post-dating bichrome figures and monochrome BRADSHAW FIGURES, and were repainted periodically.

Wando   the site of a late 11th century AD Koryo shipwreck (see KOREAN PERIODIZATION) off South Cholla Province, Korea. Nine metres long and unkeeled, the ship was constructed in traditional Korean fashion with five longitudinal timbers. Cargo consisted of 30 000 CELADON vessels from kilns in Haenam, South Cholla, destined for regional elite use.

Wangman   the name of an interloper who seized the Chinese throne, creating the Wangman Interregnum (AD 9–25) in the HAN Dynasty. Coins minted during Wangman's reign are distributed throughout East Asian archaeological sites and provide a diagnostic dating tool.

Wargata Mina   or **Judds Cavern**   a limestone cave in southwest TASMANIA, Australia. Hand stencils have been found in this and Ballawinne Cave. Human blood in red pigment on the walls has given dates of 10 730 and 9240 bp, confirming the PLEISTOCENE age of cave occupation in this region.

Wari   see HUARI.

Warka or **Uruk**   a site near the Euphrates in the southern section of the MESOPOTAMIAN ALLUVIUM, the stratigraphically-documented occupation of which begins with the 'UBAID 2 period and continues through PARTHIAN times (early 1st millennium AD). The German work at Warka begun by N. Noldeke in the 1920s provides a fundamental reference for many aspects of southern Mesopotamian archaeology. These investigations have concentrated on two temple precincts, the E-Anna and the Anu ZIGGURAT, with additional invest-igation of other major architectural units (for example, the early 2nd millennium palace of Sinkasid, the Karaindash temple of the KASSITE period, the Parthian Gareus). While the size and regional significance of Warka fluctuated through its history, the city was most important during Late URUK to EARLY DYNASTIC times, when it grew to cover some 400 ha (by the Early Dynastic I) and formed the regional demographic and probably political centre of gravity. Warka during these periods provides information central to discussion of the origins of the state in southern Mesopotamia (see EANNA SOUNDING).

warranting argument   an argument supporting the assumptions about the way the world works. Archaeologists use warranting argu-ments to support interpretations of empirical observations: e.g. the claim that certain rooms in prehistoric PUEBLOS of the American southwest were for storage can be supported by analogies concerning room features (size, presence/absence of hearth, number of means of access, location in the site) in more recent local sites. See also ACTUALISTIC STUDY, BRIDGING ARGUMENT.

Warring States   see ZHOU.

Wasserburg Buchau   see BUCHAU.

Watom Island   an island off northeast New Britain, BISMARCK ARCHIPELAGO, Melanesia, where LAPITA pottery was first reported in 1908. The most recent excavations demonstrate occupation during the middle and late phases of Lapita in the Bismarcks, 2767–1787 bp. OBSIDIAN from both TALASEA and LOU occurs, with Talasea material increasing over time. The largest sample so far of Lapita human skeletal remains comes from the Kainapirina site.

wattle and daub   the construction of walls by plastering mud over a lattice of branches and sticks.

Wayland's Smithy   a trapezoidal Neolithic long BARROW of *c*.3500 BC, in Oxfordshire, England, with a flanking kerb and MEGALITHIC PASSAGE GRAVE of cruciform plan at its southern end. Excavations beneath the mound revealed an earlier phase consisting of a wooden mortuary house with remains of 14 individuals, later covered over by an oval chalk mound. This was then in turn buried beneath the central section of the final mound.

wedge-shaped microcore   a small keel- or wedge-shaped CORE used to produce MICROBLADES. It is found in some East European Upper Palaeolithic sites (e.g. AMVROSIEVKA), but is especially common in Upper Palaeolithic cultures of Siberia and the Far East (Mongolia, northern China and Japan), and also appears in Alaska and other parts of northwestern North America at the close of the PLEISTOCENE.

wedge-shaped microcore

wedge tomb   a type of MEGALITHIC tomb common in Ireland, consisting simply of a long narrow chamber of ORTHOSTATS supporting capstones, decreasing in height towards the back and without a separate entrance passage.

Wei   see THREE KINGDOMS, CHINESE DYNASTIES.

Weichsel Glaciation   the final continental GLACIAL advance, named after the major North German icesheet, and lasting from *c*.115 000 to 10 000 bp. It corresponds broadly to the Alpine WÜRM, the North American WISCONSINAN, and the British Devensian.

Weidenreich, Franz (1873–1948)   a German anatomist and palaeoanthropologist, best known for his study of the SINANTHROPUS materials from ZHOUKOUDIAN, China.

Weipa   the site, in Cape York Peninsula, Queensland, Australia, of about 500 SHELL MOUNDS, mostly of *Anadara* shell, some of which are up to nine metres high. Excavations by Wright, and later by Bailey, demonstrated that they were human in origin and that they began forming about 1200 bp. The Weipa mounds are among the largest and best-preserved examples of shell middens anywhere in the world. Comparable sites occur in eastern Cape York and in ARNHEM LAND.

Weizhi   the *Chronicles of Wei*, compiled between AD 233–297 for the Wei Kingdom of China (see THREE KINGDOMS). One section, known as the *Gishi Wajinden* in Japanese, contains references to the Japanese islands, mentioning the country of YAMATAI. The ethnographies reported there can be correlated with YAYOI-period Japan as known archaeologically. (See also HOUHANSHU.)

were–jaguar   a creature showing both human and jaguar features. It is an important theme in OLMEC art. Were-jaguar characteristics include an infantile expression combined with fangs, a snarling mouth, and other feline facial features. The were-jaguar has been interpreted as the offspring of a woman and a jaguar, and as a priest or other ritually powerful individual with the ability to transform himself into a jaguar. Scholars suggest that various rain-gods throughout MESOAMERICA derive from it.

Wessex Culture   an Early Bronze Age culture of central southern England, essentially an aristocratic burial tradition developed from the earlier BEAKER tradition. It is represented by cemeteries of round BARROWS covering single graves in Wiltshire and adjacent areas, and is closely related to the Armorican TUMULUS Culture (see KERNONEN) with which it shares certain metal types and symbolic equipment. The Wessex I period (*c*.2000–2650 BC), associated with the major rebuilding of STONEHENGE, has richly furnished inhumations containing bronze daggers and axes, beads and buttons of amber and shale, and goldwork as in the famous BUSH BARROW. In the Wessex II period (*c*.1650–1400 BC), cremation replaces inhumation as the dominant rite, segmented FAIENCE beads appear, and goldwork largely disappears from the graves, although the RILLATON CUP is a notable exception.

Western Pluvial Lakes Tradition   a series of COMPLEXES and CULTURES found throughout Western North America, characterized by the exploitation of marshes and lakes in the early part of the POSTGLACIAL period.

Western Pueblo   see MOGOLLON.

Western Stream   see CHIFUMBAZE.

Western Zhou   see ZHOU.

West Kennet   a Neolithic long BARROW of *c*.3500 BC, in Wiltshire, England, with a MEGALITHIC chamber, part of the Avebury complex of Neolithic ritual monuments. The mound is 100 m long with a concave megalithic SARSEN façade at the eastern end, blocking an earlier entrance to the passage. This gave access to five burial chambers, arranged one at the end and two either side of a short gallery, and containing remains of at least 46 disarticulated individuals. The mound was excavated by S. Piggott.

West Slope ware   a type of HELLENISTIC pottery, named after the examples found during excavations on the west slope of the Athenian AKROPOLIS. The fabric evolved from the earlier BLACK-GLOSSED pottery produced at ATHENS, although it was enhanced by decoration in added white and yellow as well as occasional incision. It was produced in several centres in the Greek world, such as Athens, CORINTH and Crete.

Wetherill, Richard (1858–1910)   a pioneer archaeologist of the American Southwest who was responsible for locating and excavating some of the most important sites in the area, such as CLIFF PALACE in MESA VERDE and PUEBLO BONITO in CHACO CANYON, and bringing them to the attention of the public and of the profession.

Wharram Percy   a deserted mediaeval village in a valley among the rolling chalklands of the Yorkshire Wolds, England. The village consisted of rows of small rectangular WATTLE-AND-DAUB houses ranged along the principal streets, with two manor houses of more substantial construction and a 12th century AD church. Each of the ordinary houses stood within a small yard and was known as a *toft*; at the back of each toft there was an enclosed paddock or *croft*. Beyond tofts and crofts were the large open fields in which the bulk of the community's crops were grown. The village was gradually abandoned during the 14th and 15th centuries, as arable farming gave way in this area to the more profitable but less labour-intensive sheep-rearing.

Wheeler, Sir Robert Eric Mortimer (1890–1976)   a British archaeologist whose career started with excavations at COLCHESTER. He later excavated in Wales at the Roman forts of Caernarvon and Brecon as well as the legionary fortress of Caerleon. Later work was conducted at ST ALBANS and the Iron Age HILLFORT of MAIDEN CASTLE. His later British work included the exploration of the Iron Age fortress of STANWICK.

Named Director-General of Archaeology in India (1944–47), Wheeler introduced his scientific and STRATIGRAPHIC methods of excavation to the subcontinent, where they still serve as a model. He helped train a generation of Indian archaeologists, and undertook excavations at HARAPPA, MOHENJO-DARO and ARIKAMEDU. Later, with colleagues such as Glyn DANIEL, Wheeler also helped popularize archaeology through television programmes.

wheelhouse   a stone-built circular house with internal partitions radiating inwards like spokes of a wheel but leaving the central area clear. Wheelhouses are related to BROCHS, are found mainly in the Hebrides and the Shetland Islands of Scotland, and date mostly to the early centuries AD.

White, Leslie Alvin (1900–75)   an American anthropologist who helped re-introduce evolutionary thinking into American anthropology and archaeology. His views on culture as a system and on the evolutionary development of societies as mechanisms for the capture of greater amounts of energy were important precursors to the development of PROCESSUAL ARCHAEOLOGY. He proposed the term 'culturology' for the study of culture as an independent and discrete entity. See EVOLUTION.

white-ground   a technique used for ATHENIAN POTTERY especially in the 5th century BC. A white SLIP was applied to the surface of the vessel, onto which was painted the decoration in several different colours. The LEKYTHOS is the most common of the shapes to be decorated in this way, and the technique is chiefly linked to funerary vessels. Much of the iconography shows people approaching the tomb, although domestic scenes appear. In the late 5th century the technique was used on monumental funerary lekythoi, which seem to evoke their counterparts in marble. The effect is similar to that found on painted IVORY plaques, for example those from Kul Oba in Russia.

White Lady   see BRANDBERG.

Wietrzychowice   a cluster of Neolithic KUYAVIAN long BARROWS of the FUNNEL BEAKER culture, located in north-central Poland. Five of the trapezoidal long barrows have been excavated, with the longest (number 3) approximately 115 m in length. The barrows have been reconstructed as an archaeological park.

Wilburton   a Late Bronze Age metal hoard from Cambridgeshire, England, which has given its name to the Wilburton bronze industry of southern Britain, c.10th–8th centuries BC. Typical products are bronze leaf-shaped slashing swords, socketed spearheads with a peg for securing to the shaft, horse bits and socketed axes.

Wilgie Mia   a red OCHRE mine in the Weld Range, Western Australia, consisting of a large cavern with caves and galleries branching off it. Ochre from Wilgie Mia was widely traded and it is still a significant site to Aborigines. Excavations by Ian Crawford showed that it has been used for at least 1000 years.

Willandra Lakes   a chain of dry lakes in western New South Wales, Australia, which were filled periodically during the PLEISTOCENE by the Willandra Creek, an ancient distributary channel of the Lachlan River. Associated with the lakes are *lunettes,* crescent-shaped source-bordering clay, sand or GYPSUM DUNES, formed on the lee side of PLAYA lakes, characteristic of semi-arid landscapes. The lunettes provide a record of changing environment over the last 100 000 years. Human activity dates back c.35 000 years and the area is rich in archaeological material including HEARTHS, artifact scatters, freshwater SHELL MIDDENS and burials. Extinct species of MEGAFAUNA also occur. The best-known skeletal remains from the Willandra Lakes are MUNGO 1 and 3. These are gracile anatomically modern humans and are crucial to Alan Thorne's theory of a dual origin for Australian Aborigines. At least one robust individual, WLH 50, is also known, although it has not been securely dated. See also COOBOOL CREEK, KEILOR, KOW SWAMP.

Willendorf II   an Upper Palaeolithic open-air site located along the River Danube in northeastern Austria. Artifacts and faunal remains (e.g. reindeer, woolly MAMMOTH) are buried in LOESS deposits. A small assemblage of uncertain affiliation occurs in the lowest cultural layer. Layers 2–4 contain assemblages (e.g. nosed endscrapers – see SCRAPER – small RETOUCHED BLADES, bone points) assigned to the AURIGNACIAN; layer 2 recently yielded RADIOCARBON dates of 41 700–39 500 bp. Layers 5–9 contain assemblages (e.g. small BACKED BLADES) assigned to the EASTERN GRAVETTIAN; layer 5 yielded a date of 32 000 bp. Willendorf II provides evidence of early Aurignacian settlement and a classic sequence of industries in central Europe. Its Gravettian yielded several art objects including a famous obese 'VENUS' FIGURINE in 1908.

Williamsburg   see MARTIN'S HUNDRED.

willow-leaf point   an elegant and refined long thin SOLUTREAN FLAKE tool. See LAUREL-LEAF POINT.

Wilson, Daniel (1816–92)   a Scottish antiquary and author of, among other works, *The Archaeology and Prehistoric Annals of Scotland* (1851), in which the term 'PREHISTORIC' was first used. Wilson was the first to organize the available artifacts of prehistoric Scotland, following the THREE-AGE SYSTEM. He later taught at University College, Toronto, where he wrote *Prehistoric Man: Researches into the Origin of Civilization in the Old and New World* (1862).

Wilson Butte Cave   a prehistoric site located in a lava blister on the Snake River Plain of south-central Idaho, USA. Artifacts and faunal remains (e.g. camel, horse, ground sloth) are buried in deposits of clay, silt and sand. The lowest cultural layer yielded a RADIOCARBON date of 14 500 bp, and may contain one of the oldest occupations in North America. Stone artifacts are confined to a BIFACE, RETOUCHED BLADE and FLAKE. The five overlying layers contain assemblages dating to the middle–late HOLOCENE.

Wilton   a rockshelter in the eastern Cape Province of South Africa, which has given its name to a MICROLITHIC LATER STONE AGE INDUSTRY of the last 8000 years, distributed in the eastern, southern and southwestern Cape Province. Some researchers recognize a widespread Wilton complex distributed in many areas of southern Africa and encompassing Coastal and Interior Wilton Industries as well as industries such as the MATOPO/KHAMI and ZAMBIAN WILTON. In some areas of southern Africa, the appearance of pottery some 2000 years ago is associated with microlithic artifact assemblages labelled 'post-climax Wilton' or 'ceramic Wilton'.

The Wilton Industry *sensu stricto* shows changes in the relative percentages and form of certain RETOUCHED artifacts over time, especially small convex or 'thumbnail' SCRAPERS, ADZES, SEGMENTS and BACKED BLADES. It includes items made from organic materials, many decorative objects and burials, and is also associated with rock painting. Evidence for the wide range of resources exploited includes: plant remains (see MELKHOUTBOOM); faunal remains, especially of small non-gregarious browsing antelope associated with FYNBOS vegetation; and marine and freshwater resources.

Winckelmann, Johann Joachim (1717–68)   a German scholar who was appointed Prefect of the Papal Antiquities in 1763. His influential *History of Ancient Art* (1763–64), covering CLASSICAL sculpture as well as the art of Egypt and ETRURIA, provided the basis for stylistic development.

Windmill Cave, Brixham   a cave-site close to KENT'S CAVERN, Devon, England, which was discovered in 1858 and excavated by PENGELLY and a committee of fellow scientists. The site produced stone tools obviously made by humans, associated with the remains of extinct animals, and thus clearly demonstrated the true antiquity of humans in Britain. Thirty-six artifacts were reported as coming from the cave, but these were not fully published and are now mainly lost.

Windmill Hill   a Neolithic CAUSEWAYED CAMP of *c.*3350 BC, in Wiltshire, England, with three widely spaced causewayed ditch circuits, part of the AVEBURY complex of Neolithic ritual monuments. It is the type-site of the Windmill Hill culture, the earliest Neolithic of southwestern England, characterized by plain CARINATED round-based bowls.

Windover   a waterlogged site in Florida, USA, where excavations by G. Doran have uncovered America's earliest-known mass burial ground: 168 individuals buried in PEAT and dating to *c.*7400 bp. Brain tissue was preserved in 91 skeletons, including several complete brains. Studies of their DNA may reveal family relationships and shed light on how and when the New World was colonized. See also REPUBLIC GROVES and LITTLE SALT SPRING.

Winlock, Herbert Eustis (1884–1950) an American Egyptologist, best known for his excavations at DEIR EL-BAHRI and LISHT.

Wisconsinan Age a major North American geochronological subdivision of the PLEISTOCENE EPOCH, ranging from about 75 000 to 10 000 bp. See WISCONSINAN STAGE.

Wisconsinan Stage a major chronostratigraphic subdivision of the PLEISTOCENE SERIES, encompassing deposits of the last GLACIAL episode defined, in the upper American Midwest and adjacent areas of Canada, at the base by the base of material overlying the Sangamon Geosol (see SANGAMONIAN STAGE) and at the top by the top of non-glacial material overlying the youngest TILL. Remains of early humans and PALAEOINDIANS are contained in deposits belonging to the latest substages. Although the boundaries are recognized to be time-transgressive, they are conceptually placed at about 75 000 and 10 000 bp. The following substages and their general characteristics are recognized:

(a) Altonian Substage (*c.*75 000–25 000 bp) – SOIL formation early followed by LOESS SEDIMENTATION south and glacial advance and retreat north; cool climate.

(b) Farmdalian Substage (*c.*25 000–22 500 bp) – INTERSTADIAL soil formation; cool climate.

(c) Woodfordian Substage (*c.*22 500–12 500 bp) – major glacial advance and retreat; loess sedimentation and cryogenic processes; cold climate.

(d) Twocreekan Substage (*c.*12 500–11 800 bp) – interstadial, soil formation; forest beds; cool climate.

(e) Greatlakean Substage (*c.*11 800–7 000 or 10 000 bp) – minor glacial readvance; cool climate; replaces Valderan Substage (see VALDERS ADVANCE, WEICHSEL GLACIATION).

Witów an Upper Palaeolithic open-air site located in Poland. Artifacts are contained in AEOLIAN sand and associated with a buried soil dated to 11 020 bp. Tools include BLADES with arched backs, BURINS and endscrapers (see SCRAPER); remains of four dwelling structures are also present.

Wolstenholme Towne see MARTIN'S HUNDRED.

Wolstonian see SAALIAN.

wooden-chamber a form of burial chamber constructed from late Neolithic times onward in China; it was a log- or board-constructed enclosure into which nested wooden coffins, and grave-goods were packed and sealed from the top. Its use diffused to Korea and Japan in the early centuries AD. (See HEAVENLY HORSE TOMB, XIBEIGANG, MAWANGDUI, SHAFT TOMBS.)

Woodhenge a small Neolithic HENGE of *c.*2500 BC, in Wiltshire, England, lying adjacent to the major henge of DURRINGTON WALLS. Discovered by AERIAL PHOTOGRAPHY in 1925, Woodhenge consists of a series of six concentric rings of POST-HOLES within a circular ditch and bank. The post-holes may have held the supports of a roofed timber building, or perhaps an unroofed timber structure with lintels resembling STONEHENGE – hence the name.

Woodland   a STAGE in eastern North America, dated from approximately 1000 BC to AD 800, and characterized by BURIAL MOUNDS, agriculture and pottery. The term should properly be restricted to those cultures in the Eastern Woodlands of North America. The presence of Woodland-derived pottery in other areas has led to some unfortunate terminology, such as the 'Plains Woodland'. See ADENA, HOPEWELL.

Woodruff Ossuary   an ossuary in northwestern Kansas, USA, dating to about AD 600, that belongs to the Keith FOCUS of the WOODLAND stage. It comprises a series of 14 or more pits, some two metres deep. A large oval pit had then been dug across the tops of the small pits, and in the fill of both the large pit and the small ones were found at least 60 disarticulated human skeletons. Throughout the fill were thousands of beads made from locally available freshwater mussel, both randomly scattered and in lines, which suggests that they had once been strung. Other artifacts were relatively scarce.

Woolandale   a 13th century AD Late Iron Age site in central Zimbabwe which has given its name to the second phase of the LEOPARD'S KOPJE Complex in that area.

Woolley, Sir Charles Leonard (1880–1960)   a British archaeologist most widely known for his work at UR in MESOPOTAMIA between 1922 and 1934, where he revealed 5000 years of history. Woolley presented his Ur excavations in a magnificent 10-volume series, and also in several popular works. Woolley also excavated in Egypt, at CARCHEMISH (with T.E. Lawrence), at Tell ATCHANA in Syria, and at AL MINA in Turkey.

Worsaae, Jens Jacob Asmussen (1821–86)   a Danish prehistorian, Professor of Archaeology at the University of Copenhagen, Inspector-General of Antiquities in Denmark, and successor to C.J. THOMSEN as Director of the National Museum at Copenhagen. Worsaae's major contribution was the application of the THREE-AGE SYSTEM to the understanding of Danish field monuments using excavation, resulting in his influential *Danmarks Oldtid* (1843).

Wright, George Ernest (1909–74)   an American orientalist, whose best-known excavations are those at SHECHEM and GEZER.

wristguard   a long rectangular plaque, usually of stone, with one, two or three small holes at either end for tying to the wrist, as a protection from the recoil of the bowstring. In western Europe, stone wristguards are frequently found together with flint barbed and TANGED arrowheads in graves of the BEAKER tradition.

Wucheng [Wu-ch'eng]   a mid 2nd millennium BC Bronze Age site in Jiangxi Province, China, distinguished by its stone-mould casting of local styles of bronze weapons and vessels, GEOMETRIC POTTERY including GLAZED STONEWARE, and incised marks on pottery and stone moulds which are viewed as an indigenous writing system. Contemporaneous with the site of ZHENGZHOU, Wucheng represents a southern bronze civilization comparable with the Early SHANG in north-central China.

Würm Glaciation   the final Alpine GLACIAL advance which started *c.*110 000 years ago and ended with the onset of the POSTGLACIAL HOLOCENE *c.*10 000 years ago. See WEICHSEL, WISCONSINAN.

Wybalenna   a settlement established in 1833 on Flinders Island, off

TASMANIA, Australia, for the last of the Tasmanian Aborigines rounded up by ROBINSON, who was himself superintendent there in 1835–39. Wybalenna was closed in 1847 and the 47 survivors transferred to Oyster Cove. It was the site of one of the first historical excavations in Australia in the early 1970s.

Wylotne   a prehistoric rockshelter located on the Sąspówka River, north of Kraków in southern Poland. Artifacts are buried in LOESS and rubble. The three lowest cultural layers contain Middle Palaeolithic assemblages (e.g. BIFACES, SCRAPERS) that probably date to the Early GLACIAL and may be assigned to the MICOQUIAN. Upper Palaeolithic and Neolithic remains occur in the upper layers.

Wyrie Swamp   a PEAT deposit in southeast South Australia, investigated by Roger Luebbers. GAMBIERAN stone artifacts and about 25 wooden implements, including BOOMERANGS, barbed and plain spears and digging sticks, were recovered from the 10 000 year-old site. The barbed spears are the oldest known in the world. The site is significant for its extraordinary preservation.

X

X-Group   a culture of LOWER NUBIA, dated to *c*.AD 350–600, of uncertain origin but displaying some continuity with the preceding MEROITIC kingdom. The X-Group is chiefly represented archaeologically by cemeteries, especially that of the chiefs of the X-Group at BALLANA AND QUSTUL, but some settlement sites have been explored (e.g. QASR IBRIM).

Xia [Hsia]   the first of the CHINESE DYNASTIES of the SANDAI period in China, traditionally dated between 2200 and 1750 BC. Some archaeologists assign early remains of the SHANG culture – such as the ERLITOU site – to the Xia Dynasty; others maintain the Xia Dynasty is a fiction or at least not accessible in the archaeological record without direct corroboration from inscriptional remains.

Xiajiadian [Hsia–chia-tien]   a site in Chifeng, Inner Mongolia Autonomous Region of China, giving its name to two quite different cultural entities in the NORTHERN ZONE: an early local Bronze Age culture, the Lower Xiajiadian, is contemporaneous with the SHANG in the 2nd millennium BC; and a later Upper Xiajiadian agricultural society with a horse-riding aristocracy (compare XIONGNU) contemporaneous with early ZHOU. Despite the similar names, these two cultures are hypothesized to have different origins.

Xiang Khouang   'Plain of Jars', the upland region east of Luang Prabang in northern Laos, in which a series of late prehistoric burial and ceremonial sites have been found, apparently bordering old trade routes linked to northern Vietnam. These remains, the best known of which lie around the possible early crematorium site of Ban Ang, comprise large stone burial jars (containing locally made iron knives, arrowheads and spearheads, locally cast bronze jewellery, imported beads of glass and carnelian, and cowrie shells), and upright stone slabs or MENHIRS, a type of MEGALITH found more frequently in maritime Southeast Asia. Dates: *c.*300 BC–AD 300.

Xiaotun [Hsiao-t'un] the village in Hebei Province, China, where a palace/temple complex of the Late SHANG was discovered near ANYANG City. The complex consists of several building compounds oriented on a longitudinal axis, with watchtowers and altars at the southern end leading into the ancestral worship halls which were backed by residential compounds for the Shang elite. The HANGTU building foundation-platforms incorporated many burials interpreted as human sacrifices, and around the platforms occurred many other burials and some pit-house commoner dwellings.

Xibeigang [Hsi-pei-kang] the village in Hebei Province, China, where the Royal Cemetery of the Late SHANG was discovered near ANYANG City. It contains at least seven SHAFT TOMBS with WOODEN-CHAMBER burials and human sacrificial interments, and over 2000 small pit-graves of further human sacrifices. Most of the shaft tombs have been plundered, but the grave-goods probably included bronze vessels of the Anyang style, JADE and carved bone objects.

Xinle [Hsin-lo] a site in Liaoning Province, China, which has given its name to the Neolithic Xinle culture of eastern MANCHURIA, dated to the late 6th millennium BC. It is characterized by millet agriculture, coastal SHELL MIDDENS and textured-surface pottery resembling the CHULMUN tradition of the Korean peninsula.

Xiongnu [Hsiung-nu] a nomadic ethnic group occupying the Mongolian region during the HAN Dynasty and later. Constant raids by their predecessors on northern Chinese agricultural populations spurred the construction of the GREAT WALL during the ZHOU period, and the Han initiated the HEQIN system of reverse tribute to pacify them. (Compare XIAJIADIAN.)

Xochicalco an important Late CLASSIC centre in Morelos, Mexico, whose florescence coincided with the decline of TEOTIHUACÁN in the BASIN OF MEXICO. The centre of the site is on an artificially terraced hill. The sculpture and architecture at Xochicalco suggest it was in close contact with the Basin of Mexico, Gulf Coast and MAYA Lowland regions. It is one of the earliest fortified sites in the region.

x-radiography see RADIOGRAPHY.

x-ray art a style of ROCK ART characteristic of the recent period in northern Australia, especially ARNHEM LAND, in which the skeleton and internal organs of animals and humans are depicted.

x-ray diffraction analysis a physical technique used to identify the mineralogy of crystalline material such as CERAMICS, stone, and weathering products on metals. A small piece of sample is powdered and exposed to a focused beam of monochromatic x-rays that passes over the sample covering a continuous range of incident angles. The spacing between crystal lattice planes in different mineral species and the incident angle of the x-ray beam determines the series of x-ray intensities that are transmitted after passing through the sample to a recorder. Diffraction patterns are then compared with reference standards for identification. The sample can initially be mounted on a ceramic or glass slide, in which case the results are recorded on a strip chart with sharp peaks at diagnostic intervals, or it can be mounted in a camera where the diffraction pattern is projected and recorded as series of arcs on photographic film. Mineral identification is based on the spacing between arcs. Relative concentrations of constituents may also be estimated, based on the degree of darkening of the photographically recorded arcs, because the intensity is related to concentration. See also RADIOGRAPHY

x-ray fluorescence spectrometry   a physical technique used to determine the major and TRACE ELEMENTAL chemical composition of materials such as CERAMICS, OBSIDIAN and glass which may aid in identifying the material source. A sample is bombarded with x-rays; the wavelengths of the released energy, or fluorescent x-rays, are detected and measured. Constituent elements are identified based on the unique wavelengths of fluorescent x-rays they emit, and concentrations are estimated based on the intensity of the released x-rays. See also RADIOGRAPHY

x-ray microscopy   a physical technique used to identify the composition of crystalline substances by analysing atomic structure. A SCANNING or TRANSMISSION ELECTRON MICROSCOPE is used to render a greatly magnified image of sample atomic structure, based on the differential absorption and emission of x-rays produced by different elements. See RADIOGRAPHY.

x-ray milliprobe analysis   a specialized form of X-RAY FLUORESCENCE SPECTROMETRY using an instrument that directs a highly focused x-ray beam to any desired point on the sample surface. Secondary x-rays emitted from this point are directed to a detector and analysed as in x-ray fluorescence spectrometry. The great advantages of this technique are its flexibility and its ability to analyse microscopic areas.

Y

Yabrud   see JABRUD.

Yadin, Yigael (1917–84)   an Israeli archaeologist and chief of the Israeli Defence Forces, best known for his excavations at HAZOR and MASADA, and for his work on the DEAD SEA SCROLLS.

Yahya, Tepe   a 3 ha TELL in the Soghun valley of the Kirman province of southern Iran, excavated in the 1960s and 1970s by C.C. Lamberg-Karlovsky. It provides a long, if interrupted, cultural sequence of seven periods (Yahya VII–I, with subdivisions) that span the mid 5th millennium BC to early 1st millennium AD. In Period IVC (3rd millennium) occurs evidence of PROTO-ELAMITE activities, including texts, SEALS and sealings, JEMDET NASR painted wares, BEVELLED RIM BOWLS, etc., in a large building; Period IVB has evidence for the production of INTERCULTURAL STYLE CARVED CHLORITE vessels which have an extensive distribution in western Asia.

Yamatai   a POLITY in the Japanese islands known from the Chinese chronicles, the WEIZHI and HOUHANSHU. Its location was arguably in north Kyushu or the KINAI region. The queen of Yamatai is named in the chronicles as Himiko/Pimiko, who interacted with the 3rd century AD Wei court (see THREE KINGDOMS) through LELANG. This polity has not been documented archaeologically, though the YOSHINOGARI site was contemporaneous.

Yamato the former provincial name of Nara Prefecture, Japan, namesake of the emergent state of the KOFUN period. The Yamato state structure of the 5th century AD was formed through the institutionalization of the BE system for requisitioning goods and services. Yamato kings communicated with the 5th century CHINESE DYNASTIES and the elite of the KOGURYO, PAEKCHE and SILLA states on the Korean peninsula. With the adoption of the TANG administrative system from China in the late 7th century AD, Yamato was transformed into the RITSURYO state.

Yamazy-Tash see IGNATEVA CAVE.

Yamnaya culture a Late Neolithic culture (some refer to it as a 'horizon') of the lower Volga and Don steppes, sometimes also called the Pit-Grave culture. CHILDE and a number of later prehistorians including Gimbutas have viewed the Yamnaya culture as the forebear of the CORDED WARE, SINGLE GRAVE or KURGAN culture, whose dispersal was believed to coincide with the spread of INDO-EUROPEAN languages. This position has recently been questioned by Renfrew and others.

Yan see ZHOU.

Yangshao the main Neolithic culture of the LOESS area of north-central China (*c*.5000–2700 BC). It is distinguished by millet agriculture, coarse and painted pottery of innumerable regional types, sedentary organization consisting of mother–daughter villages, and kinship groups interpreted to be clans. Some marks on Yangshao pottery are considered to be incipient writing (see WUCHENG, ORACLE BONES). (Compare BANPO, HONGSHAN, MACHANG, MIAODIGOU II, DAWENKOU.)

Yanik Tepe an 8 ha site northwest of Lake Urmia near Tabriz in northwestern Iran where C. Burney's excavations in the 1960s produced evidence for Neolithic (comparable to the Hajji Firuz phase of the HASANLU sequence, dated to the late 7th/early 6th millennia BC), CHALCOLITHIC (comparable to the Pisdeli phase at Hasanlu, dated to the mid 5th millennium BC), EARLY BRONZE AGE, IRON AGE (including the initial discovery of the painted 'Triangle Ware' of the late Iron Age in the northern Zagros, dated to the second quarter of the 1st millennium BC) occupations. The Early Bronze Age settlement consists of a long sequence of KURA-ARAXES occupations, providing a detailed view of the closely packed circular dwellings equipped with benches and storage bins, the BURNISHED and ornamented pottery, and other materials typical of this culture complex. Burney's exposure also reveals changes through time in the architecture (to rectilinear dwellings) and pottery (a decrease of incised decoration) that may have relevance to the Kura-Araxes culture complex as a whole.

Yaozhou see CELADON.

Yarang a town in peninsular Thailand, the pre-modern occupation of which is represented at three moated sites ranging in date from the 6th to the 16th century AD, connected with the state of LANGKASUKA. Its style of early Buddhist art is similar to that of DVARAVATI.

yardang an erosional, streamlined LANDFORM created by AEOLIAN abrasion of bedrock residuals. Yardangs are usually associated with desert areas and may have smoothly rounded intervening troughs.

Yarim Tepe   six distinct TELLS within the Sinjar region of northern Iraq, where Soviet excavations, begun in 1969 and continued through the 1980s, produced long Neolithic sequences for two of them (Yarim 1 and Yarim 2). Yarim 1 belongs largely to the HASSUNA culture, spanning the 'Archaic', through 'Standard' Hassuna phases, and to the appearance of SAMARRAN elements; HALAF and SASSANIAN burials also occur in eroded surface sediments. The wide architectural exposure and detailed CERAMIC sequences provide considerable detail of the Hassuna phenomenon. While the Yarim 2 mound begins with traces of 'Archaic' and 'Standard' Hassuna occupation, most of the sequence belongs to the Middle Halaf period; the usual *tholos* architecture, painted pottery, and small finds appear here.

Yarmouth   see HOLSTEINIAN.

Yarmukian   see AIN GHAZAL, SHAAR HA-GOLAN.

Yayoi   a PROTOHISTORIC period in Japan (300 BC–AD 300), distinguished by wet-rice agriculture (see ITAZUKE), use of bronze (see DOTAKU) and iron, increasing warfare and social differentiation, and trade interaction with the LELANG COMMANDERY of HAN-dynasty China. Yayoi sites are often moated (see KARAKO, YOSHINOGARI, but compare TORO). Yayoi pottery succeeds JOMON but incorporates manufacturing techniques of MUMUN pottery from the Korean peninsula; it is related to the HAJI pottery of the KOFUN period. The Yayoi peoples are thought to maintain genetic continuity with the Jomon with heavy admixture from the peninsula, especially in western Japan (see DOIGAHAMA, WA). Mound-burials in Late Yayoi foreshadow the MOUNDED TOMBS of the Kofun-period rulers, in contrast to family burial grounds (see HOKEI SHUKOBO).

Yaz–depe   a 16 ha site in the Murghab delta in southeastern Turkmenia excavated by V.M. Masson in the 1950s. It is the type-site for the Iron Age Yaz complex. In its lowest level, Yaz-depe contains a citadel (monumental architecture on a massive platform) surrounded by a residential area; an extensive irrigation system runs near the settlement. Technological and formal changes in the pottery allow definition of three phases (Yaz I–III), which are roughly dated from the mid 2nd to the mid 1st millennium BC. Sites of this and related cultures are distributed between the Kopet Dagh (southeast of the Caspian Sea) and southern Bactria (northwestern Afghanistan), with settlement ranging from farmsteads to small towns (often with citadels) in association with large irrigation works.

year formula   a brief phrase in administrative CUNEIFORM documents of MESOPOTAMIA that often provides a date for a document by describing a significant event (military, cultic, public works, etc.) of a given year in a king's reign. An example of a year formula is 'year when HAMMURABI, by order of ENLIL, destroyed the walls of MARI and Malgi' (the 35th year of Hammurabi's reign). The practice of dating by year formulae, current from AKKADIAN through OLD BABYLONIAN times, provides a basic framework for the political history of southern Mesopotamia, particularly during the period of competing kingdoms in the Old Babylonian period.

Yeavering   the 7th century AD royal seat of ANGLO-SAXON Northumbria, northern England, where excavations by B. Hope-Taylor in the 1950s uncovered a series of great timber halls, and a large semicircular timber grandstand for assemblies.

Yengema   a cave in Sierra Leone with both Palaeolithic and Neolithic remains. Crudely FLAKED picks and hoe-like tools found with BACKED BLADES are considered to have been appropriate for a forested environment.

Yiewsley   a series of pits in the Yiewsley region of West Middlesex, England, which have yielded large numbers of Lower Palaeolithic artifacts, mainly recovered between 1885 and 1935. The assemblage includes over 2000 ACHEULIAN BIFACES and many LEVALLOIS FLAKES and CORES, and has been dated to *c*.200–250 000 years ago. The upper layers produced Middle Palaeolithic (MOUSTERIAN) artifacts including BOUT COUPÉ-like bifaces.

Yongnam   the region of South Korea comprising the southeastern provinces of North and South Kyongsang. The term is widely used in archaeological writings.

York (*Lat.* Eboracum, *Viking* Jorvik)   one of the three legionary fortresses in the Roman province of Britain. The thriving civilian settlement was granted the status of colony, perhaps under the emperors Septimius Severus or Caracalla. Remains of the fortress's fortifications were incorporated into the later mediaeval walls; a particularly fine stretch can be seen adjoining the Multangular Tower. Recent excavations have revealed traces of a large palace-like structure. Development in the city centre has uncovered remains of the VIKING city and these remains have been interpreted in the Jorvik reconstruction.

Yoshinogari   a site in Saga Prefecture, Japan, consisting of a double-moated YAYOI-period village containing watchtowers, pit-house remains and storage pits, with over 2000 jar burials in nearby cemeteries. A large oval mound, 30 m × 40 m, contained a jar burial with bronze dagger and beads, and is perhaps the earliest mound-burial in Japan, dating to the early 1st century BC. Discovered only in 1986, the site has been inappropriately linked to the country of YAMATAI, known from early Chinese texts; but it belongs to the time period and region of interaction with China, and so is the most important and most well-preserved western Yayoi site in Japan. (Compare TORO.)

Yuan   see CHINESE DYNASTIES.

Yuanmou   an Early Palaeolithic site in Yunnan Province, China, at which HOMO *erectus* dental remains were first reported as dated by PALAEOMAGNETISM to 1.7 million years ago. This dating is now under revision to 700 000 bp.

Yubetsu   the name of a Late Palaolithic MICROLITHIC technology for working OBSIDIAN; also known as the Shirataki technique after the type-site of Shirataki-Hattoridai in Hokkaido, Japan, dated to *c*.13 000 bp. A BIFACIAL CORE is prepared, then one lateral edge of the core is removed producing a triangular cross-sectioned SPALL; subsequent edge removals produce *ski spalls* of parallel surfaces in order to prepare the STRIKING PLATFORM of a now WEDGE-SHAPED CORE when held vertically. This technique was used from Mongolia to Alaska towards the end of the PLEISTOCENE.

Yudinovo   two Upper Palaeolithic open-air sites on the Sudost' River (Desna tributary) in European Russia. At each site, the occupation horizon is buried in slope deposits on the first TERRACE. Yudinovo I has yielded five RADIOCARBON dates between

15 660–12 300 bp. Woolly MAMMOTH remains are abundant at both sites (arctic fox is also common), and three MAMMOTH-BONE HOUSES have been uncovered (one at Yudinovo III). The non-stone artifacts include perforated marine shells from the Black Sea, 680 km to the south.

Yue [Yueh] 1. an ancient ethnic group occupying the southeastern seaboard of mainland China during the HAN Dynasty. 2. a STONEWARE of southeastern China preceding CELADON and porcelain development in the 3rd–6th centuries AD. It often has a yellowish-brown feldspathic GLAZE.

Yueh-chi see SCYTHIANS.

Yurovichi an Upper Palaeolithic site on the Pripyat' River in Belarus. The remains are buried in slope deposits on a low TERRACE, and appear to be redeposited. A RADIOCARBON date of 26 470 bp on an associated MAMMOTH tooth indicates that this may be the oldest-known Upper Palaeolithic site of the Dnepr-Desna Basin. Yurovichi was excavated by Polikarpovich in 1929–31, by Bud'ko in 1959–60 and by Ksenzov in 1976.

Z

Zakro the site of a MINOAN palace on the island of Crete, which has been excavated by Platon. Although not as large as the other palaces, Zakro shares the same basic layout of blocks of rooms arranged around a central court. The palace overlooks one of the finest harbours on the east coast of Crete, and was evidently involved, at least indirectly, in overseas trade. Zakro was destroyed by fire c.1450 BC.

Zambian Wilton a Zambian MICROLITHIC LATER STONE AGE industry of the last 6000 years from sites in the drainage basins of the Kafue and Zambezi rivers. It is akin to the better-studied WILTON Industry of South Africa (see GWISHO).

Zambujal a CHALCOLITHIC fortress near Lisbon, Portugal, with several walls strengthened by rounded bastions and a wide rock-cut ditch. Successive additions over several centuries of use resulted in walls of stones, in clay mortar, in some places over 10 m thick. The principal bastion on the inner circuit had archery slits in its base overlooking the gateways through the middle wall. Pottery included much BEAKER material along with local wares of c.2700–2200 BC.

Zaminets a settlement of the ENEOLITHIC KRIVODOL group in north-western Bulgaria, c.2800 bc, located on a promontory with palisade and bank defences. The settlement at Zaminets was rebuilt several times after episodes of destruction by fire.

Zapotec an important cultural and linguistic group in Oaxaca, Mexico, from pre-Columbian times to the present day. Zapotec cultural features noted at the time of the Spanish Conquest closely resemble aspects of the culture found at MONTE ALBÁN and other sites. It is assumed these sites were built by the Zapotecs. Monte Albán was a Zapotec centre until AD 700, when the MIXTEC began to dominate in Oaxaca. The Zapotec retained their cultural distinctiveness, however. Subsequent to the influx of the Mixtec, MITLA and other sites exhibit a Mixtec–Zapotec blend of attributes.

Zarzi   a cave in southern Kurdistan in western Iraq. GARROD'S investigations in 1928 provided the initial definition of the EPIPALAEOLITHIC Zarzian industry, which has since been studied elsewhere in the Zagros (e.g. SHANIDAR, Pa Sangar in KHORRAMABAD). The industry, dating to 10 500–6000 BC, contains high proportions of BACKED BLADELETS, a variety of geometric MICROLITHS, and notched blades.

Zaskal'naya   a group of Middle Palaeolithic sites in the Crimea, Ukraine, that consist of former (i.e. collapsed) rockshelters and caves. The most important sites are Zaskal'naya V and VI, which respectively contain seven and six occupation levels buried in layers of LOAM and rubble. The faunal remains are chiefly of saiga, MAMMOTH and horse. Some of the occupations are associated with a buried soil and appear to date to a mild climatic interval (INTERSTADIAL preceding early cold maximum of LAST GLACIAL?). The artifact assemblages are rich in BIFACIAL FOLIATES, as well as sidescrapers (see SCRAPER), and are assigned to the AK-KAYA CULTURE. Human fossil remains were found at both sites, including a minimum of five individuals ranging from 1–15 years of age at Zaskal'naya VI, and have been classified as NEANDERTHAL. These sites were discovered and excavated by Kolosov from 1969–77.

Závist   a HILLFORT of the HALLSTATT D period (c.600 BC) north of Prague in Bohemia. At its centre was an area known as the 'AKROPOLIS', where a large altar was located. Závist was abandoned during LA TÈNE B (c.300 BC) but was reconstructed as an OPPIDUM enclosing 80 ha in the 1st century BC. It was abandoned later in this century with its gate blocked by a clay wall which was destroyed by fire.

Zawi Chemi Shanidar   an open-air site near SHANIDAR Cave in the piedmont of northwestern Iraq, excavated by Ralph and Ruth Solecki in conjunction with Shanidar. It is a terminal EPIPALAEOLITHIC site (under Iron Age levels) that contains storage pits and a possible circular structure, dating to the 9th millennium BC. Although hunting was the principal source of animal protein during most of the occupation, toward its end sheep become important, and have been suggested to represent 'incipient domestication' of the species. The corresponding levels in Shanidar cave contain some 20 burials that reveal a poor state of health for this population.

Zawisza, Count Jan (1820–87)   a Polish archaeologist and Palaeolithic specialist who conducted excavations at MAMUTOWA CAVE in 1873–86, bringing to light the first evidence of Upper Palaeolithic industries containing BIFACIAL FOLIATES in this part of Europe.

Zazaragi   a Palaeolithic site in Miyagi Prefecture, Japan, with tool-yielding strata dated to between 40 000 and 45 000 bp by FISSION-TRACK and THERMOLUMINESCENCE. These dates support an early occupation of the Japanese islands.

Zebbug   a cemetery of five simple pit graves in Malta, which have given their name to the Zebbug phase of the Maltese pre-temple Neolithic c.4100–3800 BC.

Zeekoei Valley   see SEACOW VALLEY.

Zeliezovce style a late regional variant of the LINEAR POTTERY CULTURE, found in Slovakia, Moravia, and southern Poland c.4000 bc, with pottery characterized by angular incised lines relieved by lozenge-shaped incisions.

Zengővárkony a Neolithic cemetery and settlement of the LENGYEL culture in Hungary. Of the 368 graves, 47 had preserved skeletal material. Within these, the grave-goods reflect possible gender differentiation. The faunal remains from the settlement deposits have a high proportion of bones of wild animals.

Zhanguo [Chan-kuo] 'Warring States' in Chinese; see ZHOU.

Zhengzhou [Cheng-chou] a modern city in Henan Province, China, where the remains of an Early SHANG site have been recovered. A walled compound, 1.7 km × 1.9 km, contains HANGTU foundation platforms of palace buildings; and several workshops of bone, bronze and ceramic crafts are located outside the wall. Zhengzhou is thought to be one of the Shang capitals, and it has been used as the model 'ceremonial centre' by which to understand the beginnings of urbanism. The nearby village of ERLIGANG has given its name to the style of bronze vessels prevalent at Zhengzhou. (See ANYANG, PANLONGCHENG.)

Zhenla or **Chenla** the Chinese name for an early, apparently KHMER, state in southeast Cambodia and south Vietnam, which Chinese records say conquered FUNAN in the 7th century AD and subsequently broke down to form 'Land Chenla' and 'Water Chenla'. These reports probably conceal considerable fluidity amongst small pre-ANGKOR Khmer states, of which Iśanapura, with its centre at SAMBOR PREI KUK, must have been a dominant example.

Zhizo an Early Iron Age phase in western Zimbabwe and the Limpopo Valley, dating from the 8th–10th centuries AD (see SCHRODA).

Zhongyuan [Chung-yuan] the Chinese name for the 'Central Plain' of northern China.

Zhou [Chou] the name of a Bronze Age ethnic group which overthrew the SHANG c.1027 BC from QISHAN and established the Zhou Dynasty (see CHINESE DYNASTIES). The Zhou Dynasty is divided into Western or Royal Zhou (1027–771), and historic Eastern Zhou (770–221). It is further divided into the Spring and Autumn (770–476) and Warring States (475–221) periods. The Zhou period is characterized by many small competing states (e.g. Shu, Ba, Yan), organized in feudal subservience to the Royal Zhou during the early period, with hegemonies developing under successively stronger states in the later periods. The Zhou state of QIN eventually conquered its rivals and united the various states in 220 BC. The major advances during the Zhou period were the discovery and development of iron-working, construction of the GREAT WALL, coinage, and the institution of county-level administration. The earlier Zhou period is considered PROTOHISTORIC from ORACLE BONE and bronze inscriptions.

Zhoukoudian [Chou-k'ou-tien] a Palaeolithic site in Hebei Province, China, discovered by J. G. ANDERSSON in 1921. The first skullcap of HOMO *erectus* – known variously as Peking Man or Sinanthropus – was excavated in 1929 by PEI WENZHONG at Locality 1. The site has yielded the only large population (fragments of more than 40 individuals) of the species worldwide. Most of the actual bones were lost during the Second World War and only the casts have survived; these have been augmented in new excavations through to 1982. Strata at Locality 1 range in date from 700 000 to 200 000 bp, and the Upper Cave has been Radiocarbon (AMS) dated to between 13 000 and 34 000 bp. The FLAKE tools from Locality 1 typify a small-tool tradition in Palaeolithic China (see also JINNIUSH-AN), in contrast to a heavy-tool tradition manifested at the LANTIAN, KEHE and DINCUN finds. The Upper Cave remains of *Homo sapiens sapiens* comprise the first human burials and personal ornamentation known in the East Asian archaeological record.

ziggurat   a rectangular stepped temple-tower in MESOPOTAMIA. Though often confused with Egyptian PYRAMIDS in the popular imagination, the Mesopotamian ziggurat consists of one or more superimposed brick platforms, on top of which sits the temple of an individual god, with access by a central staircase. These religious structures visually dominated their cities, and form the highest point of many TELLS. Ziggurat architecture is traceable to temples on platforms built during 'UBAID times (e.g. at ERIDU), and famous later examples occur at UR, BABYLON (the 'tower of Babel') and AQAR QUF.

Zimbabwe (*Dzimbahwe* (pl. *madzimbahwe*))   the term used by Shona speakers in Zimbabwe for the court or house of a chief, or *mambo*, which traditionally consisted of a series of stone-walled enclosures built on a hill. More than 150 of these are known, mostly from the central Zimbabwe plateau, the most famous being GREAT ZIMBABWE.

Zinjanthropus   the genus name originally applied by Louis LEAKEY to a robust AUSTRALOPITHECINE found at OLDUVAI GORGE in Tanzania in 1959. It is now known as *Australopithecus boisei* or *A. robustus*.

Zinken   see HAMBURGIAN.

Złota   a late Neolithic cemetery in southeastern Poland on the Vistula River, which gives its name to the Złota culture. Many of the graves at Złota are single inhumations in niches and their grave-goods reflect a mixture of traits from a number of other cultures. The most prominent elements indicate connections to the CORDED WARE and GLOBULAR AMPHORA cultures, while cups with upturned handles are similar to those of the BADEN culture. Copper and amber ornaments are also found.

zong [tsung]   a tubular JADE artifact of unknown symbolism which appears in the southern Neolithic cultures of China such as LIANGZHU and continues into SHANG and ZHOU times. Its outside profile is square with a circular hollow through the centre. Often it is decorated with the TAOTIE design.

zooarchaeology   see ARCHAEOZOOLOGY.

zoomorph   1. an object or picture resembling an animal form.
2. In prehistoric art, a figure providing visual information recognized by contemporary humans as resembling an animal form (see also ANTHROPOMORPH).

zoomorphic, *adj.*   1. having or suggesting animal form and appearance.
2. (in prehistoric art) providing visual information recognized by contemporary humans as resembling animal form.
3. attributing the form or nature of an animal to something, especially a deity or superhuman being (see ANTHROPOMORPHOUS).

Zoser   see DJOSER.

Zürich-Utoquai   a Neolithic lake-edge settlement, in Zürich, Switzerland, with two layers of occupation separated by an abandonment phase. The lower occupation layer had flat-based 'flower pot' pottery characteristic of the HORGEN culture c.3500–2800 BC. Above was a 3rd millennium BC CORDED WARE occupation with bone and flint tools, cord-decorated BEAKERS, antler sleeves for polished stone axes, and wooden bowls and spoons.

Zvejnieki   a late Mesolithic and Neolithic cemetery located in Latvia. The 304 graves at Zvejnieki, located adjacent to a settlement, have a high degree of organic preservation and have extensive inventories that include perforated elk teeth pendants and bone points. OCHRE was used widely. The Zvejnieki cemetery shows similarities to other cemeteries of this period in northern Europe, particularly the one at VEDBAEK.

Zwoleń   a Middle Palaeolithic open-air site located on the Zwolenka River (a tributary of the Vistula) in Poland. Artifacts and faunal remains (e.g. woolly MAMMOTH, horse (predominant), reindeer) are buried in LOESS and stream deposits, dated (TL) to 115 000–80 000 bp (i.e. Early GLACIAL). The artifacts include BIFACIAL FOLIATES and side-scrapers (?) (see SCRAPER).

The maps

Each key is followed by the map or maps to which it relates. The arrangement is geographical, from West to East.

North America

Mesoamerica

South America
    South America except Peru   Peru

Western Europe: Early periods   *North*
                                      South

Western Europe: Later periods   Britain *North*
                                      Britain *South*
                                      France *North*
                                      France *South*
                                      Denmark
                                      Iberian Peninsula
                                      Italy *North*
                                      Italy *South*

Central Europe: Early periods   *North*

Eastern Europe: Early periods

Siberia: Early periods

Central and Eastern Europe, and
  Central Asia: Later periods
                                      West
                                      East
                                      Siberia

Aegean   Greece
                                      Anatolia
                                      Crete, Cyprus

The Classical World   Britain
                                      Western Europe
                                      Western Mediterranean
                                      Italy
                                      Greece
                                      Anatolia
                                      Eastern Mediterranean/Black Sea

Africa   *North*
                                      South

Egypt and the Levant   Egypt, Nubia and the Levant
                                      the Nile
                                      the Levant

The Middle East and Southern   Middle East   *West*
  Asia
                                              East
                                            South
                                   South Asia

North America

Mesoamerica

1	Ahualulco	27	Kaminaljuyú
2	Altar de Sacrificios	28	La Venta
3	Amapa	29	Matacapan
4	Basin of Mexico	30	Mayapán
5	Bonampak	31	Mitla
6	Cacaxtla	32	Monte Albán
7	Calixtlahuaca	33	Naj Tunich Cave
8	Casas Grandes	34	Nakbe
9	Cerén, Joya de	35	Palenque
10	Chalcatzingo	36	Quiriguá
11	Chiapa de Corzo	37	San Jose Mogote
12	Chichén Itzá	38	San Lorenzo
13	Cholula	39	Santa Isabel Iztapán
14	Copán	40	Sayil
15	Cozumel	41	Seíbal
16	Cuello	42	Tehuacán Valley
17	Cuicuilco	43	Tenochtitlan
18	Dainzú	44	Teotihuacán
19	Dzibilchaltún	45	Tikal
20	El Mirador	46	Tres Zapotes
21	El Tajín	47	Tula or Tollán
22	Guila Naquitz	48	Tulum
23	Iximché	49	Uaxactún
24	Ixtapalpa	50	Uxmal
25	Juxtlahuaca Cave	51	Xochicalco
26	Kabáh	52	Dos Pilas

Culture Subareas – inset

1	The Maya Highlands	6	Guerrero
2	The Maya Lowlands	7	Central Mexico
3	The Southern Periphery	8	Central Veracruz
4	Southern Veracruz-Tabasco	9	The Huasteca
5	Oaxaca	10	The West & the Northern Frontier

1	Alto Salaverry	38	Marajó Island
2	Asana	39	Marca Huamachuco
3	Asia	40	Mina Perdida
4	Aspero	41	Monte Verde
5	Batán Grande	42	Nasca
6	Caballo Muerto	43	Ollantaytambo
7	Cahuachi	44	Pacariqtambo
8	Cajamerquilla	45	Pacatnamú
9	Cerro Sechín	46	Pachacamac
10	Chancay	47	Pachamachay
11	Chan Chan	48	Pacheco
12	Chavín	49	Pampa de las Llamas
13	Chinchorro	50	Pampa Grande
14	Chiripa	51	Paracas
15	Conchopata	52	Parmana
16	Cuzco	53	Pedra Furada
17	El Inga	54	Pikillacta
18	El Paraiso	55	Pikimachay
19	Estaquería	56	Pucara
20	Fell's Cave	57	Quimbaya
21	Galindo	58	Real Alto
22	Garagay	59	Sacsayhuaman
23	Guitarrero Cave	60	San Agustín
24	Huaca la Florida	61	Sechín Alto
25	Huacaloma	62	Sipán
26	Huaca Prieta	63	Taima–Taima
27	Huánuco Pampa	64	Tairona
28	Huari	65	Tambo Colorado
29	Huaricoto	66	Tambo Viejo
30	Inca Pirca	67	Taperinha
31	Jincamocco	68	Telarmachay
32	Kotosh	69	Tiahuanaco
33	La Galgada	70	Toca de Esperanza
34	Lagoa Santa	71	Valdivia
35	Las Haldas	72	Vilcabamba
36	Lauricocha	73	Vilcas Guamán
37	Machu Picchu		

South America (except Peru)

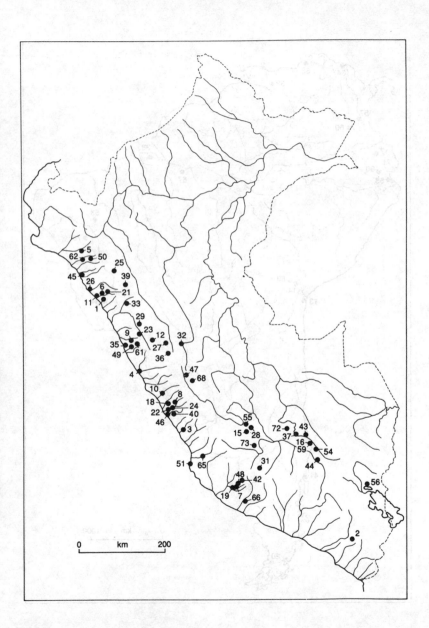

Western Europe: Early periods (alphabetical)

20	Abbeville	87	La Micoque
87	Abri Pataud	18	La Quina
42	Achenheim	32	La Riera
71	Altamira	87	Lascaux
26	Angles-sur-l'Anglin	87	Laugerie Haute
25	Arcy-sur-Cure	83	La Vache/Niaux
8	Aveline's Hole	29	Lazaret
14	Baker's Hole	59	Lehringen
45	Bockstein	82	Le Mas d'Azil
16	Boxgrove	87	Le Moustier
74	Brassempouy	54	Le Placard
3	Cass ny Hawin	87	Les Combarelles
67	Chancelade	87	Les Eyzies
52	Châtelperron	53	Les Furtins
12	Clacton	79	Lespugue
87	Combe Capelle	22	Le Tillet
87	Combe Grenal	51	Levanzo
68	Cougnac	2	Mount Sandel
5	Creswell	39	Meiendorf
87	Cro-Magnon	80	Montespan
33	Cueva Morin	86	Muge
62	Drachenloch	15	Oldbury
75	Duruthy	1	Oronsay
73	Ekain	35	Parpalló
72	El Castillo	7	Paviland Cave
33	El Juyo	87	Pech de l'Azé
23	Etiolles	69	Pech Merle
37	Ertebølle	44	Petersfels
87	Font-de-Gaume	24	Pincevent
27	Fontéchevade	4	Pontnewydd Cave
78	Gargas	38	Ringkloster
60	Geissenklösterle	49	Riparo de Romito
36	Gibraltar	63	Riparo Tagliente
55	Gönnersdorf	50	Romanelli
8	Gough's Cave	87	Rouffignac
31	Grimaldi	47	Saccopastore
65	Grotta Guattari	21	Saint Acheul
87	Grotte Vaufrey	40	Salzgitter-Lebenstedt
10	Hengistbury Head	85	Seriña
11	High Lodge	58	Skateholm
61	Hohlenstein-Stadel	41	Spy
48	Isernia la Pineta	6	Star Carr
76	Isturitz	43	Steinheim
9	Kent's Cavern	39	Stellmoor
46	Kesslerloch	14	Swanscombe
77	Labastide	84	Tautavel
87	La Chapelle-aux-Saints	28	Terra Amata
17	La Cotte de Saint-Brelade	19	Téviec
87	La Ferrassie	70	Tito Bustillo
87	La Madeleine	34	Torralba-Ambrona
66	La Marche	64	Torre in Pietra

Western Europe: Early periods (numerical)

1	Oronsay	53	Les Furtins
2	Mount Sandel	54	Le Placard
3	Cass ny Hawin	55	Gönnersdorf
4	Pontnewydd Cave	56	Vogelherd
5	Creswell	57	Vedbaek Bøgebakken
6	Star Carr	58	Skateholm
7	Paviland Cave	59	Lehringen
8	Aveline's Hole & Gough's Cave	60	Geissenklösterle
9	Kent's Cavern & Windmill Cave	61	Hohlenstein-Stadel
10	Hengistbury Head	62	Drachenloch
11	High Lodge	63	Riparo Tagliente
12	Clacton	64	Torre in Pietra
13	Yiewsley	65	Grotta Guattari
14	Baker's Hole & Swanscombe	66	La Marche
15	Oldbury	67	Chancelade
16	Boxgrove	68	Cougnac
17	La Cotte de Saint-Brelade	69	Pech Merle
18	La Quina	70	Tito Bustillo
19	Téviec	71	Altamira
20	Abbeville	72	El Castillo
21	Saint Acheul	73	Ekain
22	Le Tillet	74	Brassempouy
23	Etiolles	75	Duruthy
24	Pincevent	76	Isturitz
25	Arcy-sur-Cure	77	Labastide
26	Angles-sur-l'Anglin	78	Gargas
27	Fontéchevade	79	Lespugue
28	Terra Amata	80	Montespan
29	Lazaret	81	Volp Caves
30	Vallonnet	82	Le Mas d'Azil
31	Grimaldi	83	La Vache/Niaux
32	La Riera	84	Tautavel
33	Cueva Morin & El Juyo	85	Seriña
34	Torralba-Ambrona	86	Muge
35	Parpalló	87	Dordogne:
36	Gibraltar		Les Eyzies
37	Ertebølle		Cro-Magnon
38	Ringkloster		Abri Pataud
39	Meiendorf & Stellmoor		Font-de-Gaume
40	Salzgitter-Lebenstedt		Les Combarelles
41	Spy		Laugerie Haute
42	Achenheim		La Micoque
43	Steinheim		Grotte Vaufrey
44	Petersfels		La Ferrassie
45	Bockstein		Rouffignac
46	Kesslerloch		La Madeleine
47	Saccopastore		Le Moustier
48	Isernia la Pineta		Lascaux
49	Riparo de Romito		La Chapelle-aux-Saints
50	Romanelli		Combe Capelle
51	Levanzo		Combe Grenal
52	Châtelperron		Pech de l'Azé

Western Europe: Later periods

Please note that numerical order does not always follow alphabetical order.

1	Abeurador	50	Dissignac
2	Abingdon	51	Dowris
3	Agris	52	Durrington Walls
4	Alcalà	53	Egolzwil
5	Alésia	54	Egtved
6	Almizaraque	55	El Argar
7	Amfreville	56	El Garcel
8	Anghelu Ruju	57	Els Tudons
9	Antequera	58	Ensérune
10	Archéodrome	59	Entremont
11	Arene Candide	60	Er Lannic
12	Arras	61	Fengate
13	Artenac	62	Ferrières
14	Aulnat	63	Filitosa
15	Auvernier	64	Flag Fen
16	Avebury	65	Fontbouisse
17	Aylesford	66	Fontbrégoua
18	Barkaer	67	Fort Harrouard
19	Barnenez	68	Gaudo
20	Barumini	69	Gavrinis
21	Basse Yutz	70	Gergovia
22	Battersea	71	Glastonbury
23	Belverde	72	Glozel
24	Bibracte	79	Golasecca
25	Bougon	73	Gonvillars
26	Boussargues	74	Graig Llwyd
27	Broighter	75	Grand Pressigny
28	Bush Barrow	76	Grauballe
29	Bygholm	77	Great Langdale
30	Callanish	78	Grimes Graves
31	Carnac	80	Grotta dell'Uzzo
32	Carrowmore	81	Gundestrup
33	Castelluccio	82	Gwithian
34	Cayla de Mailhac	83	Haddenham
35	Champ Durand	84	Haguenau
36	Charavines	85	Hal Saflieni
37	Chassey	86	Hambledon Hill
38	Châteauneuf-les-Martigues	87	Hanging Grimston
39	Choisy-au-Bac	88	Hazleton
40	Ciempozuelos	89	Heathery Burn
41	Clairvaux-les-lacs	90	Hembury
42	Coppa Nevigata	91	Hengistbury Head
43	Cortaillod	92	Hjortspring
44	Cortes de Navarra	93	Hoëdic
45	Coveta de l'Or	94	Huelva
46	Crickley Hill	95	Isbister
47	Cuiry-lès-Chaudardes	96	Kernonen
48	Curacchiaghiu	97	Knowth
49	Danebury	98	La Chaussée-Tirancourt

Central Europe: Early periods (*Northern*)

1	Aggsbach	28	Nietoperzowa Cave
2	Arka	29	Nové Mesto
3	Bilzingsleben	30	Oblazowa
4	Bohunice	31	Oelknitz
5	Breitenbach	32	Ondratice
6	Býči Skala	33	Pavlov
7	Całowanie	34	Pekárna
8	Dolní Věstonice	35	Pod Hradem
9	Dzierzysław	36	Předmostí
10	Ehringsdorf	37	Přezletice
11	Erd	38	Puskaporos
12	Groitzsch	39	Ranis Cave
13	Gudenus Cave	40	Repolust Cave
14	Zwoleń	41	Sagvar
15	Istállóskö	42	Salzofen Cave
16	Jankovich	43	Stránská Skála
17	Kiskevély	44	Subalyuk
18	Kniegrotte	45	Swidry
19	Königsaue	46	Szeleta Cave
20	Kraków-Spadzista	47	Szelim
21	Kraków-Zwierzyniec	48	Tata
22	Krems-Hundssteig	49	Teufelsbrücke
23	Kůlna Cave	50	Vértesszöllös
24	Langmannersdorf	51	Willendorf II
25	Mamutowa	52	Witów
26	Markleeberg	53	Wylotne
27	Maszycka Cave		

(*Southern*)

1	Asprochaliko	10	Ohaba-Ponor
2	Bacho Kiro	11	Petralona
3	Ceahlău–Cetăţica	12	Potočka Cave
4	Crvena Stijena	13	Ripiceni-Izvor
5	Franchthi Cave	14	Samuilitsa II
6	Kastritsa	15	Sandalja I
7	Kokkinopilos	16	Stanca Ripiceni Cave
8	Krapina Cave	17	Temnata Cave
9	Muselievo	18	Vindija Cave

Eastern Europe: Early periods

1 Adzhi–Koba
2 Ak–Kaya
3 Amvrosievka
4 Ataki I
5 Avdeevo
6 Azykh Cave
7 Berdyzh
8 Betovo
9 Bol'shaya Akkarzha
10 Brynzeny I
11 Byzovaya
12 Chokurcha
13 Dobranichevka
14 Dzhruchula
15 Erevan Cave
16 Gagarino
17 Gontsy
18 Gubs Shelter No.1
19 Gvardzhilas–Klde
20 Ignateva Cave
21 Il'skaya I
22 Kapovaya
23 Ketrosy
24 Khotylevo sites
25 Khryashchi
26 Kiik–Koba
27 Kirillovskaya

28 Kodak
29 Korman' IV
30 Korolevo
31 Korpach
32 Kostenki–Borshchevo
33 Kudaro
34 Kulichivka
35 Mezhirich
36 Mezin
37 Molodova
38 Prolom II
39 Pushkari I
40 Radomyshl'
41 Rashkov VII
42 Rikhta
43 Rozhok I
44 Sagvardzhile
45 Sakazhia
46 Starosel'e
47 Sukhaya Mechetka (Volgograd)
48 Sungir'
49 Syuren' I
50 Timonovka
51 Yudinovo
52 Yurovichi
53 Zaskal'naya

Siberia: Early periods

Central and Eastern Europe, and Central Asia: Later periods

1 Aibunar
2 Anau
3 Anza
4 Ariuşd
5 Azmak
6 Băile Herculane
7 Barca
8 Bel'kachi
9 Biskupin
10 Bodrokeresztúr
11 Boian
12 Branč
13 Bronocice
14 Brześć Kujawski
15 Bubanj-Hum
16 Buchau
17 Budakalász
18 Butmir
19 Býči Skala
20 Bylany
21 Caka
22 Cascioărele
23 Cernavodă
24 Cernica
25 Chevdar
26 Cmielów
27 Coţofeni
28 Crvena Stijena
29 Cucuteni
30 Danilo
31 Dereivka
32 Divostin
33 Dölauer Heide
34 Domica
35 Dürrnberg bei Hallein
36 Eilsleben
37 Elsloo
38 Ezero
39 Glasinac
40 Gniezno
41 Goljamo Delčevo
42 Gomolava
43 Gradesnitsa
44 Gródek Nadbužny
45 Gumelniţa
46 Gura Baciului
47 Haithabu
48 Hallstatt
49 Hamangia
50 Hascherkeller
51 Heuneburg

52 Hluboke Mašûky
53 Hochdorf
54 Hohenasperg
55 Homolka
56 Janisławice
57 Jevišovice
58 Jordanów
59 Kamennaya Mogila
60 Karanovo
61 Karbuna
62 Kazanluk
63 Kietrz
64 Kiev
65 Kisapostag
66 Kökénydomb
67 Köln-Lindenthal
68 Kolomiishchina
69 Kostolac
70 Kosziderpadlás
71 Kremikovci
72 Krivodol
73 Krzemionki
74 Kunda
75 La Adam Cave
76 Lchashen
77 Łęg Piekarski
78 Łeki Małe
79 Lengyel
80 Lepenski Vir
81 Leubingen
82 Ljubljansko Blat
83 Lovčičky
84 Luka Vrublevetskaya
85 Mad'arovce
86 Magdalenska Gora
87 Maikop
88 Manching
89 Mariupol
90 Mikhajlovka
91 Mikulčice
92 Milavče
93 Mondsee
94 Mšecké Zehrovice
95 Nagyrév
96 Narva
97 Nezwiska
98 Nitra
99 Nitriansky Hrádok
100 Nové Košariská
101 Novgorod
102 Novo Mesto

Central and Eastern Europe and Central Asia: Later periods (*West*)

Aegean

Greece and Western Turkey

1	Akrotiri	50	Tiryns
2	Arapi	51	Trianda
3	Argissa	52	Tsangli
4	Argos	53	Vapheio
5	Ayia Irini	54	Volos
6	Chaironeia		
7	Chalandriani		*Crete*
8	Dendra		
9	Dhimini	1	Archanes
10	Elateia	2	Ayia Triadha
11	Eleusis	3	Chania
12	Eutresis	4	Gournia
13	Gelidonya	5	Kamares
14	Gla	6	Knossos
15	Kakovatos	7	Kommos
16	Kas	8	Lasithi
17	Kastri	9	Mallia
18	Kephala	10	Mesara
19	Kolonna	11	Mochlos
20	Korakou	12	Myrtos
21	Larissa	13	Palaikastro
22	Lefkandi	14	Phaistos
23	Leukas	15	Tylissos
24	Lerna	16	Vasiliki
25	Malthi	17	Zakro
26	Marathon		
27	Melos		*Cyprus*
28	Menelaion		
29	Mycenae	1	Alambra-Mouttes
30	Nea Nikomedeia	2	Ayios Epiktitos-Vrysi
31	Nichoria	3	Enkomi
32	Orchomenos	4	Episkopi-Phaneromeni
33	Otzaki	5	Erimi-Bamboula
34	Pefkakia	6	Hala Sultan Tekke
35	Peristeria	7	Kalavasos
36	Phylakopi	8	Khirokitia
37	Poliochni	9	Kissonerga
38	Prosymna	10	Kition
39	Pylos	11	Kouklia-Palaepaphos
40	Rachmani	12	Lemba-Lakkous
41	Routsi	13	Maa-Palaekastro
42	Saliagos	14	Maroni-Vournes
43	Sesklo	15	Myrtou-Pigadhes
44	Sitagroi	16	Nitovikla
45	Soufli	17	Philia
46	Thebes	18	Pyla-Kokkinokremos
47	Thera	19	Sinda
48	Thermi	20	Sotira-Kaminoudhia
49	Thorikos	21	Vounous

Aegean: Greece

Thrace

Macedonia

30

Epirus

40
33
3
2
45
21

Thessaly

52
9
43
54
34

Phocis
10
6
14
32

Aetolia

Boeotia
46
12

22

Achaea

Corinthia
11
26

Elis

Arcadia

20
29
38
19

Attica

15

4
8
24
50

Argolid
49
5
18

35
25

Messenia

28

7

39
41
31

53

Laconia

42

27
36

0   km   100

17

594

Aegean: Crete, Cyprus

The Classical World

Britain

1 Antonine Wall
2 Bath
3 Colchester
4 Fishbourne
5 Hadrian's Wall
6 London
7 Nene Valley
8 New Forest
9 St Albans
10 Vindolanda
11 York

Western Europe

1 Cologne
2 La Graufesenque
3 Marseilles
4 Nîmes
5 Pont du Gard
6 Saint Blaise

Western Mediterranean

1 Aleria
2 Ampurias
3 Carthage
4 Lepcis Magna
5 Sabratha

Italy

1 Agrigento
2 Apulia
3 Arrezzo
4 Campania
5 Cerveteri
6 Cumae
7 Etruria
8 Gela
9 Giglio Island
10 Gravisca
11 Herculaneum
12 Ischia
13 Lucania
14 Metaponto
15 Motya
16 Nemi
17 Oplontis
18 Ostia
19 Paestum
20 Pompeii
21 Porticello
22 Riace
23 Rome
24 Selinunte
25 Sicily
26 Spina
27 Syracuse
28 Tarentum
29 Tarquinia
30 Veii
31 Villanova
32 Vulci

Greece and western Turkey

1	Aegina	26	Phocaea
2	Aphrodisias	27	Piraeus
3	Athens	28	Priene
4	Brauron	29	Sounion
5	Byzantium	30	Sparta
6	Chios	31	Tanagra
7	Clazomenae	32	Vergina
8	Corinth		
9	Delos	*Eastern Mediterranean/Black Sea*	
10	Delphi		
11	Didyma	1	Al Mina
12	Dodona	2	Alexandria
13	Elmali	3	Baalbek
14	Ephesus	4	Berenice (Cyrenaica)
15	Epidauros	5	Berenice (Red Sea)
16	Halicarnassus	6	Berenice = Pella
17	Izmir	7	Cyrene
18	Laurion	8	Duvanli
19	Lefkandi	9	Gordion
20	Miletus	10	Naucratis
21	Myrina	11	Palmyra
22	Olympia	12	Petra
23	Olynthus	13	Salamis
24	Perachora	14	Semibratny
25	Pergamon	15	Tocra

The Classical World: Greece

Africa (excluding Egypt) (alphabetical)

22 Abu Ballas	31 Gash
20 Acacus	96 Gedi
34 Adrar Bous	81 Gobedra
39 Afunfun	87 Gogoshiis Qabe
10 Ain Hanech	132 Gokomere
53 Akjoujt	74 Gombe Point
15 Amekni	133 Great Zimbabwe
121 Apollo 11	134 Gumanye
43 Araouane	113 Gwisho
40 Arlit	83 Hadar
51 Awdaghast	12 Hassi Mouilah
38 Azelik	21 Haua Fteah
129 Bambata	90 Hyrax Hill
73 Batalimo	63 Ife
119 Benfica	67 Igbo Ukwu
66 Benin	114 Ingombe Ilede
24 Bir Kiseiba	137 Inyanga
23 Bir Tarfawi	76 Ishango
162 Boomplaas	64 Iwo Eleru
149 Border	3 Jebel Irhoud
62 Bosumpra	32 Jebel Moya
11 Bordj Mellala	26 Jebel Uweinat
72 Bouar	46 Jenne-jeno
120 Brandberg	140 K2
147 Broederstroom	29 Kadero
112 Broken Hill	108 Kalambo Falls
30 Butana	117 Kalundu
144 Cave of Hearths	57 Kamabai
165 Cederberg	79 Kamoa
89 Chesowanja	115 Kapwirimbwe
138 Chibuene	42 Karkarichinkat
7 Columnata	78 Katoto
71 Daima	104 Katuruka
9 Damous el Ahmar	88 KBS
128 Danangombe	125 Khami
2 Dar es-Soltan	106 Kilwa
33 Dhang Rial	105 Kisese
49 Dhar Tichitt	159 Klasies River Mouth
163 Die Kelders	88 Koobi Fora
151 Drakensberg	47 Koumbi Saleh
118 Dundo	48 Kourounkorokale
50 El Beyed	148 Kromdraai
16 El Guettar	116 Kumadzulo
166 Elands Bay	97 Kwale
164 Elandsfontein	101 Laetoli
100 Engaruka	82 Lalibela
27 Esh Shaheinab	17 Lalla
102 Eyasi	126 Leopard's Kopje
55 Faboura	95 Lukenya Hill
153 Florisbad	146 Lydenburg
123 Gi	144 Makapansgat
92 Gamble's	140 Mapungubwe

610

Egypt and the Levant

Egypt, Nubia and the Levant

1	Kadesh	22	Saqqara
2	Jabrud	23	Dahshur
3	Byblos	24	Qasr es-Sagha
4	Sidon	25	Karanis
5	Adlun	26	Lisht
6	Beidha	27	Meidum
7	Timna	28	el-Lahun
8	Serabit el-Khadim	29	Hawara
9	Wadi Kubbaniya	30	Oxyrhynchus
10	Kalabsha	31	Beni Hassan
11	Qasr Ibrim	32	Hermopolis Magna
12	Abu Simbel	33	Tuna el-Gebel
13	Ballana & Qustul	34	el-Bersheh
14	Arkin	35	el-Amarna
15	Buhen	36	Meir
16	Khor-Musa	37	el-Hammamiya
17	Sai	38	Abydos
18	Soleb	39	Dendera
19	Kerma	40	Naqada
20	Kurru	41	Thebes (W. Bank)
21	Napata	42	Thebes (E. Bank)
22	Gebel Barkal	43	Esna
23	Nuri	44	el-Kab
24	Meroe	45	Hierakonpolis
25	Musawwarat es-Sufra	46	Edfu
26	Axum	47	Wadi Shatt er-Rigal
		48	Kom Ombo
		49	Aswan

the Nile

1	Alexandria
2	Rosetta
3	Kellia
4	Sais
5	Behbet el-Hagar
6	Tanis
7	Minshat Abu Omar
8	Tell ed-Daba
9	Kufr Nigm
10	Bubastis
11	Athribis
12	Merimde Beni Salama
13	Tell el-Yehudieh
14	Heliopolis
15	Cairo
16	Maadi
17	Omari
18	Abu Roash
19	Giza
20	Abu Ghurab/Abusir
21	Memphis

the Levant

1	Ai
2	Arad
3	Ashdod
4	Ashkelon
5	Beersheba
6	Beit Mersim
7	Berekhat Ram
8	Beth-Shan
9	Beth-Shemesh
10	Bethel
11	Caesarea
12	el-Ajjul, Tell
13	el-Fara, Tell (N)
14	el-Fara, Tell (S)
15	el-Hesy, Tell
16	en-Nasbeh, Tell
17	Eynan
18	Gaza
19	Gezer

Egypt and the Levant Egypt, Nubia and the Levant

The Middle East and Southern Asia

Middle East: Western and Eastern regions

1	Hisarlik/Troy	51	Khorsabad
2	Dorak	52	Arpachiyah
3	Sardis	53	Balawat
4	Aphrodesias	54	Nineveh
5	Beycesultan	55	Kalhu
6	Hacilar	56	Hassuna
7	Gordion	57	Shanidar
8	Alaca Hüyük	58	Kar Tukulti Ninurta
9	Boghazköy	59	Assur
10	Alişar Hüyük	60	Zarzi
11	Kültepe	61	Jarmo
12	Suberde	62	Nuzi
13	Catal Hüyük	63	Samarra
14	Can Hasan	64	Sawwan, Tell es-
15	Mersin	65	Kheit Qasim
16	Tarsus	66	Abada, Tell
17	Karatepe	67	Choga Mami
18	'Amuq	68	Asmar, Tell
19	Atchana, Tell	69	Harmal, Tell
20	Ras Shamra/Ugarit	70	Khafadje, Tell
21	Mardikh, Tell/Ebla	71	'Aqar Quf
22	Yabrud	72	Jemdet Nasr
23	Kamid al Loz	73	Kish
24	'Aynan/Ain Mallaha	74	Babylon
25	Ein Gev	75	Abu Salabikh
26	'Ain Ghazal	76	Nippur
27	Jericho	77	Isin
28	El Khiam	78	Tello
29	Boker Tachtit	79	Hiba, Tell al-
30	Beidha	80	Warka
31	Korucutepe	81	Larsa 'Oueli, Tell
32	Norşuntepe	82	Hajji Mohammad
33	Arslantepe	83	'Ubaid, Tell al-
34	Cayönü	84	Ur
35	Nevali Cori	85	Eridu
36	Carchemish	86	Choga Zanbil
37	Habuba Kabira	87	Susa
38	Mureybit	88	Deh Luran
39	Abu Hureyrah	89	Khorramabad
40	Halaf, Tell	90	Nus-i Jan
41	'Aqab, Tell	91	Godin tepe
42	Chagar Bazar	92	Giyan tepe
43	Brak, Tell	93	Abdul Hosein, Tepe
44	Leilan, Tell	94	Ganj Dareh
45	Mari	95	Bisitun
46	Yarim Tepe Maghzalia, Tell	96	Asiab, Tepe
47	Qermez Dere	97	Hasanlu
48	Taya, Tell	98	Yanik tepe
49	Umm Dabaghiyah	99	Tilkitepe
50	Gawra, Tepe	100	Topprakale

101 Bastam
102 Metsamor
103 Karmir Blur
104 Trialeti
105 Shulaveri
106 Shomu depe
107 Kobystan

Middle East: Southern region
Southern Asia

1 Tayma
2 Marib
3 Hajjar bin Humeid
4 Hureidah
5 Maysar
6 Qurum
7 Hafit
8 Hili 8
9 Umm an Nar
10 Bahrain:
   Bahrain Tumulus Fields
   Barbar
   Qala'at al Bahrain
11 Dosariyah
12 Hissar, Tepe
13 Sialk, Tepe
14 Malyan, Tal i–
15 Persepolis
16 Yahya, Tepe
17 Iblis, Tal i–
18 Shahdad
19 Shahr i–Sokhta
20 Mundigak
21 Anau
22 Djeitun
23 Namazga depe
24 Altyn depe
25 Geoksjur
26 Kelleli
27 Yaz depe
28 Togolok
29 Gonur

30 Tillya depe
31 Dashly
32 Teshik Tash
33 Sapalli
34 Shortugai
35 Rahman Dheri
36 Taxila
37 Burzahom
38 Harappa
39 Quetta
40 Mehrgahr Sibri
41 Pirak
42 Jhukar
43 Mohenjodaro
44 Kot Diji
45 Chanhudaro
46 Amri
47 Balakot
48 Allahdino
49 Ranjpur
50 Lothal
51 Ahar
52 Kalibangan
53 Banawali
54 Mitathal
55 Alamgirpur
56 Hastinapura
57 Kausambi
58 Rajghat
59 Chirand
60 Kayatha
61 Bhimbetka
62 Navdatoli
63 Chandoli
64 Jorwe
65 Daimabad
66 Nevasa
67 Inamgaon
68 Piklihal
69 Hallur
70 Tekkalakota
71 Arikamedu

Black Sea

Halys R.

Meander R.

Mediterranean Sea

Black Sea

104
105
106

Kura R.

107

103
102

Arax R.

101

Caspian
Sea

31
Lake Van 100
32
34
99

98

Lake Urmia

40
41
42 43 44
50 51
53
47
46 48 52 54
56 55
49 58
59

57

97

60

61
62

95 92
96 94 90
93 91

63
64

65
66
67

45

Euphrates R.

68
69
70

89

Karkeh R.

71
72
74 73 75
76
77 80
78 Tigris R.
79
81

88

87

86

Karun R.

82
83
84 85

0   km   400

Persian Gulf

Black Sea

Caspian
Sea

Mediterranean Sea

22

21 ● 22

12 ●

13 ●

14 ● ● 15   17 ● ● 18

16 ●

11 ● ● 10   Persian
Gulf

9 ●

8 ● ● 7   6 ●
5 ●

Red Sea

1 ●

2 ●
3 ●   4 ●

South East Asia

Burma

1 Pagan
2 Sri Ksetra
3 Beikthano
4 Padah Lin

Thailand

5 Spirit Cave
6 Si Satchanalai
7 Sukhothai
8 Ongbah Cave
9 Sai Yok
10 Ban Kao
11 Pong Tuk
12 Ku Bua
13 U Thong
14 Nakhon Pathom
15 Ban Don Ta Phet
16 Don Noi
17 Khok Phanom Di
18 Chaiya and Leam Pho
19 Takuapa and Ko Kho Kao
20 Nakhon Si Thammarat
21 Satingpra
22 Yarang
23 Khuan Lukpad
24 Lopburi and Huai Yai
25 Ban Tha Kae
26 Chansen
27 Sab Champa
28 Khok Charoen
29 Non Pa Wai
30 Phu Lon
31 Ban Chiang
32 Ban Nadi
33 Non Nok Tha
34 Phu Wiang
35 Ban Chiang Hian
36 Kantarawichai
37 Muang Fa Daet
38 Non Chai
39 Muang Sima
40 Thamen Chai
41 Phimai
42 Non Dua

Laos

43 Xiang Khouang (Plain of Jars)

Cambodia

44 Mlu Prei
45 Angkor
46 Laang Spean
47 Samrong Sen
48 Sambor Prei Kuk
49 'Moi' forts (Mimot)

Vietnam

50 Bac Son
51 Hoa Binh
52 Son Vi
53 Cai Beo
54 Phung Nguyen
55 Go Mun
56 Dong Dau
57 Co Loa
58 Dong Son
59 Mi Son and Tra Kieu
60 Sa Huynh
61 Vo Canh and Po Nagar
62 Co Lao Rua
63 Hang Gon
64 Oc Eo and Ta Kev
65 Takeo
66 Angkor Borei

Peninsular Malaysia

67 Bukit Tengku Lembu
68 Pengkalan Bujang
69 Kambong Sungei Mas
70 Buddhagupta stone
71 Guak Kepah
72 Pasir Angin (Kuala Selinsing)
73 Kota Tampan
74 Gua Cha
75 Tembeling
76 Gua Kechil
77 Kuala Terengganu
78 Bernam–Sungkai (Slim River)
79 Kampong Sungei Lang
80 Jenderam Hilir
81 Kampong Pencu (Muar)
82 Pontian

Sumatra

83 Lhokseumawe
84 Kota Cina

85 Lobo Tuwa
86 Padang Lawas
87 Kerinci
88 Tiangko Panjang
89 Muara Jambi
90 Pasemah
91 Palembang

Java

92 Buni
93 Bandung plateau
94 Dieng
95 Borobudur
96 Prambanan
97 Pacitan
98 Sampung (Gua Lawa)
99 Sangiran
100 Trinil
101 Ngandong
102 Wajak
103 Jetis
104 Mojokerto

Borneo

105 Santubong
106 Niah
107 Kota Batu

108 Madai caves
109 Baturong caves
110 Tingkayu

Bali

111 Gilimanuk
112 Sembiran
113 Pejeng

Sulawesi

114 Ulu Leang and Leang Burung
    1 & 2
115 Cabenge
116 Kalumpang
117 Paso

Philippines

118 Tabon and Duyong
119 Batungan
120 Kalanay
121 Musang Cave
122 Cagayan valley
123 Dimolit

East Asia

Korea

1	Amsadong
2	Anapchi
3	Heavenly Horse Tomb
4	Hunam-ri
5	Kimhae
6	Kulpo-ri
7	Mongch'on
8	Muryong
9	Osan-ri
10	Sinan
11	Sokchang-ri
12	Songguk-ri
13	Tongsamdong
14	Wando

Japan

1	Akashi
2	Arava
3	Asuka, Fujiwara, Kawahara-dera
4	Babadari A, Zazaragi, Nakamine
5	Dazaifu
6	Doigahama
7	Fudodo
8	Fujinoki, Takamatsuzuka
(3)	Fujiwara
9	Fukui
10	Heijo
11	Hoshing
12	Idojiri
13	Itazuke, Magarita
14	Iwajuku
15	Kamegaoka
16	Kamikuroiwa
17	Karako
18	Kasori
(3)	Kawahara-dera
19	Kou
(13)	Magarita
	Minatogawa (on China map)
20	Nabatake
(4)	Nakamine
21	Nintoku, Ojin
22	Nishiyagi
(21)	Ojin
23	Omori
24	Oyu
25	Shirataki
26	Sozudai

(8)	Takamatsuzuka
27	Torihama
28	Toro
29	Yoshinogari
30	Yubetsu
(4)	Zazaragi

China

1	Anyang
2	Banshan
3	Chang'an
(18)	Chenjiawo
4	Cishan
5	Dapenkeng
6	Dawenkou
7	Dingcun
8	Dunhuang, Mogao
9	Erligang
10	Erlitou
11	Fengbitou
(18)	Gongwangling
12	Hemudu
13	Hongshan
14	Huashan
15	Jingdezhen
16	Jinniushan
17	Kehe
18	Lantian, Chenjiawo, Gongwangling
19	Laoguantai
20	Lelang
21	Liangzhu
22	Lijiacun
23	Maba
24	Machang
25	Mancheng
26	Mawangdui
27	Miaodigou
28	Minatogawa (Japanese island)
29	Ming tombs
(8)	Mogao
30	Panlongcheng
31	Peiligang
31	Qingliangang
33	Qishan
34	Qujialing
35	Shiyu
36	Shizhaishan
37	Shuidonggou
38	Songze

Pacific (alphabetical)

Pacific (geographical)

Australia

1 Birrigai
2 Lake George
3 Burrill Lake
4 Lime Springs
5 Mungo
6 Willandra Lakes
7 Mootwingee
8 Sturts Meadows
9 Lake Nitchie
10 Talgai
11 Kenniff Cave
12 Cathedral Cave
13 Early Man shelter
14 Mushroom Rock
15 Weipa
16 Colless Creek
17 Puritjarra
18 Cleland Hills
19 Ingaladdi
20 Malakunanja 2
21 Lindner Site, Nauwalabila 1
22 Anbangbang
23 Malangangerr
24 Ngilipitji
25 Port Essington
26 Miriwun
27 Koolan 2
28 Gallery Hill
29 Spear Hill
30 Burrup Peninsula
31 Mandu Mandu Creek
32 Wilgie Mia
33 Orchestra Shell Cave
34 Upper Swan
35 Devil's Lair
36 Cheetup
37 Koonalda Cave
38 Karolta 1
39 Devon Downs

40 Fromms Landing
41 Roonka
42 Koongine
43 Paroong Cave
44 Wyrie Swamp
45 Kow Swamp
46 Coobool Creek
47 Lancefield Swamp
48 Mount William
49 Keilor
49 Toolondo
50 Lake Condah
51 Sydney Cove
52 Wybalenna
53 Cave Bay Cave
54 Mount Cameron West
55 Rocky Cape
56 Nunamira Cave
57 Wargata Mina
58 Kutikina
59 Port Arthur
129 *Batavia* wreck

Papua New Guinea

60 Lake Santani
61 Kuk
62 Nombe
63 Kafiavana
64 Huon Peninsula
65 Kulapuari
66 Kukuba
67 Kosipe
68 Motupore
69 Mailu
70 Siassi Islands
71 Talasea
72 Lou Island
73 Watom Island

74 Eloaua Island
75 Balof
76 Matenkupkum
77 Matenbek
78 Nissan Island
79 Kilu

Solomon Is

80 Nenumbo

Vanuatu

81 Roy Mata
82 Aneityum

New Caledonia

83 Vatcha

Fiji

84 Sigatoka

W. Samoa

85 Vailele
86 Pulumelei

American Samoa

87 To'aga

Tonga

88 Ha'amonga-a-Maui
89 Mu'a

Hawaiian Is

90 Necker Island
91 Makaha Valley
92 Kaneaki
93 Bellows Beach
94 Kawakiu Bay
95 Halawa Valley
96 Kawela
97 'Ili'Ili'opae
98 'Anaeho'omalu
99 Lapakahi
100 Pu'uhonua
101 Mauna Kea

Cook Is

102 Maungaroa Valley

Society Is

103 Maupiti
104 Taputapuatea
105 Mahaiatea
106 Vaito'otia
107 Opunohu Valley
108 Maeva

Marquesas

109 Taipivai Valley
110 Vahangeku'a
111 Hane
112 Puamau Valley

Pitcairn I.

113 Pitcairn Island

Easter Island

114 Orongo
115 Puna Pau
116 Rano Raraku
117 Vinapu

New Zealand

118 Mount Camel
119 Otakanini pa
120 Mayor Island
121 Lake Mangakaware
122 Lake Ngaroto
123 Te Awanga
124 Kauri Point
125 Palliser Bay
126 Wairau Bar
127 Lake Hauroko

Micronesia (Caroline Is)

128 Nan Madol

129 *see Australia*

Kangaroo I.

Fiji

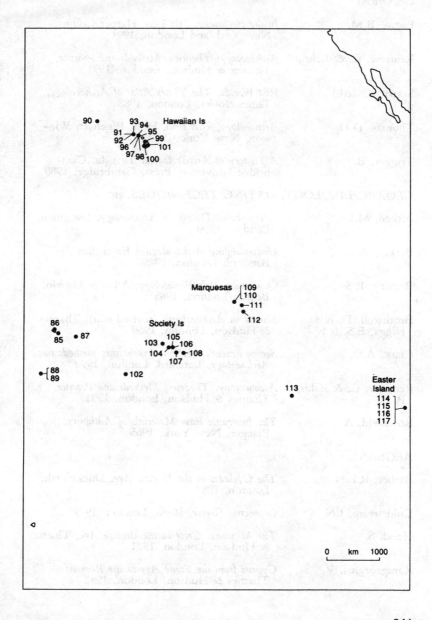

Further reading

GENERAL

Fagan, B.M.	*In the Beginning*, 7th Edn, Harper Collins, New York and London, 1991
Renfrew, C. & Bahn, P.	*Archaeology: Theories, Methods and Practice*, Thames & Hudson, London, 1991
Scarre, C. (ed.)	*Past Worlds. The Times Atlas of Archaeology*, Times Books, London, 1988
Thomas, D.H.	*Archaeology*, 2nd Edn, Holt, Rinehart, Winston, New York, 1989
Trigger, B.	*A History of Archaeological Thought*, Cambridge University Press, Cambridge, 1989

GEOARCHAEOLOGY, DATING TECHNIQUES, etc.

Aitken, M.J.	*Science-based Dating in Archaeology*, Longman, London, 1990
Barker, P.	*Understanding Archaeological Excavation*, Batsford, London, 1986
Bradley, R.S.	*Quaternary Paleoclimatology*, Allen & Unwin, Boston/London, 1985
Brothwell, D. & Higgs, E.S. (eds)	*Science in Archaeology*, (revised edn), Thames & Hudson, London, 1969
Clark, A.	*Seeing beneath the Soil. Prospecting methods in Archaeology*, Batsford, London, 1990
Renfrew, C. & Bahn, P.	*Archaeology: Theories, Methods and Practice*, Thames & Hudson, London, 1991
Rosenfeld, A.	*The Inorganic Raw Materials of Antiquity*, Praeger, New York, 1965

AEGEAN

Barber, R.L.N.	*The Cyclades in the Bronze Age*, Duckworth, London, 1987
Coldstream, J.N.	*Geometric Greece*, Benn, London, 1977
Hood, S.	*The Minoans: Crete in the Bronze Age*, Thames & Hudson, London, 1971
Karageorghis, V.	*Cyprus from the Stone Age to the Romans*, Thames & Hudson, London, 1982

Taylour, Lord W.   *The Mycenaeans*, Thames & Hudson, London, 1983

Theocharis, D.R.   *Neolithic Greece*, National Bank of Greece, Athens, 1973

Vermeule, E.   *Greece in the Bronze Age*, Chicago University Press, Chicago, 1972

AFRICA

Close, A.E. (ed.)   *Prehistory of arid North Africa. Essays in honor of Fred Wendorf*, Southern Methodist University, Dallas, 1987 (see references to works by Schild, Wendorf)

Connah, G.   *African civilization. Precolonial cities and states in tropical Africa*, Cambridge University Press, Cambridge, 1987

Hall, M.   *The changing past. Farmers, kings and traders in southern Africa, 200–1860*, David Philip, Cape Town, 1987

Klein, R.G. (ed.)   *Southern African prehistory and palaeoenvironments*, Balkema, Rotterdam, 1984

Lewis-Williams, J.D. & Dowson, T.   *Images of power. Understanding Bushman rock art*, Southern Books, Johannesburg, 1989

Phillipson, D.W.   *African archaeology*, Cambridge University Press, Cambridge, 1985

Robertshaw, P.T. (ed.)   *A history of African archaeology*, James Currey, London, 1990

van Noten, F. (ed.)   *The archaeology of central Africa*, Akademische Druck and Verlagsanstalt, Graz, 1982

AUSTRALASIA

Bahn, P. & Flenley, J.   *Easter Island, Earth Island*, Thames & Hudson, London, 1992

Bellwood, P.   *Man's conquest of the Pacific*, Collins, Auckland, 1978

Connah, G.   *'Of the hut I builded': the archaeology of Australia's history*, Cambridge University Press, Cambridge, 1988

Davidson, J.   *The prehistory of New Zealand*, Longman Paul, Auckland, 1984

Flood, J.   *Archaeology of the Dreamtime*, Revised edition, Collins, Australia, 1989

Flood, J.	*The riches of ancient Australia*, University of Queensland Press, St Lucia, 1990
Jennings, J.D. (ed.)	*The prehistory of Polynesia*, Harvard University Press, Cambridge, Mass. 1979
Kirch, P.W.	*Feathered gods and fishhooks: an introduction to Hawaiian archaeology and prehistory*, University of Hawaii Press, Honolulu, 1985
White, J.P. & O'Connell, J.F.	*A prehistory of Australia, New Guinea and Sahul*, Academic Press, New York and London, 1982

CENTRAL/EASTERN EUROPE, CENTRAL ASIA – EARLY PERIODS

Allsworth-Jones, P.	*The Szeletian*, Clarendon Press, Oxford, 1986
Boriskowskij, P.I. (ed.)	*Paleolit SSSR*, Nauka, Moskva, 1984
Boriskowskij, P.I. (ed.)	*Paleolit Kavkaza i Severnoj Azii*, Nauka, Leningrad, 1989
Chmielewski, W., Schild, R. & Wieckowska, H.	*Prahistoria Ziem Polskich, Tom I, Paleolit i Mezolit*, Polska Akademia Nauk, Wrocław, 1975
Gábori, M.	*Les Civilisations du Paléolithique Moyen entre les Alpes et l'Oural*, Akadémiai Kiadó, Budapest, 1976
Hahn, J.	*Aurignacien: Das Altere Jungpaläolithikum in Mittel- und Osteuropa*, Fundamenta Monographien zur Urgeschichte, Reihe A, Band 9, Köln, 1977
Otte, M.	*Le Gravettien en Europe Centrale* (2 vols), Dissertationes Archaeologicae Gandenses XX, De Tempel, Brugge, 1981

CENTRAL AND EASTERN EUROPE – LATER PERIODS

Barker, G.	*Prehistoric Farming in Europe*, Cambridge University Press, Cambridge, 1985
Bogucki, P.	*Forest Farmers and Stockherders. Early Agriculture and its Consequences in North-Central Europe*, Cambridge University Press, Cambridge, 1988
Chard, C.	*Northeast Asia in Prehistory*, University of Wisconsin Press, Madison, 1974
Coles, J.M. & Harding, A.F.	*The Bronze Age in Europe*, Methuen, London, 1979

Collis, J.	*The European Iron Age*, Batsford, London, 1984
Jażdżewski, K.	*Urgeschichte Mitteleuropas*, Ossolineum, Wroclaw, 1984
Sulimirski, T.	*Prehistoric Russia*, John Baker, London, 1970
Tringham, R.	*Hunters, Fishers and Farmers of Eastern Europe, 6000–3000* BC, Hutchinson, London, 1971
Wells, P.	*Farms, Villages and Cities. Commerce and Urban Origins in Late Prehistoric Europe*, Cornell University Press, Ithaca, 1984
Whittle, A.	*Neolithic Europe: a Survey*, Cambridge University Press, Cambridge, 1985

CLASSICAL

(Greece)

Lawrence, A.W. (revised Tomlinson, R.A.)	*Greek Architecture*, The Pelican History of Art, Penguin Books, London, 1983
Robertson, M.	*A History of Greek Art*, Cambridge University Press, Cambridge, 1975
Snodgrass, A.M.	*An Archaeology of Greece; the present state and future scope of a discipline*, University of California Press, London, 1987

(Etruscan)

Boëthius, A.	*Etruscan and Early Roman Architecture*, The Pelican History of Art, Penguin Books, London, 1978
Brendel, O.J.	*Etruscan Art*, The Pelican History of Art, Penguin Books, London, 1978
Spivey, N. & Stoddart, S.	*Etruscan Italy: an Archaeological History*, Batsford, London, 1990

(Roman)

Sear, F.	*Roman Architecture*, Batsford, London, 1982
Strong, D. (revised Ling, R.)	*Roman Art*, The Pelican History of Art, Penguin Books, London, 1988

EAST ASIA

(China)

Chang, K.C.   *Archaeology of Ancient China*, 4th Edn, Yale University Press, New Haven and London, 1986

Rawson, J.   *Ancient China, art and archaeology*, British Museum Publications Ltd., London, 1980

(Korea)

Kim, J.-H.   *The Prehistory of Korea*, University of Hawaii Press, Honolulu, 1978

(Japan)

Aikens, C.M. & Higuchi, T.   *Prehistory of Japan*, Academic Press, New York and London, 1982

Kidder, J.E. Jr   *Japan Before Buddhism*, 2nd Edn, Thames & Hudson, London, 1966

UNESCO Series:

Kim, W.-Y.   *Recent Archaeological Discoveries in the Republic of Korea*, 1983

Institute of Archaeology

     Recent Archaeological Discoveries in the People's Republic of China, 1984

Tsuboi, K. (ed.)   *Recent Archaeological Discoveries in Japan*, 1987

All published by UNESCO and the Centre for East Asian Cultural Studies, Paris and Tokyo

EGYPT and NUBIA

     Introduction to Ancient Egypt, British Museum, London, 1979

Adams, W.Y.   *Nubia: Corridor to Africa*, Allen Lane, London, 1977

Baines, J. & Malek, J.   *Atlas of Ancient Egypt*, Phaidon Press, Oxford, 1980

Edwards, I.E.S.   *The Pyramids of Egypt*, Penguin, Harmondsworth, 1985

Hoffman, M.   *Egypt before the Pharaohs*, Ark Paperbacks, London, 1984

Trigger, B.G., Kemp, B.J., O'Connor, D. & Lloyd, A.B.
Ancient Egypt: a Social History, Cambridge University Press, Cambridge, 1983

Trigger, B.G.
Nubia under the Pharoahs, Thames & Hudson, London 1976

MESOAMERICA

Adams, R.E.W.
Prehistoric Mesoamerica, Little, Brown and Company, Boston, 1977

Fagan, B.M.
Kingdoms of Gold, Kingdoms of Jade, The Americas before Columbus, Thames & Hudson, London, 1992

Sabloff, J.A.
The Cities of Ancient Mexico: Reconstructing a Lost World, Thames and Hudson, London, 1989

The New Archaeology and the Ancient Maya, Scientific American Library, New York, 1990

Schele, L. & Freidel, D.
A Forest of Kings: The Untold Story of the Ancient Maya, Morrow Publishing Company, New York, 1990

Townsend, R.F.
The Aztecs, Thames & Hudson, London, 1992

NORTH AMERICA

Fagan, B.M.
Ancient North America. The Archaeology of a Continent, Thames & Hudson, London, 1991

Fagan, B.M.
Kingdoms of Gold, Kingdoms of Jade. The Americas before Columbus, Thames & Hudson, London, 1992

Jennings, J. (ed.)
Ancient North Americans, W.H. Freeman, New York, 1983

McGhee, R.
Ancient Canada, Canadian Museum of Civilization, Ottawa, 1989

Willey, G. & Sabloff, J.
A History of American Archaeology, 2nd Edn, W.H. Freeman, San Francisco, 1980

SOUTH AMERICA

Donnan, C.B. (ed.)
Early Ceremonial Architecture in the Andes, Dumbarton Oaks Research Library and Collection, Washington, D.C., 1985

Fagan, B.M.   *Kingdoms of Gold, Kingdoms of Jade. The*
                               Americas before Columbus, Thames &
                               Hudson, London, 1992

Keatinge, R.W. (ed.)   *Peruvian Archaeology: an Overview of Pre-Inca*
                               and Inca Society, Cambridge University
                               Press, Cambridge and New York, 1988

Lumbreras, L.G.   *The Peoples and Cultures of Ancient Peru*
                               (transl. Betty J. Meggers), Smithsonian In-
                               stitution Press, Washington, D.C., 1974

Moseley, M.E.   *The Incas and their ancestors. The archaeology of*
                               Peru, Thames & Hudson, London, 1992

SOUTHEAST ASIA

Allen, J. Golson, J. &   *Sunda and Sahul: prehistoric studies in South-east*
Jones, R. (eds)   *Asia, Melanesia and Australia*, Academic
                               Press, London, 1977

Bellwood, P.   *Prehistory of the Indo-Malaysian Archipelago*,
                               Academic Press, London, 1985

Coèdes, G.   *The Indianized States of Southeast Asia*, East-
                               West Center Press, Honolulu, 1968

Higham, C.   *The Archaeology of Mainland Southeast Asia*,
                               Cambridge University Press, Cambridge,
                               1989

Smith, R.B. & Watson,   *Early South East Asia: essays in archaeology,*
W.   *history and historical geography*, Oxford Uni-
                               versity Press, Oxford, 1979

WEST, CENTRAL & SOUTH ASIA

Western Asia

Aharoni, Y.   *The Archaeology of the Land of Israel*, West-
                               minster Press, Philadelphia, 1982

Burney, C.   *The Ancient Near East*, Phaidon Press,
                               Oxford, 1977

Kenyon, K.   *Archaeology of the Holy Land*, 4th Edn, Benn,
                               London, 1980

Lloyd, S.   *The Archaeology of Mesopotamia: From the Old*
                               Stone Age to the Persian Conquest, Thames &
                               Hudson, London, 1984

Mellaart, J.   *The Neolithic of the Near East*, Thames &
                               Hudson, London, 1975

Nissen, H.	*The Early History of the Ancient Near East*, University of Chicago Press, Chicago, 1988
Oates, J.	*Babylon*, Thames & Hudson, London, 1986
Potts, D.	*The Arabian Gulf in Antiquity*, Clarendon Press, Oxford, 1990
Redman, C.	*The Rise of Civilization: From Early Farmers to Urban Society in the Ancient Near East*, W.H. Freeman, San Francisco, 1978
Roaf, M.	*Cultural Atlas of Mesopotamia and the Ancient Near East*, Facts on File, New York, 1990

(Central Asia)

Allchin, F.R. and Hammond, N. (eds)	*The Archaeology of Afghanistan*, Academic Press, London, 1978
Gupta, S.P.	*Archaeology of Soviet Central Asia and the Indian Borderlands*, B.R. Publishing, Delhi, 1979
Kohl, P.	*Central Asia: Palaeolithic Beginnings to the Iron Age*, Editions Recherches sur les Civilisations, Paris, 1984

(South Asia)

Agrawal, D.P.	*The Archaeology of India*, Curzon Press, London, 1982
Allchin, B. and Allchin, R.	*The Rise of Civilization in India and Pakistan*, Cambridge University Press, Cambridge, 1982

WESTERN EUROPE – EARLY PERIODS

Bordaz, J.	*Tools of the Old and New Stone Age*, David and Charles, Newton Abbot, 1971
Bordes, F.	*The Old Stone Age*, Weidenfeld & Nicolson, London, 1968
Clark, J.G.D.	*The Mesolithic Settlement of Northern Europe*, Cambridge University Press, Cambridge, 1936
Coles, J.M. & Higgs, E.S.	*The Archaeology of Early Man*, Faber & Faber, London, 1969
Gamble, C.	*The Palaeolithic Settlement of Europe*, Cambridge University Press, Cambridge, 1986

| Oakley, K.P. | *Man the Tool Maker*, 6th Edn, British Museum, London, 1972 |
| Roe, D.A. | *The Lower and Middle Palaeolithic Periods in Britain*, Routledge and Kegan Paul, London, 1981 |

WESTERN EUROPE – LATER PERIODS

Champion, T., Gamble, C., Shennan, S. & Whittle, A.	*Prehistoric Europe*, Academic Press, London, 1984
Darvill, T.	*Prehistoric Britain*, Batsford, London, 1987
Jensen, J.	*The Prehistory of Denmark*, Methuen, London, 1982
Harbison, P.	*Pre-Christian Ireland*, Thames & Hudson, London, 1988
Scarre, C. (ed.)	*Ancient France*, Edinburgh University Press, Edinburgh, 1983

Illustration Acknowledgements

The publishers have made every attempt to contact the copyright holders of material used as sources for the redrawn illustrations that appear in this title. We would be grateful to hear from any non-accredited copyright holders whom we have been unable to trace.

3   ankh: after Davies, N.M. *Picture Writing in Ancient Egypt*, Oxford University Press, 1958

5   Australopithecus: Johanson, D.C. & Edey, M.A. *Lucy. The beginnings of humankind*, Simon & Schuster, New York, 1981

6   Ban Chiang (pot): Higham, C. *The Archaeology of Mainland Southeast Asia*, Cambridge University Press, 1989

7   Ban Kao (tripod pot): ditto

8   base ring juglet: Courtois, J-C. *Alasia II*, Mission Archéologique d'Alasia, Boccard, Paris, 1981

10   bell beaker: Guilaine, J. *L'Age du Cuivre Européen ...* Editions du CNRS, 75700 Paris

12   bifacial foliate: after Allsworth-Jones, P. *The Szeletian*, Clarendon Press, Oxford, 1986

14   bulla: Le Brun A. & Vallat, F. *L'origine de l'écriture à Suse*, Cahiers de la DAFI 8, 1978

15   burin: (a) Bordes, F. *Typologie du Paléolithique Ancien et Moyen*, CNRS, 1961; (b) Bordaz, J. *Tools of the Old and New Stone Age*, David & Charles, 1970

19   chous: Kanowski, M.G. *Containers of Classical Greece*, University of Queensland Press, St Lucia, London, New York

20   cleavers (W. Eur.): *Flint Implements*, British Museum Publications 1968. (Africa): Leakey, M.D. *Olduvai Gorge*, Vol 3, Cambridge University Press, 1971

22   compartmented seal: Sarianidi, V.I. in *The Bronze Age Civilization of Central Asia*, ed. P. Kohl, Armonk, New York, 1981

23   cone mosaic: *Handbuch der Formen- und Stilkunde, Antike*, W. Kohlhammer, Stuttgart

26   cuneiform tablet: Le Brun, A. & Vallat, F. *L'origine de l'écriture à Suse*, Cahiers de la DAFI, 8, 1978

28   cylinder seal: *Handbuch der Formen- und Stilkunde, Antike*, W. Kohlhammer, Stuttgart

29   Doric order: Lawrence, A.W. *Greek Architecture*, Pelican History of Art, Penguin, 1983

30 elouera: White, J.P. & O'Connell, J.F. *A Prehistory of Australia, New Guinea and Sahul*, Academic Press, Sydney, 1982

31 emblem glyph: Weaver, M.P. *The Aztecs, Maya and their Predecessors: Archaeology of Mesoamerica*, Seminar Press, New York, 1972

32 fishtail points: Lumbreras, L.G. *The Peoples and Cultures of Ancient Peru* (trans. Meggers), Smithsonian Institution Press, Washington DC, 1974

33 flake: *Flint Implements*, British Museum, 1968

36 glyph: Weaver, M.P. *The Aztecs, Maya and their Predecessors: Archaeology of Mesoamerica*, Seminar Press, New York, 1972

37 grooved ware: *Guide Catalogue of the Neolithic and Bronze Age Collections in Devizes Museum*, Wiltshire Archaeological & Natural History Society, 1964

38 Hoabinhian: Bellwood, P. *Prehistory of the Indo-Malaysian Archipelago*, Academic Press, London, 1985

39 horsehoof core: White, J.P. & O'Connell, J.F. *A Prehistory of Australia* ... Academic Press, Sydney, 1982

40 hydria: Betancourt, P.P. *The History of Minoan Pottery*, Princeton University Press

41 Intercultural style: de Miroschedji, P. *Vases et objets en stéatite susiens* ..., Cahiers de la DAFI 3, 1973

42 Ionic order: Lawrence, A.W. *Greek Architecture*, Pelican History of Art, Penguin, 1983

44 Kimberley point: White, J.P. & O'Connell, J.F. *A Prehistory of Australia* ..., Academic Press, Sydney, 1982

45 Lerma point: Coe, M.D. *Mexico: Ancient Peoples and Places*, Praeger, New York, 1962

46 Levallois: *Flint Implements*, British Museum, 1968

47 lingling-o: Bellwood, P. *Prehistory of the Indo-Malayian Archipelago* Academic Press, London, 1985

48 livre de beurre: Bulletin de la Société Préhistorique Française, 1982, tome 79, no 10–12

49 loutrophoros: Kanowski, M.G. *Containers of Classical Greece*, University of Queensland Press, St Lucia, London, New York

50 lunula: Proceedings of the Prehistoric Society No.7, 1968

53 Mousterian: *Flint Implements*, British Museum, 1968

54 orchestra: Lawrence, A.W. *Greek Architecture*, Penguin, 1983

57 Peterborough ware: (Ebbsfleet) Keiller, A. *Windmill Hill and Avebury*, Oxford, Clarendon Press, 1965. (Fengate) Piggott, S. *The West Kennet Long Barrow ...*, HMSO, 1962

59 pirri graver: Kamminga, J. *The pirri graver*, Australian Aboriginal Studies, 1985

60 polished stone adze: Bellwood, P. *Prehistory of the Indo-Malaysian Archipelago*, Academic Press, London, 1985

61 prondnik: after Bordes, F. *The Old Stone Age*, McGraw Hill, New York, 1968

62 pyramid complex: after Edwards, I.E.S., *The Pyramids of Egypt*, Penguin, 1985

65 scraper: (both) *Flint Implements*, British Museum Publications, 1968

66 segment: Deacon, J. *The Later Stone Age of southernmost Africa*, British Archaeological Reports, Internat. Series 213, Oxford, 1984

68 shoe-last adze: Milisauskas, S. *Early Neolithic Settlement and Society at Olszanica*, Ann Arbor: Museum of Anthropology, 1986

69 shouldered point: after Boriskowskij, P.I., Paleolit SSSR, Nauka, Moskva, 1984

70 side-notched point: after Dumond, D.E., *The Eskimos and Aleuts*, Thames & Hudson, London, 1977

71 Songguk-ri: Kim, J.-H., *The Prehistory of Korea*, University of Hawaii Press, Honolulu, 1978

72 spacer plate: Piggott, S. *Ancient Europe from the beginnings of Agriculture to Classical Antiquity*, Edinburgh University Press; (necklace) Piggott, S. *Guide Catalogue of the Neolithic and Bronze Age Collections in Devizes Museum*, Wiltshire Archaeological & Natural History Society, 1964

73 stirrup jar: Betancourt, P.P. *The History of Minoan Pottery*, Princeton University Press, Princeton, NJ

74 Swiderian point: after Kozlowski, J.K. and Kozlowski, S.K., *Upper Palaeolithic and Mesolithic in Europe*, Polska Akademia Nauk, Wrocław, 1974

75 taotie: Rawson, J. *Chinese Bronzes – Art and Ritual*, British Museum & Sainsbury Centre, UEA, 1987

76 temple: Trigger, B.G. et al., *Ancient Egypt: a Social History*, Cambridge University Press, 1983

77 tholos tomb: W.G. Cavanagh, R.R. Laxton, C.D. Litton

78 Toalian: Bellwood, P. *Prehistory of the Indo-Malaysian Archipelago*, Academic Press, Sydney, London etc. 1985

79 tokens: Le Brun, A. & Vallat, F., *L'origine de l'ériture à Suse*, Cahiers de la DAFI 8, 1978

80 tula adzes: Mulvaney, D.J. *The Prehistory of Australia*, Penguin, Ringwood, 1975

81 wedge-shaped microcore: after Dumond, D.E. *The Eskimos and Aleuts*, Thames & Hudson, London, 1977

COLLINS DICTIONARY OF GEOLOGY

Dorothy Farris Lapidus

Consultant Editor: Isobel Winstanley

The *Collins Dictionary of Geology* is a new and authoritative guide to current terminology in this increasingly important field.

The Dictionary is primarily directed towards the requirements of first and second year undergraduates. Containing more than 3000 entries, it gives comprehensive coverage to the major areas of study, ranging from geophysics and geomorphology through stratigraphic terminology to palaeontology and igneous petrology. Practical applications, such as mineralogy and economic and engineering geology, are also covered, as are the principal methods of rock exploration and analysis.

Concise initial definitions for each term are supported by encyclopaedic detail where appropriate, and the extensive cross-referencing system together with the numerous illustrations facilitate access to the rich veins of information contained in the Dictionary.

The *Collins Dictionary of Geology* is thus an invaluable tool not only for students of the geological sciences but also for students and workers in related fields such as geography, surveying and environmental management.

Dorothy Farris Lapidus is a lecturer and writer from New York. Dr Isobel Winstanley tutors in Earth Sciences at the Open University.

ISBN 0 00 434148 1

COLLINS DICTIONARY OF SOCIOLOGY

David Jary & Julia Jary

The *Collins Dictionary of Sociology* is an up-to-date resource for those concerned with the complex discipline of sociology. The book is primarily directed at the undergraduate market, but is sufficiently accessible in style and organization to be useful to the 'A' level student and the general reader. However, while its breadth recommends it to a wider readership, its depth of treatment of some of the more complex issues will make it a convenient reference book for academic sociologists.

The Dictionary explains a wide range of terms and concepts from every area of sociology, and a selection of those most likely to be met from associated disciplines such as psychology, economics, anthropology and political science. It also provides a useful coveage of methodological terms and research techniques.

The treatment and organization allows the reader to build comprehensive coverage of all sociological schools, or to compare perspectives. Its coverage extends from *Social Class* to *Sexuality,* from *Functionalism* to *Feyerabend,* and from *Lumpenproletariat* to *Likert Scale.* There are also biographical entries on key figures in the development of sociology.

The *Collins Dictionary of Sociology* is an essential reference work for all who require a clear, balanced and comprehensive guide to sociology, or for anyone with an interest in contemporary society.

David Jary is Professor of Sociology at Staffordshire Polytechnic. Julia Jary teaches psychology part-time at Staffordshire Polytechnic and for the Open University. The Dictionary has been compiled with the assistance of a skilled editorial team of specialists from the main sociological fields.

ISBN 0 00 434373 5 (hardback)
ISBN 0 00 434359 X (paperback)

COLLINS DICTIONARY OF BIOLOGY

W. G. Hale and J. P. Margham

The *Collins Dictionary of Biology* is a completely new, authoritative and comprehensive guide to the complex discipline of biology. The book is directed primarily to the needs of undergraduates and advanced school students, but will also prove an invaluable source book for anyone with an interest in this wide-ranging and fascinating subject.

The Dictionary has over 5,600 entries ranging from *abdomen* to *zymogen*. There are also 285 diagrams illustrating such features as the generalized structures of animals, genetic organization, parts of plants and animals, etc., plus numerous tables.

All the major fields within biology are covered, including anatomy, biochemistry, ecology, genetics, physiology, evolutionary theory and taxonomy. The entries have been structured to provide more than an isolated definition of the term in question. An entry such as *acquired characters* is thus set in the context of the development of evolutionary theory, while the series of genetic entries guides the reader through such concepts as the basis of *genetic code* and the industrial implications of *genetic engineering*. The Dictionary also includes brief biographies of major biologists.

Professor Hale is Dean of the Faculty of Science and Head of the Department of Biology at Liverpool Polytechnic. Dr Margham is Principal Lecturer and Course Leader for the B.Sc. Honours Applied Biology Degree at Liverpool Polytechnic.

'. . . exemplary in every respect . . . a data bank of diverse facts about the science of life.' — *Literary Review*.

ISBN 0 00 434351 4

COLLINS DICTIONARY OF ENVIRONMENTAL SCIENCE

Gareth Jones, Graham Hollier, Jean Forbes and Alan Robertson

The *Collins Dictionary of Environmental Science* is the most comprehensive paperback dictionary available on the subject of environmental science.

Awareness of the effects of human activity on our planet's resources has been growing constantly over the last 20 years, and environmental science has evolved to examine the interaction of people and the environments in which they work and live. The Dictionary is a completely new guide to this important multi-disciplinary field of study and its clear, helpful definitions make it an invaluable source book as the debate over environmental issues becomes increasingly technical.

Containing over 1,800 entries, many of which are extensively cross-referenced, and more than 80 diagrams, the Dictionary draws together topics from a wide range of related fields in the biological, physical and social sciences including geology, geomorphology, climatology, botany and zoology. The Dictionary describes many facets of the natural, built and agro-socio environments. Aspects of ecology and conservation are also covered in depth, as are items of topical importance such as biosphere pollution, the nuclear industry, inner-city renewal and government management of urban and rural environments.

Gareth Jones is a senior lecturer in geography and Graham Hollier is a lecturer in geography, both at Strathclyde University, Jean Forbes is a senior lecturer at the Centre for Planning at Strathclyde University, and Alan Robertson is a chartered town planner.

ISBN 0 00 434348 4